Lyn Stringer
596 - 9705

ADDISON-WESLEY MATHEMATICS 12
BRITISH COLUMBIA EDITION

Brendan Kelly
Professor of Mathematics
Faculty of Education
University of Toronto
Ontario

Bob Alexander
Assistant Co-ordinator
of Mathematics
Toronto Board of Education
Toronto, Ontario

Paul Atkinson
Principal
Cameron Heights
Collegiate Institute
Kitchener, Ontario

Contributing Author
Robert A. Adams
Department of Mathematics
University of British Columbia
Vancouver, British Columbia

Addison-Wesley Publishers Limited

Don Mills, Ontario
Reading, Massachusetts
Menlo Park, California
Wokingham, England
Amsterdam • Bonn
Sydney • Singapore
Tokyo • Madrid
San Juan

Design
John Zehethofer
Assembly and Technical Art
Frank Zsigo
Editorial
Lesley Haynes
Typesetting
Q Composition
Printer
Ronalds Printing, Vancouver

Photographic Credits

The publisher wishes to thank the following sources for photographs and other illustrative materials used in this book. We will gladly receive information enabling us to rectify any errors or references in credits.

Cover, Richard Simpson; 1, Ministry of Fisheries and Oceans; 2, Allsport/Masterfile; N. Serba/Miller Comstock Inc; Bob Alexander; 13, Lesley Haynes; 14, Bob Alexander; 32, NASA; Carl Zeiss Canada Ltd.; 41, Province of British Columbia; 47, Schnepel Photography; 85, Paul Atkinson; 86, Gulf Canada Limited; 95, © R. Kinne/Science Source/Masterfile; 97, Addison-Wesley Photo Library; 129, Tim O'Shea; 148, Stanford News Service; 155, Nova Scotia Power Corporation; 158, Roberts/Miller Comstock Inc.; 187, Addison-Wesley Photo Library; 194, Lambert/Miller Comstock Inc.; 199, Palomar Observatory Photograph; 229, Nova Scotia Communications and Information Centre; 261, Vincent Van Gogh Foundation/National Museum, Vincent Van Gogh, Amsterdam; 303, Addison-Wesley Photo Library; 315, Roberts/Miller Comstock Inc.; 327, Masterfile; 328, Addison-Wesley Photo Library; 332, Addison-Wesley Photo Library; 339, Ministry of Agriculture and Food; 351, T. Rosenthal; 351, Government of Quebec, Tourist Branch; 365, © M.C. Escher c/o Cordon Art-Baarn Holland; 374, Yale University/M. Marsland/1989; 375, Chris D'Arcy; 382, Schnepel Photography; 427, H.E. Edgerton, M.I.T., Cambridge, Massachusettes; 435, © M.C. Escher c/o Cordon Art-Baarn Holland

Written, printed, and bound in Canada

ISBN   0-201-18646-2

A   B   C   D   E   F   – RF –   95   94   93   92   91   90

Features of Mathematics 12

CONCEPT DEVELOPMENT

Mathematics 12 is carefully sequenced to develop concepts in mathematics. Concepts are explained with several examples, each of which has a detailed solution.

4-5 SOLVING EQUATIONS AND INEQUALITIES INVOLVING ABSOLUTE VALUE

On the number line, the numbers -4 and 4 are each located 4 units from 0. Each number is said to have an absolute value of 4. We write $|-4| = 4$ and $|4| = 4$.

> Given any number x, its *absolute value* is written $|x|$, and represents the distance from x to 0 on the number line.
> - The absolute value of any number other than 0 is positive.
> - The absolute value of 0 is 0.

Example 1. Simplify.
   a) $|12|$ b) $|-7|$ c) $|1 - 4|$

Solution. a) $|12| = 12$ b) $|-7| = 7$ c) $|1 - 4| = |-3|$
                                                   $= 3$

In *Example 1c*, the expression $|1 - 4|$ represents the distance from 1 to 4 on the number line. Similarly, the expression $|x - a|$ represents the distance from x to a.

REINFORCEMENT

An abundance of exercises is provided to reinforce skills and concepts. These exercises are graded by difficulty with an appropriate balance of A, B, and C exercises. The A exercises may sometimes be completed mentally and the answers given orally or the questions may be discussed with the students. The B exercises are intended for the students to consolidate their learning of the concepts that were taught. The C exercises present a challenge and usually involve extensions of the concepts taught in that section.

Review Exercises and *Cumulative Reviews* provide additional practice. Answers to all questions are included in the text.

TECHNOLOGY

A contemporary mathematics program must reflect the impact of calculators and computers on society.

Mathematics 12 assumes that students will use scientific calculators where appropriate. It is up to the students to familiarize themselves with their calculators.

▢ COMPUTER POWER

Graphing Functions

A computer is ideally suited for graphing functions, since it can rapidly calculate the values of a function for many values of x. The graph can be displayed on the computer screen or printed on paper. The most primitive programs plot symbols on the screen, which normally consists of about 20 rows of 40 characters each. The program below is of this type, and can be used on almost any computer. For more accurate graphs, other programs must be used, but the commands are specific to particular computers.

This program can be used to obtain an approximation to the graph of any function that can be defined by an equation. When the program is run, the computer asks for the first and last values of x to be used in the

```
READ(Y1,Y2); WRITELN;
WRITELN('WHAT PLOTTING
SYMBOL DO YOU WANT? ');
S := READKEY; WRITELN;
XAXIS := TRUNC(22-(Y1*22
/ (Y2-Y1)));
YAXIS := TRUNC((-X1*40 /
(X2-X1)));
FOR X := 1 TO 40 DO BEGIN
  FOR Y := 1 TO 22 DO BEGIN
    P[X,Y] := CHR(32);
  END;
END;
FOR X := 1 TO 40 DO
P[X,XAXIS] := CHR(46);
FOR Y := 1 TO 22 DO
P[YAXIS,Y] := CHR(46);
XT := X1;
I := 0;
REPEAT
  I := SUCC(I);
  { UNCOMMENT ONE OF THESE
```

COMPUTER POWER features provide opportunities for students to explore mathematical problems using a computer. It is assumed that students know how to enter a program in PASCAL, but is not necessary for them to understand the program.

APPLICATIONS OF MATHEMATICS

Students can better understand mathematical principles when they are related to their applications. For this reason, applications are integrated throughout *Mathematics 12*.

Every chapter begins with an applied problem that is solved as an example in the chapter.

5 Trigonometric Functions

The tides in the Bay of Fundy are among the highest in the world. Suppose you know how high the water is at high tide, and the time of day this occurs, and also how high it is at low tide, and the time it occurs. How can you determine the height of the water at any other time of the day? (See Section 5-13 *Example 1.*)

Many sections begin with an application which illustrates the necessity for the mathematics that follows.

1-3 COMPOSITION OF FUNCTIONS

Consider the problem of expressing the cost of fuel, when taking a trip by car, as a function of the distance driven.

The cost of fuel, C cents, is a function of the amount of fuel consumed. If fuel costs 50 ¢/L, the cost for x litres of fuel is given by this equation.

$$C = 50x \ldots \text{①}$$

The amount of fuel consumed is a function of the distance driven. If the car consumes fuel at the rate of 8.0 L/100 km, then in travelling d kilometres the amount of fuel consumed is given by this equation.

$$x = 0.080d \ldots \text{②}$$

We can express the cost of fuel as a function of the distance driven

Applications are also included throughout the exercises.

8. The performance of a bicycle can be greatly improved by streamlining, which reduces the effective frontal area of vehicle and rider.

   a) Assuming that the riders can sustain the speeds indicated in the graph, determine the distance travelled in each position illustrated, during 8 h of cycling.

   b) State the domain and the range of the function shown in the graph.

   c) Describe what changes there would be in the graph if it were drawn to represent the speeds sustained for a much shorter period, such as one minute. What change, if any, would there be in the domain? in the range?

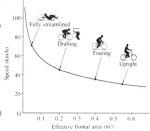

Speed sustained for 8 h by a good athlete

Fully streamlined

Drafting

Touring

Upright

Speed (km/h)

Effective frontal area (m²)

PROBLEM SOLVING

Problem solving is integrated throughout the program, with many of the exercises providing challenging problems for the students to solve. In addition, special features are included which promote the development of problem-solving skills.

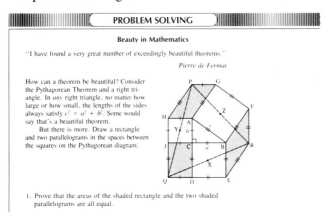

PROBLEM SOLVING

Beauty in Mathematics

"I have found a very great number of exceedingly beautiful theorems."

Pierre de Fermat

How can a theorem be beautiful? Consider the Pythagorean Theorem and a right triangle. In *any* right triangle, no matter how large or how small, the lengths of the sides always satisfy $c^2 = a^2 + b^2$. Some would say that's a beautiful theorem.

But there is more. Draw a rectangle and two parallelograms in the spaces between the squares on the Pythagorean diagram.

1. Prove that the areas of the shaded rectangle and the two shaded parallelograms are all equal.

The *PROBLEM SOLVING* feature is a two-page spread in every chapter which extends the strategies that were developed in earlier grades. The problems are graded by difficulty into B, C, and D problems. The B problems may require some ingenuity to solve. The C problems are challenging, and are similar to the problems that are found in mathematics contests. Some of the D problems are extremely difficult, and may approach the level of difficulty of the problems that occur in olympiad competitions. It is not expected that many students will solve the D problems.

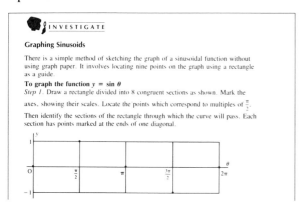

INVESTIGATE

Graphing Sinusoids

There is a simple method of sketching the graph of a sinusoidal function without using graph paper. It involves locating nine points on the graph using a rectangle as a guide.

To graph the function $y = \sin \theta$
Step 1. Draw a rectangle divided into 8 congruent sections as shown. Mark the axes, showing their scales. Locate the points which correspond to multiples of $\frac{\pi}{2}$.

Then identify the sections of the rectangle through which the curve will pass. Each section has points marked at the ends of one diagonal.

Frequent *INVESTIGATE* features are starting points for mathematical investigations to help the student develop analytic skills. These features always relate to the concepts that are developed in the sections in which they occur.

The *MATHEMATICS AROUND US* features outline applications of mathematics in the sciences, the arts, business, and industry.

MATHEMATICS AROUND US

The Waggle Dance of Honeybees

In 1973, Karl von Frisch received a Nobel Prize for his research in animal behaviour. One of his discoveries concerns a method used by honeybees to communicate the location of a food source to other bees inside a hive. Von Frisch observed bees returning to the hive when they had discovered a food source. Shortly after a bee returned, hundreds of bees left the hive, and went directly to the food source, although the bee which had found the food remained inside the hive. Somehow, the bee had informed the others where the food was located.

By marking the bees with paint, and using glass-walled hives, von Frisch learned how they do this. The bee which found the food performs a dance on the honeycomb inside the hive. It follows a figure-8 pattern and wags its body in the central part. Von Frisch observed that:
- the orientation of the central portion indicates the direction of the food source,
- the speed of the dance indicates the distance to the food.

Von Frisch made thousands of observations, comparing the speeds of the bees' dances with the distances to the food, and summarized his results on a graph like the one shown.

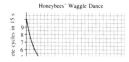

Honeybees' Waggle Dance

QUESTIONS

1. If the food is 1 km away, how many complete cycles does the bee make in

---

THE MATHEMATICAL MIND features offer insights into the work of mathematicians and the historical development of mathematics. Anecdotes of human interest that are part of history are included. In this feature, problems related to the topic are presented for the student to solve.

THE MATHEMATICAL MIND

The Cubic Equation Controversy

One of the most important mathematical achievements of the sixteenth century was the discovery by Italian mathematicians of formulas for the solution of cubic and quartic equations. This accomplishment occurred at a time when discoveries were often kept secret, and rivals were challenged to solve the same problem.

About 1510, a professor at the University of Bologna revealed to a student a method he had found of solving cubic equations without a quadratic term, such as $x^3 + 5x = 8$.

Nicolo Tartaglia
1499-1557

In 1535, when Nicolo Tartaglia claimed to have found a method of solving cubic equations without a linear term, such as $x^3 + 2x^2 = 6$, the former student challenged him to a public equation-solving contest. But before the contest, Tartaglia learned how to solve an equation of the first type as well, and he won the contest triumphantly.

Girolamo Cardano
1501-1576

Later, Girolamo Cardano urged Tartaglia to show him his method. When Cardano promised to keep it secret, Tartaglia gave it to him. But in 1545 Cardano published his *Ars Magna*, a Latin text on algebra, and included Tartaglia's solution of cubic equations. When Tartaglia protested the breach of his promise, Cardano claimed to have received his information from another party, and accused Tartaglia of plagiarism from the same source. There followed a bitter dispute between the two men over the question of who was the first to discover the formula for solving cubic equations.

Tartaglia's solution gave only one root, and later mathematicians found improved solutions. They also discovered formulas for quartic equations. Much work was done attempting to find a formula for quintic equations, but without success. This was

Contents

x

1 Functions

From studies of waves, oceanographers have learned that certain properties of waves are related. If you know its wavelength (distance between crests), how can you determine the velocity of a wave? (See Section 1–5 *Example 1.*)

1-1 REVIEW: FUNCTIONS

In everyday language, we use the word "function" to express the idea that one thing depends on another.

The time to complete the course is a function of the skipper's skill.

The time of free fall is a function of the plane's altitude.

The number appearing on the tape counter of a videocassette recorder is a function of the time of playing. The operator's manual for one machine contains the following table. Both the table and the graph show how the counter number is related to the playing time.

Graph of counter number against playing time

Time (h)	Counter Number
0	0
1	2250
2	3182
3	3897
4	4500
5	5031
6	5511

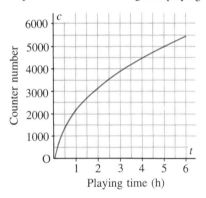

The relation between the counter number and the playing time in hours can be expressed as a set of ordered pairs.
{(0,0), (1,2250), (2,3182), (3,3897), (4,4500), (5,5031), (6,5511)}
This relation can also be expressed with an equation. The equation relating the counter number c with the playing time t hours, is $c = 2250\sqrt{t}$. You can verify that this equation is correct by substituting values for t from the table and using a calculator to calculate the values for c.

On the graph, a smooth curve was drawn through the plotted points. This curve represents the times and the corresponding counter numbers between those given. It is impossible to include all the points in the table of values or the set of ordered pairs because there are infinitely many of them. We can represent these points in a set, using a notation called *set-builder notation*, as follows.

$$\{(x,y) \mid y = 2250\sqrt{x},\ 0 \leqslant x \leqslant 6,\ x \in R\}$$

The set ... all ordered ... such $y = 2250\sqrt{x}$ ... and x is a
of ... pairs (x,y) ... that ... where x is between 0 and 6 ... real number.

Since there cannot be two different counter numbers for the same playing time, this set of ordered pairs has a special property. No two ordered pairs have the same first coordinate. A set of ordered pairs with this property is called a function.

> A *function* is a set of ordered pairs in which no two ordered pairs have the same first coordinate.

A function can be represented in different ways. The requirement that the ordered pairs must have different first coordinates can be seen in each.

- A table of values

x	y
0	0
1	2250
2	3182
3	3897
4	4500
5	5031
6	5511

All the entries in the first column are different.

- A graph

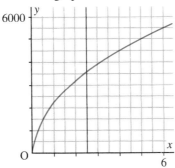

No two points can be joined by a vertical line.

- An equation

$$y = 2250\sqrt{x}$$

For any value of x, there is only one value of y.

> **Tests for a Function**   (Either of these tests is sufficient.)
>
> *Vertical-Line Test.* If no two points on a graph can be joined by a vertical line, then the graph represents a function.
>
> *Equation Test.* If a value of x can be found which produces more than one value of y when substituted in an equation, then the equation *does not* represent a function. If there is no such value of x, then the equation *does* represent a function.

Example 1. Given the equations $y = (x - 2)^2$ and $y^2 = x$

a) Graph the equations and use the graphs to determine which represents a function.

b) Use the equations to determine which represents a function.

Solution. a) $y = (x - 2)^2$

x	y
-1	9
0	4
1	1
2	0
3	1
4	4
5	9

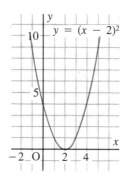

$y^2 = x$

x	y
0	0
1	± 1
4	± 2
9	± 3

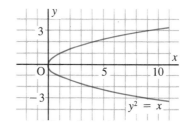

The vertical-line test shows that $y = (x - 2)^2$ is a function, and that $y^2 = x$ is not a function.

b) For the equation $y = (x - 2)^2$, only one value of y can be calculated for any value of x. Therefore, $y = (x - 2)^2$ is a function.

For the equation $y^2 = x$, there are values of x for which more than one value of y can be calculated; for example, when $x = 4$, $y = 2$ or $y = -2$. Since there is more than one value of y when $x = 4$, $y^2 = x$ is not a function.

Example 2. Determine which equations define functions.

a) $x^2 + y^2 = 10$ b) $y = 2^x$ c) $y = \dfrac{x}{x^2 - 1}$

Solution. a) $x^2 + y^2 = 10$

When $x = 0$, $y^2 = 10$
$$y = \pm\sqrt{10}$$

Since there are two values of y when $x = 0$, $x^2 + y^2 = 10$ is not a function.

b) For the equation $y = 2^x$, only one value of y can be calculated for any value of x. Therefore, $y = 2^x$ is a function.

c) The expression $\dfrac{x}{x^2 - 1}$ is not defined when $x = 1$ or when $x = -1$.
For any other value of x, there is only one value of y. Therefore, there is no value of x which produces more than one value of y when substituted in the equation. Therefore, $y = \dfrac{x}{x^2 - 1}$ defines a function if $x \neq 1$ or $x \neq -1$.

Consider again the example of the tape counter on a videocassette recorder, discussed earlier.

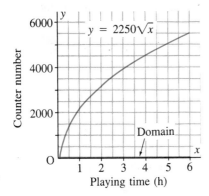

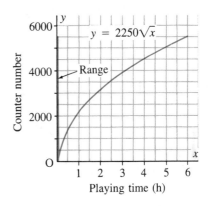

The set of first coordinates is $\{x \mid 0 \leq x \leq 6,\ x \in R\}$.
This is the set of possible playing times in hours, and is called the domain of the function.

The set of second coordinates is $\{y \mid 0 \leq y \leq 5511,\ y \in R\}$.
This is the set of counter numbers (for playing times up to 6 h), and is called the range of the function.

Given the *graph* of a function

The *domain* is the set of x-values represented by the graph.

The *range* is the set of y-values represented by the graph.

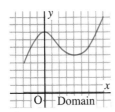

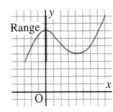

Given the *equation* of a function

The *domain* is the set of all values of x for which the equation is defined.

The *range* is the set of all values of y which are defined for values of x in the domain.

Example 3. Find the domain and the range of the function $y = \sqrt{x^2 - 1}$.

Solution. Since square roots of negative numbers are not real numbers,

$$x^2 - 1 \geq 0$$
$$x^2 \geq 1$$
$$x \geq 1 \text{ or } x \leq -1$$

The domain is the set of all real numbers greater than or equal to 1, or less than or equal to -1. In set-builder notation, the domain is $\{x \mid x \geq 1 \text{ or } x \leq -1, x \in R\}$.

Since the radical sign indicates a positive square root, the expression $\sqrt{x^2 - 1}$ is never negative. That is, $y \geq 0$. Therefore, the range is the set of all non-negative real numbers. In set-builder notation, the range is $\{y \mid y \geq 0, y \in R\}$.

EXERCISES 1-1

(A)

1. Which graphs represent functions?
   a)

Temperature of melting ice

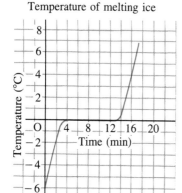

   b)

World records for the marathon run

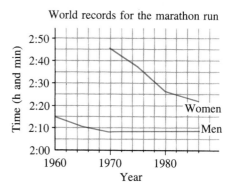

2. State the domain and the range for each function.
   a)

Value of Canadian dollar in U.S. cents

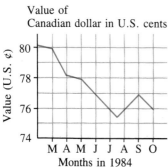

   b)

The effect of surface on air temperature

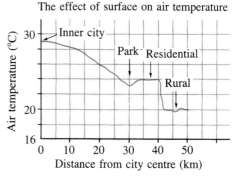

3. Determine if each graph represents a function.

a)

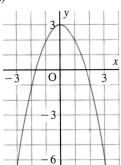

b)

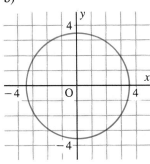

c)

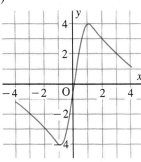

Ⓑ

4. Determine if each equation represents a function. If it does, state the domain and the range.
   a) $y = 2x - 4$
   b) $y = x^2$
   c) $y = \sqrt{x + 1}$
   d) $y^2 = x$
   e) $y = 10^x$
   f) $x^2 - y^2 = 4$

5. State the domain and the range for each function.
   a) $y = 2 - 3x$
   b) $y = x^3$
   c) $y = \sqrt{1 - x}$
   d) $y = \dfrac{1}{x}$
   e) $y = \dfrac{1}{x^2 - 1}$
   f) $y = \dfrac{x^2}{x^2 - 4}$

6. Graph each function.
   a) $y = 2x + 3$
   b) $y = 5 - 2x$
   c) $y = x^2$
   d) $y = (x + 2)^2$
   e) $y = \sqrt{x}$
   f) $y = \sqrt{x + 3}$

7. Air pressure is a function of altitude.
   a) Use the graph to find the air pressure at each location.

	Location	Altitude (m)
i)	Sea level	0
ii)	Banff, Alberta	1 383
iii)	Mexico City	2 240
iv)	Peak of Mount Everest	8 848
v)	Jet liner	12 000

   b) At what altitude is the air pressure 50% of the pressure at sea level?
   c) State the domain and the range of the function, as graphed.

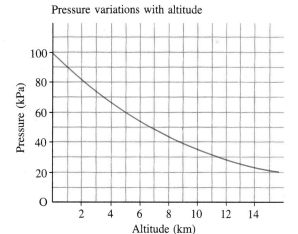

Pressure variations with altitude

8. The performance of a bicycle can be greatly improved by streamlining, which reduces the effective frontal area of vehicle and rider.
   a) Assuming that the riders can sustain the speeds indicated in the graph, determine the distance travelled in each position illustrated, during 8 h of cycling.
   b) State the domain and the range of the function shown in the graph.
   c) Describe what changes there would be in the graph if it were drawn to represent the speeds sustained for a much shorter period, such as one minute. What change, if any, would there be in the domain? in the range?

Speed sustained for 8 h by a good athlete

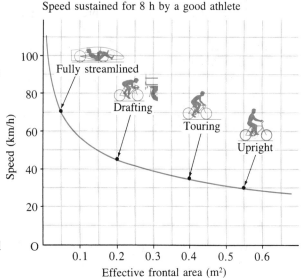

9. Graph each function.
   a) $y = 3x - 5$
   b) $y = (x + 3)^2$
   c) $y = \sqrt{2x - 4}$
   d) $y = \dfrac{1}{x}$
   e) $y = \dfrac{5}{x^2 + 1}$
   f) $y = \dfrac{5x}{x^2 + 1}$

Ⓒ

10. High-speed photographs have shown that the hand of a karate expert can reach speeds of 12 m/s or greater during certain karate manoeuvres.
    a) For each graph shown
       i) Find the speed of the hand after 0.05 s; after 0.10 s.
       ii) Find the hand's greatest speed.
    b) What happens to the speed of the hand during the forward karate punch between 0.12 s and 0.14 s? Why does this not happen during the hammer-fist strike?

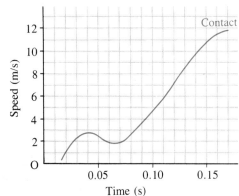

Speed of fist in hammer-fist strike

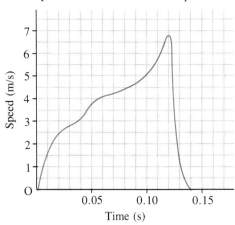

Speed of fist in forward karate punch

1-2 REVIEW: FUNCTION NOTATION

In the preceding section we saw that a function can be represented by a set of ordered pairs, a table of values, a graph, and an equation. A function can also be represented using a special notation, called *function notation*. For example, we may write:
$f(x) = 5x^2 - 6x + 1$. We say, "*f* of *x* equals $5x^2 - 6x + 1$."
This notation simplifies recording the values of the function for several values of *x*. For example, $f(-3)$ is the value of $f(x)$ when we substitute -3 for *x* everywhere *x* occurs in the expression.

$$f(x) = 5x^2 - 6x + 1$$

$$f(-3) = 5(-3)^2 - 6(-3) + 1$$
$$= 45 + 18 + 1$$
$$= 64$$

Example 1. If $f(x) = 3x + \dfrac{1}{x}$, find:

   a) $f(2)$ b) $f\left(-\dfrac{1}{2}\right)$

Solution.   a) Substitute 2 for *x*.   b) Substitute $-\dfrac{1}{2}$ for *x*.

$$f(x) = 3x + \frac{1}{x}$$

$$f(2) = 3(2) + \frac{1}{2}$$

$$= 6.5$$

$$f(x) = 3x + \frac{1}{x}$$

$$f\left(-\frac{1}{2}\right) = 3\left(-\frac{1}{2}\right) + \frac{1}{-\frac{1}{2}}$$

$$= -1.5 - 2$$
$$= -3.5$$

Algebraic expressions may be substituted for variables in the equation of a function.

Example 2. If $g(x) = \dfrac{x - 3}{x}$, $x \neq 0$, find: [*numerator* / *denominator* never = 0]

   a) $g(1 - 2x)$ never = 0   b) $g\left(\dfrac{5}{y}\right)$

Solution.   a) $g(x) = \dfrac{x - 3}{x}$ b) $g(x) = \dfrac{x - 3}{x}$

Substitute $1 - 2x$ for *x*.

$$g(1 - 2x) = \frac{(1 - 2x) - 3}{1 - 2x}$$

$$= \frac{-2 - 2x}{1 - 2x}$$

$$= \frac{2x + 2}{2x - 1}, x \neq \frac{1}{2}$$

Substitute $\dfrac{5}{y}$ for *x*.

$$g\left(\frac{5}{y}\right) = \frac{\dfrac{5}{y} - 3}{\dfrac{5}{y}} \times \frac{y}{y}$$

$$= \frac{5 - 3y}{5}, y \neq 0$$

Function notation can be used even when an equation relating the variables is not given.

Example 3. From the graph of $y = f(x)$, find:

    a) $f(1)$ b) $f(-2)$ c) $f(5)$ d) $f(0)$.

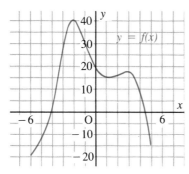

Solution.   a) $f(1)$ is the value of y when $x = 1$. To find this value, draw a vertical line, $x = 1$, to intersect the graph. Then, draw a horizontal line to intersect the y-axis.

           $f(1)$ appears to be 15.

    b) $f(-2)$ appears to be 40.

    c) $f(5)$ appears to be -15.

    d) $f(0)$ appears to be 20.

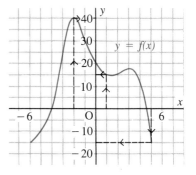

Example 4. Let n be a natural number, and let $f(n)$ represent the number of factors of n.

    a) Find $f(5)$, $f(6)$, and $f(9)$.

    b) Draw the graph of $y = f(n)$ for values of n from 1 to 12.

Solution.   a) The factors of 5 are 1 and 5.

        Since there are two factors, $f(5) = 2$.

        The factors of 6 are 1, 2, 3, and 6.

        Since there are four factors, $f(6) = 4$.

        The factors of 9 are 1, 3, and 9.

        Since there are three factors, $f(9) = 3$.

    b) Make a table of values and draw the graph.

Factors of natural numbers

n	1	2	3	4	5	6	7	8	9	10	11	12
$f(n)$	1	2	2	3	2	4	2	4	3	4	2	6

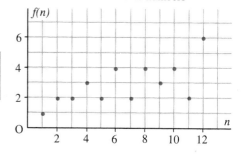

EXERCISES 1-2

1. If $f(x) = x^2 + 3$, find:
   a) $f(1)$ b) $f(2)$ c) $f(0)$ d) $f(-1)$ e) $f(-2)$ f) $f(-3)$.

2. If $g(x) = 1 - 2x$, find:
   a) $g(1)$ b) $g(-2)$ c) $g(-5)$ d) $g(0)$ e) $g(6)$ f) $g\left(-\frac{1}{2}\right)$.

3. Find $f(-3)$, $f(4)$, and $f(-0.5)$ for each function.
   a) $f(x) = 5x - 2$ b) $f(x) = x^2 - 5$ c) $f(x) = x^2 + x$

4. For each graph of $y = f(x)$, find $f(-4)$, $f(0)$, and $f(6)$.
   a)   b)

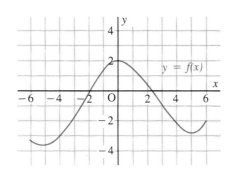
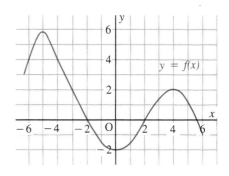

5. If $f(x) = 3x^2 - 5x + 2$, find:
   a) $f(4)$ b) $f(-2)$ c) $f(1)$ d) $f(-1)$ e) $f(0)$ f) $f(1.5)$.

6. If $g(x) = -2x^2 + 3x - 6$, find:
   a) $g(1)$ b) $g(2)$ c) $g(-2)$ d) $g(0)$ e) $g(-4)$ f) $g(-0.5)$.

7. Let n be a positive integer, and let $d(n)$ represent the number of digits of n. For example, $d(15) = 2$, since 15 has 2 digits.
   a) Find. i) $d(6)$ ii) $d(47)$ iii) $d(803)$
   b) How many positive integers n are there such that:
      i) $d(n) = 1$ ii) $d(n) = 2$ iii) $d(n) = 3$?

8. If $f(x) = 2x + 1$, and $g(x) = 3 - x$, find:
   a) $f(a)$ b) $f(3a)$ c) $f(1 + y)$ d) $f(x + 1)$
   e) $g(y)$ f) $g(2 - y)$ g) $g(z - 1)$ h) $g(2x - 3)$
   i) $2f(x)$ j) $5g(n)$ k) $-3f(x)$ l) $-2g(a)$.

9. Graph each function and state its domain and range.
   a) $f(x) = 2x + 1$ b) $f(x) = x^2$ c) $f(x) = \sqrt{x}$

10. If $f(x) = 2 - 5x$, and $g(x) = x^2 - x - 1$, evaluate each expression.
    a) $f(1) + g(1)$ b) $f(2) + g(2)$ c) $f(-1) + g(-1)$
    d) $f(-1) - g(-1)$ e) $f(-3) - g(-3)$ f) $f(0) - g(0)$

11. If $g(x) = \dfrac{x + 1}{x - 1}$, $x \neq 1$, find:

    a) $g(2x)$ b) $g(-x)$ c) $-g(x)$ d) $g\left(\dfrac{1}{x}\right)$

    e) $g(x + 1)$ f) $-g(x - 1)$ g) $g(2x + 1)$ h) $g(1 - 2x)$.

12. If $f(x) = 2x - 3$, and $g(x) = 1 - 4x$, find a value of x that satisfies each equation.
    a) $f(x) = g(x)$ b) $f(x) = g(-x)$ c) $f(-x) = g(x)$
    d) $f(x + 1) = g(x - 1)$ e) $f(2x - 1) = g(x + 1)$

13. If $f(x) = 3x - 5$, solve each equation.
    a) $f(x) = 0$ b) $f(x) = 1$ c) $f(x) = -4$
    d) $f(x) = f(-x)$ e) $f(x + 1) = f(x - 1)$

14. Let n be a positive integer, and let $s(n)$ represent the sum of the digits of n.
    a) Find.   i) $s(15)$ ii) $s(68)$ iii) $s(509)$
    b) Give examples of positive integers n such that: i) $s(n) = 1$ ii) $s(n) = 2$.
    c) How many solutions do these equations have?
        i) $s(n) = 1$ ii) $s(n) = 2$

Ⓒ

15. If $f(x) = 1 + \dfrac{1}{x}$, prove that $f(x) + f\left(\dfrac{1}{x}\right) = f(x)f\left(\dfrac{1}{x}\right)$.

16. Let n be a positive integer, and let $f(n)$ represent the number of different prime factors of n.
    a) Find.   i) $f(1)$ ii) $f(6)$ iii) $f(9)$ iv) $f(20)$
    b) What is the least number n such that: i) $f(n) = 3$ ii) $f(n) = 4$?

17. Let n be a natural number, and let $g(n)$ be the largest factor of n, other than n.
    a) Explain why $g(n) \leqslant \dfrac{1}{2}n$ for all values of n.
    b) Give an example of a natural number n such that:
        i) $g(n) = \dfrac{1}{2}n$ ii) $g(n) < \dfrac{1}{2}n$.

18. $f(x)$ is a function with the following properties.
    ● The domain of $f(x)$ is the set of real numbers.
    ● $f(0) = 0$
    ● $f(x + 1) = f(x) + 2x + 1$ for all real values of x
    a) Find.   i) $f(1), f(2), f(3), f(4)$
                ii) $f(-1), f(-2), f(-3), f(-4)$
    b) Describe the function $f(x)$.

19. Given $f(x) = 2^x$, show that:
    a) $f(x)f(y) = f(x + y)$ b) $f(nx) = [f(x)]^n$, where $n \in N$.

20. In *Exercise 19*, find another example of a function $f(x)$ such that
    $f(x)f(y) = f(x + y)$ and $f(nx) = [f(x)]^n$, $n \in N$.

MATHEMATICS AROUND US

The Waggle Dance of Honeybees

In 1973, Karl von Frisch received a Nobel Prize for his research in animal behaviour. One of his discoveries concerns a method used by honeybees to communicate the location of a food source to other bees inside a hive. Von Frisch observed bees returning to the hive when they had discovered a food source. Shortly after a bee returned, hundreds of bees left the hive, and went directly to the food source, although the bee which had found the food remained inside the hive. Somehow, the bee had informed the others where the food was located.

By marking the bees with paint, and using glass-walled hives, von Frisch learned how they do this. The bee which found the food performs a dance on the honeycomb inside the hive. It follows a figure-8 pattern and wags its body in the central part. Von Frisch observed that:

- the orientation of the central portion indicates the direction of the food source,
- the speed of the dance indicates the distance to the food.

Von Frisch made thousands of observations, comparing the speeds of the bees' dances with the distances to the food, and summarized his results on a graph like the one shown.

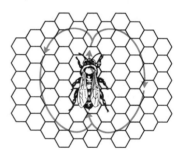

QUESTIONS

1. If the food is 1 km away, how many complete cycles does the bee make in 15 s? in 1 min?

2. If the bee makes 10 complete cycles in one minute, how far away is the food?

3. How would the graph differ if it were drawn to show the number of complete cycles in one minute instead of 15 s?

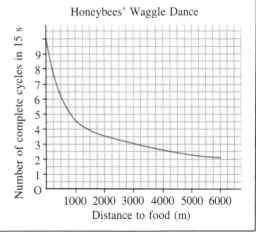

Honeybees' Waggle Dance

1-3 COMPOSITION OF FUNCTIONS

Consider the problem of expressing the cost of fuel, when taking a trip by car, as a function of the distance driven.

The cost of fuel, C cents, is a function of the amount of fuel consumed. If fuel costs 50 ¢/L, the cost for x litres of fuel is given by this equation.

$$C = 50x \ldots \text{①}$$

The amount of fuel consumed is a function of the distance driven. If the car consumes fuel at the rate of 8.0 L/100 km, then in travelling d kilometres the amount of fuel consumed is given by this equation.

$$x = 0.080d \ldots \text{②}$$

We can express the cost of fuel as a function of the distance driven by substituting $0.080d$ for x in ①.

$$C = 50x$$
$$= 50(0.080d)$$
$$C = 4.0d \ldots \text{③}$$

The cost of fuel to drive a distance of d kilometres is $C = 4.0d$, or 4 cents per kilometre.

When two functions are applied in succession, the resulting function is called the *composite* of the two given functions. The function described by equation ③ is the composite of the functions described by equations ① and ②.

Function composition can be illustrated with mapping diagrams.

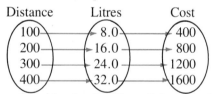

Consider the functions $f(x) = 2x + 3$ and $g(x) = x^2 - 1$. There are two different ways to form the composite of these functions.

Apply f first and g second

Double and add 3, then . . . square and subtract 1.

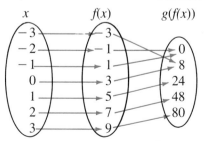

Apply g first and f second

Square and subtract 1, then . . . double and add 3.

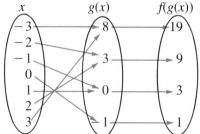

The composite function relates the numbers in the first set to those in the third, and is written as $g(f(x))$, or $g \circ f(x)$. We say, "g of f of x".

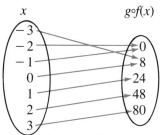

To express $g \circ f(x)$ as a function of x, substitute $f(x)$ for x in $g(x)$.

$$g(x) = x^2 - 1$$

$$g(f(x)) = (f(x))^2 - 1$$
$$= (2x + 3)^2 - 1$$
$$= 4x^2 + 12x + 9 - 1$$
$$= 4x^2 + 12x + 8$$

In this case, the composite function is written as $f(g(x))$, or $f \circ g(x)$.

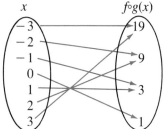

To express $f \circ g(x)$ as a function of x, substitute $g(x)$ for x in $f(x)$.

$$f(x) = 2x + 3$$

$$f(g(x)) = 2g(x) + 3$$
$$= 2(x^2 - 1) + 3$$
$$= 2x^2 - 2 + 3$$
$$= 2x^2 + 1$$

Example 1. Given $f(x) = 3x - 5$ and $g(x) = x^2 - x$
a) Find $f \circ g(3)$ and $g \circ f(3)$.
b) Express $f \circ g(x)$ and $g \circ f(x)$ as functions of x.

Solution. a)

$$g(x) = x^2 - x$$
$$g(3) = 3^2 - 3$$
$$= 6$$
$$f \circ g(3) = f(g(3))$$
$$= f(6)$$
$$= 3(6) - 5$$
$$= 18 - 5$$
$$= 13$$

$$f(x) = 3x - 5$$
$$f(3) = 3(3) - 5$$
$$= 4$$
$$g \circ f(3) = g(f(3))$$
$$= g(4)$$
$$= 4^2 - 4$$
$$= 16 - 4$$
$$= 12$$

b)

$$f \circ g(x) = f(g(x))$$
$$= 3(g(x)) - 5$$
$$= 3(x^2 - x) - 5$$
$$= 3x^2 - 3x - 5$$

$$g \circ f(x) = g(f(x))$$
$$= (f(x))^2 - f(x)$$
$$= (3x - 5)^2 - (3x - 5)$$
$$= 9x^2 - 30x + 25 - 3x + 5$$
$$= 9x^2 - 33x + 30$$

When finding the composite of two functions, it is not necessary for the functions to be different. In other words, we can find the composite of a function with itself.

Example 2. Given $f(x) = 3x - 1$, find $f \circ f(x)$.

Solution.

$$f \circ f(x) = f(f(x))$$
$$= 3(f(x)) - 1$$
$$= 3(3x - 1) - 1$$
$$= 9x - 4$$

EXERCISES 1-3

Ⓐ

1. Given $f(x) = 2x + 1$ and $g(x) = 3x + 1$, find:
   a) $f(3)$ b) $g(f(3))$ c) $g(3)$ d) $f(g(3))$.

2. For the functions in *Exercise 1*, find $g(f(x))$ and $f(g(x))$.

3. Given $f(x) = x^2 + 1$ and $g(x) = 2x$, find:
   a) $f(2)$ b) $g \circ f(2)$ c) $g(2)$ d) $f \circ g(2)$.

4. For the functions in *Exercise 3*, find $g \circ f(x)$ and $f \circ g(x)$.

5. Find $f(g(x))$ and $g(f(x))$ for each pair of functions.
   a) $f(x) = 3x + 4$; $g(x) = -2x + 5$
   b) $f(x) = x^2 + 5x$; $g(x) = 2x + 1$
   c) $f(x) = 2x^2 - 3x + 1$; $g(x) = 7 - 4x$

6. Given $f(x) = 3x^2 - 1$, find $f(g(x))$ and $g(f(x))$ for each function $g(x)$.
   a) $g(x) = x + 2$ b) $g(x) = 1 - 2x$ c) $g(x) = x^2$

   d) $g(x) = x^2 + x$ e) $g(x) = 2x^2 - 3x$ f) $g(x) = \dfrac{1}{x}, x \neq 0$

7. The area A of a circle is a function of its radius r, where $A = \pi r^2$. Express the area as a function of the diameter d.

8. The volume V of a sphere is a function of its radius r, where $V = \dfrac{4}{3}\pi r^3$. Express the volume as a function of the diameter d.

Ⓑ

9. Given $f(x) = 2x - 1$ and $g(x) = 1 - 3x$, find:
   a) $f(g(2))$ b) $g(f(2))$ c) $f(f(2))$ d) $g(g(2))$.

10. For the functions in *Exercise 9*, find:
    a) $f(g(x))$ b) $g(f(x))$ c) $f(f(x))$ d) $g(g(x))$.

11. Given $f(x) = 4 - x$ and $g(x) = x^2 + x$, find:
    a) $f \circ g(-1)$ b) $g \circ f(-1)$ c) $f \circ f(-1)$ d) $g \circ g(-1)$.

12. For the functions in *Exercise 11*, find:
    a) $f \circ g(x)$ b) $g \circ f(x)$ c) $f \circ f(x)$ d) $g \circ g(x)$.

13. For each pair of functions, find $f \circ g(x)$, $g \circ f(x)$, $f \circ f(x)$, and $g \circ g(x)$.
    a) $f(x) = \sqrt{x}$; $g(x) = 4 - 2x$ b) $f(x) = \sqrt{2x}$; $g(x) = 1 + 3x$

    c) $f(x) = \dfrac{x}{x + 1}$; $g(x) = x^2 - 1$ d) $f(x) = 2^x$; $g(x) = 3x - 4$

14. The area A and perimeter P of a square are functions of its side length S. Express the area as a function of the perimeter.

15. Express the area of a square as a function of the length of its diagonal.

16. Given $f(x) = \dfrac{1}{x}$ and $g(x) = x^2$, show that $f(g(x)) = g(f(x))$.

17. Given $f(x) = 1 - x$ and $g(x) = \dfrac{x}{1 - x}$, $x \neq 1$

   a) Show that $g(f(x)) = \dfrac{1}{g(x)}$.

   b) Does $f(g(x)) = \dfrac{1}{f(x)}$?

18. The temperature of the Earth's crust is a linear function of the depth below the surface. An equation expressing the relationship is $T = 0.01d + 20$. T is the temperature in degrees Celsius, and d is the depth in metres. If you go down the shaft in an elevator at the rate of 5 m/s, express the temperature as a function of the time of travel t seconds.

19. For each pair of functions, determine values of x such that $f(g(x)) = g(f(x))$.

   a) $f(x) = 2x + 3$; $g(x) = x^2 - x + 3$

   b) $f(x) = \dfrac{1}{x}$; $g(x) = 2x + 1$

20. From the functions listed in the box, find two whose composite function is $h(x)$.

   a) $h(x) = (x + 1)^2$

   b) $h(x) = \sqrt{x - 3}$

   c) $h(x) = x^2 - 6x + 9$

   d) $h(x) = x - 2$

   $$e(x) = x - 3 \qquad f(x) = x^2$$
   $$g(x) = \sqrt{x} \qquad k(x) = x + 1$$

21. Find two functions whose composite function is $k(x)$.

   a) $k(x) = x^6 + 2x^3 + 1$

   b) $k(x) = (x - 4)^2 + 3(x - 4) + 4$

   c) $k(x) = \sqrt{3x - 2}$

   d) $k(x) = \dfrac{1}{x + 3}$

22. Given $f(x) = x - 3$ and $g(x) = \sqrt{x}$, find:

   a) $f \circ g(x)$

   b) the domain of $f \circ g(x)$

   c) the range of $f \circ g(x)$

   d) $g \circ f(x)$

   e) the domain of $g \circ f(x)$

   f) the range of $g \circ f(x)$.

23. Given $f(x) = x^2 + 1$ and $g(x) = \sqrt{x - 1}$, find:

   a) $f \circ g(x)$

   b) the domain of $f \circ g(x)$

   c) the range of $f \circ g(x)$

   d) $g \circ f(x)$

   e) the domain of $g \circ f(x)$

   f) the range of $g \circ f(x)$.

24. Find $f(f(x))$ for each function.

   a) $f(x) = \dfrac{1}{1 - x}$, $x \neq 1$

   b) $f(x) = \dfrac{x - 1}{x + 1}$, $x \neq -1$

Ⓒ

25. Given $f(x) = 2x + 1$

   a) Find. i) $f \circ f(x)$ ii) $f \circ f \circ f(x)$ iii) $f \circ f \circ f \circ f(x)$

   b) On the basis of the results in part a), predict what these functions would be.

   i) $f \circ f \circ f \circ f \circ f(x)$

   ii) $f \circ f \circ f \circ \ldots \circ f(x)$ (n functions)

26. Repeat *Exercise 25* using $f(x) = \dfrac{x}{x + 1}$, $x \neq -1$.

27. Given $f(x) = ax + b$, $g(x) = cx + d$, and $f(g(x)) = g(f(x))$, how are a, b, c, and d related?

COMPUTER POWER

Graphing Functions

A computer is ideally suited for graphing functions, since it can rapidly calculate the values of a function for many values of *x*. The graph can be displayed on the computer screen or printed on paper. The most primitive programs plot symbols on the screen, which normally consists of about 20 rows of 40 characters each. The program below is of this type, and can be used on almost any computer. For more accurate graphs, other programs must be used, but the commands are specific to particular computers.

This program can be used to obtain an approximation to the graph of any function that can be defined by an equation. When the program is run, the computer asks for the first and last values of *x* to be used in the table of values. To reduce the length of the program, it is necessary that the first value be negative, and the second value positive. Also, the least and greatest *y*-values desired must be entered. Once again, the first must be negative, and the second positive.

To get the graph of $y = x^3 - 12x + 8$, delete the brace brackets which precede and follow the equation in the line that follows {UNCOMMENT ONE OF THESE LINES}.

```
LABEL 250;
VAR
  P : ARRAY [1..40,1..22] OF CHAR;
  S,CH : CHAR;
  X1,X2,Y1,Y2,XT : REAL;
  XAXIS,YAXIS,X,Y,I,XI :
  INTEGER;
BEGIN  { FUNCTION GRAPHS }
        WRITELN('FIRST AND LAST
        X-VALUES? ');
        READ(X1,X2); WRITELN;
        WRITELN('LEAST AND
        GREATEST Y-VALUES? ');
```

```
READ(Y1,Y2); WRITELN;
WRITELN('WHAT PLOTTING
SYMBOL DO YOU WANT? ');
S := READKEY; WRITELN;
XAXIS := TRUNC(22-(Y1*22
/ (Y2-Y1)));
YAXIS := TRUNC((-X1*40 /
(X2-X1)));
FOR X := 1 TO 40 DO BEGIN
  FOR Y := 1 TO 22 DO BEGIN
    P[X,Y] := CHR(32);
  END;
END;
FOR X := 1 TO 40 DO
P[X,XAXIS] := CHR(46);
FOR Y := 1 TO 22 DO
P[YAXIS,Y] := CHR(46);
XT := X1;
I := 0;
REPEAT
  I := SUCC(I);
  { UNCOMMENT ONE OF THESE
LINES }
  { Y := TRUNC((XT*XT*XT) -
12 * XT + 8); }
  { Y := TRUNC(XT * XT - 4 *
XT); }
  { Y := 1 SHL TRUNC(XT); }
  { Y := TRUNC(ABS(2 * XT
+ 1)); }
  { IF (XT + 3 < 0) THEN GOTO
250; Y := TRUNC(SQRT(XT +
3)); }
  IF (Y >= Y1) AND (Y<=Y2)
THEN
    P[I,TRUNC(22-((Y-Y1)
    * 22 / (Y2-Y1)))] := S;
250:  XT := XT + ((X2 - X1) /
39);
UNTIL XT >= X2;
FOR Y := 1 TO 22 DO BEGIN
  FOR X := 1 TO 40 DO BEGIN
    CH := P [X,Y];
    WRITE(CH);
  END;
  WRITELN;
END;
CH := READKEY;
END.
```

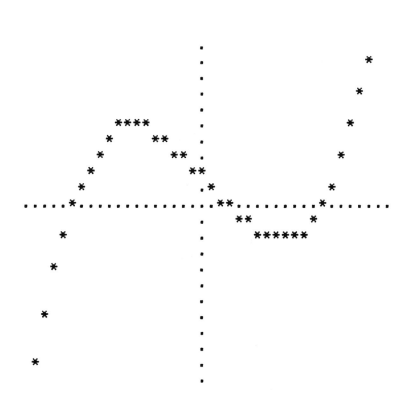

The sample output shows this function graphed for values of *x* between −5 and 5, with values of *y* between −50 and 50.

```
FIRST AND LAST X-VALUES? -5,5
LEAST AND GREATEST Y-VALUES? -50,50
WHAT PLOTTING SYMBOL DO YOU WANT? *
```

The program allows you to graph 4 other functions: $y = x^2 − 4x$; $y = 2^x$; $y = |2x + 1|$; $y = \sqrt{x + 3}$. Replace the brace brackets around the line representing $y = x^3 − 12x + 8$ and delete the brackets around the function selected. To graph any other function, insert its equation in the program without the brace brackets.

Error messages will result if values of *x* for which the function is not defined are used. For example, with reciprocal functions, a denominator of 0 must be avoided. Similarly, with square root functions, square roots of negative numbers must be avoided.

1-4 THE INVERSE OF A FUNCTION

Consider the functions $y = f(x)$ and $y = g(x)$ represented by the following mapping diagrams.

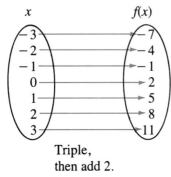

Triple,
then add 2.

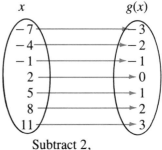

Subtract 2,
then divide by 3.

The diagram on the right reverses the mapping of the diagram on the left, and vice versa. The ordered pairs of the function $y = g(x)$ are obtained by interchanging the members of the ordered pairs of $y = f(x)$. We say that the functions $y = f(x)$ and $y = g(x)$ are inverses of each other.

> The *inverse* of a function is the set of ordered pairs obtained by interchanging the members of each ordered pair of the function.

We can compare the graphs of the functions $y = f(x)$ and $y = g(x)$ by drawing them on the same grid.

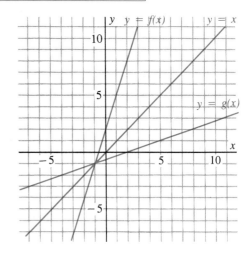

   The graphs appear to be reflections of each other in the line $y = x$. This is what we should expect since the members of the ordered pairs of one function are interchanged to obtain the ordered pairs of the other function.

> **Reflection Property**
> When the members of each ordered pair of a function are interchanged, the graph of the function is reflected in the line $y = x$.

We can prove this reflection property as follows.

Given:
The graphs of $y = f(x)$ and its inverse $y = g(x)$

Required to Prove:
$y = g(x)$ is the reflection of $y = f(x)$ in the line $y = x$.

Analysis:
If we can prove that the line $y = x$ is the perpendicular bisector of the line segment joining two corresponding points on the graphs of $y = f(x)$ and $y = g(x)$, then $y = x$ must be the line of reflection for those graphs.

Proof:
Let $P(a,b)$ be a point on the graph of $y = f(x)$.
Since $y = g(x)$ is the inverse of $y = f(x)$, $Q(b,a)$ is the corresponding point on the graph of $y = g(x)$.
Since each coordinate of the midpoint of a line segment is the mean of the corresponding coordinates of the endpoints,

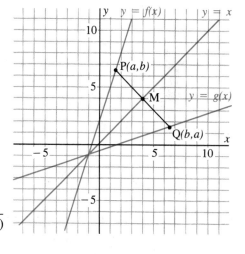

$$M\left(\frac{a + b}{2}, \frac{b + a}{2}\right) \text{ is the midpoint of PQ.}$$

Since the coordinates of M are equal, M lies on the line $y = x$.
Hence, $y = x$ bisects PQ.

Assuming $a \neq b$, the slope of PQ is $\dfrac{a - b}{b - a} = \dfrac{a - b}{-(a - b)}$
$$= -1$$

The slope of the line $y = x$ is 1.

Since their slopes are negative reciprocals, PQ is perpendicular to the line $y = x$.
We have proved that the line $y = x$ bisects PQ, and is perpendicular to PQ.
Therefore, the line $y = x$ is the perpendicular bisector of PQ.

This proves that $y = g(x)$ is the reflection of $y = f(x)$ in the line $y = x$.

When a function is defined by an equation, we can obtain its inverse by interchanging x and y in the equation rather than in the ordered pairs. In the above example, the equation of the function $y = f(x)$ is $y = 3x + 2$. We can find the equation of the inverse by interchanging x and y.

$x = 3y + 2$

It is customary to solve this equation for y.

$3y = x - 2$

$y = \dfrac{x - 2}{3}$

Therefore, the equation of the inverse function is $y = \dfrac{x - 2}{3}$.

The inverse function of a given function $y = f(x)$ is written with a special notation, $y = f^{-1}(x)$. We say, "y equals the inverse function of x." For the function $f(x) = 3x + 2$, we write $f^{-1}(x) = \dfrac{x - 2}{3}$.

Example 1. a) Find the inverse of the function $f(x) = \dfrac{1}{x + 2}$.

b) Show that the inverse is a function and write it using function notation.

c) Determine the domain and the range of the inverse.

Solution. a) Write the equation of the function.

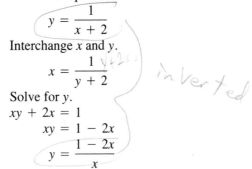

$$y = \frac{1}{x + 2}$$

Interchange x and y.

$$x = \frac{1}{y + 2}$$

inverted

Solve for y.

$$xy + 2x = 1$$
$$xy = 1 - 2x$$
$$y = \frac{1 - 2x}{x}$$

b) For each value of x, only one value of y can be calculated. Therefore, the inverse is a function.

In function notation, the inverse function is $f^{-1}(x) = \dfrac{1 - 2x}{x}$.

c) The inverse function is defined for all values of x except $x = 0$. Therefore, the domain of the inverse function is $\{x \mid x \neq 0, x \in R\}$. The domain of the given function is all values of x except $x = -2$. Since the ordered pairs are interchanged when finding the inverse, this corresponds to the range of the inverse. Therefore, the range of the inverse function is $\{y \mid y \neq -2, y \in R\}$.

Example 2. a) Find the inverse of the function $f(x) = (x - 3)^2$.

b) Graph the function $y = f(x)$ and its inverse on the same grid.

c) Is the inverse a function?

Solution. a) Write the equation of the function.

$$y = (x - 3)^2$$

Interchange x and y, and then solve for y.

$$x = (y - 3)^2$$

Take the square root of both sides, assuming $x \geqslant 0$.

$$\pm\sqrt{x} = y - 3$$
$$y = \pm\sqrt{x} + 3$$

b) We graph $f(x) = (x - 3)^2$ by making a table of values. Then we can graph the inverse by reflecting the graph of $y = f(x)$ in the line $y = x$.

$f(x) = (x - 3)^2$

x	y
0	9
1	4
2	1
3	0
4	1
5	4
6	9

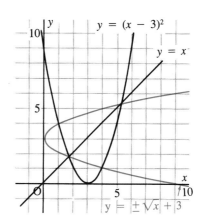

c) The inverse is not a function, since there are two values of y corresponding to a value of x. This is indicated by the term $\pm\sqrt{x}$ in the equation, and by the fact that the graph of the inverse does not pass the vertical-line test.

When the inverse of a function is not a function, we can usually restrict the domain of the given function so that its inverse is a function. Two ways of doing this for the function in *Example 2* are shown below. In principle, there are infinitely many ways of doing this.

Restrict the domain of $y = (x - 3)^2$ to values of $x \geq 3$.
Then, the inverse is $y = \sqrt{x} + 3$.

or Restrict the domain of $y = (x - 3)^2$ to values of $x \leq 3$.
Then, the inverse is $y = -\sqrt{x} + 3$.

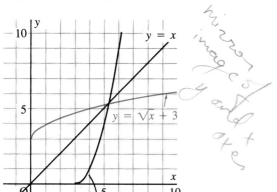

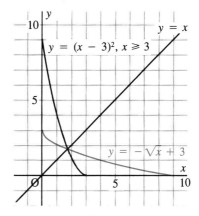

In both cases, the inverse is a function because its graph passes the vertical-line test.

Properties of the Inverse of a Function
- The inverse of a function is obtained by:
  — reversing the mapping diagram
  — interchanging the ordered pairs of the function
  — interchanging x and y in the equation, and solving for y
  — reflecting the graph of the function in the line $y = x$.
- The domain of the inverse is the range of the original function.
- The range of the inverse is the domain of the original function.
- The inverse of a function is not necessarily a function.

EXERCISES 1-4

Ⓐ

1. On each grid, is $y = g(x)$ the inverse of $y = f(x)$?

a) 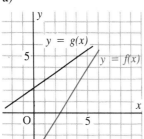   b) 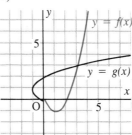   c)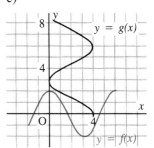

2. Find the equation for the inverse of each function. Is the inverse a function?

a) $y = 2x + 5$ b) $3x^2 - y = 4$ c) $5x + 2y = 10$

d) $f(x) = 4x^2 - 1$ e) $f(x) = \dfrac{x - 3}{x}$ f) $f(x) = \dfrac{2x + 3}{4}$

Ⓑ

3. Graph each function, its inverse, and the line $y = x$ on the same grid.

a) $f(x) = 5 - 2x$ b) $f(x) = \dfrac{1}{2}x^2 - 2, x \geqslant 0$

c) $f(x) = \dfrac{2x - 1}{x}, x > 0$ d) $f(x) = (x - 1)^2 + 2, x \geqslant 1$

4. Find the inverse of each function, and state whether the inverse is also a function. If the inverse is a function, state its domain and range.

a) $f(x) = 2x + 3$ b) $g(x) = 2x^2 - 3$ c) $h(x) = \dfrac{1}{x + 1}$

d) $f(x) = (x + 1)^2$ e) $g(x) = \dfrac{x + 1}{x}$ f) $\{(x,y) \mid y = \sqrt{x - 2}\}$

5. Restrict the domain of each function so that its inverse is a function. Illustrate the function and its inverse on a grid.
   a) $y = x^2 - 2$
   b) $y = 2(x + 1)^2 - 3$
   c) $y + x^2 = 5$
   d) $f(x) = 4 - x^2$
   e) $f(x) = (x - 1)^2 - 1$
   f) $f(x) = 4 - (x - 3)^2$

6. Find the inverse of each function.
   a) $f(x) = \dfrac{1}{1 - x}, \ x \neq 1$
   b) $f(x) = \dfrac{x - 2}{x + 2}, \ x \neq -2$
   c) $f(x) = \dfrac{2x^2}{x^2 - 4}, \ x \neq 2, -2$
   d) $f(x) = \dfrac{1}{3x^2 + 4}$

7. Two functions are described in words. Is each function the inverse of the other?
   a) i) The value of x is increased by 3.
      ii) The value of x is decreased by 3.
   b) i) Twice the value of x is decreased by 1.
      ii) Half the value of x is increased by 1.
   c) i) Twice the value of x is subtracted from 5.
      ii) The value of x is subtracted from 5, then divided by 2.
   d) i) x is reduced by 1, then squared and increased by 3.
      ii) x is reduced by 3, then the square root is found, which is then increased by 1.

8. Given $f(x) = 2x + 5$, find an expression for each function.
   a) $f^{-1}(x)$
   b) $f \circ f^{-1}(x)$
   c) $f^{-1} \circ f(x)$

9. Given $f(x) = \dfrac{x - 1}{x + 1}$, find an expression for each function.
   a) $f^{-1}(x)$
   b) $f \circ f^{-1}(x)$
   c) $f^{-1} \circ f(x)$

10. If $f(x)$ is any function which has an inverse, what do $f \circ f^{-1}(x)$ and $f^{-1} \circ f(x)$ represent?

Ⓒ

11. Show that $f(f^{-1}(x)) = x$ and $f^{-1}(f(x)) = x$, where $f^{-1}(x)$ is the inverse of $f(x)$.

12. Is the inverse of every linear function also a function? If you think it is, explain why. If you think it is not, give a counterexample.

13. Find the inverse of the inverse of each function. Is the inverse of the inverse of a given function always a function?
    a) $f(x) = \dfrac{3x - 5}{2}$
    b) $g(x) = 2(x - 1)^2 + 3$
    c) $h(x) = \dfrac{2x - 3}{x}$

14. Find two ways to restrict the domain of each function so that its inverse is a function.
    a) $g(x) = 2(x + 1)^2 - 5$
    b) $y = \dfrac{4 - x^2}{3}$
    c) $f(x) = |\,2x + 3\,| - 5$

INVESTIGATE

Find examples of functions that are equal to their own inverse functions. What property do these functions have in common?

1-5 REVIEW: QUADRATIC FUNCTIONS

When we drop a stone from a bridge over a river, a certain amount of time passes before we see it hit the water below. The time interval t seconds for a bridge 60 m high can be calculated from this equation.

$$4.9t^2 - 60 = 0$$

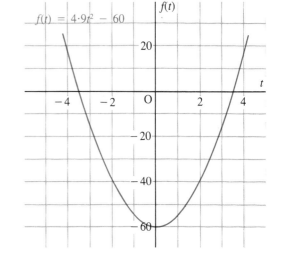

This is an example of a quadratic equation. A corresponding *quadratic function* is $f(t) = 4.9t^2 - 60$. The graph of this function has two horizontal intercepts, which we estimate to be approximately 3.5 and -3.5. We say that the zeros of the function $f(t) = 4.9t^2 - 60$ are approximately 3.5 and -3.5.

We can calculate the zeros of the function algebraically as follows.

$$4.9t^2 - 60 = 0$$
$$4.9t^2 = 60$$
$$t = \pm\sqrt{\frac{60}{4.9}}$$
$$\doteq \pm 3.5$$

The positive root represents the number of seconds for the stone to hit the water.

Example 1. In the open sea, the length of a wave is a function of its velocity. The equation $L = 0.64v^2$ expresses the wavelength L metres as a quadratic function of the velocity v metres per second.

a) If the wavelength is 15 m, what is the velocity?
b) What increase in wavelength is needed to double the velocity?

Solution. a) Substitute 15 for L in $L = 0.64v^2$.

$$15 = 0.64v^2$$
$$v = \sqrt{\frac{15}{0.64}}$$
$$\doteq 4.8$$

If the wavelength is 15 m, the velocity is approximately 4.8 m/s.

b) Substitute $2v$ for v in $L = 0.64v^2$.

$$L = 0.64(2v)^2$$
$$= 4(0.64v^2)$$

If the velocity is doubled, the wavelength increases 4-fold.

The general quadratic function is $y = ax^2 + bx + c$, where $a \neq 0$. Its zeros can be calculated by solving the corresponding quadratic equation $ax^2 + bx + c = 0$. Many quadratic equations can be solved by factoring.

Example 2. Find the zeros of each function.

a) $f(x) = x^2 - x - 12$ b) $g(t) = 4t^2 - 20t + 25$

Solution. a) Let $x^2 - x - 12 = 0$

$(x - 4)(x + 3) = 0$

Either $x - 4 = 0$ or $x + 3 = 0$

$x = 4$ $x = -3$

The zeros of f are 4 and -3.

b) Let $4t^2 - 20t + 25 = 0$

$(2t - 5)(2t - 5) = 0$

$2t - 5 = 0$

$t = 2.5$

The function g has only one zero, 2.5.

In *Example 2a*, the quadratic equation has two different roots. In *Example 2b*, we say that the equation has two equal roots.

Since the graph of every quadratic function is a parabola, we can use its zeros, if they exist, as an aid to sketch its graph.

Example 3. Sketch the graph of the quadratic function $f(x) = 2x^2 + 5x - 12$.

Solution. Let $2x^2 + 5x - 12 = 0$

$(2x - 3)(x + 4) = 0$

Either $2x - 3 = 0$ or $x + 4 = 0$

$x = 1.5$ $x = -4$

The graph is a parabola with x-intercepts -4 and 1.5.

The y-intercept is $f(0) = -12$.

We locate the points $(-4, 0)$ and $(1.5, 0)$ on the x-axis, and the point $(0, -12)$ on the y-axis. The graph is a parabola passing through these points, and with axis of symmetry midway between the two x-intercepts.

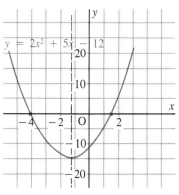

Example 4. a) Write two different quadratic functions with zeros 1 and 4.

b) Graph the functions in part a).

Solution. a) The function $y = (x - 1)(x - 4)$

or $y = x^2 - 5x + 4$

has zeros 1 and 4. Any multiple of this function also has zeros 1 and 4. For example, the function

$y = 2(x - 1)(x - 4)$

or $y = 2x^2 - 10x + 8$

also has zeros 1 and 4.

Example 4 shows that a function is not uniquely defined by its zeros. To determine the function uniquely, some additional information would be needed.

Many quadratic equations cannot be solved by factoring. But all quadratic equations can be solved using the method of *completing the square*.

Example 5. Solve $x^2 + 8x + 2 = 0$

Solution. $x^2 + 8x + 2 = 0$

Isolate the constant term.

$$x^2 + 8x = -2$$

Add the square of one-half the coefficient of x to both sides.

$$x^2 + 8x + 16 = -2 + 16$$
$$(x + 4)^2 = 14$$

Take the square root of both sides.

$$x + 4 = \pm\sqrt{14}$$
$$x = -4 \pm \sqrt{14}$$

The method of completing the square can be used to prove the formula for solving any quadratic equation.

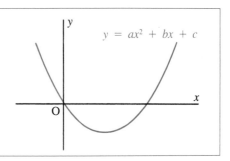

Quadratic Formula
The roots of the quadratic equation
$$ax^2 + bx + c = 0 \qquad (a \neq 0)$$
are $x = \dfrac{-b \pm \sqrt{b^2 - 4ac}}{2a}$.

These are the zeros of the corresponding quadratic function
$$f(x) = ax^2 + bx + c \qquad (a \neq 0)$$

$y = ax^2 + bx + c$

Example 6. Solve. $9x^2 - 12x + 2 = 0$

Solution. $x = \dfrac{-b \pm \sqrt{b^2 - 4ac}}{2a}$

$$= \frac{-(-12) \pm \sqrt{(-12)^2 - 4(9)(2)}}{2(9)} \qquad \begin{aligned} a &= 9 \\ b &= -12 \\ c &= 2 \end{aligned}$$

$$= \frac{12 \pm \sqrt{72}}{18}$$

$$= \frac{12 \pm 6\sqrt{2}}{18}$$

$$= \frac{2 \pm \sqrt{2}}{3}$$

The roots of the equation are $\dfrac{2 + \sqrt{2}}{3}$ and $\dfrac{2 - \sqrt{2}}{3}$.

The equation in *Example 6* has two different real roots. If the equation had been $9x^2 - 12x + 4 = 0$, the solution would differ only in the number under the radical sign, $b^2 - 4ac = (-12)^2 - 4(9)(4)$, or 0. Hence the equation $9x^2 - 12x + 4 = 0$ has two equal roots, $\frac{2}{3}$.

And, if the equation had been $9x^2 - 12x + 5 = 0$, the number under the radical sign would be $b^2 - 4ac = (-12)^2 - 4(9)(5)$, or -36. Since the square root of a negative number is not a real number, the equation $9x^2 - 12x + 5 = 0$ has no real roots.

Hence, the number under the radical sign indicates the types of roots the equation has. This number is called the *discriminant* of the equation.

Properties of Quadratic Equations
- The roots of the equation $ax^2 + bx + c = 0$, $a \neq 0$, are:
$$\frac{-b + \sqrt{b^2 - 4ac}}{2a} \text{ and } \frac{-b - \sqrt{b^2 - 4ac}}{2a}.$$
- The nature of the roots is indicated by the discriminant.
  If $b^2 - 4ac > 0$, there are two different real roots.
  If $b^2 - 4ac = 0$, there are two equal real roots.
  If $b^2 - 4ac < 0$, there are no real roots.

EXERCISES 1-5

1. Solve, expressing the roots to two decimal places.
   a) $6x^2 = 45$ b) $19m^2 = 608$ c) $5.8c^2 - 29 = 0$
   d) $37a^2 = 1776$ e) $2.7t^2 - 13.77 = 0$ f) $0.38x^2 - 5.85 = 0$

2. Solve and check.
   a) $x^2 - 9x + 14 = 0$ b) $m^2 - 2m - 15 = 0$
   c) $x^2 - 14x + 33 = 0$ d) $t^2 + 12t + 32 = 0$
   e) $y^2 + 7y - 18 = 0$ f) $x^2 + 15x + 54 = 0$

B

3. Find the zeros of each function.
   a) $f(x) = x^2 + 5x + 6$ b) $y = x^2 - 4x$
   c) $y = 2x^2 + 5x - 3$ d) $g(x) = 2 + x - 3x^2$
   e) $h(x) = 6x^2 - 7x - 3$ f) $y = 4 - 4x + x^2$

4. Sketch the graph of each quadratic function.
   a) $y = x^2 - 6x + 5$ b) $f(x) = x^2 + 3x - 4$
   c) $g(x) = 3x - x^2$ d) $y = x^2 - 4x + 4$
   e) $y = \frac{1}{2}x^2$ f) $p(x) = 0.2x^2$

5. Solve and check.
   a) $3x^2 - 5x + 2 = 0$ b) $5x^2 + 6x + 1 = 0$ c) $2x^2 - 6x - 1 = 0$
   d) $4x^2 - 24x + 36 = 0$ e) $2x^2 - 13x + 10 = 0$ f) $4x^2 - 4x - 3 = 0$

6. Solve.
   a) $x^2 + 7x - 12 = 0$ b) $x^2 - 8x + 14 = 0$ c) $3x^2 + 5x + 1 = 0$
   d) $4x^2 - 9x + 5 = 0$ e) $2x^2 + 5x + 6 = 0$ f) $5x^2 + 4x + 2 = 0$

7. Find the zeros of each function.
   a) $f(x) = 4x^2 + 20x + 10$ b) $g(x) = 4x^2 + 20x + 21$
   c) $h(x) = 4x^2 + 20x + 25$

8. Write a quadratic equation with the given roots.

   a) $3, 7$ b) $-4, 9$ c) $\frac{2}{3}, -5$

9. Write two different quadratic functions with the given zeros.

   a) $4, -1$ b) $-3, 2$ c) $\frac{3}{5}, -\frac{4}{3}$

10. A quadratic function has zeros 1 and 3. Find the equation of the function if its
    graph has a y-intercept of: a) 8   b) 4.

11. A quadratic function $y = f(x)$ has zeros -1 and 1. Find the equation of the function
    if: a) $f(0) = -2$ b) $f(0) = 1$ c) $f(2) = 12$.

12. The speed with which water flows out
    of a hole at the bottom of a reservoir
    is related to the depth of the water.
    According to Torricelli's theorem,
    $d \doteq 0.05s^2$, where d is the depth of
    the water in metres and s is the speed
    in metres per second.
    a) Solve the formula for s.
    b) What is the speed to 1 decimal place
       of the water if the depth is:
       i) 1 m   ii) 2 m   iii) 5 m?
    c) What happens to the speed if the
       depth is: i) doubled   ii) tripled?

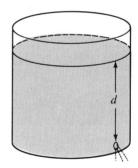

13. In a certain programming language, the instruction CALL -856 executes a delay
    loop of length t microseconds, where $t = 2.5x^2 + 13.5x + 13$, and x is a number
    stored in memory. What number x should be stored to have a delay loop of length:
    a) 1 s   b) 30 s?

14. Find the discriminant of each equation.
    a) $3x^2 + 7x + 4 = 0$ b) $2x^2 + 3x - 8 = 0$ c) $5x^2 - x + 2 = 0$
    d) $4x^2 + 12x + 9 = 0$ e) $2x^2 - 9x - 5 = 0$ f) $3x^2 + 4x + 7 = 0$

15. Which equations in *Exercise 14* have:
    a) 2 different real roots   b) 2 equal real roots   c) no real roots?

16. A square with sides of length 6 cm is divided into 3 right triangles and a larger isosceles triangle. The three right triangles have equal areas.
    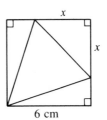
    a) Find the value of x.
    b) Find the area of the larger isosceles triangle.

17. Determine the nature of the roots of each equation.
    a) $4x^2 + 7x - 2 = 0$
    b) $2x^2 - 7x - 15 = 0$
    c) $3x^2 - 8x + 7 = 0$
    d) $7x^2 + 10x - 3 = 0$
    e) $16x^2 + 8x + 1 = 0$
    f) $12x^2 - 9x + 5 = 0$

18. Solve.
    a) $5x^2 + 4x - 1 = 0$
    b) $2x^2 - 8x + 5 = 0$
    c) $3x^2 + 5x + 1 = 0$
    d) $4x^2 + 7x + 5 = 0$
    e) $3x^2 - 8x + 4 = 0$
    f) $2x^2 - 4x + 5 = 0$

19. Solve.
    a) $5x(x + 3) = (3x + 2)(x - 1)$
    b) $(2x + 5)(x - 3) = (4x + 7)(3x - 1)$
    c) $(x + 2)(5x + 1) = 5x - (2x + 1)(2x + 2)$
    d) $(2x + 7)(x + 4) = (3x + 5)(x - 2)$

20. Solve.
    a) $\dfrac{x^2 + 5}{3} - \dfrac{7}{2} = \dfrac{x + 8}{2}$
    b) $\dfrac{4}{x + 1} - \dfrac{1}{x + 3} = \dfrac{2}{3}$
    c) $\dfrac{8}{x} + \dfrac{5}{x + 2} = 1$
    d) $\dfrac{3}{2x + 1} - \dfrac{x + 2}{3x - 1} = \dfrac{x - 3}{2x + 1}$

©

21. In $\triangle PQR$, $QR = 10\sqrt{2}$, $\angle P = 90°$, and D is a point on QR such that PD is perpendicular to QR. If $QD = 4\sqrt{2}$, find the length of PD.

22. In $\triangle ABC$, $\angle C = 60°$; the lengths of the three sides in such a triangle are related by the formula
    $c^2 = a^2 + b^2 - ab$.
    If $AC = 8$ cm and $AB = 7$ cm, find the length of BC. Explain why there are two answers.
    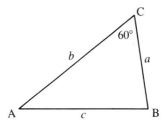

23. In *Exercise 22*, if $\angle C = 60°$ and $AC = 8$ cm, how long would side AB have to be such that there is only one value for the length of BC?

24. Determine whether or not there are any real numbers x and y with the property that the reciprocal of their sum is equal to the sum of their reciprocals.

25. a) Show that the product of two consecutive natural numbers can never be a perfect square.
    b) If n is a natural number, determine the least value of x such that $n + x$ is a rational number and $n(n + x)$ is a perfect square.

PROBLEM SOLVING

A Short History of Problem Solving

Mathematics, a product of the human mind, has been used to solve significant problems of the past and present.

What is the shape of the universe?
For centuries people believed that the world was flat. Eventually it was discovered that the Earth was round and that anyone travelling far enough in any direction would, in time, return to the starting point. In 1917, Albert Einstein made known his General Theory of Relativity which suggests that, like the Earth, the universe is finite. A space traveller covering a distance of 10^{11} light years in any given direction would eventually return to her or his original position.

What is the chance of inheriting a hereditary disease?
Genetics is the study of inherited characteristics. This important field of science relies heavily on a branch of mathematics called probability theory. Using probability, geneticists can predict the likelihood that a particular person will inherit a hereditary disease. They can also predict the likelihood that a contagious disease contracted by a given number of people will generate an epidemic.

Most significant mathematical problems that have been studied in the past have turned out to have important applications. Here is an example.

What curves result when a plane intersects a cone?
About 200 B.C. the Greek geometer Apollonius of Perga wrote a book
which described the curves that result when a plane intersects a cone,
and their properties. The curves were studied for their own sake, and
without concern for any applications they might have.

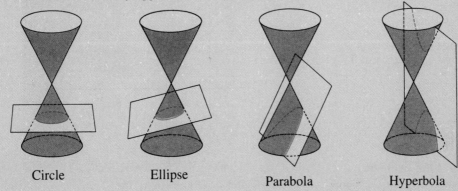

Circle	Ellipse	Parabola	Hyperbola

Who would have thought that 1800 years later the German physicist
Johannes Kepler would use Apollonius' work to describe the orbits of
the planets?

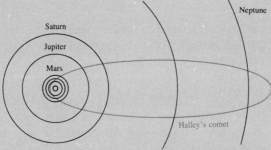

Saturn
Jupiter
Mars
Neptune
Halley's comet

To solve the problems in the *PROBLEM SOLVING* pages of this
book, you may need to use mathematical concepts from the entire cur-
riculum. Strategies you have learned in the past may be helpful. You
may have your own strategies for solving certain problems. Several
problems can be solved in more than one way, using different strategies.
Be persistent — try a problem, set it aside, try it again later, or try
another strategy. Do not be surprised if it takes several days (or even
longer) to solve a problem. Considerable ingenuity may be needed to solve
some of them. Some problems are extremely difficult. Do not be
disappointed if you never solve them.

PROBLEM SOLVING

Don't Make the Problem Harder

". . . mathematics is more than arithmetic and . . . the problem-solving process is more than a single right answer."

Jean Kerr Stenmark

Find the equation of the line which passes through the point of intersection of the lines
L_1: $5x - 3y - 6 = 0$
L_2: $3x + 4y - 12 = 0$

and which also has slope $\frac{1}{2}$.

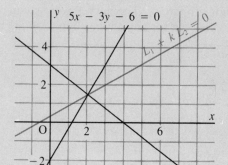

Understand the problem

● We could solve for the coordinates of the point of intersection, and then find the equation of the required line, but the solution will be encumbered with fractions with denominator 29.
● Do we have to know the point of intersection?

Think of a strategy

● According to a property of linear systems studied in earlier grades, when two lines intersect, we can add multiples of their equations together without changing the solution.
● Hence, for any value of k, the equation $L_1 + kL_2 = 0$ represents a line passing through the point of intersection of L_1 and L_2.

Carry out the strategy

● Let $5x - 3y - 6 + k(3x + 4y - 12) = 0$ represent the required line, where k is a constant to be determined.
● Write the equation in the form $Ax + By + C = 0$, and then write an expression for the slope of the line as a function of k.
● Since the slope is $\frac{1}{2}$, you should be able to determine k.
● Substitute back to find the equation of the required line.

Look back

● Check that this method is easier than solving for the point of intersection.
● Does $L_1 + kL_2 = 0$ represent every line through the point of intersection?

PROBLEMS

Ⓑ

1. a) Find a positive number that becomes its own reciprocal by subtracting 1.
   b) Show that the number in part a) also becomes its own square by adding 1.

2. Give some examples of natural numbers which can be expressed as the difference of two perfect squares. Can you find a way of telling whether or not a given natural number can be expressed as the difference of two squares?

3. What fraction of the triangular region is shaded?

4. Here is an arrangement of the natural numbers from 1 to 5: 2 4 5 3 1. Notice that the sum of any two adjacent numbers is composite.
   a) If $n < 5$, prove that it is impossible to arrange the natural numbers from 1 to n such that the sum of any two adjacent numbers is composite.
   b) If $n \geq 5$, prove that it is always possible to arrange the natural numbers from 1 to n such that the sum of any two adjacent numbers is composite.

5. Find the equation of the line which passes through the point of intersection of the lines $7x - 2y + 9 = 0$ and $6x + 5y - 2 = 0$, and which also passes through the point $(5, -1)$.

Ⓒ

6. The product of the first n natural numbers is $1 \times 2 \times 3 \times 4 \ldots \times n$. This product is called *factorial n* and is written $n!$ Find the largest power of 2 which divides 100!

7. How many natural numbers less than 1000 are divisible by 2, 3, or 5?

8. Find the equation of the line which passes through the points of intersection of the circles defined by $(x - 2)^2 + y^2 = 16$ and $x^2 + (y - 3)^2 = 16$.

Ⓓ

9. A line $y = mx + b$ and a point $A(x_1, y_1)$ are given. Determine the coordinates of the point B such that the given line is the perpendicular bisector of AB.

1-6 COMPLEX NUMBERS

Prior to the middle of the seventeenth century, when mathematicians encountered quadratic equations with negative discriminants they dismissed them as impossible or absurd. They considered that the equations had no roots because no meaning was given to square roots of negative numbers. They did not realize that meaning could be given to these quantities by extending the number system.

The idea of extending a number system to include all formally derived roots of equations was one of the important advances in mathematical thinking. Consider these examples.

● The equation $x + 3 = 0$ has no solution in the set of natural numbers. But it does have a solution, -3, in the set of integers.

● The equation $2x + 1 = 0$ has no solution in the set of integers. But it does have a solution, $-\frac{1}{2}$, in the set of rational numbers.

● The equation $x^2 - 2 = 0$ has no solution in the set of rational numbers. But it does have two solutions, $\pm\sqrt{2}$, in the set of real numbers.

Similarly, an equation such as $x^2 + 1 = 0$ has no solution in the set of real numbers. But by extending the number system, we can give meaning to the solution of this equation. We do this by defining the number i with the property that:

$$i^2 = -1, \text{ or } i = \sqrt{-1}$$

With this definition of i, $x^2 + 1 = 0$ has two roots, i and $-i$.

When $x = i$,
L.S. $= i^2 + 1$　　　　　R.S. $= 0$
　　　$= -1 + 1$, or 0
When $x = -i$,
L.S. $= (-i)^2 + 1$　　　　R.S. $= 0$
　　　$= i^2 + 1$
　　　$= -1 + 1$, or 0

Since there is no real number with the property that its square is negative, the number i is not a real number. It cannot be expressed as a decimal, and it cannot be represented by a point on the number line. For these reasons, the square roots of negative numbers were called *imaginary* numbers. This is an unfortunate name because it suggests that these numbers are somehow less valid than the real or decimal numbers to which we have become accustomed. All numbers are imaginary in the sense that they are abstractions.

Once mathematicians had learned to understand and work with this new kind of number, they found that the numbers had many applications in science, engineering, and electronics.

The number i can be used to define the square root of any negative number.

Since $\sqrt{-16} = \sqrt{16 \times (-1)}$
we can define $\sqrt{-16} = \sqrt{16} \times \sqrt{-1}$
$$= 4 \times i$$
$$= 4i$$

If $k > 0$, we define: $\sqrt{-k} = \sqrt{k} \times \sqrt{-1}$
$\qquad\qquad\qquad\qquad = \sqrt{k}i$

This definition permits us to solve quadratic equations with a negative discriminant.

Example 1. Solve. $x^2 - 6x + 13 = 0$

Solution. Use $x = \dfrac{-b \pm \sqrt{b^2 - 4ac}}{2a}$

$\qquad\qquad\qquad a = 1$
$\qquad\qquad\qquad b = -6$
$\qquad\qquad\qquad c = 13$

$$x = \frac{-(-6) \pm \sqrt{(-6)^2 - 4(1)(13)}}{2(1)}$$

$$= \frac{6 \pm \sqrt{-16}}{2}$$

$$= \frac{6 \pm 4i}{2}$$

$$= 3 \pm 2i$$

The roots of the equation are $3 + 2i$ and $3 - 2i$.

In *Example 1*, the roots of the equation are examples of complex numbers. We can check that they satisfy the equation, by using $i^2 = -1$. Check the root $x = 3 + 2i$.

L.S. $= x^2 - 6x + 13$ $\qquad\qquad$ R.S. $= 0$
$\quad = (3 + 2i)^2 - 6(3 + 2i) + 13$
$\quad = 9 + 12i + 4i^2 - 18 - 12i + 13$
$\quad = 9 - 4 - 18 + 13$
$\quad = 0$

Hence, $3 + 2i$ is a root of the equation $x^2 - 6x + 13 = 0$. We can also check the root $3 - 2i$. These two roots are called conjugates, since they differ only in the sign of the term containing i.

• An expression of the form $a + bi$, where a and b are real numbers, and $i^2 = -1$, is called a *complex number*.
• The complex numbers $a + bi$ and $a - bi$ are called *conjugates*.
• The set of complex numbers includes real numbers since any real number x can be written in the form $x + 0i$.

Example 2.   Write as a complex number.
   a) $\sqrt{-9}$ b) $\sqrt{-32}$ c) $(2 + i) + (5 - 3i)$
   d) $i(4 - 5i)$ e) i^6 f) $(1 + 2i)(1 - 2i)$

Solution.   a) $\sqrt{-9} = \sqrt{9 \times (-1)}$ b) $\sqrt{-32} = \sqrt{32 \times (-1)}$
   $\qquad\qquad = 3 \times \sqrt{-1}$ $\qquad\qquad = 4\sqrt{2} \times \sqrt{-1}$
   $\qquad\qquad = 3i$ $\qquad\qquad = 4\sqrt{2}i$

   c) $\quad (2 + i) + (5 - 3i)$ d) $\quad i(4 - 5i) = 4i - 5i^2$
   $\qquad = 2 + i + 5 - 3i$ $\qquad\qquad = 4i - 5(-1)$
   $\qquad = 7 - 2i$ $\qquad\qquad = 4i + 5$
   $\qquad\qquad\qquad\qquad\qquad\qquad = 5 + 4i$

   e) $i^6 = (i^2)^3$ f) $\quad (1 + 2i)(1 - 2i)$
   $\qquad = (-1)^3$ $\qquad = 1 - 2i + 2i - 4i^2$
   $\qquad = -1$ $\qquad = 1 - 4i^2$
   $\qquad\qquad\qquad\qquad\qquad\qquad = 1 - 4(-1)$
   $\qquad\qquad\qquad\qquad\qquad\qquad = 5$

Examples 2e and *2f* show that operations with complex numbers sometimes result in real numbers.

Example 3.   Find two numbers with a sum of 10 and a product of 40. Check the result.

Solution.   Let the numbers be represented by x and $10 - x$.
   Since their product is 40,
   $$x(10 - x) = 40$$
   $$10x - x^2 = 40$$
   $$x^2 - 10x + 40 = 0$$
   $$x = \frac{-b \pm \sqrt{b^2 - 4ac}}{2a} \qquad \begin{array}{l} a = 1 \\ b = -10 \\ c = 40 \end{array}$$
   $$x = \frac{10 \pm \sqrt{(-10)^2 - 4(40)}}{2}$$
   $$= \frac{10 \pm \sqrt{-60}}{2}$$
   $$= 5 \pm \sqrt{-15}$$
   $$= 5 \pm \sqrt{15}i$$

   The numbers are $5 + \sqrt{15}i$ and $5 - \sqrt{15}i$

Check.   Sum: $5 + \sqrt{15}i + 5 - \sqrt{15}i = 10$
   Product: $(5 + \sqrt{15}i)(5 - \sqrt{15}i) = 25 - 15i^2$
   $\qquad\qquad\qquad\qquad\qquad\qquad = 25 + 15$
   $\qquad\qquad\qquad\qquad\qquad\qquad = 40$

   The solution is correct.

EXERCISES 1-6

Ⓐ

1. Write as a complex number.
   a) $\sqrt{-5}$ b) $\sqrt{-49}$ c) $(3 + 2i) - (1 + 5i)$
   d) $i(8 + 3i)$ e) $(2 + i)(5 - 3i)$ f) $(7 - 4i)^2$

2. Show that both i and $-i$ are roots of the equation $x^2 + 1 = 0$.

3. Show that $2 + \sqrt{2}i$ and $2 - \sqrt{2}i$ satisfy the equation $x^2 - 4x + 6 = 0$.

4. Show that $\dfrac{-3 + i}{2}$ and $\dfrac{-3 - i}{2}$ are the roots of the equation $2x^2 + 6x + 5 = 0$.

5. Solve and check.
   a) $x^2 + 4 = 0$ b) $x^2 + 9 = 0$ c) $x^2 + 25 = 0$
   d) $x^2 + 12 = 0$ e) $x^2 + 18 = 0$ f) $x^2 - 2x + 2 = 0$

Ⓑ

6. Write as a complex number.
   a) $2i(3 - 5i)$ b) $(5 - 3i)(5 + 3i)$ c) $(2 - 7i) + (5 + 3i)$
   d) $(7 + 2i)(5 - 4i)$ e) $2i(3i^2 - 4i - 5)$ f) $3i(2 + 5i)^2$

7. Solve and check.
   a) $x^2 + 3x + 5 = 0$ b) $x^2 - 4x + 5 = 0$ c) $x^2 + x + 2 = 0$
   d) $x^2 - 2x + 3 = 0$ e) $x^2 - 5x + 7 = 0$ f) $2x^2 + 3x + 2 = 0$

8. Solve.
   a) $3x^2 - 4x + 2 = 0$ b) $3x^2 - 2x + 2 = 0$ c) $x^2 + \sqrt{2}x + \dfrac{1}{2} = 0$
   d) $x^2 - 2x + 5 = 0$ e) $7x^2 - 4x + 2 = 0$ f) $-7 + 4x + x^2 = 0$

9. Find two numbers which have a sum of 2 and a product of 2.

 INVESTIGATE

Dividing Complex Numbers

To divide $3 + 2i$ by $1 - 2i$ we can use either of these methods.

Using conjugates

Write $\dfrac{3 + 2i}{1 - 2i} = \dfrac{3 + 2i}{1 - 2i} \times \dfrac{1 + 2i}{1 + 2i}$

Simplify the product on the right side and write the result in the form $a + bi$.

Equating real and imaginary parts

Let $\dfrac{3 + 2i}{1 - 2i} = a + bi$

Hence, $3 + 2i = (1 - 2i)(a + bi)$
Simplify the expression on the right side and compare with the number on the left side. For what values of a and b are they equal?

Try other examples. Can these methods be used to divide any two complex numbers?

Review Exercises

1. Graph each function. State the domain and the range.
   a) $y = \dfrac{2x + 1}{3}$
   b) $y = (x - 2)^2 - 3$
   c) $y = \dfrac{x + 3}{x}$

2. If $f(x) = 5x - 2$, find:
   a) $f(-3)$
   b) $f(2a)$
   c) $f(x + 1)$
   d) $f(3n - 2)$.

3. If $f(x) = 4 - 3x$ and $g(x) = x^2 + 2x - 5$, find:
   a) $f(2)$
   b) $g(-3)$
   c) $f(2x^2 + 1)$
   d) $g(x - 1)$
   e) $f(g(x))$
   f) $g(f(x))$
   g) $2f(x) + g(x)$
   h) $g(x) - f(x)$.

4. If $f(x) = 2x^2 - 5x + 1$, solve each equation.
   a) $f(x) = -1$
   b) $f(x) = 13$
   c) $f(2a) = 13$

5. If $g(x) = \dfrac{x + 1}{x - 1}$, $x \neq 1$, find:
   a) $g(3)$
   b) $g\left(\dfrac{1}{2}a\right)$
   c) $g\left(\dfrac{2x - 1}{x}\right)$
   d) $g^{-1}(x)$.

6. Given $f(x) = 3x + 2$ and $g(x) = 2x - 1$, find:
   a) $f(g(2))$
   b) $g(f(-2))$
   c) $f(f(3))$
   d) $g(g(-1))$
   e) $f \circ g(x)$
   f) $f^{-1} \circ g(x)$
   g) $g \circ f^{-1}(x)$
   h) $g^{-1}(f(x))$.

7. If $f(x) = 2x + 5$ and $g(x) = x^2 - 3x + 2$, find:
   a) $f \circ g(x)$
   b) $g \circ f(x)$
   c) $f \circ f(x)$
   d) $g \circ g(x)$
   e) $f^{-1} \circ g(x)$
   f) $g \circ f^{-1}(x)$
   g) $f^{-1} \circ f(x)$
   h) $f^{-1} \circ f^{-1}(x)$.

8. Find the inverse of each function. Is the inverse a function?
   a) $y = \dfrac{7 - x}{3}$
   b) $y = \dfrac{2x^2 - 1}{5}$
   c) $y = \dfrac{3x + 1}{x - 2}$

9. Graph each function and its inverse on the same axes. State the domain and the range of the inverse. Is the inverse a function?
   a) $f(x) = 4 - 2x$
   b) $y = (x - 2)^2 + 3$
   c) $y = 2\sqrt{x + 1} - 2$

10. Find the zeros of each function.
    a) $f(x) = 2x^2 - 5x - 12$
    b) $g(x) = 4x^2 + 8x - 5$
    c) $h(x) = 3x^2 + 14x + 8$

11. Determine the nature of the roots of each equation.
    a) $4x^2 + 5x + 6 = 0$
    b) $5x^2 + 6x - 7 = 0$
    c) $9x^2 + 6x + 1 = 0$

12. Solve.
    a) $6x^2 - 12x + 5 = 0$
    b) $7x^2 + 3x - 6 = 0$

13. Write as a complex number.
    a) $3i(2 + 3i)$
    b) $(3 + 2i)(3 - 2i)$
    c) $7i(1 - 2i)^2$

14. Solve.
    a) $x^2 - x + 3 = 0$
    b) $3x^2 - 7x + 7 = 0$
    c) $2x^2 + 3x + 4 = 0$

2 Polynomial Functions

The Bloedel Conservatory in Vancouver, British Columbia, is an example of a geodesic dome in the shape of a spherical segment. If you know the base radius and the volume of space it encloses, how can you determine its height? (See COMPUTER POWER, page 70, *Question 4.*)

2-1 POLYNOMIAL FUNCTIONS

When we drop a stone into a well, we cannot see it hit the water, but we can hear the splash. The time interval t seconds for a well 100 m deep can be calculated from this equation.

$$0.015t^3 - 4.9t^2 + 100 = 0$$

This is an example of a cubic equation. The corresponding *cubic function* is $y = 0.015x^3 - 4.9x^2 + 100$. Quadratic and cubic functions are special cases of a more general type of function called a *polynomial function*. Here are some other examples of polynomial functions.

Quartic function (fourth degree): $f(x) = x^4 + 2x^3 - 6x^2 + 3x + 1$
Quintic function (fifth degree): $g(x) = 3x^5 + 2x^4 - 5x^2 - 3$

Polynomial equations with a cubic term, such as $x^3 - 12x + 8 = 0$, first appeared in Babylonian tablets dated about 2000 B.C. Although the Babylonians lacked a general technique for solving such equations, they developed numerical methods for solving certain types of cubic equations. During the last four thousand years, a number of different methods have been developed to solve such equations. The most useful method is one that has been employed only recently — in most practical applications, computers are now used to solve polynomial equations.

One method of solving a polynomial equation is to graph the corresponding polynomial function. The zeros of the function are the roots of the equation.

Example 1. Solve by graphing. $x^3 - 12x + 8 = 0$

Solution. Let $y = x^3 - 12x + 8$. Make a table of values for various values of x, plot the ordered pairs (x, y) on a grid, and draw a smooth curve through them.

x	y
-5	-57
-4	-8
-3	17
-2	24
-1	19
0	8
1	-3
2	-8
3	-1
4	24
5	73

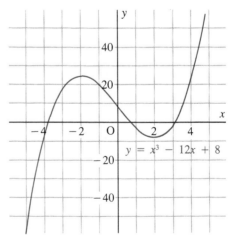

The zeros of the function $y = x^3 - 12x + 8$ are approximately -3.8, 0.7, and 3.1. These are the roots of the equation $x^3 - 12x + 8 = 0$.

Example 2. Solve graphically. a) $x^3 - 12x - 16 = 0$ b) $x^3 - 12x + 32 = 0$

Solution. Compare the given equation with the equation in *Example 1*.

a) Since the constant term in $y = x^3 - 12x - 16$ is 24 less than the constant term in $y = x^3 - 12x + 8$, the table of values can be written directly. Each y-value for $y = x^3 - 12x - 16$ is 24 less than the corresponding y-value for $y = x^3 - 12x + 8$.

b) Similarly, each y-value for $y = x^3 - 12x + 32$ is 24 greater than the corresponding y-value for $y = x^3 - 12x + 8$.

Plot the ordered pairs and draw the graphs.

	a)	b)
x	y	y
-5	-81	-33
-4	-32	16
-3	-7	41
-2	0	48
-1	-5	43
0	-16	32
1	-27	21
2	-32	16
3	-25	23
4	0	48
5	49	97

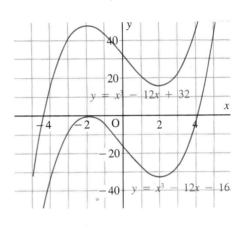

a) The graph of $y = x^3 - 12x - 16$ appears to cross the x-axis at one point and touch it at another. The equation $x^3 - 12x - 16 = 0$ has three real roots, two of which are equal: -2, -2, and 4.

b) The graph of $y = x^3 - 12x + 32$ intersects the x-axis at only one point. The equation $x^3 - 12x + 32 = 0$ has one real root, which is approximately -4.4.

Example 3. Approximate the real zeros of $f(x) = x^4 - 20x^2 + 10x + 30$.

Solution. Make a table of values for the equation $y = x^4 - 20x^2 + 10x + 30$ and graph the ordered pairs.

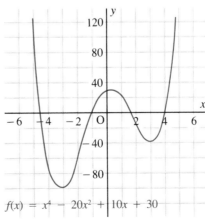

x	y
-5	105
-4	-74
-3	-99
-2	-54
-1	1
0	30
1	21
2	-14
3	-39
4	6

$f(x) = x^4 - 20x^2 + 10x + 30$

The zeros of the function $f(x) = x^4 - 20x^2 + 10x + 30$ are approximately -4.6, -1.0, 1.6, and 3.9. There are four real zeros.

EXERCISES 2-1

(A)

1. Use the graph to estimate the zero(s) of each function.
   a) $f(x) = x^3 + 2x^2 - 10$
   b) $g(x) = -x^3 - 3x^2 + 5x + 16$

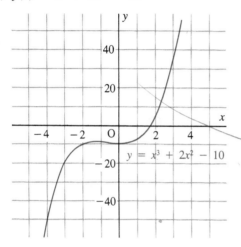

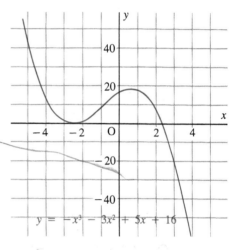

   c) $h(x) = x^4 - 10x^2 - 5x + 5$
   d) $p(x) = x^5 - 10x^3 + 15x$

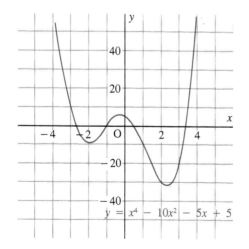

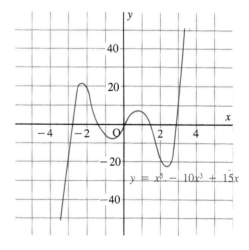

(B)

2. Solve graphically.
   a) $x^3 - 10x = 0$
   b) $x^3 - 10x + 12 = 0$
   c) $x^3 - 10x - 12 = 0$
   d) $x^3 - 10x - 24 = 0$

3. Use a graph to approximate the real zeros of each function.
   a) $p(x) = x^3 - 15x - 10$ b) $q(x) = x^3 + x - 15$
   c) $f(x) = x^4 - 15x^2 + 20$ d) $g(x) = x^4 - 5x^2 - 10x - 25$

4. Approximate the real zeros of each function.
   a) $f(x) = x^3 + 10x - 20$ b) $f(x) = x^3 - 3x^2 + x - 10$
   c) $f(x) = x^4 - 10x^2 + 5x + 7$ d) $f(x) = x^4 - 4x^3 + 16x - 25$

5. In *Exercise 1 b)*, is it possible to tell for certain if there are two equal negative zeros? If there are not two equal negative zeros, then what other possibilities are there for this function?

6. Explain why every cubic function has at least one real zero.

7. Sketch an example of a cubic function which has:
   a) three equal zeros
   b) two equal zeros and a third zero which is less than they are
   c) two equal zeros and a third zero which is greater than they are
   d) only one real zero.

8. Sketch an example of a quartic function which has:
   a) four equal zeros
   b) two pairs of two equal zeros
   c) one pair of equal zeros and two other real zeros
   d) only one pair of equal zeros.

9. Solve the equation given on page 42 to determine how long it is between dropping a stone into a well 100 m deep and hearing the stone hit the water.

10. It is given that the equations $x^3 - 12x + 16 = 0$ and $x^3 - 12x - 16 = 0$ both have two different real roots.
    a) Which of the equations below have:
       i) three different real roots   ii) only one real root?
       $$x^3 - 12x + 20 = 0 \qquad x^3 - 12x + 10 = 0 \qquad x^3 - 12x - 20 = 0$$
    b) For what values of k does the equation $x^3 - 12x + k = 0$ have:
       i) 3 different real roots   ii) 2 different real roots   iii) only 1 real root?

11. A Babylonian tablet gives the values of $n^3 + n^2$ for integral values of n from 1 to 30.
    a) Make a table of values for $n = 1$ to 10.
    b) Use your table to find a root of the equation $x^3 + 2x^2 = 441$.
    c) Determine whether or not the equation $x^3 + 2x^2 = 441$ has any other real roots.

12. Individual packets of juice measure 6.4 cm by 3.8 cm by 10.3 cm. The packets contain 250 mL of juice. The manufacturer plans to introduce a new line of juice in packets containing twice as much juice. If each dimension of the original packets is increased by the same amount, find the dimensions of the new packets.

10.3 cm

6.4 cm   3.8 cm

 **COMPUTER POWER**

Using Factoring to Evaluate Polynomials

When we make a table of values for a given polynomial, we need to evaluate the polynomial for several values of the variable. We can often simplify the calculation by factoring the polynomial before substituting. For example, suppose we evaluate $x^2 + 12x + 27$ for $x = 8$. The calculation could proceed in either of two ways.

Without factoring

$$x^2 + 12x + 27 = 8^2 + 12(8) + 27$$
$$= 64 + 96 + 27$$
$$= 187$$

This solution requires two multiplications and two additions.

With factoring

$$x^2 + 12x + 27 = (x + 9)(x + 3)$$
$$= (8 + 9)(8 + 3)$$
$$= (17)(11)$$
$$= 187$$

This solution requires two additions and only one multiplication.

Since the solution using the factored form involves one less multiplication, it is the more efficient procedure. If a polynomial is to be evaluated for many values of x, it is worth factoring the polynomial before substituting.

Not all polynomials can be factored. However, any polynomial in one variable can be expressed in a *nested form* by successive grouping and factoring. For example, the polynomial $3x^4 - 5x^3 + 7x^2 - 4x + 2$ can be expressed as follows.

$$3x^4 - 5x^3 + 7x^2 - 4x + 2 = (3x^3 - 5x^2 + 7x - 4)x + 2$$
$$= ((3x^2 - 5x + 7)x - 4)x + 2$$
$$= (((3x - 5)x + 7)x - 4)x + 2$$

When $x = 3$, the value of the polynomial can be found as follows.

Using the original form

$$3x^4 - 5x^3 + 7x^2 - 4x + 2$$
$$= 3(81) - 5(27) + 7(9) - 4(3) + 2$$
$$= 243 - 135 + 63 - 12 + 2$$
$$= 161$$

This solution requires calculating the powers, four multiplications, and four additions.

Using the nested form

$$(((3x - 5)x + 7)x - 4)x + 2$$
$$= (((9 - 5)3 + 7)3 - 4)3 + 2$$
$$= ((19)3 - 4)3 + 2$$
$$= (53)3 + 2$$
$$= 161$$

This solution requires four multiplications and four additions.

It is easier to evaluate the polynomial using the nested form than it is using the original form.

1. Write each polynomial in nested form, and then evaluate it for $x = 1, 2, 3,$ 4, and 5.
   a) $5x^3 + 2x^2 - 7x + 8$
   b) $2x^3 - 5x^2 + 3x - 9$
   c) $6x^3 + x^2 - 4x + 12$
   d) $2x^4 + 3x^3 - 5x^2 + 6x - 11$

2. a) Evaluate $f(x) = x^2 + 12x + 11$ for $x = 1, 2, 3, \ldots, 10$
   b) For what value(s) of x is $f(x)$ a perfect square?
   c) For what value(s) of x is each polynomial a perfect square?

   i) $x^2 + 7x + 6$ ii) $x^2 + 8x - 9$ iii) $x^2 - 11x + 24$

3. The program on the next page can be used to compare the time a computer takes to evaluate a polynomial, for a large number of values of x, when it is written in its usual form, with the time it takes to evaluate the polynomial, for the same values of x, when it is written in nested form. For convenience, it is assumed that the coefficient of every term is 3, and that the values of x start at 0 and increase by 0.01. The program can be used for polynomials up to the tenth degree.
   a) When the program is run, the computer prints out the times when the program starts and stops. Run the program and determine how long the computer takes to evaluate a cubic polynomial 250 times using both methods.
   b) Copy and complete the table.

Degree of polynomial	1	2	3	...	10
Time to evaluate 250 terms in original form					
Time to evaluate 250 terms in nested form					

   c) Draw a graph of the results in part b).
   d) The time required to evaluate the polynomial 250 times is a function of its degree. What kind of function does it appear to be?

```
VAR
  CH : CHAR;
  X,Y,XP : REAL;
  C,H,I,K,N : INTEGER;
  STH,STM,STS,STD : WORD;
  ETH,ETM,ETS,ETD : WORD;
BEGIN     { CALCULATING TEST }
    REPEAT
            WRITELN('WHAT IS THE DEGREE? ');
            READ(N); WRITELN;
            WRITELN('HOW MANY VALUES ARE DESIRED? ');
            READ(H); WRITELN;
            WRITELN('ENTER 1 - POLYNOMIAL, 2 - NESTED ');
            READ(C); WRITELN;

            GETTIME(STH,STM,STS,STD);
            IF C = 1 THEN BEGIN
              WRITELN('CALCULATING USING POLYNOMIAL FORM');
              X := 0;
              FOR K := 1 TO H DO BEGIN
                  Y := 3;
                  XP := X;
                  FOR I := 1 TO N DO BEGIN
                      Y := Y + 3 * XP;
                      XP := XP * X;
                  END;
                  X := X + 0.01;
              END;
            END;
            IF C = 2 THEN BEGIN
              WRITELN('CALCULATING USING NESTED FORM');
              X := 0;
              FOR K := 1 TO H DO BEGIN
                  Y := 3;
                  FOR I := 1 TO N DO BEGIN
                      Y := Y * X + 3;
                  END;
                  X := X + 0.01;
              END;
            END;
            GETTIME(ETH,ETM,ETS,ETD);

            WRITELN('STARTED AT',STH,':',STM,':',STS,':',STD);
            WRITELN('  ENDED AT',ETH,':',ETM,':',ETS,':',ETD);
            WRITELN('PRESS S TO STOP, R TO REPEAT');
            CH := READKEY;
            WRITELN;
    UNTIL CH = CHR(83);
END.
```

2-2 DIVIDING A POLYNOMIAL BY A POLYNOMIAL

Dividing a polynomial by a polynomial is similar to long division in arithmetic. Compare the steps in these two examples.

$$
\begin{array}{r}
32 \\
21\overline{)679} \\
63 \\
\hline
49 \\
42 \\
\hline
7
\end{array}
$$

Divisor — Quotient — Dividend

$$
\begin{array}{r}
3x + 2 \\
2x + 1\overline{)6x^2 + 7x + 9} \\
6x^2 + 3x \\
\hline
4x + 9 \\
4x + 2 \\
\hline
7
\end{array}
$$

Remainder

To check, multiply the divisor by the quotient and add the remainder. The result should be the dividend.

$21 \times 32 + 7 = 679 \qquad (2x + 1)(3x + 2) + 7 = 6x^2 + 7x + 9$

Example 1. Divide $2x^2 + 5x - 2$ by $x + 3$ and check. Assume that $x \neq -3$.

Solution.

$$
\begin{array}{r}
2x \\
x + 3\overline{)2x^2 + 5x - 2}
\end{array}
$$

Divide $2x^2$ by x to get $2x$.

$$
\begin{array}{r}
2x \\
x + 3\overline{)2x^2 + 5x - 2} \\
2x^2 + 6x \\
\hline
-x
\end{array}
$$

Multiply $2x$ by $x + 3$ to get $2x^2 + 6x$.
Subtract $2x^2 + 6x$ from $2x^2 + 5x$ to get $-x$.

$$
\begin{array}{r}
2x - 1 \\
x + 3\overline{)2x^2 + 5x - 2} \\
2x^2 + 6x \\
\hline
-x - 2
\end{array}
$$

Bring down the -2.
Divide $-x$ by x to get -1.

$$
\begin{array}{r}
2x - 1 \\
x + 3\overline{)2x^2 + 5x - 2} \\
2x^2 + 6x \\
\hline
-x - 2 \\
+x + 3 \\
\hline
1
\end{array}
$$

Multiply -1 by $x + 3$ to get $-x - 3$.
Subtract $-x - 3$ from $-x - 2$ to get 1.

Since the remainder has a lower degree than the divisor, the division is now complete.

Check.
$$(x + 3)(2x - 1) + 1 = 2x^2 + 5x - 3 + 1$$
$$= 2x^2 + 5x - 2$$

Example 2. Divide $-4x^3 + 6x^2 + 4x - 7$ by $2x - 3$.

Solution.

$$
\begin{array}{r}
-2x^2 \qquad + 2 \\
2x - 3\overline{)-4x^3 + 6x^2 + 4x - 7} \\
-4x^3 + 6x^2 \\
\hline
0 + 4x - 7 \\
+ 4x - 6 \\
\hline
-1
\end{array}
$$

Since the remainder is zero, bring down the next *two* terms.

The quotient is $-2x^2 + 2$ with a remainder of -1.

If a power is missing in the dividend, it must be included using zero as the coefficient.

Example 3. Divide $t^4 - 25t^2 + 62t - 36$ by $t^2 + 3t - 18$.

Solution.

$$
\begin{array}{r}
t^2 - 3t + 2 \\
t^2 + 3t - 18 \overline{)\, t^4 + 0t^3 - 25t^2 + 62t - 36 } \\
\underline{t^4 + 3t^3 - 18t^2} \\
-\,3t^3 - 7t^2 + 62t \\
\underline{-\,3t^3 - 9t^2 + 54t} \\
2t^2 + 8t - 36 \\
\underline{2t^2 + 6t - 36} \\
2t
\end{array}
$$

The quotient is $t^2 - 3t + 2$, with a remainder of $2t$.

When dividing polynomials, we must write both expressions in descending (or ascending) powers of the variable.

Example 4. Divide $-7x - 6 + x^3$ by $x + 1$ and check.

Solution. Write $-7x - 6 + x^3$ as $x^3 + 0x^2 - 7x - 6$.

$$
\begin{array}{r}
x^2 - x - 6 \\
x + 1 \overline{)\, x^3 + 0x^2 - 7x - 6 } \\
\underline{x^3 + x^2} \\
-\,x^2 - 7x \\
\underline{-\,x^2 - x} \\
-\,6x - 6 \\
\underline{-\,6x - 6} \\
0
\end{array}
$$

Check. $(x^2 - x - 6)(x + 1) = x^3 - 7x - 6$

In *Example 4*, the quotient can be factored.
We can write $x^3 - 7x - 6 = (x^2 - x - 6)(x + 1)$
$$= (x - 3)(x + 2)(x + 1)$$
This example illustrates that if one factor of a polynomial is known, other factors can be found by dividing, and then factoring the quotient.

Example 5. Show that $x - 5$ is a factor of $x^3 - 2x^2 - 33x + 90$ and use the result to factor the polynomial.

Solution.

$$
\begin{array}{r}
x^2 + 3x - 18 \\
x - 5 \overline{)\, x^3 - 2x^2 - 33x + 90 } \\
\underline{x^3 - 5x^2} \\
3x^2 - 33x \\
\underline{3x^2 - 15x} \\
-\,18x + 90 \\
\underline{-\,18x + 90} \\
0
\end{array}
$$

Since the remainder is 0, $x - 5$ is a factor of the given polynomial.
Since the quotient can be factored, we can factor the polynomial.
$$x^3 - 2x^2 - 33x + 90 = (x - 5)(x^2 + 3x - 18)$$
$$= (x - 5)(x + 6)(x - 3)$$

It is possible to reduce the amount of writing required when we divide polynomials. For example, we can delete the variables and record only the coefficients. This is called the method of *detached coefficients*.

Example 6. Divide $x^3 - 2x^2 - 33x + 90$ by $x - 5$ using detached coefficients.

Solution.

$$
\begin{array}{r}
1 + 3 - 18 \\
1 - 5 \overline{)1 - 2 - 33 + 90} \\
\underline{1 - 5} \\
3 - 33 \\
\underline{3 - 15} \\
-18 + 90 \\
\underline{-18 + 90} \\
0
\end{array}
$$

The quotient is $x^2 + 3x - 18$, and there is no remainder.

Compare the above solution with that of *Example 5*; the only difference is that the variables have been omitted. The solution of *Example 6* can be compacted even further, by using a procedure called *synthetic division*.

Example 7. Divide $x^3 - 2x^2 - 33x + 90$ by $x - 5$ using synthetic division.

Solution.

$$
\begin{array}{r|rrrr}
-5 & 1 & -2 & -33 & 90 \\
\hline
 & 1 & & &
\end{array}
$$

Write only the constant term of the divisor, and the coefficients of the dividend. Write the first coefficient under the line.

$$
\begin{array}{r|rrrr}
-5 & 1 & -2 & -33 & 90 \\
 & & -5 & & \\
\hline
 & 1 & 3 & &
\end{array}
$$

Multiply 1 by -5, record the product above the line, and subtract.

$$
\begin{array}{r|rrrr}
-5 & 1 & -2 & -33 & 90 \\
 & & -5 & -15 & \\
\hline
 & 1 & 3 & -18 &
\end{array}
$$

Multiply 3 by -5, record the product above the line, and subtract.

$$
\begin{array}{r|rrrr}
-5 & 1 & -2 & -33 & 90 \\
 & & -5 & -15 & 90 \\
\hline
 & 1 & 3 & -18 & 0
\end{array}
$$

Multiply -18 by -5, record the product above the line, and subtract.

$$\underbrace{1 \quad 3 \quad -18}_{\text{quotient}} \quad \underbrace{0}_{\text{remainder}}$$

The quotient is $x^2 + 3x - 18$, and there is no remainder.

The method illustrated above can be used when the divisor is a binomial with a leading coefficient of 1. Synthetic division can be extended to cases where the divisor is any polynomial.

EXERCISES 2-2

Ⓐ

1. Find each quotient and remainder. Assume that the divisor is not equal to zero.
   a) $(x^2 + 7x + 14) \div (x + 3)$ b) $(x^2 - 3x + 5) \div (x - 2)$
   c) $(c^2 + c - 2) \div (c + 3)$ d) $(n^2 - 11n + 6) \div (n + 5)$

2. Divide.
   a) $x^3 - 5x^2 + 10x - 15$ by $x - 3$ b) $m^3 - 5m^2 - m - 10$ by $m - 2$
   c) $3s^3 + 11s^2 - 6s - 10$ by $s + 4$ d) $2x^3 + x^2 - 27x - 36$ by $x + 3$

3. When a certain polynomial is divided by $x + 2$, the quotient is $x^2 - 4x + 1$ and the remainder is 8. What is the polynomial?

4. When a certain polynomial is divided by $x - 3$, the quotient is $x^2 + 2x - 5$ and the remainder is -3. What is the polynomial?

Ⓑ

5. Divide.
   a) $2x^2 - 1 + 5x$ by $x + 1$ b) $3x^2 - 5 + 2x$ by $x - 2$
   c) $25u^2 + 1$ by $5u + 3$ d) $6x^2 - 3$ by $2x + 4$
   e) $8x^2 + 11 - 6x$ by $2x - 3$ f) $9m^2 - 5$ by $3m + 2$

6. Divide.
   a) $c^3 + 13c^2 + 39c + 20$ by $c + 9$ b) $x^3 + x - 8x^2 + 37$ by $x - 2$
   c) $6 + 7n - 11n^2 - 2n^3$ by $6 + n$ d) $x^3 - 12x - 20$ by $2 + x$
   e) $5a^3 - 5a + 3a^2 + 3$ by $a - 1$ f) $m^3 - 19m - 24$ by $m - 3$

7. Divide.
   a) $x^3 - 10x - 15 + 7x^2$ by $x + 8$
   b) $-2a^2 + 29a - a^3 - 40$ by $-3 + a$
   c) $6m^3 + 7m + 29m^2 - 13$ by $2m - 1$
   d) $4s^3 - 13s - 6$ by $2s + 1$

8. Divide each polynomial by $x - 2$ and factor the quotient.
   a) $x^3 - 9x^2 + 26x - 24$ b) $3x^3 - 8x^2 + 3x + 2$
   c) $x^3 + 3x + 2$ d) $5x^3 - 56x + 13x^2 + 20$
   e) $16x^3 - 2x^2 - 51x - 18$ f) $-10x^3 + x - 6 + 21x^2$

9. Divide.
   a) $x^3 + 5x^2 - 2x - 24$ by $x^2 + 7x + 12$
   b) $y^3 - y^2 + 4y + 15$ by $y^2 + 2y - 3$
   c) $10a^4 - a^3 + 11a^2 + 7a + 5$ by $5a^2 + 2a - 1$
   d) $6t^4 + 4t^3 - 13t^2 - 10t - 5$ by $2t^2 - 5$

10. Find each quotient.
   a) $\dfrac{x^3 + 3x^2 - 4x - 12}{x - 2}$ b) $\dfrac{2m^3 - 3m^2 - 8m - 3}{2m + 1}$

   c) $\dfrac{3x^3 + 2x^2 - 11x - 12}{x + 1}$ d) $\dfrac{a^3 - 28a - 41}{a + 4}$

11. Find each quotient then factor it.
    a) $(x^3 + x^2y - 9xy^2 - 9y^3) \div (x + y)$
    b) $(x^3 - 5x^2y - 2xy^2 + 8y^3) \div (x - y)$
    c) $(-8a^3 + 37a^2b - 33ab^2 - 18b^3) \div (a - 2b)$
    d) $(-15m^3 + 47mn^2 + 28m^2n + 12n^3) \div (5m + 4n)$

12. Find the quotient.
    a) $(x^3 + 4x^2 - 3x - 12) \div (x + 4)$
    b) $(6a^3 + 4a^2 + 9a + 6) \div (3a + 2)$
    c) $(9m^3 + 6m - 15m^2 - 10) \div (3m - 5)$
    d) $(4x^3 - 10x^2 + 6x - 15) \div (2x - 5)$

13. One factor of $4x^3 + 15x^2 - 31x - 30$ is $x - 2$. Find the other factors.

14. Two factors of $12a^4 - 39a^2 + 8a - 8a^3 + 12$ are $a - 2$ and $2a + 1$. Find the other factors.

15. Find the quotient.
    a) $(x^4 + x^3 + 7x^2 - 6x + 8) \div (x^2 + 2x + 8)$
    b) $(-2a^3 - 10 + 16a + 39a^2 - 15a^4) \div (2 - 4a - 5a^2)$
    c) $(s^5 - 4s^3 + 19s^2 - 2s^4 + 15 - 31s) \div (s^3 - 7s + 5)$

Ⓒ

16. Find the quotient.
    a) $(x^3 + 1) \div (x + 1)$ b) $(a^5 - 1) \div (a - 1)$
    c) $(s^4 + s^2t^2 + t^4) \div (s^2 + st + t^2)$ d) $(m^4 + 4n^4) \div (m^2 + 2mn + 2n^2)$

17. When $10x^3 + mx^2 - x + 10$ is divided by $5x - 3$, the quotient is $2x^2 + nx - 2$ and the remainder is 4. Find the values of m and n.

18. Find the value of k such that when $2x^3 + 9x^2 + kx - 15$ is divided by $x + 5$, the remainder is 0.

19. Divide $x^3 + (a + b)x^2 + (ab + c)x + ac$ by $x + a$.

20. a) Divide $x^3 + (a + b + c)x^2 + (ab + bc + ac)x + abc$ by $x + a$.
    b) Using the result of part a), predict the quotient when
       $x^3 + (a + b + c)x^2 + (ab + bc + ac)x + abc$ is divided by:
       i) $x + b$ ii) $x + c$.

 INVESTIGATE

1. Let $f(x) = x^3 - 2x^2 + 7x - 4$.
   a) Divide $f(x)$ by $x - 1$, and note the remainder.
   b) Evaluate $f(1)$ and compare with the result of part a).
   c) Find the remainders when $f(x)$ is divided by $x - 2$ and by $x + 3$, and compare the results with $f(2)$ and $f(-3)$.
   d) Based on your results in parts b) and c), state a probable conclusion.

2. Investigate whether similar relations hold for other polynomials.

2-3 THE REMAINDER THEOREM

In some problems involving division, only the remainder is needed. For example, to find the day of the week 60 days from now, it is necessary to divide 60 by 7.

$$
\begin{array}{r}
8 \quad\text{------- Quotient} \\
\text{Divisor} \quad 7\overline{)60} \quad\text{------- Dividend} \\
\underline{56} \\
4 \quad\text{------- Remainder}
\end{array}
$$

Since the remainder is 4, in 60 days the day of the week will be four days after today.

In algebra, we can find remainders without actually dividing. To understand the method, it is necessary to recognize the relations among the dividend, divisor, quotient, and remainder in a division problem. For the division illustrated above, we can write:

$$
\begin{array}{ccccc}
60 & = & (7)\,(8) & + & 4 \\
\downarrow & & \downarrow\ \ \downarrow & & \downarrow \\
\end{array}
$$
dividend $=$ (divisor) (quotient) + remainder

Division Statement
In any division problem,
dividend $=$ (divisor)(quotient) + remainder

Example 1. Given $f(x) = x^3 + 4x^2 + x - 2$, find the remainder when $f(x)$ is divided by $x - 1$. Write the corresponding division statement.

Solution.

$$
\begin{array}{r}
x^2 + 5x + 6 \\
x - 1\overline{)x^3 + 4x^2 + x - 2} \\
\underline{x^3 - x^2} \\
5x^2 + x \\
\underline{5x^2 - 5x} \\
6x - 2 \\
\underline{6x - 6} \\
4
\end{array}
$$

The corresponding division statement is
$$x^3 + 4x^2 + x - 2 = (x - 1)(x^2 + 5x + 6) + 4$$

In *Example 1*, notice that the remainder is a constant, otherwise we could have continued the division. Notice also what happens if we substitute 1 for x in both sides of the division statement.

In the left side, the result is $\qquad$ In the right side, the result is
$$1^3 + 4(1)^2 + 1 - 2 = 4 \qquad (1 - 1)(1^2 + 5(1) + 6) + 4 = 0(12) + 4$$
$$= 4$$

Hence, $f(1) = 4$
Therefore, $f(1)$ is equal to the remainder. In other words, when the polynomial $x^3 + 4x^2 + x - 2$ is divided by $x - 1$, the remainder is $f(1)$.

This is an example of a general result which is true for any polynomial, and is called the remainder theorem.

Remainder Theorem
When a polynomial $f(x)$ is divided by $x - a$, the remainder is $f(a)$.

This theorem is proved below.

Given:
A polynomial $f(x)$ is divided by $x - a$.

Required to Prove:
The remainder is $f(a)$.

Analysis:
If we can write the division statement, then we can use the same reasoning that we used above. We should substitute a for x in the division statement.

Proof:
When $f(x)$ is divided by $x - a$, the division can be continued until the remainder is a constant, r.
If $q(x)$ represents the quotient, then the division statement is
$f(x) = (x - a)q(x) + r$.
Substitute a for x in both sides of the division statement.
In the left side, the result is $f(a)$.
In the right side, the result is $(a - a)q(a) + r$, or r.
Since these two results must be equal, $f(a) = r$
Therefore, the remainder is $f(a)$.

We can use the remainder theorem to find the remainder without actually dividing.

Example 2. Find the remainder when $x^3 - 4x^2 + 5x - 1$ is divided by:
a) $x - 2$ b) $x + 1$.

Solution. a) Let $f(x) = x^3 - 4x^2 + 5x - 1$.
The remainder when $f(x)$ is divided by $x - 2$ is $f(2)$.
$$f(2) = 2^3 - 4(2)^2 + 5(2) - 1$$
$$= 8 - 16 + 10 - 1$$
$$= 1$$
The remainder is 1.
b) Since $x + 1 = x - (-1)$, the remainder when $f(x)$ is divided by $x + 1$ is $f(-1)$.
$$f(-1) = (-1)^3 - 4(-1)^2 + 5(-1) - 1$$
$$= -1 - 4 - 5 - 1$$
$$= -11$$
The remainder is -11.

Example 3.   When $x^3 + 3x^2 - kx + 10$ is divided by $x - 5$, the remainder is 15.
Find the value of k.

Solution.   Let $f(x) = x^3 + 3x^2 - kx + 10$.
The remainder when $f(x)$ is divided by $x - 5$ is $f(5)$.
$f(5) = 5^3 + 3(5)^2 - 5k + 10$
$\qquad = 125 + 75 - 5k + 10$
$\qquad = 210 - 5k$
Since the remainder is 15,
$210 - 5k = 15$
$\qquad -5k = -195$
$\qquad\quad k = 39$

EXERCISES 2-3

(A)

1. Divide, and write the corresponding division statement.
   a) $a^2 - 2a - 13$ by $a + 3$
   b) $x^3 + x^2 + x + 11$ by $x + 2$
   c) $2p^3 + 5p^2 - 2p - 3$ by $p + 1$
   d) $2s^3 - 7s^2 + 16s - 22$ by $2s - 3$

2. Find the remainder when $x^3 + 3x^2 - 5x + 4$ is divided by each binomial.
   a) $x - 1$
   b) $x - 2$
   c) $x - 3$
   d) $x + 1$
   e) $x + 2$
   f) $x + 3$

3. Find the remainder when each polynomial is divided by $x - 2$.
   a) $x^2 - 5x + 2$
   b) $x^3 + x^2 - 2x + 3$
   c) $-x^3 - x^2 + 10x - 8$
   d) $3x^3 - 5x^2 + 2x + 8$
   e) $2x^3 + x^2 + 4x - 7$
   f) $-x^4 - 3x^3 + 2x^2 - 5x - 1$

4. Without using long division, find each remainder.
   a) $(2a^2 + 6a + 8) \div (a + 1)$
   b) $(n^2 + 4n + 12) \div (n - 4)$
   c) $(y^3 + 6y^2 - 4y + 3) \div (y + 2)$
   d) $(-p^3 + 2p^2 + 5p + 9) \div (p + 1)$
   e) $(3m^3 + 7m^2 - 2m - 11) \div (m - 2)$
   f) $(-c^4 + 3c^2 - c + 1) \div (c + 2)$

5. What is the remainder when each polynomial is divided by x?
   a) $x^2 + 3x$
   b) $x^3 - 2x + 8$
   c) $-x^3 - 7x^2 + 4x - 6$
   d) $-x^4 + 2x^2 + 1$
   e) $x^3 - x^2 + 5x$
   f) $-x^4 - 3x^3 + 2$

(B)

6. Find each remainder.
   a) $(2m^2 + m - 6) \div (m + 3)$
   b) $(-a^3 + 2a^2 - 5a + 1) \div (a - 2)$
   c) $(2x^3 + 7x^2 - 3x + 10) \div (1 + x)$
   d) $(n^3 - n^2 + 7n + 4) \div (n - 3)$
   e) $(-3y^3 - 9y^2 + 12) \div (2 + y)$
   f) $(-2x^4 + 3x^2 - 5x + 14) \div (-2 + x)$

7. Find k.
   a) When $x^3 + kx^2 + 2x - 3$ is divided by $x + 2$, the remainder is 1.
   b) When $x^4 - kx^3 - 2x^2 + x + 4$ is divided by $x - 3$, the remainder is 16.
   c) When $2x^3 - 3x^2 + kx - 1$ is divided by $x - 1$, the remainder is 1.

8. When $kx^3 + px^2 - x + 3$ is divided by $x - 1$, the remainder is 4. When this polynomial is divided by $x - 2$, the remainder is 21. Find the values of k and p.

9. When $x^3 + kx^2 + 2x + 9$ is divided by $x - 1$, the remainder is 7. What is the remainder when $x^3 + kx^2 + 2x + 9$ is divided by $x + 1$?

Ⓒ

10. $f(x)$ is a polynomial which leaves a remainder of 3 when it is divided by $x + 2$. Find the remainder when each polynomial is divided by $x + 2$.
    a) $f(x) + 1$ b) $f(x) + x + 2$ c) $2f(x)$

11. When the polynomial $f(x)$ is divided by $x - a$, the quotient is $q(x)$ and the remainder is r. Show that the remainder is equal to each of these expressions.
    a) $f(0) + aq(0)$ b) $f(a + 1) - q(a + 1)$ c) $f(a - 1) + q(a - 1)$
    Illustrate your answers with an example in which $f(x)$ is a cubic polynomial and $q(x)$ is a quadratic polynomial.

12. Without using long division, find the remainder.
    a) $(6x^2 - 10x + 7) \div (3x + 1)$ b) $(-8a^2 - 2a - 3) \div (4a - 1)$
    c) $(-4x^3 - 9x + 10) \div (1 - 2x)$ d) $(6m^3 - 15m^2 + 3) \div (2m + 1)$

13. a) If a fourth-degree polynomial is divided by a quadratic polynomial, would it be possible for the remainder to be: i) a cubic polynomial
    ii)   a quadratic polynomial   iii)   a linear polynomial?
    b) Use the result of part a) to find the remainder when $x^4 + 2x^3 - 5x^2 + x + 3$ is divided by $x^2 + x - 2$.

14. Without using long division, find the remainder.
    a) $(x^3 + 3x^2 - x - 2) \div (x + 3)(x + 1)$
    b) $(2x^3 + x^2 - 4x + 12) \div (x^2 + x - 2)$
    c) $(x^4 - 4x^2 + 2) \div (x - 1)(x + 1)(x - 2)$

15. Find the remainder if the polynomial $f(x)$ is divided by each expression.
    a) $ax + b$ b) $(x - a)(x - b)$

16. If $f(x) = (x - a)q(x) + r$, where r is a constant, what multiples of $x - a$ are closest to $f(x)$? Illustrate your answer with an example in which $f(x)$ is a cubic polynomial and $q(x)$ is a quadratic polynomial.

 INVESTIGATE

The remainder theorem was proved by substituting a for x in the division statement $f(x) = (x - a)q(x) + r$. Investigate what happens if values of x other than a are substituted in this statement. Illustrate your results with specific examples.

2-4 THE FACTOR THEOREM

According to the remainder theorem, if a number a is substituted for x in a polynomial, the value obtained is the remainder when the polynomial is divided by $x - a$. If this remainder is 0, then $x - a$ is a factor of the polynomial. This special case of the remainder theorem is called the factor theorem.

> **Factor Theorem**
> If $x = a$ is substituted into a polynomial in x, and the resulting value is 0, then $x - a$ is a factor of the polynomial.

Example 1. a) Find the remainder when $x^3 - 4x^2 + x + 6$ is divided by $x - 3$.
b) State a factor of $x^3 - 4x^2 + x + 6$.

Solution. a) Let $f(x) = x^3 - 4x^2 + x + 6$.
The remainder when $f(x)$ is divided by $x - 3$ is $f(3)$.
$$f(3) = 3^3 - 4(3)^2 + 3 + 6$$
$$= 27 - 36 + 3 + 6$$
$$= 0$$
b) By the factor theorem, $x - 3$ is a factor of $x^3 - 4x^2 + x + 6$.

The factor theorem provides a simple method for determining whether a binomial of the form $x - a$ is a factor of a given polynomial.

Example 2. Determine which binomials are factors of $x^3 - 6x^2 + 3x + 10$.
a) $x - 2$ b) $x - 3$ c) $x + 1$ d) $x - 5$

Solution. Let $f(x) = x^3 - 6x^2 + 3x + 10$.
a) $f(2) = 2^3 - 6(2)^2 + 3(2) + 10$
$= 8 - 24 + 6 + 10$
$= 0$
Since $f(2) = 0$, $x - 2$ is a factor of $x^3 - 6x^2 + 3x + 10$.
b) $f(3) = 3^3 - 6(3)^2 + 3(3) + 10$
$= 27 - 54 + 9 + 10$
$= -8$
Since $f(3) \neq 0$, $x - 3$ is not a factor of $x^3 - 6x^2 + 3x + 10$.
c) $f(-1) = (-1)^3 - 6(-1)^2 + 3(-1) + 10$
$= -1 - 6 - 3 + 10$
$= 0$
Since $f(-1) = 0$, $x + 1$ is a factor of $x^3 - 6x^2 + 3x + 10$.
d) $f(5) = 5^3 - 6(5)^2 + 3(5) + 10$
$= 125 - 150 + 15 + 10$
$= 0$
Since $f(5) = 0$, $x - 5$ is a factor of $x^3 - 6x^2 + 3x + 10$.

In *Example 2*, we found three factors of $x^3 - 6x^2 + 3x + 10$. The product of these three factors must be $x^3 - 6x^2 + 3x + 10$. This can be checked by multiplication.

$(x - 5)(x + 1)(x - 2) = x^3 - 6x^2 + 3x + 10$

Notice that the product of the constant terms in the factors is $(-5)(+1)(-2)$, or 10. This is also the constant term in the polynomial. This suggests the following property of the factors of a polynomial.

> **Factor Property**
> If a polynomial has any factor of the form $x - a$, then the number a is a factor of the constant term of the polynomial.

The factor property indicates which factors to test when attempting to factor a polynomial.

Example 3. Find one factor of the polynomial $x^3 + 2x^2 - 5x - 6$.

Solution. Let $f(x) = x^3 + 2x^2 - 5x - 6$.

We must find a value of x such that $f(x)$ has a value of 0.

According to the factor property, the numbers to test are the factors of -6: that is, 1, 2, 3, 6, -1, -2, -3, and -6.

Try $x = 1$.
$$f(1) = 1^3 + 2(1)^2 - 5(1) - 6$$
$$= 1 + 2 - 5 - 6$$
$$\neq 0$$

$x - 1$ is not a factor of $x^3 + 2x^2 - 5x - 6$.

Try $x = -1$.
$$f(-1) = (-1)^3 + 2(-1)^2 - 5(-1) - 6$$
$$= -1 + 2 + 5 - 6$$
$$= 0$$

$x + 1$ is a factor of $x^3 + 2x^2 - 5x - 6$.

Therefore, one factor of $x^3 + 2x^2 - 5x - 6$ is $x + 1$.

From *Example 3*, we know that $x + 1$ is one factor of $x^3 + 2x^2 - 5x - 6$. The other factors can be found using either of the following strategies.

Using long division

$$
\require{enclose}
\begin{array}{r}
x^2 + x - 6 \\
x + 1 \enclose{longdiv}{x^3 + 2x^2 - 5x - 6} \\
\underline{x^3 + x^2} \\
x^2 - 5x \\
\underline{x^2 + x} \\
- 6x - 6 \\
\underline{- 6x - 6} \\
0
\end{array}
$$

The other factor is $x^2 + x - 6$. Therefore,
$$x^3 + 2x^2 - 5x - 6 = (x + 1)(x^2 + x - 6)$$
$$= (x + 1)(x + 3)(x - 2)$$

By equating coefficients

One factor of $x^3 + 2x^2 - 5x - 6$ is $x + 1$. Let the other factor be $x^2 + bx + c$. Then,

$$(x + 1)(x^2 + bx + c) = x^3 + 2x^2 - 5x - 6$$

When the product on the left side is expanded, the constant term must equal the constant term on the right side. Also, the term containing x must equal the term containing x on the right side. These terms are found as follows.

The constant term: $(x + 1)(x^2 + bx + \underbrace{c}) = x^3 + 2x^2 - 5x - 6$
                                        $\underbrace{ + 1c }$

$$c = -6$$

The x term: $(\overbrace{x + 1)(x^2 + bx + c}^{cx}) = x^3 + 2x^2 - 5x - 6$
                       $\underbrace{+ 1bx }$

$$cx + bx = -5x$$
$$(c + b)x = -5x$$

Since this equation is true for all values of x, the coefficients are equal.

$$c + b = -5$$
$$-6 + b = -5$$
$$b = 1$$

The other factor of $x^3 + 2x^2 - 5x - 6$ is $x^2 + x - 6$. Therefore,

$$x^3 + 2x^2 - 5x - 6 = (x + 1)(x^2 + x - 6)$$
$$= (x + 1)(x + 3)(x - 2)$$

Example 4.   Factor fully. $x^3 - 6x^2 - x + 30$

Solution.   Let $f(x) = x^3 - 6x^2 - x + 30$.

Since the constant term 30 is much larger than the coefficients of the other terms, we can see that substituting $x = 1$ or $x = -1$ would not give zero.

Try $x = 2$. $f(2) = 2^3 - 6(2)^2 - 2 + 30$
                              $= 8 - 24 - 2 + 30$
                              $\neq 0$

Try $x = -2$. $f(-2) = (-2)^3 - 6(-2)^2 - (-2) + 30$
                                 $= -8 - 24 + 2 + 30$
                                 $= 0$

Therefore, $x + 2$ is one factor of $x^3 - 6x^2 - x + 30$.

The other factor can be found using long division or by equating coefficients. We use the method of equating coefficients.

Let the other factor be $x^2 + bx + c$. Then,

$$(x + 2)(x^2 + bx + c) = x^3 - 6x^2 - x + 30$$

Equate coefficients.

Since the constant term is 30, $2c = 30$
                                                    $c = 15$

Since the term containing x is $-x$, $2b + c = -1$
                                                          $2b + 15 = -1$
                                                          $b = -8$

Therefore, the other factor of $x^3 - 6x^2 - x + 30$ is $x^2 - 8x + 15$.
$$x^3 - 6x^2 - x + 30 = (x + 2)(x^2 - 8x + 15)$$
$$= (x + 2)(x - 3)(x - 5)$$

Example 5. Factor fully. $2x^3 + 7x^2 + 2x - 3$

Solution. Let $f(x) = 2x^3 + 7x^2 + 2x - 3$.
Try $x = -1$. $f(-1) = 2(-1)^3 + 7(-1)^2 + 2(-1) - 3$
$$= -2 + 7 - 2 - 3$$
$$= 0$$
Therefore, $x + 1$ is one factor of $2x^3 + 7x^2 + 2x - 3$.

We use the method of equating coefficients to find the other factor.

Let the other factor be $ax^2 + bx + c$. Then,
$(x + 1)(ax^2 + bx + c) = 2x^3 + 7x^2 + 2x - 3$
Equate coefficients.
Since the term containing x^3 is 2, $a = 2$
Since the term containing x^2 is 7, $a + b = 7$
$$2 + b = 7$$
$$b = 5$$
Since the constant term is -3, $c = -3$
Therefore, the other factor of $2x^3 + 7x^2 + 2x - 3$ is $2x^2 + 5x - 3$.
$$2x^3 + 7x^2 + 2x - 3 = (x + 1)(2x^2 + 5x - 3)$$
$$= (x + 1)(2x - 1)(x + 3)$$

In *Example 5*, since $2x - 1$ is a factor of $2x^3 + 7x^2 + 2x - 3$, substituting $x = \frac{1}{2}$ into the polynomial should give a value of zero.

That is, $f(x) = 2x^3 + 7x^2 + 2x - 3$

$$f\left(\frac{1}{2}\right) = 2\left(\frac{1}{2}\right)^3 + 7\left(\frac{1}{2}\right)^2 + 2\left(\frac{1}{2}\right) - 3$$

$$= \frac{1}{4} + \frac{7}{4} + 1 - 3$$
$$= 0$$

EXERCISES 2-4

Ⓐ

1. Given $f(x) = x^3 + x^2 - 9x - 9$
   a) Show that $f(3) = 0$.
   b) Use long division to show that $x - 3$ is a factor of $f(x)$.

2. Given $g(x) = x^3 + 4x^2 + 5x + 2$
   a) Show that $g(-2) = 0$.
   b) Use long division to show that $x + 2$ is a factor of $g(x)$.

3. Given $p(x) = 2x^3 + x^2 - 27x - 36$
   a) Show that $p(-3) = 0$.
   b) Use long division to show that $p(x)$ is divisible by $x + 3$.

4. If $x + 7$ is a factor of $f(x)$, then what is the value of $f(-7)$?

5. If $f(5) = 0$, then what must be a factor of $f(x)$?

6. Which polynomials have $x - 2$ as a factor?
   a) $x^3 - 3x^2 - 4x + 12$
   b) $x^3 + x^2 - 16x + 20$
   c) $-x^3 + 3x - 2$
   d) $x^4 - 8x^3 + 24x^2 - 32x + 16$

7. Which polynomials have $x + 3$ as a factor?
   a) $x^3 + 2x^2 - 9x - 18$
   b) $-x^3 - 2x^2 + 21x - 18$
   c) $x^3 + 6x^2 + 9x$
   d) $-x^4 - 8x^3 - 14x^2 + 8x + 15$

8. Which of the following polynomials has $x - 2$ as a factor?
   a) $x^3 - 5x^2 - 17x + 21$
   b) $-x^3 - 5x^2 + 2x + 24$
   c) $x^3 - x^2 - 17x - 15$
   d) $x^3 + 7x^2 + 7x - 15$

9. a) Which polynomial in *Exercise 8* has $x + 5$ as a factor?
   b) Which polynomial in *Exercise 8* has $x - 7$ as a factor?

10. If $y^3 + 2y^2 - 5y - 6$ has a value of 0 when -1, 2, and -3 are substituted for y, then what are the factors of $y^3 + 2y^2 - 5y - 6$? $(x+1)(y-2)(x+3)$

11. Determine which binomials are factors of $x^3 - 4x^2 + x + 6$ without dividing.
    a) $x - 2$
    b) $x + 2$
    c) $x - 3$

12. Given $f(x) = x^3 - 3x^2 - 6x + 8$, determine which binomials are factors of $f(x)$.
    a) $x + 1$
    b) $x - 2$
    c) $x - 4$
    d) $x - 1$

13. Given $p(x) = 2x^3 + 11x^2 - 7x - 6$, determine if $p(x)$ is divisible by each binomial.
    a) $x - 1$
    b) $x + 6$
    c) $x + 2$

Ⓑ

14. Show that the first two binomials are factors of the cubic polynomial, and use the results to factor the polynomial.
    a) $a - 2, a - 1; a^3 - 6a^2 + 11a - 6$
    b) $a + 2, a - 2; a^3 + 3a^2 - 4a - 12$
    c) $x + 3, x + 2; x^3 + 4x^2 + x - 6$

15. Determine whether each binomial is a factor of the higher-degree polynomial, without dividing.
    a) $x - 1; x^2 - 7x + 6$
    b) $x + 2; x^2 + 8x + 6$
    c) $x - 2; x^3 - 3x^2 - 4x + 12$
    d) $x - 3; x^3 + 6x^2 - 2x + 3$
    e) $x + 1; x^7 - 5x^4 - 4x + 2$
    f) $2x - 1; 4x^3 - 6x^2 + 8x - 3$

16. Find a linear factor of each polynomial.
    a) $x^3 - 4x + 3$
    b) $x^3 + x^2 + x + 1$
    c) $-y^3 - 19y^2 - 19y - 1$
    d) $x^3 - 27$
    e) $-y^3 + y^2 + y + 2$
    f) $x^3 + 2x^2 + 5x + 4$

17. a) Show that both $x - 1$ and $x + 2$ are factors of $x^3 - 3x^2 - 6x + 8$.
    b) Find another factor of $x^3 - 3x^2 - 6x + 8$.

18. a) Show that both $x - 2$ and $x - 3$ are factors of $2x^3 - 11x^2 + 17x - 6$.
    b) Find another factor of $2x^3 - 11x^2 + 17x - 6$.

19. Three students were discussing their methods of factoring cubic polynomials.

    Scott, "After finding one factor by the factor theorem, I always use long division to get another factor."

    Megan, "I don't like using long division, so I always use the method of equating coefficients."

    Ivan, "I have found a faster method. I try to use the factor theorem three times. If I can get three values of x which make the expression equal 0, then I know what the three factors are."

    Megan, "But that method won't work for all cubic polynomials."

    a) Factor $x^3 - 8x^2 + 19x - 12$ using Ivan's method.

    b) Give two examples which show that Megan is correct.

20. Factor completely.

    a) $x^3 + 5x^2 + 2x - 8$ b) $x^3 + 9x^2 + 23x + 15$

    c) $x^3 + 2x^2 - 19x - 20$ d) $x^3 - 7x - 6$

    e) $5x^3 - 7x^2 - x + 3$ f) $x^3 - 9x^2 + 17x - 6$

    g) $x^3 + 8x^2 + 17x + 10$ h) $2x^3 - x^2 - 13x - 6$

21. Factor completely.

    a) $x^3 - 8x^2 + 17x - 6$ b) $x^3 - 3x^2 - 24x - 28$

    c) $x^3 + 6x^2 - 31x - 36$ d) $x^3 - 28x - 48$

    e) $3x^3 + 2x^2 - 11x - 10$ f) $10x^3 - 21x^2 - x + 6$

    g) $x^3 - 39x - 70$ h) $3x^3 + 4x^2 - 35x - 12$

22. Find k.

    a) $x - 2$ is a factor of $x^3 - 6x^2 + kx - 6$.

    b) $x + 4$ is a factor of $3x^3 + 11x^2 - 6x + k$.

    c) $x - 3$ is a factor of $x^3 + kx^2 + kx + 21$.

ⓒ

23. Is $2x + 1$ a factor of $2x^3 - x^2 - 13x - 6$?

24. Is $x^2 - 1$ a factor of $2x^4 - 3x^3 + 3x^2 + 3x - 5$?

25. Is $x^3 - 6x^2 + 3x + 10$ divisible by $x^2 - x - 2$?

26. Solve by factoring.

    a) $x^3 - 2x^2 - 19x + 20 = 0$ b) $x^3 - 8x^2 + x + 42 = 0$

    c) $6x^3 + 13x^2 - 16x - 3 = 0$ d) $5x^3 - 13x^2 - 56x - 20 = 0$

27. Prove that $x - y$ is a factor of $x^n - y^n$ for all values of $n \in$ N.

28. Prove that $x + a$ is a factor of $(x + a)^5 + (x + c)^5 + (a - c)^5$.

29. Show that for any polynomial $f(x)$ there exists a polynomial $g(x)$ such that $f(x) = xg(x) + c$, where c is a constant.

 INVESTIGATE

Investigate whether or not $x + y$ is a factor of $x^n + y^n$ for all values of $n \in$ N. If it is not, then for what values of n is $x + y$ a factor of $x^n + y^n$?

2-5 SOLVING POLYNOMIAL EQUATIONS BY FACTORING

Although there are formulas for solving cubic and quartic equations, they involve cube and fourth roots, and are too complicated to be of practical significance. There are no formulas for solving polynomial equations of degree higher than the fourth.

Some polynomial equations can be solved by factoring.

Example 1. Solve for x. $x^3 - x = 0$

Solution. The left side of the equation has a common factor.
$$x^3 - x = 0$$
$$x(x^2 - 1) = 0$$
$$x(x - 1)(x + 1) = 0$$
Either $x = 0$ or $x - 1 = 0$ or $x + 1 = 0$
$$x = 1 \qquad x = -1$$

Example 2. Solve for x. $x^3 - 3x^2 - 4x + 12 = 0$

Solution. We recognize that the left side can be factored by grouping because a factor of $x - 3$ remains when common factors are removed from the first two terms and from the last two terms.
$$x^3 - 3x^2 - 4x + 12 = 0$$
$$x^2(x - 3) - 4(x - 3) = 0$$
$$(x - 3)(x^2 - 4) = 0$$
$$(x - 3)(x + 2)(x - 2) = 0$$
Either $x - 3 = 0$ or $x + 2 = 0$ or $x - 2 = 0$
$$x = 3 \qquad x = -2 \qquad x = 2$$

Example 3. Solve for x. $x^3 + 9x^2 + 13x + 5 = 0$

Solution. Since grouping does not produce a common factor, we try the factor theorem.
Let $f(x) = x^3 + 9x^2 + 13x + 5$.
The factors of 5 are ± 1 and ± 5.
By inspection, we see that $f(1) \neq 0$. All the terms are positive and hence cannot have a sum of zero.
$$f(-1) = (-1)^3 + 9(-1)^2 + 13(-1) + 5$$
$$= -1 + 9 - 13 + 5$$
$$= 0$$
Since $f(-1) = 0$, $x + 1$ is a factor of the left side of the given equation. Also, 5 is the last term in the quadratic factor. The quadratic factor can be found by long division, or by equating coefficients.

$$\text{Let } (x + 1)(x^2 + bx + 5) = x^3 + 9x^2 + 13x + 5.$$

The term containing x is $5x + bx$ on the left side, and $13x$ on the right side. Since the coefficients are equal,

$5 + b = 13$

$b = 8$

Therefore, the given equation can be written in the form

$(x + 1)(x^2 + 8x + 5) = 0$

Either $x + 1 = 0$ or $x^2 + 8x + 5 = 0$

$$x = -1 \qquad x = \frac{-8 \pm \sqrt{8^2 - 4(1)(5)}}{2}$$

$$= \frac{-8 \pm \sqrt{64 - 20}}{2}$$

$$= \frac{-8 \pm \sqrt{44}}{2}$$

$$= -4 \pm \sqrt{11}$$

Example 4. Solve for x. $x^3 + 1 = 0$

Solution. The left side of the equation is a sum of cubes.

$$x^3 + 1 = 0$$

$(x + 1)(x^2 - x + 1) = 0$

Either $x + 1 = 0$ or $x^2 - x + 1 = 0$

$$x = -1 \qquad x = \frac{1 \pm \sqrt{(-1)^2 - 4(1)(1)}}{2}$$

$$= \frac{1 \pm \sqrt{-3}}{2}$$

There is only one root, $x = -1$, in the set of real numbers.

Example 5. A rectangular piece of cardboard measuring 10 cm by 8 cm is made into an open box by cutting squares from the corners and turning up the sides. If the box is to hold a volume of 48 cm³, what size of square must be removed?

Solution. Draw a diagram.

Let the side of the square to be removed be represented by x centimetres. Then the volume of the box is given by this expression.

$V = x(10 - 2x)(8 - 2x)$

Since the volume is 48 cm³,

$x(10 - 2x)(8 - 2x) = 48$

$4x(5 - x)(4 - x) = 48$

$x(20 - 9x + x^2) = 12$

$x^3 - 9x^2 + 20x = 12$

$x^3 - 9x^2 + 20x - 12 = 0$ ... ①

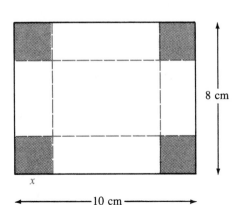

Solve using the factor theorem.

Let $f(x) = x^3 - 9x^2 + 20x - 12$.

$$f(1) = 1^3 - 9(1)^2 + 20(1) - 12$$
$$= 1 - 9 + 20 - 12$$
$$= 0$$

Since $f(1) = 0$, $x - 1$ is a factor of the left side of equation ①. The other factors can be found by division, by inspection, or by using the factor theorem again.

$$f(2) = 2^3 - 9(2)^2 + 20(2) - 12$$
$$= 8 - 36 + 40 - 12$$
$$= 0$$

Since $f(2) = 0$, $x - 2$ is a factor of the left side of equation ①.

Since $x - 1$ and $x - 2$ are factors, using the factor property the third factor has the form $x - a$, where

$$(-1)(-2)(-a) = -12$$
$$a = 6$$

Therefore, the third factor is $x - 6$.

That is, the equation may be written $(x - 1)(x - 2)(x - 6) = 0$.
Either $x = 1$, $x = 2$, or $x = 6$

When $x = 1$, the dimensions of the box are 8 cm by 6 cm by 1 cm, and it has a volume of 48 cm³.

When $x = 2$, the dimensions are 6 cm by 4 cm by 2 cm, and the volume is also 48 cm³.

It is impossible for x to be 6 since four squares with sides of this length cannot be cut from the cardboard.

Therefore, four squares with 1 cm sides, or four squares with 2 cm sides can be removed to form a box with a volume of 48 cm³.

As the above examples suggest, only certain polynomial equations can be solved by factoring. More general methods are needed to solve other polynomial equations.

EXERCISES 2-5

Ⓐ

1. Solve for x.
   a) $x(x - 2)(x + 5) = 0$
   b) $x(2x + 3)(x - 4) = 0$
   c) $x(x^2 + 10x + 21) = 0$
   d) $x(6x^2 + 5x - 21) = 0$
   e) $x^3 - 4x = 0$
   f) $2x^3 + 10x^2 + 12x = 0$

2. a) One root of each equation below is the same for every equation. What is this root?
   i) $10x^3 - 25x^2 - 15x = 0$
   ii) $12x^3 = 27x$
   iii) $6x^3 + 45x = 33x^2$
   iv) $3x^4 + 14x^3 + 8x^2 = 0$
   v) $18x^4 - 50x^2 = 0$
   vi) $35x^2 - 5x^3 = 60x$
   b) Find the other roots of each equation in part a).

(B)

3. Solve.
   a) $x^3 - 2x^2 + 3x - 6 = 0$ b) $x^3 + 5x^2 - 9x - 45 = 0$
   c) $2x^3 - 3x^2 - 11x + 6 = 0$ d) $3x^3 - 2x^2 - 12x + 8 = 0$

4. Solve.
   a) $x^3 + 3x^2 - 10x - 24 = 0$ b) $x^3 - x^2 + 9x - 9 = 0$
   c) $2x^3 - 3x^2 - 5x + 6 = 0$ d) $8x^3 + 4x^2 - 18x - 9 = 0$

5. Solve.
   a) $x^3 + x - 10 = 0$ b) $2x^3 - 4x^2 - 18x + 36 = 0$
   c) $2x^3 + 10x^2 + 13x + 5 = 0$ d) $3x^3 + 2x^2 + 75x - 50 = 0$

6. Find three consecutive integers with a product of: a) -24 b) -120.

7. What number and its cube differ by: a) 24   b) -120?

8. A rectangular piece of cardboard measuring 12 cm by 8 cm is made into an open box by cutting squares from the corners and turning up the sides. If the volume of the box is 60 cm³, what are its dimensions?

(C)

9. The product of the squares of two consecutive integers is 256 036. Find the integers.

10. Write a polynomial equation with these roots.
    a) 2, 5, 1   b) $-1, 2 + \sqrt{3}, 2 - \sqrt{3}$
    c) $-\dfrac{1}{2}, 3, -3, 1$ d) $-1, \dfrac{3 + 2\sqrt{5}}{2}, \dfrac{3 - 2\sqrt{5}}{2}$

11. If one root is 2, find each value of k, and the other roots.
    a) $2x^3 - 13x^2 + kx + 10 = 0$ b) $25x^4 + kx^2 + 16 = 0$
    c) $3x^3 - 15x^2 + kx - 4 = 0$ d) $3x^4 - kx^3 + 49x^2 - 23x - 14 = 0$

12. Solve.
    a) $3x^4 - 15x^2 + 12 = 0$ b) $\dfrac{3}{x^2} + \dfrac{2x}{x + 2} = \dfrac{3x}{x + 2} + \dfrac{1}{x^2}$

13. The diagrams show the first four pyramidal numbers. The number of balls in each layer of the pyramids is a perfect square. An expression for the nth pyramidal number is $\dfrac{n(n + 1)(2n + 1)}{6}$.

    a) Verify that the expression is correct by using it to find the number of balls in the pyramids shown in the diagrams.
    b) The only pyramidal number (other than 1) which is a perfect square is 4900. How many layers are in the pyramid for this number?

COMPUTER POWER

Solving Polynomial Equations

The computer is an ideal tool for solving polynomial equations such as $x^3 - 12x + 8 = 0$ (see *Example 1* in Section 2-1). The program below can be used to find decimal approximations to the roots of polynomial equations up to the tenth degree.

```
VAR
  CH : CHAR;
  I,N,K,Q : INTEGER;
  D,DT,T,X,XT,Y,Y1,Y2 : REAL;
  A : ARRAY [0..255] OF REAL;
BEGIN      { POLYNOMIAL EQUATIONS }
        WRITELN('WHAT IS THE DEGREE? ');
        READ(N); WRITELN;
        WRITELN('ENTER ',N+1,' COEFFICIENTS');
        FOR I := 0 TO N DO READ(A[I]);
        WRITELN('WHAT IS THE FIRST VALUE OF X? ');
        READ(X); WRITELN;
        T := 0;
        WRITELN('WHAT IS THE INCREMENT? ');
        READ(D);
        Y1 := 0; Y2 := 0;
        CH := CHR(1);
        REPEAT
          FOR K := 1 TO 11 DO BEGIN
            Y := A[0];
            FOR I := 1 TO N DO Y := Y * X + A[I];
            Y2 := Y1; Y1 := Y;
            WRITELN(X:5:8,' ',Y:5:8);
            IF Y = 0 THEN BEGIN
              WRITELN; WRITELN(X:5:8,'IS A ROOT');
            END;
            IF (Y1 * Y2) < 0 THEN BEGIN
              WRITELN;
              WRITELN('THERE IS A ROOT BETWEEN ',X-D:5:8,'
              AND ',X:5:8);
              WRITELN('ENTER 1 - FOR A MORE ACCURATE
              APPROXIMATION');
              WRITELN('        2 - TO CONTINUE');
              WRITELN('        3 - TO REPEAT');
              WRITELN('        4 - TO STOP');
              READ (Q);

              IF T = 0 THEN BEGIN
                XT := X;
                DT := D;
              END;
```

```
        CASE Q OF
            1:
                BEGIN
                T := T + 1; Y1 := 0; Y2 := 0;
                X := X - D; D := D / 10;
                END;
            2:
                BEGIN
                T := 0; X := XT; D := DT;
                END;
            3:
                T := 0;
            4:
                CH := CHR(0);
            END;
        END;
            X := X + D;
        END;
    UNTIL CH = CHR(0);
END.
```

When the program is run, the computer first asks for the degree of the polynomial, and then for the coefficients. These must be entered in descending order, including zero coefficients for missing terms. For example, to solve the equation $x^3 - 12x + 8 = 0$, the degree is 3 and the coefficients are 1, 0, -12, and 8.

The program instructs the computer to evaluate the polynomial for eleven successive values of x. You must enter the first value of x desired, and the increment. For example, if you enter -5 for the first value of x, and 1 for the increment, the computer will evaluate the polynomial for these values of x: -5, -4, -3, . . ., 5. For the polynomial $x^3 - 12x + 8 = 0$, the computer is calculating the table of values shown on page 42. In this table, notice that some of the y-values are negative, while others are positive. Also, a root of the equation occurs between the values of x for which the corresponding values of y change sign. The program uses this fact to calculate the root of the equation.

When the computer encounters two consecutive values of y with opposite signs, it indicates that a root exists between the two corresponding values of x. At this point, four options are given. Simply follow the instructions on the screen. For example, if you indicate that a more accurate approximation is desired, the computer will calculate values of x between those found, using a smaller increment. If this option is chosen several times in succession, the root can be found very accurately.

The following result was obtained for the root of the equation $x^3 - 12x + 8 = 0$ which lies between -4 and -3.

```
THERE IS A ROOT BETWEEN -3.8 AND -3.7
THERE IS A ROOT BETWEEN -3.76 AND -3.75
THERE IS A ROOT BETWEEN -3.759 AND -3.758
THERE IS A ROOT BETWEEN -3.7588 AND -3.7587
THERE IS A ROOT BETWEEN -3.75878 AND -3.75877
THERE IS A ROOT BETWEEN -3.758771 AND -3.75877
THERE IS A ROOT BETWEEN -3.7587705 AND -3.7587704
```

This shows that one root of the equation is $-3.758\ 770$, to six decimal places.

Use the program to answer these questions.

1. Find the other roots of the equation $x^3 - 12x + 8 = 0$, to six decimal places.

2. Each equation has a root between -3 and $+3$. Find this root to four decimal places.
   a) $x^3 + 6x^2 + 5x - 15 = 0$
   b) $x^5 + 5x^4 + 5x^3 - 5x^2 - 6x - 40 = 0$
   c) $x^3 - 3x - 5 = 0$

3. Find all the real roots of each equation, to four decimal places.
   a) $x^3 + 2x^2 - 11x - 5 = 0$
   b) $x^4 - 4x^3 - 4x^2 + 16x - 1 = 0$
   c) $x^5 - 2x^3 + x^2 - 10x + 25 = 0$

4. The volume V of a spherical segment with base radius a and height h is given by this formula.
   $$V = \frac{1}{6}\pi h(3a^2 + h^2)$$

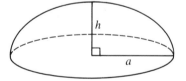

   A domed stadium is designed to be in the shape of a spherical segment with a base radius of 150 m. If the dome is to contain a volume of 3 500 000 m³, find the height of the dome at its centre, to the nearest tenth of a metre.

5. Give an example of a polynomial equation which has a real root that would not likely be found by the program. Use the program to illustrate that it cannot be found this way.

THE MATHEMATICAL MIND

The Cubic Equation Controversy

One of the most important mathematical achievements of the sixteenth century was the discovery by Italian mathematicians of formulas for the solution of cubic and quartic equations. This accomplishment occurred at a time when discoveries were often kept secret, and rivals were challenged to solve the same problem.

About 1510, a professor at the University of Bologna revealed to a student a method he had found of solving cubic equations without a quadratic term, such as $x^3 + 5x = 8$.

Nicolo Tartaglia
1499-1557

In 1535, when Nicolo Tartaglia claimed to have found a method of solving cubic equations without a linear term, such as $x^3 + 2x^2 = 6$, the former student challenged him to a public equation-solving contest. But before the contest, Tartaglia learned how to solve an equation of the first type as well, and he won the contest triumphantly.

Tartaglia knew that, by substituting $y - \dfrac{b}{3a}$ for x, any cubic equation

$ax^3 + bx^2 + cx + d = 0$ could be reduced to the form $y^3 + my = n$.
He proved that a root of this equation is

$$y = \sqrt[3]{\sqrt{\left(\frac{m}{3}\right)^3 + \left(\frac{n}{2}\right)^2} + \frac{n}{2}} - \sqrt[3]{\sqrt{\left(\frac{m}{3}\right)^3 + \left(\frac{n}{2}\right)^2} - \frac{n}{2}}.$$

Girolamo Cardano
1501-1576

Later, Girolamo Cardano urged Tartaglia to show him his method. When Cardano promised to keep it secret, Tartaglia gave it to him. But in 1545 Cardano published his *Ars Magna*, a Latin text on algebra, and included Tartaglia's solution of cubic equations. When Tartaglia protested the breach of his promise, Cardano claimed to have received his information from another party, and accused Tartaglia of plagiarism from the same source. There followed a bitter dispute between the two men over the question of who was the first to discover the formula for solving cubic equations.

Tartaglia's solution gave only one root, and later mathematicians found improved solutions. They also discovered formulas for quartic equations. Much work was done attempting to find a formula for quintic equations, but without success. This was proved to be impossible in 1824 by the Norwegian mathematician, Niels Henrik Abel.

QUESTIONS

1. Use a calculator and the formula given above to solve these cubic equations. Verify each solution.
   a) $y^3 + 6y = 2$
   b) $y^3 + 4y + 3 = 0$
   c) $x^3 - 3x^2 + 5x + 4 = 0$

2-6 THE ROOTS OF POLYNOMIAL EQUATIONS

During the last two centuries, mathematicians have devoted much time
and effort to the problem of solving polynomial equations. In this work
it is often possible to prove something about the roots of an equation
without knowing what they are. For example, if we calculate the value
of the discriminant $b^2 - 4ac$, we can determine the nature of the roots
of a quadratic equation $ax^2 + bx + c = 0$ without solving the
equation.

The graphs of some cubic functions are shown below.

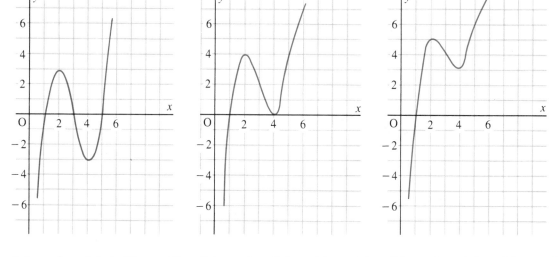

$$f(x) = x^3 - 9x^2 + 23x - 15 \qquad f(x) = x^3 - 9x^2 + 24x - 16 \qquad f(x) = x^3 - 9x^2 + 25x - 17$$

In each case, the graph intersects the x-axis at least once. These examples
suggest that the graph of every cubic function intersects the x-axis at
least once. There is a simple reason for this.

If x is a negative number with a large absolute value, such as -100
or -1000, the value of the cubic term will be a very large negative
number. This dominates the other terms, leaving a negative number for
the value of the polynomial. Conversely, if x is a very large positive
number, the value of the cubic term will be a very large positive number.
This dominates the other terms, leaving a positive number for the value
of the polynomial. Therefore, the graph of a cubic function proceeds from
the lower left to the upper right, and must cross the x-axis.

This reasoning applies to all cubic functions whose coefficient of
x^3 is positive. If the coefficient is negative, the analysis is similar, but
the graph proceeds from the upper left to the lower right.

Since the graph of every cubic function intersects the x-axis at least once, we conclude that every cubic equation has at least one real root. Then, what are the possibilities for the other roots?

Consider the equations below. These correspond to the three graphs on the opposite page. Each equation has $x = 1$ as a root. The other roots are found by dividing each polynomial by $x - 1$.

Equation 1. $x^3 - 9x^2 + 23x - 15 = 0$
$(x - 1)(x^2 - 8x + 15) = 0$
In addition to $x = 1$, there are two other roots, which are the roots of this quadratic equation.
$x^2 - 8x + 15 = 0$
$(x - 3)(x - 5) = 0$
$x = 3$ or $x = 5$
This equation has three different real roots. These occur at the points where the graph of the corresponding function intersects the x-axis.

Equation 2. $x^3 - 9x^2 + 24x - 16 = 0$
$(x - 1)(x^2 - 8x + 16) = 0$
In addition to $x = 1$, there are two other roots, which are the roots of this quadratic equation.
$x^2 - 8x + 16 = 0$
$(x - 4)^2 = 0$
$x = 4$
The cubic equation has three real roots, two of which are equal. These equal roots occur at the point where the graph of the corresponding function touches the x-axis.

Equation 3. $x^3 - 9x^2 + 25x - 17 = 0$
$(x - 1)(x^2 - 8x + 17) = 0$
In addition to $x = 1$, there may be two other real roots, which are the roots of this quadratic equation.
$x^2 - 8x + 17 = 0$
Use the quadratic formula.
$$x = \frac{-b \pm \sqrt{b^2 - 4ac}}{2a}$$
$$= \frac{8 \pm \sqrt{64 - 4(17)}}{2}$$
$$= \frac{8 \pm \sqrt{-4}}{2}$$
There are no other real roots. The one real root occurs at the point where the graph of the corresponding function crosses the x-axis.

These examples suggest the following properties of cubic equations.

> **Property of Cubic Equations**
> ● Every cubic equation has one, two, or three roots.

We can analyze higher-order polynomial equations in a similar manner. The graph of a 4th degree polynomial may intersect the x-axis up to four times. Hence, a 4th degree polynomial equation has at most four real roots. If the graph intersects the x-axis less than four times, then two or more of the roots are real and equal. Similar results occur for polynomial equations of the 5th degree and higher degrees.

> **Property of Polynomial Equations**
> ● Every polynomial equation of degree n has at most n real roots.

Example 1. Write a polynomial equation with these four roots: -3, 4, and a double root of $-\frac{1}{2}$.

Solution. By the factor theorem, the factors of the polynomial are $(x + 3)$, $(x - 4)$, $\left(x + \frac{1}{2}\right)$, and $\left(x + \frac{1}{2}\right)$. Hence, the equation is:

$$(x + 3)(x - 4)\left(x + \frac{1}{2}\right)^2 = 0$$

or $\quad (x + 3)(x - 4)(2x + 1)^2 = 0$

The equation in *Example 1* is a 4th degree equation. Although it is not necessary to do so, the factors may be multiplied and the equation written as

$$4x^4 - 51x^2 - 49x - 12 = 0 \ ... \ ①$$

If we had left the equation as $(x + 3)(x - 4)\left(x + \frac{1}{2}\right)^2$ and multiplied the factors, the result would have been

$$x^4 - \frac{51}{4}x^2 - \frac{49}{4}x - 3 = 0 \ ... \ ②$$

Equations ① and ② are equivalent because ① can be obtained from ② by multiplying by 4. These equations have the same roots. That is, multiplying both sides of an equation by a constant does not change the roots of the equation.

Similarly, multiplying a function by a constant does not change its zeros, but it does yield a different function. For example, the polynomial functions corresponding to ① and ② are

$$p(x) = 4x^4 - 51x^2 - 49x - 12$$

$$q(x) = x^4 - \frac{51}{4}x^2 - \frac{49}{4}x - 3$$

Both $p(x)$ and $q(x)$ have the same zeros; that is, -3, 4, and a double zero of $-\frac{1}{2}$.

But $p(x)$ and $q(x)$ are different functions. The graph of $p(x)$ is expanded vertically by a factor of 4 relative to the graph of $q(x)$. Since the coefficients of $p(x)$ are integers, $p(x)$ is an example of an *integral polynomial function*.

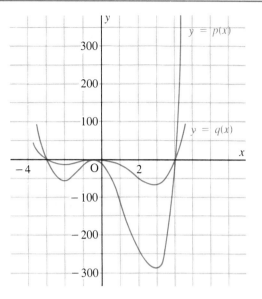

Hence, we can see that a polynomial function is not uniquely defined by its zeros. That is, the zeros alone are not sufficient to determine a polynomial function. Some additional information must be given, such as another point on its graph.

Example 2. A cubic function has zeros -3, -1, and 2. The y-intercept of its graph is 12.

a) Sketch the graph of the function.
b) Determine the function.

Solution. a) The x-intercepts of the graph are -3, -1, and 2. Infinitely many cubic curves can be drawn through these points, but only one of them has a y-intercept of 12.

b) Let $f(x) = a(x + 3)(x + 1)(x - 2)$
Since the y-intercept is 12, $f(0) = 12$
Hence, $a(0 + 3)(0 + 1)(0 - 2) = 12$
$$-6a = 12$$
$$a = -2$$

$$f(x) = -2(x + 3)(x + 1)(x - 2)$$

Therefore, the function is $f(x) = -2(x + 3)(x + 1)(x - 2)$
or $f(x) = -2x^3 - 4x^2 + 10x + 12$

In *Example 2* the zeros of the polynomial $f(x)$ are -3, -1, and $+2$. These zeros are factors of the constant term of the polynomial, 12. This is a direct consequence of the factor theorem, and is known as the Integral Zero Theorem.

Integral Zero Theorem
Let $p(x)$ be an integral polynomial function which has an integral zero $x = a$. Then, a is a factor of the constant term of the polynomial.

Proof: Since $x = a$ is a zero of the polynomial, $p(a) = 0$.
Hence, by the factor theorem, $p(x) = (x - a)q(x)$, where $q(x)$ is an integral polynomial. Therefore, the constant term of $p(x)$ is $-a$ times the constant term of $q(x)$. That is, a is a factor of the constant term of $p(x)$.

Corollary   Rational Zero Theorem
Let $p(x)$ be an integral polynomial function which has a rational

zero $x = \dfrac{a}{b}$, $a \in I$, $b \in I$, $b \neq 0$. Then, a is a factor of the

constant term of the polynomial, and b is a factor of the coefficient of the highest-degree term.

Example 3. List the possible rational roots of the equation
$$2x^3 + 11x^2 + 17x + 5 = 0.$$

Solution.   If the equation has a rational root $\dfrac{a}{b}$, then by the rational zero theorem, a

is a factor of the constant term 5, and b is a factor of the coefficient of x^3, 2. The only possibilities for a and b are $a = \pm 1, \pm 5$, and $b = \pm 1, \pm 2$. Hence, the only possible rational roots are $1, -1, 5,$
$-5, \dfrac{1}{2}, -\dfrac{1}{2}, \dfrac{5}{2},$ and $-\dfrac{5}{2}$.

In *Example 3*, to determine which if any of the possible rational roots are, in fact, roots of the equation, we would have to substitute each one in turn into the left side and see if the expression simplifies to 0. For this particular equation, the work is simplified considerably if we observe that it is impossible for the equation to have a positive root, since the left side of the equation is positive if $x > 0$. Hence, we would only need to check the possible negative roots. If we did this, we would find that $x = -\dfrac{5}{2}$ is the only rational root of the equation.

EXERCISES 2-6

1. What is the greatest number of real roots each equation could have?
   a) $x^3 + 5x^2 - 6x - 3 = 0$ b) $7x^2 - 12x + 4 = 0$
   c) $2x^3 - x^2 + 8x - 9 = 0$ d) $5x^4 + 3x^2 - x - 12 = 0$
   e) $3x^3 + 17x + 15 = 0$ f) $x^3 + 10x = 3x^5 - 8x^2 + 4$

2. Write a cubic equation with the given roots.
   a) 1, 2, 3   b) 2, 2, 5   c) −4, 1, 0   d) 2, 2, 2

3. Write a polynomial equation with the given roots.
   a) 1, 2, 3, 4   b) 5, −2, 1, 2   c) 1, 1, 2, 2, 3, 3

4. Polynomial functions of degree 2, 3, 4, 5, 6, and 7 are graphed below. What is the degree of the function in each graph?

a)
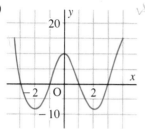

b)
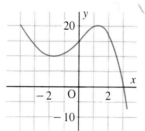

c)
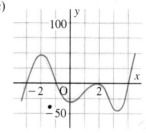

d)
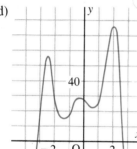

e)
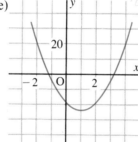

f)
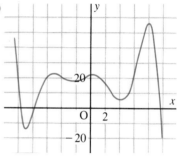

Ⓑ

5. A cubic function has zeros −2, 1, and 4. The *y*-intercept of its graph is 24.
   a) Sketch the graph of the function.
   b) Determine the function.

6. Sketch the graph of each polynomial function and determine the function.
   a) zeros −2, 2, 2; graph has *y*-intercept −16.
   b) zeros −3, 2, 5; graph has *y*-intercept 45.
   c) zeros −2, −1, 1, 2; graph has *y*-intercept 20.
   d) zeros 0, 2, 4; graph passes through (3, 9).

7. a) Find an integral root of the cubic equation $x^3 - 10x + 9 = 0$.
   b) Show that the equation in part a) has only one integral root.

8. List the possible integral roots of each equation.
   a) $x^3 - 2x^2 + 6x - 5 = 0$ b) $x^3 - x^2 - 4x + 4 = 0$
   c) $x^3 - x^2 - 3x - 9 = 0$ d) $2x^3 - 7x - 6 = 0$

9. List the possible integral zeros of each polynomial.
   a) $x^3 - 3x^2 - x + 3$ b) $2x^3 + x^2 - 13x + 6$
   c) $3x^3 - 20x^2 + 23x + 10$ d) $4x^4 + 3x^2 - 1$

10. Prove that the equation $x^5 + 9x^3 + 7x^2 + x + 1 = 0$ has no positive roots.

11. Prove that the equation $x^4 - 4x^3 + 5x^2 - 3x + 6 = 0$ has no negative roots.

12. List the possible rational roots of each equation.
    a) $5x^3 + 13x^2 + 9x + 1 = 0$
    b) $2x^5 - x^4 - 2x + 1 = 0$
    c) $2x^3 - 3x^2 - x - 2 = 0$
    d) $4x^3 + 2x^2 + 2x + 1 = 0$
    e) $5x^3 + 17x^2 - 17x + 3 = 0$
    f) $6x^4 - 4x^3 + 3x^2 - 8x + 4 = 0$

13. State which of the five equations listed has:
    a) a root of 2
    b) a root of -5
    c) a root of $\frac{2}{3}$
    d) at least one real root
    e) no positive root.

    i) $3x^3 - 4x^2 + x = 0$
    ii) $3x^3 - 5x^2 - 4x + 4 = 0$
    iii) $x^3 + 8x^2 + 16x + 5 = 0$
    iv) $x^3 + 8x^2 + 17x + 10 = 0$
    v) $x^4 + 3x^3 - 11x^2 - 3x + 10 = 0$

14. Find all three roots of each cubic equation.
    a) $2x^3 + x^2 - 13x + 6 = 0$
    b) $x^3 - 1 = 0$
    c) $2x^3 + 11x^2 + 17x + 5 = 0$
    d) $6x^3 + 7x^2 - 7x - 6 = 0$

Ⓒ

15. Explain why a polynomial equation of degree n has at least one real root if n is odd.

16. Consider the three cubic functions graphed on page 72.
    $y = x^3 - 9x^2 + 23x - 15$
    $y = x^3 - 9x^2 + 24x - 16$
    $y = x^3 - 9x^2 + 25x - 17$
    a) Note the pattern in the coefficients. Assuming that this pattern is continued, write the next three functions in the list.
    b) Describe what happens to the shape of the graph of the function
    $f(x) = x^3 - 9x^2 + (24 + k)x - (16 + k)$ as k increases through positive values.
    c) If the pattern is continued in the opposite direction, write the preceding three functions in the list.
    d) Describe what happens to the shape of the graph of the function
    $f(x) = x^3 - 9x^2 + (24 + k)x - (16 + k)$ as k decreases through negative values.

2-7 SOLVING POLYNOMIAL INEQUALITIES

The graph below shows the polynomial function $y = x^3 - 2x^2 - 5x + 6$.
The graph divides the x-axis into three different sets of values of x.

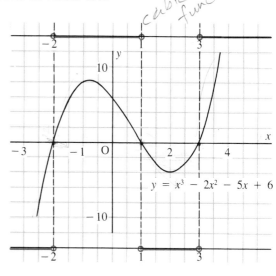

- The values of x which satisfy the inequality $x^3 - 2x^2 - 5x + 6 > 0$; these are the values of x where the graph is above the x-axis. We say that the solution set of the inequality is $\{x \mid -2 < x < 1 \text{ or } x > 3\}$.

- The values of x which satisfy the equation $x^3 - 2x^2 - 5x + 6 = 0$; these are the values of x where the graph intersects the x-axis. The roots of the equation are -2, 1, and 3.

- The values of x which satisfy the inequality $x^3 - 2x^2 - 5x + 6 < 0$; these are the values of x where the graph is below the x-axis. The solution set of the inequality is $\{x \mid x < -2 \text{ or } 1 < x < 3\}$.

Any polynomial inequality can be solved by graphing. But notice in the above example that the roots of the corresponding equation determine the endpoints of the intervals in the solutions of the inequalities. Hence, a more efficient method of solving a polynomial inequality is to solve the corresponding equation and test values of x in the intervals defined by the roots of the equation.

Example 1. Solve the inequality $6 - 5x^2 < 13x$.

Solution. *Step 1.* Solve the equation $6 - 5x^2 = 13x$.

By factoring, or using the quadratic formula, we find that the roots are -3 and $\frac{2}{5}$. These divide the x-axis into three intervals: A, B, and C.

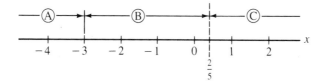

Step 2. Select a value of x in each interval, and substitute it in both sides of the given inequality. If the inequality is satisfied, all values of x in the interval are solutions of the inequality.

A value of x in interval A is -10. Substitute -10 for x.

Left side $= -494$ Right side $= -130$

This value of x satisfies the inequality.

A value of x in interval B is 0. Substitute 0 for x.

Left side $= 6$ Right side $= 0$

This value of x does not satisfy the inequality.

A value of x in interval C is 1. Substitute 1 for x.

Left side $= 1$ Right side $= 13$

This value of x satisfies the inequality.

Step 3. Write the solution set of the inequality, or illustrate the solution set on a number line.

The solution set is $\left\{ x \mid x < -3 \text{ or } x > \frac{2}{5} \right\}$.

In *Example 1*, the numbers -3 and $\frac{2}{5}$ are not part of the solution set. If the inequality had been $6 - 5x^2 \le 13x$, these numbers would satisfy the inequality, and the solution set would be written as

$$\left\{ x \mid x \le -3 \text{ or } x \ge \frac{2}{5} \right\}$$

Polynomial inequalities of higher degree can be solved in the same way. The initial step of solving the corresponding equation can be carried out by factoring or by using a computer.

EXERCISES 2-7

(A)

1. Use each graph to write the solution set of the inequalities given below it.

   a)

   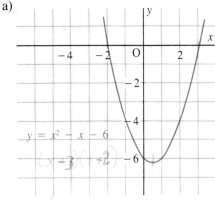

   i) $x^2 - x - 6 < 0$

   ii) $x^2 - x - 6 > 0$

   b)

   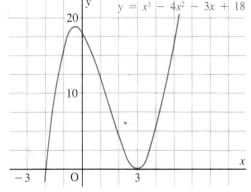

   i) $x^3 - 4x^2 - 3x + 18 < 0$

   ii) $x^3 - 4x^2 - 3x + 18 > 0$

2. Solve each inequality.

   a) $(x - 2)(x + 2) > 0$

   b) $(x + 1)(x + 2) \le 0$

   c) $x(x - 5) > 0$

   d) $x(x - 2)(x - 4) \le 0$

   e) $(a - 1)(a - 2)(a - 3) < 0$

   f) $(n + 1)(n - 3)(n + 5) \ge 0$

Ⓑ

3. Solve each inequality.
   a) $(x - 2)(x + 2)(x - 6) > 0$
   b) $(c + 4)(c - 3)^2 < 0$
   c) $s(s + 3)(s + 5) \geq 0$
   d) $x(x - 2)(x^2 - 16) \leq 0$
   e) $(x + 2)^2 (x - 5)^2 > 0$
   f) $(u - 1)(u - 2)(u - 3) < (u - 1)(u - 3)$

4. Solve each inequality.
   a) $x^2 - 5x < 0$ b) $m^2 - 2m \geq 8$
   c) $18 - 3y - y^2 \geq 0$ d) $x^2 + 4 > 4x$
   e) $x^3 - 4x^2 > 0$ f) $a^2 + 15 \leq 17a - a^3$

5. Solve each inequality.
   a) $2z^3 - z^2 - 8z + 4 > 0$ b) $x^3 + 3x^2 - 9x - 27 < 0$
   c) $2x^3 + x^2 + 2x < 0$ d) $n^2 - 6n + 11 > 0$
   e) $x^4 - 10x^2 + 9 \geq 0$ f) $r^4 - r \leq 3r^3 - 3$

6. For what values of x does the parabola $y = x^2 - 4x$ lie above the line $y = 2x - 5$?

7. For what values of x does the graph of the cubic function $y = x^3 + 2x^2 + 3x + 4$ lie above the parabola $y = x^2 + 2x + 3$?

8. Which real numbers are less than their square roots?

Ⓒ

9. Prove that every cubic inequality has infinitely many real solutions.

10. Give an example of a polynomial inequality that has no real solution.

11. Give an example of a polynomial inequality whose solution set is the set of all real numbers except:
    a) 3   b) 3 and -3.

12. Write a polynomial inequality whose solution set is each given graph.
    a)
    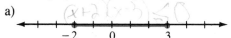
    b)
    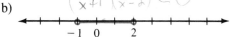

    c)
    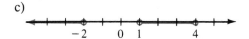
    d)
    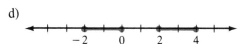

    e)
    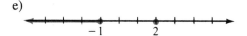
    f)
    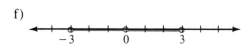

 **PROBLEM SOLVING**

The Crossed Ladders Problem

"Not all problems can be solved within the confines of one mathematics lesson; some need to be "mulled over" for longer periods of time."

Marilyn N. Suydam

In an alley, two ladders, 6 m and 9 m long, lean against opposite walls, and cross at a point 3 m above the ground. Determine the distance between the walls.

Think of a strategy
- Try using similar triangles.

Carry out the strategy
- If x represents the length of BC, can you use similar triangles to find an equation in x? If not, try letting x represent the length of BE.
- Since some of the triangles are right triangles, the Pythagorean Theorem may be useful.
- Can you use similar triangles and the Pythagorean Theorem to obtain an equation in x? Do not be surprised if it is a polynomial equation of the fourth degree.

Look back
- If you can obtain a polynomial equation in x, the problem about the ladders is essentially solved. You can use systematic trial or the computer program on page 68 to solve the equation.
- In the past, this problem was popular because it leads to a fourth degree equation. Since there were no computers, the challenge of solving the problem was replaced with the challenge of solving the equation!
- Does the equation have any negative roots? Only a positive root can be a solution of the crossed ladders problem.
- Is there any way to check the answer?

PROBLEMS

Ⓑ

1. Two cardboard strips with small holes in each end are linked with a paper fastener at P. Point A is held fixed and a pencil is placed at point B.

   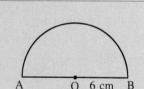

   a) If AP $= x$ cm and PB $= y$ cm, describe the region in which B is free to move.
   b) Describe the region if point B is held fixed and the pencil is placed at point A.

2. Given $ab = cd$ and $bc = ad$
   a) Prove that either $a^2 = c^2$ or $b^2 = d^2$ or both.
   b) Give a numerical example in which $a^2 = c^2$ and $b^2 = d^2$, and another numerical example in which $a^2 = c^2$ and $b^2 \neq d^2$.

3. Two consecutive odd numbers that are powers of positive integers are $25 = 5^2$ and $27 = 3^3$. Determine whether or not it is possible for two consecutive even numbers to be powers of positive integers. If it is possible, give a numerical example. Otherwise, prove that it is impossible.

Ⓒ

4. A semicircular piece of paper has a radius of 6 cm. Edges OA and OB are joined to form a cone. Find the height of the cone.

   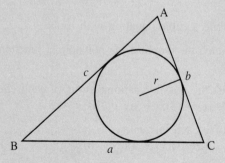

5. There is only one two-digit number that becomes a perfect square when it is doubled, and a perfect cube when it is tripled. What is this number?

6. Prove that the area A of any $\triangle ABC$ is given by the formula $A = rs$, where r is the radius of the inscribed circle, and s is the *semi-perimeter*,

   $$s = \frac{1}{2}(a + b + c).$$

Ⓓ

7. Prove that the graph of every cubic function has *point symmetry*. That is, a point F can be found such that for every other point P on the graph, there is a point Q on the graph such that F is the midpoint of PQ.

Review Exercises

1. Solve graphically.

   a) $x^3 - 5x + 9 = 0$ b) $\dfrac{x^3}{3} - 3x = 0$

2. Divide, then factor the quotient if possible.
   a) $2a^3 - 5a^2 - 9a + 18$ by $a + 2$
   b) $2x^3 - 13x + 5x^2 - 30$ by $x + 3$
   c) $6x^3 + 17x^2y - 26xy^2 + 8y^3$ by $x + 4y$
   d) $32x^3 - 18x - 16x^2 + 9$ by $2x + 1$

3. Find the remainder when $x^3 + 2x^2 - x + 3$ is divided by each binomial.
   a) $x - 1$ b) $x + 3$ c) $x + 2$

4. When $x^4 - 3x^3 - kx^2 + 5x - 2$ is divided by $x - 3$, the remainder is -5. Find the value of k.

5. Which polynomials have $x - 3$ as a factor?
   a) $x^3 - 29x + 2x^2 + 40$
   b) $x^3 - 9x^2 + 26x - 24$
   c) $5x^3 - 18x^2 - 5x + 42$
   d) $8x^3 + 33x - 37x^2 + 18$

6. Factor completely.
   a) $x^3 + 3x^2 - 4x - 12$
   b) $x^3 - 3x - 2$
   c) $x^3 + 5x^2 + 2x - 8$
   d) $x^3 + x^2 - 9x - 9$

7. Find k if $x + 2$ is a factor of $x^3 - 5x^2 + kx - 4$.

8. Solve.
   a) $(x^2 + 4x)^2 - 9(x^2 + 4x) - 36 = 0$
   b) $x^3 - 4x^2 + x + 6 = 0$
   c) $x^3 - x^2 - 4x + 4 = 0$
   d) $x^4 - 3x^3 - 2x^2 + 12x - 8 = 0$

9. Write a cubic equation with roots -4, 2, and 5.

10. Sketch the graph of the polynomial function with zeros -2, 1, and 4, and y-intercept 16.

11. List the possible rational roots of each equation.
    a) $3x^3 - 4x^2 + 6x - 10 = 0$ b) $4x^4 + 7x^3 - 6x + 3 = 0$

12. Solve each inequality.
    a) $(x + 3)(x - 4)(x + 6) > 0$ b) $(a - 1)(a + 2)(a - 5) \leq 0$

3 Quadratic Relations

Some bridges have curved arches like this one. If the type of arch is known, and if the height and the width at its base are known, how can the height be determined at any other point under the arch? (See Section 3-6, *Example 1*.)

3-1 DISTANCE AND MIDPOINT

In the Cartesian coordinate system, the positions of points in the plane are represented by ordered pairs (x,y). One advantage of this system is that the distance between any two points is easily found.

Length of a Line Segment

In the Hibernia Oil Fields off the coast of Newfoundland, the Canadian coast guard sights an iceberg on a possible collision course with an oil rig. On a map, the navigator uses ordered pairs to plot the positions of the rig $R(-4,3)$ and the iceberg $I(6,8)$. If the units are kilometres, how far is the iceberg from the oil rig?

On the grid, line segments RC and IC are parallel to the x- and y-axes respectively. Therefore,

$$RC = |6 - (-4)| \qquad \text{and} \qquad IC = |8 - 3|$$
$$= 10 \qquad\qquad\qquad\qquad = 5$$

The length of RI is found using the Pythagorean Theorem.

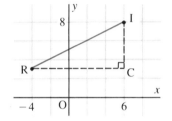

$$RI^2 = RC^2 + IC^2$$
$$= 10^2 + 5^2$$
$$= 125$$
$$RI = \sqrt{125}$$
$$\doteq 11.2$$

The negative root is ignored since distances cannot be negative.

The iceberg is about 11.2 km from the oil rig.

The distance between any two points $P_1(x_1,y_1)$ and $P_2(x_2,y_2)$ is given by this formula.
$$P_1P_2 = \sqrt{(x_2 - x_1)^2 + (y_2 - y_1)^2}$$

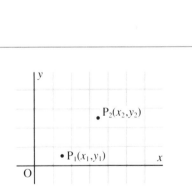

Example 1. A triangle has vertices R($-2,4$), S($4,1$), and T($2,-3$).

 a) Graph △RST and find the lengths of its sides to one decimal place.

 b) Determine if △RST is a right triangle.

Solution. a) RS $= \sqrt{[4-(-2)]^2 + (1-4)^2}$

$= \sqrt{45}$

$\doteq 6.7$

ST $= \sqrt{(2-4)^2 + (-3-1)^2}$

$= \sqrt{20}$

$\doteq 4.5$

RT $= \sqrt{[2-(-2)]^2 + (-3-4)^2}$

$= \sqrt{65}$

$\doteq 8.1$

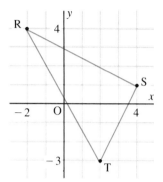

 b) If △RST is a right triangle, the longest side RT will be the hypotenuse and RT^2 = RS^2 + ST^2.

RT$^2 = (\sqrt{65})^2$

$= 65$

RS^2 + ST$^2 = (\sqrt{45})^2 + (\sqrt{20})^2$

$= 45 + 20$

$= 65$

Since RT^2 = RS^2 + ST^2, △RST is a right triangle.

Example 2. Find the coordinates of the point on the *x*-axis which is equidistant from A($5,8$) and B($-3,4$). Check the result.

Solution. Let P($x,0$) be the required point.

Then PA $= \sqrt{(5-x)^2 + (8-0)^2}$

and PB $= \sqrt{(-3-x)^2 + (4-0)^2}$

Since P is equidistant from A and B,

PA = PB

$\sqrt{(5-x)^2 + (8-0)^2} = \sqrt{(-3-x)^2 + (4-0)^2}$

Square both sides.

$(5-x)^2 + 64 = (-3-x)^2 + 16$

$25 - 10x + x^2 + 64 = 9 + 6x + x^2 + 16$

$16x = 64$

Therefore, $x = 4$

The point P($4,0$) is equidistant from A($5,8$) and B($-3,4$).

Check. PA $= \sqrt{1^2 + 8^2}$

$= \sqrt{65}$

PB $= \sqrt{7^2 + 4^2}$

$= \sqrt{65}$

The solution is correct.

Midpoint of a Line Segment

The coast guard sights another iceberg M halfway between two other oil rigs S(2,7) and T(10,3). What are the coordinates of M?

M is the midpoint of line segment ST. Perpendiculars are drawn from T, M, and S to the axes. It appears that the coordinates of M are the means of the coordinates of S and T.

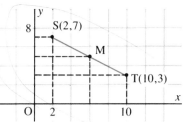

x-coordinate of M: $\dfrac{2 + 10}{2} = 6$

y-coordinate of M: $\dfrac{7 + 3}{2} = 5$

The coordinates of M are (6,5).

If M is the midpoint of a line segment with endpoints $P_1(x_1, y_1)$ and $P_2(x_2, y_2)$, the coordinates of M are: $\left(\dfrac{x_1 + x_2}{2}, \dfrac{y_1 + y_2}{2}\right)$. That is, the coordinates of M are the means of the coordinates of P_1 and P_2.

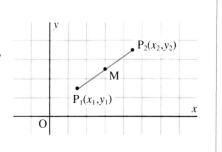

Example 3. A triangle has vertices D(7,5), E(1, − 3), and F(9, − 1). The midpoints of DE and EF are M and N respectively.
a) Find the coordinates of M and N.
b) Compare the lengths of MN and DF.

Solution. a) The coordinates of M are:
$$\left(\frac{7 + 1}{2}, \frac{5 - 3}{2}\right), \text{ or } (4,1).$$
The coordinates of N are:
$$\left(\frac{1 + 9}{2}, \frac{-3 - 1}{2}\right), \text{ or } (5, -2).$$

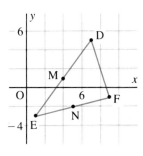

b) $MN = \sqrt{(5 - 4)^2 + (-2 - 1)^2}$
  $= \sqrt{10}$
  $DF = \sqrt{(9 - 7)^2 + (-1 - 5)^2}$
  $= \sqrt{40}$
  $= 2\sqrt{10}$
  DF is twice as long as MN.

EXERCISES 3-1

Ⓐ

1. Plot each pair of points and find the distance between them.
   a) A(3,1), B(9,9)
   b) C(−2,4), D(7,−1)
   c) E(−5,−2), F(10,6)
   d) G(−2,5), H(−4,−3)
   e) J(8,4), K(2,−7)
   f) L(−3,5), M(7,−3)

2. Find the length of each line segment with the given endpoints.
   a) N(7,12), P(−1,3)
   b) Q(−9,5), R(6,−2)
   c) S(−4,−8), T(1,−13)
   d) U(6,−7), V(−5,8)
   e) W(−3,−1), A(4,−11)
   f) B(14,9), C(−6,−6)

3. Find the coordinates of the midpoint of each line segment with the given endpoints.
   a) D(4,2), E(−8,−6)
   b) F(5,6), G(13,−4)
   c) H(−6,3), J(4,−5)
   d) K(4,2), L(12,−7)
   e) M(−3,7), N(6,2)
   f) P(−4,−3), Q(10,9)

Ⓑ

4. A triangle has vertices A(−2,8), B(2,−6), and C(6,2).
   a) Find the coordinates of the midpoints D, E, and F of the sides AB, BC, and AC respectively.
   b) Compare the lengths of the sides of △DEF with those of △ABC.

5. A triangle has vertices P(−1,−3), Q(1,−1), and R(−5,5). Show that:
   a) the triangle is a right triangle
   b) the midpoint of the hypotenuse is equidistant from all three vertices.

6. Find the coordinates of the point on: i) the x-axis   ii) the y-axis
   that is equidistant from each pair of points.
   a) R(5,5) and S(4,−4)
   b) T(2,−6) and U(−5,−1)
   c) V(7,5) and W(3,8)
   d) A(−4,2) and B(9,−6)

7. The coordinates of the vertices of a triangle are given. Graph the triangle and classify it as scalene, isosceles, or equilateral. State whether it is a right triangle.
   a) A(7,−3), B(2,6), C(−2,2)
   b) D(0,−3), E(5,2), F(−1,0)
   c) G(2,−3), H(6,2), J(0,3)
   d) K(−6,6), L(−3,−3), M(6,0)
   e) N(1,−2), P(9,5), Q(−3,3)
   f) R(−3,−1), S(6,−4), T(6,2)

8. The coordinates of the vertices of a rectangle are given. Find:
   i)   the lengths of the sides
   ii) the lengths of the diagonals
   iii) the perimeter
   iv) the area
        a) A(−3,3), B(−2,−1), C(6,1), D(5,5)
        b) E(8,5), F(−4,−1), G(−2,−5), H(10,1)
        c) J(2,1), K(6,−5), L(12,−1), M(8,5)
        d) P(6,10), Q(3,9), S(6,0), T(9,1)

9. The coordinates of the endpoints of a line segment are given. Find the coordinates of the three points that divide each segment into four equal parts.
   a) $A(-6,4)$, $B(10,-4)$ b) $C(2,9)$, $D(-14,-3)$
   c) $E(-7,5)$, $F(11,9)$ d) $G(-4,-9)$, $H(9,-1)$

10. M is the midpoint of line segment AB. Find the coordinates of B if those of A and M are:
   a) $A(-2,4)$, $M(3,1)$ b) $A(-5,-2)$, $M(6,3)$
   c) $A(4,7)$, $M\left(-\frac{3}{2}, 2\right)$ d) $A(8,-3)$, $M\left(-\frac{1}{2}, \frac{5}{2}\right)$.

11. P has coordinates $(9,3)$ and Q is a point on the y-axis. If the midpoint M of PQ is on the x-axis, find the coordinates of Q and M.

12. The vertices of a parallelogram are $A(-4,-1)$, $B(5,-6)$, $C(11,-3)$, and $D(2,2)$. Show that the diagonals bisect each other.

13. A triangle has vertices $E(-4,3)$, $F(2,-5)$, and $G(6,5)$. Find the lengths of its three medians.

14. A triangle has vertices $P(3,6)$, $Q(-5,0)$, and $R(3,-4)$.
   a) Classify the triangle according to the lengths of its sides.
   b) If the median from P meets QR at S, what is the measure of $\angle PSR$?
   c) What is the area of $\triangle PQR$?

15. Boats in a regatta are required to sail a triangular course with vertices on a map grid $H(25,-25)$, $J(100,150)$, and $K(200,25)$. If the units are kilometres, how long is the course?

16. A fishing boat sends out a distress signal giving its location by the grid reference $B(-50,175)$. A yacht at $Y(100,-400)$ and a freighter at $F(225,100)$ hear and respond. If the yacht travels twice as fast as the freighter, which arrives first?

17. Three booster transmitters are to be located equally spaced between two towers at grid references $B(-240,-160)$ and $T(560,800)$. Find the positions of the booster transmitters.

Ⓒ

18. Two vertices of a triangle are $P(3,4)$ and $Q(6,-2)$. Find the possible coordinates of the third vertex if its distances from the given vertices are 5 units and $\sqrt{40}$ units.

19. A quadrilateral has vertices $J(-5,5)$, $K(11,-5)$, $L(7,7)$, and $M(-1,9)$. Show that the segments joining the midpoints of opposite sides:
   a) bisect each other
   b) bisect the line segment joining the midpoints of the diagonals.

3-2 LOCUS

To make this photograph, a point source of
light was mounted on a wheel. A camera
recorded the light at split-second intervals as
the wheel rolled along a flat surface. The
path traced out by the light is an example of
a locus. Another example of a locus is the
path traced out by a pencil point when
compasses are used to construct a circle.

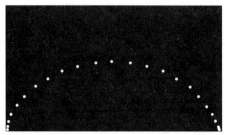

A *locus* is the path traced out by a point which moves according
to a given condition. If the given condition is simple enough, we can find
an equation which represents the path.

Example 1.   A point moves such that it is always 3 units from the point A(2, 0).
   a) Identify the locus.
   b) Find the equation of the locus.

Solution.   a) The locus is a circle with centre (2, 0)
      and radius 3.
   b) Let P(x, y) be any point on the locus.
      Then,

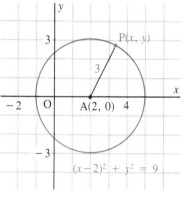

$$AP = 3$$
$$\sqrt{(x - 2)^2 + (y - 0)^2} = 3$$

Square both sides.

$$(x - 2)^2 + y^2 = 9$$

The equation of the locus is
$(x - 2)^2 + y^2 = 9$,
or $x^2 + y^2 - 4x - 5 = 0$

Example 2.   Let N be the point (1, -2). A point P moves such that the slope of the
segment NP is always $\frac{3}{4}$.

   a) Identify the locus.
   b) Find the equation of the locus.

Solution.   a) The locus is a straight line with slope
      $\frac{3}{4}$, passing through N(1, -2).

   b) Let P(x, y) be any point on the locus.
      Then, since the slope of NP is $\frac{3}{4}$,

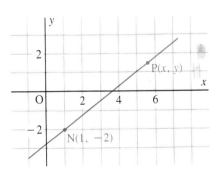

$$\frac{y + 2}{x - 1} = \frac{3}{4}$$
$$3x - 3 = 4y + 8$$
$$3x - 4y - 11 = 0$$

The equation of the locus is
$3x - 4y - 11 = 0$

In *Examples 1* and *2* we could identify the locus before we found its equation. If the given condition is more complicated, it may not be possible to do this.

Example 3. A point P moves such that it is always the same distance from the point F(5, 1) as it is from the line defined by $y = -1$.

a) Find the equation of the locus.

b) Identify the locus and sketch its graph.

c) Find the value of y_1 if T(11, y_1) is on the graph.

Solution.   a) Let P(x, y) be any point on the locus.
Then according to the given condition,
$$PF = PN$$
$$\sqrt{(x - 5)^2 + (y - 1)^2} = y + 1$$
Square both sides.
$$(x - 5)^2 + (y - 1)^2 = (y + 1)^2$$
$$x^2 - 10x + 25 + y^2 - 2y + 1 = y^2 + 2y + 1$$
$$4y = x^2 - 10x + 25$$
$$y = \frac{1}{4}(x - 5)^2$$

b) The locus is a parabola with vertex (5, 0), and axis of symmetry $x = 5$. The parabola opens up, and is congruent to the parabola defined by $y = \frac{1}{4}x^2$.

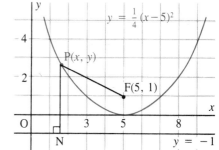

c) Substitute 11 for x and y_1 for y in the equation.
$$y = \frac{1}{4}(x - 5)^2$$
$$y_1 = \frac{1}{4}(11 - 5)^2$$
$$= 9$$

Hence, if T(11, y_1) is on the graph, $y_1 = 9$.

In the above examples we used the following fundamental properties of a locus.

Properties of a Locus

● The coordinates of every point on a locus satisfy the equation of the locus.

● Every point whose coordinates satisfy the equation of a locus is on the locus.

EXERCISES 3-2

Ⓐ

1. Describe each graph as a locus.

a)

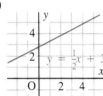

$x^2 + y^2 = 4$

b)

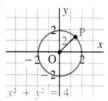

$x^2 + (y - 2)^2 = 4$

c)

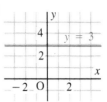

$y = 3$

d)

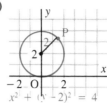

$y = \frac{1}{2}x + 3$

e)

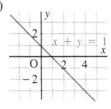

$x + y = 1$

f)

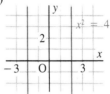

$x^2 = 4$

2. Describe the graph of each equation as a locus.
   a) $y = -5$ b) $x = -2$ c) $x^2 + y^2 = 49$
   d) $y = x + 2$ e) $(x - 1)^2 + (y + 4)^2 = 16$ f) $(x - 1)^2 + y^2 = 1$

Ⓑ

3. A point P moves such that it is always 6 units from the point B(0,3).
   a) Identify the locus.
   b) Find the equation of the locus.

4. A point P moves such that it is always 5 units from the point C(-1,2).
   a) Find the equation of the locus.
   b) Identify the locus and sketch its graph.
   c) Find the value of y_1 if A(3,y_1) is on the graph.

5. Find the equation of the locus of P. Identify the locus and sketch its graph.

   a) The slope of the line through P and M(3, -1) is $\frac{2}{3}$.

   b) P is equidistant from the point F(0,1) and the line defined by $y = -1$.
   c) P is equidistant from the point F(3, -1) and the line defined by $y = 1$.

6. A point P moves such that it is always equidistant from the point G(2,5) and the
   line defined by $y = 3$.
   a) Find the equation of the locus.
   b) Identify the locus and sketch its graph.
   c) Find the value of y_1 if B(-4,y_1) is on the graph.

7. Find the equation of the locus of P. Identify the locus and sketch its graph.
   a) P is always the same distance from A(-2,3) as it is from B(8, -1).
   b) P is always twice as far from A(8,0) as it is from B(2,0).
   c) The slope of the line through P and A(2,1) is equal to the slope of the line
      through P and B(-1,4).

8. A point P moves such that the slope of the line through P and S(2,0) is always 2 greater than the slope of the line through P and T(-2,0).
   a) Find the equation of the locus.
   b) Identify the locus and sketch its graph.
   c) Find the value of x_1 if M(x_1,16) is on the graph.

9. A point P moves such that the product of the slopes of the line segments joining P to Q(-5,0) and to R(5,0) is -1.
   a) Find the equation of the locus.
   b) Identify the locus and sketch its graph.
   c) Find the value of y_1 if the point D(2,y_1) lies on the graph.

10. Perpendicular lines are drawn through A(4,0) and B(-4,0).
    a) Find the equation of the locus of the point of intersection of these lines.
    b) Identify the locus and draw its graph.

11. A line segment 10 units long has its endpoints on the *x*- and *y*-axes. Find the equation of the locus of its midpoint, and sketch its graph.

12. Find the equation of the locus of P. Sketch the graph of the locus.
    a) P is 3 units from the *x*-axis.
    b) The product of the distances from P to the *x*- and *y*-axes is 6.
    c) The sum of the distances from P to the *x*- and *y*-axes is 5.
    d) The difference of the distances from P to the *x*- and *y*-axes is 3.
    e) P is equidistant from the *x*- and *y*-axes.
    f) P is always twice as far from the *x*-axis as it is from the point V(0,3).

13. Find the equation of the locus of a point P which moves such that the slope of the line segment joining P to A(-3,0) is half the slope of the line segment joining P to B(3,0). Identify the locus and sketch its graph.

14. Find the equation of the locus of P.
    a) The sum of the distances from P to A(2,0) and B(-2,0) is 8.
    b) The difference of the distances from P to C(4,0) and D(-4,0) is 2.

15. In △ABC, ∠C = $90°$ and C is the point (5,3). If A is on the *x*-axis and B is on the *y*-axis, find the equation of the locus of the midpoint of AB.

INVESTIGATE

A circle can be defined as the locus of a point which moves such that its distance to a given point is constant. By examining the examples and exercises of this section:
a) list some other possible definitions of a circle
b) list some possible definitions of: a straight line; a parabola.

3-3 INTRODUCTION TO QUADRATIC RELATIONS

The ancient Greeks defined a cone as the surface generated when a line is rotated about a fixed point P on the line. Notice that the cone has two symmetric parts on either side of P.

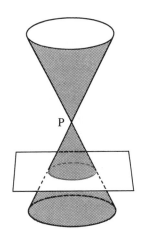

The curves that result when a plane intersects a cone are called *conic sections*, or *conics*. The Greeks discovered many properties of conics, but they were not interested in practical applications. In the seventeenth century, Isaac Newton proved that the orbit of a body revolving around another in accordance with the law of gravitation is a conic.

When a plane intersects a cone, the angle of inclination of the plane with respect to the cone determines the shape of the curve that results.

The Circle

In the drawing above, the plane is parallel to the base of the cone. In this case the curve of intersection is a *circle*. Hence, a circle is a conic.

The orbits of satellites and planets are nearly circular. The spectacular photographs we see of a total solar eclipse are caused by the fact that both the sun and the moon appear to us as circular discs of about the same size.

Although the conics are defined as sections of a cone, they also occur as the graphs of certain equations in *x* and *y*.

Example 1.   Graph the relation $x^2 + y^2 = 16$.

Solution.   We could use a table of values to draw the graph. A more efficient method is to observe that the equation expresses the condition that the distance from a point $P(x,y)$ to $O(0,0)$ be 4 units. Hence, the graph is a circle, with centre (0,0) and radius 4.

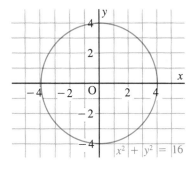

The Ellipse

If the intersecting plane is inclined to the base of the cone as shown, an *ellipse* results. As the angle of the intersecting plane increases, the shape of the ellipse changes from circular to long and elongated.

Satellites, planets, and some comets travel in elliptical orbits. Halley's comet, which returns to the sun approximately every 76 years, has a very long elliptical orbit.

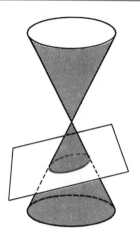

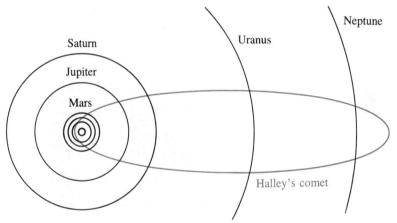

Example 2. Graph the relation $4x^2 + 9y^2 = 36$ using a table of values.

Solution. To prepare a table of values, we first solve the equation for y.

$$4x^2 + 9y^2 = 36$$
$$9y^2 = 36 - 4x^2$$
$$y = \frac{\pm\sqrt{36 - 4x^2}}{3}$$

x	y
0	± 2.00
0.5	± 1.97
1.0	± 1.89
1.5	± 1.73
2.0	± 1.49
2.5	± 1.11
3.0	0

x	y
0	± 2.00
-0.5	± 1.97
-1.0	± 1.89
-1.5	± 1.73
-2.0	± 1.49
-2.5	± 1.11
-3.0	0

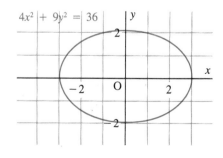

The Parabola

In this diagram, the intersecting plane is parallel to the line AB on the cone. The resulting curve is a *parabola*. Hence, a parabola is a conic.

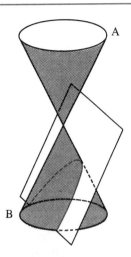

    Parabolas have many applications in astronomy. The mirrors in some telescopes have surfaces whose cross sections are parabolas. Many comets have orbits which extend far beyond the outermost planets. In the vicinity of the sun, these orbits are nearly parabolic. Also, as the photograph below suggests, a parabolic shape is sometimes formed by the coma and dust tail of a comet.

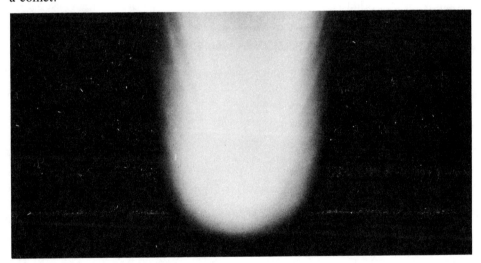

Example 3.   Graph the relation $x^2 - 4y = 0$.

Solution.   We could use a table of values to draw the graph. A more efficient method is to solve the equation for y and use our knowledge of the transformations of functions.

$$x^2 - 4y = 0$$
$$y = \frac{1}{4}x^2$$

The graph is a parabola with vertex $(0,0)$, axis of symmetry the y-axis, and opens up. It is a vertical compression of the parabola $y = x^2$.

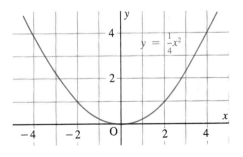

The Hyperbola

If the plane intersects the cone as shown, the resulting curve is called a *hyperbola*. Note that a hyperbola intersects both parts of the cone. Hence, a hyperbola has two distinct parts, or branches.

Some comets travel along paths which are slightly hyperbolic. As a result, they only appear once near the sun, and do not return. If a star passes another star, each is deflected along a hyperbolic path by the other. Another example of a hyperbolic path is provided by the Voyager 2 space probe which was launched to the outer planets in August, 1977. The diagram shows Voyager's path as it passed by Uranus in January, 1986.

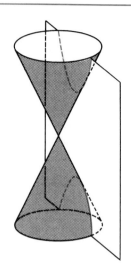

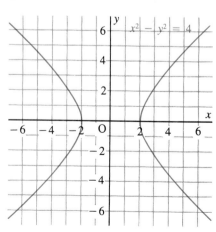

Uranus

Voyager 2

Example 4. Graph the relation $x^2 - y^2 = 4$ using a table of values.

Solution. To prepare a table of values, we first solve the equation for y.

$$x^2 - y^2 = 4$$
$$y^2 = x^2 - 4$$
$$y = \pm\sqrt{x^2 - 4}$$

x	y
2	0
3	± 2.24
4	± 3.46
5	± 4.58
6	± 5.66

x	y
-2	0
-3	± 2.24
-4	± 3.46
-5	± 4.58
-6	± 5.66

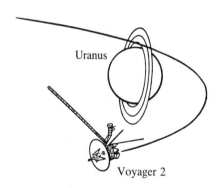

Each equation in the above examples has terms of the second degree in x or y. Any relation whose defining equation contains terms of the second degree, but no terms of higher degree, is called a *quadratic relation*.

These are quadratic relations.

$x^2 + 9y^2 = 18$

$2x^2 + xy - 2x = 14$

These are not quadratic relations.

$y = x^3$

$x^2 + 2xy^2 + 3y = 6$

In this chapter we will develop techniques for graphing certain quadratic relations without making tables of values.

EXERCISES 3-3

Ⓐ

1. Which of these are quadratic relations?
   a) $x^2 - y^2 = 9$
   b) $2x^3 + y^3 = 24$
   c) $3x^2 + 2y^2 = 12$
   d) $x^2 + 3x^2y = 6$
   e) $x^2 - 2y^2 + x - y = 7$
   f) $xy = 12$

Ⓑ

2. Graph each relation and identify the curve.
   a) $x^2 + y^2 = 9$
   b) $4x^2 + y^2 = 16$
   c) $4x^2 - y^2 = 16$
   d) $y = \dfrac{x^2}{8}$
   e) $4x^2 + 25y^2 = 100$
   f) $4x^2 - 25y^2 = 100$

3. a) Graph each relation.
   i) $x^2 + y^2 = 0$
   ii) $x^2 - y^2 = 0$
   iii) $(x - y)^2 = 0$
   b) Explain how the graphs of the relations in part a) could result when a plane intersects a cone.

4. A jet breaking the sound barrier creates a shock wave which has the shape of a cone. Describe the shape of the shock wave on the ground if the jet is:
   a) flying parallel to the ground
   b) gaining altitude
   c) losing altitude.

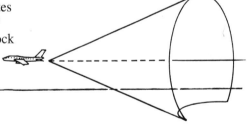

 INVESTIGATE

Models of the Conics

You can make models of the conics using styrofoam cones, which can be obtained from a craft store. Cut some styrofoam cones with a fine-toothed saw to create a circle, an ellipse, a parabola, and a hyperbola. Paint the surfaces.

Can you make four cuts in one cone to show a circle, an ellipse, a parabola, and a hyperbola?

3-4 THE RECTANGULAR HYPERBOLA

An equation such as $x^2 + y^2 = 9$ represents a circle. A similar equation
is $x^2 - y^2 = 9$. Since the squared terms are subtracted, this equation
cannot represent a circle. But it is a quadratic relation, and it represents
a conic.

Example 1.   Graph the relation $x^2 - y^2 = 9$, and identify the conic it represents.

Solution.   First, solve the equation for y.
$$x^2 - y^2 = 9$$
$$y^2 = x^2 - 9$$
$$y = \pm\sqrt{x^2 - 9}$$

We could graph the relation by making a table of values. But a more
efficient method is to consider how the values of y are related to the values
of x.

Since $x^2 - 9$ occurs under the radical sign, then $x^2 - 9 \geq 0$. Hence,
values of y are defined only when $x \geq 3$ or when $x \leq -3$.

If $x = \pm 3$, then $y = \pm\sqrt{(\pm 3)^2 - 9}$
$$= 0$$
Hence, $(3,0)$ and $(-3,0)$ are on the graph.

For each value of $x > 3$, or $x < -3$, there are two values of y, one
positive and the other negative. If $|x|$ is large, then x^2 is very large compared
with 9, and so

$y = \pm\sqrt{x^2 - 9}$

$\doteq \pm\sqrt{x^2}$

$\doteq x$ or $-x$

Hence, the graph comes
closer to the lines defined
by $y = x$ and $y = -x$.
The graph is a hyperbola.

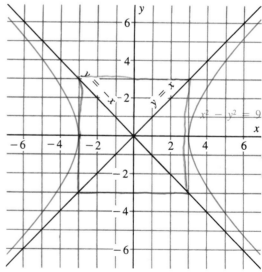

In *Example 1* the point $(0, 0)$ is called the *centre* of the hyperbola.
The points $(3, 0)$ and $(-3, 0)$ are called the *vertices*. The line segment
joining the vertices is called the *transverse axis*. The lines defined by
$y = x$ and $y = -x$ are called the *asymptotes*. Since the asymptotes are
perpendicular, we say that the hyperbola is *rectangular*.

The above example suggests that any equation of the form $x^2 - y^2 = a^2$ represents a rectangular hyperbola with centre $(0,0)$ and vertices on the x-axis. A rectangular hyperbola with vertices on the y-axis will have a different form of equation. To discover this form, we can interchange x and y in the equation of the hyperbola in *Example 1*. This has the effect of reversing the coordinates of the points which satisfy the equation. Hence, the graph of the relation is reflected in the line defined by $y = x$.

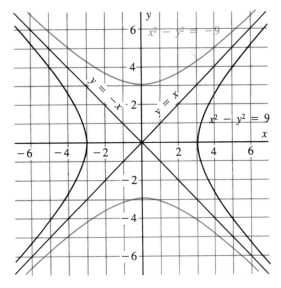

If we interchange x and y in $x^2 - y^2 = 9$, we obtain $y^2 - x^2 = 9$.

It is customary to write this equation as $x^2 - y^2 = -9$. The graph of this relation is shown. It was obtained by reflecting the graph of *Example 1* in the line defined by $y = x$.

Using the methods of the above examples, we can write the equation of any rectangular hyperbola with centre $(0,0)$ and vertices on the coordinate axes. The form of the equation depends on whether the vertices are on the x-axis or the y-axis.

Standard Equations of a Rectangular Hyperbola with Centre $(0,0)$

The equation of a rectangular hyperbola with centre $(0,0)$ and vertices on the x-axis is $x^2 - y^2 = a^2$.

The equation of a rectangular hyperbola with centre $(0,0)$ and vertices on the y-axis is $x^2 - y^2 = -a^2$.

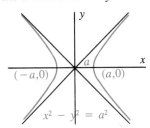

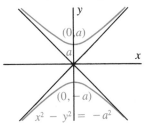

Vertices: $(a,0)$ and $(-a,0)$
Asymptotes: $y = x$ and $y = -x$

Vertices: $(0,a)$ and $(0,-a)$
Asymptotes: $y = x$ and $y = -x$

We can always tell whether the vertices are on the x-axis or the y-axis from the standard equation. If the constant term on the right side is positive, the vertices are on the x-axis; if it is negative, the vertices are on the y-axis.

EXERCISES 3-4

(A)

1. Determine if each point is on the rectangular hyperbola defined by $x^2 - y^2 = 15$.
   a) $(-4,1)$ b) $(7,8)$ c) $(8,7)$ d) $(0,\sqrt{15})$

2. State the coordinates of the centre, the coordinates of the vertices, and the equations of the asymptotes of the rectangular hyperbola defined by each equation.
   a) $x^2 - y^2 = 25$ b) $x^2 - y^2 = 64$ c) $x^2 - y^2 = -81$
   d) $x^2 - y^2 = 2$ e) $x^2 - y^2 = -5$ f) $x^2 - y^2 = -20$

3. The coordinates of one vertex of a rectangular hyperbola are given. If the centre is $(0,0)$, write an equation of the rectangular hyperbola.
   a) $(7,0)$ b) $(0,4)$ c) $(0,-6)$ d) $(-10,0)$

(B)

4. Sketch the rectangular hyperbolas defined by these equations on the same grid.
   a) $x^2 - y^2 = 4$ b) $x^2 - y^2 = 16$ c) $x^2 - y^2 = 36$
   d) $x^2 - y^2 = -4$ e) $x^2 - y^2 = -16$ f) $x^2 - y^2 = -36$

5. When a square is cut from another square as shown, the area of the remaining portion is 144 cm².
   a) Find the relation between x and y.
   b) Graph the relation.

6. A rectangular hyperbola has centre $(0,0)$ and vertices on the x-axis.
   a) Find an equation of the hyperbola if it passes through $(8,2)$.
   b) Find the value of x_1 if $(x_1,14)$ is on the hyperbola.

7. A rectangular hyperbola has centre $(0,0)$ and vertices on the y-axis.
   a) Find an equation of the hyperbola if it passes through $(7,-8)$.
   b) Find the value of y_1 if $(1,y_1)$ is on the hyperbola.

8. A bridge over a river is supported by a hyperbolic arch which is 200 m wide at the base. The maximum height of the arch is 50 m.
   a) Write an equation to represent the arch.
   b) How high is the arch at a point 30 m from the centre?

(C)

9. Given the equation $Ax^2 + By^2 + C = 0$, what conditions must be satisfied by A, B, and C if this equation represents a rectangular hyperbola with vertices on:
   a) the x-axis b) the y-axis?

10. $P(x_1,y_1)$ is a point on the right branch of the rectangular hyperbola defined by $x^2 - y^2 = 4$. $D(\sqrt{2},y_1)$ is the corresponding point to the left of P on the line defined by $x = \sqrt{2}$.
    a) If F is the point $(2\sqrt{2},0)$ prove that $PF = \sqrt{2}PD$ for any position of P on the right branch of the hyperbola.
    b) Obtain a similar result if P is a point on the left branch.

3-5 GRAPHING QUADRATIC RELATIONS: PART ONE

The graphs of the conics are of essentially three different types.

circular or elliptical (closed curve)	*hyperbolic* (two branches and two asymptotes)	*parabolic* (only one branch and no asymptotes)
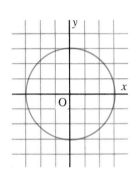	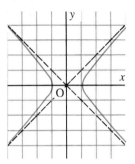	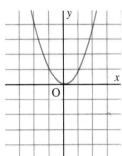

If the curves are drawn in a central position on a coordinate grid, as shown, their equations have certain characteristic forms.

Circle with centre (0, 0)	Rectangular hyperbola with centre (0, 0) and	Parabola with vertex (0, 0) and axis of symmetry:
	● vertices on *x*-axis	● the *y*-axis
$x^2 + y^2 = r^2$	$x^2 - y^2 = a^2$	$y = x^2$
	● vertices on *y*-axis	● the *x*-axis
	$x^2 - y^2 = -a^2$	$x = y^2$
Squared terms separated by a + sign	Squared terms separated by a − sign	Only one squared term

To obtain the graphs of the other conics, we take these basic graphs and expand or compress them vertically or horizontally. We can also change their positions relative to the axes. When these changes are made to the graphs, corresponding changes occur in the equations. In this section and in a later section, we will see how the changes in the equations are related to the changes in the graphs. Then we will be able to sketch graphs of the conics without making tables of values.

For example, we can obtain an ellipse graphically by expanding a circle horizontally or vertically. We can also expand it by different amounts both horizontally and vertically. And, if we know the equation of the circle, we can determine the equation of the ellipse.

Compare these two equations.

$$x^2 + y^2 = 1 \quad \ldots \text{①}$$

$$\left(\frac{x}{3}\right)^2 + \left(\frac{y}{2}\right)^2 = 1 \quad \ldots \text{②}$$

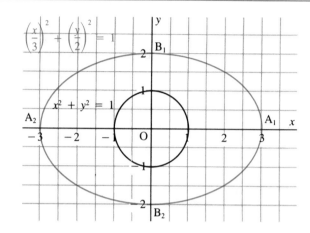

Each equation states that the sum of the squares of two numbers is 1. In equation ① these numbers are the coordinates of points on a unit circle. In equation ②, to give the same numbers whose squares add to 1 as in equation ①, the values of x must be 3 *times* those in equation ①. Similarly, the values of y must be 2 *times* those in equation ①.

Every point whose coordinates satisfy equation ② must be 3 times as far from the y-axis, and 2 times as far from the x-axis, as the corresponding point whose coordinates satisfy equation ①. Hence, the graph of equation ② is *expanded horizontally* by a factor of 3 and *expanded vertically* by a factor of 2 relative to the graph of equation ①. Equation ② represents an ellipse with x-intercepts 3 and -3, and with y-intercepts 2 and -2.

(0, 0) is the *centre* of the ellipse. The line segment A_1A_2 is the *major axis*; it is the longest line segment joining two points on the ellipse. The line segment B_1B_2 is the *minor axis*; it is the shortest line segment through the centre which joins two points on the ellipse. Points $A_1(3, 0)$ and $A_2(-3, 0)$ are the *vertices*; these are the endpoints of the major axis.

Equation ② may be written as

$$\frac{x^2}{9} + \frac{y^2}{4} = 1$$

or as $\quad 4x^2 + 9y^2 = 36$

Compare either of these equations with equation ①. Observe that the squared terms are separated by a $+$ sign. This is the distinguishing property of the equation of a circle or an ellipse, and it was not affected by the expansion.

The above analysis can be applied to the equation of any relation and its graph.

Expansion Property of a Relation

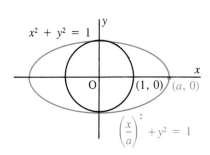

- If x is replaced with $\dfrac{x}{a}$ in the equation of a relation, the graph is expanded horizontally by a factor of a.

- If y is replaced with $\dfrac{y}{b}$ in the equation of a relation, the graph is expanded vertically by a factor of b.

- These replacements do not change the distinguishing properties of the equations:
  ellipse: squared terms separated by a $+$ sign
  hyperbola: squared terms separated by a $-$ sign
  parabola: only one squared term.

Example 1. Describe and sketch the graph of each relation.
a) $25x^2 - 4y^2 = 100$ b) $4x^2 - y^2 = -16$

Solution. Since the squared terms are separated by a $-$ sign, each equation represents a hyperbola.
a) $25x^2 - 4y^2 = 100$
   Divide both sides of the equation by 100.

$$\frac{25x^2}{100} - \frac{4y^2}{100} = 1$$

$$\frac{x^2}{4} - \frac{y^2}{25} = 1$$

or $\left(\dfrac{x}{2}\right)^2 - \left(\dfrac{y}{5}\right)^2 = 1$

The graph of the hyperbola is expanded horizontally by a factor of 2 and vertically by a factor of 5 relative to the graph of the rectangular hyperbola defined by $x^2 - y^2 = 1$.
Centre: $(0, 0)$
Vertices: $(2, 0)$ and $(-2, 0)$
Asymptotes: $y = \pm\dfrac{5}{2}x$, or $y = \pm 2.5x$

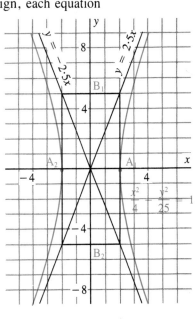

b) $4x^2 - y^2 = -16$

Divide both sides of the equation by 16.

$$\frac{x^2}{4} - \frac{y^2}{16} = -1$$

or $\left(\dfrac{x}{2}\right)^2 - \left(\dfrac{y}{4}\right)^2 = -1$

The graph of the hyperbola is expanded horizontally by a factor of 2 and vertically by a factor of 4 relative to the graph of the rectangular hyperbola defined by $x^2 - y^2 = -1$.

Centre: (0, 0)

Vertices: (0, 4) and (0, −4)

Asymptotes: $y = \pm 2x$

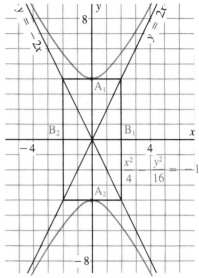

In *Example 1a*, the line segment A_1A_2 is the transverse axis. Since there was a vertical expansion by a factor of 5, we indicate the points $B_1(0, 5)$ and $B_2(0, -5)$ on the y-axis. The line segment B_1B_2 is called the *conjugate axis*. In *Example 1b*, the conjugate axis joins the points $B_1(2, 0)$ and $B_2(-2, 0)$. Observe that the points A_1, A_2, B_1, and B_2 determine a rectangle centred at (0, 0). The diagonals of this rectangle determine the asymptotes, which serve as guides for graphing the hyperbola.

Example 2.   Describe and sketch the graph of each relation.

a) $9x^2 + y^2 = 36$ b) $y = 2x^2$

Solution.   a) $9x^2 + y^2 = 36$

Since the squared terms are separated by a + sign, the equation represents an ellipse.

$9x^2 + y^2 = 36$

Divide both sides by 36.

$$\frac{x^2}{4} + \frac{y^2}{36} = 1$$

or $\left(\dfrac{x}{2}\right)^2 + \left(\dfrac{y}{6}\right)^2 = 1$

The graph of the ellipse is expanded horizontally by a factor of 2 and vertically by a factor of 6 relative to the graph of the circle defined by $x^2 + y^2 = 1$.

Centre: (0, 0)

Vertices: $(0, \pm6)$

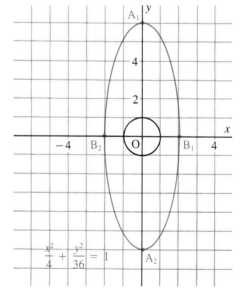

b) Since there is only one squared term, the equation represents a parabola. In a previous grade we saw that the graph of $y = 2x^2$ is expanded vertically by a factor of 2 relative to the graph of $y = x^2$. (This is consistent with the development in this section, since the equation can be written as

$$\frac{y}{2} = x^2.)$$

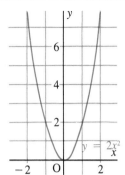

In *Examples 1* and *2* the equations were written in *standard form*.

Equations of Conics in Standard Form Centred at (0, 0)

Ellipse with centre (0, 0)

Major axis on the *x*-axis

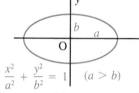

$$\frac{x^2}{a^2} + \frac{y^2}{b^2} = 1 \quad (a > b)$$

Major axis on the *y*-axis

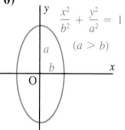

$$\frac{x^2}{b^2} + \frac{y^2}{a^2} = 1$$

$$(a > b)$$

The squared terms are separated by a + sign. The term in which the larger denominator occurs indicates which axis contains the major axis. If $a = b$, the equation represents a circle.

Hyperbola with centre (0, 0)

Transverse axis on the *x*-axis

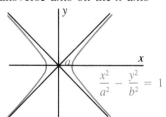

$$\frac{x^2}{a^2} - \frac{y^2}{b^2} = 1$$

Transverse axis on the *y*-axis

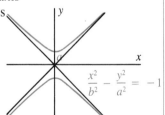

$$\frac{x^2}{b^2} - \frac{y^2}{a^2} = -1$$

The squared terms are separated by a − sign. The term having the same sign as the constant term indicates which axis contains the transverse axis.

Parabola with vertex (0, 0)

Axis of symmetry the *x*-axis

Opens right if $a > 0$

Opens left if $a < 0$

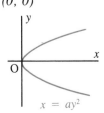

$$x = ay^2$$

Axis of symmetry the *y*-axis

Opens up if $a > 0$

Opens down if $a < 0$

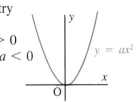

$$y = ax^2$$

EXERCISES 3-5

1. State which equations represent each curve.

   i) a circle   ii) an ellipse   iii) a hyperbola   iv) a parabola

   a) $\dfrac{x^2}{9} + \dfrac{y^2}{36} = 1$ b) $\dfrac{x^2}{5} - \dfrac{y^2}{10} = 1$ c) $x^2 + 4y^2 - 8 = 0$

   d) $3x^2 + 3y^2 - 5 = 0$ e) $x = 6y^2$ f) $2x^2 - 3y^2 + 6 = 0$

2. Describe and sketch the graph of each relation.

   a) $\dfrac{x^2}{25} + \dfrac{y^2}{16} = 1$ b) $\dfrac{x^2}{16} + \dfrac{y^2}{36} = 1$ c) $\dfrac{x^2}{16} - \dfrac{y^2}{9} = -1$

   d) $\dfrac{x^2}{36} - \dfrac{y^2}{16} = 1$ e) $\dfrac{x^2}{9} + \dfrac{y^2}{6} = 1$ f) $\dfrac{x^2}{49} - \dfrac{y^2}{25} = -1$

   g) $x = 3y^2$ h) $y = -2x^2$ i) $9x^2 + y^2 = 9$

3. Describe and sketch the graph of each relation.

   a) $16x^2 + 9y^2 = 144$ b) $4x^2 - 25y^2 = 100$ c) $9x^2 - 25y^2 = -400$

   d) $x^2 + 3y^2 = 12$ e) $4x^2 + y^2 = 20$ f) $3x^2 + 4y^2 = 36$

   g) $3x^2 - y^2 = 18$ b) $5x^2 - 4y^2 = 40$ i) $8x^2 - 6y^2 = -48$

4. An ellipse has centre $(0, 0)$ and major axis on the x-axis. Write the equation of the ellipse if:

   a) the x-intercepts are ± 6 and the y-intercepts are ± 3

   b) one vertex is $A_1(5, 0)$ and one y-intercept is 2

   c) the major axis has length 10 and the minor axis has length 4.

5. A hyperbola has centre $(0, 0)$ and transverse axis on the x-axis. Write the equation of the hyperbola if:

   a) the transverse axis has length 6 and the conjugate axis has length 4

   b) the transverse axis has length 4 and the conjugate axis has length 6

   c) the transverse axis has length 12 and one asymptote is defined by $y = 2x$.

6. Repeat *Exercise 5* if the transverse axis is on the y-axis.

7. The equation of an ellipse may be written in the form $b^2x^2 + a^2y^2 = a^2b^2$. Observe that the constant term is equal to the product of the coefficients of x^2 and y^2. Does this mean that an equation that does not have this property, such as $2x^2 + 3y^2 = 24$, does not represent an ellipse? Explain.

8. a) Find the area of a square inscribed in the ellipse defined by $\dfrac{x^2}{a^2} + \dfrac{y^2}{b^2} = 1$.

   b) Investigate whether or not a square can be inscribed in the hyperbola defined by $\dfrac{x^2}{a^2} - \dfrac{y^2}{b^2} = 1$. If it can, determine its area.

3-6 APPLICATIONS OF QUADRATIC RELATIONS

Quadratic relations have many applications in astronomy, and in construction and design. The problems are usually solved by using the given data to determine an equation of a conic in standard form, and then using the equation to determine some unknown quantity.

Example 1. A bridge over a river is supported by a parabolic arch which is 40 m wide at water level. The maximum height of the arch is 16 m.
a) Write an equation to represent the arch.
b) How high is the arch at a point 10 m from the centre?

Solution.   a) Use a coordinate system as shown.
Let the equation of the arch be $y = ax^2$. From the given information, and the diagram, the point $M(20, -16)$ is on the parabola. Hence, these coordinates satisfy the equation. Substitute 20 for x and -16 for y in $y = ax^2$.

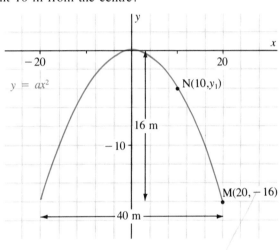

$$-16 = a(20)^2$$
$$-16 = 400a$$
$$a = -\frac{16}{400}$$
$$= -0.04$$

The equation of the parabola is $y = -0.04x^2$.

b) Let $N(10, y_1)$ represent a point on the arch which is 10 m from the centre. Then these coordinates satisfy the equation. Substitute 10 for x and y_1 for y in $y = -0.04x^2$.
$$y_1 = -0.04(10)^2$$
$$= -4$$

A point 10 m from the centre is 4 m below the highest point, and therefore 12 m above the water level. Hence, the arch is 12 m high at a point 10 m from the centre.

In *Example 1* we used the standard form of the equation of a parabola given in the previous section, $y = ax^2$. We could also have used the standard form, $x^2 = 4py$. Both forms are equivalent, because they are derived from the equation $y = x^2$ by multiplying one side of the equation by a constant.

Example 1 was solved using the fundamental property of a locus. That is, the coordinates of every point on the graph of a relation satisfy its equation; and, every point whose coordinates satisfy the equation of a relation is on its graph.

Example 2. The arch of a bridge has the shape of a rectangular hyperbola. The base is 120 m wide, and the vertex is 30 m above the base.
a) Find an equation of the hyperbola.
b) Find the height of the arch at a point 25 m from the centre.

Solution. a) Let the equation of the hyperbola be $x^2 - y^2 = -a^2$. The coordinates of vertex A_2 are $(0, -a)$. Let P be a point 60 m to the right of A_2 and 30 m below A_2. Hence, the coordinates of P are $(60, -a - 30)$. Since P is on the hyperbola, its coordinates satisfy the equation. Substitute 60 for x and $-a - 30$ for y in $x^2 - y^2 = -a^2$.

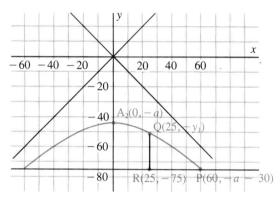

$$3600 - (-a - 30)^2 = -a^2$$
$$3600 - (a^2 + 60a + 900) = -a^2$$
$$a = \frac{2700}{60}$$
$$= 45$$

Hence, the equation of the hyperbola is $x^2 - y^2 = -45^2$, or $x^2 - y^2 = -2025$.

b) Let $Q(25, -y_1)$ represent a point on the arch 25 m from the centre. Then these coordinates satisfy the equation. Substitute 25 for x and $-y_1$ for y.

$$x^2 - y^2 = -2025$$
$$625 - y_1^2 = -2025$$
$$y_1^2 = 2650$$
$$y_1 = \sqrt{2650}$$
$$\doteq 51.5$$

The coordinates of Q are $(25, -51.5)$. From part a), the coordinates of P are $(60, -75)$. Hence, the coordinates of R are $(25, -75)$, and the length of segment QR is $75 - 51.5$, or 23.5. Hence, the arch is 23.5 m high at a point which is 25 m from the centre.

EXERCISES 3-6

(B)

1. The cables of a suspension bridge hang in a curve which approximates a parabola. The road bed passes through the vertex. If the supporting towers are 720 m apart and 60 m high, find:
   a) an equation of the parabola
   b) the height of the cables at a point 30 m from the vertex.

2. A stone thrown horizontally from a bridge 25 m above a river splashes in the water 40 m from the base of the bridge. If the stone falls in a parabolic path, find its equation relative to the position from which it was thrown.

3. The supporting structure for the roof of a curling rink has parabolic arches anchored at ground level. If the arches are 15.3 m high, and span 70 m, find:
   a) an equation of the parabola
   b) the height of the arches at a point 10 m from the centre.

4. A pool has the shape of an ellipse. The major axis has length 10 m and the minor axis has length 6 m.
   a) Write an equation of the ellipse.
   b) Find the width of the pool at a point on the major axis which is 2 m from the centre.

5. A retractable dome on a sports stadium has the shape of an ellipse. Its height is 125 m and it spans 300 m.
   a) Write an equation of the ellipse.
   b) Calculate the height of the dome at a point on the major axis which is 20 m from the centre.

6. A tunnel is built under a river for a road 12 m wide with a 2 m sidewalk on either side. The top of the tunnel is semi-elliptical. A local bylaw stipulates that there must be a clearance of at least 3.6 m at all points on the road. If the smallest possible ellipse is used, find the clearance at the centre of the road.

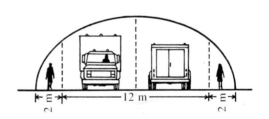

7. A bridge over a river is supported by a hyperbolic arch which is 200 m wide at the base. The maximum height of the arch is 50 m. How high is the arch at a point 30 m from the centre?

(C)

8. The orbit of a satellite is an ellipse with the centre of the Earth on its major axis. One satellite has an orbit with major axis 15 540 km and minor axis 15 490 km. The centre of the orbit is 600 km from the centre of the Earth. The radius of the Earth is 6370 km. Calculate the height of the satellite at:
   a) its lowest point (the *perigee*)   b) its highest point (the *apogee*).

All Parabolas Have the Same Shape

"When I use a word," Humpty Dumpty said in a rather scornful tone, "it means just what I choose it to mean — neither more nor less."

Lewis Carroll

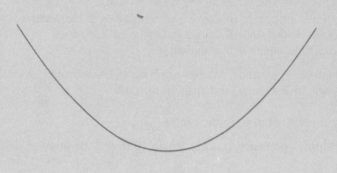

Prove that all parabolas have the same shape.

Understand the problem
- Do these parabolas look like they have the same shape?
- What does "have the same shape" mean?

The diagrams below suggest a general definition for "same shape".

All circles have the same shape.	All squares have the same same shape.	Similar triangles have the same shape.

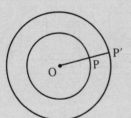

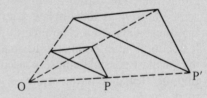

$$\frac{OP'}{OP} = k \qquad \frac{OP'}{OP} = k \qquad \frac{OP'}{OP} = k$$

Two curves C and C′ have the *same shape* if there is a point O such that $\frac{OP'}{OP} = k$ for every point P on C and a corresponding point P′ on C′, where O, P, and P′ are collinear and k is a constant.

Think of a strategy

- If it is true that all parabolas have the same shape, then we should be able to prove this using the defining property of a parabola. Since the defining property involves the focus, the point O is probably the focus.
- Draw two parabolas with the same focus, O.
- Draw a line through O to intersect the parabolas at P and Q. We must prove that $\dfrac{OQ}{OP}$ is constant.

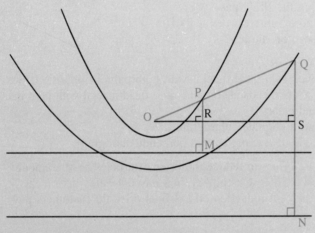

Carry out the strategy

- Drop perpendiculars PM and QN to the corresponding directrices. Then, according to the defining property of a parabola, OP = PM and OQ = QN.
- The proof will probably involve △OPR and △OQS. What properties do these triangles have?
- Since OQ = QN = QS + SN and OP = PM = PR + RM, we may write $\dfrac{OQ}{OP} = \dfrac{QS + SN}{PR + RM}$. Use this equation, and the fact that △OPR ~ △OQS to prove that $\dfrac{OQ}{OP} = \dfrac{SN}{RM}$.
- Explain why this proves that $\dfrac{OQ}{OP}$ is a constant.

Look back

- Do the parabolas on page 112 have the same shape? Do they look like they have the same shape? Explain this apparent inconsistency.

PROBLEMS

Ⓑ

1. If this pattern is cut out and folded to make a polyhedron, how many edges will it have? How many vertices will it have?

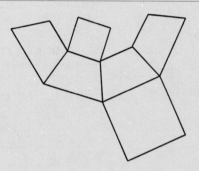

2. An airplane leaves Calgary in the evening and arrives in London, England early the next morning. During the flight passengers see a sunset and a sunrise. Explain why both are seen on the left side of the plane.

3. A parallelogram is defined as a quadrilateral with both pairs of opposite sides parallel. We can define a "perpendicularogram" as a quadrilateral with both pairs of opposite sides perpendicular.
   a) Sketch an example of a perpendicularogram.
   b) State a property of one of the angles of a perpendicularogram.

4. To promote sales, a store offers to reduce the price of articles by the amount of the provincial sales tax, 6%. Customers then pay 6% sales tax on the reduced amount. What percent reduction on the final price do customers pay as a result?

Ⓒ

5. In $\triangle ABC$, points D and E are located on AB and AC such that DE $\parallel$ BC. If DE bisects the area of $\triangle ABC$, and if BC has length x, express the length of DE as a function of x.

6. Any chord of an ellipse which passes through the centre is called a *diameter*. Let P be any point on the ellipse $b^2x^2 + a^2y^2 = a^2b^2$.
   a) Prove that the product of the slopes of the segments joining P to the endpoints of any diameter is constant.
   b) Discuss how the result in part a) is a generalization of the theorem in geometry that the angle in a semicircle is a right angle.

Ⓓ

7. In a semicircle, three connected chords have lengths 1, 2, and 3 respectively. Calculate the radius of the semicircle.

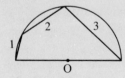

3-7 GRAPHING QUADRATIC RELATIONS: PART TWO

In *Section 3-5* we investigated the effect of dividing x or y in the equation of a relation by a constant. This resulted in an expansion of its graph in the horizontal or vertical directions respectively. In this section we investigate the effect of adding or subtracting a constant to the variables in the equation.

Compare these two equations.

$$\frac{x^2}{9} + \frac{y^2}{4} = 1 \dots \text{①}$$

$$\frac{(x-5)^2}{9} + \frac{(y+1)^2}{4} = 1 \dots \text{②}$$

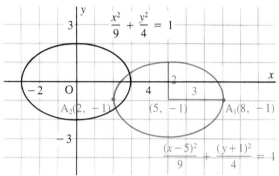

Equation ① represents an ellipse with centre (0, 0).
For this ellipse, $a = 3$ and $b = 2$
The major axis has length $2a$, or 6.
The minor axis has length $2b$, or 4.
The coordinates of the vertices are (3, 0) and (−3, 0)
We can use this information to sketch the graph of equation ②. Both equation ① and equation ② state that the sum of two numbers is 1.

In equation ②, to give the same numbers adding to 1 as in equation ①, the values of x must be 5 *greater* than those in equation ①. Similarly, the values of y must be 1 *less* than those in equation ①. Every point whose coordinates satisfy equation ② must be 5 units to the *right* of, and 1 unit *below* the corresponding point whose coordinates satisfy equation ①. Hence, equation ② represents an ellipse that has been translated 5 units to the right and 1 unit down relative to the first ellipse. Therefore, its centre is (5, −1). Since the major axis has length 6, the coordinates of the vertices are (5 ± 3, −1); that is, (8, −1) and (2, −1). The minor axis has length 4, and the coordinates of its endpoints are (5, −1 ± 2); that is, (5, 1) and (5, −3).

Equations ① and ② may be written as follows.

$$4x^2 + 9y^2 = 36 \dots \text{③}$$

and

$$4(x-5)^2 + 9(y+1)^2 = 36$$

$$4x^2 + 9y^2 - 40x + 18y - 73 = 0 \dots \text{④}$$

Observe that equations ③ and ④ contain the same quadratic terms. That is, the quadratic terms were not affected by the translation.

The above analysis can be applied to the equation of any quadratic relation and its graph.

Translation Property of a Relation

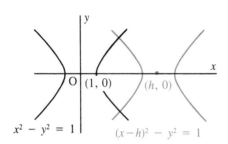

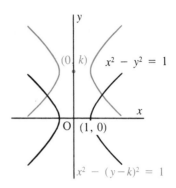

- If x is replaced with $x - h$ in the equation of a relation, the graph is translated h units horizontally.
- If y is replaced with $y - k$ in the equation of a relation, the graph is translated k units vertically.
- These replacements do not change the quadratic terms in the equation.

Example 1. Describe and sketch the graph of each relation.

a) $\dfrac{(x-3)^2}{25} + \dfrac{(y+4)^2}{4} = 1$ b) $y - 3 = \dfrac{(x-2)^2}{4}$

Solution. a) Since the squared terms are separated by a $+$ sign, the equation represents an ellipse. Its graph is translated 3 units to the right and 4 units down relative to the graph of the ellipse defined by $\dfrac{x^2}{25} + \dfrac{y^2}{4} = 1$.

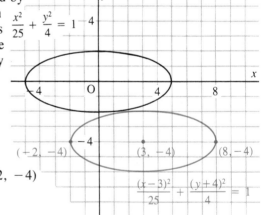

Length of major axis: $2a$, or 10
Length of minor axis: $2b$, or 4
Centre: $(3, -4)$
Vertices: $(3 + 5, -4)$ or $(8, -4)$
       and $(3 - 5, -4)$ or $(-2, -4)$

b) Since there is only one squared term, the equation represents a parabola. Its graph is translated 2 units to the right and 3 units up relative to the graph of the parabola defined by $y = \left(\dfrac{x}{2}\right)^2$, or $y = \dfrac{1}{4}x^2$.

Vertex: $(2, 3)$
Axis: $x - 2 = 0$

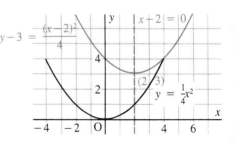

The equations in the above examples were written in standard form.

Equations of Conics in Standard Form Centred at (*h*, *k*)

Ellipse with centre (h,k)

Major axis horizontal

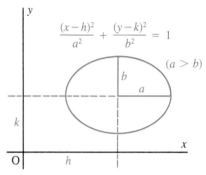

$$\frac{(x-h)^2}{a^2} + \frac{(y-k)^2}{b^2} = 1$$

$(a > b)$

Major axis vertical

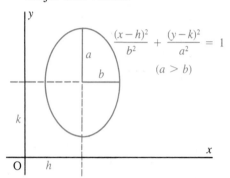

$$\frac{(x-h)^2}{b^2} + \frac{(y-k)^2}{a^2} = 1$$

$(a > b)$

Hyperbola with centre (h,k)

Transverse axis horizontal

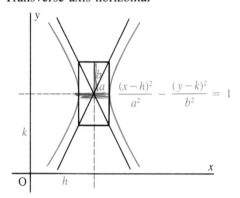

$$\frac{(x-h)^2}{a^2} - \frac{(y-k)^2}{b^2} = 1$$

Transverse axis vertical

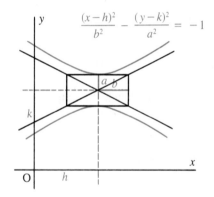

$$\frac{(x-h)^2}{b^2} - \frac{(y-k)^2}{a^2} = -1$$

Parabola with vertex (h,k)

Axis of symmetry horizontal

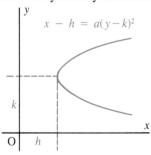

$$x - h = a(y-k)^2$$

Axis of symmetry vertical

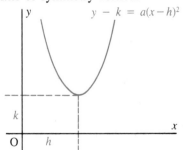

$$y - k = a(x-h)^2$$

$$\frac{(x-h)^2}{a^2} + \frac{(y-k)^2}{b^2} = 1$$

EXERCISES 3-7

(A)

1. Write an equation to represent each conic.

h=3 k=2

a)

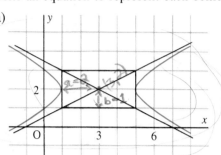

b)

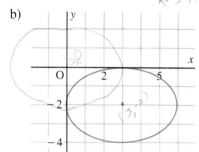

(B)

2. Describe and sketch the graph of each relation.

a) $\dfrac{(x-2)^2}{16} + \dfrac{(y+3)^2}{49} = 1$

b) $\dfrac{(x+5)^2}{16} + \dfrac{(y-3)^2}{4} = 1$

c) $\dfrac{(x-4)^2}{9} - \dfrac{(y+6)^2}{4} = 1$

d) $\dfrac{(x-2)^2}{9} - \dfrac{y^2}{25} = 1$

e) $\dfrac{(x+3)^2}{18} + \dfrac{(y+3)^2}{9} = 1$

f) $\dfrac{(x-5)^2}{36} - \dfrac{(y-1)^2}{9} = -1$

g) $y + 2 = (x-3)^2$

h) $y - 4 = \dfrac{(x+1)^2}{4}$ parabola

3. Describe and sketch the graph of each relation.

a) $4(x-3)^2 + 9(y-2)^2 = 36$

b) $4(x+1)^2 - (y-3)^2 = 16$

c) $(x+5)^2 - 4(y+4)^2 = -36$

d) $3(x-2)^2 + 4(y+2)^2 = 24$

e) $3x^2 - (y-2)^2 = 27$

f) $(x+5)^2 + 6y^2 = 36$

g) $4(y-1) = (x-2)^2$

h) $4(x+2) = (y-5)^2$

❚ INVESTIGATE

Degenerate Conics

1. In *Section 3-3*, diagrams were shown illustrating four ways in which a plane can intersect a cone. In what other ways can a plane intersect a cone?

2. *Question 1* suggests that a second-degree equation in *x* and *y* may have a graph which is not a circle, ellipse, parabola, or hyperbola. What other possible graphs are there? Write an example of an equation to represent each possibility.

3-8 WRITING EQUATIONS IN STANDARD FORM

When the equation of a quadratic relation is written in standard form, the numbers in the equation indicate certain properties of its graph. For example, we can tell that the equation

$$\frac{(x - 2)^2}{9} + \frac{(y - 1)^2}{16} = 1$$

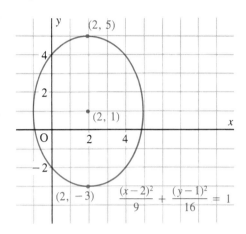

represents an ellipse with these properties.

Centre: (2, 1)
Length of major axis: $2a$, or 8
Length of minor axis: $2b$, or 6
The major axis is vertical.
Vertices: (2, 1 + 4), or (2, 5)
        and (2, 1 − 4), or (2, −3)

The above equation can also be written as follows.

$$16(x - 2)^2 + 9(y - 1)^2 = 144$$
$$16(x^2 - 4x + 4) + 9(y^2 - 2y + 1) = 144$$
$$16x^2 + 9y^2 - 64x - 18y - 71 = 0$$

This form of writing the equation is called the *general form*. When an equation is written in general form we cannot read the properties of the graph from the equation. To determine the properties we must first write the equation in standard form.

Example 1. Given the conic defined by $4x^2 - 9y^2 + 32x + 18y + 91 = 0$
a) Write the equation in standard form.
b) Describe and sketch the graph of the conic.

Solution. a) We collect the terms containing x, and the terms containing y.

$$4x^2 - 9y^2 + 32x + 18y + 91 = 0$$
$$4x^2 + 32x - 9y^2 + 18y + 91 = 0$$
$$4(x^2 + 8x) - 9(y^2 - 2y) + 91 = 0$$

Complete each square.

$$4(x^2 + 8x + 16 - 16) - 9(y^2 - 2y + 1 - 1) + 91 = 0$$
$$4(x + 4)^2 - 64 - 9(y - 1)^2 + 9 + 91 = 0$$
$$4(x + 4)^2 - 9(y - 1)^2 = -36$$
$$\frac{(x + 4)^2}{9} - \frac{(y - 1)^2}{4} = -1$$

b) The equation represents a
   hyperbola.
   Centre: $(-4, 1)$
   Length of transverse axis:
   $2a$, or 4
   Length of conjugate axis:
   $2b$, or 6
   The transverse axis is
   vertical.
   Vertices:
   $(-4, 1 + 2)$, or $(-4, 3)$;
   $(-4, 1 - 2)$, or $(-4, -1)$

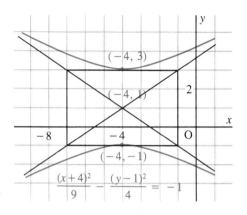

In *Example 1* we could have predicted that the given equation represents a hyperbola since the quadratic terms are separated by a $-$ sign.

Equations that represent a parabola contain only one squared term; hence, only one square can be completed.

Example 2.   Given the conic defined by $x^2 + 10x + 4y + 13 = 0$
a) Write the equation in standard form.
b) Describe and sketch the graph of the conic.

Solution.   a)
$$x^2 + 10x + 4y + 13 = 0$$
$$x^2 + 10x + 25 - 25 + 4y + 13 = 0$$
$$(x + 5)^2 + 4y - 12 = 0$$
$$4(y - 3) = -(x + 5)^2$$
$$y - 3 = -\left(\frac{x + 5}{2}\right)^2$$

b) The equation represents a parabola.
   Vertex: $(-5, 3)$
   Direction of opening: down
   Axis: $x = -5$

   Congruent to $y = \frac{1}{4}x^2$

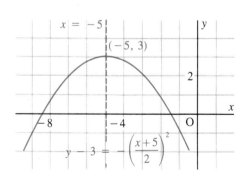

The equations in the above examples are examples of the general equation $Ax^2 + By^2 + 2Gx + 2Fy + C = 0$. Such an equation does not always have a graph. For example, if $A = 3$, $B = 2$, $C = 1$, and $G = F = 0$, the equation becomes $3x^2 + 2y^2 + 1 = 0$ which is not satisfied by any values of x and y since the left side is always greater than or equal to 1. When the graph of the general equation exists, it is a conic with its axes (or axis) parallel to the coordinate axes. The nature of the conic depends only on the quadratic terms, $Ax^2 + By^2$.

Properties of the Equation $Ax^2 + By^2 + 2Gx + 2Fy + C = 0$
We assume that A and B are not both 0.
- If the graph of this equation exists, it is a conic.
- The axes (or axis) of the conic are parallel to the coordinate axes.
- If $AB > 0$, the conic is an ellipse (a circle if $A = B$).
  If $AB < 0$, the conic is a hyperbola.
  If $A = 0$ or $B = 0$, the conic is a parabola.

EXERCISES 3-8

Ⓐ

1. Write each equation in general form.
   a) $3(x - 1)^2 + (y + 2)^2 = 9$
   b) $(x + 5)^2 - 2(y - 1)^2 = 10$
   c) $y - 2 = 3(x - 4)^2$
   d) $\dfrac{(x + 2)^2}{9} + \dfrac{(y - 3)^2}{4} = 1$
   e) $\dfrac{(x + 1)^2}{6} - \dfrac{(y + 2)^2}{3} = -1$
   f) $x + 4 = -2(y - 3)^2$

2. Each equation represents a conic. State which represents each conic.
   i) a circle   ii) an ellipse   iii) a hyperbola   iv) a parabola
   a) $9x^2 + 4y^2 - 54x + 16y + 61 = 0$
   b) $2x^2 - 3y^2 - 8x - 6y + 11 = 0$
   c) $y^2 - 4x + 6y - 23 = 0$
   d) $x^2 + y^2 + 4x + 5y = 0$

(B)

3. Given the conic defined by each equation, write the equation in standard form, and then sketch the conic.
   a) $2x^2 + y^2 + 12x - 2y + 15 = 0$
   b) $4x^2 + 9y^2 - 8x + 36y + 4 = 0$
   c) $x^2 - 9y^2 - 4x + 18y - 14 = 0$
   d) $x^2 - 4y^2 - 2x - 3 = 0$
   e) $y^2 - 4x + 8y + 3 = 0$
   f) $x^2 + 2x + 3y + 4 = 0$

4. Describe the graph of each equation.
   a) $x^2 + y^2 - 8x + 6y + 9 = 0$
   b) $x^2 + 4y^2 - 2x + 16y + 13 = 0$
   c) $3x^2 + 4y^2 + 18x - 16y + 31 = 0$
   d) $3x^2 - 2y^2 - 36x + 96 = 0$
   e) $y^2 - 8x - 8y = 0$
   f) $6x^2 + 24x - y + 19 = 0$

5. The diagram shows three overlapping squares.
   a) If the colored region has the same area as the shaded square, what is the relation between x and y?
   b) Graph the relation between x and y.

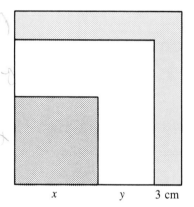

x y 3 cm

6. Find the equation of the locus of a point P which moves such that it is equidistant from the point F(3, 2) and the line defined by $y = 6$.

(C)

7. Find the equation of the locus of a point P which moves such that the sum of its distances from (0, 3) and (8, 3) is 10.

8. Describe the graph of each equation.
   a) $3x^2 + 2y^2 - 6x + 16y + 35 = 0$
   b) $2x^2 + y^2 - 12x - 8y + 36 = 0$
   c) $4x^2 - y^2 + 16x - 4y + 12 = 0$
   d) $x^2 + 2xy + y^2 + 2x + 2y + 1 = 0$

3-9 THE GENERAL QUADRATIC EQUATION IN x AND y

Up to now in this chapter we have encountered quadratic relations with defining equations such as $4x^2 + 9y^2 = 36$ and $x^2 + 10x + 4y + 13 = 0$, which contain terms in x^2 and/or y^2. Furthermore, the axes of the conics have always been parallel to the coordinate axes.

Observe that none of the equations considered so far has contained an xy term. A conic whose defining equation contains an xy term has axes which are inclined to the coordinate axes. A study of its properties involves trigonometry, and requires an analysis of the effect on the equation of a relation when its graph is rotated about the origin through an angle θ, which is beyond the scope of this book. Hence, in this section, we will simply state some of the results and verify them in particular examples.

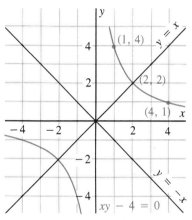

A simple example of an equation with an xy term is $xy - 4 = 0$. Three points on the graph of this equation are $(2, 2)$, $(4, 1)$, and $(1, 4)$. As x increases beyond 4, y decreases and becomes closer and closer to 0. Similarly, as y increases beyond 4, x decreases and becomes closer and closer to 0. A similar situation occurs when x and y are both negative. Hence, we can sketch the graph as shown. The graph is a rectangular hyperbola with centre $(0, 0)$ and vertices $(2, 2)$ and $(-2, -2)$. The asymptotes are the x- and y-axes. The line $y = x$ contains the transverse axis, and the line $y = -x$ contains the conjugate axis.

This example suggests that an xy term occurs in the equation of a quadratic relation when the graph is rotated such that the axes (or axis) of the conic are inclined to the coordinate axes. We can verify this in an example such as the following.

Example 1. Find the equation of the locus of a point P which moves such that it is always the same distance from the point $F(5,1)$ as it is from the line defined by $y = x$.

Solution. Let $P(x, y)$ be any point on the locus, and let D be the foot of the perpendicular from P to the line $y = x$. To obtain an expression for the length of PD, let N be the point on the line $y = x$ such that PN is parallel to the x-axis.

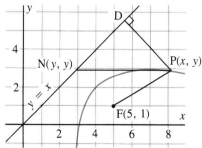

Then $\triangle PDN$ is an isosceles right triangle, and, $PN = \sqrt{2}\, PD$,

or, $\quad PD = \dfrac{PN}{\sqrt{2}}$

Since P is any point on the locus,

$$PF = PD$$

$$PF = \dfrac{PN}{\sqrt{2}}$$

$$\sqrt{(x-5)^2 + (y-1)^2} = \dfrac{\sqrt{(x-y)^2 + 0^2}}{\sqrt{2}}$$

Square both sides.

$$x^2 - 10x + 25 + y^2 - 2y + 1 = \dfrac{x^2 - 2xy + y^2}{2}$$

This equation simplifies to $x^2 + 2xy + y^2 - 20x - 4y + 52 = 0$, which is the equation of the locus.

In *Example 1*, the equation $x^2 + 2xy + y^2 - 20x - 4y + 52 = 0$ represents a parabola. Its axis of symmetry is the line through $(5, 1)$ with slope -1. Its equation is $y - 1 = -1(x - 5)$, or $x + y - 6 = 0$. This result provides further evidence that an xy term is introduced when a conic is rotated such that its axes (or axis) are inclined to the coordinate axes. We will assume that this property is true for all quadratic relations, without proof.

The equation in *Example 1* has the form $Ax^2 + 2Hxy + By^2 + 2Gx + 2Fy + C = 0$. This equation is called the *general quadratic equation in x and y*. Such an equation does not always have a graph, but when it does, the nature of the graph depends only on the quadratic terms $Ax^2 + 2Hxy + By^2$. In particular, it depends on the value of the expression $AB - H^2$. The table below gives the value of this expression for the examples in this section and in *Section 3-8*.

Equation	Conic	Value of $AB - H^2$
$16x^2 + 9y^2 - 64x - 18y - 71 = 0$	ellipse	$(16)(9) - 0^2 = 144$
$4x^2 - 9y^2 + 32x + 18y + 91 = 0$	hyperbola	$(4)(-9) - 0^2 = -36$
$x^2 + 10x + 4y + 13 = 0$	parabola	$(1)(0) - 0^2 = 0$
$xy = 0$	hyperbola	$(0)(0) - \left(\frac{1}{2}\right)^2 = -\frac{1}{4}$
$x^2 + 2xy + y^2 - 20x - 4y + 52 = 0$	parabola	$(1)(1) - 1^2 = 0$

Observe that, in these examples, the value of $AB - H^2$ is positive for the ellipse, negative for the hyperbolas, and 0 for the parabolas. This property is true in general.

> **Properties of the Equation** $Ax^2 + 2Hxy + By^2 + 2Gx + 2Fy + C = 0$
> We assume that A, B, and C are not all 0.
> ● If the graph of this equation exists, it is a conic.
> ● If $H = 0$, the axes (or axis) of the conic are parallel to the coordinate axes.
> ● If $H \neq 0$, the axes (or axis) are not parallel to the coordinate axes.
> ● If $AB - H^2 > 0$, the conic is an ellipse.
>   If $AB - H^2 < 0$, the conic is a hyperbola.
>   If $AB - H^2 = 0$, the conic is a parabola.

EXERCISES 3-9

1. Only one of these equations represents a conic with axes parallel to the coordinate axes. Which equation is this?
   $x^2 - 2xy + y^2 - 6x - 14y + 19 = 0$
   $xy + 2x - 2y + 4 = 0$
   $3x^2 + 2y^2 - 6x + 8y - 1 = 0$
   $3x^2 - 4xy + 16x - 8y + 16 = 0$

2. Only one of these equations represents an ellipse. Which equation is this?
   $7x^2 + 6xy - y^2 - 54x - 14y + 63 = 0$
   $x^2 - 6xy + 9y^2 + 130x + 10y - 575 = 0$
   $4xy + 3y^2 - 8x - 16y + 4 = 0$
   $5x^2 - 4xy + 8y^2 + 2x - 44y + 29 = 0$

3. State which equations could represent each conic.
   i) an ellipse   ii) a hyperbola   iii) a parabola
   a) $9x^2 - 24xy + 16y^2 - 125y + 355 = 0$
   b) $8x^2 + 12xy + 17y^2 - 4x + 22y - 7 = 0$
   c) $x^2 - 16xy - 11y^2 + 135 = 0$
   d) $4x^2 - 36xy + 31y^2 + 28x - 26y - 21 = 0$
   e) $16x^2 + 24xy + 9y^2 - 120x + 160y + 600 = 0$
   f) $41x^2 + 4xy + 44y^2 - 720 = 0$

4. Describe and sketch the graph of each relation.
   a) $xy - 6 = 0$ b) $xy + 6 = 0$
   c) $(x - 4)(y + 3) - 6 = 0$ d) $xy - 3x + 4y - 18 = 0$

5. Find the equation of the locus of a point P which moves such that it is always the same distance from the point F(3,0) as it is from the line defined by $y = x + 5$.

6. The diagram shows three overlapping squares. The smallest square has sides of length 5 cm. If the colored region has the same area as the shaded region, what is the relation between x and y?

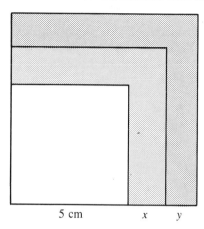

5 cm x y

7. The general quadratic equation can be written as
   $Ax^2 + Bxy + Cy^2 + Dx + Ey + F = 0$.
   a) In this form, what expression would be used to test if the equation represents an ellipse, a hyperbola, or a parabola?
   b) Discuss the advantages and disadvantages of the two forms of the general quadratic equation.

8. Find the equation of the locus of a point which moves such that:
   a) the sum of its distances from $(1, 1)$ and $(-1, -1)$ is 4
   b) the sum of its distances from $(0, 0)$ and $(2, 2)$ is 4.

9. Given any conic with equation $Ax^2 + 2Hxy + By^2 + 2Gx + 2Fy + C = 0$, prove that the quadratic terms $Ax^2 + 2Hxy + By^2$ do not change if the graph of the conic is translated.

10. If the graph of a circle was rotated, would an xy term be introduced in its equation? Explain.

11. Given the equation $Ax^2 + 2Hxy + By^2 + 2Gx + 2Fy + C = 0$, what conditions must be satisfied if this equation represents:
    a) a circle
    b) an ellipse with major axis on: i) the x-axis   ii) the y-axis
    c) a hyperbola with transverse axis on: i) the x-axis   ii) the y-axis
    d) a parabola with: i) a horizontal axis   ii) a vertical axis?

1. Find the length of each line segment with the given endpoints.
   a) A(0,0), B(−3,4) b) C(−3,−7), D(9,−2) c) E(−6,−4), F(−2,7)

2. Find the coordinates of the midpoint of each line segment in *Exercise 1*.

3. Find the equation of the locus of a point P which moves according to each condition. Identify the locus and sketch its graph.
   a) P is always 3 units from Q(−2,1).
   b) The slope of the segment from P to S(5,−3) is $-\frac{3}{4}$.
   c) P is the same distance from F(3,2) as it is from the line $y = -2$.
   d) P is the same distance from A(2,−5) as it is from B(−6,1).

4. Graph each relation and identify the curve.
   a) $\dfrac{x^2}{16} + \dfrac{y^2}{9} = 1$
   b) $x^2 = 4y$
   c) $x^2 + y^2 = 25$
   d) $x^2 - y^2 = 9$
   e) $4x^2 + 4y^2 = 49$
   f) $9x^2 - 16y^2 = -144$

5. A rectangular hyperbola with centre (0,0) and vertices on the *y*-axis passes through (6,−9). Is (−2,7) on the hyperbola?

6. An ellipse has centre (0,0) and major axis on the *y*-axis. Write the equation of the ellipse if:
   a) the *x*- and *y*-intercepts are ±3 and ±5 respectively
   b) the major axis is 12 units and the minor axis is 6 units.

7. Find the equation of the hyperbola, centre (0,0), conjugate axis on the *y*-axis, and:
   a) vertices at (±4,0), and an asymptote defined by $y = 2x$
   b) a transverse axis of 8 units, and a conjugate axis of 14 units.

8. A stone thrown horizontally from a bridge 25 m above the river splashes in the water 40 m from the base of the bridge. If the stone falls in a parabolic path, find its equation.

9. One of the supports in a retractable roof of a sports complex is semi-elliptical. If it is 25 m high and spans 60 m, find its equation.

10. The base of a bridge arch is 80 m wide and 25 m high. Find its equation if the arch is in the shape of a rectangular hyperbola.

11. Describe and sketch the graph of each relation.
    a) $y + 3 = \frac{1}{2}(x + 2)^2$
    b) $\dfrac{(x - 1)^2}{16} + \dfrac{(y + 2)^2}{9} = 1$
    c) $\dfrac{(x + 5)^2}{25} - \dfrac{(y - 2)^2}{16} = 1$
    d) $(x - 2)^2 - 3(y + 1)^2 = -27$

12. Describe the graph of each relation.
    a) $x^2 + y^2 + 4x - 10y - 20 = 0$
    b) $9x^2 + 16y^2 - 18x + 96y + 9 = 0$
    c) $y^2 - 4y - 6x = 38$
    d) $5x^2 - 4y^2 - 30x - 16y + 49 = 0$

1. Graph each function. State its domain and range.

   a) $3x - 4y = 12$ b) $y = 2(x - 3)^2 + 5$ c) $y = \dfrac{2x - 1}{x}$

2. If $f(x) = 3x - 2$ and $g(x) = x^2 + 3x - 1$, find:
   a) $f(5)$ b) $g(-2)$ c) $f(4a)$
   d) $f(x^2 - 1)$ e) $g(2x - 1)$ f) $f(g(x))$.

3. Graph each function and its inverse on the same grid. State the domain and range of the inverse. Is the inverse a function?

   a) $f(x) = \dfrac{6 - 3x}{2}$ b) $g(x) = \dfrac{3x + 2}{x}, x \neq 0$

4. Determine the nature of the roots of each equation.
   a) $2x^2 + 7x - 5 = 0$ b) $4x^2 - 3x + 2 = 0$ c) $16x^2 - 24x + 9 = 0$

5. Solve each equation.
   a) $x^2 - 5x - 8 = 0$ b) $2x^2 + 3x + 4 = 0$ c) $2.5x^2 + 2x - 4.5 = 0$

6. Solve graphically.
   a) $x^2 + 2x - 5 = 0$ b) $2x^3 + 2x = 0$

7. If $x - 3$ is a factor of each polynomial, find the other factors.
   a) $x^3 - 6x^2 - x + 30$ b) $4x^3 - x - 12x^2 + 3$ c) $x^4 - x^3 - 7x^2 + x + 6$

8. Which polynomials have $x + 2$ as a factor? If $x + 2$ is not a factor, find the remainder when the polynomial is divided by $x + 2$.
   a) $x^4 - x^3 - 5x^2 + 7x + 10$ b) $2x^4 + 4x^3 - x^2 + 2x + 6$

9. Factor completely.
   a) $x^3 + 7x^2 + 7x - 15 = 0$ b) $x^4 + 2x^3 - 7x^2 - 8x + 12 = 0$

10. List the possible rational roots of each equation.
    a) $x^3 - 5x^2 + 7x - 12 = 0$ b) $2x^3 - 9x + 3 = 0$

11. Solve each inequality.
    a) $(x + 2)(x + 3)(x - 1) < 0$ b) $(x^2 - 1)(x^2 - x - 6) \geq 0$

12. Find the length, and the coordinates of the midpoint of each line segment whose endpoints are given.
    a) $P(-2,1), Q(5,-3)$ b) $R(4,9), S(-8,-2)$ c) $T(5,-7), W(8,-4)$

13. Identify the locus of each point P and sketch its graph.
    a) P is the same distance from $A(-3,-5)$ as it is from $B(2,3)$.
    b) P is always 4 units from $Q(-2,-3)$.

14. Find the equation of an ellipse with major axis on the x-axis if:
    a) the x- and y-intercepts are ±4 and ±1 respectively
    b) the semimajor axis is 6 units and the minor axis is 8 units.

15. A rectangular hyperbola with centre $O(0,0)$ and vertices on the y-axis passes through $P(-6,8)$. Find the equation of the hyperbola.

4 Systems of Quadratic Equations, and Inequalities

A sky diver jumped from an airplane and fell freely
for several seconds before releasing her parachute. If
the equations giving her height above the ground
before and after opening her parachute are known, how
may her height at the time of releasing the parachute
be determined? (See Section 4-2 *Example 2.*)

4-1 SOLVING SYSTEMS OF EQUATIONS BY GRAPHING

To solve a system, or pair of equations means to find all the ordered pairs (x, y), if any, that satisfy both equations. These may be estimated by graphing both equations on the same grid. In a system of equations, one or both of the equations may be quadratic.

Linear-Quadratic Systems
From a lighthouse, the range of visibility on a clear day determines a circle with the lighthouse at the centre. Any ship on or inside the circle can be seen from the lighthouse. Suppose a ship travels on a straight-line course through this circle. Then, the ship can be seen between the two points on its course where the line intersects the circle.

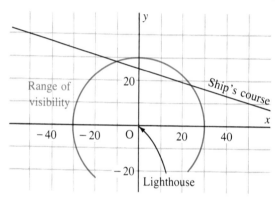

A system of equations consisting of a linear relation and a quadratic relation is called a *linear-quadratic* system. We can estimate the solutions of a linear-quadratic system by graphing.

Example 1. Solve graphically.

    a) $3x - 4y + 15 = 0$ b) $3x - 4y + 25 = 0$
           $x^2 + y^2 = 25$ $x^2 + y^2 = 25$

    c) $3x - 4y + 35 = 0$
           $x^2 + y^2 = 25$

Solution. $x^2 + y^2 = 25$ is a circle, centre $(0,0)$ and radius 5.

    a) $3x - 4y + 15 = 0$ is a straight line.
        When $x = -1$, $y = 3$
        When $y = 0$, $x = -5$
        Since the line intersects the circle
        in two points, there are two solutions.
        One solution is $(-5, 0)$. The other,
        estimated from the graph, is about
        $(1.5, 4.7)$.

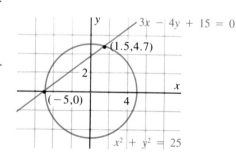

b) $3x - 4y + 25 = 0$ is a straight line.
When $x = -3$, $y = 4$; when $x = -7$, $y = 1$
The line appears to touch the circle in only one point, $(-3, 4)$
(below left).

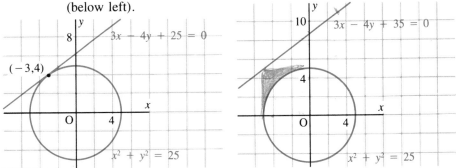

c) $3x - 4y + 35 = 0$ is a straight line.
When $x = -1$, $y = 8$; when $x = -5$, $y = 5$
There is no solution because the line does not intersect the circle (above right).

Example 1 illustrates that the exact coordinates of a point of intersection cannot always be read from a graph. In part b), it is not certain that the line intersects the curve at one point. It may intersect the curve at two points which are close together, or it may not intersect the curve at all.

Quadratic-Quadratic Systems

In the LORAN system of navigation, transmitters send out radio signals simultaneously from beacons on the coast. Equipment on a ship measures the difference in time taken for the signals to reach it. This locates the ship on a hyperbola. A second pair of beacons is used to locate the ship on a second hyperbola. Hence, the ship's position is at the point of intersection of the two hyperbolas. Since there may be more than one such point, a third pair of beacons may be needed.

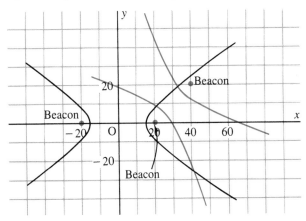

A system of equations consisting of two quadratic relations is called a *quadratic-quadratic* system. We can estimate the solutions of a quadratic-quadratic system by graphing.

Example 2.   Solve graphically.
$$4x^2 + 9y^2 = 36$$
$$y = x^2 - 2$$

Solution.   The first equation may be written as $\dfrac{x^2}{9} + \dfrac{y^2}{4} = 1$.

This is an ellipse with intercepts $(\pm 3, 0)$ and $(0, \pm 2)$. The second equation is a parabola with vertex $(0, -2)$ and opening up. There are three solutions: $(0, -2)$ and approximately $(\pm 1.9, 1.6)$.

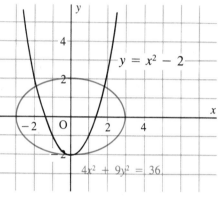

Solving systems of equations by graphing is time-consuming and not very accurate. Algebraic methods of solution will be given in the next section.

EXERCISES 4-1

(A)

1. The graph of the circle $x^2 + y^2 = 5$ is shown below left. Which of these lines intersect it in: i) two points   ii) one point   iii) no points?
   a) $y = x + 1$ b) $y = x + 5$ c) $y = 2x$ d) $y = 2x + 5$

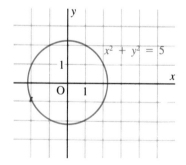
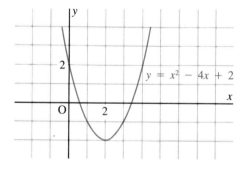

2. The graph of the parabola $y = x^2 - 4x + 2$ is shown above right. Which of these lines intersect it in: i) two points   ii) one point   iii) no points?
   a) $y = \dfrac{1}{2}x + 3$ b) $y = \dfrac{1}{2}x - 4$ c) $y = -2x$ d) $x - 3 = 0$

(B)

3. Find the coordinates of the points of intersection of the circle defined by
   $x^2 + y^2 = 25$ with each line.
   a) $4x - 3y = 0$ b) $4x - 3y + 25 = 0$ c) $4x - 3y + 50 = 0$

4. Find the coordinates of the points of intersection of the parabola defined by
   $y = x^2$ with each line.
   a) $y = 2x + 3$ b) $y = 2x - 1$ c) $y = 2x - 5$

5. Solve ~~graphically~~.
   a) $x^2 + y^2 = 100$ b) $x^2 + y^2 = 9$ c) $x - 2y + 1 = 0$
         $y = x - 2$ $x + 3y = 12$ $xy = 6$
   d) $2x - y + 1 = 0$ e) $x^2 + 4y^2 = 16$ f) $x^2 - y^2 = 9$
          $y = x^2 + 2$ $y = 2 - x^2$ $xy = 4$

6. Given the circle $x^2 + y^2 = 20$, write the equation of any line such that the circle
   and the line form a system with:
   a) two different solutions   b) no solution.

7. Given the ellipse $4x^2 + 9y^2 = 36$, write the equation of any parabola such that
   the ellipse and the parabola form a system with:
   a) four different solutions   b) three different solutions
   c) two different solutions   d) only one solution
   e) no solution.

8. State whether each system has a solution.
   a) $x^2 + y^2 = 29$ b) $y = x^2 + 4x + 3$
       $2x - 3y + 12 = 0$ $x + 3y = -5$
   c) $x^2 + y^2 = 50$ d) $xy = 18$
        $6x + 5y = 60$ $5x + 3y = 15$
   e) $y = x^2 - 4x + 7$ f) $(x - 2)^2 + (y + 5)^2 = 10$
       $2x + y = 6$ $x + 3y + 5 = 0$

(C)

9. a) If $k > 0$, for what values of k does the system $x^2 + (y - 5)^2 = 9$ have:
                                                  $y = x^2 + k$
   i) 4 solutions   ii) 3 solutions   iii) 2 solutions   iv) 1 solution   v) no solution?
   b) What is the reason for the condition $k > 0$ in part a)?

10. For what values of r does the system $4x^2 - 9y^2 = 36$ have:
                                     $(x - 1)^2 + y^2 = r^2$
    a) no solution   b) 1 solution   c) 2 solutions
    d) 3 solutions   e) 4 solutions?

11. What condition(s) must be satisfied by r, a, and b if the circle defined by
    $x^2 + y^2 = r^2$ intersects each curve?
    a) the ellipse $\dfrac{x^2}{a^2} + \dfrac{y^2}{b^2} = 1$ b) the hyperbola $\dfrac{x^2}{a^2} - \dfrac{y^2}{b^2} = 1$

MATHEMATICS AROUND US

MATHEMATICS AROUND US

The Law of Supply and Demand

Many different crops are grown in Canada, and Canadian factories produce a wide variety of goods. Whatever is grown or made is produced in a certain quantity and sold at a certain price. These are determined by the supply of, and demand for, the product.

Supply

Suppose that the quantity of grapes s kilograms that growers are willing to harvest is given by this formula $s = 5000p - 5000$, where p is the price of grapes in dollars per kilogram. The table and graph show the relation between s and p.
Can you give reasons why the supply increases as the price increases?

Grapes	
Price p ($/kg)	Supply s (1000 kg)
2	5
3	10
4	15
5	20

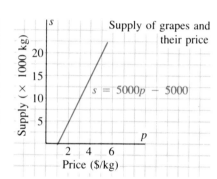

Demand

Suppose that the quantity of grapes d kilograms that shoppers are willing to buy is given by this formula $d = -4000p + 26\,000$, where p is the price of grapes in dollars per kilogram. The table and graph show the relation between d and p.

Can you give reasons why the demand decreases as the price increases?

Grapes	
Price p ($/kg)	Demand d (1000 kg)
2	18
3	14
4	10
5	6

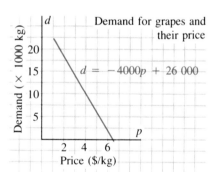

The two graphs are shown on the same axes.

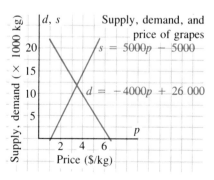

The point of intersection indicates that at about $3.50/kg, the quantity of grapes that people are willing to buy is equal to the quantity that growers are willing to harvest. This is the best selling price for grapes.

Since the supply equals the demand at this price, we can find the exact price by solving this equation.

$$5000p - 5000 = -4000p + 26\ 000$$
$$9000p = 31\ 000$$
$$p = \frac{31}{9}$$
$$\doteq 3.44$$

At a price of $3.44/kg, the supply of grapes equals the demand. What happens when the price is not $3.44/kg?

At $2.50/kg, from the graph $s = 7500$ and $d = 16\ 000$; that is, the demand exceeds the supply. Many people would be willing to pay a higher price. The price would rise.

At $4.50/kg, from the graph $s = 17\ 500$ and $d = 8000$; that is, the supply exceeds the demand. Sellers would have to reduce the price to get rid of the surplus. The price would fall.

Law of Supply and Demand
If demand exceeds supply, the price should rise.
If supply exceeds demand, the price should fall.

QUESTIONS

s, d, and p represent supply, demand, and price respectively.

1. Assume that $s = 4000p - 2000$.
   a) Find the supply if the price is: i) 3   ii) 4   iii) 5.
   b) Find the price if the supply is: i) 12 000   ii) 17 000   iii) 22 800.
   c) What is the lowest price at which the product will be supplied?

2. Assume that $d = -3000p + 7500$.
   a) Find the demand if the price is: i) 1   ii) 1.5   iii) 2.
   b) Find the price if the demand is: i) 5100   ii) 3750   iii) 900.
   c) What is the highest price anyone will pay for the product?
   d) What is the demand if the product is free?

3. Assume that for a particular product, $s = 8000p - 2000$ and $d = -2000p + 6000$.
   a) What is the best selling price?
   b) What amount should be produced at this price?

4-2 SOLVING LINEAR-QUADRATIC SYSTEMS ALGEBRAICALLY

To solve a linear-quadratic system algebraically, we always follow these
steps.

Step 1. Solve the linear equation for either variable.

Step 2. Substitute into the quadratic equation and solve for the other
variable.

Step 3. Substitute the results from *Step 2* into the linear equation, and
solve for the first variable.

Example 1. Find the coordinates of the points of intersection of the circle $x^2 + y^2 = 10$
and the line $3x + y = 6$. Check the solution.

Solution. $x^2 + y^2 = 10$ . . . ①

$3x + y = 6$ . . . ②

Solve ② for y.

$y = 6 - 3x$ . . . ③

Substitute this expression for y in ① and solve for x.

$$x^2 + (6 - 3x)^2 = 10$$
$$x^2 + 36 - 36x + 9x^2 = 10$$
$$10x^2 - 36x + 26 = 0$$
$$5x^2 - 18x + 13 = 0$$
$$(x - 1)(5x - 13) = 0$$

Either $x - 1 = 0$ or $5x - 13 = 0$

$x = 1$

$x = \dfrac{13}{5}$, or 2.6

Substitute in the linear equation ③ to find y for each value of x.

When $x = 1$, $y = 6 - 3(1)$
                    $= 3$

When $x = 2.6$, $y = 6 - 3(2.6)$
                        $= -1.8$

The system has two solutions: $(1, 3)$ and $(2.6, -1.8)$. These are the
coordinates of the points of intersection.

Check.   When $x = 1$ and $y = 3$

$x^2 + y^2 = 1^2 + 3^2$ $3x + y = 3(1) + 3$
            $= 10$ $= 6$

When $x = 2.6$ and $y = -1.8$

$x^2 + y^2 = (2.6)^2 + (-1.8)^2$ $3x + y = 3(2.6) - 1.8$
            $= 6.76 + 3.24$ $= 7.8 - 1.8$
            $= 10.00$ $\doteq 6.0$

The solutions are correct.

The procedure in *Example 1* may be better seen graphically.

Given the linear-quadratic system $\quad x^2 + y^2 = 10$
$$3x + y = 6$$

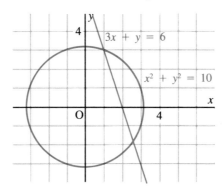

Substitute $6 - 3x$ for y
in $x^2 + y^2 = 10$ to get
$x = 1$ and $x = 2.6$.

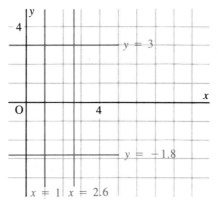

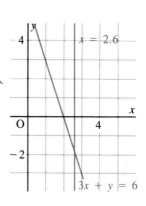

We have the
related system
$x = 1$
$y = 6 - 3x$.

We have the
related system
$x = 2.6$
$y = 6 - 3x$.

The solutions of the
related systems are:

| $x = 1$ | and | $x = 2.6$ |
| $y = 3$ | | $y = -1.8$ |

The reason why the values found for x must be substituted in the linear equation and not in the quadratic equation may be seen from this graph.

If, for example, $x = 1$ were substituted in the equation of the circle, two values of y would result, 3 and -3. One might think that $(1,3)$ and $(1,-3)$ are both solutions of the linear-quadratic system. But, as the graph shows, $(1,-3)$ is not on the given line, and therefore $(1,-3)$ is not a solution of the system.

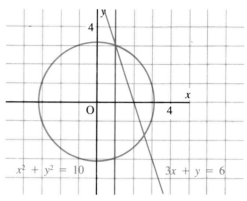

Example 2. A sky diver jumped from an airplane and fell freely for several seconds before releasing her parachute. Her height h metres above the ground at any time is given by:
$h = -4.9t^2 + 5000$ before she released her parachute, and
$h = -4t + 4000$ after she released her parachute.
a) How long after jumping did she release her parachute?
b) How high was she above the ground at that time?

Solution.   a) At the moment of releasing her parachute, both equations apply. Therefore, solve this system.

$$h = -4.9t^2 + 5000 \quad \ldots \textcircled{1}$$
$$h = -4t + 4000 \quad \ldots \textcircled{2}$$

Substitute $-4t + 4000$ for h in $\textcircled{1}$.

$$-4t + 4000 = -4.9t^2 + 5000$$
$$4.9t^2 - 4t - 1000 = 0$$

Use the quadratic formula, $t = \dfrac{-b \pm \sqrt{b^2 - 4ac}}{2a}$

$$t = \frac{4 \pm \sqrt{(-4)^2 - 4(4.9)(-1000)}}{2(4.9)} \qquad \begin{array}{l} a = 4.9 \\ b = -4 \\ c = -1000 \end{array}$$

$$= \frac{4 \pm \sqrt{19\,616}}{9.8}$$

$$\doteq \frac{4 \pm 140.1}{9.8} \qquad \text{Since the time is positive,}$$

$$\doteq 14.7 \text{ or } -13.9 \qquad \text{the negative root is rejected.}$$

The sky diver released her parachute after about 14.7 s.
b) To find her height at this time, substitute 14.7 for t in $\textcircled{2}$.

$$h \doteq -4(14.7) + 4000$$
$$\doteq 3941.2$$

She released her parachute when she was about 3940 m above the ground.

EXERCISES 4-2

Ⓐ

1. Find the coordinates of the points of intersection of each line and circle.

   a) $y = 2x$
   $x^2 + y^2 = 5$

   b) $y = 2x - 5$
   $x^2 + y^2 = 5$

   c) $y = 2x - 5$
   $x^2 + y^2 = 10$

   d) $x - y = 8$
   $x^2 + y^2 = 25$

2. Solve each system.

   a) $x^2 + y^2 = 25$
   $y = 3x - 5$

   b) $y = x^2$
   $x - y = -2$

   c) $x^2 + y^2 = 20$
   $y = 2x - 10$

   d) $xy = 12$
   $y = 2x - 2$

Ⓑ

3. The sum of two numbers is 10 and the sum of their squares is 58. Find the numbers.

4. The perimeter of a rectangle is 13 cm and its area is 10 cm². Find its length and width.

5. A movie stunt man jumped from the CN Tower and fell freely for several seconds before releasing his parachute. His height h metres t seconds after jumping is given by:

   $h = -4.9t^2 + t + 350$ before he released his parachute, and
   $h = -4t + 141$ after he released his parachute.

   a) How long after jumping did he release his parachute?
   b) How high was he when he released his parachute?

6. Solve each system.

   a) $x^2 + y^2 = 13$
   $2x + 3y = 5$

   b) $x^2 + y^2 = 13$
   $2x + 3y = 13$

   c) $y = x^2 + 6x + 5$
   $x + 3y + 15 = 0$

   d) $x^2 - y^2 = 4$
   $x + 2y = 0$

   e) $(x - 4)^2 + (y + 2)^2 = 10$
   $2x - y = 2$

   f) $xy = -4$
   $3x - 2y + 10 = 0$

7. Point P is on the line $3x + y = 26$ and is 10 units from the origin. Find the coordinates of P, and illustrate your solution with a graph.

8. From a lighthouse, the range of visibility on a clear day is 40 km. On a coordinate system, where $(0,0)$ represents the lighthouse, a ship is travelling on a course represented by $y = 2x + 80$. Between what two points on the course can the ship be seen from the lighthouse?

9. Show that the graphs of $2x + 5y = 11$ and $x^2 + y^2 = 4$ do not intersect.

10. What two numbers differ by 4 and have squares that differ by 80?

11. What two numbers differ by 4 and have squares with a sum of 136?

12. A rectangular field has a perimeter of 500 m and an area of 14 400 m². Find the lengths of its sides.

13. A right triangle has a hypotenuse 10 cm long. If the perimeter is 22 cm, find the lengths of the other two sides.

14. A line through (6,2) forms a triangle with the positive arms of the coordinate axes. If the area of the triangle is 27 units², find the equation of the line.

15. A(−3,4) and B(5,3) are two points.
    a) Find the coordinates of a point P on $y = x + 4$ such that $\angle APB = 90°$. Illustrate your solution with a graph.
    b) Show that there is no point P on $y = x − 4$ such that $\angle APB = 90°$.

16. a) Solve each system graphically.
    i) $5x + 4y − 32 = 0$ ii) $y = x + 9$
         $x^2 + y^2 = 25$ $x^2 + y^2 = 40$
    b) Check the results of part a) by solving algebraically.

17. A(−3,4), B(3,4), and C(4,3) are points on $x^2 + y^2 = 25$ (below left). P(5,10) is a point outside the circle.
    a) Show that line AP intersects the circle in only one point.
    b) Lines PB and PC intersect the circle again at D and E respectively. Find the coordinates of D and E.
    c) Show that $PA^2 = PB \times PD = PC \times PE$.

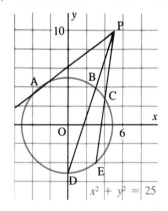 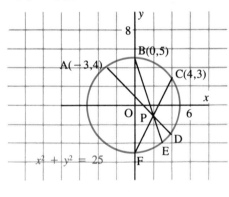

18. Chords AD, BE, and CF of the circle $x^2 + y^2 = 25$ (above right) intersect at point P(2, −1).
    a) If A, B, and C have the coordinates shown, find the coordinates of D, E, and F.
    b) Show that $PA \times PD = PB \times PE = PC \times PF$.

Is it possible for a linear-quadratic system to have infinitely many solutions?

4-3 SOLVING QUADRATIC-QUADRATIC SYSTEMS ALGEBRAICALLY

To solve a quadratic-quadratic system, we combine the equations algebraically to eliminate one of the variables.

Example 1. Find the coordinates of the points of intersection of the circle $x^2 + y^2 = 65$ and the hyperbola $x^2 - y^2 = 33$.

Solution.
$$x^2 + y^2 = 65 \ldots ①$$
$$x^2 - y^2 = 33 \ldots ②$$
Add. $\quad 2x^2 \qquad = 98$
$$x^2 = 49$$
$$x = \pm 7$$

Substitute each value of x in ① to find the corresponding value of y.

When $x = 7$, ① becomes: $\qquad$ When $x = -7$, ① becomes:
$$7^2 + y^2 = 65 \qquad\qquad (-7)^2 + y^2 = 65$$
$$y^2 = 16 \qquad\qquad\qquad y^2 = 16$$
$$y = \pm 4 \qquad\qquad\qquad y = \pm 4$$

Hence, two solutions are $\qquad$ Hence, two solutions are
$(7, 4)$ and $(7, -4)$. $\qquad\qquad$ $(-7, 4)$ and $(-7, -4)$.

We can illustrate the system in *Example 1* and its solution graphically.

The given quadratic-quadratic system
$x^2 + y^2 = 65$
$x^2 - y^2 = 33$
represents a circle and a hyperbola.

The right branch of the hyperbola intersects the circle in two points with x-coordinate 7. Substituting 7 for x in ① gives the y-coordinates of those points.

The left branch of the hyperbola intersects the circle in two points with x-coordinate -7. Substituting -7 for x in ① gives the y-coordinates of those points.

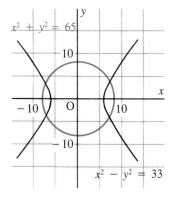

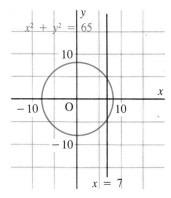

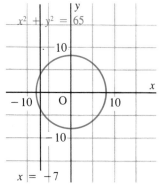

The system in *Example 1* has four real solutions. Quadratic-quadratic systems can have any number of real solutions from 0 to 4. The solutions correspond to the points of intersection of the corresponding graphs. For example, in *Example 1*, the radius of the circle is $\sqrt{65}$, and the semi-transverse axis of the hyperbola is $\sqrt{33}$.

If the radius of the circle were $\sqrt{33}$, the system would have two solutions.

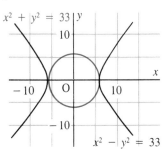

If the radius of the circle were less than $\sqrt{33}$, the system would have no real solutions.

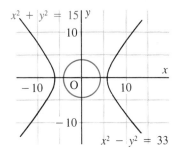

Example 2. Solve the system.
$$4x^2 + 9y^2 = 36$$
$$y = x^2 - 2$$

Solution.
$$4x^2 + 9y^2 = 36 \quad \dots \; \text{①}$$
$$y = x^2 - 2 \quad \dots \; \text{②}$$

Solve ② for x^2. $x^2 = y + 2$

Substitute this expression for x^2 in ① to obtain a quadratic equation in y.
$$4(y + 2) + 9y^2 = 36$$
$$4y + 8 + 9y^2 = 36$$
$$9y^2 + 4y - 28 = 0$$

Solve using either the quadratic formula or by factoring.
$$(y + 2)(9y - 14) = 0$$
Either $y + 2 = 0$ or $9y - 14 = 0$
$$y = -2 \qquad\qquad y = \frac{14}{9}$$

Substitute to find corresponding values of x.

When $y = -2$, $x^2 = -2 + 2$
$$= 0$$

When $y = \frac{14}{9}$, $x^2 = \frac{14}{9} + \frac{18}{9}$
$$= \frac{32}{9}$$
$$x = \frac{\pm 4\sqrt{2}}{3}$$

The system has three solutions: $(0, -2)$, $\left(\dfrac{4\sqrt{2}}{3}, \dfrac{14}{9}\right)$, and $\left(-\dfrac{4\sqrt{2}}{3}, \dfrac{14}{9}\right)$.

Compare the above results with the graphical solution of this system given in Section 4-1, *Example 2*.

Solving a quadratic-quadratic system can sometimes be difficult. There is no simple general method as there is for solving a linear-quadratic system. The equations must be combined in some way to eliminate a variable. Although the elimination was straightforward in *Examples 1* and *2*, some ingenuity may be needed to solve other systems.

EXERCISES 4-3

Ⓐ

1. Keeping in mind that there may be as many as four real solutions, or no real solution, solve each quadratic-quadratic system by inspection.

a) $x = y^2$
   $y = x^2$

b) $x^2 + y^2 = 4$
   $x^2 + y^2 = 9$

c) $x^2 + y^2 = 9$
   $x^2 - y^2 = 16$

d) $x^2 + y^2 = 16$
   $x^2 - y^2 = 16$

e) $x^2 + y^2 = 1$
   $y = x^2 - 1$

f) $x^2 + 2y^2 = 12$
   $2x^2 + y^2 = 12$

Ⓑ

2. a) Find the coordinates of the points of intersection of the ellipse defined by $x^2 + 3y^2 = 12$ with each circle.

   i) $x^2 + y^2 = 4$ ii) $x^2 + y^2 = 10$ iii) $x^2 + y^2 = 12$

   b) Write the equation of any circle which does not intersect the ellipse in part a).

3. Solve each system.

a) $x^2 + y^2 = 20$
   $y = x^2$

b) $4x^2 + y^2 = 16$
   $y = x^2 - 4$

c) $x^2 + 4y^2 = 20$
   $x^2 - y^2 = 15$

d) $3x^2 - 2y^2 = 10$
   $y = 5 - x^2$

e) $y^2 = x$
   $x^2 = -8y$

f) $9x^2 + 4y^2 = 36$
   $xy - 3 = 0$

4. Solve each system.

a) $4x^2 + y^2 = 20$
   $4x = y^2 - 12$

b) $x^2 + y^2 - 4x - 5 = 0$
   $x^2 - y^2 = 1$

c) $x^2 + y^2 - 6y - 1 = 0$
   $xy + 6 = 0$

d) $y^2 = -27x$
   $x^2 = 8y$

e) $4x^2 + 9y^2 = 36$
   $y = x^2 - 2$

5. Given the system $x^2 + 4y^2 = 4$
   $y = x^2 - 4$

a) Solve the system graphically. How many solutions do there appear to be?

b) Solve the system algebraically, and compare with part a).

6. a) Show that the ellipse defined by $x^2 + 9y^2 = 36$ and the hyperbola defined by $xy - 6 = 0$ intersect at only two points.

   b) Illustrate the system in part a) on a graph.

7. By comparing the signals from two beacons, a ship's position is located on the hyperbola $5x^2 - 3y^2 - 3000 = 0$. Using another pair of beacons, the position is located on the hyperbola $2x^2 - 3y^2 - 360x + 13\ 200 = 0$. Determine the coordinates of the ship's position, assuming that it is in the first quadrant.

8. The length of the diagonal of a rectangle is $\sqrt{20}$ cm, and its area is 10 cm². Determine the length and the width of the rectangle.

9. The sum of the squares of two numbers is 100. Find the numbers if one number is double the other number.

10. The difference of the squares of two numbers is 15. Find the numbers if their product is 18.

11. Pat can travel 30 km to his cottage by car or by bicycle. By bicycle, his average speed is 40 km/h slower than by car, and it takes one hour longer. How long does it take him to go to his cottage by bicycle?

12. Find x and y in each diagram.

a)

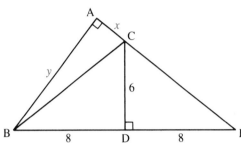

b)

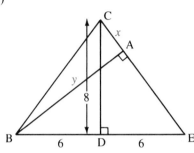

13. *Exercise 12* suggests a theorem. State the theorem, and prove it.

14. Determine the condition that the circle defined by $x^2 + y^2 = r^2$ and the rectangular hyperbola defined by each equation intersect.
    a) $x^2 - y^2 = a^2$
    b) $xy = k$

15. Find the coordinates of the point on the circle defined by $x^2 + y^2 = 5$ which is closest to each point.
    a) $(6, 3)$
    b) $(6, 4)$

16. Solve each system.
    a) $\quad x^2 - 4x - 2y - 4 = 0$
    $\qquad\qquad\quad x^2 + y^2 = 20$
    b) $\quad x^2 + 4y^2 - 4x - 16y = 0$
    $\qquad\quad x^2 - 4x - 4y = 0$

4-4 SOLVING SYSTEMS OF INEQUALITIES

The rectangular hyperbola defined by $x^2 - y^2 = 9$ divided the plane into three sets of points.

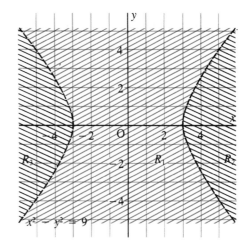

- the points on the hyperbola
  These are the points whose coordinates satisfy the equation $x^2 - y^2 = 9$.
- the points in the region R_1 between the branches
  The coordinates of any point in R_1, for example, $(0, 0)$ satisfy the inequality $x^2 - y^2 < 9$. Hence, R_1 is the graph of the inequality $x^2 - y^2 < 9$.
- the points in the regions R_2 and R_3 contained within each branch
  The coordinates of any point in R_2 such as $(4, 0)$, and any point in R_3 such as $(-4, 0)$, satisfy the inequality $x^2 - y^2 > 9$. Hence, R_2 and R_3 form the graph of the inequality $x^2 - y^2 > 9$.

In general, the graph of an equation in x and y is a line or a curve on the coordinate grid. The line or curve divides the plane into two or more regions which are the graphs of the corresponding inequalities. As the example above shows, the graph of an inequality may consist of more than one region.

To graph an inequality, follow these steps.
Step 1. Graph the corresponding equation.
Step 2. Find the coordinates of a point in each region bounded by the graph.
Step 3. Determine if the coordinates of each point found in *Step 2* satisfy the inequality. If so, the point is located in the graph of the region.

To graph a system of inequalities, graph each inequality on the same grid. The solution of the system consists of all points in the regions where the graphs of the inequalities overlap.

Example 1. Show the solution of this system as a region on the plane.
$$x^2 - y^2 < 9 \quad \text{...} \; \textcircled{1}$$
$$x - 2y + 3 > 0 \quad \text{...} \; \textcircled{2}$$

Solution. The graph of $\textcircled{1}$ is the region
R_1 shown above.
To graph $\textcircled{2}$, first graph the
line defined by
$x - 2y + 3 = 0$. It is convenient to solve the equation
for y and use the slope y-
intercept form, $y = \frac{1}{2}x + \frac{3}{2}$.

Hence, the line has slope $\frac{1}{2}$ and

y-intercept $\frac{3}{2}$. A point below

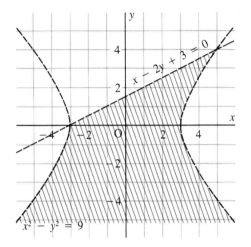

the line, such as $(0, 0)$, has
coordinates which satisfy the
inequality, while a point above the line, such as $(0, 4)$, has coordinates
which do not satisfy the inequality. Hence, the graph of $\textcircled{2}$ is the half-plane
below the line.
    The solution of the given system of inequalities in *Example 1* is
the region shown in color, where the region between the branches of the
hyperbola overlaps the region below the line. Notice that the hyperbola
and the line are dotted because they are not part of the regions defined
by the inequalities.

Example 2. Show the solution of this system on a graph.
$$x^2 + 4y^2 < 16 \quad \text{...} \; \textcircled{1}$$
$$x^2 - y \geq 2 \quad \text{...} \; \textcircled{2}$$

Solution. Equation $\textcircled{1}$ represents an
ellipse, and $\textcircled{2}$ represents a
parabola.
The equation corresponding to

$\textcircled{1}$ is $\dfrac{x^2}{16} + \dfrac{y^2}{4} = 1$.

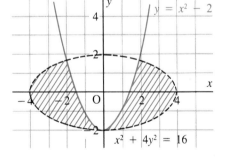

The graph of $\textcircled{1}$ is the region
inside the ellipse.
The equation corresponding to
$\textcircled{2}$ is $y = x^2 - 2$. Since
$(0, 0)$ does not satisfy $\textcircled{2}$,
while $(0, -5)$ does, the graph
of $\textcircled{2}$ is the region below the parabola, including points on the parabola.
    The solution of the given system of inequalities is the region shown
in color.
    In *Example 2*, the parabola is shown as a solid curve, because it is
part of the region defined by the inequality $x^2 - y \geq 2$.

EXERCISES 4-4

Ⓐ

1. Write an inequality to represent each shaded region.

a)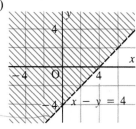

b)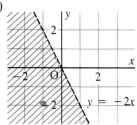

c)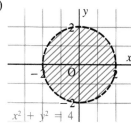

d)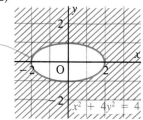

e)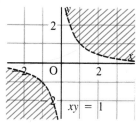

f)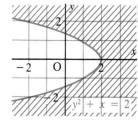

Ⓑ

2. Graph each inequality.
   a) $x - 3y \leq 6$ b) $2x + 3y \leq 0$ c) $x^2 + y^2 \leq 16$
   d) $9x^2 + y^2 > 9$ e) $4x^2 + 9y^2 \leq 36$ f) $x^2 - 4y^2 > 16$

3. Show the solution of each system on a graph.
   a) $x + y < 6$ b) $2x + y \geq 6$ c) $4x - y + 8 > 0$
        $x < 4$ $x - y \geq 2$ $x + 3y + 3 \leq 0$
   d) $x^2 + y^2 \leq 25$ e) $x^2 + y^2 \geq 9$ f) $\quad y \leq x^2$
        $y \leq 3$ $y \geq x$ $x + y \geq 5$

4. Show the solution of each system on a graph.
   a) $9x^2 + 4y^2 \leq 36$ b) $\quad x^2 - y^2 \leq -4$ c) $x^2 + y^2 < 25$
        $2x + y \leq 1$ $x^2 - y - 2 > 0$ $x^2 + y^2 \geq 9$
   d) $x^2 + 4y^2 \leq 36$ e) $\quad x^2 + 4y^2 \geq 16$ f) $\qquad xy > 4$
        $x^2 - y^2 > 4$ $x - y^2 + 6 \geq 0$ $x^2 - y - 6 > 0$

Ⓒ

5. Write an example of a system of inequalities that has:
   a) no solution   b) exactly one solution   c) exactly two different solutions.

6. We have graphed an inequality by first graphing the corresponding equation, and then using test points to determine the regions corresponding to the inequality. Formulate some rules you could use to identify the region from the inequality itself, without using test points. Your rules should apply to any given inequality, whose corresponding equation has a graph which is a line, an ellipse, a hyperbola, or a parabola.

PROBLEM SOLVING

Extend the Problem

"(No) problem whatever is completely exhausted. There remains always something to do; with sufficient study and penetration, we can improve any solution, and, in any case, we can always improve our understanding of the solution."

George Polya

George Polya, a former professor of mathematics at Stanford University, gained worldwide recognition for his skills as a teacher. Polya is suggesting that when we have solved a problem, we may also think of related problems. These may often be obtained by generalizing some condition of the problem, or changing some part of the problem to make a new problem. For example, some of the ways in which the Pythagorean Theorem can be extended are given below.

The Pythagorean Theorem states that the areas of the squares constructed on the sides of a right triangle are related:

area of the square on the hypotenuse = sum of the areas of the squares on the other two sides

$$a^2 = b^2 + c^2$$

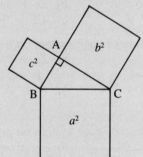

First extension

The lengths of the sides of a right triangle satisfy the equation $x^2 + y^2 = z^2$. Find integral values of x, y, and z which satisfy this equation. These are called *Pythagorean triples*.

Second extension
Can you find integral values of x, y, and z which satisfy equations such as these?

$$x^2 + y^2 + z^2 = w^2$$
$$x^2 + y^2 = z^2 + w^2$$
$$x^{-1} + y^{-1} = z^{-1}$$

$$x^3 + y^3 + z^3 = w^3$$
$$x^3 + y^3 = z^3 + w^3$$
$$x^{\frac{1}{2}} + y^{\frac{1}{2}} = z^{\frac{1}{2}}$$

Third extension
The Pythagorean Theorem can be used to find the distance between any two points in the plane. How could you find the distance between any two points in three dimensions?

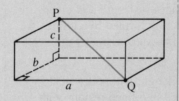

Fourth extension
The Pythagorean Theorem relates the lengths of the sides of any right triangle. If $\triangle ABC$ is not a right triangle, how are the lengths of its sides related?

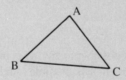

Fifth extension
If figures other than squares are constructed on the sides of a right triangle, does the area relation still hold for these figures?

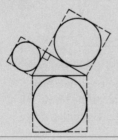
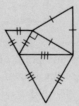
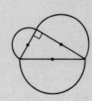

PROBLEMS

Ⓑ

1. The Earth's equatorial diameter is 12 756 km. The polar diameter is about 0.33% less than this. What is the polar diameter?

2. Given any three natural numbers, prove that at least two of them have a sum which is even.

3. Let k be a positive rational number. Prove that $k + \frac{1}{k}$ is a natural number if, and only if, $k = 1$.

4. A square with sides of length s is given. A regular octagon is formed by cutting off four corner isosceles triangles as shown. Express x as a function of s.

5. An equilateral triangle with sides of length s is divided into three regions with equal areas by two segments of lengths x and y parallel to one of the sides. Find equations expressing x and y as functions of s.

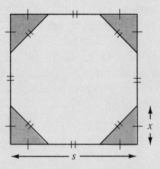

Ⓒ

6. Determine if it is possible to find two prime numbers p and q such that $pq + 1$ is a perfect square. If it is possible, find out as much as you can about primes which have this property.

7. Two vertices of an equilateral triangle are A(1, 8) and B(5, 2). Find the possible coordinates of the third vertex.

8. Four quarter circles are inscribed in a square with sides of 6 cm using the vertices as centres. Calculate the areas of the regions x, y, and z.

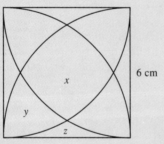

Ⓓ

9. A triangle is inscribed in a circle, and P is any point on the circle. Prove that the distance from P to the farthest vertex of the triangle is equal to the sum of its distances to the other two vertices if, and only if, the triangle is equilateral.

4-5 SOLVING EQUATIONS AND INEQUALITIES INVOLVING ABSOLUTE VALUE

On the number line, the numbers -4 and 4 are each located 4 units from 0. Each number is said to have an absolute value of 4. We write $|-4| = 4$ and $|4| = 4$.

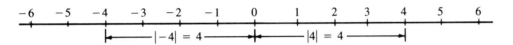

> Given any number x, its *absolute value* is written $|x|$, and represents the distance from x to 0 on the number line.
> - The absolute value of any number other than 0 is positive.
> - The absolute value of 0 is 0.

Example 1. Simplify.

    a) $|12|$ b) $|-7|$ c) $|1 - 4|$

Solution.   a) $|12| = 12$ b) $|-7| = 7$ c) $|1 - 4| = |-3|$
$$= 3$$

    In *Example 1c)*, the expression $|1 - 4|$ represents the distance from 1 to 4 on the number line. Similarly, the expression $|x - a|$ represents the distance from x to a.

> The expression $|x - a|$ represents the distance from x to a on the number line.

    We can use the above ideas to solve equations and inequalities involving absolute value.

Example 2. Solve for x.

    a) $|x| = 3$ b) $|x - 2| = 3$ c) $|x + 2| = 3$

Solution.   a) $|x| = 3$

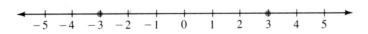

Both 3 and -3 are 3 units from 0 on the number line. Therefore, the equation $|x| = 3$ has two roots, 3 and -3.

    b) $|x - 2| = 3$

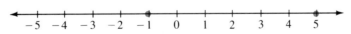

The distance from x to 2 must be 3 units. Hence, the roots of the equation are -1 and 5.

c) $|x + 2| = 3$

Write the equation in the form $|x - (-2)| = 3$.

The distance from x to -2 must be 3 units. Hence, the roots are -5 and 1.

Example 3. Solve for x.

    a) $|x - 5| < 3$ b) $|2x + 3| \geq 4$

Solution.   a) $|x - 5| < 3$

The solution consists of all numbers that are less than 3 units from 5 on the number line. These are the numbers between 2 and 8. The solution set is $\{x \mid 2 < x < 8,\ x \in R\}$.

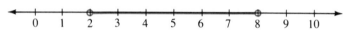

The open dots at 2 and 8 indicate that these numbers are not part of the solution set.

b) $|2x + 3| \geq 4$

Divide both sides by 2 and write the inequality in the form $|x - (-1.5)| \geq 2$.

The solution consists of those numbers that are 2 or more units from -1.5 on the number line. These are the numbers which are less than -3.5 or greater than 0.5.

The solution set is $\{x \mid x \leq -3.5 \text{ or } x \geq 0.5,\ x \in R\}$.

The closed dots at -3.5 and 0.5 indicate that these numbers are part of the solution set.

We can use the method of the above examples to solve any equation or inequality in which the variable x occurs only within the absolute-value signs. Different methods are required to solve an equation such as $|x - 3| = 2x$ or an inequality such as $|x - 2| < 2x$.

EXERCISES 4-5

1. Solve for x.

  a) $|x| = 5$ b) $|x| = 0$ c) $|x - 2| = 7$

  d) $|x - 4| = 2$ e) $|x + 1| = 5$ f) $0 = |x - 5|$

2. Solve for x.

  a) $|x| < 3$ b) $|x| \geq 4$ c) $|x - 2| < 5$

  d) $|x - 1| \leq 2$ e) $|x + 1| \geq 7$ f) $|x + 1| < 9$

Ⓑ

3. Solve and check.

a) $|x - 5| = 2$ b) $|x - 2| = 5$ c) $|x + 1| = 2$
d) $|x + 2| = 1$ e) $|x - 3| = 9$ f) $4 = |3 - x|$

4. Solve and graph the solution set on the number line.

a) $|x - 3| \leq 1$ b) $|x - 3| > 2$ c) $|x + 2| < 6$
d) $|x - 5| \geq 4$ e) $|x + 1| \geq 10$ f) $|x + 5| \leq 9$

5. Solve.

a) $|2x - 3| = 4$ b) $|2x + 1| = 3$ c) $|3x - 5| = 2$
d) $|4x + 3| = 6$ e) $|2 - 3x| = 1$ f) $1 = |1 + 4x|$

6. Solve.

a) $|2x + 1| \leq 9$ b) $|3x - 2| < 6$ c) $|4 + 2x| > 3$

d) $|5x + 2| \geq 3$ e) $\left|\frac{1}{2}x + 1\right| \leq 2$ f) $3 > |2 - 3x|$

7. Write an absolute-value inequality whose solution set is each given graph.

a)

b)

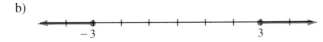

c)

d)

Ⓒ

8. Write an absolute-value inequality for each solution set.

a) $\{x \mid 1 \leq x \leq 7\}$ b) $\{x \mid -2 \leq x \leq 4\}$ c) $\{x \mid -1 < x < 2\}$
d) $\{x \mid x < 2 \text{ or } x > 6\}$ e) $\{x \mid x < 0 \text{ or } x > 4\}$ f) $\{x \mid x \neq 2\}$

9. Write an absolute-value inequality which has:

a) no solution
b) every real number as a solution
c) only one solution.

10. a) If the area of a rectangle, in square centimetres, is represented by $7x - x^2 - 9$, and its width in centimetres is represented by $x - 2$, find an expression for its length.

b) Assuming that the length is greater than or equal to the width, for what values of x does the expression found in part a) represent the length of the rectangle?

Review Exercises

1. State which of the lines listed below intersects the circle $x^2 + y^2 = 9$ in:
   a) 2 points
   b) 1 point
   c) 0 points.

   i) $y = -\frac{2}{3}x + 2$
   ii) $x - 2y + 8 = 0$
   iii) $x = -3$

2. Solve graphically.
   a) $x^2 + y^2 = 16$
      $y = 2x - 1$

   b) $y = x^2 - 4x + 1$
      $y = \frac{2}{3}x + 2$

   c) $x + 2y = 5$
      $xy = 6$

   d) $x^2 + 9y^2 = 36$
      $y = x^2 + 2x - 2$

   e) $x^2 - y^2 = 9$
      $2x - 3y = 0$

   f) $4x^2 + y^2 = 16$
      $xy = 1$

3. Solve each system. Give the answers to 2 decimal places where necessary.
   a) $x^2 + y^2 = 4$
      $2x + y = 3$

   b) $y = x^2 - 2x - 2$
      $x + 3y = 6$

   c) $x^2 - y^2 = -9$
      $xy = 4$

   d) $4x^2 + 9y^2 = 36$
      $x - 2y = 1$

4. Which two numbers differ by 3 and have squares that total 65?

5. A radar station located at $O(0,0)$ can track aircraft up to 400 km away. The flight path of a small plane is given by $y = \frac{1}{4}x^2 + 5$. For what values of x can it be tracked by the radar station?

6. In a rectangle of area 18 cm², the length of the diagonal is $3\sqrt{5}$ cm. Find the dimensions of the rectangle.

7. Show the solution of each system on a graph.
   a) $x^2 + y^2 \leq 16$
      $y \geq (x + 2)^2 - 3$

   b) $x^2 + 9y^2 < 36$
      $4x + 3y < 12$

   c) $x^2 - 4y^2 \geq 4$
      $9x^2 + 16y^2 < 144$

8. Solve for x.
   a) $|x + 2| = 5$
   b) $|x - 4| = 2$
   c) $|2x + 3| = 8$

9. Solve for x.
   a) $|x - 1| \leq 4$
   b) $|x + 3| \geq 7$
   c) $|2x + 1| < 5$
   d) $|4x + 1| \leq 13$
   e) $|3x - 8| > 4$
   f) $|5 - 2x| \leq 1$

5 Trigonometric Functions

The tides in the Bay of Fundy are among the highest in the world. Suppose you know how high the water is at high tide, and the time of day this occurs, and also how high it is at low tide, and the time it occurs. How can you determine the height of the water at any other time of the day? (See Section 5-13 *Example 1*.)

5-1 INTRODUCTION TO PERIODIC FUNCTIONS

In this chapter we will describe many applications of mathematics involving quantities that change in a regular way. Applications concerned with the sun and human physiology are shown on these pages.

The time of the sunset
In summer, the sun sets later than it does in winter. The graph below shows how the time of the sunset at Ottawa varies during a two-year period. The times are given on a 24 h clock in hours and decimals of hours. For example, on June 21 the sun sets at 20.3 h. This means 20 h and 0.3 × 60 min, or 20 h 18 min.

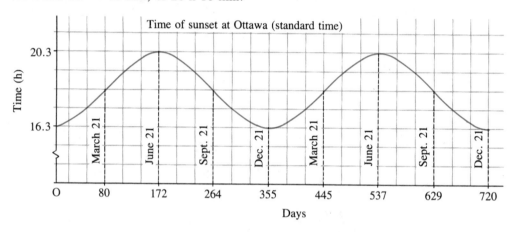

1. a) Estimate the time of the sunset at Ottawa on these dates.
   i) February 2   ii) July 25   iii) October 30
   b) Estimate the dates when the sun sets at these times.
   i) 8 P.M.   ii) 7 P.M.   iii) 6 P.M.   iv) 5 P.M.

2. Suppose similar graphs were drawn for Yellowknife and Mexico City. In what ways would the graphs for these cities differ from the graph above? In what ways would they be similar?

	Approximate time of sunset on			
	March 21	June 21	September 21	December 21
Mexico City	18.8 h	19.3 h	18.6 h	17.9 h
Yellowknife	18.9 h	22.4 h	18.7 h	15.2 h

Sunspots
Sunspots are dark spots that appear from time to time on the surface of the sun. The periodic variation in the number of sunspots has been recorded for hundreds of years. The following graph shows how the number of sunspots varied from 1944 to 1986.

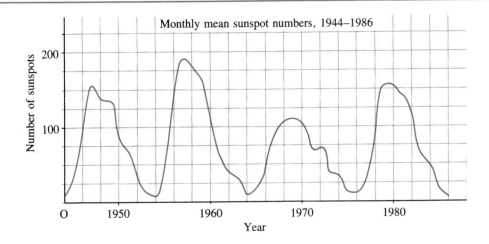

Monthly mean sunspot numbers, 1944–1986

3. The graph shows that sunspot activity increases and decreases at fairly regular intervals. Estimate the number of years, on the average, between the times when there is a maximum number of sunspots.

Lengths of shadows
The graph below shows how the length of the shadow of a 100-m building varies during a three-day period. It is assumed that the sun is directly overhead at noon.

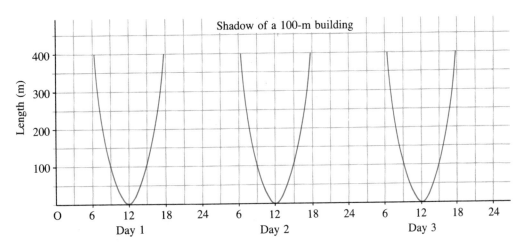

Shadow of a 100-m building

4. a) How long is the shadow at 8 A.M.? at 2 P.M.?
   b) For about how many hours during the day is the shadow longer than 100 m?

5. In many localities the sun is never directly overhead. What change would be needed in the graph if it were drawn for such a locality?

Blood pressure and volume

There are two significant phases to a heart-beat. During the systolic phase, the heart contracts, and pumps blood into the arteries. This phase is marked by a sudden increase in the pressure and a decrease in the volume of blood in the heart. The second phase is the diastolic phase, when the heart relaxes. The pressure decreases and the volume increases as more blood is drawn into the heart from the veins.

Graphs showing how the pressure and volume of blood in the left ventricle of the heart vary during five consecutive heartbeats are shown below. The time scale is the same for both graphs.

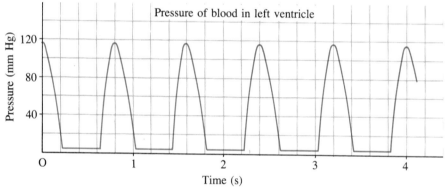

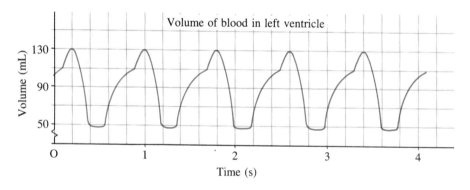

6. During intense physical activity the heart beats faster to satisfy the body's demand for more oxygen. Suppose graphs showing the variation of blood pressure and volume were drawn in this situation. How would the graphs differ from those above? In what ways would they be similar?

Volume of air in the lungs

The volume of air in your lungs is a periodic function of time. This graph shows how the volume of air in the lungs varies during normal breathing.

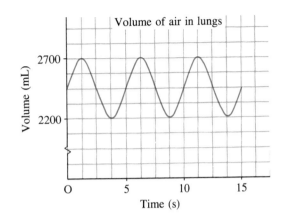

7. According to the graph, how long does it take to inhale and exhale once?

8. When the average person takes a deep breath, about 5000 mL of air can be inhaled. But only about 4000 mL of this air can be exhaled. Suppose that such a breath takes twice as much time as a normal breath. If a graph similar to the one shown were drawn for deep breathing, in what ways would it differ?

Summary

The graphs in this section suggest what is meant by a *periodic function*. The graph of such a function repeats in a regular way. The length of the part that repeats, measured along the horizontal axis, is called the *period* of the function.

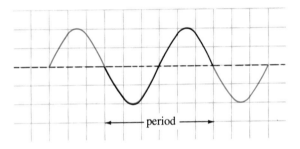

9. All periodic functions have a period. Estimate the period for the functions illustrated above.

10. State the period of this function.

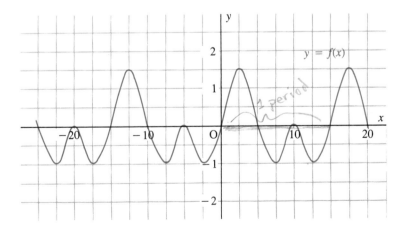

11. One of the examples in this section suggests a periodic function, but it is not a periodic function. Which example is this?

5-2 RADIAN MEASURE

When we construct a circle graph, we assume that the area of a *sector* of a circle is proportional to the *sector angle*. The length of the arc bounding the sector is proportional to the sector angle and is called the *arc length*.

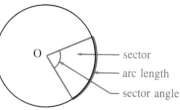

Example 1.   Calculate the arc length of a sector of a circle of radius 20 cm if the sector angle is 140°.

Solution.   Since the angle subtended at the centre of the circle by the circumference is 360°,

the arc length of the sector shown is $\frac{140}{360}$ of the circumference.

$$\frac{\text{Arc length}}{\text{Circumference}} = \frac{140}{360}$$

The circumference of the circle is $2\pi(20)$, or 40π.

Therefore, arc length $= \frac{140}{360}(40\pi)$

$\doteq 48.9$

The arc length is about 49 cm.

Example 1 illustrates the following relationship.

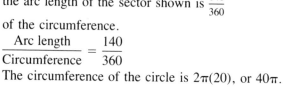

$$\frac{\text{Arc length of a sector}}{\text{Circumference}} = \frac{\text{Sector angle}}{\text{Full-turn angle}}$$

Using this relationship, we can calculate the sector angle that corresponds to a given arc length.

Example 2.   Find the measure of the angle, to the nearest tenth of a degree, subtended at the centre of a circle, radius R, by an arc of each length.
a) R b) $2R$ c) $3R$

Solution.   a) Rewrite the proportion above.

$$\frac{\text{Sector angle}}{\text{Full-turn angle}} = \frac{\text{Arc length}}{\text{Circumference}}$$

For an arc length R

$$\frac{\text{Sector angle}}{360°} = \frac{R}{2\pi R}$$

Therefore, sector angle $= \frac{360°}{2\pi}$

$= \frac{180°}{\pi}$

$\doteq 57.3°$

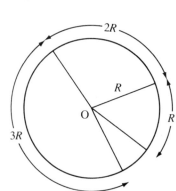

b) Since the sector angle is proportional to the arc length, for an arc length $2R$ the sector angle is twice as large as in part a).

$$\text{Sector angle} = 2\left(\frac{180°}{\pi}\right)$$
$$\doteq 114.6°$$

c) Similarly, for an arc length $3R$

$$\text{Sector angle} = 3\left(\frac{180°}{\pi}\right)$$
$$\doteq 171.9°$$

In *Example 2* we discovered that an angle of $\dfrac{180°}{\pi}$ (approximately 57°) is subtended at the centre of a circle by an arc of length R, where R is the radius.

Definition: One *radian* is the measure of an angle which is subtended at the centre of a circle by an arc equal in length to the radius of the circle.

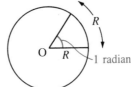

From this definition, $1 \text{ radian} = \dfrac{180°}{\pi}$

Multiply both sides by π, to get the following result.

$$\pi \text{ radians} = 180°$$

Hence, a full-turn angle, 360°, is equal to 2π radians.

We can use this result to derive a simple relation between the arc length, the radius, and the sector angle measured in radians. Let a represent the arc length which subtends an angle θ radians at the centre of a circle, radius R.

Substitute in this proportion.

$$\frac{\text{Arc length of a sector}}{\text{Circumference}} = \frac{\text{Sector angle}}{\text{Full-turn angle}}$$

$$\frac{a}{2\pi R} = \frac{\theta}{2\pi}$$

$$a = R\theta$$

This formula can be used to find an arc length if the angle it subtends at the centre of the circle is measured in radians.

The arc length a subtended by an angle θ radians in a circle with radius R is given by the formula: $a = R\theta$

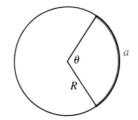

The fact that π radians is equal to $180°$ can be used to convert from radians to degrees, and vice versa.

Example 3. Express each angle to 2 decimal places.

    a) 4 radians in degrees   b) $138°$ in radians

Solution.   a) π radians $= 180°$ b) $180° = \pi$ radians

$$1 \text{ radian} = \frac{180°}{\pi}$$

$$1° = \frac{\pi}{180} \text{ radians}$$

$$4 \text{ radians} = 4\left(\frac{180°}{\pi}\right)$$

$$138° = 138\left(\frac{\pi}{180}\right) \text{ radians}$$

$$\doteq 229.18°$$

$$\doteq 2.41 \text{ radians}$$

Most scientific calculators have keys which enable you to convert from radians to degrees, and vice versa. Read your calculator manual to determine how to make these conversions. Verify the answers in *Example 3*.

Example 4. A circle has radius 6.5 cm. Calculate the length of an arc of this circle subtended by each angle.

    a) 2.4 radians   b) $75°$

Solution.   a) $a = R\theta$

$$a = (6.5)(2.4)$$
$$= 15.6$$

The arc length is 15.6 cm.

    b) To use the formula $a = R\theta$, the angle must be in radians.

$$180° = \pi \text{ radians}$$

$$1° = \frac{\pi}{180} \text{ radians}$$

$$75° = 75\left(\frac{\pi}{180}\right) \text{ radians}$$

$$\doteq 1.309 \text{ radians}$$

Substitute in the formula $a = R\theta$.

$$a = R\theta$$
$$\doteq (6.5)(1.309)$$
$$\doteq 8.5085$$

The arc length is approximately 8.5 cm.

EXERCISES 5-2

Ⓐ

1. Convert from degrees to radians. Express the answer in terms of π.

    a) $30°$ b) $45°$ c) $60°$ d) $90°$ e) $120°$ f) $135°$

    g) $150°$ h) $180°$ i) $210°$ j) $225°$ k) $240°$ l) $270°$

    m) $300°$ n) $315°$ o) $330°$ p) $360°$ q) $390°$ r) $405°$

2. Convert from radians to degrees.

a) $\frac{\pi}{2}$ radians
b) $\frac{3\pi}{4}$ radians
c) $-\frac{2\pi}{3}$ radians
d) $\frac{7\pi}{6}$ radians

e) $\frac{\pi}{4}$ radians
f) $-\frac{3\pi}{2}$ radians
g) $\frac{7\pi}{4}$ radians
h) 2π radians

i) $-\frac{5\pi}{3}$ radians
j) $\frac{5\pi}{4}$ radians
k) $\frac{\pi}{6}$ radians
l) $-\frac{11\pi}{6}$ radians

3. Convert from degrees to radians. Give the answers to 2 decimal places.

a) $100°$
b) $225°$
c) $57.3°$
d) $-125°$
e) $75x°$
f) $\frac{60°}{\pi}$

g) $-65°$
h) $24.5x°$
i) $150°$
j) $30°$
k) $\frac{180°}{\pi}$
l) $-90x°$

4. Convert from radians to degrees. Give the answers to 1 decimal place.
   a) 2 radians
   b) -5 radians
   c) 3.2 radians
   d) 1.8 radians
   e) -0.7 radians
   f) 1.4θ radians
   g) 6.7 radians
   h) $-2\pi x$ radians

5. Find the length of the arc which subtends each angle at the centre of a circle of radius 5 cm. Give the answers to 1 decimal place.
   a) 2.0 radians
   b) 3.0 radians
   c) 1.8 radians
   d) 6.1 radians
   e) 4.2 radians
   f) 0.6 radians

6. Find the length of the arc of a circle with radius 12 cm that subtends each sector angle. Give the answers to 1 decimal place where necessary.
   a) $135°$
   b) $75°$
   c) $105°$
   d) $165°$
   e) $240°$
   f) $180°$
   g) $310°$
   h) $200°$

7. Find the arc length to the nearest centimetre of the sector of a circle with radius:
   a) 7 m, if the sector angle is   i) $120°$ ii) $210°$
   b) 90 cm, if the sector angle is i) $30°$ ii) $225°$
   c) 216 mm, if the sector angle is i) $135°$ ii) $300°$.

(B)

8. How many radians are there in:
   a) a full turn
   b) a half turn
   c) a quarter turn?

9. Calculate the arc length to the nearest metre of a sector of a circle with radius 6 m if the sector angle is $140°$.

10. Two sectors of the same circle have sector angles of $35°$ and $105°$ respectively. The arc length of the smaller sector is 17 cm. What is the arc length of the larger sector?

11. Write an expression for the measure in radians of the sector angle of a sector, in a circle graph with radius r, which represents $x\%$ of the total area.

12. The Earth travels in a nearly circular
    orbit around the sun. The radius of the
    orbit is about 149 000 000 km.
    a) What is the measure in radians of
       the angle subtended at the sun by the
       positions of the Earth at two differ-
       ent times 24 h apart?
    b) About how far does the Earth travel
       in one day in its orbit around the sun?

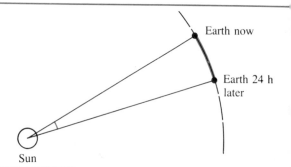

13. The *angular velocity* of an object is the angle per unit time through which an object
    rotates about a rotation centre.
    a) What is the angular velocity in radians per second of a car tire of diameter
       64 cm when the car is travelling at 100 km/h?
    b) Write an expression for the angular velocity in radians per second for a car tire
       of diameter *d* centimetres when the car is travelling at *x* kilometres per hour?

14. a) Write expressions for the distance
       from A to B:
       i) along the line segment AB
       ii) along the circular arc from A to B.
    b) How many times as long as the
       straight-line distance is the distance
       along the circular arc from A to B?
    c) Write an expression for the area of
       the shaded segment of the circle.
    d) Write an expression for the shortest
       distance from the vertex of the
       right angle to the line segment AB.

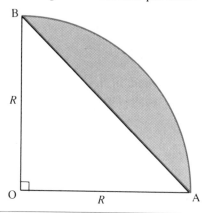

 INVESTIGATE

A Reason for Introducing Radian Measure

1. The formula $a = R\theta$ for the arc length subtended by an angle θ radians
   in a circle with radius R was derived in this section. Derive a similar formula
   if the measure of the angle is degrees instead of radians. Then compare
   the two formulas.

2. a) Derive a formula for the area of a sector formed by an angle θ radians
      in a circle with radius R.
   b) Derive a similar formula if the measure of the angle is degrees. Then
      compare the two formulas.

3. Suggest an advantage of using radian measure instead of degree measure
   for angles.

5-3 TRIGONOMETRIC FUNCTIONS OF ANGLES IN STANDARD POSITION

Perhaps the simplest example of periodic motion is motion in a circle. To study motion in a circle, we define the standard position of an angle.

Let $P(x,y)$ represent a point which moves around a circle with radius r and centre $(0,0)$. P starts at the point $A(r,\theta)$ on the x-axis. For any position of P, an angle θ is defined, which represents the amount of rotation about the origin. We say that the angle θ is in *standard position*, where OA is the *initial arm* and OP is the *terminal arm*. If $\theta > 0°$, the rotation is counterclockwise. If $\theta < 0°$, the rotation is clockwise. The measure of the angle may be in degrees or in radians.

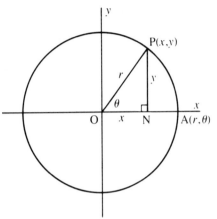

For any position of P on the circle, we define the *primary trigonometric functions* of θ as follows.

$$\sin \theta = \frac{y}{r} \qquad \cos \theta = \frac{x}{r} \qquad \tan \theta = \frac{y}{x} \qquad x \neq 0$$

where $r = \sqrt{x^2 + y^2}$

We can use these definitions to determine the sine, cosine, or tangent of any angle θ in standard position.

Example 1. The point $P(-1,2)$ is on the terminal arm of an angle θ.
   a) Draw a diagram showing θ in standard position.
   b) Calculate the values of $\sin \theta$, $\cos \theta$, and $\tan \theta$ to five decimal places.

Solution.   a)

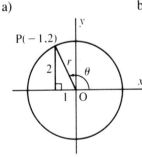

b) From the diagram,
$$r = \sqrt{(-1)^2 + 2^2}$$
$$= \sqrt{5}$$
Therefore,

$$\sin \theta = \frac{y}{r} \qquad\qquad \cos \theta = \frac{x}{r} \qquad\qquad \tan \theta = \frac{y}{x}$$

$$= \frac{2}{\sqrt{5}} \qquad\qquad = \frac{-1}{\sqrt{5}} \qquad\qquad = -2$$

$$\doteq 0.894\ 43 \qquad\qquad \doteq -0.447\ 21$$

In *Example 1*, notice that sin θ is positive, while both cos θ and tan θ are negative. This is because θ is in the second quadrant, where x is negative. The table below summarizes the possible combinations of signs for each function. Since $r = \sqrt{x^2 + y^2}$, its sign is always positive.

	Quadrant I	Quadrant II	Quadrant III	Quadrant IV
	(x,y)	$(-x,y)$	$(-x,-y)$	$(x,-y)$
Sign of $\sin \theta = \dfrac{y}{r}$	$+$	$+$	$-$	$-$
Sign of $\cos \theta = \dfrac{x}{r}$	$+$	$-$	$-$	$+$
Sign of $\tan \theta = \dfrac{y}{x}$	$+$	$-$	$+$	$-$

We can use a scientific calculator to find the sine, cosine, or tangent of any angle when its measure is given in degrees or radians. When the angle is in radians, it is customary to indicate no unit.

Example 2. Find each value to five decimal places.
    a) tan 125°   b) cos 2.4

Solution.   a) First be sure that the calculator is in *degree mode*.
          tan 125° $\doteq$ $-1.428\ 15$
      b) Since there is no unit for the angle, the angle is in radians. Be sure that the calculator is in *radian mode*.
          cos 2.4 $\doteq$ $-0.737\ 39$

As θ rotates around the circle, past 360° or 2π, the same values of x and y are encountered as before. Hence, in *Example 2*, there are infinitely many other angles which have the same tangent as 125°, or the same cosine as 2.4 radians.

Use your calculator to verify that these expressions are also equal to tan 125°.
tan (125° + 360°), or tan 485°
tan (125° + 720°), or tan 845°
tan (125° − 360°), or tan (−235°)

Use your calculator to verify that these expressions are also equal to cos 2.4.
cos (2.4 + 2π)
cos (2.4 + 4π)
cos (2.4 − 2π)

Conversely, if an equation such as sin θ = 0.75 is given, there are infinitely many values of θ which satisfy the equation. These are called the *roots* of the equation. We are normally interested only in the roots between 0° and 360° (if θ is in degrees) or between 0 and 2π (if θ is in radians).

Example 3. Solve the equation sin θ = 0.85 for θ in radians, to two decimal places, where $0 \leqslant \theta \leqslant 2\pi$.

Solution. Since sin θ is positive, and sin $\theta = \frac{y}{r}$, θ lies in the quadrants in which

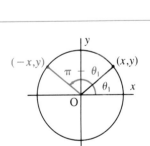

y > 0, namely, Quadrants I and II.
In radian mode, use the inverse sine key
to obtain 1.015 985 3.

Hence, one root is 1.02. Since 1.02 < $\frac{\pi}{2}$,

this root is in Quadrant 1.
To find the root in Quadrant II,
consider the diagram.
P'($-x,y$) is the reflection of P(x,y)
in the y-axis.
By symmetry, $\angle$P'OB = $\angle$POA,
or approximately 1.02
Hence, $\angle$P'OA = π − 1.015 985 3
                            $\doteq$ 2.125 607 3
To two decimal places, the equation sin θ = 0.85 has two roots between 0 and 2π: θ_1 = 1.02 and θ_2 = 2.13.

In *Example 3*, notice that when the values of the angle are subtracted from π, more than two decimal places are used. This avoids rounding errors.

Example 3 illustrates the following general result.

Property of sine functions
If k is a constant between − 1 and + 1, the
equation sin θ = k has infinitely many roots.

If θ_1 is one root, then another root is:
$\theta_2 = \pi - \theta_1$ (in radians)

All other roots can be found by adding multiples
of 2π to θ_1 or θ_2.

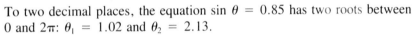

Example 4.   Solve the equation $\sin \theta = -0.428$ in radians, to two decimal places, where $0 \leqslant \theta \leqslant 2\pi$.

Solution.   Since $\sin \theta$ is negative, and $\sin \theta = \frac{y}{r}$, θ lies in the quadrants in which $y < 0$, namely, Quadrants III and IV.
In radian mode, use the inverse sine key to obtain $-0.442\ 278\ 7$.
Hence, one root of the equation is approximately -0.44. Although this is not between 0 and 2π, we can use it to obtain two roots which are between 0 and 2π.
To obtain one root, add 2π: $-0.442\ 278\ 7 + 2\pi \doteq 5.840\ 906\ 6$.
This is the root in Quadrant IV.
To obtain the other root, use the property of sine functions.
Another angle that satisfies the equation is:
$\pi - (-0.442\ 278\ 7) = 3.583\ 871\ 3$.   This is the root in Quadrant III.
To two decimal places, the equation $\sin \theta = -0.428$ has two roots between 0 and 2π: $\theta_1 = 3.58$ and $\theta_2 = 5.84$.
Check these results with your calculator.

Example 5.   Solve the equation $\cos \theta = -0.375$ in radians, to two decimal places, where $0 \leqslant \theta \leqslant 2\pi$.

Solution.   Since $\cos \theta$ is negative, and $\cos \theta = \frac{x}{r}$, θ lies in the quadrants in which $x < 0$, namely, Quadrants II and III.
Use the inverse cosine key to obtain $1.955\ 193\ 1$.
Hence, one root is 1.96, which is in Quadrant II.
To find the root in Quadrant III, consider the diagram. $P'(x, -y)$ is the reflection of $P(x, y)$ in the x-axis. By symmetry, $\angle P'OA = \angle POA$, or approximately 1.96.
Hence, as an angle in standard position,
$\angle P'OA = 2\pi - 1.955\ 193\ 1$
$\doteq 4.327\ 992\ 2$
This is the root in Quadrant III.
To two decimal places, the equation $\cos \theta = -0.375$ has two roots between 0 and 2π: $\theta_1 = 1.96$ and $\theta_2 = 4.33$.

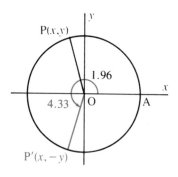

Example 5 illustrates the following general result.

Property of cosine functions
If θ_1 is any value of θ such that $\cos \theta = k$, then another value of θ that satisfies this equation is:

$\theta_2 = 2\pi - \theta_1$ (in radians)

All other roots can be found by adding multiples of 2π to θ_1 or θ_2.

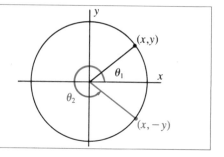

Example 6. Solve the equation $\tan \theta = 1.75$ in radians, to four decimal places, where $0 < \theta < 2\pi$.

Solution.   Since $\tan \theta$ is positive, and $\tan \theta = \frac{y}{x}$, θ lies in the quadrants in which

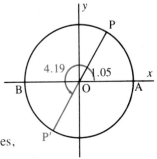

$y > 0$ and $x > 0$, or $y < 0$ and $x < 0$, namely, Quadrants I and III.
Use the inverse tangent key to obtain 1.051 650 2.
Hence, one root is 1.0517, which is in Quadrant I.
To find the root in Quadrant III, consider
the diagram. $P'(-x, -y)$ is the reflection
of $P(x,y)$ in the origin. By symmetry,
$\angle P'OB = \angle POA$, or approximately 1.0517.
Hence, as an angle in standard position,
$\angle P'OA = \pi + 1.051\ 650\ 2$
$\doteq 4.193\ 242\ 9$
This is the root in Quadrant III. To four decimal places,
the equation $\tan \theta = 1.75$ has two roots between 0
and 2π: $\theta_1 = 1.0517$ and $\theta_2 = 4.1932$.

Example 6 illustrates the following general result.

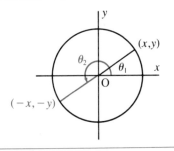

Property of tangent functions
If θ_1 is any value of θ such that $\tan \theta = k$,
then another value of θ which satisfies this
equation is:
$\theta_2 = \pi + \theta_1$ (in radians)
All other roots can be found by adding
multiples of π to θ_1.

Note: After this section, all angle measures in this book will be in radians,
unless stated otherwise.

EXERCISES 5-3

(A)

1. Use a scientific calculator in degree mode. Find each value to 5 decimal places.
   a) $\sin 110°$ b) $\cos 154°$ c) $\tan 103°$ d) $\sin 202°$
   e) $\cos 216°$ f) $\sin 352°$ g) $\tan 337°$ h) $\cos 543°$

2. Use a scientific calculator in radian mode. Find each value to 5 decimal places.
   a) $\sin 0.3$ b) $\cos 0.7$ c) $\tan 1.4$ d) $\sin 1.6$
   e) $\cos 3.2$ f) $\tan 5.05$ g) $\sin 5.93$ h) $\cos 8.57$

3. The point $P(4, -2)$ is on the terminal arm of an angle θ.
   a) Draw a diagram showing θ in standard position.
   b) Calculate $\sin \theta$, $\cos \theta$, and $\tan \theta$ to 5 decimal places.

4. The point P($-2,3$) is on the terminal arm of an angle θ.
   a) Draw a diagram showing θ in standard position.
   b) Calculate sin θ, cos θ, and tan θ to 5 decimal places.

5. Solve for θ in radians to 2 decimal places, if $0 < \theta < 2\pi$.
   a) cos $\theta = 0.73$ b) tan $\theta = 0.512$ c) cos $\theta = 0.165$
   d) tan $\theta = 0.1976$ e) sin $\theta = 0.3324$ f) cos $\theta = 0.6215$

Ⓑ

6. Each point P is on the terminal arm of an angle θ. Use a diagram to calculate sin θ, cos θ, and tan θ.
   a) P($11,-6$)   b) P($-5,-1$)   c) P($-4,2$)   d) P($-4,-5$)
   e) P($5,-3$)   f) P($3,8$)   g) P($0,3$)   h) P($-4,0$)

7. a) Find sin 135° to 5 decimal places.
   b) Find three other angles which have the same sine as 135°, and verify with a calculator.

8. a) Find tan 5.6 to 5 decimal places.
   b) Find three other angles which have the same tangent as 5.6 radians, and verify with a calculator.

9. Solve for θ to the nearest degree, if $0° < \theta < 360°$.
   a) sin $\theta = -0.3926$ b) cos $\theta = -0.7515$ c) tan $\theta = 0.3125$
   d) tan $\theta = -0.8642$ e) cos $\theta = -0.4875$ f) sin $\theta = 0.2425$

10. Solve for θ in radians to 2 decimal places, if $0 < \theta < 2\pi$.
    a) tan $\theta = -0.318$ b) sin $\theta = -0.525$ c) cos $\theta = -0.8076$
    d) cos $\theta = 0.2599$ e) tan $\theta = -0.6741$ f) sin $\theta = 0.4892$

11. Solve for θ:
    a) to the nearest degree, if $0° < \theta < 360°$
    b) in radians to 2 decimal places, if $0 < \theta < 2\pi$.
       i) tan $\theta = 0.92$ ii) tan $\theta = -1.425$ iii) tan $\theta = -2.0217$

12. The angle θ is in the first quadrant, and tan $\theta = \dfrac{4}{5}$.
    a) Draw a diagram showing the angle in standard position and a point P on its terminal arm.
    b) Determine possible coordinates for P.
    c) Find the other two primary trigonometric functions of θ.

13. Repeat *Exercise 12* if θ is in the second quadrant, and tan $\theta = -\dfrac{5}{3}$.

14. Repeat *Exercise 12* if θ is in the second quadrant, and sin $\theta = \dfrac{3}{\sqrt{10}}$.

Ⓒ

15. You can use a scientific calculator to find the sine, the cosine, or the tangent of any angle in standard position.
    a) Determine the largest angle your calculator will accept: in degrees; in radians.
    b) Are these two angles equal?

5-4 THE RECIPROCAL TRIGONOMETRIC RATIOS

To this point, we have defined the three primary trigonometric ratios of an angle θ.

$$\sin \theta = \frac{\text{opposite}}{\text{hypotenuse}} \qquad \cos \theta = \frac{\text{adjacent}}{\text{hypotenuse}} \qquad \tan \theta = \frac{\text{opposite}}{\text{adjacent}}$$

The reciprocals of these ratios are respectively called the *cosecant*, *secant*, and *cotangent ratios* and are abbreviated as *csc*, *sec*, and *cot*. These *reciprocal trigonometric ratios* are defined as follows.

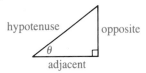

$$\csc \theta = \frac{\text{hypotenuse}}{\text{opposite}} \qquad \sec \theta = \frac{\text{hypotenuse}}{\text{adjacent}} \qquad \cot \theta = \frac{\text{adjacent}}{\text{opposite}}$$

It follows from these definitions that:

$$\csc \theta = \frac{1}{\sin \theta} \qquad \sec \theta = \frac{1}{\cos \theta} \qquad \cot \theta = \frac{1}{\tan \theta}.$$

Since we can readily compute the value of a reciprocal ratio by taking the reciprocal of a primary ratio, most scientific calculators have keys for only the primary trigonometric ratios. For example, to obtain csc 36° on a calculator, we find sin 36° and use the reciprocal key $\boxed{1/x}$.

Example 1. Find the values of the six trigonometric ratios for 47°.

Solution. Use a calculator.

$\sin 47° \doteq 0.731\ 353\ 7$
$\csc 47° \doteq 1.367\ 327\ 5$
$\cos 47° \doteq 0.681\ 998\ 4$
$\sec 47° \doteq 1.466\ 279\ 2$
$\tan 47° \doteq 1.072\ 368\ 7$
$\cot 47° \doteq 0.932\ 515\ 1$

Example 2. Write the six trigonometric ratios for the two acute angles in the right triangle with sides of length 12, 35, and 37 units.

Solution. Let α and β represent the acute angles. From the definition of the trigonometric ratios

$$\sin \alpha = \frac{12}{37} \quad \cos \alpha = \frac{35}{37} \quad \tan \alpha = \frac{12}{35}$$

$$\csc \alpha = \frac{37}{12} \quad \sec \alpha = \frac{37}{35} \quad \cot \alpha = \frac{35}{12}$$

$$\sin \beta = \frac{35}{37} \quad \cos \beta = \frac{12}{37} \quad \tan \beta = \frac{35}{12}$$

$$\csc \beta = \frac{37}{35} \quad \sec \beta = \frac{37}{12} \quad \cot \beta = \frac{12}{35}$$

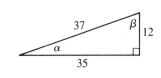

Example 2 not only shows the relationship between the primary and reciprocal ratios, but the diagram suggests a relationship between the trigonometric ratios of two angles which total 90°.

Since $\sin \alpha = \cos \beta = \frac{12}{37}$, and $\beta = 90° - \alpha$

then $\sin \alpha = \cos (90° - \alpha)$

Similarly, $\cos \alpha = \sin (90° - \alpha)$ and $\tan \alpha = \cot (90° - \alpha)$

Just as we can calculate all primary trigonometric ratios given any one primary trigonometric ratio, so also we can calculate all trigonometric ratios given any one trigonometric ratio.

Example 3. If $\cot \theta = \frac{b}{a}$, write expressions for the six trigonometric ratios for θ.

Solution. Sketch a right triangle with side a opposite θ and side b adjacent θ.
From the Pythagorean Theorem, the hypotenuse has length $\sqrt{a^2 + b^2}$.
From the definition of the trigonometric ratios

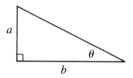

$$\sin \theta = \frac{a}{\sqrt{a^2 + b^2}} \qquad \cos \theta = \frac{b}{\sqrt{a^2 + b^2}} \qquad \tan \theta = \frac{a}{b}$$

$$\csc \theta = \frac{\sqrt{a^2 + b^2}}{a} \qquad \sec \theta = \frac{\sqrt{a^2 + b^2}}{b} \qquad \cot \theta = \frac{b}{a}$$

Example 4. Find each value of θ to the nearest degree.
      a) $\cot \theta = 1.234$ b) $\sec \theta = 2.561$ c) $\csc \theta = 4.032$

Solution.   a) Since $\tan \theta = \dfrac{1}{\cot \theta}$

$$\tan \theta = \frac{1}{1.234}$$
$$\doteq 0.810\ 372\ 8$$
$$\theta \doteq 39°$$

b) Since $\cos \theta = \dfrac{1}{\sec \theta}$

$$\cos \theta = \frac{1}{2.561}$$
$$\doteq 0.390\ 472\ 5$$
$$\theta \doteq 67°$$

c) Since $\sin \theta = \dfrac{1}{\csc \theta}$

$$\sin \theta = \frac{1}{4.032}$$
$$\doteq 0.248\ 015\ 9$$
$$\theta \doteq 14°$$

EXERCISES 5-4

Ⓐ

1. Find the value to 3 decimal places of each trigonometric ratio.
   a) csc 17°   b) cot 29°   c) sec 64°   d) cot 81°   e) sec 57°   f) csc 71°
   g) cot 11°   h) sec 9°   i) cot 53°   j) csc 39°   k) sec 23°   l) csc 84°

2. Find the values to 3 decimal places of the six trigonometric ratios for each angle.
   a) 25°   b) 50°   c) 75°   d) 30°   e) 45°   f) 60°

3. Find each value of θ to the nearest ~~degree~~, if θ is acute.
   RADIAN
   a) csc θ = 1.624   b) cot θ = 0.675   c) sec θ = 1.058   d) cot θ = 0.554
   e) sec θ = 1.325   f) csc θ = 1.305   g) cot θ = 3.732   h) sec θ = 3.628
   i) csc θ = 2.591   j) sec θ = 2.591   k) cot θ = 4.915   l) csc θ = 1.267

Ⓑ

4. Write expressions for the six
   trigonometric ratios of each angle.
   a) ∠A   b) ∠B

5. Match each ratio in the first row with
   an equivalent ratio from the second
   row if ∠A + ∠B = 90°.

   | sin A | cos A | tan A | csc A | sec A | cot A |
   | sin B | cos B | tan B | csc B | sec B | cot B |

6. Solve each triangle. Give the answers to 1 decimal place.
   a)   b)   c)

   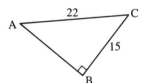
   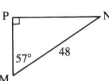

7. Write expressions for the other five trigonometric ratios for each acute angle.

   a) csc $\theta = \dfrac{p}{q}$ b) sec $\phi = \dfrac{x+1}{x-1}$, $x \neq 1$ c) cot $\alpha = \dfrac{2a}{a+1}$, $a \neq -1$

Ⓒ

8. The departure d kilometres of the Earth's surface
   from the line of sight is approximated by this
   formula.

   $d = 6370\left(1 - \cos\left(\dfrac{18a}{637\pi}\right)\right)$ where a kilometres

   is the distance measured along the Earth's surface
   Find the value of d for each given value of a.
   a) 2 km   b) 10 km   c) 50 km   d) 350 km

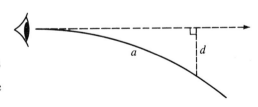

5-5 FUNCTION VALUES OF SPECIAL ANGLES

This diagram illustrates the angle $\frac{\pi}{4}$ in standard position. If PN is perpendicular to OA, then $\triangle$PON is an isosceles triangle with

$\angle$OPN $= \angle$PON $= \frac{\pi}{4}$.

Let PN $=$ ON $= 1$
Then, OP $= \sqrt{1^2 + 1^2}$, or $\sqrt{2}$

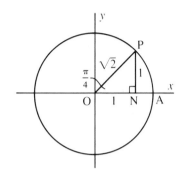

This diagram illustrates the angle $\frac{\pi}{3}$ in standard position. If PN is perpendicular to OA, then $\angle$OPN $= \frac{\pi}{6}$, and $\triangle$OPN is

a $\frac{\pi}{6}, \frac{\pi}{3}, \frac{\pi}{2}$ triangle.

Hence, if OP $= 2$, then ON $= 1$, and PN $= \sqrt{3}$.

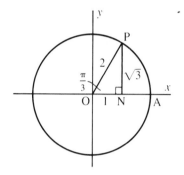

The trigonometric ratios of the angles in the diagrams above can now be calculated. They are shown in the chart below; each angle is in radians.

	sin	**cos**	**tan**	**csc**	**sec**	**cot**
$\frac{\pi}{6}$	$\frac{1}{2}$	$\frac{\sqrt{3}}{2}$	$\frac{1}{\sqrt{3}}$	2	$\frac{2}{\sqrt{3}}$	$\sqrt{3}$
$\frac{\pi}{4}$	$\frac{1}{\sqrt{2}}$	$\frac{1}{\sqrt{2}}$	1	$\sqrt{2}$	$\sqrt{2}$	1
$\frac{\pi}{3}$	$\frac{\sqrt{3}}{2}$	$\frac{1}{2}$	$\sqrt{3}$	$\frac{2}{\sqrt{3}}$	2	$\frac{1}{\sqrt{3}}$

The diagrams above can be used to determine the trigonometric ratios for 0 and $\frac{\pi}{2}$.

As OP rotates clockwise, $\angle$PON decreases to 0 radians, OP approaches ON in length, and PN approaches 0.

As OP rotates counterclockwise, $\angle$PON increases to $\frac{\pi}{2}$, PN approaches OP in length, and ON approaches 0.

The trigonometric ratios of 0 radians and $\frac{\pi}{2}$ radians are shown below.

	sin	**cos**	**tan**	**csc**	**sec**	**cot**
0	0	1	0	∞	1	∞
$\dfrac{\pi}{2}$	1	0	∞	1	∞	0

In the previous section, we learned how to find the trigonometric ratios for angles in any quadrant. Recall that the primary ratios, and their reciprocals are all positive in the first quadrant. Only one primary ratio, and its reciprocal are positive in each of the other quadrants.

Example 1. Find the exact values of sin θ, cos θ, and tan θ, for each value of θ.

a) $\frac{3}{4}\pi$ b) $\frac{4}{3}\pi$

Solution.   a) Since $\angle POA = \frac{3}{4}\pi$, $\angle PON = \pi - \frac{3}{4}\pi$, or $\frac{1}{4}\pi$

$\triangle PON$ is an isosceles right triangle, with sides 1, 1, and $\sqrt{2}$.
    In Quadrant II, only the sine ratio is positive.

$$\sin \frac{3}{4}\pi = \frac{1}{\sqrt{2}}$$

$$\cos \frac{3}{4}\pi = -\frac{1}{\sqrt{2}}$$

$$\tan \frac{3}{4}\pi = -1$$

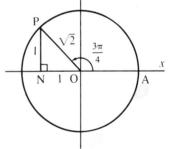

b) Since reflex $\angle POA = \frac{4}{3}\pi$, $\angle PON = \frac{4}{3}\pi - \pi$, or $\frac{\pi}{3}$

$\triangle PON$ is a $\frac{\pi}{6}, \frac{\pi}{3}, \frac{\pi}{2}$ triangle, with sides 1, 2, and $\sqrt{3}$.
    In Quadrant III, only the tangent ratio is positive.

$$\sin \frac{4}{3}\pi = -\frac{\sqrt{3}}{2}$$

$$\cos \frac{4}{3}\pi = -\frac{1}{2}$$

$$\tan \frac{4}{3}\pi = \sqrt{3}$$

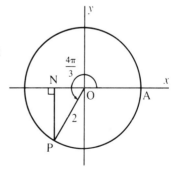

In *Example 1*, each value of $\angle PON$ is called the *reference angle*; that is, the acute angle between OP and the x-axis.

Example 2. Find the exact values of the six trigonometric ratios for each angle.

a) $\dfrac{11\pi}{6}$ b) $\dfrac{3\pi}{2}$

Solution.   a) Since $\angle POA = \dfrac{11\pi}{6}$, the reference

angle $\angle PON = 2\pi - \dfrac{11\pi}{6}$, or $\dfrac{\pi}{6}$

The sides of $\triangle PON$ are 1, 2, and $\sqrt{3}$.

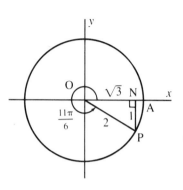

In Quadrant IV, the cosine and secant ratios are positive.

$$\sin \frac{11\pi}{6} = -\frac{1}{2} \qquad \csc \frac{11\pi}{6} = -2$$

$$\cos \frac{11\pi}{6} = \frac{\sqrt{3}}{2} \qquad \sec \frac{11\pi}{6} = \frac{2}{\sqrt{3}}$$

$$\tan \frac{11\pi}{6} = -\frac{1}{\sqrt{3}} \qquad \cot \frac{11\pi}{6} = -\sqrt{3}$$

b) For an angle of $\dfrac{3\pi}{2}$, the terminal arm lies along the negative y-axis.

The "reference angle" is $\dfrac{\pi}{2}$.

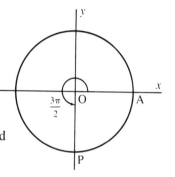

$$\sin \frac{3\pi}{2} = -1 \qquad \csc \frac{3\pi}{2} = -1$$

$$\cos \frac{3\pi}{2} = 0 \qquad \sec \frac{3\pi}{2} \text{ is undefined}$$

$$\tan \frac{3\pi}{2} \text{ is undefined} \qquad \cot \frac{3\pi}{2} = 0$$

The value of a trigonometric ratio may be raised to a power. For example, $(\sin \theta)^2$ means $(\sin \theta)(\sin \theta)$, and it is written $\sin^2\theta$.

Example 3. Evaluate. a) $\tan^2 \dfrac{5}{6}\pi$ \qquad\qquad b) $\sec^3 \dfrac{5\pi}{4}$

Solution.   a) $\tan^2 \dfrac{5}{6}\pi = \left(\tan \dfrac{5}{6}\pi\right)^2$ \qquad b) $\sec^3 \dfrac{5\pi}{4} = \left(\sec \dfrac{5\pi}{4}\right)^3$

$\qquad\qquad = \left(-\dfrac{1}{\sqrt{3}}\right)^2$ \qquad\qquad\qquad\qquad $= (-\sqrt{2})^3$

$\qquad\qquad = \dfrac{1}{3}$ \qquad\qquad\qquad\qquad\qquad\qquad $= -2\sqrt{2}$

Example 4. If $\cos^2\theta = \dfrac{3}{4}$, find $\sin \theta$ and $\tan \theta$.

Solution.   If $\cos^2\theta = \dfrac{3}{4}$, then $\cos \theta = \pm\dfrac{\sqrt{3}}{2}$

The reference angle is $\dfrac{\pi}{6}$.

For $\cos \theta = \dfrac{\sqrt{3}}{2}$, θ is in Quadrants I or IV.

Hence, $\sin\theta = \pm\dfrac{1}{2}$ and $\tan\theta = \pm\dfrac{1}{\sqrt{3}}$

For $\cos\theta = -\dfrac{\sqrt{3}}{2}$, θ is in Quadrants II or III.

Hence, $\sin\theta = \pm\dfrac{1}{2}$ and $\tan\theta = \pm\dfrac{1}{\sqrt{3}}$

EXERCISES 5-5

Ⓐ

1. State the exact value of each ratio.

a) $\sin\dfrac{\pi}{2}$ b) $\csc\dfrac{\pi}{3}$ c) $\cos\dfrac{\pi}{6}$ d) $\tan 0$ e) $\sec\dfrac{\pi}{3}$ f) $\cot\dfrac{\pi}{4}$

g) $\csc\dfrac{\pi}{4}$ h) $\cos\dfrac{\pi}{4}$ i) $\tan\dfrac{\pi}{3}$ j) $\sin\dfrac{\pi}{3}$ k) $\cot\dfrac{\pi}{2}$ l) $\sec 0$

2. State the exact value of each ratio, where possible.

a) $\sec\dfrac{3\pi}{4}$ b) $\sin\dfrac{5\pi}{6}$ c) $\tan\pi$ d) $\cos\dfrac{7\pi}{3}$ e) $\cot\dfrac{5\pi}{4}$ f) $\csc 2\pi$

g) $\cos\dfrac{9\pi}{4}$ h) $\sec\dfrac{10\pi}{3}$ i) $\csc\dfrac{8\pi}{3}$ j) $\sin\dfrac{3\pi}{2}$ k) $\tan\dfrac{11\pi}{6}$ l) $\cot\dfrac{7\pi}{3}$

3. Evaluate.

a) $\tan^2\dfrac{\pi}{3}$ b) $\csc^2\dfrac{5\pi}{6}$ c) $\cos^2\dfrac{2\pi}{3}$ d) $\sec^2\dfrac{11\pi}{6}$ e) $\sin^3\dfrac{7\pi}{4}$ f) $\cot^2\dfrac{4\pi}{3}$

Ⓑ

4. Find each value of θ for $0 < \theta < 2\pi$.

a) $\sin\theta = -\dfrac{1}{2}$ b) $\cos\theta = \dfrac{1}{\sqrt{2}}$ c) $\tan\theta = -\sqrt{3}$ d) $\csc\theta = 2$

e) $\sec\theta = \sqrt{2}$ f) $\tan\theta = -1$ g) $\sin\theta = \dfrac{1}{\sqrt{2}}$ h) $\cot\theta = \sqrt{3}$

i) $\cos\theta = -\dfrac{1}{2}$ j) $\csc\theta = -1$ k) $\sec\theta = -2$ l) $\cot\theta = -\dfrac{1}{\sqrt{3}}$

5. Find the values of each angle θ if $0 < \theta < 2\pi$.

a) $\sin^2\theta = \dfrac{1}{2}$ b) $\tan^2\theta = 3$ c) $\sec^2\theta = 2$ d) $\cot^2\theta = \dfrac{1}{3}$

e) $\csc^2\theta = \dfrac{4}{3}$ f) $\sec^3\theta = -8$ g) $\sin^3\theta = -\dfrac{1}{8}$ h) $\tan^2\theta = 1$

6. State the values of the other five trigonometric ratios for each angle θ.

a) $\sin\theta = -\dfrac{\sqrt{3}}{2}$ b) $\tan\theta = \sqrt{3}$ c) $\sec\theta = -\dfrac{2}{\sqrt{3}}$

Ⓒ

7. θ is an acute angle defined by a point $P(x, y)$ in the first quadrant. Use x, y, and r to define the six trigonometric ratios of each angle.

a) $\pi + \theta$ b) $2\pi - \theta$

5-6 GRAPHING THE SINE AND COSINE FUNCTIONS

To draw graphs of the functions $y = \sin \theta$ and $y = \cos \theta$, recall their definitions. If $P(x,y)$ is any point on a circle of radius r and centre $(0,0)$, then

$$\sin \theta = \frac{y}{r} \qquad \cos \theta = \frac{x}{r}.$$

Imagine that P rotates around the circle counterclockwise starting at $A(r,0)$. As θ increases, the values of x and y change periodically. This causes a periodic change in the values of $\sin \theta$ and $\cos \theta$.

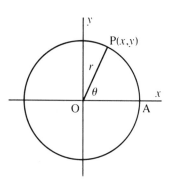

Graphing the function $y = \sin \theta$

The function values are independent of the radius of the circle. Therefore, for convenience, we assume that $r = 2$.
Suppose θ starts at 0 and increases to π. Then $\sin \theta$ changes as follows.

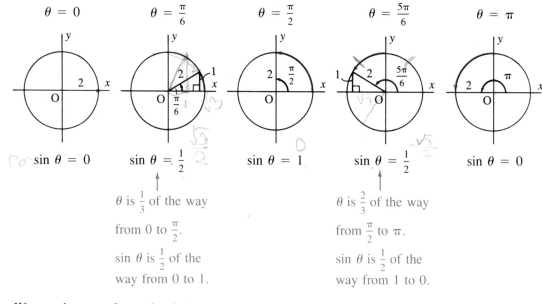

$\theta = 0$ $\theta = \dfrac{\pi}{6}$ $\theta = \dfrac{\pi}{2}$ $\theta = \dfrac{5\pi}{6}$ $\theta = \pi$

$\sin \theta = 0$ $\sin \theta = \dfrac{1}{2}$ $\sin \theta = 1$ $\sin \theta = \dfrac{1}{2}$ $\sin \theta = 0$

θ is $\dfrac{1}{3}$ of the way from 0 to $\dfrac{\pi}{2}$.

$\sin \theta$ is $\dfrac{1}{2}$ of the way from 0 to 1.

θ is $\dfrac{2}{3}$ of the way from $\dfrac{\pi}{2}$ to π.

$\sin \theta$ is $\dfrac{1}{2}$ of the way from 1 to 0.

We use these results to sketch the graph for $0 \leqslant \theta \leqslant \pi$.

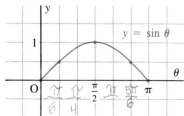

Suppose θ continues from π to 2π. Then $\sin\theta$ changes as follows.

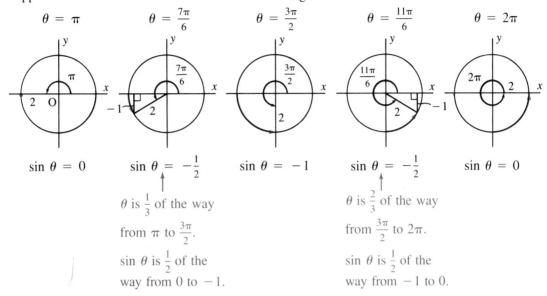

$\theta = \pi$	$\theta = \dfrac{7\pi}{6}$	$\theta = \dfrac{3\pi}{2}$	$\theta = \dfrac{11\pi}{6}$	$\theta = 2\pi$

$\sin\theta = 0$ $\qquad$ $\sin\theta = -\dfrac{1}{2}$ $\qquad$ $\sin\theta = -1$ $\qquad$ $\sin\theta = -\dfrac{1}{2}$ $\qquad$ $\sin\theta = 0$

θ is $\dfrac{1}{3}$ of the way from π to $\dfrac{3\pi}{2}$.

$\sin\theta$ is $\dfrac{1}{2}$ of the way from 0 to -1.

θ is $\dfrac{2}{3}$ of the way from $\dfrac{3\pi}{2}$ to 2π.

$\sin\theta$ is $\dfrac{1}{2}$ of the way from -1 to 0.

We use these results to sketch the graph for $\pi \le \theta \le 2\pi$.

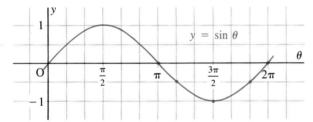

As θ continues beyond 2π, P rotates around the circle again, and the same values of $\sin\theta$ are encountered. Hence, the graph can be continued to the right. Similarly, the graph can be continued to the left, corresponding to a rotation in the opposite direction. Hence, the patterns in the graph repeat every 2π in both directions.

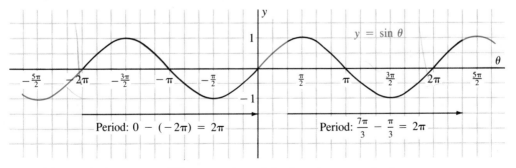

This graph shows two different cycles of the function $y = \sin\theta$. When θ is in radians, the period of this function is 2π.

A *cycle* of a periodic function is a part of its graph from any point to the first point where the graph starts repeating.

The *period* of a periodic function of θ may be expressed as the difference in the values of θ for the points at the ends of a cycle.

Graphing the function $y = \cos \theta$

We can graph the function $y = \cos \theta$ using the same method as we used to graph the function $y = \sin \theta$. The result is shown below.

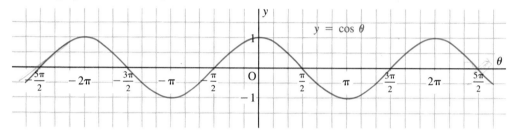

The function $y = \cos \theta$ has a period of 2π. Its graph is congruent to the graph of $y = \sin \theta$, but it is shifted horizontally so that it intersects the y-axis at $(0,1)$ instead of $(0,0)$.

Properties of the function $y = \sin \theta$

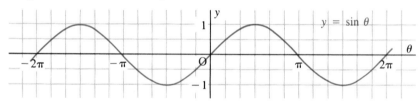

Period: 2π Maximum value of y: 1   Minimum value of y: -1
Domain : θ may represent any angle in standard position
Range: $\{y \mid -1 \leq y \leq 1\}$
θ-intercepts: $\ldots, -\pi, 0, \pi, 2\pi, \ldots$ y-intercept: 0

Properties of the function $y = \cos \theta$

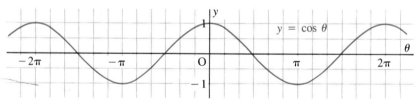

Period: 2π Maximum value of y: 1   Minimum value of y: -1
Domain: θ may represent any angle in standard position
Range: $\{y \mid -1 \leq y \leq 1\}$

θ-intercepts: $\ldots, -\dfrac{\pi}{2}, \dfrac{\pi}{2}, \dfrac{3\pi}{2}, \dfrac{5\pi}{2}, \ldots$ y-intercept: 1

These curves are called *sinusoids*, meaning "like sine curves". To use sinusoidal functions in applications involving quantities that change periodically, we must be able to work with them when their maximum and minimum values are different from 1 and -1, and their periods are different from 2π. This involves taking the basic graphs described in this section, and expanding or compressing them in the vertical or horizontal directions, as well as changing their positions relative to the axes. When changes such as these are made to the graphs of these functions, corresponding changes occur in the equations. In the following sections we will investigate how the changes in the equations are related to the changes in the graphs.

EXERCISES 5-6

(A)

1. In the following diagrams, graphs of $y = \sin \theta$ have been started using different scales. Copy each graph on graph paper, and then extend it for the number of cycles indicated.

   a) 2 cycles   b) 2 cycles   c) 1 cycle

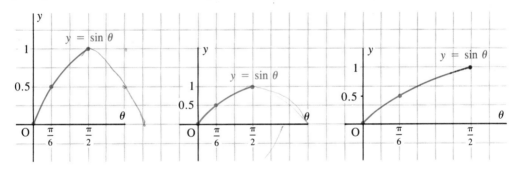

2. **Graphing the function $y = \cos \theta$**

   Let P be a point on the terminal arm of an angle θ in standard position on a circle with radius $r = 2$.

   a) Suppose θ starts at 0 and increases to π. Use diagrams like those on page 178 corresponding to $\theta = 0, \frac{\pi}{3}, \frac{\pi}{2}, \frac{2\pi}{3}$, and π to determine values of $\cos \theta$, and use the results to sketch the graph of $y = \cos \theta$ for $0 \leq \theta \leq \pi$.

   b) Suppose θ continues from π to 2π. Determine values of $\cos \theta$ for $\theta = \frac{4\pi}{3}, \frac{3\pi}{2}, \frac{5\pi}{3}$, and 2π, and use the results to continue the graph from π to 2π.

   c) Continue the graph of $y = \cos \theta$ for values of θ greater than 2π and less than 0.

3. In the following diagrams, graphs of $y = \cos \theta$ have been started using different scales. Copy each graph on graph paper, and then extend it for the number of cycles indicated.

   a) 2 cycles

   b) 2 cycles

   c) 4 cycles

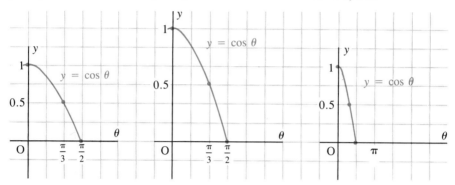

Ⓑ

4. Without making a table of values, draw graphs of $f(\theta) = \sin \theta$ and $f(\theta) = \cos \theta$ for $-2\pi \le \theta \le 2\pi$.

5. For the graph of $y = \sin \theta$
   a) What is the maximum value of y? For what values of θ does this occur?
   b) What is the minimum value of y? For what values of θ does this occur?
   c) What is the range of the function?
   d) What is the y-intercept?
   e) What are the θ-intercepts?

6. Repeat *Exercise 5* for the graph of $y = \cos \theta$.

7. Compare the graphs of $f(\theta) = \sin \theta$ and $f(\theta) = \cos \theta$. In what ways are they alike? In what ways are they different?

Ⓒ

8. A function $y = f(x)$ is defined to be *periodic* if there is a number p such that $f(x + p) = f(x)$ for all values of x in the domain. Use this definition to prove that the functions $y = \sin \theta$ and $y = \cos \theta$ are periodic.

9. a) A function $y = f(x)$ is defined to be an *even* function if $f(-x) = f(x)$ for all values of x in the domain. Use this definition to prove that $y = \cos \theta$ is an even function.
   b) A function $y = f(x)$ is defined to be an *odd* function if $f(-x) = -f(x)$ for all values of x in the domain. Use this definition to prove that $y = \sin \theta$ is an odd function.

10. Graph each function.
    a) $y = |\sin \theta|$
    b) $y = \sin |\theta|$
    c) $y = |\cos \theta|$
    d) $y = \cos |\theta|$

Graphing Sinusoids

There is a simple method of sketching the graph of a sinusoidal function without using graph paper. It involves locating nine points on the graph using a rectangle as a guide.

To graph the function $y = \sin \theta$

Step 1. Draw a rectangle divided into 8 congruent sections as shown. Mark the axes, showing their scales. Locate the points which correspond to multiples of $\frac{\pi}{2}$.

Then identify the sections of the rectangle through which the curve will pass. Each section has points marked at the ends of one diagonal.

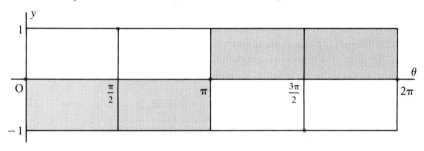

The curve will pass through the unshaded sections.

Step 2. Divide each section into 6 congruent rectangles, as shown. Locate the vertex in each section, which is closest to the point where the graph crosses the θ-axis. Draw a smooth curve through the marked points.

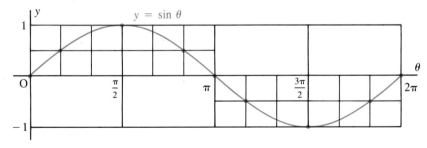

By extending the rectangles to the left or the right, we can sketch additional cycles of $y = \sin \theta$.

1. a) Use the above method to sketch the graph of $f(\theta) = \sin \theta$ for
   $-2\pi \leqslant \theta \leqslant 2\pi$.
   b) Use the method to sketch the graph of $f(\theta) = \cos \theta$ for
   $-2\pi \leqslant \theta \leqslant 2\pi$.

5-7 GRAPHING THE TANGENT FUNCTION

To draw a graph of the tangent function
$f(\theta) = \tan \theta$, recall the definition. If $P(x,y)$
is a point on a circle of radius r and centre
$(0,0)$, then $\tan \theta = \frac{y}{x}$.

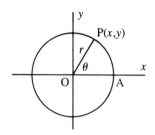

Imagine that P rotates around the circle
counterclockwise, starting at $A(r,0)$. As θ
increases, the values of x and y change
periodically. This causes a periodic change
in the values of $\tan \theta$.

Step 1. Consider values of θ from 0 to $\frac{\pi}{2}$.

When $\theta = 0$, $y = 0$ and $x = r$, so $\tan 0 = \frac{0}{r}$, or 0.

Thus, $(0,0)$ is a point on the graph. As θ increases
from 0 to $\frac{\pi}{4}$, y increases and x decreases.

Hence, $\tan \theta$ increases.

When $\theta = \frac{\pi}{4}$, x and y are equal, so $\tan \frac{\pi}{4} = 1$.

Hence, $\left(\frac{\pi}{4},1\right)$ is a point on the graph. As θ increases

further, $\tan \theta$ continues to increase.

When $\theta = \frac{\pi}{2}$, $y = r$ and $x = 0$. Hence, $\tan \frac{\pi}{2}$ is

undefined. When θ is close to $\frac{\pi}{2}$, $\tan \theta$ is very large.

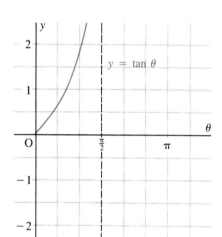

Step 2. Consider values of θ from $\frac{\pi}{2}$ to π.

When θ is close to $\frac{\pi}{2}$, y is very large and positive. But
x is negative, and has a small absolute value. Hence,
$\tan \theta$ is negative and has a very large absolute value.
As θ increases, y decreases and the absolute value of
x increases.
Since $\tan \theta$ is negative, $\tan \theta$ increases.

When $\theta = \frac{3\pi}{4}$, x and y differ only in sign, so

$\tan \frac{3\pi}{4} = -1$. As θ increases further, $\tan \theta$ continues

to increase.

When $\theta = \pi$, $y = 0$ and $x = -r$. Hence,
$\tan \pi = 0$.

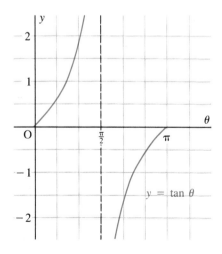

Step 3. This completes one cycle. Other cycles can be graphed similarly.

From the graph, we see that the period of the tangent function is π.

The graph of the tangent function illustrates many properties of this function.

Properties of the function $y = \tan \theta$

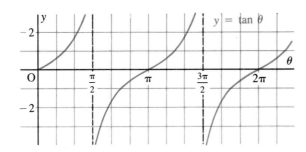

Period: π

Domain: θ may represent any angle in standard position, *except*

$$\cdots \ -\frac{3\pi}{2}, \ -\frac{\pi}{2}, \frac{\pi}{2}, \frac{3\pi}{2}, \cdots$$

Range: All real numbers

θ-intercepts: $\cdots \ -2\pi, \ -\pi, \ 0, \ \pi, \ 2\pi, \ \cdots$

y-intercept: 0

EXERCISES 5-7

(A)

1. In the following diagrams, graphs of $y = \tan \theta$ have been started using different scales. Copy each graph on graph paper, and then extend it for at least two cycles.

a)

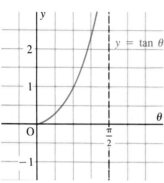

b)

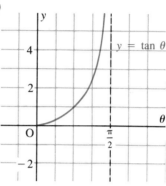

c)

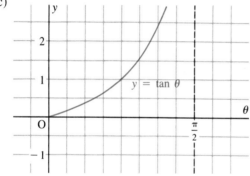

(B)

2. Without making a table of values, draw a graph of $f(\theta) = \tan \theta$ for $-2\pi \le \theta \le 2\pi$.

3. For the graph of $y = \tan \theta$
   a) Are there any maximum or minimum values of y? Explain your answer.
   b) What are the domain and the range?
   c) What is the y-intercept?
   d) What are the θ-intercepts?

4. Compare the graph of $f(\theta) = \tan \theta$ with the graphs of $f(\theta) = \sin \theta$ and $f(\theta) = \cos \theta$. In what ways are they alike? In what ways are they different?

(C)

5. Use the definition in Exercise 8, page 182, to prove that the function $f(\theta) = \tan \theta$ is periodic.

6. Is the function $f(\theta) = \tan \theta$ an even function or an odd function? Use the definition in Exercise 9, page 182.

7. Graph each function.
   a) $y = |\tan \theta|$ b) $y = \tan |\theta|$

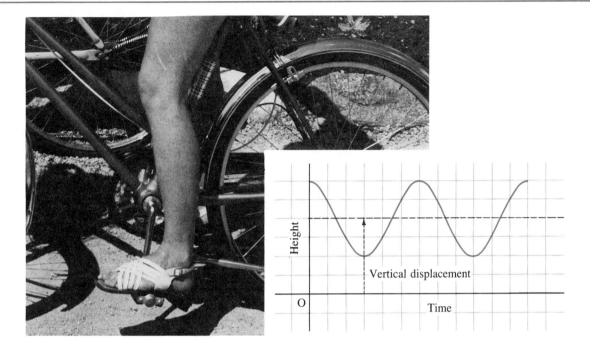

Vertical displacement

Height

O   Time

5-8 VARYING THE VERTICAL DISPLACEMENT AND THE AMPLITUDE OF SINE AND COSINE FUNCTIONS

In this section and the following sections we shall develop a technique for graphing a sinusoidal function without making a table of values.

Varying the Vertical Displacement
As you pedal a bicycle, the heights of the pedals above the ground change periodically. A graph of the height of a pedal against time is a sinusoidal curve with a vertical displacement corresponding to the mean height of the pedal above the ground.

To introduce the vertical displacement of a cosine function, we investigate the effect of q on the graph of $y = \cos \theta + q$. We substitute different values for q, and graph the resulting functions.

If $q = 0$, the equation is $y = \cos \theta$ ... ①
If $q = 1$, the equation is $y = \cos \theta + 1$ ... ②
The y-coordinates of all points on the graph of ② are 1 *greater* than those on the graph of ①. Therefore, the graph of ② is 1 unit *above* the graph of ①. We say that the *vertical displacement* of the function $y = \cos \theta + 1$ is 1.

If $q = -0.5$, the equation is $y = \cos \theta - 0.5$ ... ③
The values of y will all be 0.5 less than those in ①. Therefore, the graph of ③ is 0.5 units *below* the graph of ①. The vertical displacement is -0.5.

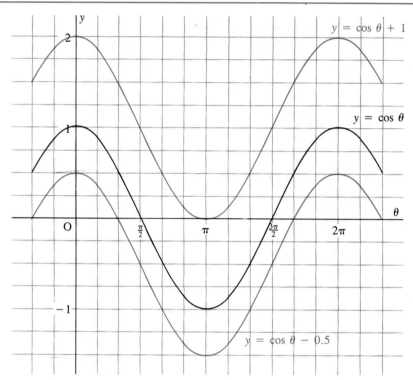

Similar results will be found for other values of q, and for sine functions.

In general, adding a constant to $\sin \theta$ or $\cos \theta$ in the equations of the functions $y = \sin \theta$ or $y = \cos \theta$ causes a vertical translation of the graph. The sign of the constant indicates whether the graph is translated up or down. A positive constant causes a translation up; a negative constant causes a translation down.

The graph of $y = \cos \theta + q$ is related to that of $y = \cos \theta$ by a vertical translation. The vertical displacement is q.

The graph of $y = \sin \theta + q$ is related to that of $y = \sin \theta$ by a vertical translation. The vertical displacement is q.

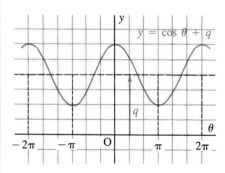

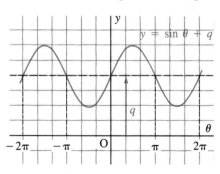

We can draw the graph of an equation in this form without making a table of values.

Example 1. State the vertical displacement for the function $y = \sin \theta + 2$, and draw its graph.

Solution. The vertical displacement is 2.
Draw a graph of $y = \sin \theta$, and then draw its image when translated 2 units up.

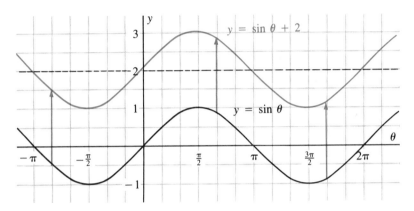

Varying the Amplitude

This graph shows how the top of a building sways in a high wind. The distance the building sways from the centre is called the amplitude of the vibration.

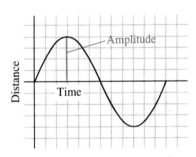

To introduce the amplitude of a sine function, we investigate the effect of a on the graph of $y = a \sin \theta$. We will assume that $a > 0$, since there is no need to consider negative values of a in applications.

If $a = 1$, the equation is $y = \sin \theta$ ... ①
If $a = 2$, the equation is $y = 2 \sin \theta$ ... ②
The y-coordinates of all points on the graph of ② are *two times* those on the graph of ①. Therefore, the graph of ② is *expanded* vertically relative to the graph of ①. The factor 2 is called the amplitude of the function.

If $a = \frac{1}{2}$, the equation is $y = \frac{1}{2} \sin \theta$ ... ③
The values of y will all be one-half of those in ①. Therefore, the graph of ③ is *compressed* vertically relative to the graph of ①.

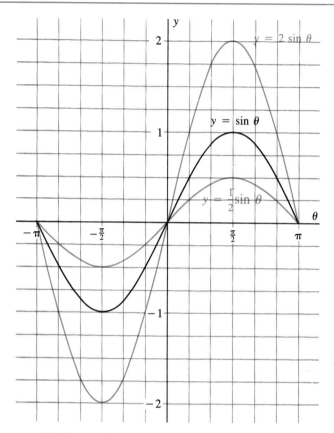

Similar results will be found for other positive values of a, and for cosine functions.

In general, multiplying $\sin \theta$ or $\cos \theta$ by a positive constant a causes a vertical expansion or compression of the graphs of $y = \sin \theta$ or $y = \cos \theta$. That is, for $0 < a < 1$, there is a compression; for $a > 1$, there is an expansion.

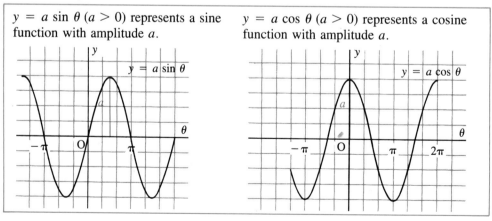

$y = a \sin \theta \ (a > 0)$ represents a sine function with amplitude a.

$y = a \cos \theta \ (a > 0)$ represents a cosine function with amplitude a.

Since we know that $y = a \sin \theta$ and $y = a \cos \theta$ represent sinusoidal functions with the above properties, we can draw the graph of an equation in this form without making a table of values.

Example 2. Draw a graph of the function $f(\theta) = 0.75 \cos \theta$, and state its amplitude.

Solution. Draw a graph of $y = \cos \theta$, then compress it vertically by a factor of 0.75. This means that the y-coordinate of each point on the image is 0.75 times the y-coordinate of the corresponding point on the graph of $y = \cos \theta$.
The amplitude of $f(\theta) = 0.75 \cos \theta$ is 0.75.

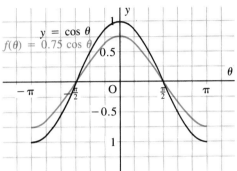

Vertical displacement and amplitude can be combined in the same function.

Example 3. Draw a graph of the function $f(\theta) = 2 \sin \theta + 3$ over two cycles.

Solution. Draw a graph of $y = \sin \theta$, and expand it vertically by a factor of 2. Then translate the image 3 units up.

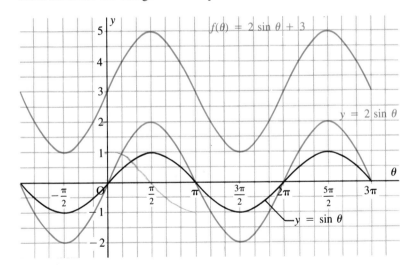

We can use the graph in *Example 3* to derive a definition for the amplitude of a periodic function. In this graph, the maximum value of the function is 5, and the minimum value is 1. The amplitude is one-half the way from the minimum to the maximum, measured in the vertical direction. For this function, the amplitude is $\frac{1}{2}(5 - 1)$, or 2.

If M represents the maximum value of a periodic function in any cycle, and m represents the minimum value in that cycle, then the *amplitude A* of the function is

$$A = \frac{M - m}{2}$$

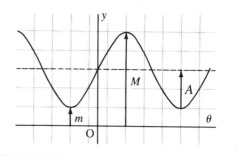

EXERCISES 5-8

Ⓐ

1. a) Graph each set of functions on the same grid for $-\pi \leq \theta \leq \pi$.
   i) $f(\theta) = \sin \theta$ $f(\theta) = \sin \theta + 1.5$ $f(\theta) = \sin \theta - 2$
   ii) $f(\theta) = \cos \theta$ $f(\theta) = \cos \theta - 3$ $f(\theta) = \cos \theta + 4$
   b) Graph each set of functions on the same grid for $-\pi \leq \theta \leq \pi$.

   i) $f(\theta) = 2 \cos \theta$ $f(\theta) = \cos \theta$ $f(\theta) = \frac{1}{2} \cos \theta$

   ii) $f(\theta) = 3 \sin \theta$ $f(\theta) = \sin \theta$ $f(\theta) = \frac{1}{4} \sin \theta$

2. Each function graphed below is sinusoidal. Write an equation for each function. State the maximum and minimum values of y, and the amplitude.
   a)   b)

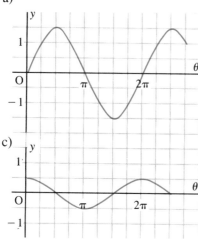

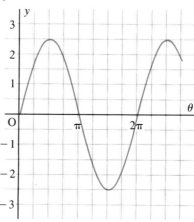

3. Write an equation to represent each function. State the vertical displacement, the maximum value of y, the minimum value of y, and the y-intercept.

a)

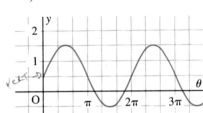

b)

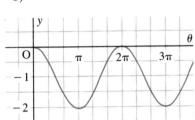

(B)

4. Graph each sinusoidal function over two complete cycles. Determine the maximum and minimum values of the function, and its range.

a) $y = 5 \sin \theta$

b) $y = 3 \cos \theta$

c) $y = 3 \sin \theta + 4$

d) $f(\theta) = 2 \cos \theta - 3$

e) $f(\theta) = 4 \sin \theta - 2$

f) $f(\theta) = \frac{1}{2} \cos \theta + 3$

g) $f(\theta) = \frac{1}{2} \sin \theta - 1$

h) $f(\theta) = 2 + 2 \sin \theta$

i) $f(\theta) = 3 + 3 \cos \theta$

5. Given the function $f(\theta) = a \sin \theta + q$
   a) What is the maximum value of $f(\theta)$? For what values of θ does this occur?
   b) What is the minimum value of $f(\theta)$? For what values of θ does this occur?

6. Repeat *Exercise 5* for the function $g(\theta) = a \cos \theta + q$.

(C)

7. Find the equation of a function of the form $f(\theta) = \sin \theta + p$ whose graph just touches the θ-axis. How many such functions are there?

INVESTIGATE

Negative values of a in $y = a \sin \theta$ and $y = a \cos \theta$

1. a) Draw graphs of these functions.

   i) $y = -\sin \theta$
   ii) $y = -2 \sin \theta$
   iii) $y = -\frac{1}{2} \sin \theta$

   b) How are the graphs of the functions in part a) related to the graph of the function $y = \sin \theta$?
   c) Draw diagrams to illustrate how the graphs of $y = a \sin \theta$ and $y = a \cos \theta$ are related to the graphs of $y = \sin \theta$ and $y = \cos \theta$ if $a < 0$.
   d) Do negative values of a affect the amplitude? In what way?

2. Graph each function over two cycles, and state the amplitude.

   a) $y = -4 \sin \theta$
   b) $y = -0.2 \sin \theta$
   c) $y = -9 \cos \theta$
   d) $y = -3 \sin \theta + 2$
   e) $y = 4 - 2 \cos \theta$
   f) $y = 5 - 10 \sin \theta$

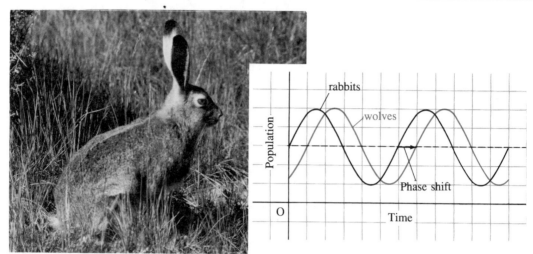

5-9 VARYING THE PHASE SHIFT OF SINE AND COSINE FUNCTIONS

In a certain region the number of rabbits increases and decreases periodically. This variation is caused by wolves which feed on the rabbits. If the number of wolves is small, the rabbits will flourish. But then the number of wolves will increase, since food is easy to find. This, in turn, causes a decrease in the number of rabbits, which causes the number of wolves to decrease, and the cycle begins all over again. The population graph for the wolves is shifted horizontally relative to the population graph for the rabbits.

In $y = \sin \theta$, if θ is replaced with $\theta - p$, we obtain $y = \sin (\theta - p)$. To investigate the effect of this on the graph of the function $y = \sin \theta$, we substitute different values for p, and graph the resulting functions.

If $p = 0$, the equation is $y = \sin \theta$ ...... ①

If $p = \frac{\pi}{2}$, the equation is $y = \sin \left(\theta - \frac{\pi}{2}\right)$ ...... ②

If we were to graph this function using a table of values, we would start with values of θ, subtract $\frac{\pi}{2}$, and then find the sines of the results. To give the same y-coordinates as in ①, the values of θ must be $\frac{\pi}{2}$ units greater than in ①. That is, the θ-coordinates of all points on the graph of ② are $\frac{\pi}{2}$ *greater* than those on the graph of ①. Therefore, the graph of ② is shifted $\frac{\pi}{2}$ units to the *right* relative to the graph of ①.

We say that the phase shift of the function $y = \sin \left(\theta - \frac{\pi}{2}\right)$ is $+\frac{\pi}{2}$.

If $p = -\frac{\pi}{3}$, the equation is $y = \sin\left(\theta + \frac{\pi}{3}\right)$ ...... ③

To give the same y-coordinates as in ①, the values of θ must be $\frac{\pi}{3}$ *less*

than those in ①. Therefore, the graph of ③ is shifted $\frac{\pi}{3}$ units to the

left relative to the graph of ①. The phase shift is $-\frac{\pi}{3}$.

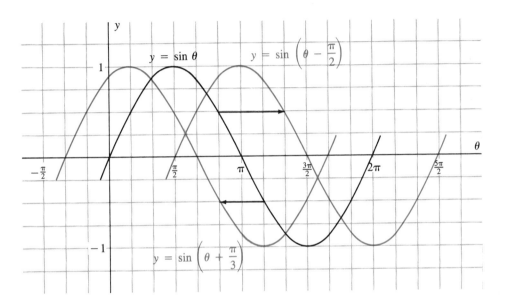

The graph of $y = \sin\left(\theta + \frac{\pi}{3}\right)$ is the image of the graph of $y = \sin\theta$, which has been translated $\frac{\pi}{3}$ to the *left*.

The graph of $y = \sin\left(\theta - \frac{\pi}{2}\right)$ is the image of the graph of $y = \sin\theta$, which has been translated $\frac{\pi}{2}$ to the *right*.

The *phase shift* of a periodic function is the amount by which the graph of the function is translated horizontally with respect to the basic function. A negative phase shift corresponds to a translation to the left. A positive phase shift corresponds to a translation to the right.

Similar results will be found for other values of θ, and for cosine functions. In general, adding a constant to the variable θ in the equations of the functions $y = \sin\theta$ or $y = \cos\theta$ causes a horizontal translation of the graph. A positive constant causes a translation to the left; a negative constant causes a translation to the right.

The graph of $y = \sin(\theta - p)$ is the image of the graph of $y = \sin\theta$ under a horizontal translation of p units.

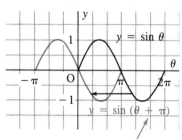

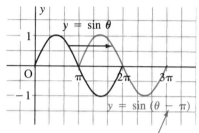

Positive sign, graph moved π units to the *left*

Negative sign, graph moved π units to the *right*

The graph of $y = \cos(\theta - p)$ is the image of the graph of $y = \cos\theta$ under a horizontal translation of p units.

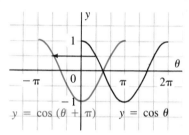

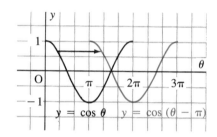

We can draw the graph of an equation in this form without making a table of values.

Example 1. Draw a graph of the function $y = \cos\left(\theta + \dfrac{2\pi}{3}\right)$ over two cycles, and state its phase shift.

Solution. Draw a graph of $y = \cos\theta$, then translate it $\dfrac{2\pi}{3}$ units to the left. The phase shift is $-\dfrac{2\pi}{3}$.

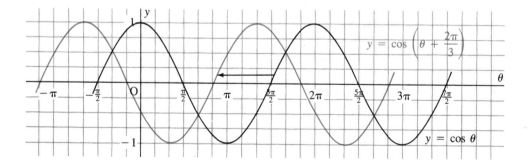

In general, the phase shift of $y = \sin(\theta - p)$ or $y = \cos(\theta - p)$ is the value of θ for which $\theta - p = 0$; that is, p.

Vertical displacement, phase shift, and amplitude are often combined in the same function.

Example 2. Draw a graph of the function $f(\theta) = 3 \sin\left(\theta - \dfrac{2\pi}{3}\right) + 2$ over two cycles. State the vertical displacement, the phase shift, and the amplitude.

Solution. Draw a graph of $y = \sin\theta$, and expand it vertically by a factor of 3. Then translate the image $\dfrac{2\pi}{3}$ units to the right and 2 units up.

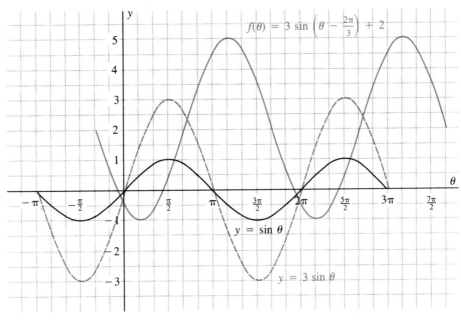

The vertical displacement is 2, the phase shift is $\dfrac{2\pi}{3}$, and the amplitude is 3.

EXERCISES 5-9

(A)

1. a) Graph these functions on the same grid for $-\pi \le \theta \le \pi$.

$$y = \sin\theta \qquad y = \sin\left(\theta - \frac{\pi}{6}\right) \qquad y = \sin\left(\theta - \frac{\pi}{3}\right) \qquad y = \sin\left(\theta + \frac{\pi}{4}\right)$$

b) Graph these functions on the same grid for $-\pi \le \theta \le \pi$.

$$y = \cos\theta \qquad y = \cos\left(\theta + \frac{\pi}{3}\right) \qquad y = \cos\left(\theta - \frac{\pi}{3}\right) \qquad y = \cos\left(\theta - \frac{\pi}{4}\right)$$

2. The function graphed below can be considered as a sine function. Find two possible values for the phase shift. What is the equation of the function for each phase shift?

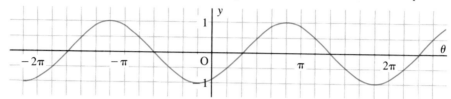

3. The function in *Exercise 2* can also be considered as a cosine function. Find two possible values for the phase shift. What is the equation of the function for each phase shift?

Ⓑ

4. Graph each sinusoidal function over two cycles.

   a) $y = \sin\left(\theta - \frac{\pi}{4}\right)$
   b) $y = \sin\left(\theta - \frac{4\pi}{3}\right)$
   c) $y = 2\sin\left(\theta + \frac{5\pi}{6}\right)$
   d) $y = 3\cos\left(\theta - \frac{\pi}{6}\right)$
   e) $y = 2\cos\left(\theta + \frac{5\pi}{3}\right)$
   f) $y = 5\cos\left(\theta - \frac{7\pi}{6}\right)$

5. Graph each sinusoidal function, and determine its domain and range.

   a) $f(\theta) = 2\sin\left(\theta - \frac{\pi}{4}\right) + 3$
   b) $g(\theta) = 2\cos\left(\theta - \frac{\pi}{6}\right) + 2$
   c) $h(\theta) = 4\cos\left(\theta - \frac{4\pi}{3}\right) - 1$
   d) $k(\theta) = 4\sin\left(\theta + \frac{2\pi}{3}\right) - 2$

6. a) Graph the function $f(\theta) = \sin\left(\theta + \frac{\pi}{2}\right)$. What conclusion can you make?

   b) Graph the function $g(\theta) = \cos\left(\theta - \frac{\pi}{2}\right)$. What conclusion can you make?

7. Find values of p for which the graph of $y = \sin(\theta - p)$ coincides with the graph of:

   a) $y = \sin\theta$
   b) $y = \cos\theta$.

8. Repeat *Exercise 7* for the function $y = \cos(\theta - p)$.

Ⓒ

9. Given the function $f(\theta) = a\sin(\theta - p) + q$, where $a > 0$
   a) What is the maximum value of $f(\theta)$? For what values of θ does this occur?
   b) What is the minimum value of $f(\theta)$? For what values of θ does this occur?

10. Repeat *Exercise 9* for the function $f(\theta) = a\cos(\theta - p) + q$, where $a > 0$.

11. Find an equation of a function of the form $f(\theta) = \sin(\theta - p) + q$ which has a maximum value of 3 when $\theta = 0$.

12. Find an equation of a function of the form $f(\theta) = \cos(\theta - p) + q$ which has a minimum value of -5 when $\theta = 0$.

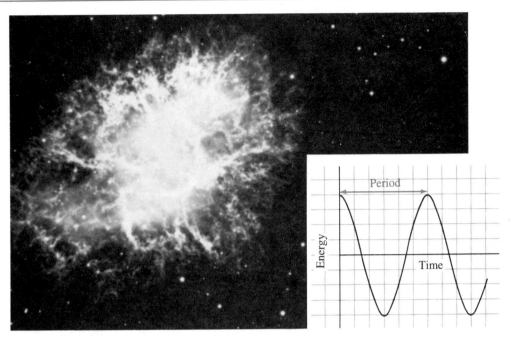

5-10 VARYING THE PERIOD OF SINE AND COSINE FUNCTIONS

In 1968 the scientific world was astonished when two astronomers detected extremely massive stars which spin on their axes in a fraction of a second. Since a pulse of radio energy is sent out on each rotation, these stars are called pulsating stars, or pulsars. One pulsar, in the Crab Nebula, pulses every 0.033 s. This time is called the period.

In $y = \cos \theta$, if θ is replaced with $k\theta$, we obtain $y = \cos k\theta$. To investigate the effect of this on the graph of the function $y = \cos \theta$, we substitute different values for k, and graph the resulting functions. We will assume that k is positive, since there is no need to consider negative values of k in applications.

If $k = 1$, the equation is $y = \cos \theta$ ...... ①
Since one cycle is completed in 2π units along the θ-axis, the period of $y = \cos \theta$ is 2π.

If $k = 2$, the equation is $y = \cos 2\theta$ ...... ②
If we were to graph this function using a table of values, we would start with values of θ, multiply by 2, and then find the cosines of the results. To give the same y-coordinates as in ①, the values of θ must be one-half of those in ①. That is, the θ-coordinates of all points on the graph of ② are *one-half* of those on the graph of ①. Therefore, the graph of ② is *compressed* horizontally relative to the graph of ①. The period of $y = \cos 2\theta$ is π, since one cycle is completed in π units along the θ-axis.

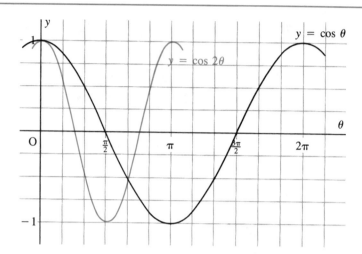

The graph of $y = \cos 2\theta$ is the image of the graph of $y = \cos \theta$ which has been compressed horizontally by a factor of $\frac{1}{2}$.

If $k = \frac{1}{2}$, the equation is $y = \cos \frac{1}{2}\theta$ ...... ③

To give the same *y*-coordinates as in ①, the values of θ must be *two times* those in ①. Therefore, the graph of ③ is *expanded* horizontally relative to the graph of ①. The period of $y = \cos \frac{1}{2}\theta$ is 4π.

The graph of $y = \cos \frac{1}{2}\theta$ is the image of the graph of $y = \cos \theta$ which has been expanded horizontally by a factor of 2.

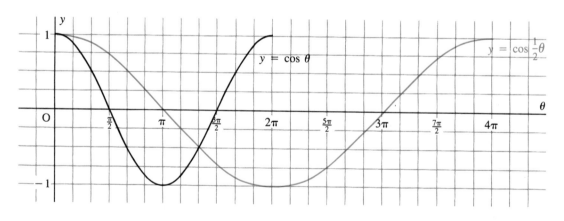

Similar results will be found for other positive values of k, and for sine functions.

In general, multiplying the variable θ in the equations of the functions $y = \cos \theta$ or $y = \sin \theta$ by a positive constant k affects the period and causes a horizontal expansion or compression of its graph. If $0 < k < 1$, there is an expansion; if $k > 1$, there is a compression.

To discover how k is related to the period, we compare the three functions graphed on the previous page with their periods.

Function	Value of k	Period
$y = \cos \theta$	1	2π
$y = \cos 2\theta$	2	π
$y = \cos \dfrac{1}{2}\theta$	$\dfrac{1}{2}$	4π

In each case, if we multiply the value of k by the period, the product is 2π.

$$(k)(\text{period}) = 2\pi$$
$$\text{period} = \frac{2\pi}{k}$$

The graphs of $y = \cos k\theta$ and $y = \sin k\theta$ $(k > 0)$ are related to the graphs of $y = \cos \theta$ and $y = \sin \theta$ by a horizontal expansion or compression. The period of each function is $\dfrac{2\pi}{k}$.

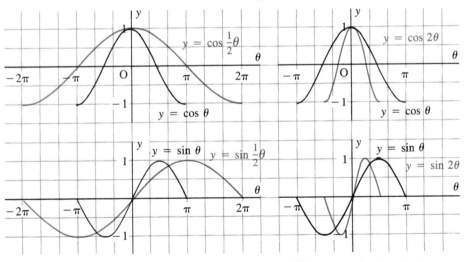

If $0 < k < 1$, there is a horizontal expansion.

If $k > 1$, there is a horizontal compression.

Since we know that $y = \sin k\theta$ and $y = \cos k\theta$ represent sinusoidal functions with the above properties, we can draw the graph of an equation in this form without making a table of values.

Example 1. Draw a graph of the function $y = \sin 3\theta$ over two cycles, and state its period.

Solution. Graph $y = \sin \theta$, then compress horizontally by a factor of $\frac{1}{3}$.

If (θ, y) is any point on the graph of $y = \sin \theta$, then $\left(\frac{1}{3}\theta, y\right)$ is the image point on the graph of $y = \sin 3\theta$. For example, the image of $A(2\pi, 0)$ is $A'\left(\frac{2\pi}{3}, 0\right)$.

The period of this function is $\frac{2\pi}{3}$.

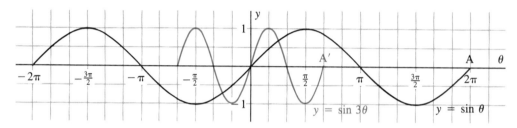

Very often, horizontal expansions or compressions are combined with horizontal translations. The result depends on the order in which these two transformations are applied. With sinusoidal functions we will assume that the expansion or compression is applied first, since there is no need to consider the reverse order in applications.

Suppose the graph of the function $y = \cos \theta$ is compressed horizontally by a factor of $\frac{1}{2}$. To find the equation of the image, replace θ with 2θ. The equation becomes $y = \cos 2\theta$.

Now suppose the resulting graph is translated $\frac{\pi}{3}$ units to the right. To find the image equation after the translation, replace θ with $\left(\theta - \frac{\pi}{3}\right)$. The equation becomes $y = \cos 2\left(\theta - \frac{\pi}{3}\right)$.

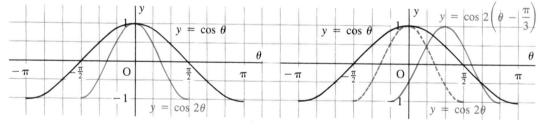

In the above example, the magnitude and direction of the translation give the phase shift. Also, the translation does not affect the period.

The phase shift of $y = \cos 2\left(\theta - \frac{\pi}{3}\right)$ is $\frac{\pi}{3}$. The period of $y = \cos 2\left(\theta - \frac{\pi}{3}\right)$ is $\frac{2\pi}{2}$, or π.

Similar results will be found for other functions.

> The graphs of $y = \cos k(\theta - p)$ and $y = \sin k(\theta - p)$ are related to the graphs of $y = \cos \theta$ and $y = \sin \theta$ by a horizontal expansion or compression followed by a horizontal translation. For $y = \cos k(\theta - p)$ and $y = \sin k(\theta - p)$:
>
> - the phase shift is p
> - the period is $\frac{2\pi}{k}$.

Example 2. Graph the function $y = 2 \cos 3\left(\theta - \frac{\pi}{2}\right)$ over two cycles, and state its amplitude, phase shift, and period.

Solution. Graph $y = 2 \cos \theta$, then compress horizontally by a factor of $\frac{1}{3}$. At this point, the equation of the curve is $y = 2 \cos 3\theta$.

Then translate the image $\frac{\pi}{2}$ units to the right.

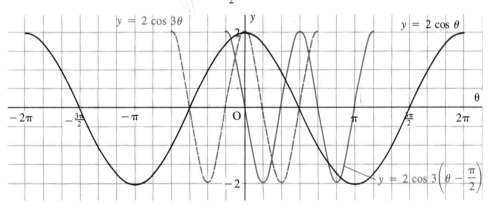

The amplitude of the function is 2.

The phase shift is $\frac{\pi}{2}$.

The period is $\frac{2\pi}{3}$.

EXERCISES 5-10

1. a) Graph these functions on the same grid for $-\pi \leqslant \theta \leqslant \pi$.

$$y = \sin 2\theta \qquad y = \sin \theta \qquad y = \sin \frac{1}{2}\theta$$

b) Graph these functions on the same grid for $-\pi \leqslant \theta \leqslant \pi$.

$$y = \cos 3\theta \qquad y = \cos \theta \qquad y = \cos \frac{1}{3}\theta$$

c) Describe the effect on the graphs of $y = \sin k\theta$ and $y = \cos k\theta$ as the value of k varies.

2. Each function graphed below is sinusoidal. Write an equation for each function.

a)

b)

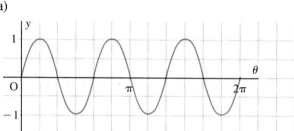

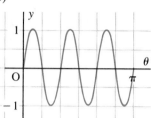

(B)

3. Graph each sinusoidal function, and state its amplitude and period.

a) $y = 2 \sin 2\theta$ b) $y = 3 \sin \frac{1}{2}\theta$ c) $y = 4 \sin 2\theta$

d) $y = 4 \cos \frac{1}{2}\theta$ e) $y = 5 \cos 2\theta$ f) $y = 3 \cos 3\theta$

4. State the amplitude, the period, and the phase shift for each function.

a) $f(\theta) = 5 \cos 3(\theta - \pi)$ b) $f(\theta) = 2 \sin 4\left(\theta + \frac{\pi}{2}\right)$

c) $f(\theta) = 2.5 \sin 6\left(\theta - \frac{2\pi}{3}\right)$ d) $f(\theta) = 0.5 \cos 5\left(\theta + \frac{5\pi}{4}\right)$

5. Graph each function over two cycles, and state its amplitude, period, and phase shift.

a) $y = \sin 2\left(\theta - \frac{\pi}{3}\right)$ b) $y = 2 \cos 3\left(\theta - \frac{\pi}{2}\right)$

c) $y = 4 \cos \frac{1}{2}(\theta + \pi)$ d) $y = 0.5 \sin \frac{1}{2}\left(\theta - \frac{5\pi}{4}\right)$

(C)

6. **Negative values of k in $y = \sin k\theta$ and $y = \cos k\theta$**
   a) Draw graphs of these functions.

   i) $y = \sin(-\theta)$ ii) $y = \sin(-2\theta)$ iii) $y = \sin\left(-\frac{1}{2}\theta\right)$

   b) How are the graphs of the functions in part a) related to the graph of the function $y = \sin \theta$?
   c) Draw diagrams to illustrate how the graphs of $y = \sin k\theta$ and $y = \cos k\theta$ are related to the graphs of $y = \sin \theta$ and $y = \cos \theta$ if $k < 0$.
   d) Do negative values of k affect the period? In what way?

7. Graph each function over two cycles, and state the period.

a) $y = \sin(-3\theta)$ b) $y = 4 \cos\left(-\frac{1}{2}\theta\right)$ c) $y = 3 \sin(-2\theta) + 3$

8. Compare the graphs of each pair of functions. What conclusions can you make?
   a) $y = \sin \theta$ and $y = \sin(-\theta)$ b) $y = \cos \theta$ and $y = \cos(-\theta)$

THE MATHEMATICAL MIND

Evaluating Trigonometric Functions

To keep pace with progress in navigation and astronomy in the 17th and 18th centuries, mathematicians required increasingly more accurate values of certain functions, including trigonometric functions. Credit goes to the Englishman, Brook Taylor (1685-1731) and the Scotsman, Colin Maclaurin (1698-1746) for showing that under certain conditions a function $f(x)$ can be expressed as an infinite series of powers of x. Two important series are the series for $\sin x$ and $\cos x$, where x is a real number.

$$\sin x = \frac{x}{1!} - \frac{x^3}{3!} + \frac{x^5}{5!} - \frac{x^7}{7!} + \ldots \qquad \cos x = 1 - \frac{x^2}{2!} + \frac{x^4}{4!} - \frac{x^6}{6!} + \ldots$$

The denominators in these series use a special notation called *factorial notation*. The factorial sign ! following a number means the product of all natural numbers up to and including the number. For example, $4! = 4 \times 3 \times 2 \times 1$, or 24

We can regard these series as formulas for calculating values of the trigonometric functions for all real values of x. The formulas are valid only when x is in radians. Hence, to calculate $\cos 60°$, we substitute $\frac{\pi}{3}$ for x in the second formula. Taking the first four terms, we obtain:

$$\cos \frac{\pi}{3} \doteq 1 - \frac{1}{2}\left(\frac{\pi}{3}\right)^2 + \frac{1}{24}\left(\frac{\pi}{3}\right)^4 - \frac{1}{720}\left(\frac{\pi}{3}\right)^6$$

$$\doteq 1 - 0.548\ 311\ 4 + 0.050\ 107\ 6 - 0.001\ 831\ 6$$

$$\doteq 0.499\ 964\ 6$$

This is very close to the actual value of 0.5. For a more accurate result, additional terms of the series can be used.

QUESTIONS

1. Simplify each factorial.
   a) 3! b) 5! c) 7! d) 8! e) 9! f) 10!

2. Write the first six terms of the series for $\sin x$ and $\cos x$.

3. Use the result of *Question 2* to calculate each value. Check using the $\boxed{\sin}$ or $\boxed{\cos}$ key on your calculator.

   a) $\cos \frac{\pi}{6}$ b) $\sin \frac{\pi}{2}$ c) $\sin \frac{\pi}{5}$ d) $\cos \pi$

4. How many terms of the series are needed to obtain a value of $\cos \frac{\pi}{5}$:

   a) to 2 decimal places b) to 4 decimal places c) to 6 decimal places?

5-11 GRAPHING GENERAL TRIGONOMETRIC FUNCTIONS

When we graph a function, we customarily draw the axes before we draw the curve. Then we make the curve fit the scales on the axes we have already drawn. We have used this method in previous sections of this book. However, with sinusoidal functions, it is easier to draw the curve first and then add the axes later. In other words, we make the axes fit the curve.

For example, consider the function $y = 3 \cos 2\left(\theta - \frac{\pi}{3}\right) + 4$.

We can graph this function as follows.

Step 1. Draw a sinusoidal curve, without axes.

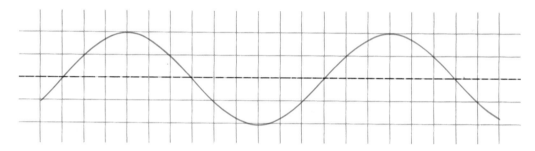

Step 2. Find the phase shift and the period, and use them to establish a horizontal scale.

The phase shift is $\frac{\pi}{3}$, and the period is $\frac{2\pi}{2}$, or π.

Since the function is a cosine function, the phase shift $\frac{\pi}{3}$ is the θ-coordinate of a maximum point. Since the period is π, the θ-coordinate of the next maximum point is $\frac{\pi}{3} + \pi$, or $\frac{4\pi}{3}$. Label these points.

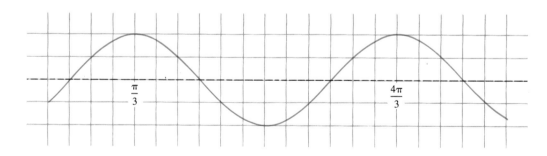

Step 3. Complete the graph by drawing the axes and their scales.

The graph was drawn such that the period corresponds to 12 squares. Therefore, the horizontal scale is:

12 squares correspond to π

4 squares correspond to $\dfrac{\pi}{3}$.

The position of O is 4 squares to the left of the first maximum point. Draw the y-axis through this point.

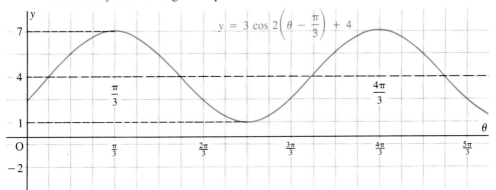

The vertical displacement is 4. Since the amplitude is 3, the maximum value of y is 7 and the minimum value is 1. Use these values to mark the vertical scale. Draw the θ-axis and mark its scale.

The method illustrated above may be used to graph any sinusoidal function.

Example 1. Draw a graph of the function $y = 5 \sin 3\left(\theta + \dfrac{\pi}{4}\right) + 3$ over two cycles.

Solution. *Step 1.*

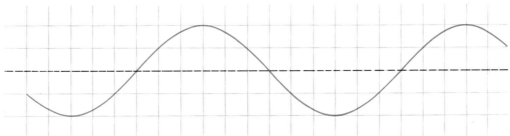

Step 2. The phase shift is $-\dfrac{\pi}{4}$, and the period is $\dfrac{2\pi}{3}$. Since the function is a sine function, the phase shift $-\dfrac{\pi}{4}$ is the θ-coordinate of a point on the axis preceding a maximum point. Then, since the period is $\dfrac{2\pi}{3}$, the θ-coordinate of the next point preceding a maximum point is

$-\dfrac{\pi}{4} + \dfrac{2\pi}{3}$, or $\dfrac{5\pi}{12}$.

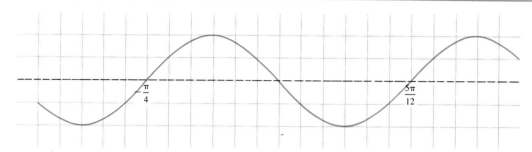

Step 3. The graph was drawn such that the period corresponds to 12 squares. Therefore, the horizontal scale is:

12 squares correspond to $\frac{2\pi}{3}$, so 1 square corresponds to $\frac{\pi}{18}$.

Mark the horizontal scale as shown. The position of O is halfway between $-\frac{\pi}{12}$ and $\frac{\pi}{12}$. Draw the y-axis through this point.

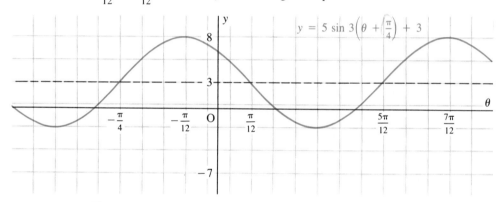

The vertical displacement is 3. Since the amplitude is 5, the maximum value of y is 8 and the minimum value is -2. Use these values to mark the vertical scale.

We can also find an equation of a sinusoidal function from its graph.

Example 2. A sinusoidal function is shown in the graph below.
    a) Determine the vertical displacement and the amplitude.
    b) Determine a possible phase shift, and the period.
    c) Write an equation of the function.

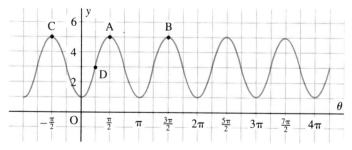

Solution.   a) The vertical displacement is 3.
The amplitude is 2.

b) There are many possible phase shifts, depending on whether we regard
the function as a cosine function or a sine function, and on which
point is taken to correspond to the phase shift.

For example, if we consider the function to be a cosine function,
the phase shift is the θ-coordinate of any maximum point. Using point
A, the phase shift is $\frac{\pi}{2}$.

The period is the difference in the values of θ for two consecutive
maximum points. Using points A and B, the period is $\frac{3\pi}{2} - \frac{\pi}{2}$, or π.

c) An equation of the function is $y = 2 \cos 2\left(\theta - \frac{\pi}{2}\right) + 3$.

In *Example 2*, there are other functions with the same graph.

Using point B and its θ-coordinate $\frac{3\pi}{2}$ as the phase shift: $y = 2 \cos 2\left(\theta - \frac{3\pi}{2}\right) + 3$

Using point C and its θ-coordinate $-\frac{\pi}{2}$ as the phase shift: $y = 2 \cos 2\left(\theta + \frac{\pi}{2}\right) + 3$

Considering the function as a sine function, and using point D and its
θ-coordinate $\frac{\pi}{4}$ as the phase shift: $y = 2 \sin 2\left(\theta - \frac{\pi}{4}\right) + 3$

EXERCISES 5-11

(A)

1. For each graph below, state:
    i) the amplitude   ii) the period   iii) a possible phase shift
    iv) the maximum value of y, and the values of θ for which it occurs
    v) the minimum value of y, and the values of θ for which it occurs
    vi) the vertical displacement.
    a)   b)

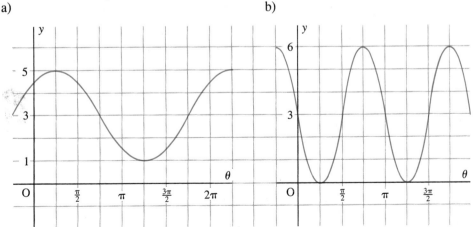

c)

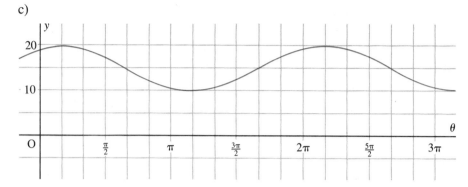

2. Write an equation to represent each function in *Exercise 1*.

⑧

3. Given the function $y = 2 \cos 2\left(\theta - \frac{\pi}{3}\right) + 4$

   taller ↑*squished* → *phase shift right* → *vertically displaced up 4*
   amplitude *period*

   a) Find the phase shift and the period.
   b) Determine the vertical displacement and the amplitude.
   c) Graph the function by graphing a sinusoidal curve first, and making the axes fit the curve.

4. Given the function $y = 3 \sin 2\left(\theta - \frac{\pi}{4}\right) + 3$

   a) Find the phase shift and the period.
   b) Determine the vertical displacement and the amplitude.
   c) Graph the function by graphing a sinusoidal curve first, and making the axes fit the curve.

5. Determine the phase shift and the period for each function. Then graph the function by graphing a sinusoidal curve first, and making the axes fit the curve.

   a) $y = 4 \cos 3\left(\theta - \frac{\pi}{2}\right) + 4$ b) $y = 2 \cos 4(\theta + \pi) + 3$

   c) $y = 3 \sin 2\left(\theta + \frac{\pi}{6}\right) + 6$ d) $y = 4 \sin 3\left(\theta - \frac{\pi}{6}\right) + 2$

6. Graph each function.

   a) $y = \sin 2\left(\theta - \frac{\pi}{2}\right)$ b) $y = 2 \sin 3\left(\theta - \frac{\pi}{3}\right) + 5$

   c) $y = 3 \cos 2\left(\theta + \frac{\pi}{4}\right) + 1$ d) $y = 3 \cos 3\left(\theta - \frac{2\pi}{3}\right) + 4$

7. Describe what happens to each graph.

   a) $y = a \sin 2\left(\theta - \frac{\pi}{6}\right) + 5$ as a varies

   b) $y = 3 \sin k\left(\theta - \frac{\pi}{6}\right) + 5$ as k varies

   c) $y = 3 \sin 2(\theta - p) + 5$ as p varies

   d) $y = 3 \sin 2\left(\theta - \frac{\pi}{3}\right) + q$ as q varies

8. Determine the phase shift and the period of each function, and draw the graph.

a) $y = \sin(2\theta - \pi)$

b) $y = 2\cos(3\theta - \pi) + 1$

c) $y = 2\cos(3\theta - \pi) + 4$

d) $y = 5\sin(4\theta + \pi) - 3$

9. Graph each function.

a) $y = 2\sin\left(2\theta + \dfrac{\pi}{3}\right)$

b) $y = 5\cos\left(2\theta - \dfrac{\pi}{2}\right)$

c) $y = 3\cos\left(2\theta - \dfrac{\pi}{2}\right)$

d) $y = 5\sin\left(2\theta + \dfrac{\pi}{3}\right)$

Ⓒ ──

10. Two of these equations represent the same function. Which two are they?

a) $y = 3\sin 2\left(\theta + \dfrac{\pi}{2}\right)$

b) $y = 3\cos 2\theta$

c) $y = 3\cos 2\left(\theta + \dfrac{\pi}{4}\right)$

d) $y = 3\sin 2(\theta + \pi)$

11. Two of these equations represent the same function. Which two are they?

a) $y = 3\sin(2\theta + \pi)$

b) $y = 3\cos\left(2\theta + \dfrac{\pi}{2}\right)$

c) $y = 3\cos 2\theta$

d) $y = 3\sin(2\theta + 2\pi)$

12. a) Find three different roots of the equation $2\cos\left(\theta + \dfrac{\pi}{2}\right) = 0$.

b) Write a general expression which could be used to represent all the roots of the equation in part a).

13. a) Find three different roots of the equation $3\sin 2\left(\theta - \dfrac{\pi}{4}\right) = 0$.

b) Write a general expression which could be used to represent all the roots of the equation in part a).

14. Two students discussed their methods of graphing sinusoidal functions. Their discussion went as follows.

Kwan: "I always draw the curve first and make the axes fit the curve. That method is very easy."

Marc: "But then all your graphs are going to look the same, even if they have different amplitudes and different periods."

Kwan: "Not really. I have two different ways of getting around that problem."

What methods might Kwan have been using so that her graphs do not all look like they have the same amplitude and the same period?

15. Given the function $y = \cos 2\pi\theta$

a) Find the phase shift and the period.

b) Graph the function.

16. Repeat *Exercise 15* for these functions.

a) $y = \sin 2\pi\theta$

b) $y = \cos \dfrac{\pi}{2}\theta$

c) $y = \sin \dfrac{\pi}{2}\theta$

5-12 SCALING THE HORIZONTAL AXIS

In the first section of this chapter several graphs were shown illustrating some examples of sinusoidal functions.

- time of the sunset
- number of sunspots
- lengths of shadows
- blood pressure
- volume of blood in the heart
- volume of air in the lungs

These graphs differ from the trigonometric graphs we studied in the preceding sections in one major way. They show periodic functions without the use of angles.

Up to now the horizontal axis has been scaled in degrees or in radians. These scales are not very useful in applications such as those above, where the horizontal axis is usually marked in time intervals. To use sinusoidal functions in applications we must change their graphs in two ways.

- We will no longer use θ as the variable on the horizontal axis. Instead, we will use t to indicate time. This involves nothing more than changing the letter on the axis and in the equations.
- We will scale the horizontal axis with whole numbers such as 1, 2, 3, or their multiples. We do this by adjusting the period of the functions.

For example, the graphs below show cosine and sine functions with period 1. Their equations can be written in the form $y = \cos kt$ and $y = \sin kt$. Since the period of each function is $\frac{2\pi}{k}$, we can write

$$\frac{2\pi}{k} = 1$$

$$k = 2\pi$$

The equations of the functions are $y = \cos 2\pi t$ and $y = \sin 2\pi t$.

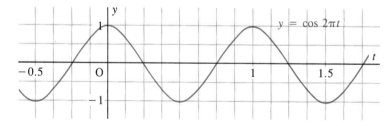

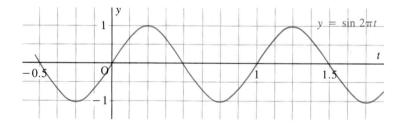

The examples on the previous page show that if π occurs in the equation as a factor of the quantity whose sine or cosine is to be found, then it does not appear on the horizontal axis. The fact that π does not occur on the axis means that it must occur in the equation.

Example 1. a) Find the period of the function $y = \sin \dfrac{2\pi t}{5}$.

b) Graph the function in part a).

Solution. a) The equation is in the form $y = \sin kt$, which has period $\dfrac{2\pi}{k}$.

Since $k = \dfrac{2\pi}{5}$, we see that the period of the function is $\dfrac{2\pi}{\frac{2\pi}{5}}$, or 5.

b) Draw the graph of a sine function with period 5.

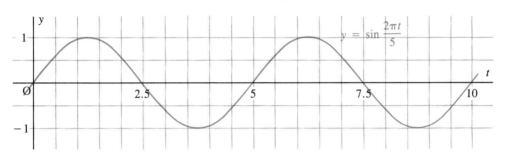

In *Example 1*, notice that the coefficient of t in the equation can be expressed in the form of a fraction, $\dfrac{2\pi}{k}$. When the coefficient is written in this form, the denominator is the period of the function.

$y = \cos \dfrac{2\pi t}{k}$ represents a cosine function with period k.

$y = \sin \dfrac{2\pi t}{k}$ represents a sine function with period k.

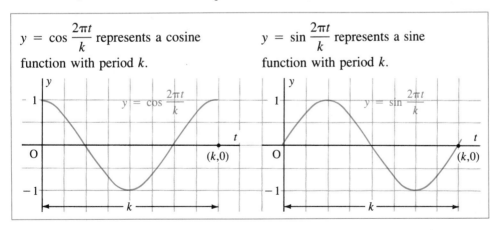

This scaling of the horizontal axis affects only the period, as shown above. It does not affect the vertical displacement, amplitude or how the phase shift is found.

Example 2.   Graph the function $y = 3 \sin 2\pi \dfrac{(t-2)}{4} + 6$.

Solution.   *Step 1*. Draw a sinusoidal curve.

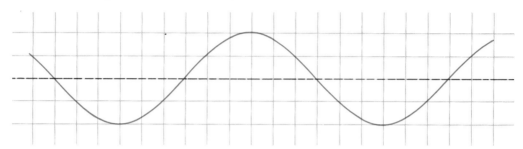

Step 2. Find the phase shift and the period, and use them to establish a horizontal scale.

The phase shift is 2. The period is 4.

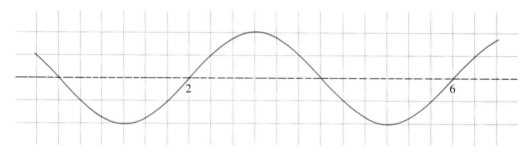

Step 3. Complete the graph by drawing the axes and their scales. We use the fact that the amplitude is 3 and the vertical displacement is 6.

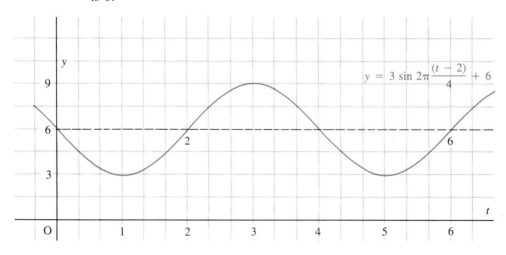

In *Example 2*, the period, amplitude, phase shift, and vertical displacement are all represented by numbers in the equation.

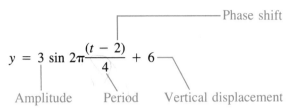

Notice the factor 2π in the equation. This factor must be present for the period to be as indicated. We can use this pattern to write the equation when these data are given or when they can be read from a graph.

Example 3. Write an equation of this sinusoidal function.

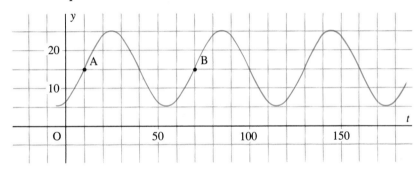

Solution.   The vertical displacement is 15.
The amplitude is 10.
For a sine function, the phase shift is the horizontal coordinate of A: 10.
The period is the difference between the horizontal coordinates of A and B:
$70 - 10$, or 60.

An equation of the function is $y = 10 \sin 2\pi\dfrac{(t - 10)}{60} + 15$.

In *Example 3*, the function can also be expressed as a cosine function. The only difference is the phase shift. Since the first maximum occurs when $t = 25$, the phase shift is 25. An equation of the function is $y = 10 \cos 2\pi\dfrac{(t - 25)}{60} + 15$. What are other equations for this function?

Example 4.   The volume of air in the lungs is a sinusoidal function of time. A graph illustrating this variation for normal breathing is shown on page 159. Write an equation for this function.

Solution.   The vertical displacement is 2450 mL. The amplitude is 250 mL. The period is 5 s. If V millilitres represents the volume of air in the lungs at time t seconds, then an equation for the function is:

$$V = 250 \sin \frac{2\pi t}{5} + 2450.$$

EXERCISES 5-12

1. State the amplitude, period, phase shift, and vertical displacement for each function.

   a) $y = 3 \sin 2\pi \dfrac{(t - 1)}{5} + 4$

   b) $y = 2 \cos 2\pi \dfrac{(t - 5)}{4} + 6$

2. For each graph, determine the amplitude, period, phase shift, and vertical displacement.

   a)

   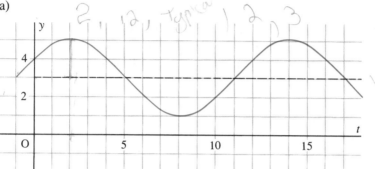

   b)

   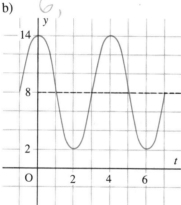

   c)

   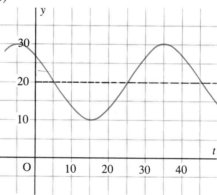

3. Write an equation to represent each function in *Exercise 2*.

4. Write an equation to represent each function.

   a)   b)

   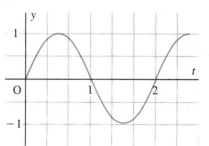
   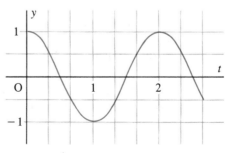

c)

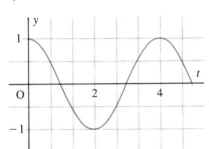

d)

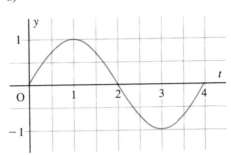

5. Write an equation for a cosine function with the following properties.
   a) amplitude: 5   period: 1   phase shift: 9   vertical displacement: 4
   b) amplitude: 12   period: $\frac{1}{2}$ phase shift: -3 vertical displacement: 1.5
   c) amplitude: 2.4   period: 27   phase shift: 19   vertical displacement: 15.1

(B)

6. Draw a graph of each function.

   a) $y = 2 \cos 2\pi\dfrac{(t - 1)}{3} + 4$

   b) $y = 3 \cos 2\pi\dfrac{(t - 4)}{2} + 3$

   c) $y = 2.4 \cos 2\pi\dfrac{(t + 3)}{12} + 3.6$

   d) $y = 3.5 \sin 2\pi\dfrac{(t - 8.4)}{9.2} + 10$

7. Draw a graph of each function.

   a) $y = \sin 2\pi t$

   b) $y = \sin \dfrac{2\pi t}{3}$

   c) $y = \sin 2\pi(t - 2)$

   d) $y = \sin 2\pi\dfrac{(t - 2)}{3}$

   e) $y = \cos 2\pi t$

   f) $y = \cos \dfrac{2\pi t}{3}$

   g) $y = \cos 2\pi(t - 2)$

   h) $y = \cos 2\pi\dfrac{(t - 2)}{3}$

60%

8. State the maximum and minimum values of y, and the values of t for which they occur, where $-5 \leqslant t \leqslant 5$.

   a) $y = 2 \cos 2\pi\dfrac{(t - 1)}{3} + 3$

   b) $y = 4 \sin 2\pi\dfrac{(t + 2)}{5} - 4$

   c) $y = 2 \sin 2\pi\dfrac{(t - 1)}{3} + 6$

   d) $y = 5 \cos 2\pi\dfrac{(t + 3)}{6} + 2$

9. Write an equation to represent a sine function with the following properties.
   a) maximum: 23   minimum: 11   period: 5   phase shift: 9
   b) maximum: 17.2   minimum: 8.6   period: 3.9   phase shift: 4.7

10. Write an equation for the volume of air in the lungs during deep breathing, when the variation is from 1000 mL to 5000 mL. Assume that the period is 10 s.

11. The twin towers of the World Trade Center in New York were once the tallest buildings in the world. During a strong wind, the top of each tower swings back and forth as much as 80 cm, with a period of 10 s.
    a) Draw a graph showing the departure of the top of one of the buildings from the normal position as a function of time, for 20 s.
    b) Write an equation for the function in part a).

12. A piston in an engine moves up and down in the cylinder, as shown in the diagram. The height h centimetres of the piston at time t seconds is given by this formula.

    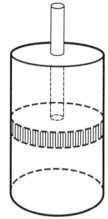

    $$h = 20 \sin \frac{2\pi t}{0.05} + 20$$

    a) State the piston's:
       i) maximum height
       ii) minimum height
       iii) period.
    b) If the piston operates for exactly one hour, how many complete cycles does it make?

13. The fundamental tone of a guitar string with length L is associated with a sinusoidal function with a period of $2L$.

    The period of the first overtone is $\frac{2L}{2}$;

    the period of the second overtone is $\frac{2L}{3}$;

    and so on.
    a) Assuming that the string is 50 cm long, and that the amplitude of the vibration is 0.5 cm, write the equations of the functions associated with the fundamental tone and the first three overtones.
    b) Draw the graphs of the functions in part a) on the same axes.

    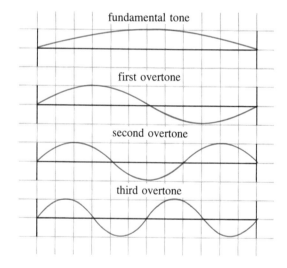

    fundamental tone

    first overtone

    second overtone

    third overtone

Ⓒ

14. Two of these equations represent the same function. Which two are they?

    a) $y = 3 \sin 2\pi \dfrac{(t - 1)}{8} + 2$
    b) $y = 3 \cos 2\pi \dfrac{(t - 5)}{8} + 2$

    c) $y = 3 \sin 2\pi \dfrac{(t - 3)}{8} + 2$
    d) $y = 3 \cos 2\pi \dfrac{(t + 1)}{8} + 2$

5-13 APPLYING GENERAL TRIGONOMETRIC FUNCTIONS

The tides are the periodic rise and fall of the water in the oceans, caused almost entirely by the gravitational attraction of the moon and the sun. An equation expressing the depth of the water as a function of time is extremely complicated, since the distances and relative positions of the moon and sun are constantly changing. However, the depth can be approximated by a sinusoidal function. The amplitude of the function depends on the location, and at any particular location it varies considerably at different times of the year.

Some of the highest tides in the world occur in the Bay of Fundy, where the Annapolis Tidal Generating Station has been in operation since 1984. The graph below shows how the depth of the water at the station varies during a typical day. Notice that times are given in decimal form using a 24 h clock.

When we work with sinusoidal functions involving time in hours, a fractional part of an hour must be expressed in decimal form. For example, the period of the tidal motion (below) is 12 h 25 min. Converting to decimal form,

$$12 \text{ h } 25 \text{ min} = \left(12 + \frac{25}{60} \right) \text{ h}$$
$$\doteq 12.4 \text{ h}$$

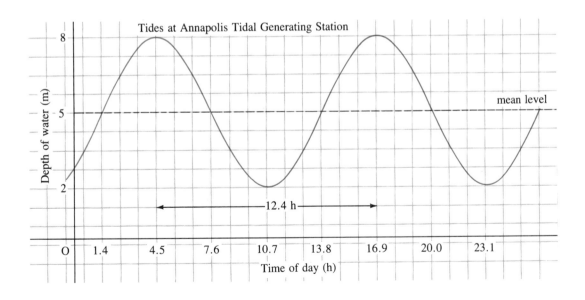

We can find the vertical displacement, the phase shift, the period, and the amplitude of the function from the graph, and use these to write an equation of the function.

Since the mean level is 5 m, the vertical displacement is 5 m.

The amplitude is the difference between high tide level and mean level, 3 m.

The first high tide occurs at 4.5 h. If we think of the function as a cosine function, then the phase shift is 4.5 h.

The period is the time between two high tides, 12.4 h.

Therefore, if h metres represents the depth, and t hours represents the time, an equation of the function is:

$$h = \underset{\text{Amplitude}}{3} \cos 2\pi \underset{\text{Period}}{\frac{(t - 4.5)}{12.4}} + \underset{\text{Mean level}}{5} \quad \begin{array}{l} \text{Phase shift} \\ \text{(time at first} \\ \text{high tide)} \end{array}$$

We can use this equation to calculate the depth of the water at any time during the day.

Example 1. Calculate the depth of the water to the nearest tenth of a metre at:

        a) 9:30 A.M.   b) 6:45 P.M.

Solution. Convert the times to decimals of hours, on a 24 h clock.

    9:30 A.M = 09.50 h   6:45 P.M. = (12 + 6.75) h

                                                   = 18.75 h

a) Substitute $t = 9.5$ in the above equation.

$$h = 3 \cos 2\pi \frac{(t - 4.5)}{12.4} + 5$$

$$= 3 \cos 2\pi \frac{(9.5 - 4.5)}{12.4} + 5$$

Use a scientific calculator in *radian mode* to evaluate this expression.

$$h \doteq 2.537\ 709\ 7$$

At 9:30 A.M., the depth of the water is approximately 2.5 m.

b) Substitute $t = 18.75$ in the above equation.

$$h = 3 \cos 2\pi \frac{(t - 4.5)}{12.4} + 5$$

$$= 3 \cos 2\pi \frac{(18.75 - 4.5)}{12.4} + 5$$

$$\doteq 6.775\ 631$$

At 6:45 P.M., the depth of the water is approximately 6.8 m.

If your calculator requires the function key to be pressed first you may need to use the memory or brackets to evaluate expressions such as those in *Example 1*.

The pattern suggested by *Example 1* can be used to solve other problems involving quantities which change periodically. In each case, we use a sinusoidal function to approximate the data. The general pattern in the equation of the function is shown below.

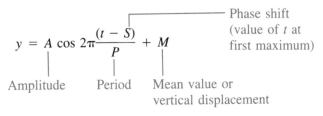

$$y = A \cos 2\pi\frac{(t - S)}{P} + M$$

Phase shift
(value of t at
first maximum)

Amplitude   Period   Mean value or
vertical displacement

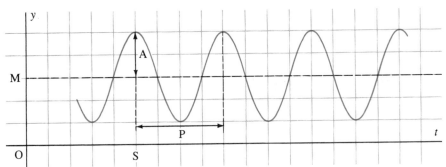

Example 2. A Ferris wheel with a radius of 20 m rotates once every 40 s. Passengers get on at point S, which is 1 m above level ground. Suppose you get on at S and the wheel starts to rotate.
  a) Draw a graph showing how your height above the ground varies during the first two cycles.
  b) Write an equation which expresses your height as a function of the elapsed time.
  c) Calculate your height above the ground after 15 s.

Solution. a) *Step 1*. Draw a sinusoidal curve.

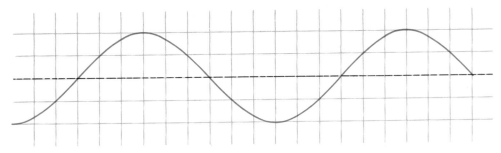

Step 2. Find the phase shift and the period, and use them to establish a horizontal scale.

For a cosine function, the phase shift is the *t*-coordinate of the first maximum, point A. Since you take 20 s to reach A, the phase shift is 20 s. Since the Ferris wheel rotates once every 40 s, the period is 40 s. Hence, the *t*-coordinates of two consecutive maximum points are 20 and 60.

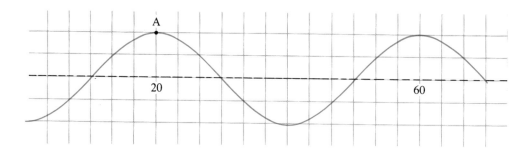

Step 3. Complete the graph by drawing the axes and their scales. The vertical displacement is 21 m, and the amplitude is 20 m. Since the people get on at the bottom, draw the vertical axis as shown.

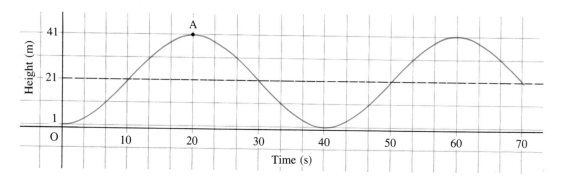

b) An equation which expresses your height as a function of time is:
$$h = 20 \cos 2\pi\frac{(t - 20)}{40} + 21.$$

c) To calculate your height above the ground after 15 s, substitute 15 for *t* in the above equation.
$$h = 20 \cos 2\pi\frac{(t - 20)}{40} + 21$$
$$= 20 \cos 2\pi\frac{(15 - 20)}{40} + 21$$
$$\doteq 35.142\ 136$$
After 15 s you will be about 35 m above the ground.

EXERCISES 5-13

Ⓐ

1. At a seaport, the depth of the water h metres at time t hours during a certain day is given by this formula.

   $$h = 1.8 \sin 2\pi\frac{(t - 4.00)}{12.4} + 3.1$$

   a) Calculate the depth of the water at 5 A.M. and at 12 noon.
   b) What is the maximum depth of the water? When does it occur?

2. The equation below gives the depth of the water h metres at an ocean port at any time t hours during a certain day.

   $$h = 2.5 \sin 2\pi\frac{(t - 1.5)}{12.4} + 4.3$$

   Calculate the approximate depth of the water at 9:30 A.M.

Ⓑ

3. At an ocean port, the water has a maximum depth of 4 m above the mean level at 8 A.M., and the period is 12.4 h.
   a) Assuming that the relation between the depth of the water and time is a sinusoidal function, write an equation for the depth of the water at any time t.
   b) Find the depth of the water at 10 A.M.

4. Tidal forces are greatest when the Earth, the sun, and the moon are in line. When this occurs at the Annapolis Tidal Generating Station, the water has a maximum depth of 9.6 m at 4:30 A.M. and a minimum depth of 0.4 m 6.2 h later.
   a) Write an equation for the depth of the water at any time t.
   b) Calculate the depth of the water at 9:30 A.M. and at 6:45 P.M.
   c) Compare the results of part b) with *Example 1*.

5. Repeat *Exercise 4* when the tidal forces are weakest. The maximum and minimum depths of the water at this time are 6.4 m and 3.6 m.

6. A certain mass is supported by a spring so that it is at rest 0.5 m above a table top. The mass is pulled down 0.4 m and released at time $t = 0$, creating a periodic up and down motion, called *simple harmonic motion*. It takes 1.2 s for the mass to return to the low position each time.

   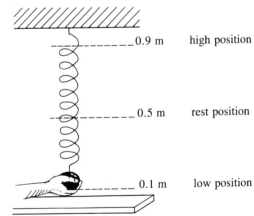

   0.9 m   high position

   0.5 m   rest position

   0.1 m   low position

   a) Draw a graph showing the height of the mass above the table top as a function of time for the first 2.0 s.
   b) Write an equation for the function in part a).
   c) Use your equation to determine the height of the mass above the table top after: i) 0.3 s ii) 0.7 s iii) 1.2 s.

7. A Ferris wheel has a radius of 25 m, and its centre is 26 m above the ground. It rotates once every 50 s. Suppose you get on at the bottom at $t = 0$.
   a) Draw a graph showing how your height above the ground changes during the first two minutes.
   b) Write an equation for the function in part a).
   c) Use your equation to determine how high you will be above the ground after:
      i)   10 s   ii)   20 s   iii) 40 s   iv) 60 s.

8. The pedals of a bicycle are mounted on a bracket whose centre is 29.0 cm above the ground. Each pedal is 16.5 cm from the bracket. Assume that the bicycle is pedalled at the rate of 12 cycles per minute.

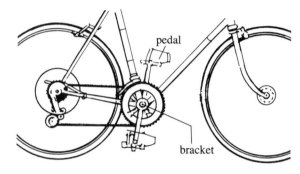

   a) Draw a graph showing the height of a pedal above the ground for the first few cycles. Assume that the pedal starts at the topmost position at $t = 0$.
   b) Write an equation for the function in part a).
   c) Use your equation to determine the height of the pedal after:
      i)   5 s   ii)   12 s   iii) 18 s.

9. The graph shows how the time of the sunset at Edmonton varies during the year.
   a) Write an equation which gives the time of the sunset on the nth day of the year.
   b) Use the equation found in part a) to calculate, to the nearest minute, the time of the sunset on:
      i) May 10 (day 130)
      ii) June 12 (day 163)
      iii) September 17 (day 260)
      iv) December 2 (day 336).

10. A graph showing the time of the sunset at Ottawa was shown on page 304.
    a) Write an equation which can be used to find the time of the sunset at Ottawa on the nth day of the year. (Assume it is not a leap year.)
    b) Use the equation to find the time of the sunset at Ottawa on:
       i)   February 20   ii)   April 14
       iii) July 25   iv)   November 5.

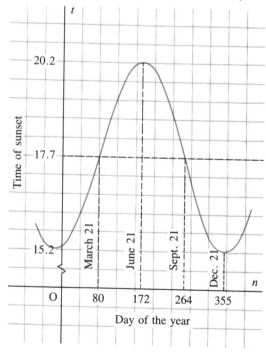

Time of sunset at Edmonton (standard time)

Day of the year

11. At St. John's, the time of the sunrise on the *n*th day of the year is given by this formula.

$$t = 1.89 \sin 2\pi \frac{(n - 80)}{365} + 6.41$$

   a) Calculate the time the sun rises on October 20 (day 293).
   b) Give one significant reason why the actual time of the sunrise on October 20 may differ somewhat from your answer in part a).

12. On December 21 each year, the sun is closest to the Earth, at approximately 147.2 million kilometres. On June 21 the sun is at its greatest distance, approximately 152.2 million kilometres.

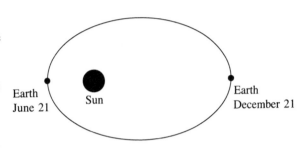

Earth June 21   Sun   Earth December 21

   a) Express the distance *d* from the Earth to the sun as a sinusoidal function of the number of the day of the year.
   b) Use the function to calculate the approximate distance from the Earth to the sun on:
   i) March 1   ii) April 30   iii) September 2.

Ⓒ

13. a) In *Example 1*, if the calculator is in *degree mode*, what change would have to be made in the equation?
   b) Solve *Example 1* using your calculator in degree mode.

14. In the solution of *Example 1*, a cosine function was used. Solve *Example 1* using a sine function.

15. On the *n*th day of the year, the number of hours of daylight at Victoria is given by this formula.

$$h = 3.98 \sin 2\pi \frac{(n - 80)}{365} + 12.16$$

   a) About how many hours of daylight should there be today?
   b) On what dates should there be about 10 h of daylight?

16. In *Example 1*, calculate to the nearest minute the first time after 4:30 A.M. when the depth of the water is: a) 6.0 m   b) 3.0 m.

 INVESTIGATE

1. From an almanac or newspaper files, determine the approximate time the sun rises and sets in your locality on June 21 and December 21.

2. Determine equations which represent the time the sun rises and sets on the *n*th day of the year.

3. Use the equations to predict the time the sun rises and sets today, and check your results in the newspaper.

Beauty in Mathematics

"I have found a very great number of exceedingly beautiful theorems."

Pierre de Fermat

How can a theorem be beautiful? Consider the Pythagorean Theorem and a right triangle. In *any* right triangle, no matter how large or how small, the lengths of the sides always satisfy $c^2 = a^2 + b^2$. Some would say that's a beautiful theorem.

But there is more. Draw a rectangle and two parallelograms in the spaces between the squares on the Pythagorean diagram.

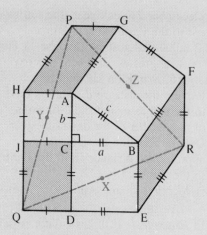

1. Prove that the areas of the shaded rectangle and the two shaded parallelograms are all equal.

2. $\triangle PQR$ is formed by the outer vertices of the rectangle and the parallelograms. Prove that the centres of the squares are the midpoints of the sides of $\triangle PQR$.

3. Prove that the area of $\triangle PQR$ is $(a + b)^2$.

Think of a strategy and carry it out
- What other segments in the diagram have lengths represented by a or b?
- Can you construct other segments with these lengths?
- Try to use this information to solve each problem.

Look back
- Prove that XY, YZ, and ZX divide $\triangle PQR$ into four congruent triangles.
- If $\triangle ABC$ is isosceles, what is the ratio of the areas of $\triangle PQR$ and $\triangle ABC$?
- Prove that the area of $\triangle PQR$ is never less than 8 times the area of $\triangle ABC$.
- If you think that these results are rather "neat", that's what Pascal meant when he wrote that some theorems are beautiful.

PROBLEMS

Ⓑ

1. Let B be any point on the parabola $y^2 = 4px$, and let A be the fixed point $(-2a^2, 0)$. Find the equation of the locus of the midpoint of AB.

2. Calculate the perpendicular distance from the point P(5, 4) to the line $4x - 3y + 12 = 0$.

3. Given the line $Ax + By + C = 0$ and the point $P(x_1, y_1)$, determine an expression for the perpendicular distance from the point to the line.

4. Find, to the nearest degree, the measures of the angles of the triangle formed by the lines $5x - 2y - 13 = 0$, $3x + 2y - 11 = 0$, $x - 2y + 7 = 0$.

Ⓒ

5. Prove that one root of the equation $ax^2 + bx + c = 0$ is double the other if and only if $2b^2 - 9ac = 0$.

6. In $\triangle$ABC, the bisector of $\angle$A intersects BC at D. Prove that $\dfrac{BD}{DC} = \dfrac{BA}{AC}$.

7. a) D is any point on side BC of $\triangle$ABC. If m, n, and d are as defined on the diagram, prove that $mb^2 + nc^2 = a(mn + d^2)$.
   b) Determine whether the result of part a) holds for points D on line BC, but not between B and C.
   c) Express d in terms of a, b, and c only, if AD is:
      i) the median from A to BC
      ii) the bisector of $\angle$A
      iii) the altitude from A to BC.

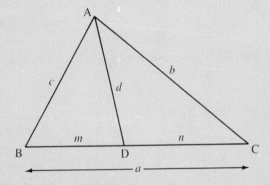

8. Points P, Q, R, and S are the midpoints of the sides of square ABCD. Find the ratio of the area of the shaded square to the area of square ABCD.

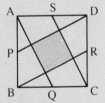

Ⓓ

9. In $\triangle$ABC, the bisectors of $\angle$B and $\angle$C meet at M and N respectively. If segments BM and CN have the same length, prove that $\triangle$ABC is isosceles.

Review Exercises

1. Convert from radians to degrees. Give the answers to 1 decimal place where necessary.

   a) $\frac{\pi}{3}$ radians
   b) $-\frac{7\pi}{4}$ radians
   c) $\frac{5\pi}{6}$ radians
   d) 4.7 radians

2. Convert from degrees to radians. Give the answers to 2 decimal places where necessary.

   a) 135°
   b) 270°
   c) 330°
   d) −47°

3. Calculate the arc length to the nearest centimetre of a sector of a circle with radius 9 cm if the sector angle is 220°.

4. Each point P is on the terminal arm of angle θ. Find sin θ, cos θ, and tan θ to 3 decimal places.

   a) P(4,9)
   b) P(8, − 15)
   c) P(− 4,7)
   d) P(− 6, − 5)

5. Find each value of θ in *Exercise 4*:
   i)   in degrees to 1 decimal place
   ii)   in radians to 3 decimal places.

6. Solve for θ to the nearest degree, $0° \leqslant \theta \leqslant 360°$.

   a) sin θ = 0.7295
   b) cos θ = −0.3862
   c) tan θ = −5.1730

7. Solve for θ in radians to 2 decimal places, $0 \leqslant \theta \leqslant 2\pi$.

   a) cos θ = 0.2681
   b) tan θ = 1.0744
   c) sin θ = −0.4683

8. Given θ is an acute angle, find expressions for the other five trigonometric ratios.

   a) $\sin \theta = \frac{a}{b}$
   b) $\tan \theta = \frac{p}{p + q}$
   c) $\sec \theta = \frac{2m - 1}{m + 3}$

9. State the exact values of the six trigonometric ratios of each angle.

   a) $\frac{5\pi}{6}$
   b) $\frac{\pi}{3}$
   c) $\frac{7\pi}{4}$
   d) $\frac{4\pi}{3}$
   e) $\frac{11\pi}{6}$

10. Draw graphs of $y = \sin \theta$ and $y = \cos \theta$ for $-2\pi \leqslant \theta \leqslant 2\pi$. For each graph
    a) State the maximum value of y, and the values of θ for which it occurs.
    b) State the minimum value of y, and the values of θ for which it occurs.
    c) State the θ- and y-intercepts.

11. Find the amplitude, the period, the phase shift, and the vertical displacement for each function.

    a) $y = 3 \sin 2\left(\theta - \frac{\pi}{4}\right) - 4$
    b) $y = 2 \cos 5\left(\theta + \frac{\pi}{3}\right) + 1$

12. Sketch the graphs of each set of functions on the same grid for $-2\pi \leqslant \theta \leqslant 2\pi$.
    a) $y = \sin \theta$ $y = 3 \sin \theta$ $y = 3 \sin \theta + 2$
    b) $y = \frac{1}{2} \cos \theta$ $y = \frac{1}{2} \cos \left(\theta + \frac{\pi}{3}\right)$ $y = \frac{1}{2} \cos \left(\theta + \frac{\pi}{3}\right) + 2$

13. Sketch the graph of each function.

    a) $y = \frac{1}{2} \sin 2\pi \frac{(t + 1)}{2} - 3$
    b) $y = 3 \sin 2\pi \frac{(t - 2)}{4} + 3$

6 Trigonometric Identities and Equations

Suppose you have an equation which expresses the depth of water as a trigonometric function of the time on a particular day. How can you determine the time if the depth is given? (See Section 6-5 *Example 4*.)

6-1 PYTHAGOREAN, RECIPROCAL, AND QUOTIENT IDENTITIES

Let $P(x,y)$ be any point on a circle of radius r, corresponding to an angle θ in standard position. Recall that the six trigonometric functions are defined as follows.

$$\sin \theta = \frac{y}{r} \qquad \cos \theta = \frac{x}{r} \qquad \tan \theta = \frac{y}{x}, x \neq 0$$

$$\csc \theta = \frac{r}{y}, y \neq 0 \qquad \sec \theta = \frac{r}{x}, x \neq 0 \qquad \cot \theta = \frac{x}{y}, y \neq 0$$

where $r = \sqrt{x^2 + y^2}$

These definitions apply for any angle θ in any quadrant.

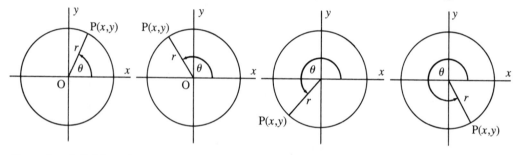

First Quadrant *Second Quadrant* *Third Quadrant* *Fourth Quadrant*

Since the definitions involve only three quantities x, y, and r, and since $r^2 = x^2 + y^2$, the trigonometric functions are related in a wide variety of different ways. For example, the following identities are direct consequences of the definitions.

Reciprocal Identities

$$\csc \theta = \frac{1}{\sin \theta} \qquad \sec \theta = \frac{1}{\cos \theta} \qquad \cot \theta = \frac{1}{\tan \theta}$$

Quotient Identities

$$\frac{\sin \theta}{\cos \theta} = \tan \theta \qquad \frac{\cos \theta}{\sin \theta} = \cot \theta$$

Equations such as those above are called *identities*. They are satisfied for all values of the variable for which they are defined. The reciprocal and quotient identities can be used to prove other identities, such as those in the following example.

Example 1.   Prove each identity.

a) $\sec \theta (1 + \cos \theta) = 1 + \sec \theta$

b) $\sec \theta = \tan \theta \csc \theta$

Solution.   a) $\sec \theta (1 + \cos \theta) = 1 + \sec \theta$

Left side	Reason
$\sec \theta (1 + \cos \theta)$	
$= \sec \theta + \sec \theta \cos \theta$	Expanding
$= \sec \theta + 1$	Reciprocal identity
$=$ Right side	

Since the left side simplifies to the right side, the identity is correct.

b) $\sec \theta = \tan \theta \csc \theta$

Left side	Reason
$\sec \theta$	
$= \dfrac{1}{\cos \theta}$	Reciprocal identity

Right side	Reason
$\tan \theta \csc \theta$	
$= \dfrac{\sin \theta}{\cos \theta} \times \dfrac{1}{\sin \theta}$	Quotient and reciprocal identities
$= \dfrac{1}{\cos \theta}$	

Since both sides simplify to the same expression, the identity is correct.

Observe the methods used in *Example 1* to prove the identities. We use the reciprocal and quotient identities, along with algebraic simplification, to show that one side of the identity is equal to the other side, or that both sides of the identity are equal to the same expression.

The reciprocal and quotient identities are rather like theorems in geometry, because they are used to prove other identities.

Another useful set of identities is called the *Pythagorean identities* because the identities are established by applying the Pythagorean Theorem to △PON in the diagram shown.

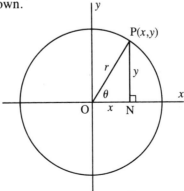

$x^2 + y^2 = r^2$

Divide both sides by r^2.

$\dfrac{x^2}{r^2} + \dfrac{y^2}{r^2} = 1$

$(\cos \theta)^2 + (\sin \theta)^2 = 1$

An expression such as $(\cos \theta)^2$ occurs so frequently that it is abbreviated as $\cos^2\theta$. Similarly, $(\sin \theta)^2$ is written as $\sin^2\theta$. Hence, we obtain the identity

$\cos^2\theta + \sin^2\theta = 1$.

We can obtain two additional Pythagorean identities from the equation $x^2 + y^2 = r^2$.

Divide both sides by x^2.

$$1 + \frac{y^2}{x^2} = \frac{r^2}{x^2}$$
$$1 + (\tan \theta)^2 = (\sec \theta)^2$$
$$1 + \tan^2\theta = \sec^2\theta$$

Divide both sides by y^2.

$$\frac{x^2}{y^2} + 1 = \frac{r^2}{y^2}$$
$$(\cot \theta)^2 + 1 = (\csc \theta)^2$$
$$\cot^2\theta + 1 = \csc^2\theta$$

Pythagorean Identities

$$\sin^2\theta + \cos^2\theta = 1 \qquad 1 + \tan^2\theta = \sec^2\theta \qquad 1 + \cot^2\theta = \csc^2\theta$$

Example 2.   Prove the identity $1 - \cos^2\theta = \cos^2\theta \tan^2\theta$.

Solution.

Left side	Reason
$1 - \cos^2\theta$ $= \sin^2\theta$	Pythagorean identity

Right side	Reason
$\cos^2\theta \tan^2\theta$ $= \cos^2\theta \times \dfrac{\sin^2\theta}{\cos^2\theta}$ $= \sin^2\theta$	Quotient identity

Since both sides simplify to the same expression, the identity is correct.

Example 3.   a) Prove the identity $\dfrac{\sin \theta}{1 + \cos \theta} = \dfrac{1 - \cos \theta}{\sin \theta}$.

b) Predict a similar identity for the expression $\dfrac{\cos \theta}{1 + \sin \theta}$, and prove that it is correct.

Solution.   a)

Left side	Reason
$\dfrac{\sin \theta}{1 + \cos \theta}$ $= \dfrac{\sin \theta}{1 + \cos \theta} \times \dfrac{1 - \cos \theta}{1 - \cos \theta}$ $= \dfrac{\sin \theta(1 - \cos \theta)}{1 - \cos^2\theta}$	Multiplying by 1
$= \dfrac{\sin \theta(1 - \cos \theta)}{\sin^2\theta}$	Pythagorean identity
$= \dfrac{1 - \cos \theta}{\sin \theta}$	Dividing numerator and denominator by $\sin \theta$
$=$ Right side	

Since the left side simplifies to the right side, the identity is correct.

b) The pattern of the terms sin θ and cos θ in part a) suggests that a similar identity might be:
$$\frac{\cos\theta}{1 + \sin\theta} = \frac{1 - \sin\theta}{\cos\theta}.$$
We can prove this identity in a similar way.
Another way to prove this identity (and the one in part a)) is to start with the Pythagorean identity $\sin^2\theta + \cos^2\theta = 1$ and perform the same operation to both sides. That is, we may write
$$\sin^2\theta + \cos^2\theta = 1$$
$$\cos^2\theta = 1 - \sin^2\theta$$
$$\cos^2\theta = (1 - \sin\theta)(1 + \sin\theta)$$
Hence, $\dfrac{\cos\theta}{1 + \sin\theta} = \dfrac{1 - \sin\theta}{\cos\theta}$

EXERCISES 6-1

(A)

1. Prove each identity.
   a) $\tan\theta\cos\theta = \sin\theta$
   c) $\sin\theta\cot\theta = \cos\theta$
   e) $\sin\theta = \dfrac{\tan\theta}{\sec\theta}$

   b) $\cot\theta\sec\theta = \csc\theta$
   d) $\tan\theta\csc\theta = \sec\theta$
   f) $\dfrac{\cot\theta}{\csc\theta} = \cos\theta$

2. Prove each identity.
   a) $\csc\theta(1 + \sin\theta) = 1 + \csc\theta$
   c) $\cos\theta(\sec\theta - 1) = 1 - \cos\theta$
   e) $\dfrac{1 - \tan\theta}{1 - \cot\theta} = -\tan\theta$

   b) $\sin\theta(1 + \csc\theta) = 1 + \sin\theta$
   d) $\sin\theta\sec\theta\cot\theta = 1$
   f) $\cot\theta = \dfrac{1 + \cot\theta}{1 + \tan\theta}$

(B)

3. Prove each identity.
   a) $\sin\theta\tan\theta + \sec\theta = \dfrac{\sin^2\theta + 1}{\cos\theta}$
   c) $\dfrac{1 + \sin\theta}{1 - \sin\theta} = \dfrac{\csc\theta + 1}{\csc\theta - 1}$
   e) $\dfrac{1 + \sin\theta}{1 + \csc\theta} = \sin\theta$

   b) $\dfrac{1 + \cos\theta}{1 - \cos\theta} = \dfrac{1 + \sec\theta}{\sec\theta - 1}$
   d) $\dfrac{1 + \tan\theta}{1 + \cot\theta} = \dfrac{1 - \tan\theta}{\cot\theta - 1}$
   f) $\dfrac{\sin\theta + \tan\theta}{\cos\theta + 1} = \tan\theta$

4. Prove each identity.
   a) $\sin^2\theta\cot^2\theta = 1 - \sin^2\theta$
   c) $\sin^2\theta = \dfrac{\tan^2\theta}{1 + \tan^2\theta}$
   e) $\sin\theta\cos\theta\tan\theta = 1 - \cos^2\theta$

   b) $\csc^2\theta - 1 = \csc^2\theta\cos^2\theta$
   d) $\dfrac{\sin\theta + \cos\theta\cot\theta}{\cot\theta} = \sec\theta$
   f) $\dfrac{\cos\theta}{1 + \sin\theta} + \dfrac{\cos\theta}{1 - \sin\theta} = 2\sec\theta$

5. a) Prove this identity. $\dfrac{\sin\theta + \cos\theta}{\csc\theta + \sec\theta} = \sin\theta\cos\theta$

   b) Predict a similar identity for the expression $\dfrac{\sin\theta + \tan\theta}{\csc\theta + \cot\theta}$, and prove that it is
      correct.

   c) Establish another identity like those in parts a) and b).

6. a) Prove this identity. $\dfrac{\tan\theta}{\sec\theta + 1} = \dfrac{\sec\theta - 1}{\tan\theta}$

   b) Predict a similar identity for the expression $\dfrac{\cot\theta}{\csc\theta + 1}$, and prove that it is correct.

7. a) Prove this identity. $\dfrac{1}{1 + \sin\theta} + \dfrac{1}{1 - \sin\theta} = 2\sec^2\theta$

   b) Establish a similar identity for this expression. $\dfrac{1}{1 + \cos\theta} + \dfrac{1}{1 - \cos\theta}$

8. a) Prove this identity. $\tan^2\theta\,(1 + \cot^2\theta) = \sec^2\theta$

   b) Predict a similar identity for the expression $\cot^2\theta\,(1 + \tan^2\theta)$, and prove that
      it is correct.

9. a) Prove each identity.
      i) $(1 - \cos^2\theta)(1 + \tan^2\theta) = \tan^2\theta$ ii) $(1 - \sin^2\theta)(1 + \cot^2\theta) = \cot^2\theta$

   b) Establish another identity like those in part a).

10. Prove each identity.
    a) $\tan\theta + \cot\theta = \sec\theta\csc\theta$ b) $\sec^2\theta + \csc^2\theta = \sec^2\theta\csc^2\theta$
    c) $\sec^2\theta + \csc^2\theta = (\tan\theta + \cot\theta)^2$ d) $\sin^2\theta = \cos\theta\,(\sec\theta - \cos\theta)$

11. Let P be any point on the unit circle,
    and construct the tangent to the circle at
    P. Let the tangent intersect the *x*-axis
    at A and the *y*-axis at B.
    a) Show that:
       i) PN $= \sin\theta$ ii) ON $= \cos\theta$
       iii) OB $= \csc\theta$ iv) OA $= \sec\theta$
       v) AP $= \tan\theta$ vi) BP $= \cot\theta$.
    b) Use the results of part a) and similar
       triangles on the diagram to illus-
       trate these identities.
       i) $1 + \tan^2\theta = \sec^2\theta$
       ii) $\sin^2\theta = \cos\theta\,(\sec\theta - \cos\theta)$
       iii) $\tan\theta\cot\theta = 1$
    c) What other identities can you find
       that can be illustrated by this
       diagram?

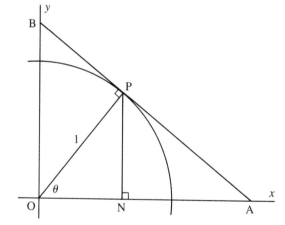

Ⓒ

12. In *Exercise 7*, identities for $\dfrac{1}{1 + f(x)} + \dfrac{1}{1 - f(x)}$, where $f(x) = \sin x$ and $f(x) = \cos x$, were established. Establish similar identities where $f(x)$ represents each of the other four trigonometric functions.

13. Establish an identity which involves all six trigonometric functions.

14. Prove each identity.

a) $\dfrac{1}{1 + \cos \theta} = \csc^2\theta - \dfrac{\cot \theta}{\sin \theta}$

b) $\tan \theta + \tan^3\theta = \dfrac{\sec^2\theta}{\cot \theta}$

c) $\dfrac{1 + \csc \theta}{\cot \theta} - \sec \theta = \tan \theta$

d) $\dfrac{(1 - \cos^2\theta)(\sec^2\theta - 1)}{\cos^2\theta} = \tan^4\theta$

15. Let $P(x,y)$ be any point on a circle of radius r, corresponding to an angle θ in standard position. Let A and C be the points shown on the diagram.

a) Express the lengths AP and CP as functions of r and θ.

b) Check the results of part a) when $\theta = 0, \dfrac{\pi}{2}, \pi$, and $\dfrac{3\pi}{2}$.

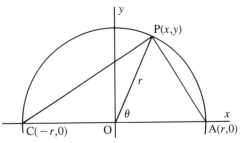

16. Solve for x. $\sin x - \tan x = 0, 0 \le x \le 2\pi$

17. Prove that the following expressions are *not* identities.

a) $\sin 2\theta = 2 \sin \theta$ b) $\cos 2\theta = 2 \cos \theta$ c) $\tan 2\theta = 2 \tan \theta$

 INVESTIGATE

Identities for $\sin 2\theta$, $\cos 2\theta$, and $\tan 2\theta$ can be established using the diagram of the unit circle shown. Since $\triangle ONP$ is a right triangle with hypotenuse 1 unit, then $ON = \cos 2\theta$ and $PN = \sin 2\theta$. Similarly, since $\triangle MCO$ is a right triangle with hypotenuse 1 unit, then $CM = \cos \theta$ and $MO = \sin \theta$.

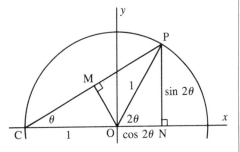

1. If $\angle MCO = \theta$, explain why $\angle PON = 2\theta$.

2. Write two different expressions for the length of CP. Use the results to establish an identity for $\cos 2\theta$ in terms of $\cos \theta$.

3. Use the results of *Question 2* to establish identities for $\sin 2\theta$ and $\tan 2\theta$ in terms of functions of θ.

6-2 ODD-EVEN, RELATED-ANGLE, AND COFUNCTION IDENTITIES

In addition to the reciprocal, quotient, and Pythagorean identities, and identities that can be derived from them, there are many other identities relating the trigonometric functions.

Odd-Even Identities

Let $P(x, y)$ be any point which is on a circle with radius r, and on the terminal arm of an angle θ. Then,

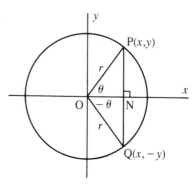

$$\sin \theta = \frac{y}{r} \dots ① \qquad \cos \theta = \frac{x}{r} \dots ②$$

Let $Q(x, -y)$ be the other point on the circle with the same x-coordinate as P. Then, by the SAS congruence theorem, $\triangle QON \cong \triangle PON$. Since the triangles are congruent, $\angle QON = \angle PON$. Therefore, Q is on the terminal arm of an angle $-\theta$. Hence, by definition,

$$\sin (-\theta) = \frac{-y}{r} \dots ③ \qquad \cos (-\theta) = \frac{x}{r} \dots ④$$

Comparing ① and ③, we obtain the identity
$\sin (-\theta) = -\sin \theta$.
Comparing ② and ④, we obtain $\cos (-\theta) = \cos \theta$.

These identities are called *odd-even identities*, because they are similar to a property of powers: if n is a natural number, then $(-x)^n = -x^n$ if n is odd, and $(-x)^n = x^n$ if n is even. Odd-even identities for the other trigonometric functions can be proved in the same way.

Odd-Even Identities

$$\sin (-\theta) = -\sin \theta \qquad \cos (-\theta) = \cos \theta \qquad \tan (-\theta) = -\tan \theta$$
$$\csc (-\theta) = -\csc \theta \qquad \sec (-\theta) = \sec \theta \qquad \cot (-\theta) = -\cot \theta$$

The identities $\cos (-\theta) = \cos \theta$ and $\sin (-\theta) = -\sin \theta$ can be seen on the graphs of the cosine and sine functions.

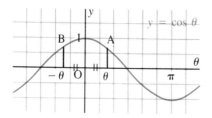

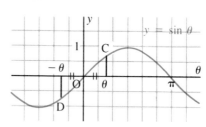

$\cos \theta$ is the y-coordinate of A.
$\cos (-\theta)$ is the y-coordinate of B.
Since these y-coordinates are equal,
$\cos (-\theta) = \cos \theta$.

$\sin \theta$ is the y-coordinate of C.
$\sin (-\theta)$ is the y-coordinate of D.
Since these y-coordinates are equal in absolute value, but have opposite signs,
$\sin (-\theta) = -\sin \theta$.

Related-Angle Identities

Let $Q(-x,y)$ be the reflection of P in the
y-axis. Then, Q is on the terminal arm of an
angle in standard position equal to $\pi - \theta$.
We apply the definitions of the
trigonometric functions to Q.

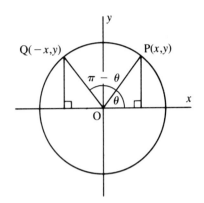

$\sin (\pi - \theta) = \dfrac{y}{r}$ . . . ⑤

$\cos (\pi - \theta) = -\dfrac{x}{r}$ . . . ⑥

Comparing ① and ⑤, we obtain
$\sin (\pi - \theta) = \sin \theta$
Comparing ② and ⑥, we obtain
$\cos (\pi - \theta) = -\cos \theta$

These identities are called *related-angle identities.*
    Similar identities relating the other trigonometric functions can be
proved in the same way.

Related-Angle Identities

$\sin (\pi - \theta) = \sin \theta$	$\csc (\pi - \theta) = \csc \theta$
$\cos (\pi - \theta) = -\cos \theta$	$\sec (\pi - \theta) = -\sec \theta$
$\tan (\pi - \theta) = -\tan \theta$	$\cot (\pi - \theta) = -\cot \theta$

These identities can be seen on graphs.

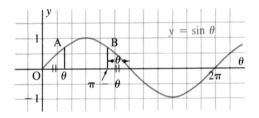

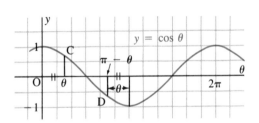

$\sin \theta$ is the y-coordinate of A.
$\sin (\pi - \theta)$ is the y-coordinate of B.
Since these y-coordinates are equal,
$\sin (\pi - \theta) = \sin \theta$.

$\cos \theta$ is the y-coordinate of C.
$\cos (\pi - \theta)$ is the y-coordinate of D.
Since these y-coordinates are equal in
absolute value, but have opposite signs,
$\cos (\pi - \theta) = -\cos \theta$

Cofunction Identities

Let Q(y,x) be the reflection of P in the line $y = x$. Then, Q is on the terminal arm of an angle in standard position equal to $\frac{\pi}{2} - \theta$. We apply the definitions of the trigonometric functions to Q.

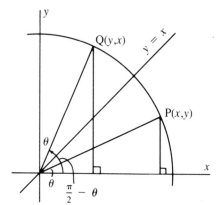

$\sin\left(\frac{\pi}{2} - \theta\right) = \frac{x}{r} \ldots \; ⑦$

$\cos\left(\frac{\pi}{2} - \theta\right) = \frac{y}{r} \ldots \; ⑧$

Comparing ② and ⑦, we obtain

$\sin\left(\frac{\pi}{2} - \theta\right) = \cos\theta.$

Comparing ① and ⑧, we obtain

$\cos\left(\frac{\pi}{2} - \theta\right) = \sin\theta.$

These identities are called *cofunction identities* because they involve complementary angles and the *co*sine and sine functions. They state that:
- the *co*sine of an angle is equal to the sine of the *co*mplementary angle.
- the sine of an angle is equal to the *co*sine of the *co*mplementary angle.

Similar identities relating the other trigonometric functions can be proved in the same way.

Cofunction Identities

$\sin\left(\frac{\pi}{2} - \theta\right) = \cos\theta$ $\csc\left(\frac{\pi}{2} - \theta\right) = \sec\theta$

$\cos\left(\frac{\pi}{2} - \theta\right) = \sin\theta$ $\sec\left(\frac{\pi}{2} - \theta\right) = \csc\theta$

$\tan\left(\frac{\pi}{2} - \theta\right) = \cot\theta$ $\cot\left(\frac{\pi}{2} - \theta\right) = \tan\theta$

The cofunction identities can be seen on graphs. For example, on the graph (below left), $\cos\theta$ is the y-coordinate of A. On the other graph, $\sin\left(\frac{\pi}{2} - \theta\right)$ is the y-coordinate of B. Since these y-coordinates are equal, $\sin\left(\frac{\pi}{2} - \theta\right) = \cos\theta.$

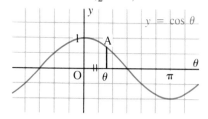

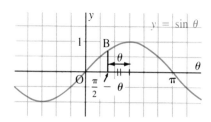

Example 1. Simplify.   a) $\cos\left(-\frac{\pi}{3}\right)$ b) $\sin\left(-\frac{\pi}{4}\right)$

Solution.   a) $\cos\left(-\frac{\pi}{3}\right) = \cos\frac{\pi}{3}$ b) $\sin\left(-\frac{\pi}{4}\right) = -\sin\frac{\pi}{4}$

$$= \frac{1}{2} \qquad\qquad\qquad\qquad = -\frac{1}{\sqrt{2}}$$

Example 2. Simplify.   a) $\sin\frac{5\pi}{6}$ b) $\cos\frac{3\pi}{4}$

Solution.   a) $\sin\frac{5\pi}{6} = \sin\left(\pi - \frac{\pi}{6}\right)$ b) $\cos\frac{3\pi}{4} = \cos\left(\pi - \frac{\pi}{4}\right)$

$$= \sin\frac{\pi}{6} \qquad\qquad\qquad = -\cos\frac{\pi}{4}$$

$$= \frac{1}{2} \qquad\qquad\qquad\qquad = -\frac{1}{\sqrt{2}}$$

Example 3. Use your calculator to check.

a) $\cos 2.4 = -\cos(\pi - 2.4)$ b) $\sin 1.5 = \cos\left(\frac{\pi}{2} - 1.5\right)$

Solution.   Be sure the calculator is in radian mode.

a) $\cos 2.4 \doteq -0.737\ 393\ 7$ and $\cos(\pi - 2.4) \doteq 0.737\ 393\ 7$

b) $\sin 1.5 \doteq 0.997\ 495$ and $\cos\left(\frac{\pi}{2} - 1.5\right) \doteq 0.997\ 495$

The identities established in this section are special cases of more general identities involving trigonometric functions of the sum or the difference of two angles. These identities will be developed in the next section.

EXERCISES 6-2

Ⓐ

1. Simplify.

   a) $\sin\left(-\frac{\pi}{6}\right)$ b) $\cos\left(-\frac{\pi}{4}\right)$ c) $\sin\left(-\frac{\pi}{2}\right)$ d) $\cos(-\pi)$

   e) $\cos\frac{5\pi}{6}$ f) $\sin\frac{3\pi}{4}$ g) $\sin\frac{2\pi}{3}$ h) $\cos\frac{2\pi}{3}$

2. Use your calculator to check that:
   a) $\sin 1 = \sin(\pi - 1)$ b) $\cos 1 = -\cos(\pi - 1)$
   c) $\cos 0.8 = -\cos(\pi - 0.8)$ d) $\sin 1 = \cos\left(\frac{\pi}{2} - 1\right)$
   e) $\cos 1 = \sin\left(\frac{\pi}{2} - 1\right)$ f) $\sin 0.8 = \cos\left(\frac{\pi}{2} - 0.8\right)$

(B)

3. Simplify.

   a) $\tan\left(-\dfrac{\pi}{3}\right)$ b) $\sec\left(-\dfrac{\pi}{4}\right)$ c) $\csc\left(-\dfrac{\pi}{6}\right)$ d) $\cot\left(-\dfrac{\pi}{3}\right)$

   e) $\tan\dfrac{5\pi}{6}$ f) $\cot\dfrac{3\pi}{4}$ g) $\csc\dfrac{2\pi}{3}$ h) $\sec\dfrac{5\pi}{6}$

4. On the graph, the y-coordinates of A and B are equal; the y-coordinates of C and B are equal in absolute value but opposite in sign. State the corresponding identities.

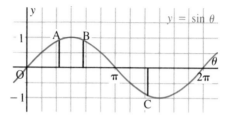

5. a) Related-angle identities for the sine and cosine functions were developed on page 237. Establish the related-angle identities for the other four trigonometric functions.

   b) Cofunction identities for the sine and cosine functions were developed on page 238. Establish the cofunction identities for the other four trigonometric functions.

6. In the identity $\sin\left(\dfrac{\pi}{2} - \theta\right) = \cos\theta$, substitute $\dfrac{\pi}{2} - \theta$ for θ and simplify the result. What do you notice?

(C)

7. a) Prove each identity.

   i) $\sin\left(\dfrac{\pi}{2} + \theta\right) = \sin\left(\dfrac{\pi}{2} - \theta\right)$ ii) $\cos\left(\dfrac{\pi}{2} + \theta\right) = -\cos\left(\dfrac{\pi}{2} - \theta\right)$

   b) Establish similar identities involving π, $\dfrac{3\pi}{2}$, and 2π.

 **INVESTIGATE**

Relations Among the Identities

A variety of other identities can be obtained from the related-angle identities and the cofunction identities, by substitution. For example, in *Exercise 6* the expression $\dfrac{\pi}{2} - \theta$ was substituted for θ in one of the cofunction identities.

This substitution can be made in any of the identities of this section. Similarly, other expressions such as $-\theta$ and $\pi + \theta$ can also be substituted for θ in the identities.

1. Investigate the effect of substituting expressions such as those above in the identities of this section. Look for patterns in the results, and classify the results in some way.

6-3 SUM AND DIFFERENCE IDENTITIES

In mathematics we often combine the operation of evaluating a function with the operations of addition or subtraction. These operations frequently give different results if they are carried out in different orders.

For example:

1. Triple a sum

   The sum of the numbers tripled

   $3(a + b)$ $3a + 3b$

2. The square of a sum

   The sum of the squares

   $(a + b)^2$ $a^2 + b^2$

3. The square root of a sum

   The sum of the square roots

   $\sqrt{a + b}$ $\sqrt{a} + \sqrt{b}$

4. The reciprocal of a sum

   The sum of the reciprocals

   $\dfrac{1}{a + b}$ $\dfrac{1}{a} + \dfrac{1}{b}$

5. The sine of a sum

   The sum of the sines

   $\sin(\alpha + \beta)$ $\sin\alpha + \sin\beta$

6. The cosine of a sum

   The sum of the cosines

   $\cos(\alpha + \beta)$ $\cos\alpha + \cos\beta$

The first pair of expressions are equal for all values of the variables. That is, we can write $3(a + b) = 3a + 3b$. We say that the operation of multiplication is *distributive* over addition.

   In general, function operations are not distributive over addition. For example, the next three pairs of expressions above are not equal.

$$(a + b)^2 \neq a^2 + b^2; \quad \sqrt{a + b} \neq \sqrt{a} + \sqrt{b}; \quad \text{and} \quad \frac{1}{a + b} \neq \frac{1}{a} + \frac{1}{b}$$

We can show that $\cos(\alpha + \beta) \neq \cos\alpha + \cos\beta$ by using a counter-example. Suppose $\alpha = \dfrac{\pi}{6}$ and $\beta = \dfrac{\pi}{3}$.

Then $\cos(\alpha + \beta) = \cos\left(\dfrac{\pi}{6} + \dfrac{\pi}{3}\right)$ but $\cos\alpha + \cos\beta = \cos\dfrac{\pi}{6} + \cos\dfrac{\pi}{3}$

$$= \cos\frac{\pi}{2} \qquad\qquad\qquad\qquad = \frac{\sqrt{3}}{2} + \frac{1}{2}$$

$$= 0 \qquad\qquad\qquad\qquad\qquad \neq 0$$

Therefore, $\cos\left(\dfrac{\pi}{6} + \dfrac{\pi}{3}\right) \neq \cos\dfrac{\pi}{6} + \cos\dfrac{\pi}{3}$

Hence, $\cos(\alpha + \beta) \neq \cos\alpha + \cos\beta$

Similarly, $\sin(\alpha + \beta) \neq \sin\alpha + \sin\beta$

   Therefore, in general, the operation of evaluating a sine or a cosine is not distributive over addition or subtraction. Hence, we now consider the problem of finding expressions for $\cos(\alpha + \beta)$ and $\sin(\alpha + \beta)$. To do this, we must use the definitions of the trigonometric functions as given in *Section 5-3*.

The trigonometric functions were defined using a circle with radius r. If the circle is a unit circle, then $r = 1$, and an important special case of the definitions results. Let $P(x, y)$ represent any point on a unit circle. Then P is on the terminal arm of an angle θ in standard position. By definition,

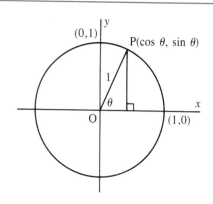

$$\sin \theta = \frac{y}{r} \qquad \cos \theta = \frac{x}{r}$$

$$= \frac{y}{1} \qquad\qquad = \frac{x}{1}$$

$$= y \qquad\qquad = x$$

Hence, $x = \cos \theta$ and $y = \sin \theta$. That is, the coordinates of P are $(\cos \theta, \sin \theta)$. Hence, the coordinates of any point P on a unit circle can be represented by $(\cos \theta, \sin \theta)$, where θ is the angle in standard position corresponding to P. We can use this property to derive identities for $\cos (\alpha - \beta)$ and $\sin (\alpha - \beta)$.

Deriving Identities for cos ($\alpha - \beta$) and sin ($\alpha - \beta$)

Let A($\cos \alpha$, $\sin \alpha$) and B($\cos \beta$, $\sin \beta$) be points on a unit circle, where α and β are the angles in standard position corresponding to A and B, respectively. Let C be on the circle such that OC is perpendicular to OB. Since the slopes of OC and OB are negative reciprocals, the coordinates of C may be represented by $(-\sin \beta, \cos \beta)$.

Rotate quadrilateral OBAC clockwise about the origin through angle β. Then B coincides with E(1, 0), C coincides with F(0, 1), and A coincides with D, where $\angle DOE = \alpha - \beta$. Hence, the coordinates of D are $(\cos (\alpha - \beta), \sin (\alpha - \beta))$.

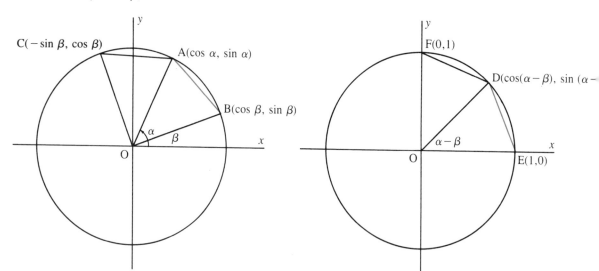

Since $\angle AOB = \angle DOE$, $\triangle AOB \cong \triangle DOE$.
Since the triangles are congruent,
$$AB = DE$$
$$\sqrt{(\cos \alpha - \cos \beta)^2 + (\sin \alpha - \sin \beta)^2} = \sqrt{(\cos (\alpha - \beta) - 1)^2 + (\sin (\alpha - \beta) - 0)^2}$$
Square both sides to eliminate the radicals.
$$(\cos \alpha - \cos \beta)^2 + (\sin \alpha - \sin \beta)^2 = (\cos (\alpha - \beta) - 1)^2 + \sin^2(\alpha - \beta)$$
Expand the binomial squares and use the Pythagorean identity.
$$\cos^2\alpha - 2 \cos \alpha \cos \beta + \cos^2\beta + \sin^2\alpha - 2 \sin \alpha \sin \beta + \sin^2\beta$$
$$= \cos^2(\alpha - \beta) - 2 \cos (\alpha - \beta) + 1 + \sin^2(\alpha - \beta)$$
$$(\cos^2\alpha + \sin^2\alpha) + (\cos^2\beta + \sin^2\beta) - 2 (\cos \alpha \cos \beta + \sin \alpha \sin \beta)$$
$$= (\cos^2(\alpha - \beta) + \sin^2(\alpha - \beta)) + 1 - 2 \cos (\alpha - \beta)$$
$$2 - 2(\cos \alpha \cos \beta + \sin \alpha \sin \beta) = 2 - 2 \cos (\alpha - \beta)$$

Hence, $\cos (\alpha - \beta) = \cos \alpha \cos \beta + \sin \alpha \sin \beta$ . . . ①

Similarly, using $AC = DF$, we can derive the following identity for $\sin (\alpha - \beta)$.

$$\sin (\alpha - \beta) = \sin \alpha \cos \beta - \cos \alpha \sin \beta \text{ . . . } ②$$

Equations ① and ② are the identities for $\cos (\alpha - \beta)$ and $\sin (\alpha - \beta)$ we have been seeking.

Example 1.   Use a calculator to verify identities ① and ② for $\alpha = 1.2$ and $\beta = 0.9$.

Solution.   Substitute $\alpha = 1.2$ and $\beta = 0.9$ into each identity.
Using identity ①:
$\cos (1.2 - 0.9) = \cos 1.2 \cos 0.9 + \sin 1.2 \sin 0.9$
or $\cos 0.3 = \cos 1.2 \cos 0.9 + \sin 1.2 \sin 0.9$
Be sure the calculator is in radian mode.
Both sides of this equation are equal to approximately 0.955 336 5.

Using identity ②:
$\sin (1.2 - 0.9) = \sin 1.2 \cos 0.9 - \cos 1.2 \sin 0.9$
or $\sin 0.3 = \sin 1.2 \cos 0.9 - \cos 1.2 \sin 0.9$
Both sides of this equation are equal to approximately 0.295 520 2.

Deriving Identities for cos $(\alpha + \beta)$ and sin $(\alpha + \beta)$
It is possible to obtain identities for $\cos (\alpha + \beta)$ and $\sin (\alpha + \beta)$ using diagrams similar to those on page 242. However, it is simpler to apply the odd-even identities to the identities ① and ② we already have. We can do this because the sum of two angles can also be expressed as a difference. That is, $\alpha + \beta = \alpha - (-\beta)$. Hence, we can write:
$$\cos (\alpha + \beta) = \cos (\alpha - (-\beta))$$
$$= \cos \alpha \cos (-\beta) + \sin \alpha \sin (-\beta)$$
$$= \cos \alpha \cos \beta - \sin \alpha \sin \beta$$
Similarly, we can obtain $\sin (\alpha + \beta) = \sin \alpha \cos \beta + \cos \alpha \sin \beta$.

Sum and Difference Identities
$$\sin (\alpha + \beta) = \sin \alpha \cos \beta + \cos \alpha \sin \beta$$
$$\sin (\alpha - \beta) = \sin \alpha \cos \beta - \cos \alpha \sin \beta$$
$$\cos (\alpha + \beta) = \cos \alpha \cos \beta - \sin \alpha \sin \beta$$
$$\cos (\alpha - \beta) = \cos \alpha \cos \beta + \sin \alpha \sin \beta$$

We can use the sum and difference identities to find expressions for the sine or cosine of an angle obtained by adding or subtracting multiples of $\frac{\pi}{6}$ or $\frac{\pi}{4}$. For example, since $\frac{5\pi}{12} = \frac{\pi}{4} + \frac{\pi}{6}$, we can find an expression for $\sin \frac{5\pi}{12}$ without using a calculator.

Example 2. Find an exact expression for $\sin \frac{5\pi}{12}$, and check with a calculator.

Solution.
$$\sin \frac{5\pi}{12} = \sin \left(\frac{\pi}{4} + \frac{\pi}{6}\right)$$
$$= \sin \frac{\pi}{4} \cos \frac{\pi}{6} + \cos \frac{\pi}{4} \sin \frac{\pi}{6}$$
$$= \frac{1}{\sqrt{2}} \left(\frac{\sqrt{3}}{2}\right) + \frac{1}{\sqrt{2}}\left(\frac{1}{2}\right)$$
$$= \frac{\sqrt{3} + 1}{2\sqrt{2}}$$

Both sides of this equation are equal to approximately 0.965 925 8.

We can use the sum and difference identities to prove the cofunction identities, and many other related identities.

Example 3. Prove each identity.

    a) $\cos \left(\frac{\pi}{2} + \theta\right) = -\sin \theta$ b) $\sin (\pi - \theta) = \sin \theta$

Solution.
    a) $\cos \left(\frac{\pi}{2} + \theta\right) = \cos \frac{\pi}{2} \cos \theta - \sin \frac{\pi}{2} \sin \theta$
$$= (0)\cos \theta - (1)\sin \theta$$
$$= -\sin \theta$$
    b) $\sin (\pi - \theta) = \sin \pi \cos \theta - \cos \pi \sin \theta$
$$= (0) \cos \theta - (-1)\sin \theta$$
$$= \sin \theta$$

To use the sum and difference identities, we must know both the sine and the cosine of the two angles involved in the expression.

Example 4. Given $\cos \theta = \frac{3}{5}$, where θ is in Quadrant I, evaluate $\cos \left(\theta + \frac{\pi}{6}\right)$.

Solution. The two angles are θ and $\frac{\pi}{6}$. Hence, we need to know the sine and the cosine of each angle.

We know that $\sin \frac{\pi}{6} = \frac{1}{2}$ and $\cos \frac{\pi}{6} = \frac{\sqrt{3}}{2}$.

The value of $\cos \theta$ is given, and we can obtain the value of $\sin \theta$ from a diagram.

Since θ is in Quadrant I, let $P(x,y)$ be a point in the first quadrant. Compare the general value of $\cos \theta = \frac{x}{r}$ with the given value of $\cos \theta = \frac{3}{5}$. Hence, $x = 3$ and $r = 5$.

Then, from the Pythagorean theorem,
$$r^2 = x^2 + y^2$$
$$25 = 9 + y^2$$
$$y = \pm 4$$

Since P is in Quadrant I, $y = 4$

Hence, $\sin \theta = \frac{4}{5}$

$$\cos \left(\theta + \frac{\pi}{6}\right) = \cos \theta \cos \frac{\pi}{6} - \sin \theta \sin \frac{\pi}{6}$$

$$= \frac{3}{5}\left(\frac{\sqrt{3}}{2}\right) - \frac{4}{5}\left(\frac{1}{2}\right)$$

$$= \frac{3\sqrt{3} - 4}{10}$$

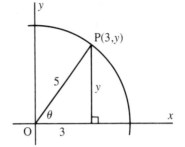

EXERCISES 6-3

(A)

1. Use a calculator to verify the sum and difference identities for $\alpha = 2.2$ and $\beta = 1.4$.

2. Expand and simplify each expression.

a) $\sin \left(\frac{\pi}{6} + \frac{\pi}{3}\right)$ b) $\cos \left(\frac{\pi}{4} + \frac{\pi}{4}\right)$ c) $\sin \left(\frac{\pi}{3} - \frac{\pi}{6}\right)$ d) $\cos \left(\frac{\pi}{2} - \frac{\pi}{6}\right)$

3. Evaluate $\cos \frac{2\pi}{3}$ by expanding and simplifying each expression.

a) $\cos \left(\frac{\pi}{3} + \frac{\pi}{3}\right)$ b) $\cos \left(\frac{\pi}{2} + \frac{\pi}{6}\right)$ c) $\cos \left(\pi - \frac{\pi}{3}\right)$

4. Evaluate $\sin \frac{3\pi}{4}$ by expanding and simplifying each expression.

a) $\sin \left(\frac{\pi}{2} + \frac{\pi}{4}\right)$ b) $\sin \left(\pi - \frac{\pi}{4}\right)$

(B)

5. a) Use the fact that $\frac{\pi}{12} = \frac{\pi}{3} - \frac{\pi}{4}$ to prove that $\sin \frac{\pi}{12} = \frac{\sqrt{3} - 1}{2\sqrt{2}}$.
   b) Find a similar expression for $\cos \frac{\pi}{12}$.
   c) Check the results in parts a) and b) with a calculator.

6. Find an exact expression for each sine or cosine.

a) $\cos \frac{7\pi}{12}$ b) $\sin \frac{11\pi}{12}$ c) $\cos \frac{5\pi}{12}$ d) $\sin \frac{5\pi}{12}$

7. Show that the cofunction identities provide counterexamples to prove that $\cos(\alpha - \beta) \neq \cos\alpha - \cos\beta$ and $\sin(\alpha - \beta) \neq \sin\alpha - \sin\beta$.

8. Prove each identity.

a) $\sin\left(\frac{\pi}{2} + \theta\right) = \cos\theta$

b) $\cos(\pi + \theta) = -\cos\theta$

c) $\cos\left(\frac{3\pi}{2} + \theta\right) = \sin\theta$

d) $\sin\left(\frac{3\pi}{2} - \theta\right) = -\cos\theta$

9. Simplify each expression.

a) $\cos(\pi - \theta)$ b) $\sin\left(\frac{\pi}{2} - \theta\right)$ c) $\sin(\pi - x)$ d) $\cos\left(x - \frac{\pi}{2}\right)$

10. Given $\sin\theta = \frac{4}{5}$, where θ is in Quadrant I, evaluate each expression.

a) $\sin\left(\theta + \frac{\pi}{6}\right)$ b) $\sin\left(\theta + \frac{\pi}{4}\right)$ c) $\cos\left(\theta - \frac{\pi}{3}\right)$

11. Given $\cos\theta = -\frac{2}{3}$, where θ is in Quadrant II, evaluate each expression.

a) $\sin\left(\theta + \frac{\pi}{6}\right)$ b) $\cos\left(\theta + \frac{\pi}{3}\right)$ c) $\cos\left(\theta - \frac{\pi}{4}\right)$

12. Given $\sin\theta = 0.75$, where $\frac{\pi}{2} < \theta < \pi$, evaluate each expression.

a) $\sin\left(\theta + \frac{\pi}{3}\right)$ b) $\cos\left(\theta - \frac{\pi}{6}\right)$ c) $\cos\left(\theta + \frac{\pi}{4}\right)$

13. a) Prove that $\sin\left(\frac{\pi}{4} + \theta\right) + \sin\left(\frac{\pi}{4} - \theta\right) = \sqrt{2}\cos\theta$.

b) Find a similar expression for:

i) $\sin\left(\frac{\pi}{6} + \theta\right) + \sin\left(\frac{\pi}{6} - \theta\right)$ ii) $\sin\left(\frac{\pi}{3} + \theta\right) + \sin\left(\frac{\pi}{3} - \theta\right)$.

c) State a general result suggested by parts a) and b), and prove it.

14. Given that $\sin\alpha = \frac{3}{5}$ and $\cos\beta = \frac{5}{13}$, where both α and β are in Quadrant I, evaluate each expression.

a) $\cos(\alpha + \beta)$ b) $\cos(\alpha - \beta)$ c) $\sin(\alpha + \beta)$ d) $\sin(\alpha - \beta)$

15. Given that $\cos\alpha = -\frac{4}{5}$ and $\sin\beta = \frac{2}{3}$, where both α and β are in Quadrant II, evaluate each expression.

a) $\cos(\alpha + \beta)$ b) $\cos(\alpha - \beta)$ c) $\sin(\alpha + \beta)$ d) $\sin(\alpha - \beta)$

16. Determine whether or not there are any values of α and β such that:

a) $\sin(\alpha + \beta) = \sin\alpha + \sin\beta$ b) $\cos(\alpha + \beta) = \cos\alpha + \cos\beta$

c) $\tan(\alpha + \beta) = \tan\alpha + \tan\beta$.

17. Derive the identity $\sin(\alpha - \beta) = \sin\alpha\cos\beta - \cos\alpha\sin\beta$ in two ways.

a) using the diagram on page 242

b) using the identity for $\cos(\alpha + \beta)$ and a cofunction identity

6-4 DOUBLE-ANGLE IDENTITIES

In *Section 6-3* we developed identities for the sine and cosine of the sum of two angles.

$\sin (\alpha + \beta) = \sin \alpha \cos \beta + \cos \alpha \sin \beta$

$\cos (\alpha + \beta) = \cos \alpha \cos \beta - \sin \alpha \sin \beta$

If the two angles α and β are equal, then these identities reduce to identities for $\sin 2\alpha$ and $\cos 2\alpha$.

$$\begin{aligned}\sin 2\alpha &= \sin (\alpha + \alpha) \\ &= \sin \alpha \cos \alpha + \cos \alpha \sin \alpha \\ &= 2 \sin \alpha \cos \alpha\end{aligned} \qquad \begin{aligned}\cos 2\alpha &= \cos (\alpha + \alpha) \\ &= \cos \alpha \cos \alpha - \sin \alpha \sin \alpha \\ &= \cos^2\alpha - \sin^2\alpha \quad \dots \text{①}\end{aligned}$$

We can use the Pythagorean identity $\sin^2\alpha + \cos^2\alpha = 1$ to express the identity for $\cos 2\alpha$ in two other forms.

Since $\sin^2\alpha + \cos^2\alpha = 1$, then

$$\sin^2\alpha = 1 - \cos^2\alpha$$

Substitute this expression in ①

$$\begin{aligned}\cos 2\alpha &= \cos^2\alpha - \sin^2\alpha \\ &= \cos^2\alpha - (1 - \cos^2\alpha) \\ &= 2 \cos^2\alpha - 1\end{aligned}$$

Since $\sin^2\alpha + \cos^2\alpha = 1$, then

$$\cos^2\alpha = 1 - \sin^2\alpha$$

Substitute this expression in ①

$$\begin{aligned}\cos 2\alpha &= \cos^2\alpha - \sin^2\alpha \\ &= (1 - \sin^2\alpha) - \sin^2\alpha \\ &= 1 - 2 \sin^2\alpha\end{aligned}$$

Double-Angle Identities

$$\sin 2\alpha = 2 \sin \alpha \cos \alpha \qquad \begin{aligned}\cos 2\alpha &= \cos^2\alpha - \sin^2\alpha \\ &= 2 \cos^2\alpha - 1 \\ &= 1 - 2 \sin^2\alpha\end{aligned}$$

Example 1. Use a calculator to verify that $\sin 1.2 = 2 \sin 0.6 \cos 0.6$.

Solution. Both sides of the equation are equal to approximately 0.932 039 1.

Example 2. If $\cos \theta = -\dfrac{1}{3}$, and $\dfrac{\pi}{2} < \theta < \pi$, evaluate each expression.

a) $\sin 2\theta$ b) $\cos 2\theta$ c) $\tan 2\theta$

Solution. To find the values of these expressions, we need the value of $\sin \theta$ in addition to the given value of $\cos \theta$.

Since $\dfrac{\pi}{2} < \theta < \pi$, the point P lies in the second quadrant where $x < 0$ and $y > 0$.

Compare the general value of $\cos \theta = \dfrac{x}{r}$

with the given value of $-\dfrac{1}{3}$.

The *x*-coordinate of P is -1 and $r = 3$.

Since $r^2 = x^2 + y^2$

$$9 = 1 + y^2$$

$$y = \sqrt{8} \qquad \text{(since } y > 0\text{)}$$

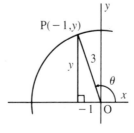

Hence, $\sin \theta = \dfrac{y}{r}$

$$= \frac{\sqrt{8}}{3}$$

a) $\sin 2\theta = 2 \sin \theta \cos \theta$

$$= 2 \left(\frac{\sqrt{8}}{3} \right) \left(-\frac{1}{3} \right)$$

$$= -\frac{2\sqrt{8}}{9}$$

b) We can find $\cos 2\theta$ using the Pythagorean identity, or any of the three identities for $\cos 2\theta$. For example,
$\cos 2\theta = 2 \cos^2 \theta - 1$

$$= 2 \left(-\frac{1}{3} \right)^2 - 1$$

$$= -\frac{7}{9}$$

c) To find $\tan 2\theta$ we use the quotient identity.

$$\tan 2\theta = \frac{\sin 2\theta}{\cos 2\theta}$$

$$= \frac{-\dfrac{2\sqrt{8}}{9}}{-\dfrac{7}{9}}$$

$$= \frac{2\sqrt{8}}{7}$$

The patterns in the double-angle identities can be used to simplify certain trigonometric expressions.

Example 3. Write each expression in terms of a single trigonometric function.

  a) $2 \sin 0.45 \cos 0.45$ b) $\cos^2 5 - \sin^2 5$

Solution.   a) $2 \sin 0.45 \cos 0.45$

     This expression can be obtained by substituting 0.45 for α in the right side of the identity $\sin 2\alpha = 2 \sin \alpha \cos \alpha$. Hence, we substitute 0.45 for α in the left side of the identity. Therefore, $2 \sin 0.45 \cos 0.45 = \sin 0.90$

   b) $\cos^2 5 - \sin^2 5$

     Similarly, by substituting 5 for α in the identity $\cos 2\alpha = \cos^2 \alpha - \sin^2 \alpha$, we obtain $\cos^2 5 - \sin^2 5 = \cos 10$.

Example 4. Prove the identity $\dfrac{1 + \cos 2\theta}{\sin 2\theta} = \cot \theta$.

Solution. In the left side, we use the double-angle identities for $\sin 2\theta$ and $\cos 2\theta$. There are three expressions we could substitute for $\cos 2\theta$. We choose the one which eliminates the 1 from the numerator.

Left side	Reason
$\dfrac{1 + \cos 2\theta}{\sin 2\theta}$	
$= \dfrac{1 + (2\cos^2\theta - 1)}{2 \sin \theta \cos \theta}$	Double-angle identities
$= \dfrac{2\cos^2\theta}{2 \sin \theta \cos \theta}$	
$= \dfrac{\cos \theta}{\sin \theta}$	Dividing numerator and denominator by $2 \cos \theta$
$= \cot \theta$	Reciprocal identity
$=$ Right side	

Since the left side simplifies to the right side, the identity is correct.

In *Example 4*, the expression $\dfrac{1 + \cos 2\theta}{\sin 2\theta}$ on the left side is not defined for values of θ such that $\sin 2\theta = 0$. Hence, the identity holds for all values of θ except those for which $\sin 2\theta = 0$.

EXERCISES 6-4

Ⓐ

1. Use a calculator to verify the double-angle identities for $\alpha = 0.45$.

2. Use a calculator to verify the double-angle identities for $\alpha = 5$.

3. Write each expression in terms of a single trigonometric function.
   a) $2 \sin 0.6 \cos 0.6$ b) $2 \sin 3 \cos 3$ c) $2 \sin 2 \cos 2$
   d) $\cos^2 0.45 - \sin^2 0.45$ e) $2 \cos^2 5 - 1$ f) $1 - 2 \sin^2 3$

4. Write each expression in terms of a single trigonometric function.
   a) $2 \sin \dfrac{\pi}{6} \cos \dfrac{\pi}{6}$ b) $\cos^2 \dfrac{\pi}{10} - \sin^2 \dfrac{\pi}{10}$ c) $2 \cos^2 0.5 - 1$

5. Given that $\sin \dfrac{\pi}{3} = \dfrac{\sqrt{3}}{2}$ and $\cos \dfrac{\pi}{3} = \dfrac{1}{2}$, use the double-angle identities to determine the values of $\sin \dfrac{2\pi}{3}$ and $\cos \dfrac{2\pi}{3}$.

6. Given that $\sin \dfrac{\pi}{4} = \dfrac{1}{\sqrt{2}}$ and $\cos \dfrac{\pi}{4} = \dfrac{1}{\sqrt{2}}$, use the double-angle identities to determine the values of $\sin \dfrac{\pi}{2}$ and $\cos \dfrac{\pi}{2}$.

(B)

7. The identity $\cos 2\theta = 2\cos^2\theta - 1$ was used to prove the identity in *Example 4*. Prove the identity using one of the other identities for $\cos 2\theta$.

8. If $\sin \theta = \frac{1}{3}$, and θ is in Quadrant I, evaluate each expression.

   a) $\sin 2\theta$ b) $\cos 2\theta$ c) $\tan 2\theta$

9. A value of θ is defined. Evaluate the expressions $\sin 2\theta$, $\cos 2\theta$, and $\tan 2\theta$.

   a) $\cos \theta = -\frac{1}{2}$, and θ is in Quadrant II

   b) $\sin \theta = -\frac{2}{3}$, and θ is in Quadrant III

   c) $\tan \theta = 0.75$ and $\pi < \theta < \frac{3\pi}{2}$

10. Prove each identity.

   a) $1 + \sin 2\theta = (\sin \theta + \cos \theta)^2$ b) $\sin 2\theta = 2\cot \theta \sin^2\theta$

   c) $\cos 2\theta = \dfrac{1 - \tan^2\theta}{1 + \tan^2\theta}$ d) $\sec^2\theta = \dfrac{2}{1 + \cos 2\theta}$

11. a) Show that the expression $\dfrac{1 - \cos 2\theta}{2}$ is equivalent to $\sin^2\theta$.

   b) Find a similar expression equivalent to $\cos^2\theta$. Try to do this in more than one way.

12. Show that the expression $\dfrac{\sin^2\theta + \cos^2\theta}{\sin^2\theta - \cos^2\theta}$ is equivalent to $-\sec 2\theta$, provided that $\sin^2\theta \neq \cos^2\theta$.

13. a) Show that the expression $\dfrac{(\sin \theta + \cos \theta)^2}{\sin 2\theta}$ is equivalent to the expression $\csc 2\theta + 1$, provided that $\sin 2\theta \neq 0$.

   b) Find a similar expression equivalent to $\csc 2\theta - 1$.

14. In *Example 4*, an identity for $\dfrac{1 + \cos 2\theta}{\sin 2\theta}$ was proved. Establish similar identities for each expression.

   a) $\dfrac{1 - \cos 2\theta}{\sin 2\theta}$ b) $\dfrac{\sin 2\theta}{1 + \cos 2\theta}$ c) $\dfrac{\sin 2\theta}{1 - \cos 2\theta}$

15. a) If $\sin \theta + \cos \theta = \frac{1}{2}$, find the value of $\sin 2\theta$.

   b) Check the result of part a) with your calculator.

(C)

---

16. a) Sketch the graphs of the functions $y = \sin 2\theta$ and $y = 2\sin \theta$.

   b) Use the graphs to explain why $\sin 2\theta \neq 2\sin \theta$.

   c) Are there any values of θ such that $\sin 2\theta$ is equal to $2\sin \theta$?

17. Repeat *Exercise 16* using the cosine function.

6-5 SOLVING TRIGONOMETRIC EQUATIONS

In *Section 5-3*, we solved equations such as $\sin \theta = 0.75$ and $\cos \theta = -0.275$ for θ. These equations are examples of trigonometric equations.

An equation involving one or more trigonometric functions of a variable is called a *trigonometric equation*.

These are trigonometric equations.

$2 \sin 2x - \cos x = 0$

$x + \tan x = 1$

There are *not* trigonometric equations.

$4x - 2 \sin 4.5 = 3$

$x^2 + \cos \pi = 0$

Since trigonometric functions are periodic, a trigonometric equation usually has infinitely many roots. Sometimes, only the roots in a particular domain are required.

Example 1. Solve the equation $3 \cos^2 \theta + \cos \theta - 1 = 0$ for θ, to two decimal places, where $0 \le \theta < 2\pi$.

Solution. $3 \cos^2 \theta + \cos \theta - 1 = 0$ is a quadratic equation in $\cos \theta$.
Use the quadratic formula.

$$\cos \theta = \frac{-b \pm \sqrt{b^2 - 4ac}}{2a} \qquad \begin{matrix} a = 3 \\ b = 1 \\ c = -1 \end{matrix}$$

$$= \frac{-1 \pm \sqrt{1^2 - 4(3)(-1)}}{2(3)}$$

$$= \frac{-1 \pm \sqrt{13}}{6}$$

$$\doteq 0.434\ 258\ 5 \text{ or } -0.767\ 591\ 9$$

When $\cos \theta \doteq 0.434\ 258\ 5$

$$\theta \doteq 1.121\ 581\ 3,$$

which is one root of the equation
By the property of cosine functions in *Section 5-3*, another root is
$2\pi - 1.121\ 581\ 3 = 5.161\ 604$.
When $\cos \theta \doteq -0.767\ 591\ 9$

$$\theta \doteq 2.445\ 871\ 8,$$

which is a root of the equation
Another root is $2\pi - 2.445\ 871\ 8 = 3.837\ 313\ 5$.
Hence, the given equation has four roots between 0 and 2π. To two decimal places, these roots are 1.12, 2.45, 3.84, and 5.16.

In *Example 1*, notice that when the values of θ are subtracted from 2π, more than two decimal places are used. This avoids rounding errors. For example, if the root 2.445 871 8 had been rounded to two decimal places as 2.45 and then subtracted from 2π, the result would have been 3.83. This value is not correct to two decimal places.

In *Example 1*, only one trigonometric function was present in the equation. Other equations contain two or more trigonometric functions.

Example 2. Solve the equation $2 \sin x = 3 + 2 \csc x$ over the domain $0 \leqslant x < 2\pi$.

Solution. Since the sine and cosecant functions are reciprocal functions, we can write $\csc x$ in terms of $\sin x$.

$2 \sin x = 3 + 2 \csc x$

$2 \sin x = 3 + \dfrac{2}{\sin x}$

Multiply both sides by $\sin x$.

$2 \sin^2 x - 3 \sin x - 2 = 0$

$(2 \sin x + 1)(\sin x - 2) = 0$

Either $2 \sin x + 1 = 0$ or $\sin x - 2 = 0$

           $\sin x = -0.5$ $\sin x = 2$

One value of x satisfying this   There are no real values of

equation is $x = -\dfrac{\pi}{6}$. x satisfying this equation.

The root $x = -\dfrac{\pi}{6}$ is not in the domain. By the property of sine functions in *Section 5-3*, a root in the domain is $\pi - \left(-\dfrac{\pi}{6}\right)$, or $\dfrac{7\pi}{6}$. Since the sine function has period 2π, another root in the domain is $-\dfrac{\pi}{6} + 2\pi$, or $\dfrac{11\pi}{6}$.

Hence, for $0 \leqslant x < 2\pi$, the equation has two roots: $\dfrac{7\pi}{6}$ and $\dfrac{11\pi}{6}$.

     No general methods exist for solving trigonometric equations, but the strategy used in *Example 2* is often helpful. The given equation involved both the sine and the cosecant function. We used a trigonometric identity to reduce the equation to one involving only the sine function, which we solved using algebraic methods.

Example 3. Solve over the real numbers. $4 \sin x \cos x - 1 = 0$

Solution. A product of the form $\sin x \cos x$ occurs in the double-angle identity $\sin 2\theta = 2 \sin \theta \cos \theta$. Hence, we write the equation as follows.

$2 (2 \sin x \cos x) - 1 = 0$

         $2 \sin 2x - 1 = 0$

            $\sin 2x = 0.5 \ldots \textcircled{1}$

Since $\sin \dfrac{\pi}{6} = 0.5$, one value is   By the property of sine functions, another value is

$2x = \dfrac{\pi}{6}$ $2x = \pi - \dfrac{\pi}{6}$

$x = \dfrac{\pi}{12}$ $x = \dfrac{5\pi}{12}$

These are two roots of the equation. Since the function in equation $\textcircled{1}$ is periodic with period π, we can find infinitely many other roots by adding multiples of the period to these roots.

There are infinitely many roots   And, there are infinitely many of the form   roots of the form

$x = \dfrac{\pi}{12} + n\pi$, where $n \in I$. $x = \dfrac{5\pi}{12} + n\pi$, where $n \in I$.

In *Example 3*, the expressions $\frac{\pi}{12} + n\pi$ and $\frac{5\pi}{12} + n\pi$ form what is called the *general solution* of the equation. Particular solutions can be obtained by substituting integers for n. For example, if $n = 2$, we obtain the roots $\frac{25\pi}{12}$ and $\frac{29\pi}{12}$. You can check that these are correct by substituting them for x into the left side of the original equation and using your calculator.

In *Section 5-13* we expressed the depth of the water at Annapolis Tidal Generating Station as a function of the time on a particular day, by the equation $h = 3 \cos 2\pi \dfrac{(t - 4.5)}{12.4} + 5$. We used this equation to calculate the depth at different times. The graph of this function is repeated below.

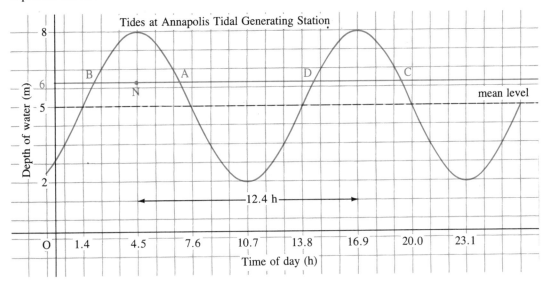

We now ask the inverse question — if we know the depth of the water, how can we calculate the time? For example, if the depth is 6.0 m, we would write this equation.

$$3 \cos 2\pi \dfrac{(t - 4.5)}{12.4} + 5 = 6$$

This is an example of a trigonometric equation with the variable t. We can see from the graph that this equation has more than one solution. That is, the times when the water is 6.0 m deep are represented by the points A, B, C, and D. This is what we should expect, because the water will be 6.0 m deep at different times during the day.

Example 4. a) Calculate, to the nearest minute, one of the times when the water is 6.0 m deep on the day represented by the graph.

b) Calculate the other times on the same day when the water is 6.0 m deep.

Solution.   a) $3 \cos 2\pi \dfrac{(t - 4.5)}{12.4} + 5 = 6$

$$3 \cos 2\pi \dfrac{(t - 4.5)}{12.4} = 1$$

$$\cos 2\pi \dfrac{(t - 4.5)}{12.4} = \dfrac{1}{3}$$

To solve this equation, we must find a number whose cosine is $\frac{1}{3}$.

Since the cosine function is periodic, there are infinitely many numbers with this property. Using a calculator, one of these numbers is approximately 1.230 959 4.

Hence, we can write

$$2\pi\dfrac{(t - 4.5)}{12.4} \doteq 1.230\ 959\ 4$$

To solve this equation for t, we multiply both sides by 12.4, then divide both sides by 2π, and finally add 4.5 to both sides. We do these steps with the calculator and get 6.929 324 6. This is one root of the equation.

To convert to minutes, multiply the fractional part by 60 and get 55.759 477. Hence, to the nearest minute, the water was 6 m deep at 6:56 A.M.

b) The time found in part a) is represented by point A on the graph. The other times when the water is 6 m deep are represented by B, C, and D.

To calculate the t-coordinate of B, we use the fact that the segments AN and BN have the same length.

Since 6.929 324 6 − 4.5 = 2.429 324 6, the t-coordinate of B is 4.5 − 2.429 324 6, or 2.070 675 4. As before, we convert to minutes by multiplying the fractional part by 60. The water was 6 m deep at 2:04 A.M.

To calculate the t-coordinates of C and D, we add the period to the t-coordinates of A and B. The results are:

Point C: $t = 6.929\ 324\ 6 + 12.4$

$\qquad\quad = 19.329\ 324\ 6$

The corresponding time is 19:20, or 7:20 P.M.

Point D:

$t = 2.070\ 675\ 4 + 12.4$

$\ = 14.470\ 675\ 4$

The corresponding time is 14:28, or 2:28 P.M.

Hence, during the day represented by the graph, the water was 6.0 m deep at 2:04 A.M., 6:56 A.M., 2:28 P.M., and 7:20 P.M.

EXERCISES 6-5

Ⓑ

1. Solve for θ to 2 decimal places, $0 \leqslant \theta < 2\pi$.
   a) $2 \sin^2\theta - 3 \sin \theta + 1 = 0$
   b) $2 \cos^2\theta + 5 \cos \theta - 3 = 0$
   c) $2 \tan^2\theta = 3 \tan \theta - 1$
   d) $3 \tan^2\theta = 2 \tan \theta + 4$

2. Solve for x to 2 decimal places, $0 \leqslant x < 2\pi$.
   a) $2 \cos^2x + \cos x - 1 = 0$
   b) $3 \sin^2x + \sin x - 1 = 0$
   c) $4 \cos x = 6 \sec x - 5$
   d) $\sec x - 7 \cos x = \dfrac{5}{6}$

3. Solve over the domain $0 \leqslant x < 2\pi$.
   a) $2 \cos x = 7 - 3 \sec x$
   b) $\csc x = 2 \sin x + 1$
   c) $2 \sin x \cos x + 1 = 0$
   d) $\cos^2x - \sin^2x = 1$

4. Solve over the real numbers.
   a) $4 \sin x \cos x + 1 = 0$
   b) $4 \sin 2x \cos 2x + 1 = 0$
   c) $\dfrac{\sin x + 1}{\csc x} = 3$
   d) $4 \tan x + \cot x = 5$

5. At a seaport, the depth of the water h metres at time t hours during a certain day is given by this formula.
$$h = 2.4 \cos 2\pi \frac{(t - 5.00)}{12.4} + 4.2$$
   Calculate, to the nearest minute, at least two different times during this day when the water is 5.0 m deep.

6. a) On the same grid, draw the graphs of $y = \cos x$ and $y = \cos 2x$ over the domain $0 \leqslant x < 2\pi$. Then use the graph to determine the roots of the equation $\cos x + \cos 2x = 0$ over this domain.
   b) Give an algebraic solution of the equation in part a).
   c) Repeat parts a) and b) for the sine function.

Ⓒ

7. A carpenter makes the triangular framework shown, in which AC = 2000 mm, BC = 1000 mm, and $\angle$ACB = 90°. The framework is reinforced by segments BD and DE, where DE $\perp$ AB. If the total length of material to be used for the segments BD and DE is 1875 mm, calculate $\angle$DBC to the nearest degree.

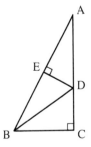

8. Write an example of a trigonometric equation, with domain the set of real numbers, that has:
   a) no real roots
   b) only one real root
   c) exactly three real roots.

9. Determine the root of each equation as accurately as you can, where $0 \leqslant \theta < \dfrac{\pi}{2}$.
   a) $\sin \theta = \theta$
   b) $\cos \theta = \theta$
   c) $\tan \theta = \theta$

PROBLEM SOLVING

The Golden Ratio

"Geometry has two great treasures: one is the theorem of Pythagoras; the other, the division of a line segment into extreme and mean ratio. The first we may compare to a measure of gold; the second we may name a precious jewel."

Johannes Kepler

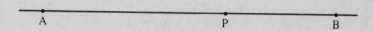

Given any line segment AB, there is a point P which divides the segment into two parts such that the length of the longer part is to the length of the shorter part as the length of the entire segment is to the length of the longer part. That is, $\dfrac{AP}{PB} = \dfrac{AB}{AP}$. This is what Kepler meant by "division . . . into extreme and mean ratio". The ratio is now known as the *golden ratio*.

The golden ratio occurs frequently and unexpectedly in a wide variety of problems. The problems below and in the problems section provide only a glimpse of this variety.

Problem 1. Find the numerical value of the golden ratio.

Understand the problem
- How can a ratio have a numerical value?

Think of a strategy and carry it out
- On the diagram above, let $AP = x$ and $PB = 1$.
- Use the definition of the golden ratio to write an equation in x, then solve the equation.
- The golden ratio is the positive root of this equation.

Look back
- Did you get the equation $x^2 - x - 1 = 0$?
- Did you obtain the root $\dfrac{1 + \sqrt{5}}{2}$? This is the golden ratio expressed as a real number.
- Why is the golden ratio the positive root rather than the negative root?
- Use a calculator to express the golden ratio in decimal form.

Problem 2. Prove that the diagonals of a regular pentagon divide each other in the golden ratio.

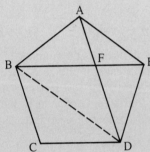

Understand the problem
- What is a regular pentagon?
- Do all the diagonals have the same length?

Think of a strategy
- Since the pentagon is regular, what properties would certain angles and segments have in a diagram like the one above?
- Could you prove these properties?
- There is no loss of generality in letting the sides of the pentagon have length 1. Hence, let the diagonals have length x.
- Write what is required to prove about point F and the diagonal BE. Are some of the segments involved sides of triangles?
- What kind of triangles might they be?

Carry out the strategy
- BF and FE are sides of △BFD and △EFA. Use properties of a regular pentagon to prove that these triangles are similar.
- Then use the result to prove that F divides BE in the same ratio that a diagonal bears to a side.
- Is this true about every diagonal and every side?
- Complete the proof that F divides BE in the golden ratio.

Look back
- Did you obtain the equation $x^2 - x - 1 = 0$?
- Does F divide DA in the golden ratio?
- What is the ratio of a diagonal to a side?
- Why is there no loss of generality in assuming that the sides of the pentagon have length 1?

PROBLEMS

Ⓑ

1. Prove each identity.
   a) $\sin 3\theta = 3 \sin \theta - 4 \sin^3\theta$ b) $\cos 3\theta = 4 \cos^3\theta - 3 \cos \theta$

2. The function $z(n)$ is defined as the number of zeros at the end of $n!$. For example, since $5! = 120$, which ends in one zero, then $z(5) = 1$.
   a) Determine. i) $z(10)$ ii) $z(20)$ iii) $z(30)$
   b) Is it possible to find a value of n such that $z(n) = 5$?
   c) Given any natural number n, describe a method you could use to determine the value of $z(n)$.

3. If $\triangle ABC$ is a right triangle, prove that
   $\sin^2 A + \sin^2 B + \sin^2 C = 2(\cos^2 A + \cos^2 B + \cos^2 C)$.

4. Prove that $\cos 36° = \dfrac{\sqrt{5} + 1}{4}$ and $\cos 72° = \dfrac{\sqrt{5} - 1}{4}$.

5. Find the equations of the lines with slope $\dfrac{3}{4}$ that are 2 units from the point P(5, −1).

Ⓒ

6. Find the equations of two parallel lines passing through A(0, 2) and B(0, 7) which are 3 units apart.

7. Triangle ABC has vertices A(4, 9), B(1, 2), and C(9, 6). Find the area of $\triangle ABC$.

8. T is any point on a circle with centre C. P is a point on the tangent at T such that PT = 2CT. With centre P a second circle is drawn tangent to the given circle to intersect PT at N.
   a) Prove that N divides PT in the golden ratio.
   b) Use the result of part a) to construct a regular pentagon with one side PN.

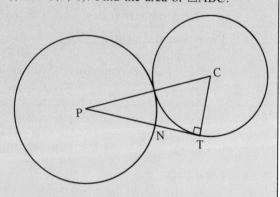

Ⓓ

9. In $\triangle ABC$, $\angle B = 90°$, and the ratio of the sides is AB : BC : CA = 3 : 4 : 5. O is the point of intersection of BC and the bisector of $\angle A$. With centre O and radius OB, a circle is drawn to intersect AO at P and Q. Prove that P divides QA in the golden ratio.

1. Prove each identity.
   a) $\sec \theta (1 + \sin \theta) = \tan \theta (1 + \csc \theta)$
   b) $\csc \theta - \dfrac{\cot \theta}{\sec \theta} = \sin \theta$

   c) $\cos^2\theta = \sin \theta (\csc \theta - \sin \theta)$
   d) $\sec^2\theta - 1 = (\sin \theta \sec \theta)^2$

2. Prove each identity.
   a) $\cos^2\theta = \dfrac{\cot^2\theta}{1 + \dfrac{1}{\tan^2\theta}}$
   b) $\dfrac{\sin \theta}{1 - \cos \theta} + \dfrac{\sin \theta}{1 + \cos \theta} = 2 \csc \theta$

   c) $\sin \theta \cot^2\theta + \cos \theta \tan^2\theta = \dfrac{\sin^3\theta + \cos^3\theta}{\sin \theta \cos \theta}$
   d) $\dfrac{\tan^2\theta + 1}{\cot^2\theta + 1} = \dfrac{1 - \cos^2\theta}{\cos^2\theta}$

3. Simplify.
   a) $\sin \left(-\dfrac{\pi}{3}\right)$
   b) $\sec \left(-\dfrac{\pi}{4}\right)$
   c) $\tan \left(-\dfrac{2\pi}{3}\right)$
   d) $\cos \left(-\dfrac{5\pi}{6}\right)$

4. Expand and simplify.
   a) $\cos \left(\dfrac{\pi}{6} + \dfrac{\pi}{4}\right)$
   b) $\cos \left(\dfrac{3\pi}{4} - \dfrac{\pi}{3}\right)$
   c) $\sin \left(\dfrac{\pi}{2} + \dfrac{\pi}{6}\right)$
   d) $\sin \left(\dfrac{5\pi}{6} - \dfrac{\pi}{6}\right)$

5. Find an exact expression for each trigonometric ratio.
   a) $\sin \dfrac{\pi}{12}$
   b) $\cos \dfrac{13\pi}{12}$
   c) $\cos \dfrac{7\pi}{12}$
   d) $\sin \dfrac{23\pi}{12}$

6. Given $\cos \theta = -\dfrac{2}{5}$ and θ is in Quadrant II, evaluate:
   a) $\sin \left(\theta + \dfrac{\pi}{6}\right)$
   b) $\cos \left(\theta - \dfrac{\pi}{4}\right)$.

7. If $\sin \alpha = \dfrac{3}{4}$ and $\cos \beta = -\dfrac{3}{5}$, where α and β are in Quadrant II, evaluate:
   a) $\cos (\alpha + \beta)$
   b) $\cos (\alpha - \beta)$
   c) $\sin (\alpha + \beta)$
   d) $\sin (\alpha - \beta)$.

8. Write each expression as a single trigonometric ratio.
   a) $\cos^2 \dfrac{\pi}{6} - \sin^2 \dfrac{\pi}{6}$
   b) $2 \sin 0.8 \cos 0.8$
   c) $2 \cos^2 0.35 - 1$

9. If $\sin \theta = \dfrac{1}{4}$ and θ is in Quadrant II, evaluate:
   a) $\sin 2\theta$
   b) $\cos 2\theta$
   c) $\tan 2\theta$.

10. Prove each identity.
    a) $\dfrac{(\sin \theta + \cos \theta)^2}{\sin 2\theta} = 1 + \csc 2\theta$
    b) $\dfrac{\sin 2\theta}{1 - \cos 2\theta} = \dfrac{1}{\tan \theta}$

    c) $2 \cos^2\theta - 1 = \cos^4\theta - \dfrac{1}{\csc^4\theta}$
    d) $\dfrac{\cos 2\theta}{\sin 2\theta + 1} = \dfrac{1 - \tan \theta}{1 + \tan \theta}$

11. Solve for θ to 2 decimal places, where $0 < \theta < 2\pi$.
    a) $8 \sin^2\theta - 6 \sin \theta + 1 = 0$
    b) $3 \cos^2\theta = 4 \cos \theta + 4$
    c) $\sin 2\theta + \cos \theta = 0$
    d) $3 \cos^2\theta - 3 \sin^2\theta + 2 = 0$

1. Solve.
   a) $x^2 - 9y^2 = 36$
      $x - 3y = 3$
   b) $x^2 + 4y = 16$
      $4x^2 + y^2 = 16$
   c) $y = x^2 - 4x + 3$
      $2x - y = 2$

2. Which two numbers have a product of 24, and a difference of squares of 55?

3. Find the dimensions of a rectangle with an area of 60 cm² and a perimeter of 34 cm.

4. Solve.
   a) $|2x + 1| = 7$
   b) $|3x - 2| \leq 10$
   c) $|5 - 2x| \geq 11$

5. Convert from radians to degrees. Give each answer to 2 decimal places where necessary.
   a) $\frac{3\pi}{4}$
   b) $-\frac{7\pi}{6}$
   c) 2.7 radians
   d) $-\frac{11\pi}{3}$

6. Convert from degrees to radians. Give each answer to 2 decimal places where necessary.
   a) $210°$
   b) $-225°$
   c) $147°$
   d) $270°$

7. Each point P is on the terminal arm of an angle θ.
   a) Find $\sin \theta$, $\cos \theta$, and $\tan \theta$.
      i) P(3,1)   ii) P($-5, -2$)   iii) P(6, -4)
   b) Find each value of θ in degrees to 1 decimal place.

8. Solve for θ in radians to 2 decimal places, if $0 \leq \theta \leq 2\pi$.
   a) $\sin \theta = 0.7642$
   b) $\tan \theta = -1.4950$
   c) $\sec \theta = 1.1541$

9. If θ is an acute angle, find expressions for the other 5 trigonometric ratios.
   a) $\sin \theta = \dfrac{a}{b - c}$
   b) $\cot \theta = \dfrac{2p}{q}$

10. State the amplitude, period, phase shift, and vertical displacement for each function.
    a) $y = 2 \sin 3\left(\theta - \frac{\pi}{6}\right)$
    b) $y = \frac{1}{2} \cos \left(2\theta + \frac{\pi}{2}\right) - 1$

11. Prove each identity.
    a) $\sin^4\theta - \cos^4\theta = 2 \sin^2\theta - 1$
    b) $\dfrac{\csc \theta}{\sec^2\theta} = \csc \theta - \sin \theta$
    c) $\dfrac{\sin \theta + \tan \theta}{1 + \cos \theta} = \tan \theta$
    d) $\dfrac{\cos \theta}{1 - \sin \theta} + \dfrac{\cos \theta}{1 + \sin \theta} = 2 \sec \theta$

12. Expand and simplify.
    a) $\sin \left(\frac{\pi}{6} + \frac{\pi}{4}\right)$
    b) $\cos \left(\frac{\pi}{3} - \frac{\pi}{4}\right)$
    c) $\tan \left(\frac{\pi}{3} + \frac{\pi}{4}\right)$

13. If $\sin \alpha = \frac{2}{3}$ and $\cos \beta = -\frac{1}{4}$, where α and β are in Quadrant II, evaluate:
    a) $\cos (\alpha + \beta)$
    b) $\sin (\alpha - \beta)$
    c) $\cos 2\alpha$
    d) $\cos (\alpha - \beta)$.

14. Solve for θ to 2 decimal places where necessary, if $0 \leq \theta \leq 2\pi$.
    a) $6 \sin^2\theta + \sin \theta - 2 = 0$
    b) $12 \cos^2\theta = 13 \cos \theta - 3$

7 Exponential and Logarithmic Functions

In 1947 an investor bought Van Gogh's painting *Irises* for $84 000. In 1987 she sold it for $49 million. What annual rate of interest corresponds to an investment of $84 000 which grows to $49 million in 40 years? (See Section 7-10 *Example 2*.)

7-1 INTRODUCTION TO EXPONENTIAL FUNCTIONS

Exponents were originally introduced into mathematics as a shorthand for repeated multiplication. Repeated multiplication occurs frequently in applications involving growth and decay.

Compound Interest

Compound interest provides a simple example of *exponential growth*. Suppose you make a long-term investment of $500 at a fixed interest rate of 8% per annum compounded annually. We can calculate the value of your investment at the end of each year.

Value in dollars of the investment after

year 1: $500(1.08) = 540$

year 2: $500(1.08)(1.08) = 500(1.08)^2$, or 583.20

year 3: $500(1.08)(1.08)(1.08) = 500(1.08)^3$, or 629.86

$$\vdots \qquad \vdots$$

year n: $500(1.08)^n$

Hence, the value of an investment A dollars can be expressed as a function of the number of years n by this equation.

$$A = 500(1.08)^n$$

In this equation, n is a natural number since it indicates how many factors of 1.08 there are in the expression. Using values of n from 1 to 25, we obtain values of A and draw the graph shown. The fact that we can draw a smooth curve through the plotted points on the graph suggests that an expression such as $(1.08)^n$ can be defined for values of n that are not natural numbers. We will see how to do this in the next section.

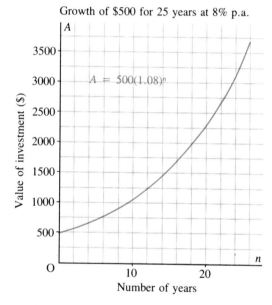

Growth of $500 for 25 years at 8% p.a.

Growth of Populations

In 1987 the world population reached 5 billion, and was increasing at the rate of approximately 1.6% per year. If we assume that this rate of growth is maintained, we can write an equation expressing the predicted population P billion as a function of the number of years n since 1987.

$$P \doteq 5(1.016)^n$$

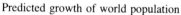

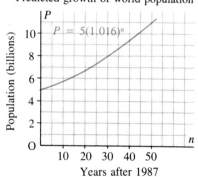

Predicted growth of world population

The graph on the facing page shows this equation plotted for values of n from 0 to 50 corresponding to the years from 1987 to 2037. In this equation, n is also a natural number, but since the graph represents as many as 50 values of n, the graph is drawn as a smooth curve.

A Bouncing Ball

A bouncing ball provides a simple example of *exponential decay*. In this picture, on each bounce the ball rises to 70% of the height from which it fell. Suppose that the ball originally fell from a height of 2.00 m. We can calculate the height to which the ball rises on each successive bounce.
Height in metres of the ball after
bounce 1: $2.00(0.7) = 1.4$
bounce 2: $2.00(0.7)(0.7) = 2.0(0.7)^2$, or 0.98
bounce 3: $2.00(0.7)(0.7)(0.7) = 2.0(0.7)^3$, or 0.69

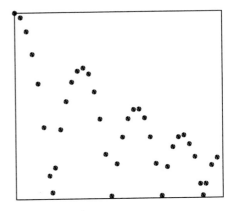

. . .
. . .
. .

bounce n: $2.00(0.7)^n$

Hence, the height h metres can be expressed as a function of the number of bounces n by this equation.

$$h = 2.00(0.7)^n$$

The graph shows the values of n for $0 \leq n \leq 10$. Since it is not meaningful to have a fractional number of bounces, the points are not joined by a smooth curve.

Light Penetration Under Water

For every metre a diver descends below the surface, the light intensity is reduced by 2.5%. Hence, the percent P of surface light present can be expressed as a function of the depth d metres by this equation.

$$P = 100(1 - 0.025)^d$$
$$\text{or} \quad P = 100(0.975)^d$$

The graph shows P as a function of d for $0 \leq d \leq 100$. Although d is understood to represent a natural number in the expression above, we have drawn a smooth curve to indicate light intensity at all depths to 100 m, including those depths that are not whole numbers of metres.

Height of bouncing ball

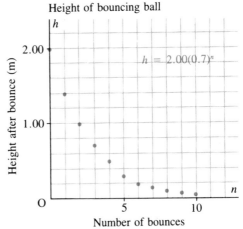

Number of bounces

Light penetration under water

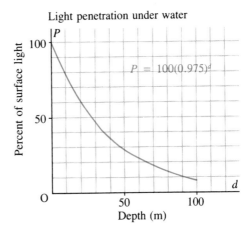

Depth (m)

In each of the above equations, the variable in the expression on the right side appears in an exponent. Functions whose defining equation have this property are called exponential functions.

> An *exponential function* has an equation which can be written in the form $f(x) = ca^x$, where c and a are constants, and $a > 0$.

Note the following properties of the variable x, and the constants a and c.
- In this section, x is understood to represent a natural number, since it represents the number of times the constant a occurs as a factor. This restriction will be removed in the next section.
- Since all the applications of exponential functions are ones in which the base is positive, we will assume that $a > 0$.
- The constant c is any real number, though in most applications we shall encounter this number is usually positive also.

In the following example an exponential function is defined by a statement describing how variables are related.

Example.   In favorable breeding conditions, a colony of insects can multiply 10-fold every 3 weeks. If there are now 500 insects in the colony, express the number of insects N as a function of the elapsed time w weeks.

Solution.   "Multiply 10-fold every 3 weeks" means that every time 3 weeks elapse, there are 10 times as many insects as before.
Number of insects after:
3 weeks: 500(10)
6 weeks: $500(10)^2$ Each exponent is $\frac{1}{3}$ of
9 weeks: $500(10)^3$ the number of weeks.

.   .
.   .
.   .

w weeks: $500(10)^{\frac{w}{3}}$
Hence, $N(w) = 500(10)^{\frac{w}{3}}$

EXERCISES 7-1
Note: Exercises 1 to 8 refer to the above examples.

Ⓑ

1. Use the graph on page 262 to estimate how many years it takes, at 8%, for the original investment:
   a) to double in value   b) to triple in value.

2. Describe how the graph would differ if:
   a) the interest rate were
      i) greater than 8%   ii) less than 8%;
   b) the original investment were
      i) greater than $500   ii) less than $500.

3. Use the graph on page 262 to estimate the number of years required for the population of the world to double.

4. Describe how the population graph would differ for a country such as:
   a) Mexico which has a growth rate of approximately 3.5%
   b) Japan which has a growth rate of approximately 1.1%.

5. Use the graph on page 263 to estimate how many bounces are needed before the ball bounces to only 10% of the original height from which it was dropped.

6. Describe how both the graph and the equation on page 263 would differ for a ball which is:
   a) more resilient, and bounces higher than the one shown
   b) less resilient, and does not bounce as high as the one shown.

7. Use the graph on page 263 to estimate the depth where the light intensity is only 50% of that at the surface.

8. The depth to which light penetrates under water depends on the color of the light. The graph was drawn for yellow light. How would the graph differ for:
   a) red light which penetrates about 20% as far as yellow light
   b) blue light which penetrates about 4 times as far as yellow light?

9. At current growth rates, the population of Mexico is doubling about every 20 years. The population in 1985 was 80 million. Write an expression for the population P million as an exponential function of the time n years since 1985.

10. There are now 300 insects in a colony. The population of the colony doubles every 5 days. Express the population P of the colony as an exponential function of the elapsed time d days.

11. Several layers of glass are stacked together, as shown. Each layer reduces the light passing through it by 5%. Write an expression for the percent P of light that passes through n panes of glass.

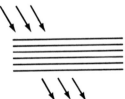

12. Most cars have a plastic container which holds fluid for cleaning the windshield. Throughout the winter, a motorist used 100% pure solvent in the container. One day in the spring, when the container was half full of solvent, she topped up the container with water. From then on throughout the summer, whenever the container was half full, she topped it up with water. Write an equation that expresses the concentration C of the solvent in the container as an exponential function of the number of times n it was topped up with water.

7-2 REVIEW: THE LAWS OF EXPONENTS

By counting the bacteria in a culture, scientists can learn how bacteria grow under controlled conditions. The growth of a certain bacteria is shown in the table. The number of bacteria doubles every hour, over several hours. The number of bacteria N is an exponential function of the time t hours. We can represent this function by the equation

$N(t) = 1000(2)^t$ ... ①

with the graph shown below.

Time t hours	Number of bacteria N
−3	125
−2	250
−1	500
0	1 000
1	2 000
2	4 000
3	8 000
4	16 000

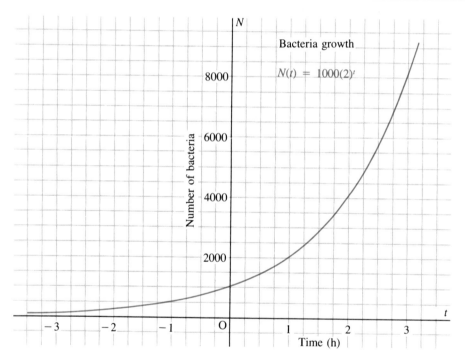

Bacteria growth

$N(t) = 1000(2)^t$

We can use the following definitions to approximate the number of bacteria at any time.

Definition of Integral and Rational Exponents

$a^0 = 1$ where $a \neq 0$ $\qquad$ $a^{-n} = \dfrac{1}{a^n}$ where $n \in \mathbb{N}, a \neq 0$

$a^{\frac{m}{n}} = (\sqrt[n]{a})^m$ and $a^{-\frac{m}{n}} = \dfrac{1}{a^{\frac{m}{n}}} = \dfrac{1}{(\sqrt[n]{a})^m}$ where $m, n \in \mathbb{N}, a > 0$

Example 1. How many bacteria are in the culture when:

a) $t = 0$ h   b) $t = -2$ h   c) $t = \frac{1}{2}$ h   d) $t = 1$ h 40 min?

Solution. Substitute each value of t into equation ①.

a) $N(0) = 1000(2)^0$
$= 1000(1)$
$= 1000$

b) $N(-2) = 1000(2)^{-2}$
$= 1000\left(\frac{1}{2^2}\right)$
$= 250$

c) $N\left(\frac{1}{2}\right) = 1000(2)^{\frac{1}{2}}$
$= 1000\sqrt{2}$
$\doteq 1414$

d) 1 h 40 min $= 1\frac{2}{3}$ h, or $\frac{5}{3}$ h

$N\left(\frac{5}{3}\right) = 1000(2)^{\frac{5}{3}}$
$= 1000(\sqrt[3]{2})^5$
$\doteq 3175$

Example 2. Evaluate each expression without using a calculator.

a) $(0.75)^{-2}$ b) $9^{1.5}$ c) $8^{-\frac{2}{3}}$

Solution.

a) $(0.75)^{-2} = \left(\frac{3}{4}\right)^{-2}$

$= \frac{1}{\left(\frac{3}{4}\right)^2}$

$= \frac{16}{9}$

b) $9^{1.5} = 9^{\frac{3}{2}}$
$= (\sqrt{9})^3$
$= 27$

c) $8^{-\frac{2}{3}} = \frac{1}{8^{\frac{2}{3}}}$

$= \frac{1}{(\sqrt[3]{8})^2}$

$= \frac{1}{4}$

The definition of a positive integral exponent, as indicating repeated multiplication, leads to the five exponent laws shown below. It can be shown that the definitions of integral and rational exponents are consistent with these laws. In fact, the definition of an exponent and the laws of exponents can even be extended to include irrational exponents such as π and $\sqrt{2}$.

Laws of Exponents for Real Exponents

If m and n are any real numbers, then

1. $a^m \times a^n = a^{m+n}$

2. $\dfrac{a^m}{a^n} = a^{m-n}$ $(a \neq 0)$

3. $(a^m)^n = a^{mn}$

4. $(ab)^n = a^n b^n$

5. $\left(\dfrac{a}{b}\right)^n = \dfrac{a^n}{b^n}$ $(b \neq 0)$

The laws of exponents are useful for simplifying expressions involving exponents.

Example 3. Simplify each expression.

a) $\dfrac{a^2 b^{-1}}{a^{-3} b}$

b) $\left(\dfrac{a^{\frac{1}{2}}}{b^{-2}}\right)^{\frac{2}{3}}$

c) $\left(\dfrac{x}{y^2}\right)^{\frac{1}{2}} (xy^2)^{-\frac{1}{2}}$

Solution. a) $\dfrac{a^2 b^{-1}}{a^{-3} b} = a^{2-(-3)} b^{-1-1}$

$= a^5 b^{-2}$, or $\dfrac{a^5}{b^2}$

b) $\left(\dfrac{a^{\frac{1}{2}}}{b^{-2}}\right)^{\frac{2}{3}} = (a^{\frac{1}{2}} b^2)^{\frac{2}{3}}$

$= a^{\frac{1}{3}} b^{\frac{4}{3}}$

c) $\left(\dfrac{x}{y^2}\right)^{\frac{1}{2}} (xy^2)^{-\frac{1}{2}} = (xy^{-2})^{\frac{1}{2}}(xy^2)^{-\frac{1}{2}}$

$= x^{\frac{1}{2}} y^{-1} x^{-\frac{1}{2}} y^{-1}$

$= x^0 y^{-2}$

$= \dfrac{1}{y^2}$

Example 4. If $x = 4$ and $y = \dfrac{1}{9}$, evaluate this expression. $(x^2 y^{-\frac{1}{2}})^{-2}(x^{-3}y)^{-\frac{1}{2}}$

Solution. Simplify the expression before substituting.

$(x^2 y^{-\frac{1}{2}})^{-2}(x^{-3}y)^{-\frac{1}{2}} = (x^{-4}y^1)(x^{\frac{3}{2}} y^{-\frac{1}{2}})$

$= x^{-\frac{5}{2}} y^{\frac{1}{2}}$

Substitute. $= 4^{-\frac{5}{2}} \left(\dfrac{1}{9}\right)^{\frac{1}{2}}$

$= \dfrac{1}{(\sqrt{4})^5} \left(\dfrac{1}{3}\right)$

$= \left(\dfrac{1}{32}\right)\left(\dfrac{1}{3}\right)$

$= \dfrac{1}{96}$

Example 5. a) Evaluate $3.2^{2.57}$ to the nearest thousandth.

b) Explain the meaning of the result.

Solution. a) Using the $\boxed{y^x}$ key on a calculator, we obtain
$3.2^{2.57} \doteq 19.872$

b) To explain the meaning of the result, write the exponent 2.57 in fractional form.

$2.57 = \dfrac{257}{100}$

Hence, $3.2^{2.57} = 3.2^{\frac{257}{100}}$

$= (\sqrt[100]{3.2})^{257}$

Hence, $(\sqrt[100]{3.2})^{257} \doteq 19.872$

EXERCISES 7-2

Ⓐ

1. Evaluate.

a) 7^0　　b) 5^{-1}　　c) $\left(\dfrac{2}{5}\right)^3$　　d) 2^{-3}　　e) 4^{-2}　　f) $\left(\dfrac{4}{9}\right)^0$

g) $\left(\dfrac{1}{2}\right)^{-2}$　h) $\left(\dfrac{3}{2}\right)^{-4}$　i) 8^{-2}　　j) $\left(\dfrac{5}{3}\right)^{-2}$　k) 3^4　　l) $\left(\dfrac{3}{4}\right)^{-3}$

2. Evaluate.

a) $27^{\frac{1}{3}}$　　b) 3^{-2}　　c) $(0.4)^{-1}$　　d) $25^{\frac{1}{2}}$　　e) $(0.008)^{-\frac{1}{3}}$　f) $16^{-\frac{1}{4}}$

g) 10^{-3}　h) $64^{\frac{1}{6}}$　i) $\left(\dfrac{25}{49}\right)^{-\frac{1}{2}}$　　j) $81^{-\frac{1}{2}}$　k) $(0.125)^{-\frac{1}{3}}$　l) $32^{\frac{1}{5}}$

3. Evaluate.

a) $36^{-\frac{3}{2}}$　　b) $27^{\frac{2}{3}}$　　c) $(0.125)^{-\frac{2}{3}}$　　d) $16^{-\frac{5}{4}}$　e) $9^{-\frac{5}{2}}$　f) $(2.25)^{\frac{3}{2}}$

g) $(0.6)^{-3}$　h) $100^{-\frac{3}{2}}$　i) $\left(\dfrac{8}{125}\right)^{\frac{2}{3}}$　　j) $(0.36)^{-\frac{3}{2}}$　k) $64^{\frac{5}{6}}$　l) $81^{-\frac{3}{4}}$

4. Evaluate.

a) $4^{2.5}$　　　　b) $25^{-1.5}$　　　c) $81^{-1.25}$　　　d) $400^{1.5}$

e) $32^{0.6}$　　　f) $\left(\dfrac{1}{16}\right)^{-0.75}$　　g) $\left(\dfrac{27}{49}\right)^0$　　h) $(6.25)^{-2.5}$

i) $(0.0625)^{-\frac{1}{4}}$　j) $\left(\dfrac{32}{243}\right)^{0.8}$　　k) $\left(\dfrac{9}{4}\right)^{-1.5}$　　l) $(5.25)^0$

5. Evaluate to the nearest thousandth.

a) $2.1^{1.6}$　　b) $3.7^{2.14}$　　c) $7.4^{0.85}$　　d) $16^{0.75}$　　e) $4.5^{3.19}$　　f) $1.9^{1.9}$

g) $1.4^{-2.2}$　h) $2.8^{-1.7}$　i) $4.65^{2.75}$　j) $0.52^{-3.61}$　k) $3.82^{-1.44}$　l) $1.75^{-0.64}$

6. Simplify.

a) $m^2 \times m^{-8}$　　　b) $\dfrac{x^{-4}}{x^{-9}}$　　　　　　c) $-15a^{-3} \times 3a^{10}$

d) $\dfrac{42s^4}{-3s^{-11}}$　　　e) $-3m^4 \times 12m^{-6} \times \dfrac{1}{4}m^7$　f) $\dfrac{(16n^{-2})(12n^{-3})}{15n^{-6}}$

7. Simplify.

a) $x^{\frac{2}{3}} \times x^{-\frac{5}{3}}$　　　　b) $\dfrac{s^{-\frac{3}{4}}}{s^{-\frac{1}{2}}}$　　　　c) $\dfrac{-12m^{-\frac{8}{5}}}{4m^{\frac{2}{5}}}$

d) $\dfrac{18a^{\frac{2}{5}}}{-6a^{-\frac{1}{5}}}$　　　e) $n^{\frac{3}{4}} \times n^{-\frac{3}{5}} \times n^{\frac{2}{3}}$　　f) $\dfrac{-5x^{-\frac{1}{2}} \times 8x^{-\frac{3}{4}}}{10x^{-2}}$

Ⓑ

8. Simplify.
   a) $3^2 - 16^{\frac{1}{2}}$
   b) $2^5 - 5^2$
   c) $3^{-2} + 2^{-3}$

   d) $2^{-4} - 4^{-2}$
   e) $3^3 - \left(\frac{1}{2}\right)^{-4}$
   f) $12^0 - 4^{-\frac{1}{2}}$

   g) $(8^{\frac{2}{3}})(16^{\frac{3}{2}})$
   h) $4^{\frac{1}{2}} + \left(\frac{1}{2}\right)^4$
   i) $\left(\frac{4}{9}\right)^{-\frac{3}{2}} \div \left(\frac{16}{25}\right)^{-\frac{1}{2}}$

9. A colony of insects doubles in size every 6 days. If there are now 2000 insects in the colony, how many
   a) will there be in: i) 12 days ii) 21 days iii) 3 days;
   b) were there: i) 6 days ago ii) 3 days ago iii) 10 days ago?

10. During the twentieth century, the population of Canada has been growing at the rate of approximately 1.85% per annum. The population in 1981 was 24.3 million.
    a) Write an equation representing the population P million as a function of the time t years relative to 1981.
    b) Use this equation to approximate the population in 1971.

11. In 1940, a large computer could perform about 100 operations per second. Since then, the speed of computers has multiplied 10-fold about every 7 years.
    a) Express the number of operations per second N as an exponential function of the time t years since 1940.
    b) About how many operations per second could computers perform in 1986?

12. Simplify.
    a) $\dfrac{-28a^2b^{-5}}{4a^{-7}b^3}$
    b) $4m^{-3}n^9 \times 5m^{-4}n^{-6}$
    c) $\dfrac{12x^{-2}y^4 \times 15x^7y^{-11}}{20x^{-4}y^5}$

    d) $\dfrac{6a^3b^{-7}c^0 \times 18a^{-5}b^2}{-9a^{-5}b^{-1}c^4}$
    e) $\dfrac{(14m^{-3}n)(-15m^4n^{-2})}{-21mn^{-5}}$
    f) $\dfrac{(24x^3z^{-4})(-35x^{-7}z^3)}{(-8x^5z^0)(-14x^{-5}z^{-6})}$

13. Simplify.
    a) $\dfrac{-12a^{-\frac{1}{3}}b}{3a^{-\frac{1}{3}}b^{\frac{2}{3}}}$
    b) $\dfrac{-25m^{\frac{3}{4}}n^{-\frac{1}{2}}}{-10m^{-\frac{1}{4}}n^{\frac{1}{3}}}$
    c) $\left(\dfrac{x^{\frac{2}{3}}}{y^{-\frac{1}{2}}}\right)^{\frac{6}{5}}$

    d) $\left(\dfrac{a^2}{b^{\frac{1}{3}}}\right)^{\frac{3}{4}}(a^2b^{-1})^{-3}$
    e) $\left(\dfrac{m^{\frac{3}{4}}n^{\frac{4}{3}}}{m^2}\right)^{\frac{2}{3}}$
    f) $\dfrac{(a^{-5}b^3)^{\frac{1}{2}}}{a^{-\frac{2}{3}}b^{-\frac{1}{2}}}$

14. Simplify.
    a) $\dfrac{-21m^{\frac{5}{6}}n^{-\frac{1}{3}}}{7m^{\frac{1}{2}}n^{\frac{1}{6}}}$
    b) $-7a^{\frac{2}{3}}b^{-\frac{1}{2}} \times 6a^{-\frac{1}{2}}b^{\frac{2}{3}}$

    c) $\dfrac{-8x^{-\frac{4}{3}}y^{\frac{1}{2}} \times 6x^{-\frac{3}{4}}y^{-\frac{2}{3}}}{24x^{-\frac{5}{6}}y^{-\frac{1}{6}}}$
    d) $\dfrac{(9a^{-\frac{1}{3}}b^{-\frac{4}{5}}c^{-\frac{4}{5}})(-4a^{-\frac{1}{2}}b^{\frac{3}{5}}c^0)}{-18a^{\frac{1}{6}}b^{-\frac{1}{2}}c^{-\frac{1}{3}}}$

e) $\dfrac{(13a^{-\frac{3}{4}}c^{-\frac{1}{2}})(-6a^{-\frac{1}{2}}c^{-\frac{3}{2}})}{(-21c^{\frac{1}{4}})(-39a^{-\frac{3}{2}}c^{\frac{3}{4}})}$

f) $\dfrac{(25x^{\frac{1}{4}}z^{\frac{1}{2}})(-16x^{-\frac{3}{4}}z^{\frac{3}{2}})}{(-6x^{-\frac{1}{4}}z^{-\frac{1}{2}})(-15x^{\frac{3}{2}}z^{\frac{3}{4}})}$

15. If $a = \dfrac{1}{8}$ and $b = 4$, evaluate each expression.

   a) $a^{-1}b^{\frac{1}{2}}$ b) $(a^{-2}b^{\frac{1}{2}})(a^{\frac{1}{3}}b^{\frac{3}{2}})^{-1}$ c) $(a^{\frac{4}{3}}b^{-\frac{3}{2}})^{3}(a^{-2}b^{\frac{5}{2}})$ d) $(a^{\frac{2}{3}}b^{-2})^{2}(a^{-\frac{2}{3}}b^{-1})^{-3}$

16. If $x = \dfrac{4}{9}$ and $y = 27$, evaluate each expression.

   a) $-x^{2}y^{\frac{2}{3}}$ b) $(3x^{-1}y^{\frac{1}{3}})(-4x^{\frac{3}{2}})^{-2}$ c) $\dfrac{6x^{-\frac{3}{2}}y^{-\frac{2}{3}}}{16x^{-\frac{5}{2}}y^{-\frac{4}{3}}}$ d) $\dfrac{-16x^{-\frac{5}{2}}y^{\frac{4}{3}}}{-9x^{-\frac{1}{2}}y^{-\frac{1}{3}}}$

17. If $x = 2a^{4}$, $y = a^{3}$, and $z = \dfrac{1}{2}a^{2}$, write each expression as an exponential function of a.

   a) $(xyz)^{\frac{1}{2}}$ b) $xy^{-2}z^{-1}$ c) $(3x^{2}yz)^{3}$

18. If $p = 3x$, $q = \dfrac{2}{3}x^{2}$, and $r = x^{5}$, write each expression as an exponential function of x.

   a) $p^{2}qr$ b) $p^{-1}q^{2}r^{-3}$ c) $(9p^{-2}q^{2}r^{-1})^{-1}$

19. Simplify.

   a) $\dfrac{(x^{2a})(x^{-5a})}{x^{-3a}}$ b) $\dfrac{(s^{2n})(s^{-n})}{(s^{-3n})(s^{-4n})}$ c) $\dfrac{(a^{x-1})(a^{x+1})}{a^{2x-1}}$

   d) $\dfrac{(m^{-ac})(m^{-ab})}{m^{-bc}}$ e) $\dfrac{(x^{-3})^{a}(x^{a})^{2}}{x^{a-2}}$ f) $\dfrac{(a^{2x-y})(a^{x-y})}{(3a^{x+y})^{2}}$

   g) $\dfrac{(x^{\frac{a}{4}})(x^{-\frac{a}{3}})}{x^{\frac{a}{12}}}$ h) $\dfrac{(m^{-\frac{n}{2}})(n^{-\frac{m}{4}})}{(m^{\frac{n}{3}})(n^{\frac{m}{2}})}$ i) $\dfrac{(a^{-\frac{x}{2}})^{3}(a^{-\frac{x}{3}})^{4}}{(a^{\frac{x}{4}})^{2}}$

Ⓒ

20. Use your calculator to evaluate to the nearest thousandth.
   a) 3^{π} b) π^{π} c) $10^{\sqrt{2}}$ d) $(\sqrt{2})^{\sqrt{3}}$
   e) $4^{-\pi}$ f) $7^{-\sqrt{2}}$ g) $2^{\sqrt{\pi}}$ h) $2^{\sqrt{2}} + 2^{-\sqrt{2}}$

21. a) Evaluate each power.
   i) 2^{2} ii) $(0.5)^{2}$ iii) 2^{-2} iv) $(0.5)^{-2}$
   v) $4^{\frac{1}{2}}$ vi) $(0.25)^{\frac{1}{2}}$ vii) $4^{-\frac{1}{2}}$ viii) $(0.25)^{-\frac{1}{2}}$
   b) Using the results of part a) as a guide, make a conjecture about how you can tell, given the values of x and y ($y > 0$), if:
   i) $y^{x} > 1$ ii) $0 < y^{x} < 1$.

22. Write as a single power.

   a) $3(5)^{\frac{1}{3}} + 2(5)^{\frac{1}{3}}$ b) $(2^{x})^{2} + 2^{2x}$ c) $3(4)^{x} + 2^{2x}$

 **PROBLEM SOLVING**

Look for a Pattern

"One cannot escape the feeling that these mathematical formulas have an independent existence and an intelligence of their own, that they are wiser than we are, wiser even than their discoverers, that we get more out of them than was originally put into them."

Heinrich Hertz

Find a function $f(x)$ such that $f(x + 2) = 9f(x)$ for all values of x.

Understand the problem
- What does $f(x + 2)$ mean?
- What does $9f(x)$ mean?

Think of a strategy
- The left side involves addition, and the right side involves multiplication. What kinds of functions relate addition and multiplication?
- The numbers in the given equation are 2 and 9. What kind of natural number is 9? How might this be related to the 2?
- What kind of function might $f(x)$ be?

Carry out the strategy
- The function $f(x)$ might be an exponential function.
- Let $f(x) = a^x$, where x is a constant to be determined.
- If $f(x) = a^x$, then what does $f(x + 2)$ equal? What does $9f(x)$ equal?
- Since $f(x + 2) = 9f(x)$, can you find the value of a?
- What is the function $f(x)$?

Look back
- For the function $f(x)$ you found, check that $f(x + 2) = 9f(x)$.
- Is the function $f(x)$ unique?
- Write similar relations involving $f(x + 3)$, $f(x + 4)$, ..., $f(x + n)$.
- Find a function $f(x)$ such that $f(x + n) = kf(x)$ for all values of x.

PROBLEMS

(B)

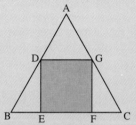

1. Triangle ABC is an equilateral triangle with sides 6 cm long. Calculate the area of the shaded square, to the nearest hundredth of a square centimetre.

2. The natural number 64 is both a perfect square (since $64 = 8^2$) and a perfect cube (since $64 = 4^3$).
   a) Find other natural numbers which are both perfect squares and perfect cubes.
   b) Find a natural number which is a perfect square, a perfect cube, and a perfect fourth power.

3. Three cylindrical logs with radius 10 cm are piled as shown. Determine the distance from the top of the pile to the ground.

4. Find the equations of the lines which are parallel to the line $3x - 4y + 12 = 0$, and 2 units from it.

(C)

5. If the sides of a triangle are in the ratio 3 : 4 : 5, the triangle is right-angled. Find out something about a triangle whose sides are in the ratio 4 : 5 : 6, and prove your result.

6. The double factorial symbol !! is defined as follows.
   $n!! = n(n - 2)(n - 4) \ldots 5 \times 3 \times 1$ if n is odd
   $\quad\quad n(n - 2)(n - 4) \ldots 6 \times 4 \times 2$ if n is even
   a) Simplify $n!!(n - 1)!!$ b) Prove that $(2n)!! = 2^n(n!)$
   c) Find a similar expression for $(2n - 1)!!$

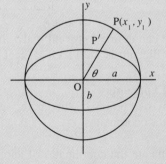

7. The ellipse $b^2x^2 + a^2y^2 = a^2b^2$ is inscribed in the circle $x^2 + y^2 = a^2$. $P(x_1, y_1)$ is any point on the circle, forming an angle θ with the major axis. If P′ is the corresponding point on the ellipse, determine the ratio $\dfrac{OP'}{OP}$ in terms of a, b, and θ.

(D)

8. Prove that it is impossible to fill a rectangular box completely with cubes no two of which are congruent.

7-3 GRAPHING EXPONENTIAL FUNCTIONS

Some of the properties of exponential functions that we have studied can be illustrated on a graph. For example, we can graph the function $f(x) = 2^x$ using a table of values.

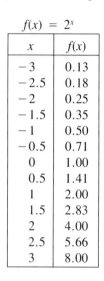

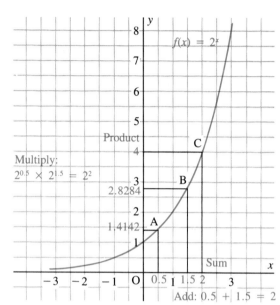

We can use the graph to illustrate the following properties of the function $f(x) = 2^x$.

Vertical intercept

$f(0) = 2^0$
$\quad\ \ = 1$

The vertical intercept is 1.

Horizontal intercept

Let $f(x) = 0$.
Then $2^x = 0$
This equation has no real solution since $2^x > 0$ for all real values of x. Hence, there is no horizontal intercept.

Domain

Since we can define 2^x for all real values of x, the domain is the set of all real numbers.

Range

Since there is a value of x for all positive real values of 2^x, the range is the set of all positive real numbers.

Law of Exponents

Select any two points on the curve, such as $A(0.5, 2^{0.5})$ and $B(1.5, 2^{1.5})$.
Add their x-coordinates.   *Multiply* their y-coordinates.
$0.5 + 1.5 = 2$ $(2^{0.5})(2^{1.5}) = 2^2$
The results are the coordinates of another point $C(2, 2^2)$ on the graph.
Is this true for any two points on the graph?

    We can graph other exponential functions using tables of values, but it is more efficient to sketch the graphs by considering how they are related to the graph of $f(x) = 2^x$, which we have already drawn.

Example 1. Sketch these functions on the same grid.

a) $f(x) = 2^x$ b) $g(x) = 1.5^x$ c) $h(x) = 1^x$ d) $k(x) = 0.5^x$

Solution. All four graphs pass through the point (0,1).

a) The graph of $f(x) = 2^x$ is shown.

b) If $x > 0$, then $1.5^x < 2^x$. Hence, in the first quadrant, the graph of $g(x) = 1.5^x$ lies below that of $f(x) = 2^x$. To judge how far below, use a test point. Substitute $x = 2$ into 1.5^x to get 2.25. Hence, the point (2, 2.25) lies on the graph.

Conversely, if $x < 0$, then $1.5^x > 2^x$. Hence, in the second quadrant, the graph of $g(x) = 1.5^x$ lies above that of $f(x) = 2^x$. To judge how far above, use a test point. Substitute $x = -2$ into 1.5^x to get approximately 0.44. Hence, (−2, 0.44) lies on the graph.

c) Since $1^x = 1$ for all values of x, the graph of $h(x) = 1^x$ is a horizontal line 1 unit above the x-axis.

d) If $x > 0$, 0.5^x is less than 1. Also, as x increases, 0.5^x becomes closer and closer to 0. If $x < 0$, 0.5^x becomes larger and larger, without limit.

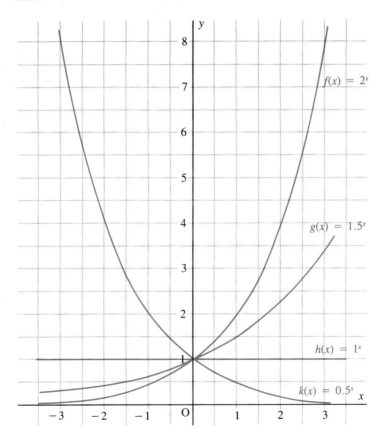

Example 1 illustrates properties of the graph of the exponential function $f(x) = a^x$.

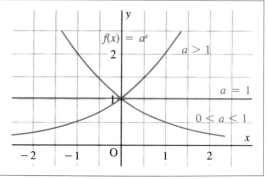

Properties of the graph of the function $f(x) = a^x$

Vertical intercept: 1

Horizontal intercept: none

Domain: all real numbers

Range: all positive real numbers

Example 2. Prove that if (x_1, y_1) and (x_2, y_2) are points on the graph of $f(x) = a^x$, then $(x_1 + x_2, y_1y_2)$ is also a point on the graph.

Solution. Since (x_1, y_1) is on the graph of $f(x) = a^x$, its coordinates satisfy the equation $y = a^x$.

Hence, $y_1 = a^{x_1}$ ... ①

Similarly, $y_2 = a^{x_2}$ ... ②

Multiply equations ① and ②, and use the law of exponents.

$$y_1y_2 = (a^{x_1})(a^{x_2})$$
$$= a^{x_1+x_2}$$

Hence, the coordinates of the point $(x_1 + x_2, y_1y_2)$ also satisfy the equation $y = a^x$. That is, $(x_1 + x_2, y_1y_2)$ is also a point on the graph of $f(x) = a^x$.

The result of *Example 2* is a consequence of the law of exponents for multiplication. Adding the horizontal coordinates of points on the graph of $f(x) = a^x$ corresponds to multiplying their vertical coordinates.

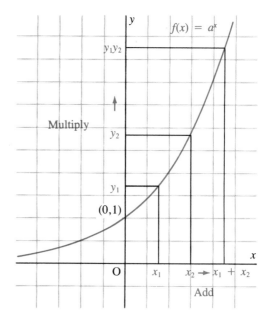

EXERCISES 7-3

1. Identify the graph which best represents each function.

   a) $f(x) = 3^x$ b) $g(x) = 10^x$ c) $h(x) = \left(\dfrac{3}{4}\right)^x$ d) $k(x) = \left(\dfrac{1}{4}\right)^x$

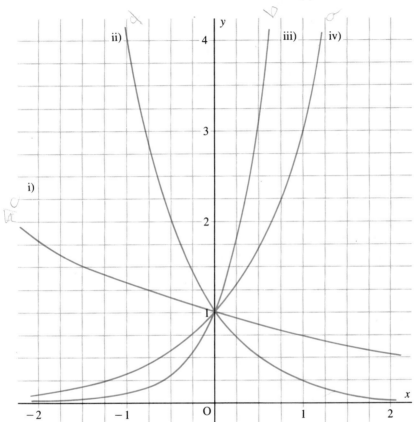

2. Describe how the graph of $f(x) = a^x$ varies as a varies.

3. a) Make tables of values and graph these functions on the same grid.

   $$f_1(x) = 3^x \text{ for } -2 \le x \le 2 \qquad f_2(x) = \left(\frac{1}{3}\right)^x \text{ for } -2 \le x \le 2$$

   b) On the same grid as in part a), sketch the graph of each function.

   $$f_1(x) = 4^x \qquad g_1(x) = 2^x \qquad f_2(x) = \left(\frac{1}{2}\right)^x \qquad g_2(x) = \left(\frac{1}{4}\right)^x$$

4. Draw the graphs of these functions on the same grid.

   $$f_1(x) = 2^x \qquad g_1(x) = 5^x \qquad h_1(x) = 10^x$$
   $$f_2(x) = \left(\frac{1}{2}\right)^x \qquad g_2(x) = \left(\frac{1}{5}\right)^x \qquad h_2(x) = \left(\frac{1}{10}\right)^x$$

5. Find each value of a if the graph of $f(x) = a^x$ passes through each point.
   a) A(3, 216)   b) B(5, 32)   c) C(3, 512)   d) D(4, 256)
   e) E(-2, 64)   f) F$\left(-3, \dfrac{1}{216}\right)$ g) G(3, 343)   h) H$\left(\dfrac{1}{3}, 3\right)$

6. Prove that if $f(x) = a^x$, then $f(x)f(y) = f(x + y)$.

7. a) Prove that if (x_1, y_1) and (x_2, y_2) are two points on the graph of $f(x) = a^x$, then
      both $(x_1 + x_2, y_1y_2)$ and $\left(x_1 - x_2, \dfrac{y_1}{y_2}\right)$ are points on the graph.
   b) Prove that if (x_1, y_1) is a point on the graph of $f(x) = a^x$, then both $(2x_1, y_1{}^2)$
      and $\left(-x_1, \dfrac{1}{y_1}\right)$ are points on the graph.

8. a) Graph the function $f(x) = 2^x$.
   b) On the same grid as in part a), sketch the graph of each function.
      i) $y = f(x) - 1$ ii) $y = f(x - 1)$ iii) $y = f(x + 1)$
      iv) $y = f(0.5x)$ v) $y = f(2x)$ vi) $y = f(-x)$

9. If $a > 0$, for what values of a and x is each statement true?
   a) $a^x = 1$ b) $a^x > 1$ c) $0 < a^x < 1$

10. a) Graph the function $f(x) = 2^x$ for $-3 \leqslant x \leqslant 3$.
    b) By expressing 5 as a power of 2, show that the graph of $g(x) = 5^x$ is a horizontal
       compression of the graph of $f(x) = 2^x$.
    c) Similarly, show that the graph of $h(x) = 1.5^x$ is a horizontal expansion of the
       graph of $f(x) = 2^x$.
    d) Use the results of parts b) and c) to graph the functions $g(x) = 5^x$ and $h(x) = 1.5^x$
       on the same grid as in part a).

11. Explain why the graphs of all exponential functions can be regarded as
    transformations of the graph of $f(x) = 2^x$.

12. Graph each function.
    a) $f(x) = 2^{|x|}$ b) $f(x) = x(2^x)$ c) $f(x) = x^x$

 INVESTIGATE

The ⬚log⬚ key on a Calculator

Find out what the ⬚log⬚ key on your calculator does. Try a wide variety of
numbers such as those below. Look for patterns in the results.
- Numbers selected at random, for example, 3, 65, 239, 4772
- Powers of 10; for example, 10, 100, 1000, 10 000, 1, 0.1, 0.01, 0.001
- Multiples of 10; for example, 20, 200, 2000, 30, 300, 3000
- Zero and negative numbers; for example, 0, -2, -3, -10

Write a report of your findings.

7-4 COMMON LOGARITHMS

In *Exercises 7-1* we encountered problems such as these.

In how many years will an investment of $500 double in value at 8% per annum compounded annually?

The answer to this question is the solution of this equation.

$$1000 = 500(1.08)^n$$
or $(1.08)^n = 2$

At what depth under water is the light level 50% of the light level at the surface?

The answer to this question is the solution of this equation.

$$50 = 100(0.975)^d$$
or $(0.975)^d = 0.5$

In these equations the variable appears in an exponent. Such equations are called *exponential equations*, and they can be solved to any degree of accuracy by systematic trial. However, exponential equations occur so frequently in applications that mathematicians have developed a more direct method of solution. This method involves logarithms. After defining a logarithm and introducing some of its properties, we will show how the above equations can be solved using logarithms.

In the preceding investigation you may have discovered that the ⌊log⌋ key of a calculator gives exponents for powers of 10.

Using a calculator: $\log 100 = 2$
2 is the exponent that 100 has when it is expressed as a power of 10.
Since $100 = 10^2$
we write $\log 100 = 2$

Using a calculator: $\log 0.001 = -3$
-3 is the exponent that 0.001 has when it is expressed as a power of 10.
Since $0.001 = 10^{-3}$
we write $\log 0.001 = -3$

These logarithms are called *common logarithms* since they are the exponents of numbers written as powers with base 10. In a later section we will study logarithms with bases other than 10.

Definition of a Logarithm
- $\log x$ is the exponent that x would have if it were written as a power with base 10.
- $\log x = y$ means that $x = 10^y$.

Since $10^y > 0$ for all real values of y, then $x > 0$. Hence, $\log x$ is defined as a real number only when $x > 0$.

Example 1. Use the definition of a logarithm to evaluate each expression.
a) $\log 100\ 000$ b) $\log 0.01$ c) $\log \sqrt{10}$ d) $\log 1$

Solution.   a) Since $100\ 000 = 10^5$, then $\log 100\ 000 = 5$
b) Since $0.01 = 10^{-2}$, then $\log 0.01 = -2$
c) Since $\sqrt{10} = 10^{0.5}$, then $\log \sqrt{10} = 0.5$
d) Since $1 = 10^0$, then $\log 1 = 0$

The answers in *Example 1* can be checked with a calculator.

We can use the $\boxed{\log}$ key of a calculator to find approximations to the logarithm of any positive number. Hence, we can write any positive number as a power of 10.

Example 2. Use your calculator to evaluate each logarithm. Then write the result in exponential form.

a) log 7   b) log 500   c) log 0.4

Solution. a) $\log 7 \doteq 0.845\ 098$
This means that $10^{0.845098} \doteq 7$
b) $\log 500 \doteq 2.698\ 97$
This means that $10^{2.69897} \doteq 500$
c) $\log 0.4 \doteq -0.397\ 94$
This means that $10^{-0.39794} \doteq 0.4$

The results in *Example 2* can be checked using the $\boxed{10^x}$ or $\boxed{y^x}$ keys.

Since log x is defined as a real number only when $x > 0$, you will get an error message if you attempt to find the logarithm of 0, or of a negative number.

log $0 = y$ means $10^y = 0$, which is impossible.   log $(-2) = y$ means $10^y = -2$, which is impossible.

Example 3. Simplify each expression.

a) log 10^x b) $10^{\log x}$

Solution. a) log 10^x is the exponent that 10^x would have if it were written as a power of 10. But, 10^x *is* written as a power of 10, and has exponent x. Hence, log $10^x = x$
b) $10^{\log x}$ is 10 raised to the exponent that x would have if x were written as a power of 10. Hence, $10^{\log x} = x$

Example 3 shows that taking a common logarithm of a number and raising the number to a power of 10 are inverse operations, just as squaring a number and taking the square root of the number are inverse operations. If your calculator has a $\boxed{10^x}$ key, you can illustrate this by using the $\boxed{10^x}$ and $\boxed{\log}$ keys in succession in either order. For example, $\log\left(10^{4.5}\right) = 4.5$ and $10^{\log 4.5} = 4.5$

Summary
- A logarithm is an exponent.
- log $x = y$ means that $x = 10^y$, $x > 0$.
- log x is defined only when $x > 0$.
- log $10^x = x$ and $10^{\log x} = x$

EXERCISES 7-4

(A)

1. Use the definition to evaluate each logarithm.
   a) log 100
   b) log 1000
   c) log 1 000 000
   d) log 10
   e) log 0.1
   f) log 0.001
   g) log 1
   h) log $\sqrt[3]{10}$
   i) log 10^5
   j) log $10^{\frac{1}{5}}$
   k) log $10^{\frac{2}{3}}$
   l) log 10^n

2. Use your calculator to evaluate each logarithm to 4 decimal places. Then write each result in exponential form, and check it with the calculator.
   a) log 5
   b) log 18
   c) log 62.4
   d) log 4877
   e) log 0.25
   f) log 0.8
   g) log 0.02
   h) log 0.006

3. In 1987, the Canadian astronomer Ian Shelton discovered a supernova, or exploding star, from an observatory in Chile. State the common logarithm of each number.
   a) The supernova was more than 100 000 light years, or 10^{20} m, from the Earth.
   b) At its brightest, a supernova is about 10^9 times as bright as a star like the sun.
   c) Throughout recorded history only about 10 supernovas have been visible to the unaided eye.

4. On a single optical disk, an amount of data equivalent to all the text appearing in 15 years of daily newspapers can be recorded. State the common logarithm of each number.
   a) More than 10^{12} bytes of data are recorded on each disk.
   b) To avoid errors, a laser beam is focused within 10^{-7} m of dead centre for each pit on the surface of the disk.
   c) The error rate for a typical disk is 10^{-12}.

(B)

5. Write in exponential form.
   a) log 10 000 = 4
   b) log 10 = 1
   c) log 0.01 = -2

6. Write in logarithmic form.
   a) 10^3 = 1000
   b) 10^0 = 1
   c) 10^{-3} = 0.001

7. One centillion is defined as the 100th power of 1 000 000. What is the common logarithm of one centillion?

8. Solve each equation.
   a) log x = 2
   b) log x = 5
   c) log x = -3
   d) log x = 0
   e) log x = 1
   f) log log x = 1

9. Simplify each expression.
   a) log 10^4
   b) log 10^5
   c) log 10^{-3}
   d) $10^{\log 100}$
   e) $10^{\log 20}$
   f) $10^{\log 0.2}$

10. a) Use your calculator to evaluate each logarithm.
    i) log 2
    ii) log 20
    iii) log 200
    iv) log 2000
    v) log 0.2
    vi) log 0.02
    vii) log 0.002
    viii) log 0.0002
    b) Account for the pattern in the results.

7-5 THE LAWS OF LOGARITHMS (BASE 10)

A logarithm is an exponent. Hence, it should be possible to write the laws of exponents in logarithmic form.

Consider an example of the law of exponents for multiplication, such as $10^2 \times 10^3 = 10^5$. Since $\log 10^2 = 2$, $\log 10^3 = 3$, and $\log 10^5 = 5$, we can write this equation as:

$$\log 10^2 + \log 10^3 = \log 10^5$$
or $\qquad \log 10^5 = \log 10^2 + \log 10^3$

This example suggests that a possible law of logarithms for multiplication might be $\log xy = \log x + \log y$. This equation states that the exponent that xy would have if it were expressed as a power of 10 is equal to the sum of the exponents that x and y would have if they were expressed as powers of 10.

Theorem   **Law of Logarithms for Multiplication (Base 10)**

If x and y are any positive real numbers, then $\log xy = \log x + \log y$

Given: Two real numbers x and y
Required to Prove: $\log xy = \log x + \log y$
Proof: Let $\log x = M$ and $\log y = N$
$$x = 10^M \qquad y = 10^N$$
Hence, $xy = (10^M)(10^N)$
$$= 10^{M+N}$$
Therefore, $\log xy = \log (10^{M+N})$
$$= M + N$$
$$= \log x + \log y$$

Corollary   **Law of Logarithms for Division (Base 10)**

If x and y are any positive real numbers, then $\log \left(\dfrac{x}{y}\right) = \log x - \log y$

Example 1.   Write $\log 6$ as:
  a) a sum of two logarithms   b) a difference of two logarithms.

Solution.   a) Since $6 = 2 \times 3$, then by the law of logarithms for multiplication,
  $\log 6 = \log 2 + \log 3$
  b) Since $6 = 12 \div 2$, then by the law of logarithms for division,
  $\log 6 = \log 12 - \log 2$

In *Example 1*, $\log 6$ can be expressed as a sum or a difference of logarithms in infinitely many other ways, such as:
$\log 6 = \log 1.5 + \log 4 \qquad \log 6 = \log 18 - \log 3$
$\log 6 = \log 10 + \log 0.6 \qquad \log 6 = \log 60 - \log 10$
Check these results with your calculator.

Example 2. Write each expression as a single logarithm.

        a) $\log 5 + \log 4$ b) $\log 21 - \log 3$

Solution.   a) $\log 5 + \log 4 = \log (5 \times 4)$ b) $\log 21 - \log 3 = \log \left(\dfrac{21}{3}\right)$

                               $= \log 20$ $= \log 7$

Example 3. Given that $\log 5 \doteq 0.698\ 97$, find an approximation for each logarithm.

        a) $\log 50$ b) $\log 500$ c) $\log 0.5$ d) $\log 0.05$

Solution.   a) $\log 50 = \log 10 + \log 5$ b) $\log 500 = \log 100 + \log 5$

                        $\doteq 1 + 0.698\ 97$ $\doteq 2 + 0.698\ 97$

                        $\doteq 1.698\ 97$ $\doteq 2.698\ 97$

    c) $\log 0.5 = \log 5 - \log 10$ d) $\log 0.05 = \log 5 - \log 100$

                      $\doteq 0.698\ 97 - 1$ $\doteq 0.698\ 97 - 2$

                      $\doteq -0.301\ 03$ $\doteq -1.301\ 03$

Check the results of *Examples 2* and *3* with your calculator.

The law of logarithms for products may be applied when the factors are equal. For example, if $x = y$, then the law:

    $\log xy = \log x + \log y$ may be written

  $\log (x)(x) = \log x + \log x$

or $\log (x^2) = 2 \log x$

This example suggests that a possible law of logarithms for powers might be $\log (x^n) = n \log x$. This equation states that the exponent that x^n would have if it were expressed as a power of 10 is n times the exponent that x would have if it were expressed as a power of 10.

Theorem   **Law of Logarithms for Powers (Base 10)**

If x and n are real numbers, and $x > 0$, then $\log (x^n) = n \log x$

Given: Two real numbers x and n, where $x > 0$

Required to Prove: $\log (x^n) = n \log x$

Proof: Let $\log x = M$

        $x = 10^M$

  Hence, $x^n = (10^M)^n$

           $= 10^{nM}$

  Therefore, $\log (x^n) = \log (10^{nM})$

                $= nM$

                $= n \log x$

Corollary   **Law of Logarithms for Roots (Base 10)**

If x and n are real numbers, and $x > 0$, then $\log \sqrt[n]{x} = \dfrac{1}{n} \log x$

Example 4. a) Write log 125 as a product of a whole number and a logarithm.
b) Write 4 log 3 as a single logarithm.

Solution. a) Since $125 = 5^3$, then $\log 125 = \log (5^3)$
$$= 3 \log 5$$
b) $4 \log 3 = \log (3^4)$, or log 81

Example 5. Given that $\log 2 \doteq 0.301\ 03$, find an approximation for each logarithm.
a) log 8
b) $\log \sqrt[3]{2}$

Solution. a) $\log 8 = \log (2^3)$
$$= 3 \log 2$$
$$\doteq 3(0.301\ 03)$$
$$\doteq 0.903\ 09$$

b) $\log \sqrt[3]{2} = \log (2^{\frac{1}{3}})$
$$= \frac{1}{3} \log 2$$
$$\doteq \frac{1}{3}(0.301\ 03)$$
$$\doteq 0.100\ 34$$

Check the results of *Examples 4* and *5* with your calculator.

Laws of Logarithms (Base 10)
- Multiplication $\log xy = \log x + \log y$ $x, y > 0$
- Division $\log \left(\frac{x}{y}\right) = \log x - \log y$ $x, y > 0$
- Powers $\log (x^n) = n \log x$ $x > 0$
- Roots $\log \sqrt[n]{x} = \frac{1}{n} \log x$ $x > 0$

These laws are the laws of exponents (with base 10) restated in logarithmic form.

Example 6. Write in terms of log *a* and log *b*.
a) $\log (100ab^2)$
b) $\log \left(\frac{a^2}{\sqrt{b}}\right)$

Solution. a) $\log (100ab^2) = \log 100 + \log a + \log (b^2)$
$$= 2 + \log a + 2 \log b$$
b) $\log \left(\frac{a^2}{\sqrt{b}}\right) = \log (a^2) - \log (\sqrt{b})$
$$= 2 \log a - \frac{1}{2} \log b$$

Example 7. Write as a single logarithm.
a) $\log a + \log b - \log c$
b) $\log a + 3 \log b - \frac{1}{2} \log c$

Solution. a) $\log a + \log b - \log c = \log ab - \log c$
$$= \log \left(\frac{ab}{c}\right)$$
b) $\log a + 3 \log b - \frac{1}{2} \log c = \log a + \log (b^3) - \log \sqrt{c}$
$$= \log \left(\frac{ab^3}{\sqrt{c}}\right)$$

An important application of the laws of logarithms is to the problem of expressing any positive number as a power of any other positive number (except 1).

Example 8. Express 19 as a power of 2 and check with a calculator.

Solution. Let $19 = 2^x$

Take the logarithm of each side.

$\log 19 = \log (2^x)$

$\log 19 = x \log 2$

Hence, $x = \dfrac{\log 19}{\log 2}$

$\doteq 4.247\ 927\ 5$

Therefore, $19 \doteq 2^{4.2479275}$

To check, use the $\boxed{y^x}$ key on your calculator.

EXERCISES 7-5

(A)

1. Write as a single logarithm, and check with your calculator.
   a) $\log 6 + \log 7$ b) $\log 24 - \log 6$ c) $\log 3 + \log 8$
   d) $\log 35 - \log 5$ e) $\log 12 + \log 7$ f) $\log 1 - \log 2$
   g) $\log 5 + \log 8 - \log 4$ h) $\log 6 + \log 3 + \log 5$
   i) $\log 12 - \log 4 + \log 7$ j) $\log 7 + \log 8 - \log 2$

2. Write as a sum of logarithms, and check with your calculator.
   a) $\log 10$ b) $\log 21$ c) $\log 28$ d) $\log 36$
   e) $\log 9$ f) $\log 44$ g) $\log 57$ h) $\log 121$

3. Write as a difference of logarithms, and check with your calculator.
   a) $\log 5$ b) $\log 8$ c) $\log 12$ d) $\log 13$
   e) $\log 10$ f) $\log 21$ g) $\log 17$ h) $\log 40$

4. Write as a product of a whole number and a logarithm, and check with your calculator.
   a) $\log 9$ b) $\log 25$ c) $\log 8$ d) $\log 27$
   e) $\log 1000$ f) $\log 32$ g) $\log 343$ h) $\log 128$

5. Write as a single logarithm, and check with your calculator.
   a) $2 \log 6$ b) $3 \log 4$ c) $2 \log 9$ d) $2 \log 7$
   e) $5 \log 3$ f) $4 \log 2$ g) $3 \log 6$ h) $5 \log 10$

(B)

6. Given $\log 3 \doteq 0.477\ 12$, find an approximation for each logarithm.
   a) $\log 30$ b) $\log 3000$ c) $\log 0.3$ d) $\log 0.003$
   e) $\log 9$ f) $\log 81$ g) $\log \sqrt{3}$ h) $\log \sqrt[5]{3}$

7. Given that $\log 5 \doteq 0.698\ 97$, find an approximation for each logarithm.
   a) $\log 625$ b) $\log \sqrt[3]{5}$ c) $\log 0.2$ d) $\log 0.04$

8. If $\log 70 \doteq 1.8451$, find an approximation for each logarithm.
   a) $\log 7$
   b) $\log 700$
   c) $\log 0.07$
   d) $\log 0.7$
   e) $\log 700\,000$
   f) $\log 0.007$

9. Write in terms of $\log a$ and $\log b$.
   a) $\log (1000ab)$
   b) $\log (a^2b)$
   c) $\log (a\sqrt{b})$
   d) $\log \left(\dfrac{a}{b^2}\right)$
   e) $\log \left(\dfrac{\sqrt{a}}{b}\right)$
   f) $\log \left(\dfrac{\sqrt[3]{a}}{b^2}\right)$

10. Write each expression in terms of $\log x$.
    a) $\log (10x^2)$
    b) $\log \sqrt{x}$
    c) $\log \sqrt{10x}$
    d) $\log \sqrt{10x}$
    e) $\log 10\sqrt{x}$

11. Write as a single logarithm.
    a) $\log x + \log y - \log z$
    b) $\log m - (\log n + \log p)$
    c) $\log a + \log b - \log c - \log d$
    d) $\log a + \log (a + b) - \log (a - b)$

12. Write as a single logarithm.

    a) $2 \log a + 5 \log b$

    b) $3 \log x + \dfrac{1}{2} \log y$

    c) $2 \log m + \log n - 5 \log p$

    d) $\dfrac{1}{2} \log x - 2 \log y - \log z$

    e) $3 \log a + \dfrac{1}{2} \log b - \dfrac{5}{4} \log c$

    f) $10 \log a - 3 \log b + \dfrac{1}{2} \log c - \log d$

13. Write as a single logarithm. For what values of the variable is each expression not defined?
    a) $\log (x + 3) - \log (x - 1)$
    b) $\log (2x - 7) - \log (x + 3)$
    c) $-\log (a - 2) + \log (a + 2)$
    d) $\log (8a + 15) - \log (2a + 3)$

14. If $\log 2 = x$ and $\log 3 = y$, write each logarithm as an expression in x and y.
    a) $\log 6$
    b) $\log 1.5$
    c) $\log 60$
    d) $\log 12$
    e) $\log 18$
    f) $\log 36$
    g) $\log 3.6$
    h) $\log \left(\dfrac{1}{6}\right)$

15. Express.
    a) 7 as a power of 3
    b) 5 as a power of 2
    c) 29 as a power of 2
    d) 77 as a power of 8
    e) 3 as a power of 0.5
    f) 0.45 as a power of 6

16. Solve to the nearest thousandth.
    a) $2^x = 11$
    b) $3^x = 17$
    c) $6^x = 5$
    d) $5^{x-1} = 9$
    e) $2^{x+3} = 6$
    f) $5^{1+x} = 2^{1-x}$

17. Solve.
    a) $3^x = 2$
    b) $4^x = 5$
    c) $7^{-x} = 3$
    d) $3^{1-x} = 5$
    e) $\left(\dfrac{1}{8}\right)^x = 25$
    f) $5^{3x} = 41$

18. x and y are two positive numbers. How are $\log x$ and $\log y$ related if:

   a) $y = 10x$

   b) $y = \dfrac{1}{x}$

   c) $y = x^2$

   d) $y = \sqrt{x}$

   e) $y = 10\sqrt{x}$

   f) $y = \sqrt{10x}$?

Ⓒ

19. Prove each identity, and state the value(s) of x for which the identity is true.

   a) $\log (x - 1) + \log (x - 2) = \log (x^2 - 3x + 2)$

   b) $\log x + \log (x + 3) = \log (x^2 + 3x)$

   c) $\log (x - 5) + \log (x + 5) = \log (x^2 - 25)$

20. Solve and check.

   a) $\log (x + 2) + \log (x - 1) = 1$

   b) $\log (3x + 2) + \log (x - 1) = 2$

   c) $2 \log (x - 1) = 2 + \log 100$

21. Express y as a function of x. What is the domain?

   a) $\log 3 + \log y = \log (x + 2) - \log x$

   b) $\log y - 2 + \log x - \log (x + 1) = 0$

   c) $\log 4y = x + \log 4$

22. The table shows some large prime numbers that were discovered using computers. How many digits does each prime number have?

	Prime Number	Year	Computer
a)	$2^{11213} - 1$	1963	ILLIAC-II
b)	$2^{21701} - 1$	1978	CDC-CYBER-174
c)	$2^{132049} - 1$	1983	CRAY-1
d)	$2^{216091} - 1$	1985	CRAY-1

23. In 1938, the physicist Sir Arthur Eddington calculated that the number of particles in the universe is 33×2^{259}. He called this number the *cosmical number*.

   a) Write the cosmical number in scientific notation.

   b) How many digits are there in this number?

24. If n is a natural number, find the least value of n such that:

   a) $1.1^n > 10^9$

   b) $1.01^n > 10^9$

   c) $1.001^n > 10^9$

   d) 1.001^n exceeds the capacity of your calculator's display.

25. Let N be any positive number, no matter how large. Prove that no matter how small the positive number x is, it is always possible to find a value of n such that $(1 + x)^n > N$.

MATHEMATICS AROUND US

Orders of Magnitude

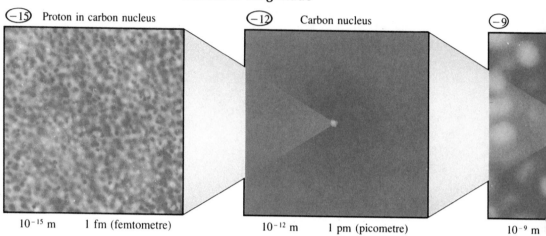

−15   Proton in carbon nucleus   −12   Carbon nucleus   −9

10^{-15} m   1 fm (femtometre) 10^{-12} m   1 pm (picometre) 10^{-9} m

Scientists have always wanted to extend our range of observation of the world around us, from the microscopic scale to the astronomic scale. What might we see if we could take an imaginary journey along a straight line beginning at the nucleus of an atom and ending at the farthermost reaches of outer space?

The first illustration shows part of the nucleus of a carbon atom. As we get farther and farther away, greater and greater distances are brought into view. The steps we take in this journey are not regular steps, but rather, each step is 1000 times as great as the previous one.

Hence, the dimensions of each illustration represent a distance 1000 times as long as the one before it. And, each illustration shows a 1000× enlargement of a small portion at the centre of the next one. Although it can be seen in only the first illustration, the nucleus of the carbon atom where we started the journey is at the centre of all of them.

The journey covers four pages in this book. Study the illustrations on all four pages before you begin the questions.

QUESTIONS

1. Notice the circled number in the upper left corner of each illustration.
   a) How is this number related to the distance represented by the illustration?
   b) As you move from one illustration to the next, compare the change in the circled number with the change in the distance represented by the illustration.

2. A factor of 10 is called one *order of magnitude*. Hence, a factor of 100, or 10 × 10, represents two orders of magnitude. How many orders of magnitude are represented by the change from:
   a) any illustration to the next
   b) the first illustration to the last?

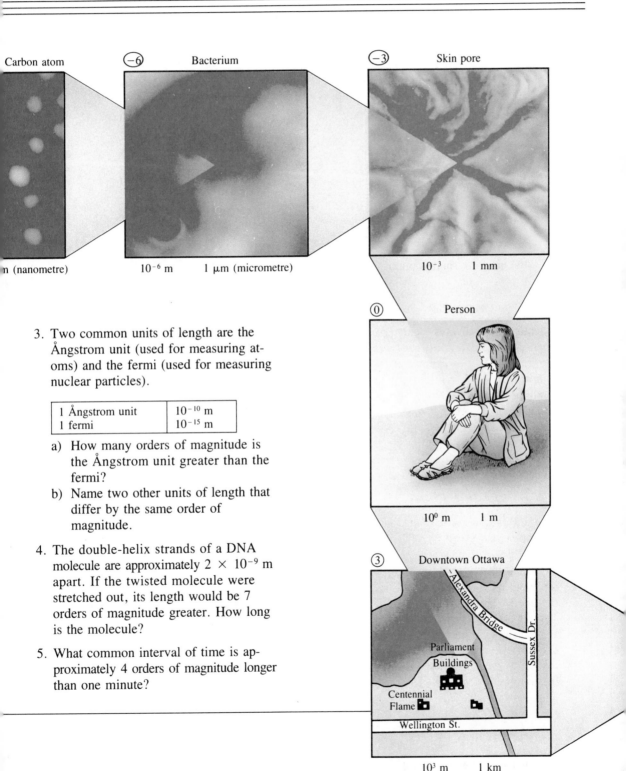

Carbon atom

−6 Bacterium

−3 Skin pore

n (nanometre) 10^{-6} m 1 μm (micrometre) 10^{-3} 1 mm

0 Person

10^0 m 1 m

3 Downtown Ottawa

Alexandra Bridge

Sussex Dr.

Parliament Buildings

Centennial Flame

Wellington St.

10^3 m 1 km

3. Two common units of length are the Ångstrom unit (used for measuring atoms) and the fermi (used for measuring nuclear particles).

| 1 Ångstrom unit | 10^{-10} m |
| 1 fermi | 10^{-15} m |

a) How many orders of magnitude is the Ångstrom unit greater than the fermi?

b) Name two other units of length that differ by the same order of magnitude.

4. The double-helix strands of a DNA molecule are approximately 2×10^{-9} m apart. If the twisted molecule were stretched out, its length would be 7 orders of magnitude greater. How long is the molecule?

5. What common interval of time is approximately 4 orders of magnitude longer than one minute?

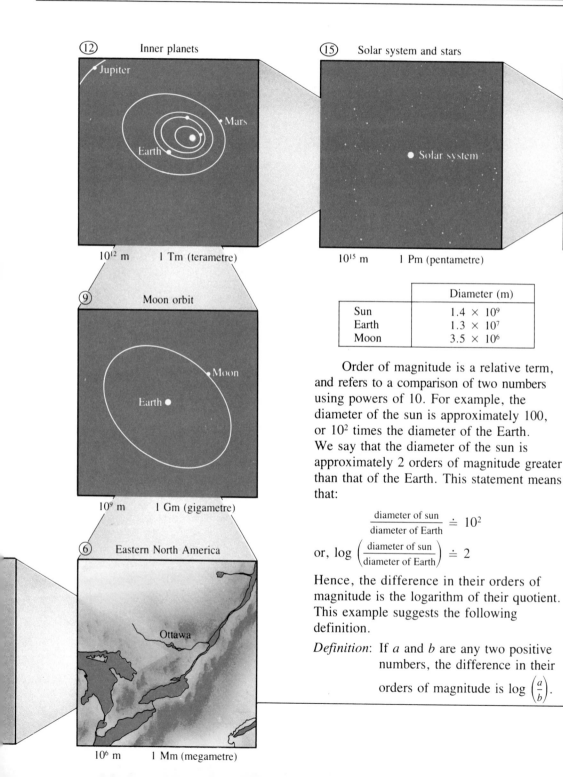

⑫ Inner planets

Jupiter

Mars

Earth

10^{12} m   1 Tm (terametre)

⑮ Solar system and stars

Solar system

10^{15} m   1 Pm (pentametre)

⑱

10^{18} m

⑨ Moon orbit

Moon

Earth

10^9 m   1 Gm (gigametre)

⑥ Eastern North America

Ottawa

10^6 m   1 Mm (megametre)

	Diameter (m)
Sun	1.4×10^9
Earth	1.3×10^7
Moon	3.5×10^6

Order of magnitude is a relative term, and refers to a comparison of two numbers using powers of 10. For example, the diameter of the sun is approximately 100, or 10^2 times the diameter of the Earth. We say that the diameter of the sun is approximately 2 orders of magnitude greater than that of the Earth. This statement means that:

$$\frac{\text{diameter of sun}}{\text{diameter of Earth}} \doteq 10^2$$

or, $\log\left(\dfrac{\text{diameter of sun}}{\text{diameter of Earth}}\right) \doteq 2$

Hence, the difference in their orders of magnitude is the logarithm of their quotient. This example suggests the following definition.

Definition: If *a* and *b* are any two positive numbers, the difference in their orders of magnitude is $\log\left(\dfrac{a}{b}\right)$.

Stars

㉑ Milky Way galaxy

㉔ Galactic cluster

m (exametre) 10^{21} m 10^{24} m

6. Show that the diameter of the sun is approximately 2.6 orders of magnitude greater than that of the moon.

7. Two common units of length are the astronomical unit (used for measuring planetary distances) and the light year (used for measuring stellar and galactic distances).

| 1 astronomical unit | 1.5×10^{11} m |
| 1 light year | 9.5×10^{15} m |

How many orders of magnitude is the light year greater than the astronomical unit?

8. The planets Neptune and Pluto are approximately 5×10^{12} m from the Earth. How many orders of magnitude greater than this are these distances?
   a) The nearest star, Proxima Centauri, 4×10^{18} m from Earth
   b) The centre of the Milky Way Galaxy, 6.7×10^{20} m from Earth
   c) A chain of galaxies 7×10^{24} m from Earth

9. In 1989, the space probe *Voyager II* will photograph the planet Neptune, about 5×10^{12} m from the Earth. The *Space Telescope* will be able to examine objects 13.4 orders of magnitude farther than this. What is the limit of observation of the Space Telescope?

10. The limit of the known universe is about 2.3 orders of magnitude greater than the distance represented by the last illustration above. How many metres is this?

11. Now that we have finished our journey from the nucleus of the carbon atom to outer space, suppose we reverse our direction and take the return trip back to the nucleus of the carbon atom where we started. What percent of the remaining distance would we cover from one illustration to the next?

7-6 INTRODUCTION TO LOGARITHMIC FUNCTIONS

Many examples of exponential functions were given in the previous sections of this chapter. Associated with each of these functions there is a corresponding function whose equation we can obtain by solving for the variable in the exponent.

Growth of Populations

In 1987 the world population reached 5 billion. At the time, the population was increasing at the rate of approximately 1.6% per year. If the rate of growth remains constant, then the population P billion is expressed as an exponential function of the number of years n relative to 1987 by this equation.

$$P = 5(1.016)^n \ldots \text{①}$$

Suppose we ask in how many years will the population reach P billion? We express the number of years n as a function of P by solving equation ① for n. Hence, we take the logarithm of each side.

$$\log P = \log 5 + n \log 1.016$$

Solve for n.

$$n \log 1.016 = \log P - \log 5$$

$$n = \frac{\log \left(\dfrac{P}{5} \right)}{\log 1.016}$$

The coefficient of the expression on the right side is $\frac{1}{\log 1.016}$, or about 145.

Hence, the equation for n becomes

$$n \doteq 145 \log \left(\frac{P}{5} \right) \ldots \text{②}$$

Equation ② expresses the number of years n as a logarithmic function of the population P. The graph shows the values of n for $3 \leqslant P \leqslant 10$. Compare this graph with the one on page 262.

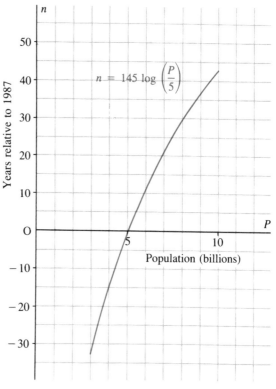

In this example, notice that n is not defined if P is 0, or if P is negative. This is reasonable, since the population P must be a positive number. Hence, the domain of the function is the set of positive integers.

Light Penetration Under Water

For every metre a diver descends below the surface, the light intensity is reduced by 2.5%. The percent P of surface light present is expressed as an exponential function of the depth d metres by this equation.

$$P = 100(0.975)^d \ldots \text{①}$$

Suppose we ask at what depth is the light intensity $P\%$? We express d as a function of P by solving equation ① for d. Take the logarithm of each side.

$$\log P = \log 100 + d \log 0.975$$

Solve for d.

$$d = \frac{\log\left(\dfrac{P}{100}\right)}{\log 0.975}$$

$$d \doteq -90.9 \log\left(\frac{P}{100}\right) \ldots \text{②}$$

Equation ② expresses the depth d metres as a logarithmic function of the light intensity P. The graph shows the values of d for $0 < P \leq 100$. Compare this graph with the one on page 263.

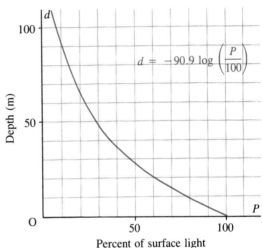

$$d = -90.9 \log\left(\frac{P}{100}\right)$$

Depth (m)

Percent of surface light

In the final equations of the above examples, the expression on the right side involves the logarithm of the variable. Functions whose defining equation have this property are called logarithmic functions.

> A *logarithmic function* has an equation which can be written in the form $f(x) = k \log x$, where k is a constant, and $x > 0$.

Example. Given the exponential function $f(x) = 10^x$
    a) Determine the inverse function $f^{-1}(x)$.
    b) Graph $f(x)$ and $f^{-1}(x)$ on the same grid.

Solution.   a) Recall that to obtain the inverse of a function from its equation, we interchange x and y in the equation and solve for y. Hence, to find the inverse of $f(x) = 10^x$:
    Step 1. Let $y = 10^x$, then interchange x and y. $x = 10^y$
    Step 2. Solve for y. $y = \log x$
    Hence, the inverse of the exponential function $f(x) = 10^x$ is the logarithmic function $f^{-1}(x) = \log x$.

b) We graph $f(x) = 10^x$ using a table of values. Recall that we can graph the inverse by reflecting the graph of $y = 10^x$ in the line $y = x$. This is equivalent to interchanging the ordered pairs in the table of values for $y = f(x)$.

$f(x) = 10^x$

x	y
-2	0.01
-1.5	0.03
-1	0.10
-0.5	0.32
-0.2	0.63
0	1.00
0.1	1.26
0.2	1.58
0.3	2.00

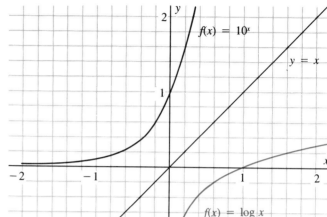

Recall that in *Section 7-4* we observed that taking a common logarithm of a number and raising the number to a power of 10 are inverse operations. This is consistent with the above *Example*, which shows that the logarithmic function $y = \log x$ can be defined as the inverse of the exponential function $y = 10^x$.

EXERCISES 7-6

(A)

1. Solve each equation for x, thus expressing x as a logarithmic function of y.
   a) $y = 5(2)^x$
   b) $y = 1.3(10)^x$
   c) $y = 8.2(1.03)^x$
   d) $y = 6.4\left(\frac{1}{2}\right)^x$
   e) $y = 3.5(2.7)^x$
   f) $y = 2.75\left(\frac{2}{3}\right)^x$

(B)

2. An investment of $500 at 8% per annum compounded annually grows to A dollars in n years. In Section 7-1, page 262, we showed that an equation expressing the amount A dollars as an exponential function of the time n years is $A = 500(1.08)^n$.
   a) Solve this equation for n, thus expressing n as a logarithmic function of A.
   b) Calculate the value of n for each value of A and interpret the result.
      i) $A = 1250$ ii) $A = 350$

c) Graph the function in part a) for $0 < A \leqslant 1250$. Compare your graph with the one on page 262.

d) State the domain and the range of the function.

3. A ball is dropped from a height of 2.00 m. On each bounce the ball rises to 70% of the height from which it fell. In Section 7-1, page 263, we showed that an equation expressing the bounce height h metres as an exponential function of the number of bounces n is $h = 2.00(0.7)^n$.

a) Solve this equation for n, thus expressing n as a logarithmic function of h.

b) Calculate the value of n for each value of h and interpret the result.
   i) 0.7 m   ii) 0.12 m

c) Graph the function in part a) for $0 < h \leqslant 2.00$. Compare your graph with the one on page 263.

d) What is the range of the function?

4. a) The population of the town of Elmira was 6800 in 1987. If the population is growing at the rate of 1.8% per annum, write an equation expressing the population P as a function of n, the number of years relative to 1987.

b) Solve this equation for n.

c) Find the value of n if P is: i) 9200   ii) 5500.

d) Graph the functions in parts a) and b). How are these functions related?

5. On bright sunny days, the amount of bromine in a municipal swimming pool decreases by 10% each hour. If there was 145 g of bromine in the pool at noon on a sunny day, when would the pool contain: a) 102 g b) 85 g c) 200 g?

6. Given the exponential function $f(x) = 3^x$, graph $y = f(x)$ and $y = f^{-1}(x)$ on the same grid.

7. Graph each function and its inverse on the same grid.

a) $f(x) = 2^x$

b) $g(x) = \left(\frac{2}{3}\right)^x$

INVESTIGATE

At the beginning of this section, the equation $n \doteq 145 \log\left(\frac{P}{5}\right)$ was derived to represent the number of years for the world population to grow to P billion, assuming a constant growth rate of 1.6% per year. Notice that the coefficient 145 is the reciprocal of the logarithm of the base of the corresponding exponential function; that is, $\frac{1}{\log 1.016} \doteq 145$. This suggests that the form of the equation of the logarithmic function will be simpler if the base of the corresponding exponential function is 10, for then that coefficient will be 1, since $\log 10 = 1$.

Investigate whether this is true by first changing the base of the corresponding exponential function, $P = 5(1.016)^n$, to base 10, and then solving for n to obtain the corresponding logarithmic function.

7-7 DEFINING AND GRAPHING LOGARITHMIC FUNCTIONS

In the *Example* of the preceding section we saw that the logarithmic function $y = \log x$ can be defined as the inverse of the exponential function $y = 10^x$. This suggests that other logarithmic functions can be defined as inverses of exponential functions with bases other than 10. In fact, for each choice of base for the exponential function $g(x) = a^x$, $a > 0$, there is an associated logarithmic function. Hence, we define the function $f(x) = \log_a x$, $a > 0$, as follows.

> The logarithmic function $f(x) = \log_a x$ $(a > 0, a \neq 1)$ is the inverse of the exponential function $g(x) = a^x$.

We say, "$f(x)$ equals log to the base a of x".

Recall that we can graph the inverse of any function by reflecting its graph in the line $y = x$. This is equivalent to interchanging the ordered pairs in the table of values of the function. For example, the graph below shows the function $g(x) = 2^x$ and its inverse $g^{-1}(x) = \log_2 x$. Compare this graph with the one on page 294.

$g(x) = 2^x$

x	y
-3	0.13
-2	0.25
-1	0.50
-0.5	0.71
0	1.00
0.5	1.41
1	2.00
1.5	2.83
2	4.00

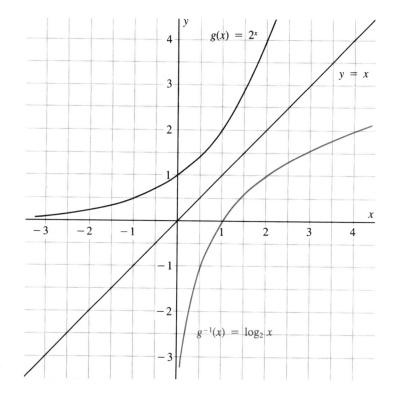

$g^{-1}(x) = \log_2 x$

x	y
0.13	-3
0.25	-2
0.50	-1
0.71	-0.5
1.00	0
1.41	0.5
2.00	1
2.83	1.5
4.00	2

The graph illustrates the following properties of the function $g^{-1}(x) = \log_2 x$. These properties are consequences of the corresponding properties of $y = 2^x$.

Vertical intercept

There is no vertical intercept since the function $g(x) = 2^x$ has no horizontal intercept.

Horizontal intercept

The horizontal intercept is 1, since the vertical intercept of $g(x) = 2^x$ is 1. Hence, $\log_2 1 = 0$

Domain

The domain of $g^{-1}(x) = \log_2 x$ is the set of positive real numbers, since this is the range of $g(x) = 2^x$.

Range

The range of $g^{-1}(x) = \log_2 x$ is the set of all real numbers, since this is the domain of $g(x) = 2^x$.

If any exponential function is given, we can sketch its graph. The graph of the inverse is then the graph of the corresponding logarithmic function.

Example 1. a) Sketch the graph of the exponential function $f(x) = \left(\dfrac{1}{3}\right)^x$

b) Sketch the graph of the inverse of the function in part a) on the same grid.

c) Write the equation of the inverse function.

Solution. a) $f(x) = \left(\dfrac{1}{3}\right)^x$

When x is very large and positive, $f(x)$ is very small and positive.

$f(0) = 1$

When x is negative and has a large absolute value, $f(x)$ is very large.

b) Reflect $y = \left(\dfrac{1}{3}\right)^x$ in the line $y = x$. The image is $y = \log_{\frac{1}{3}} x$.

c) The equation of the inverse function is $f^{-1}(x) = \log_{\frac{1}{3}} x$.

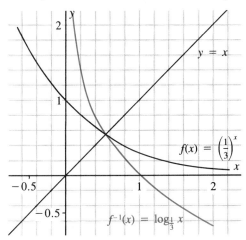

The graphs in the above examples illustrate properties of the logarithmic function $f(x) = \log_a x$.

Properties of the graph of the
function $f(x) = \log_a x$
Vertical intercept: none
Horizontal intercept: 1
Domain: all positive real numbers
Range: all real numbers

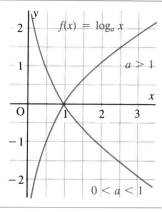

Example 2.   Prove that if (x_1, y_1) and (x_2, y_2) are points on the graph of
$f(x) = \log_a x$, then $(x_1x_2, y_1 + y_2)$ is also a point on the graph.

Solution.   Since (x_1, y_1) is on the graph of $f(x) = \log_a x$, its coordinates satisfy the
equation $y = \log_a x$.
Hence, $y_1 = \log_a x_1$ ... ①
Similarly, $y_2 = \log_a x_2$ ... ②
Add equations ① and ②, and use the law of logarithms.
$y_1 + y_2 = \log_a x_1 + \log_a x_2$
$= \log_a (x_1x_2)$
Hence, the coordinates of the point $(x_1x_2, y_1 + y_2)$ also satisfy the equation
$y = \log_a x$. That is, $(x_1x_2, y_1 + y_2)$ is also a point on the graph of
$f(x) = \log_a x$.

The result of *Example 2* is a
consequence of the law of
logarithms for multiplication.
Multiplying the horizontal
coordinates of points on the
graph of $f(x) = \log_a x$ corresponds
to adding their vertical coordinates.
Compare this example with
Example 2, page 276.

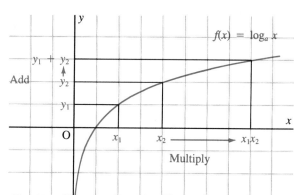

EXERCISES 7-7

(A)

1. Write the inverse of each exponential function.
   a) $f(x) = 10^x$ b) $g(x) = 3^x$ c) $h(x) = 7^x$
   d) $f(x) = (0.4)^x$ e) $g(x) = \left(\dfrac{3}{2}\right)^x$ f) $h(x) = 15^x$

2. Write the inverse of each logarithmic function.
   a) $f(x) = \log x$
   b) $g(x) = \log_2 x$
   c) $h(x) = \log_6 x$
   d) $f(x) = \log_{\frac{1}{2}} x$
   e) $g(x) = \log_{\frac{5}{4}} x$
   f) $h(x) = \log_{21} x$

Ⓑ

3. Copy each graph and sketch the graph of the inverse of the given function on the same grid. Then write the equation of the inverse function.
   a)
   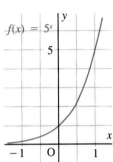
   b)
   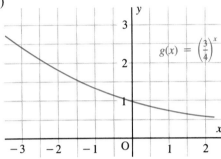

4. a) Sketch the graph of the exponential function $f(x) = 3^x$.
   b) Sketch the graph of the inverse of the function in part a) on the same grid.
   c) Write the equation of the inverse function.

5. Repeat *Exercise 4*, starting with the function $g(x) = \left(\dfrac{1}{2}\right)^x$

6. Graph each function.
   a) $f(x) = \log_4 x$
   b) $g(x) = \log_6 x$
   c) $h(x) = \log_{\frac{1}{2}} x$
   d) $f(x) = \log_{0.8} x$
   e) $g(x) = \log_{1.5} x$
   f) $h(x) = \log_{\frac{2}{5}} x$

7. Prove that if $f(x) = \log_a x$, then $f(xy) = f(x) + f(y)$.

8. a) Prove that if (x_1, y_1) and (x_2, y_2) are two points on the graph of $y = \log_a x$, then $\left(\dfrac{x_1}{x_2}, y_1 - y_2\right)$ is also a point on the graph.
   b) Prove that if (x_1, y_1) is a point on the graph of $y = \log_a x$, then $(x_1{}^2, 2y_1)$ and $\left(\dfrac{1}{x_1}, -y_1\right)$ are also points on the graph.

Ⓒ

9. In *Example 1*, the graphs of $f(x) = \left(\dfrac{1}{3}\right)^x$, $f^{-1}(x) = \log_{\frac{1}{3}} x$, and $y = x$ are shown. Determine the coordinates of their point of intersection to 3 decimal places.

10. Given the function $f(x) = a^x$ and its inverse $f^{-1}(x) = \log_a x$, where $a > 0$
    a) For what values of a do the graphs of $y = f(x)$ and $y = f^{-1}(x)$ intersect?
    b) Find out as much as you can about the point of intersection of the graphs in part a).

7-8 LOGARITHMS AS EXPONENTS

Recall that to find the inverse of a function from its equation, we interchange x and y in the equation and solve for y. Hence, to find the inverse of $y = a^x$:

Step 1. Interchange x and y.　　$x = a^y$ ... ①

Step 2. Solve for y. We can do this using common logarithms, but it is preferable to use the definition on page 296. According to the definition, the inverse is
$$y = \log_a x \dots ②$$
　　Hence, this is the equation that results when equation ① is solved for y.
Comparing equations ① and ②, we see that

$$\log_a x = y \qquad \text{means that} \qquad x = a^y, x > 0.$$
　base　exponent

Hence, $\log_a x$ is an exponent. It is the exponent that x would have if it were written in power form with base a ($a > 0$, $a \neq 1$). If the base is omitted, it is understood to be base 10.

Example 1.　Evaluate each logarithm.

　　　a) $\log_5 25$　　b) $\log_7 \sqrt{7}$　　c) $\log_{\frac{1}{3}} 9$　　d) $\log_a a$

Solution.　a)　Since $25 = 5^2$, then $\log_5 25 = 2$

　　b)　Since $\sqrt{7} = 7^{\frac{1}{2}}$, then $\log_7 \sqrt{7} = \frac{1}{2}$

　　c)　Write 9 as a power of $\frac{1}{3}$. Since $\left(\frac{1}{3}\right)^2 = \frac{1}{9}$, then $\left(\frac{1}{3}\right)^{-2} = 9$
　　　　Hence, $\log_{\frac{1}{3}} 9 = -2$

　　d)　Since $a = a^1$, then $\log_a a = 1$

　　Since any positive number can be expressed as a power of any other positive number (except 1), we can find approximations to the logarithm of any positive number to any positive base (except 1).

Example 2.　Find $\log_5 9$ to the nearest thousandth.

Solution.　To find $\log_5 9$ means to find the exponent that 9 would have if it were expressed as a power of 5.
　　Let $9 = 5^x$
　　Take the logarithm of each side to base 10.
　　$\log 9 = \log (5^x)$
　　$\log 9 = x \log 5$
　　$x = \dfrac{\log 9}{\log 5}$
　　　$\doteq 1.365\ 212\ 4$
　　To the nearest thousandth, $9 \doteq 5^{1.365}$
　　Therefore, $\log_5 9 \doteq 1.365$

Example 3. Simplify each expression.
a) $\log_a a^x$ b) $a^{\log_a x}$

Solution.   a) $\log_a a^x$ is the exponent that a^x would have if it were written as a power of a. This exponent is x. Hence, $\log_a a^x = x$
b) $a^{\log_a x}$ is a raised to the exponent that x would have if x were written as a power of a. Hence, $a^{\log_a x} = x$

Summary
- $\log_a x = y$ means that $x = a^y$, where $a > 0$, $a \neq 1$, and $x > 0$
- $\log_a a^x = x$ and $a^{\log_a x} = x$
- $\log_a a = 1$

Example 4. Write each expression in exponential form.
a) $\log_2 16 = 4$ b) $\log_2 0.5 = -1$

Solution.   a) $\log_2 16 = 4$ b) $\log_2 0.5 = -1$
$\qquad 16 = 2^4$ $\qquad 0.5 = 2^{-1}$

Example 5. Write each expression in logarithmic form.
a) $3^5 = 243$ b) $a^b = c$

Solution.   a) $3^5 = 243$ b) $a^b = c$
$\qquad 5 = \log_3 243$ $\qquad b = \log_a c$

EXERCISES 7-8

Ⓐ

1. Write in exponential form.
   a) $\log_2 8 = 3$ b) $\log_2 32 = 5$ c) $\log_2 \left(\frac{1}{4}\right) = -2$

   d) $\log_5 625 = 4$ e) $\log_3 9 = 2$ f) $\log_9 3 = \frac{1}{2}$

2. Evaluate each logarithm.
   a) $\log_2 16 = y$ b) $\log_2 4$ c) $\log_3 27$ d) $\log_5 25$
   e) $\log_5 \left(\frac{1}{5}\right)$ f) $\log_7 7$ g) $\log_3 1$ h) $\log_3 3^4$

3. In geography, sediments are classified by particle size, as shown.
   a) Write the logarithm to base 2 of each number.
   b) Write the logarithm to base 4 of each number.

Type of sediment	Size (mm)
Boulder	256
Cobble	64
Pebble	4
Granule	2
Sand	$\frac{1}{16}$
Silt	$\frac{1}{256}$

4. Evaluate each logarithm.

a) $\log_5 \sqrt{5}$　　b) $\log_{\frac{1}{2}}\left(\frac{1}{16}\right)$　　c) $\log_{\frac{3}{2}}\left(\frac{9}{4}\right)$　　d) $\log_{\sqrt{3}} 9$

e) $\log_{\frac{1}{2}} 8$　　f) $\log_{\frac{2}{5}}\left(\frac{25}{4}\right)$　　g) $\log_3 (\sqrt{3})^3$　　h) $\log_{\sqrt{5}} 125$

5. Evaluate each logarithm to the nearest thousandth.

a) $\log_3 5$　b) $\log_7 4$　c) $\log_2 50$　d) $\log_5 12$　e) $\log_4 27$　f) $\log_{16} 8$

6. Write in logarithmic form.

a) $6^2 = 36$　　　　b) $4^{-2} = \frac{1}{16}$　　　　c) $3^5 = 243$

d) $7^3 = 343$　　　e) $8^{\frac{1}{3}} = 2$　　　f) $2^0 = 1$

g) $5^{-2} = 0.04$　　h) $4^{-\frac{1}{2}} = \frac{1}{2}$　　i) $\left(\frac{1}{2}\right)^2 = \frac{1}{4}$

j) $\left(\frac{2}{3}\right)^{-1} = \frac{3}{2}$　　k) $\left(\frac{1}{9}\right)^2 = \frac{1}{81}$　　l) $x^y = z$

7. Write in exponential form.

a) $\log_{20} 400 = 2$　　b) $\log_7\left(\frac{1}{49}\right) = -2$　　c) $\log_8 4 = \frac{2}{3}$

d) $\log_6 36^2 = 4$　　e) $\log_{0.5} 8 = -3$　　f) $\log_r s = t$

8. Solve for x.

a) $x = \log_5 25$　　b) $\log_4 1 = x$　　c) $\log_x 16 = 2$

d) $\log_x 3 = \frac{1}{2}$　　e) $\log_2 x = 3$　　f) $\log_3 x = 4$

9. Solve for x.

a) $\log_2 x = 9$　　b) $\log_2 x = -2$　　c) $\log_3\left(\frac{1}{3}\right) = x$

d) $\log_{\sqrt{2}} 32 = x$　　e) $\log_x 16 = -2$　　f) $\log_x 125 = -3$

10. If $\log_8 3 = x$ and $\log_4 7 = y$, find an expression in terms of x and y for:

a) $\log_2 21$　　　　b) $\log_2 63$.

11. Given that $f(x) = x - \log_2 x$ and $g(x) = 2^x$, find: a) $f(g(x))$　b) $g(f(x))$.

12. If a telephone network is designed to carry N telephone calls simultaneously, then the number of switches needed per call must be at least $\log_2 N$. If the network can carry 10 000 calls simultaneously, how many switches would be needed:

a) for one call　　　　　　　　b) for 10 000 simultaneous calls?

13. a) Evaluate each logarithm.　i) $\log_2 8$ and $\log_8 2$　　ii) $\log_5 25$ and $\log_{25} 5$

b) On the basis of the results of part a), make a conjecture about how $\log_a b$ and $\log_b a$ are related, where $a, b > 0$. Prove your conjecture.

14. Let a and b be any two positive numbers. Prove that for all positive values of x, $\log_b x$ is directly proportional to $\log_a x$.

MATHEMATICS AROUND US

The Logarithmic Spiral

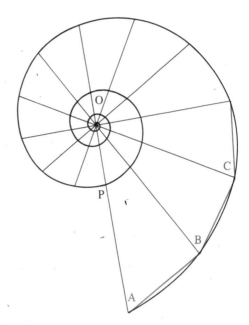

Some living creatures exhibit exponential growth in their dimensions.
A well-known example is the chambered nautilus of the Indian
and Pacific Oceans. As it grows, the shell extends continuously,
generating a natural spiral.

QUESTIONS

1. The diagram shows a series of equally-spaced radii drawn from the centre of
   the spiral. The radii are spaced every 30°.
   a) Measure and record the length of each radius, starting with OP and pro-
      ceeding clockwise around the spiral.
   b) Verify that the length of the radius L centimetres satisfies the equation
      $L = 1.5(1.0034)^\theta$, where θ degrees is the angle of rotation measured
      clockwise starting at OP.

2. a) Measure the angles represented by A, B, C, . . ., on the diagram.
   b) Prove that if the length of the radius is an exponential function of the angle
      of rotation, then the angles A, B, C, . . ., are all equal.

3. a) Suggest why the spiral is called a *logarithmic spiral*.
   b) The spiral is also referred to as an *equiangular spiral*. Suggest why.

7-9 THE LAWS OF LOGARITHMS (BASE *a*)

In *Section 7-5* we developed the laws of logarithms for logarithms with base 10. The restriction to base 10 is not necessary, and the laws can be extended to logarithms with any positive base (except 1).

   For example, an equation such as $2^3 \times 2^4 = 2^7$ can be written in logarithmic form as $\log_2 8 + \log_2 16 = \log_2 128$. This equation states that the sum of the exponents that 8 and 16 have when expressed as powers of 2 is equal to the exponent that 128 has when expressed as a power of 2.

Theorem   Law of Logarithms for Multiplication (Base *a*)
If x and y are positive real numbers, then
$$\log_a xy = \log_a x + \log_a y \qquad a > 0, a \neq 1$$

Given: Two positive real numbers x and y
Required to Prove: $\log_a xy = \log_a x + \log_a y \qquad a > 0, a \neq 1$
Proof: Let $\log_a x = M$ and $\log_a y = N$
$$x = a^M \qquad\qquad y = a^N$$
Hence, $xy = (a^M)(a^N)$
$$= a^{M+N}$$
Therefore, $\log_a xy = \log_a (a^{M+N})$
$$= M + N$$
$$= \log_a x + \log_a y$$

Corollary   Law of Logarithms for Division (Base *a*)
If x and y are positive real numbers, then
$$\log_a \left(\frac{x}{y}\right) = \log_a x - \log_a y \qquad a > 0, a \neq 1$$

Example 1.   Write $\log_2 15$ as:
   a) a sum of two logarithms   b) a difference of two logarithms.

Solution.   a) Since $15 = 5 \times 3$, then $\log_2 15 = \log_2 5 + \log_2 3$
   b) Since $15 = 30 \div 2$, then $\log_2 15 = \log_2 30 - \log_2 2$

   What other answers can you find for *Example 1*?

Example 2.   Write each expression as a single logarithm and simplify it.
   a) $\log_3 6 + \log_3 1.5$ b) $\log_5 50 - \log_5 0.4$

Solution.   a) $\log_3 6 + \log_3 1.5 = \log_3 (6 \times 1.5)$
$$= \log_3 9$$
$$= 2$$

   b) $\log_5 50 - \log_5 0.4 = \log_5 \left(\frac{50}{0.4}\right)$
$$= \log_5 125$$
$$= 3$$

> **Theorem**   **Law of Logarithms for Powers (Base *a*)**
>
> If x and n are real numbers, and $x > 0$, then
>
> $\log_a (x^n) = n \log_a x$ $a > 0, a \neq 1$

Given: Two real numbers x and n, where $x > 0$

Required to Prove: $\log_a (x^n) = n \log_a x$

Proof: Let $\log_a x = M$

$$x = a^M$$

Hence, $x^n = (a^M)^n$

$$= a^{nM}$$

Therefore, $\log_a (x^n) = \log_a (a^{nM})$

$$= nM$$

$$= n \log_a x$$

> **Corollary**   **Law of Logarithms for Roots (Base *a*)**
>
> If x and n are real numbers, and $x > 0$, then
>
> $\log_a \sqrt[n]{x} = \dfrac{1}{n} \log_a x$ $a > 0, a \neq 1$

Example 3. a) Write $\log_5 16$ as a product of a whole number and a logarithm.

b) Write as a single logarithm. i) $2 \log_6 5$ ii) $\dfrac{1}{3} \log_4 125$

Solution. a) Since $16 = 2^4$, then $\log_5 16 = \log_5 (2^4)$

$$= 4 \log_5 2$$

b) i) $2 \log_6 5 = \log_6 (5^2)$

$$= \log_6 25$$

ii) $\dfrac{1}{3} \log_4 125 = \log_4 (\sqrt[3]{125})$

$$= \log_4 5$$

Example 4. Given that $\log_2 7 \doteq 2.8074$, find an approximation for each logarithm.

a) $\log_2 14$ b) $\log_2 49$ c) $\log_2 \left(\dfrac{4}{7}\right)$ d) $\log_2 \sqrt[3]{7}$

Solution. a) $\log_2 14 = \log_2 (7 \times 2)$ b) $\log_2 49 = \log_2 (7^2)$

$ = \log_2 7 + \log_2 2$ $ = 2 \log_2 7$

$ \doteq 2.8074 + 1$ $ \doteq 2(2.8074)$

$ \doteq 3.8074$ $ \doteq 5.6148$

c) $\log_2 \left(\dfrac{4}{7}\right) = \log_2 4 - \log_2 7$ d) $\log_2 \sqrt[3]{7} = \dfrac{1}{3} \log_2 7$

$ \doteq 2 - 2.8074$ $\phantom{d) \log_2 \sqrt[3]{7}} \doteq \dfrac{1}{3} (2.8074)$

$ \doteq -0.8074$ $\phantom{d) \log_2 \sqrt[3]{7}} \doteq 0.9358$

Laws of Logarithms (Base *a*) $a > 0, a \neq 1$

- Multiplication $\log_a xy = \log_a x + \log_a y$ $x, y > 0$

- Division $\log_a \left(\dfrac{x}{y} \right) = \log_a x - \log_a y$ $x, y > 0$

- Powers $\log_a (x^n) = n \log_a x$ $x > 0$

- Roots $\log_a \sqrt[n]{x} = \dfrac{1}{n} \log_a x$ $x > 0$

We can solve equations involving logarithms by using the laws of logarithms and the definition of a logarithm.

Example 5.   Solve each equation, and check.

   a) $2 \log x = \log 8 + \log 2$ b) $\log_8 (2 - x) + \log_8 (4 - x) = 1$

Solution.   a) $2 \log x = \log 8 + \log 2$

   $\log x^2 = \log 16$

Hence, $x^2 = 16$

   $x = \pm 4$

To check, substitute each value of x into the original equation.
When $x = 4$,
L.S. $= 2 \log 4$ R.S. $= \log 8 + \log 2$
   $= \log 16$ $= \log 16$
4 is a root.
When $x = -4$, the left side is not defined since $\log x$ is defined only when $x > 0$. Hence, -4 is an extraneous root.

   b) $\log_8 (2 - x) + \log_8 (4 - x) = 1$

Simplify the left side using the law of logarithms for multiplication.
   $\log_8 (2 - x)(4 - x) = 1$
Use the definition of a logarithm.
   $(2 - x)(4 - x) = 8^1$
   $8 - 6x + x^2 = 8$
   $-6x + x^2 = 0$
   $x = 0 \text{ or } x = 6$

When $x = 0$,
L.S. $= \log_8 2 + \log_8 4$ R.S. $= 1$
   $= \log_8 8$
   $= 1$
0 is a root.
When $x = 6$, the left side is not defined. Hence, 6 is an extraneous root.

In *Example 5b* we may ask, if 6 is an extraneous root, then where did it come from? The key to the answer is the quadratic equation $(2 - x)(4 - x) = 8$ which occurred in the solution. This equation may also be written as $(x - 2)(x - 4) = 8$ without changing the two roots. But then the associated logarithmic equation would be $\log_8 (x - 2) + \log_8 (x - 4) = 1$. Hence, if this equation were solved using the method of *Example 5b* the same two roots 0 and 6 would result, but this time 6 would be the root and 0 would be extraneous.

EXERCISES 7-9

Ⓐ

1. Write each expression as a single logarithm, and simplify it.
   a) $\log_6 9 + \log_6 4$ b) $\log_5 15 - \log_5 3$ c) $\log_4 2 + \log_4 32$
   d) $\log_2 48 - \log_2 6$ e) $\log_3 54 - \log_3 2$ f) $\log_3 9 + \log_3 9$

2. Write as a sum of logarithms.
   a) $\log_3 20$ b) $\log_7 45$ c) $\log_5 90$ d) $\log_{12} 6$ e) $\log_8 75$ f) $\log_{20} 39$

3. Write as a difference of logarithms.
   a) $\log_4 11$ b) $\log_3 12$ c) $\log_9 5$ d) $\log_6 7$ e) $\log_{11} 21$ f) $\log_2 13$

4. Write each expression as a single logarithm and simplify it.
   a) $\log_6 4 + \log_6 3 + \log_6 3$ b) $\log_4 8 + \log_4 6 + \log_4 \left(\dfrac{4}{3}\right)$
   c) $\log_3 18 + \log_3 5 - \log_3 10$ d) $\log_2 20 - \log_2 5 + \log_2 8$

5. Simplify.
   a) $\log_2 (8 \times 16)$ b) $\log_3 (27 \times 81)$ c) $\log_5 (625 \times 25)$
   d) $\log_2 \left(\dfrac{32}{4}\right)$ e) $\log_3 \left(\dfrac{27}{3}\right)$ f) $\log_5 \left(\dfrac{125}{25}\right)$

6. Write each logarithm as a product of a whole number and a logarithm.
   a) $\log_3 8$ b) $\log_5 36$ c) $\log_2 27$ d) $\log_6 32$ e) $\log_{12} 81$ f) $\log_4 125$

7. Write as a single logarithm.
   a) $3 \log_2 5$ b) $2 \log_7 4$ c) $6 \log_3 8$ d) $5 \log_{12} 4$ e) $15 \log_2 3$

Ⓑ

8. Write as a single logarithm and simplify it.
   a) $\log_4 48 + \log_4 \left(\dfrac{2}{3}\right) + \log_4 8$ b) $\log_8 24 + \log_8 4 - \log_8 3$
   c) $\log_9 36 + \log_9 18 - \log_9 24$ d) $\log_4 20 - \log_4 5 + \log_4 8$
   e) $\log_3 \sqrt{45} - \log_3 \sqrt{5}$ f) $\log_2 \sqrt{5} - \log_2 \sqrt{40}$
   g) $\log_5 \sqrt{10} + \log_5 \sqrt{\dfrac{25}{2}}$ h) $\log_4 \sqrt{40} + \log_4 \sqrt{48} - \log_4 \sqrt{15}$

9. Given $\log_2 5 \doteq 2.3219$, find an approximation for each logarithm.
   a) $\log_2 20$ b) $\log_2 25$ c) $\log_2 2.5$ d) $\log_2 \sqrt{5}$

10. Simplify.

  a) $\log_2 24 - \log_2 \left(\frac{3}{4}\right)$

  b) $\log_2 20 + \log_2 0.4$

  c) $\log_8 48 + \log_8 4 - \log_8 3$

  d) $\log_{21} 7 + \log_{21} 9 + \log_{21} \left(\frac{1}{3}\right)$

11. Given $\log_3 10 \doteq 2.0959$, find an approximation for each logarithm.

  a) $\log_3 1000$
  b) $\log_3 30$
  c) $\log_3 \sqrt{0.3}$
  d) $\log_3 \left(\frac{100}{9}\right)$

12. Express y as a function of x. What is the domain?

  a) $\log_2 xy = 3 \log_2 x$

  b) $\log_5 y = 2 \log_5 (x + 1) + \log_5 (x - 1)$

  c) $\log_3 (y - 3) = 1 + 2 \log_3 (x + 3)$

13. Use your calculator to evaluate each expression.

  a)   i) $\log_2 3000$ ii) $\log_2 300$ iii) $\log_2 30$ iv) $\log_2 3$
      v) $\log_2 0.3$ vi) $\log_2 0.03$ vii) $\log_2 0.003$ viii) $\log_2 0.0003$
  b) Can you find a pattern in the results of part a)? Account for the pattern.

14. If $\log_3 2 = x$, simplify each logarithm.

  a) $\log_3 8$
  b) $\log_3 24$
  c) $\log_3 \sqrt{2}$
  d) $\log_3 6\sqrt{2}$

15. If $\log_2 5 = x$, simplify each logarithm.

  a) $\log_2 20$
  b) $\log_2 100$
  c) $\log_2 10\sqrt{5}$
  d) $\log_2 \left(\frac{\sqrt[3]{5}}{2}\right)$

16. Given that $\log_2 x = 5$, evaluate each logarithm.

  a) $\log_2 2x$
  b) $\log_2 \left(\frac{x}{2}\right)$
  c) $\log_2 (x^2)$
  d) $\log_2 (4x^2)$

17. Given that $\log_3 x = 2$ and $\log_3 y = 5$, evaluate each logarithm.

  a) $\log_3 xy$
  b) $\log_3 (9x^2y)$
  c) $\log_3 \left(\frac{3x^2}{y}\right)$
  d) $\log_3 (27x^{-2}y)$

18. Solve and check.

  a) $2 \log x = \log 32 + \log 2$
  b) $2 \log x = \log 3 + \log 27$
  c) $\log_4 (x + 2) + \log_4 (x - 1) = 1$
  d) $\log_2 (x - 5) + \log_2 (x - 2) = 2$
  e) $\log_2 x + \log_2 (x + 2) = 3$
  f) $\log_6 (x - 1) + \log_6 (x + 4) = 2$

19. Solve and check.

  a) $2 \log m + 3 \log m = 10$
  b) $\log_3 x^2 - \log_3 2x = 2$
  c) $\log_3 s + \log_3 (s - 2) = 1$
  d) $\log (x - 2) + \log (x + 1) = 1$
  e) $\log_7 (x + 4) + \log_7 (x - 2) = 1$
  f) $\log_2 (2m + 4) - \log_2 (m - 1) = 3$

20. Solve each equation to the nearest thousandth.

  a) $\log_2 x + \log_4 x = 5$
  b) $\log_5 x + \log_{10} x = 5$

21. a) Show that: i) $\dfrac{1}{\log_3 10} + \dfrac{1}{\log_4 10} = \dfrac{1}{\log_{12} 10}$ ii) $\dfrac{1}{\log_3 x} + \dfrac{1}{\log_4 x} = \dfrac{1}{\log_{12} x}$.

  b) Using the results of part a) as a guide, state a general result and prove it.

7-10 APPLICATIONS OF EXPONENTIAL AND LOGARITHMIC FUNCTIONS: PART ONE

Exponential functions have defining equations of the form $y = ca^x$. In many applied problems, we are given three of the quantities c, a, x, and y, and are required to calculate the fourth quantity.

Compound Interest

Example 1.   What amount of money would grow to $1000 in 5 years if it is invested at 9% per annum compounded annually?

Solution.   Let the amount of money be P dollars. Then,

$P(1.09)^5 = 1000$

$$P = \frac{1000}{(1.09)^5}$$

$ = 1000(1.09)^{-5}$

$ \doteq 649.93$

Hence, $649.93 would grow to $1000 in 5 years at 9% per annum.

Solving an equation of the form $y = ca^x$ for the base a amounts to taking a root of both sides. We illustrate this in the next example.

Example 2.   In 1947 an investor bought Van Gogh's painting *Irises* for $84 000. In 1987 she sold it for $49 million. What annual rate of interest corresponds to an investment of $84 000 which grows to $49 million in 40 years?

Solution.   Let i represent the rate of interest. Then,

$84\ 000(1 + i)^{40} = 49\ 000\ 000$

$$(1 + i)^{40} = \frac{49\ 000}{84}$$

Take the 40th root of each side.

$$1 + i = \left(\frac{49\ 000}{84}\right)^{\frac{1}{40}}$$

$1 + i \doteq 1.173$

$\phantom{1 + {}} i \doteq 0.173$

The annual rate of interest is approximately 17.3%.

Example 3.   Suppose you invest $500 at 8% per annum compounded annually. How many years would it take for your investment to double?

Solution.   Let n represent the number of years. Then,

$500(1.08)^n = 1000$

$(1.08)^n = 2$

Take the logarithm of each side (base 10).

$n \log 1.08 = \log 2$

$$n = \frac{\log 2}{\log 1.08}$$

$ \doteq 9.0$

Hence, $500 earning interest at 8% per annum will double in approximately 9 years.

In many applications of exponential functions it is necessary to solve an equation of the form $y = ca^x$ for the exponent x. This was illustrated in *Example 3*.

Light Penetration

Example 4. For every metre a diver descends below the water surface, the light intensity is reduced by 2.5%. At what depth is the light intensity only 50% of that at the surface?

Solution. Let d metres represent the required depth.
Then,
$$50 = 100(0.975)^d$$
$$(0.975)^d = 0.5$$
Take the logarithm of each side (base 10).
$$d \log 0.975 = \log 0.5$$
$$d = \frac{\log 0.5}{\log 0.975}$$
$$\doteq 27.4$$

The light intensity is only 50% of that at the surface at a depth of approximately 27 m.

Nuclear Fallout

Exponential functions occur in the study of nuclear fallout. This refers to the contamination of the atmosphere and the ground from radioactive particles released in a nuclear accident or explosion. The harmful effects arise when these particles decay into other particles and release radiation. Each radioactive substance decays with a characteristic *halflife*. This is the time required for one-half of the material to decay.

Example 5. In a nuclear test explosion, some strontium-90 is released. This substance has a halflife of 28 years.
a) Draw a graph showing the percent of strontium-90 remaining up to 140 years.
b) Express the percent P of strontium-90 remaining as a function of:
  i) the number of halflives elapsed, n
  ii) the number of years elapsed, t.
c) What percent of strontium-90 remains after 50 years?

Solution. a) Make a table of values for time intervals of 1 halflife. Plot the percent remaining against the time in years.

Halflives (n)	0	1	2	3	4	5
Years (t)	0	28	56	84	112	140
Percent remaining (P)	100	50	25	12.5	6.25	3.13

b) i) After each half life, the percent remaining is halved. Hence, the percent remaining after n half lives have elapsed is:

$$P = 100\left(\frac{1}{2}\right)^{n} \ldots \text{①}$$

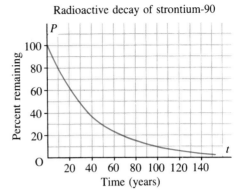

Radioactive decay of strontium-90

ii) Since $t = 28n$, we can write equation ① in terms of t.

Substitute $\frac{t}{28}$ for n.

$$P = 100\left(\frac{1}{2}\right)^{\frac{t}{28}} \ldots \text{②}$$

c) Substitute 50 for t in equation ②.

$$P = 100\left(\frac{1}{2}\right)^{\frac{50}{28}}$$
$$\doteq 29.003\ 235$$

Hence, about 29% of the strontium-90 remains after 50 years.

Example 6. In April 1986 there was a major nuclear accident at the Chernobyl power plant in the Soviet Union. The atmosphere was contaminated with quantities of radioactive iodine-131, which has a half life of 8.1 days. How long did it take for the level of radiation to reduce to 1% of the level immediately after the accident?

Solution. Let P represent the percent of the original radiation that was present after t days. Then, since the half life is 8.1 days,

$$P = 100\left(\frac{1}{2}\right)^{\frac{t}{8.1}}$$

Substitute 1 for P and solve for t by taking the logarithm of each side.

$$1 = 100(0.5)^{\frac{t}{8.1}}$$

$$\log 1 = \log 100 + \frac{t}{8.1}\log 0.5$$

$$0 = 2 + \frac{t}{8.1}\log 0.5$$

$$t = -\frac{16.2}{\log 0.5}$$

$$\doteq 54$$

It took about 54 days for the level of radiation to reduce to 1% of the level immediately after the accident.

EXERCISES 7-10

Compound Interest

1. How much should you invest at 7% per annum compounded annually so that $5000 will be available in 4 years?

2. The 50¢ Bluenose is one of Canada's most famous postage stamps. In 1930 it could be bought at the post office for 50¢. In 1987 a superb copy was sold at an auction for $500. What annual rate of interest corresponds to an investment of 50¢ in 1930 which grows to $500 in 1987?

3. In 1626, Manhattan Island was sold for $24. If that money had been invested at 8% per annum compounded annually, what would it have amounted to today?

4. Suppose you invest $200 at 9% per annum compounded annually. How many years would it take for your investment to grow to $500?

5. Mary invests $2500 at 11% per annum compounded annually. How many years will it take for her investment to double in value?

Light Penetration

6. For every metre a diver descends under water, the intensity of three colors of light is reduced as shown.
   a) For each color, write an equation which expresses the percent P of surface light as a function of the depth d metres.

Color	Percent Reduction per metre
Red	35%
Green	5%
Blue	2.5%

   b) For each color, determine the depth at which about half the light has disappeared.
   c) Let us agree that, for all practical purposes, the light has disappeared when the intensity is only 1% of that at the surface. At what depth would this occur for each color?

7. Several layers of glass are stacked together. Each layer reduces the light passing through it by 5%.
   a) What percent of light passes through 10 layers of glass?
   b) How many layers of glass are needed to reduce the intensity to only 1% of the original light?

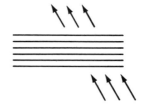

Growth of Populations

8. The town of Springfield is growing at a rate of 6.5% per annum. How many people are there in Springfield now, if there will be 15 000 in 4.5 years?

9. In 1950 the world population was approximately 2.5 billion. The population doubled to 5 billion in 1987. What was the average annual growth rate of the world population from 1950 to 1987?

10. A culture has 750 bacteria. The number of bacteria doubles every 5 h. How many bacteria are in the culture after 12 h?

11. A colony of bees increases by 25% every three months. How many bees should Raiman start with if he wishes to have 10 000 bees in 18 months?

12. If the population of a colony of bacteria doubles every 30 min, how long would it take for the population to triple?

13. Prove that if the growth rate is constant, the time required for a population to double is independent of the population size.

Nuclear Fallout

14. When strontium-90 decays, the percent P remaining is expressed as a function of the time t years by the equation $P \doteq 100(2)^{-0.0357t}$. How long is it until the percent remaining is: a) 10% b) 1%?

15. The halflives of two products of a nuclear explosion are shown. For each substance
    a) Draw a graph showing the percent remaining during the first five halflives.

Substance	Halflife
Iodine-131	8.1 days
Cesium-144	282 days

    b) Express the percent remaining as a function of:
       i) the number of halflives elapsed, n ii) the number of days elapsed, t.
    c) What percent of the substance remains after:
       i) one week   ii) 30 days   iii) one year?
    d) How long is it until the percent remaining of each substance is:
       i) 10%   ii) 0.1%?

16. Another product of a nuclear explosion is plutonium-239, which has a halflife of 24 000 years. What percent of plutonium-239 remains after:
    a) 100 years   b) 1000 years   c) 10 000 years   d) 100 000 years?

17. Polonium-210 is a radioactive element with a halflife of 20 weeks. From a sample of 25 g, how much would remain after:
    a) 30 weeks   b) 14 weeks   c) 1 year   d) 511 days?

Other Applications

18. Jacques bought a new car for $15 000. Each year the value of the car depreciates to 70% of its value the previous year. In how many years will the car be worth only $500?

19. A pan of water is brought to a boil and then removed from the heat. Every 5 min thereafter the difference between the temperature of the water and room temperature is reduced by 50%.
    a) Room temperature is 20°C. Express the temperature of the water as a function of the time since it was removed from the heat.
    b) How many minutes does it take for the temperature of the water to reach 30°C?

20. A cup of coffee contains approximately 100 mg of caffeine. When you drink the coffee, the caffeine is absorbed into the bloodstream, and is eventually metabolized by the body. Every 5 h the amount of caffeine in the bloodstream is reduced by 50%.
    a) Write an equation which expresses the amount of caffeine c milligrams in the bloodstream as an exponential function of the elapsed time t hours since drinking one cup of coffee.
    b) How many hours does it take for the amount of caffeine to be reduced to:
       i) 10 mg   ii) 1 mg?

21. In a steel mill, red-hot slabs of steel are pressed many times between heavy rollers. The drawings show two stages in rolling a slab.

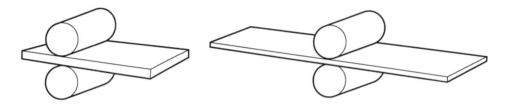

    A slab is 2.00 m long and 0.120 m thick. On each pass through the rollers, its length increases by 20%.
    a) Write the equation which expresses the length L metres of the slab as an exponential function of the number of passes n through the rollers.
    b) How many passes are needed to increase the length of the slab to 50 m?

22. a) For the slab in *Exercise 21*, by what factor does the thickness of the slab decrease on each pass through the rollers? Assume the width is constant.
    b) Write an equation which expresses the thickness t metres of the slab as an exponential function of the number of passes n through the rollers.
    c) How many passes are needed to reduce the thickness of the slab to 0.001 m?
    d) How long would the slab be when its thickness is 0.001 m?

ⓒ

23. The total amount of arable land in the world is about 3.2×10^9 ha. At current population rates, about 0.4 ha of land is required to grow food for each person in the world.
    a) Assuming a 1987 world population of 5 billion and a constant growth rate of 1.5%, determine the year when the demand for arable land exceeds the supply.
    b) Compare the effect of each comment on the result of part a).
       i) doubling the productivity of the land so that only 0.2 ha is required to grow food for each person
       ii) reducing the growth rate by one-half, to 0.75%
       iii) doubling the productivity of the land *and* reducing the growth rate by 50%

7-11 APPLICATIONS OF EXPONENTIAL AND LOGARITHMIC FUNCTIONS: PART TWO

Growth of Populations

Occasionally we see statements such as this, in magazines and newspapers.

In favorable breeding conditions, the population of a swarm of desert locusts can multiply 10-fold in 20 days.

This information is not sufficient to calculate the population of a swarm of locusts, since an initial population figure is not given. But we can still use the statement to compare the populations of a swarm at two different times.

Example 1. Use the information above to compare the population of a swarm of locusts after 30 days with its population after 20 days.

Solution. Let P_0 represent the population of a swarm at $t = 0$. Then we can use the fact that the population is multiplied 10-fold in 20 days to express the population P as an exponential function of the time t days.

$$P = P_0(10)^{\frac{t}{20}}$$
$$\text{or} \qquad P = P_0(10)^{0.05t} \quad \ldots \text{①}$$

Let P_{20} and P_{30} represent the populations after 20 and 30 days, respectively. Then, using equation ①, we obtain

$$P_{20} = P_0(10)^{0.05(20)}$$
$$= P_0(10) \quad \ldots \text{②}$$
$$P_{30} = P_0(10)^{0.05(30)}$$
$$= P_0(10)^{1.5} \quad \ldots \text{③}$$

Since we do not know the value of P_0, we cannot calculate P_{20} or P_{30}. But we can find their ratio by dividing equation ③ by equation ②.

$$\frac{P_{30}}{P_{20}} = \frac{P_0(10)^{1.5}}{P_0(10)}$$
$$= 10^{0.5}$$
$$\doteq 3.162\ 277\ 7$$

A swarm is about 3.2 times as large after 30 days as it was after 20 days.

Calculations such as those in *Example 1* are used in many applications of exponential and logarithmic functions.

Earthquakes

A scale for comparing the intensities of earthquakes was devised by Charles Richter about 50 years ago. The intensity of an earthquake is measured by the amount of ground motion as recorded on a seismometer.

When we use the Richter scale, we do not need to know the actual intensities, or seismometer readings. The scale is used simply to compare the intensities of two earthquakes using the following rule.

Each increase of 1 unit in magnitude on the Richter scale represents a 10-fold increase in intensity as measured on a seismometer.

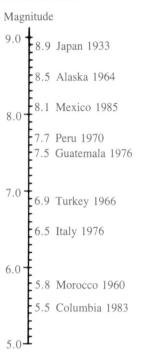

The Richter Scale

Magnitude

9.0 — 8.9 Japan 1933

8.5 Alaska 1964

8.1 Mexico 1985

8.0 — 7.7 Peru 1970

7.5 Guatemala 1976

7.0 — 6.9 Turkey 1966

6.5 Italy 1976

6.0 — 5.8 Morocco 1960

5.5 Columbia 1983

5.0 —

Consider, for example, the Italy earthquake of 1976 which had a magnitude of 6.5 on the Richter scale. Notice that the Guatemala earthquake the same year had a magnitude of 7.5, which is exactly 1 unit greater. This means that the second earthquake was *10 times* as intense as the first. Similarly, the Alaska earthquake in 1964 was 10×10, or *100 times* as intense as the 1976 Italy earthquake, and $10 \times 10 \times 10$, or *1000 times* as intense as the 1983 earthquake in Colombia. But, how do we compare the intensities of earthquakes such as the Alaska earthquake in 1964 and the Turkey earthquake in 1966, whose magnitudes do not differ by a whole number?

Example 2. Use the information above to compare the intensity of the 1964 Alaska earthquake with the intensity of the 1966 Turkey earthquake.

Solution. Let I_0 represent the intensity of an earthquake with a magnitude of 0 on the Richter scale. Then we can use the fact that the intensity is multiplied 10-fold for each increase in 1 unit of magnitude to express the intensity I as an exponential function of the magnitude M.

$$I = I_0(10)^M \quad \ldots \text{①}$$

Let I_A and I_T represent the intensities of the Alaska and Turkey earthquakes, respectively. Then, using equation ①, we obtain

$$I_A = I_0(10)^{8.5} \quad \ldots \text{②}$$
$$I_T = I_0(10)^{6.9} \quad \ldots \text{③}$$

Since we do not know the value of I_0, we cannot calculate I_A or I_T. But we can find their ratio by dividing equation ② by equation ③.

$$\frac{I_A}{I_T} = \frac{I_0(10)^{8.5}}{I_0(10)^{6.9}}$$
$$= 10^{8.5 - 6.9}$$
$$= 10^{1.6}$$
$$\doteq 39.810\ 717$$

The Alaska earthquake was about 40 times as intense as the Turkey earthquake.

Acid Rain

Acid rain has become a major environmental problem. The acidity of rainwater is measured on a special scale called a *pH scale*. Each 1 unit decrease in pH represents a 10-fold *increase* in acidity. For example, the pH of vinegar is 2 units less than that of tomatoes. Hence, vinegar is 10^2, or 100 times more acidic than tomatoes.

Let A represent the acid content of a substance with a pH of P. Then, since each increase of 1 unit in P represents a 10-fold decrease in A,

$$A = A_0(0.1)^P \dots \text{①}$$

where A_0 represents the acid content of a substance with pH 0.
To express P as a function of A, solve equation ① for P.

$$\log A = \log A_0 + P \log 0.1$$
$$P \log 0.1 = \log A - \log A_0$$
$$P = \frac{\log \left(\frac{A}{A_0}\right)}{\log 0.1}$$

or $$P = -\log \left(\frac{A}{A_0}\right) \dots \text{②}$$

Equation ② expresses the pH of a substance as a logarithmic function of its acid content.

In the equation for pH, $P = -\log \left(\frac{A}{A_0}\right)$, notice that the value of A_0 is not given. Despite this, we can still use this equation to obtain useful information. This involves a comparison of the acid content, or pH of two substances.

Example 3. A lake in the Muskoka region of Ontario has a pH of 4.0. How many times as acidic as clean rain water, which has a pH of 5.6, is the water in this lake?

Solution. Use the equation developed above. $P = -\log \left(\frac{A}{A_0}\right)$

Let P_1 and A_1 represent the pH and acid content of clean rain water, and let P_2 and A_2 represent the pH and acid content of the lake. Then,

$$P_1 = -\log \left(\frac{A_1}{A_0}\right)$$
$$P_2 = -\log \left(\frac{A_2}{A_0}\right)$$

Subtract and then use the law of logarithms for division.

$$P_1 - P_2 = -\log \left(\frac{A_1}{A_0}\right) + \log \left(\frac{A_2}{A_0}\right)$$
$$= \log \left(\frac{A_2}{A_0}\right) - \log \left(\frac{A_1}{A_0}\right)$$
$$= \log \left(\frac{A_2}{A_1}\right)$$

Substitute 5.6 for P_1 and 4.0 for P_2.

$$5.6 - 4.0 = \log\left(\frac{A_2}{A_1}\right)$$

$$1.6 = \log\left(\frac{A_2}{A_1}\right)$$

By the definition of a logarithm

$$\frac{A_2}{A_1} = 10^{1.6}$$

$$\doteq 39.8$$

Hence, the lake is about 40 times as acidic as clean rain water.

EXERCISES 7-11

Ⓑ

Growth of Populations

1. The population of a swarm of insects can multiply 5-fold in 4 weeks. Let P_0 represent the population at time $t = 0$.
   a) Write expressions to represent the population after:
      i) 4 weeks   ii) 6 weeks.
   b) How many times as great is the population after 6 weeks as it was after 4 weeks?

2. The population of a nest of ants can multiply 3-fold in 5 weeks. After 8 weeks, how many times as great is the population as it was after 5 weeks?

3. The population of a colony of bacteria can double in 25 min. After one hour, how many times as great is the population as it was after 25 min?

Earthquakes

4. On July 26, 1986, an earthquake with magnitude 5.5 hit California. The next day a second earthquake with magnitude 6.2 hit the same region. How many times as intense as the first earthquake was the second earthquake?

5. In 1985/86, three earthquakes hit Mexico City. How many times as intense as:
   a) the second earthquake was the first
   b) the third earthquake was the second
   c) the third earthquake was the first?

Mexico City Earthquakes	
Date	**Magnitude**
Sept. 19, 1985	8.1
Sept. 21, 1985	7.5
April 30, 1986	7.0

6. It has been observed that for every decrease of 1 unit in magnitude, earthquakes are about 6 or 7 times as frequent. In a given year, how should the number of earthquakes with magnitudes between 4.0 and 4.9 compare with the number of earthquakes with magnitudes between:
   a) 5.0 and 5.9   b) 6.0 and 6.9   c) 7.0 and 7.9?

Acid Rain

7. Between 1956 and 1976 the annual average pH of precipitation at Sault Ste. Marie, Ontario, dropped from 5.6 to 4.3. How many times as acidic as the precipitation in 1956 was the precipitation in 1976?

8. In the spring, the pH of a stream dropped from 6.5 to 5.5 during a 3-week period in April.
   a) How many times as acidic did the stream become?
   b) Why would this happen in April?
   c) The mean pH of Lake Huron is 8.2. How many times as acidic was the stream:
      i) before the 3-week period   ii) after the 3-week period?

9. When the pH of the water in a lake falls below 4.7, nearly all species of fish in the lake are deformed or killed. How many times as acidic as clean rainwater, which has a pH of 5.6, is such a lake?

Other Applications

10. If the temperature is constant, the pressure of the Earth's atmosphere decreases by 5% for every 300 m increase in altitude.
    a) Let P_1 and P_2 represent the pressures at altitudes h_1 and h_2 respectively. Derive an equation which expresses the ratio $\dfrac{P_2}{P_1}$ as an exponential function of the difference in altitudes $h_2 - h_1$.
    b) A jet gains 1000 m in altitude. By what percent did the atmospheric pressure decrease?

11. One of the most remarkable technological trends ever recorded is the growth of the number of components on a silicon chip. Since 1970, the number of components on each chip has quadrupled every three years. It is expected that this level should persist until the early 1990s.
    a) Let N_1 and N_2 represent the numbers of components on a chip in the years t_1 and t_2 respectively. Derive an equation which expresses the ratio $\dfrac{N_2}{N_1}$ as an exponential function of the time difference $t_2 - t_1$.
    b) How did the number of components on a chip in 1985 compare with the number in: i) 1980   ii) 1975   iii) 1970?

 **INVESTIGATE**

The $\boxed{\text{ln}}$ key on a Calculator

Your calculator should have a key marked $\boxed{\text{ln}}$. This key calculates logarithms of numbers to a base different from 10. Find the base of these logarithms as accurately as you can.

THE MATHEMATICAL MIND

Natural Logarithms

Logarithms were introduced into mathematics almost four hundred years ago by the Scotsman, John Napier. The invention was enthusiastically hailed throughout Europe as a great breakthrough in computation. This was because logarithms can be used to reduce multiplication and division to the simpler operations of addition and subtraction. For example, the law of logarithms, $\log xy = \log x + \log y$, can be applied to multiply two numbers x and y by adding their logarithms. In the past, extensive tables of logarithms were prepared for this purpose. Of course, modern technology has rendered this method of computation obsolete.

Originally, Napier's logarithms had a certain base which was different from 10. These logarithms are called *natural logarithms*.

You can evaluate natural logarithms using the $\boxed{\ln}$ key on your calculator. For example, key in: 3 $\boxed{\ln}$ to display 1.0986123. We write $\ln 3 \doteq 1.098\ 612\ 3$, and we say "lawn 3 is approximately 1.098 612 3". To explain what this means, we need to know the base of the logarithms. The base of the natural logarithms is always represented by the letter e.

You can use your calculator to find the value of e. Key in: 1 $\boxed{e^x}$ or 1 $\boxed{INV}$ $\boxed{\ln}$ to display 2.7182818. Hence, $e \doteq 2.718\ 281\ 8$

Therefore, $\ln 3 \doteq 1.098\ 612\ 3$ means that $e^{1.0986123} \doteq 3$, where $e \doteq 2.718\ 281\ 8$.

Natural logarithms are a particular case of logarithms to base a, which were studied earlier in this chapter. Hence, natural logarithms have all the properties of logarithms to base a. This means that we can use natural logarithms to solve problems like those solved earlier.

For example, to solve the equation $e^x = 3.5$ for x, take the natural logarithm of both sides, and write $x \ln e = \ln 3.5$. Since $\ln e = 1$, then $x = \ln 3.5$. Key in: 3.5 $\boxed{\ln}$ to display 1.2527630. Hence, $x \doteq 1.252\ 763$.

QUESTIONS

1. Use your calculator to evaluate each logarithm. Then write the result in exponential form and check with the calculator.
   a) ln 2   b) ln 4   c) ln 30   d) ln 100
   e) ln 8750   f) ln 0.5   g) ln 0.1   h) ln 0.000 44

2. Solve for x.
   a) $e^x = 5$ b) $e^x = 15$ c) $e^x = 53.9$ d) $e^x = 266$
   e) $e^x = 1$ f) $e^x = 0.25$ g) $e^x = 0.092$ h) $e^x = 0.0003$

3. Solve for x.
   a) $\ln x = 1$ b) $\ln x = 1.6$ c) $\ln x = 3$ d) $\ln x = 4.5$
   e) $\ln x = 0.33$ f) $\ln x = -1$ g) $\ln x = -1.4$ h) $\ln x = -2.2$

4. Write as a single logarithm, and check with your calculator.
   a) $\ln 5 + \ln 3$ b) $\ln 2 + \ln 10$ c) $2 \ln 6$

   d) $\ln 18 - \ln 2$ e) $\ln 21 - \ln 3$ f) $\frac{1}{2} \ln 25$

5. a) Simplify each expression.
      i) $\ln e$ ii) $\ln e^2$ iii) $\ln e^{-3}$ iv) $\ln e^{0.2}$
   b) Based on the results of part a), state a general result.

6. About 200 years ago, at age 15, Carl Friedrich Gauss noticed that the number of primes less than a given natural number n can be approximated by $\dfrac{n}{\ln n}$.
   Use this expression to approximate the number of primes less than:
   a) 10   b) 100   c) 1000   d) 10^6 e) 10^9

7. Although it has never been proved, mathematicians have observed that the number of twin primes less than a given number n is approximately equal to $\dfrac{2n}{(\ln n)^2}$. Use this result to approximate the number of twin primes less than:
   a) 10   b) 100   c) 1000   d) 10^6 e) 10^9

8. It has been proved that the average spacing of the prime numbers near a given natural number n is approximately equal to $\ln n$. For example, the six prime numbers closest to 50, and the successive differences between them are:

   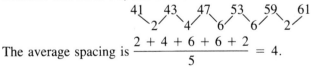

   The average spacing is $\dfrac{2 + 4 + 6 + 6 + 2}{5} = 4$.

   a) Find ln 50, and compare it with the above result.
   b) Check that the average spacing of the six primes closest to:
      i) 100 is approximately ln 100   ii) 150 is approximately ln 150.

MATHEMATICS AROUND US

Applications of Natural Logarithms

In the applications of exponential and logarithmic functions studied in *Sections 7-10* and *7-11*, many different bases were used. For example, in compound interest applications the base depended on the interest rate. In other applications we used bases 2, $\frac{1}{2}$, and 10.

It would simplify matters to use the same base every time, and mathematicians have found that there is an advantage to using base e.

For example, consider population growth. In 1987 the world population reached 5 billion, and was increasing at about 1.6% per annum. Hence, an equation expressing the population P billion as a function of time t years relative to 1987 is

$$P = 5(1.016)^t \ldots \text{①}$$

Let's investigate what would happen if we express this equation with base e instead of base 10. To do this, we must write 1.016 as a power of e.

Let $1.016 = e^k$. Then, by definition, $k = \ln 1.016$
Key in: 1.016 $\boxed{\ln}$ to display 0.0158733
To two significant figures, $k \doteq 0.016$
Hence, $1.016 \doteq e^{0.016}$, and equation ① can be written as follows.

$$P = 5e^{0.016t}$$

Initial population   Growth rate

Look at that! The constant in the exponent is 0.016, which is the growth rate. We now see an advantage of using base e. When an exponential function is expressed with base e, the constant in the exponent is the rate of growth. e is the only number with this property. Hence, it is the natural base to use in problems involving exponential growth and decay.

There is another advantage. Notice that the value of k obtained was not exactly 0.016. This slight discrepancy is caused by the way in which e is defined in higher mathematics. The definition assumes that the population grows continuously, and that the new members are not added all at once at the end of the year. In this case, the growth rate is called *instantaneous*. In the above example, the instantaneous rate of growth is 0.015 873 3, whereas the annual rate is 0.016. In some applications the difference may not be significant. Since a rigorous development of instantaneous rates of growth requires calculus, we will ignore its effect.

Example 1. In 1986 the population of Canada was 25.5 million, and was growing at the rate of approximately 1.0% per annum.
a) Write an equation for the population P million after t years.
b) Assuming that the growth rate remains constant, use the equation to determine:
   i) the predicted population in the year 2000
   ii) the number of years required for the population to reach 40 million.

Solution.
a) The equation is $P = 25.5e^{0.01t}$.
b) i) The year 2000 is 14 years later than 1986. Hence, substitute 14 for t.

$$P = 25.5e^{0.01(14)}$$
$$= 25.5e^{0.14}$$
$$\doteq 29.331\ 982$$

The population will be approximately 29.3 million in the year 2000.

   ii) Substitute 40 for P.

$$40 = 25.5e^{0.01t}$$

To solve for t, take the natural logarithm of each side.

$$\ln 40 = \ln 25.5 + 0.01t$$
$$t = \frac{\ln 40 - \ln 25.5}{0.01}$$
$$\doteq 45.020\ 100$$

The population will reach 40 million 45 years after 1986, or in the year 2031.

Example 2. In 1987 the world population reached 5 billion. According to United Nations forecasts, the population will reach 6.1 billion in the year 2001. Calculate the average annual rate of growth from 1987 to 2001.

Solution. Let $P = P_0 e^{kt}$
Substitute 5 for P_0, 6.1 for P, and 14 for t.

$$6.1 = 5e^{14k}$$

Take the natural logarithm of each side.

$$\ln 6.1 = \ln 5 + 14k$$
$$k = \frac{\ln 6.1 - \ln 5}{14}$$
$$\doteq 0.014\ 203\ 6$$

Hence, the average annual rate of growth is about 1.42%.

The conventions of writing log x to mean the logarithm to base 10 of x, and ln x to mean the logarithm to base e of x are by no means universal. In higher mathematics, natural logarithms are usually the only logarithms that are used, and log x often refers to the natural logarithm of x. Also, many computer languages use LOG(X) for the natural logarithm function.

QUESTIONS

1. Each equation represents the population P million of a country t years after 1985. State the 1985 population and the growth rate for each country.
   a) Italy $\qquad P = 57e^{0.007t}$
   b) Kenya $\qquad P = 20e^{0.030t}$
   c) Costa Rica $\quad P = 2.6e^{0.038t}$

2. In 1985 the population of India was 770 million, and was growing at approximately 1.6% per annum.
   a) Write an equation for the population P million after t years, using an exponential function with base e.
   b) Assuming that the growth rate is constant, determine:
      i) the predicted population in 1995
      ii) when the population will reach 1 billion
      iii) when the population was 500 million.

3. When uranium-238 decays, the percent P remaining after t years is given by the equation $P = 100e^{-1.53 \times 10^{-10}t}$.
   a) What percent remains after 10 million years?
   b) Determine the halflife of uranium-238.

4. The altitude of an aircraft can be determined by measuring the air pressure. In the stratosphere (between 12 000 m and 30 000 m) the pressure P kilopascals is expressed as an exponential function of the altitude h metres by the equation $P = 130e^{-0.000155h}$.
   a) What is the altitude if the pressure is 8.5 kPa; 2.5 kPa?
   b) What is the pressure at an altitude of 20 000 m?
   c) Solve the equation for h to obtain an equation expressing the altitude as a logarithmic function of the pressure.

5. A rule of thumb which is used to approximate the time required for an investment to double in value is to divide 70 by the interest rate. For example, if the interest rate is 8%, then an investment will double in approximately $\dfrac{70}{8}$, or 9 years. Explain why the rule of thumb works.

1. Evaluate.

   a) $8^{-\frac{2}{3}}$

   b) $27^{\frac{1}{3}}$

   c) $32^{\frac{3}{5}}$

   d) $\left(\dfrac{1}{125}\right)^{-\frac{2}{3}}$

   e) $(2.25)^{1.5}$

   f) $\left(\dfrac{16}{81}\right)^{-0.75}$

   g) $(0.0144)^0$

   h) $(0.0016)^{1.25}$

2. A bacteria culture doubles in size every 8 h. If there are now 1000 bacteria in the culture, how many:
   a) will there be in   i) 16 h   ii) 44 h
   b) were there   i) 24 h ago   ii) 1.5 days ago?

3. Simplify.

   a) $\dfrac{-15x^{-3}y^2 \times 8x^5y^3}{-24x^{-1}y^7}$

   b) $\dfrac{18m^2n^{-5} \times (-5m^{-4}n^2)}{-15m^3n^{-4} \times 12m^{-7}n^0}$

   c) $(2a^2b)^{-3}(5ab^{-2})^2$

   d) $(x^{\frac{1}{2}}y^{-\frac{2}{3}})^3 \times \left(\dfrac{3}{5}x^{-\frac{3}{4}}y^{\frac{1}{3}}\right)^2$

   e) $\dfrac{21a^{-\frac{3}{4}}b^{\frac{2}{3}}}{-35a^{-\frac{1}{2}}b}$

   f) $\dfrac{6m^{\frac{1}{4}}n^{-\frac{1}{3}} \times 35m^{-\frac{3}{4}}n^{\frac{1}{2}}}{14m^{\frac{1}{2}}n^{\frac{5}{6}} \times 10m^{\frac{3}{2}}n^{-\frac{1}{2}}}$

4. Simplify.

   a) $\dfrac{(x^{3a})(x^{-5a})}{x^{-2a}}$

   b) $\dfrac{(m^{3x+y})(2m^{x-2y})}{(3m^{-2x+3y})}$

   c) $\dfrac{(a^{\frac{x}{4}})(b^{\frac{2x}{3}})^3}{(a^{\frac{3x}{2}})^{-\frac{1}{2}}(b^{\frac{3x}{4}})^2}$

5. How much must be invested at 7.5% interest compounded annually, so that there will be $5600 in 12 years?

6. There are 5400 red ants in a particular colony. If there were 1200 ants in the colony 8 months ago, what is the monthly rate of growth?

7. A diamond ring worth $12 500 increases in value by 12% per year. In how many years will it be worth $50 000?

8. Write in exponential form.

   a) $\log 1000 = 3$

   b) $\log \sqrt{10} = \dfrac{1}{2}$

   c) $\log_3 81 = 4$

9. Write in logarithmic form.
   a) $10^4 = 10\ 000$

   b) $10^{-3} = 0.001$

   c) $5^4 = 625$

10. Solve for x.
    a) $\log x = 2$

    b) $\log x = -5$

    c) $\log_x 64 = 2$

    d) $\log_3 x = 3$

    e) $\log_5 0.04 = x$

    f) $\log_2 x = 5$

11. Write in terms of $\log x$ and $\log y$.
    a) $\log (xy^2)$

    b) $\log (x\sqrt{y})$

    c) $\log (10x^3y^2)$

    d) $\log (\sqrt[3]{xy^2})$

    e) $\log \left(\dfrac{x}{\sqrt{y}}\right)$

    f) $\log \left(\dfrac{x^2}{\sqrt[3]{y}}\right)$

12. Write as a single logarithm.
    a) $\log x + \log y - \log z$
    b) $2 \log x - \log y$
    c) $3 \log x + 5 \log y$
    d) $\dfrac{1}{2} \log x + 3 \log y$
    e) $\log (2x - 3) + \log (y + 5)$
    f) $3 \log (x + y) - \log (x - y)$

13. Express.
    a) 8 as a power of 3
    b) 24 as a power of 6
    c) 12 as a power of 1.3
    d) 0.78 as a power of 2

14. Solve for x. Give the answers to 4 decimal places.
    a) $5^x = 9$
    b) $14^x = 8$
    c) $3^{2x-1} = 25$
    d) $4^{5-x} = 45$
    e) $7^{3-x} = 4$
    f) $8^{5x-2} = 69$
    g) $2^{1-x} = 9^{x+1}$
    h) $5^{3x+1} = 12^{x+4}$

15. Evaluate.

    a) $\log 10\ 000$
    b) $\log_2 16$
    c) $\log_3 243$
    d) $\log_2 \left(\dfrac{1}{8}\right)$

    e) $\log_{\frac{1}{3}} 27$
    f) $\log_{\sqrt{2}} 32$
    g) $\log_5 0.008$
    h) $\log_7 343$

16. Solve and check.
    a) $3 \log x = \log 512 - \log 8$
    b) $\log_2 x + \log_2 (x - 3) = 2$
    c) $\log_{\sqrt{2}} (x - 2) + \log_{\sqrt{2}} (x + 1) = 4$
    d) $\log_6 (x + 3) + \log_6 (x - 2) = 1$

17. Graph each function and its inverse on the same grid.
    a) $y = 3^x$
    b) $y = \log_5 x$
    c) $y = \log_{\frac{1}{3}} x$

18. The halflife of a radioactive substance is 23 days. How long is it until the percent remaining is:
    a) 10%
    b) 3% ?

19. a) An air filter loses about 0.3% of its effectiveness each day. What is its effectiveness after 145 days as a percent of its initial effectiveness?
    b) The filter should be replaced when its effectiveness has decreased to 20% of its initial value. After how long should it be replaced?

20. In 1951 the UNIVAC computer performed approximately 1000 arithmetic operations per second. Since then, the speed of computers has doubled, on the average, about every 2 years.
    a) Express the number of operations per second N as an exponential function of the time n years since 1951.
    b) Predict when computers will be able to perform a billion operations per second. What assumption are you making?

21. On each bounce a ball rises to 70% of the height from which it fell. Let us agree that, for all practical purposes, the ball stops bouncing when the height to which it rises is only 0.1% of the height from which it was dropped originally. How many bounces will this take?

The Olympic Games are held every four years. The dates form an arithmetic sequence. Were they held the year you were born? (See Section 8-2 *Example 4*.)

8-1 WHAT IS A SEQUENCE?

"Sequence" and "series" are two words which are often used inter-
changeably in everyday language. In mathematics, however, they have
precise and different meanings. We shall consider sequence first, and
series in a later section.

In a sequence, the order in which the events or numbers occur is
important. Here are some examples of sequences.

In football, the quarterback uses a
sequence of audible signals which informs
and directs his team but confuses the
defensive team. One such sequence might
be:

Red 5 29 6 Blue 4 14 2 Green 3 21 5

This tells player 4 to use play 14 and
carry the ball through hole 2.

A computer program is a sequence of instructions. You will find
several programs in this text.

IQ tests sometimes contain problems in which a sequence of letters,
numbers, or geometric figures is given. The problem is to discover the
pattern. Can you determine the next diagram?

In mathematics, many sequences involve numbers. These numbers
are called the *terms* of the sequence. Frequently, there is a pattern that
is used to write the terms of the sequence.

Example 1. Describe each pattern, and predict the next term.
  a) 3, 7, 11, 15, . . .   b) 2, 6, 18, 54, . . .   c) 1, 1, 2, 3, 5, 8, . . .

Solution. a) 3, 7, 11, 15, . . .
      Add 4 to the preceding term. The next term is 19.
  b) 2, 6, 18, 54, . . .
      Multiply the preceding term by 3. The next term is 162.
  c) 1, 1, 2, 3, 5, 8, . . .
      Add the two preceding terms. The next term is 13.

Several sequences may begin with the same three or four terms. It
is therefore necessary, when describing a sequence, to list enough terms
to show the pattern which generates the succeeding terms.

The symbols, t_1, t_2, t_3, . . . are used to represent the terms of a
sequence. Thus for the sequence of square numbers: 1, 4, 9, 16, . . .
$t_1 = 1$, or 1^2 $t_2 = 4$, or 2^2 $t_3 = 9$, or 3^2 $t_4 = 16$, or 4^2
The *general term* is n^2; that is, $t_n = n^2$

In many sequences, the formula for the general term can be used
to generate the terms of the sequence.

Example 2. Write the first four terms and the 10th term for the sequence defined
by $t_n = \dfrac{n}{n + 1}$.

Solution. Substitute 1, 2, 3, 4, and 10 for n in the formula for t_n.

$$t_1 = \frac{1}{1 + 1}, \text{ or } \frac{1}{2} \qquad t_2 = \frac{2}{2 + 1}, \text{ or } \frac{2}{3} \qquad t_3 = \frac{3}{3 + 1}, \text{ or } \frac{3}{4}$$

$$t_4 = \frac{4}{4 + 1}, \text{ or } \frac{4}{5} \qquad t_{10} = \frac{10}{10 + 1}, \text{ or } \frac{10}{11}$$

The sequence is: $\dfrac{1}{2}, \dfrac{2}{3}, \dfrac{3}{4}, \dfrac{4}{5}, \dots, \dfrac{10}{11}, \dots$

When a few terms of a sequence are given, a formula for the general
term can sometimes be found.

Example 3. Describe each sequence and write an expression for the general term t_n.
a) 101, 102, 103, 104, . . .   b) 2, 4, 6, 8, . . .
c) 6, 11, 16, 21, 26, . . .   d) 3, 9, 27, 81, . . .
e) 0, 3, 8, 15, 24, . . .

Solution. a) 101, 102, 103, 104, . . .
The sequence is the positive integers greater than 100.
$t_n = 100 + n$
b) 2, 4, 6, 8, . . .
The sequence is the even numbers. $t_n = 2n$
c) 6, 11, 16, 21, 26, . . .
The sequence is the multiples of 5 increased by 1. $t_n = 5n + 1$
d) 3, 9, 27, 81, . . .
The sequence is the powers of 3. $t_n = 3^n$
e) 0, 3, 8, 15, 24, . . .
The sequence is the square numbers decreased by 1. $t_n = n^2 - 1$

EXERCISES 8-1

(A)

1. Explain how a sequence is involved in each operation.
   a) Opening a combination lock   b) Dialing a telephone number
   c) Starting a car   d) Writing a computer program
   e) Baking a cake   f) Finding a word in a dictionary

2. What are the next three letters in each sequence?
   a) A C E G I . . .   b) A B D G . . .   c) A B C B D B E B . . .

3. Describe each pattern and predict the next 3 terms.
   a) 2, 4, 6, 8, . . .   b) 1, 3, 9, 27, . . .   c) 5, 10, 15, 20, . . .
   d) 1, 2, 4, 7, 11, . . .   e) 16, 8, 4, 2, . . .   f) 2, 5, 8, 11, . . .

Ⓑ

4. The general term of a sequence is given. Write the first 5 terms.
   a) $t_n = 2n$ b) $t_n = 10 + n$ c) $t_n = 3n$
   d) $t_n = 2^n$ e) $t_n = 10 - n$ f) $t_n = n$

5. Describe each sequence and write an expression for its general term t_n.
   a) 1, 3, 5, 7, 9, . . .   b) 5, 10, 15, 20, 25, . . .
   c) 4, 9, 14, 19, 24, . . .   d) 10, 100, 1000, 10 000, . . .

6. The general term of a sequence is given. Write the first 5 terms.
   a) $t_n = 3n - 2$ b) $t_n = 2^n - 1$ c) $t_n = 21 - 3n$
   d) $t_n = 2n + 5$ e) $t_n = \dfrac{n}{3n + 1}$ f) $t_n = 3 - \dfrac{1}{n}$

7. Find the indicated terms in each sequence.
   a) $t_n = 10 + 2n$, t_7 and t_{12} b) $t_n = 6n + 5$, t_2 and t_8
   c) $t_n = n^2 - 5$, t_4 and t_9 d) $t_n = (-2)^n$, t_2 and t_5

8. Which of the general terms listed is the general term for each sequence?
   i) $t_n = 5n - 1$ ii) $t_n = 22 - 2n$ iii) $t_n = 10^{n-1}$
   iv) $t_n = 2n - 20$ v) $t_n = 4n - 3$ vi) $t_n = 2(4^{n-1})$
   a) 1, 5, 9, 13, . . .   b) 20, 18, 16, 14, . . .
   c) 2, 8, 32, 128, . . .   d) 1, 10, 100, 1000, . . .

9. Find an expression for the general term of each sequence.
   a) 2, 4, 6, 8, 10, . . .   b) 5, 7, 9, 11, 13, . . .
   c) $-3, -1, 1, 3, 5, . . .$ d) 2, 4, 8, 16, 32, . . .
   e) 1, 3, 7, 15, 31, . . .   f) 16, 13, 10, 7, 4, . . .
   g) $1, \dfrac{2}{3}, \dfrac{3}{5}, \dfrac{4}{7}, \dfrac{5}{9}, . . .$ h) $\dfrac{1}{2}, \dfrac{2}{3}, \dfrac{3}{4}, \dfrac{4}{5}, \dfrac{5}{6}, . . .$

10. Create as many different patterns as you can that start with 1, 2, 3, . . .

Ⓒ

11. Is each statement a correct definition of a sequence of numbers?
    a) A sequence is a set of numbers.
    b) A sequence is a set of numbers written in a definite order.
    c) A sequence is a function with domain the real numbers.
    d) A sequence is a function with domain the positive integers.

12. Write the next 2 terms of each sequence.
    a) Power functions: $f(x) = x^2$, $f(x) = x^3$, $f(x) = x^4$, . . .
    b) Polynomial functions: $f(x) = ax + b$, $f(x) = ax^2 + bx + c$,
       $f(x) = ax^3 + bx^2 + cx + d$, . . .

13. The least number of diagonals needed to divide a sequence of regular polygons into triangles forms a sequence.
    a) List the next three terms of the sequence shown for the number of diagonals.
    b) Find a formula for the general term.

Regular Polygon	Number of		Angle
	sides	diagonals	
Equilateral triangle	3	0	60°
Square	4	1	90°
Pentagon	5	2	108°

14. The angle measures in a sequence of regular polygons also form a sequence.
    a) List the next three terms of the sequence shown in *Exercise 13*.
    b) Find a formula for the general term.

15. The diagram shows a system of one-way streets.
    a) How many different routes are there from A:
       i) to B   ii) to C   iii) to D   iv) to E?
    b) Explain how you could find the number of routes if there were more squares in the diagram.

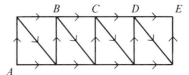

INVESTIGATE

These sequences all start with the same 3 terms. What is the pattern in each sequence?
a) 2, 3, 5, 7, 11, 13, . . .   b) 2, 3, 5, 8, 12, 17, . . .
c) 2, 3, 5, 8, 13, 21, . . .   d) 2, 3, 5, 10, 20, 40, . . .
e) 2, 3, 5, 6, 7, 8, 10, . . .   f) 2, 3, 5, 14, 69, 965, . . .

INVESTIGATE

The first 6 terms of this sequence are prime; the next term is not. Find other sequences like this. Write a report of your findings.
7,   37,   337,   3337,   33 337,   333 337,   3 333 337, . . .

8-2 ARITHMETIC SEQUENCES

Throughout recorded history, comets have been associated with significant events such as famine, plague, and floods. In 1705, the English astronomer, Edmund Halley, noticed striking similarities in the records of major comets which had appeared in 1531, 1607, and 1682. He noticed also that these dates were almost the same number of years apart.

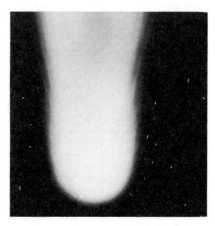

1531   1607   1682
76 years   75 years

Halley concluded that the three appearances represented return visits of the same comet, which was in an extremely elongated orbit around the sun. He predicted it would return in 1758. The comet, now known as Halley's comet, returned in 1759, and records have since been found for every appearance of the comet since 239 B.C.

If it were not for the gravitational influence of the planets, the comet would always reappear every 77 years.

1531   1608   1685   1762 . . .
+77   +77   +77

The sequence of numbers 1531, 1608, 1685, 1762, . . . is an example of an *arithmetic sequence*. Each successive term is formed by adding the same number, 77. In an arithmetic sequence, the difference between consecutive terms is a constant. This constant is called the *common difference*.

These are arithmetic sequences:

3, 7, 11, 15, . . .	common difference 4
9, 4, -1, -6, . . .	common difference -5
1, 1.25, 1.5, 1.75, 2, . . .	common difference 0.25
$a, a + d, a + 2d, a + 3d,$ . . .	common difference d

If the first term and the common difference of an arithmetic sequence are known, any other term can be found.

Example 1.   In the arithmetic sequence 2, 5, 8, . . ., find each term.

a) t_5 b) t_{20} c) t_n

Solution.   By inspection, the common difference is 3.

a) t_5 can be found by extending the sequence two more terms.

2, 5, 8, 11, 14

t_5 is 14.

t_5 can also be found by adding 4 differences to the first term:

$2 + 3 + 3 + 3 + 3 = 14$

The number of differences is 1 less than the term number.

b) To find t_{20}, add 19 differences to the first term.

$$t_{20} = 2 + (19)3$$
$$= 2 + 57$$
$$= 59$$

c) An expression for t_n can be found by adding $(n - 1)$ differences to the first term.

$$t_n = 2 + (n - 1)3$$
$$= 2 + 3n - 3$$
$$= 3n - 1$$

The general arithmetic sequence has the first term represented by a and the common difference by d. The first few terms are shown here.

$$t_1 = a$$
$$t_2 = a + d$$
$$t_3 = a + 2d$$
$$t_4 = a + 3d$$

.   .
.   .
.   .

$$t_n = a + (n - 1)d$$

The general term of an arithmetic sequence is given by:

$t_n = a + (n - 1)d$,

where a is the first term, n is the number of the term, and d is the common difference.

Example 2. Given the arithmetic sequence 8, 14, 20, 26, . . .
   a) Find the 20th term.   b) Which term is 236?

Solution.   By inspection, the common difference is 6.
   Use the formula. $t_n = a + (n - 1)d$
   a) $t_{20} = 8 + (20 - 1)6$
   $$= 8 + (19)6$$
   $$= 122$$
   The 20th term is 122.
   b) $236 = 8 + (n - 1)6$
   $$= 2 + 6n$$
   $$6n = 234$$
   $$n = 39$$
   236 is the 39th term of the sequence.

Given the position of any two terms of an arithmetic sequence, the first term and the common difference can be found.

Example 3.   In an arithmetic sequence, the third term is 8 and the tenth term is 4.5. Find the sequence.

Solution.   Let the first term be a and the common difference d.
Since the third term is 8: $8 = a + 2d$ . . . ①
Since the tenth term is 4.5: $4.5 = a + 9d$ . . . ②
Solve equations ① and ② to find a and d.
Subtract ② from ①. $3.5 = -7d$
$d = -0.5$
Substitute -0.5 for d in ①. $8 = a + 2(-0.5)$
$a = 9$
The first term is 9 and the common difference is -0.5.
The sequence is 9, 8.5, 8, 7.5, ...

Example 4.   The Olympic Games are held every four years. The dates form an arithmetic sequence. Were they held the year you were born?

Solution.   The Olympic Games were held in Seoul, Korea, in 1988. Write the sequence 1988, 1984, 1980, 1976, . . . as far as necessary to determine if they were held in the year you were born.

EXERCISES 8-2

Ⓐ

1. Is each sequence arithmetic? If it is, what is the common difference?
   a) 3, 5, 9, 15, 23, . . .
   b) $-4, -1, 2, 5, 8, 11, . . .$
   c) 2, 1, 0, -1, -2, . . .
   d) $1, \frac{1}{2}, \frac{1}{3}, \frac{1}{4}, . . .$
   e) 4, 4, 4, 4, 4, . . .
   f) 3, 11, 19, 27, 35, . . .

2. State the common difference and list the next 3 terms of each arithmetic sequence.
   a) 1, 4, 7, 10, . . .
   b) $-5, -1, 3, 7, . . .$
   c) 16, 14, 12, 10, . . .
   d) $-2, -8, -14, -20, . . .$
   e) 2, 7, 12, 17, . . .
   f) 6, 3, 0, -3, . . .

3. Write the first 5 terms of each arithmetic sequence with the given values of a and d.
   a) $a = 2, d = 3$
   b) $a = 7, d = 4$
   c) $a = -1, d = -3$
   d) $a = 12, d = -4$
   e) $a = -8, d = 5$
   f) $a = 25, d = -5$

Ⓑ

4. In the arithmetic sequence 3, 5, 7, 9, ..., find each term.
   a) t_8
   b) t_{25}
   c) t_n

5. In the arithmetic sequence 11, 8, 5, 2, ..., find each term.
   a) t_6
   b) t_{20}
   c) t_n

6. The disappearance of the dinosaurs about 65 million years ago is one of the great mysteries of science. Scientists have recently found that mass extinctions of the Earth's creatures are separated by periods of roughly 26 million years.
   a) About when did other mass extinctions occur?
   b) If the theory is correct, estimate when the next mass extinction should occur.

7. The years in which the Olympic Games are held form an arithmetic sequence. The sequence since 1968 is 1968, 1972, 1976, 1980, 1984, 1988, . . .
   a) Will the Olympic Games be held: i) in 1998   ii) in 2000?
   b) The modern Olympics began in 1896. Explain why the 1988 Olympics, in Seoul, is referred to as the XXIV Olympiad.

8. Which of the general terms listed is the general term of each arithmetic sequence?
   i) $t_n = 3 + 2n$ ii) $t_n = 2 + 3n$ iii) $t_n = 1 + 4n$
   iv) $t_n = 20 - 3n$ v) $t_n = 12 - 2n$ vi) $t_n = 1 + 3n$
        a) 5, 8, 11, 14, . . .   b) 17, 14, 11, 8, . . .
        c) 5, 7, 9, 11, . . .   d) 10, 8, 6, 4, . . .

9. Write the first 5 terms of each arithmetic sequence defined by the given terms.
   a) $t_1 = 3$, $t_2 = 10$ b) $t_1 = -3$, $t_2 = 1$ c) $t_n = 2n + 3$
   d) $t_n = -5n + 21$ e) $t_n = -7 + 3n$ f) $t_n = -4n - 6$

10. For the arithmetic sequence 2, 5, 8, 11, 14, . . ., find:
    a) t_{24} and t_{35} b) which term is 152.

11. For the arithmetic sequence -8, -3, 2, 7, . . ., find:
    a) t_{17} and t_{43} b) which term is 322.

12. For each arithmetic sequence, write a formula for t_n and use it to find each indicated term.
    a) 1, 5, 9, 13, . . ., t_{17} b) 3, 6, 9, 12, . . ., t_{21}
    c) -4, 1, 6, 11, . . ., t_{13} d) 41, 35, 29, 23, . . ., t_{18}
    e) -2, -5, -8, -11, . . ., t_{10} f) 9, 1, -7, -15, . . ., t_{46}

13. In an arithmetic sequence, the third term is 11 and the eighth term is 46. Find the first 2 terms of the sequence.

14. The 10th term of an arithmetic sequence is 39. If the first term is 3, find the next 3 terms.

15. The 8th term of an arithmetic sequence is 45. If the common difference is -6, find the first 3 terms.

16. In an arithmetic sequence, the 11th term is 53 and the sum of the 5th and 7th terms is 56. Find the first 3 terms of the sequence.

17. The sum of the first 2 terms of an arithmetic sequence is 15, and the sum of the next 2 terms is 43. Find the first 3 terms of the sequence.

18. How many terms are in each sequence?
    a) 2, 6, 10, . . ., 94   b) -9, -4, 1, . . ., 171
    c) 4, 15, 26, . . ., 213   d) 18, 13, 8, . . ., -102

19. Find the missing terms in each arithmetic sequence.
    a) $-, 9, 16, -, -$
    b) $-, -, 8, 2, -$
    c) $12, -, 22, -, -$
    d) $3, -, -, 24, -$
    e) $-, 4, -, -, -8$
    f) $15, -, -, -, -21$

20. If $5 + x$, 8, and $1 + 2x$ are consecutive terms in an arithmetic sequence, find x.

21. If $2x + y + 3$, $4x - y - 2$, and $x + 5y - 8$ are consecutive terms in an arithmetic sequence, find the relation between x and y.

22. Every appearance of Halley's comet has been recorded since 239 B.C. How many times has it been recorded?

Ⓒ

23. The sum of the first three terms of an arithmetic sequence is 12. The sum of their squares is 66. Find the fourth term.

24. Find an expression for the general term of each sequence. Is the sequence arithmetic?
    a) $1 \times 1, 3 \times 4, 5 \times 7, 7 \times 10, \ldots$
    b) $2 \times 3, 4 \times 6, 6 \times 9, 8 \times 12, \ldots$
    c) $\dfrac{1}{3}, \dfrac{2}{5}, \dfrac{3}{7}, \dfrac{4}{9}, \ldots$
    d) $\dfrac{1 \times 3}{2 \times 4}, \dfrac{3 \times 5}{4 \times 6}, \dfrac{5 \times 7}{6 \times 8}, \dfrac{7 \times 9}{8 \times 10}, \ldots$

25. The diagram shows a pattern of positive integers in five columns. If the pattern is continued, in which columns will these numbers appear?
    a) 49
    b) 117
    c) 301
    d) 8725

		Columns		
1	**2**	**3**	**4**	**5**
1		2		3
	5		4	
6		7		8
	10		9	
11		12		13
			14	

26. The diagram shows a pattern of positive integers in four rows. If the pattern is continued:
    a) what are the first ten numbers in row 3
    b) in which row will these numbers appear?
        i) 75
        ii) 93
        iii) 259
        iv) 3267

Rows					
1	1	8	9	16	17
2	2	7	10	15	18
3	3	6	11	14	
4	4	5	12	13	

INVESTIGATE

Find, if possible, three or more perfect squares in arithmetic sequence.

COMPUTER POWER

Prime Sequences

Prime numbers have always interested mathematicians. This interest has increased in recent years because many investigations can now be carried out with a computer. One of these investigations concerns prime numbers which are in arithmetic sequence; 11, 17, 23, 29 is an example. In this sequence, $a = 11$ and $d = 6$

In 1983, Paul A. Pritchard of Cornell University programmed a computer to find, in its free time, long arithmetic sequences of prime numbers. After about a month, the longest sequence the computer had found was one with 18 terms. The first term of this sequence is 107 928 278 317 and the common difference is 9 922 782 870. At the time, this was the longest known arithmetic sequence of primes.

1. Using primes less than 100, find some that are in arithmetic sequence.

2. The following program can be used to find primes in arithmetic sequence.

```
LABEL 140,150,200;
VAR
  CH : CHAR;
  A,D : REAL;
  I : INTEGER;
BEGIN  { PRIME SEQUENCES }
     REPEAT
       WRITELN('WHAT IS THE FIRST NUMBER? ');
       READ(A); WRITELN;
       WRITELN('WHAT IS THE COMMON DIFFERENCE? ');
       READ(D); WRITELN;
       IF A = 3 THEN BEGIN
         WRITELN(A:5:0);
          A := A + D;
         END;
```

```
140:    IF (A > 2) AND ((A / 2.0) = TRUNC(A / 2.0)) THEN GOTO
        200;
        {IF (A / 2.0) = INT(A / 2.0) THEN GOTO 200;}
        I := 3;
150:    IF ABS(A / I - TRUNC(A / I)) < 0.0000001 THEN GOTO
        200;
        I := I + 2;
        IF I < TRUNC(SQRT(A)) THEN GOTO 150;
        WRITELN(A:5:0);
        A := A + D;
        GOTO 140;
200:    WRITELN(A:5:0,' IS COMPOSITE');
        WRITELN('PRESS S TO STOP, C TO CONTINUE');
        CH := READKEY;
     UNTIL CH = CHR(83);
END.
```

  a) Run the program several times and try to find sequences with 6 or more terms.
  b) What is the longest arithmetic sequence of primes you can find?

3. The first term of an arithmetic sequence of 7 primes is less than 10. Find the sequence if its common difference is a multiple of 30 and less than 200.

4. Primes which differ by 2, such as 29 and 31, are called twin primes.
  a) Find two arithmetic sequences of twin primes in primes less than 100.
  b) Two long arithmetic sequences of twin primes have first terms less than 50 and common differences that are multiples of 210. Find the sequences.

The next two questions concern the arithmetic sequence of 18 primes found by the computer in Paul Pritchard's investigation.

5. Find the last prime in the longest known arithmetic sequence of primes.

6. Express the common difference 9 922 782 870 as a product of prime factors. Do the same with the suggested differences given above. The results may suggest possible differences to use in your search for long arithmetic sequences of primes.

8-3 GEOMETRIC SEQUENCES

More potatoes are grown on Prince Edward Island than in any other province of Canada. The industry is so large that an entire farm is devoted to producing the seed potatoes for the other farms in the province.

Part of the eye of a potato is allowed to grow and is then cut to produce six more. When this is done again and again, the number of potato plants increases according to this pattern.

$$1, \quad 6, \quad 36, \quad 216, \quad 1296, \quad 7776, \quad 46\,656, \quad 279\,936, \ldots$$
$$\times 6 \quad \times 6 \quad \times 6 \quad \times 6 \quad \times 6 \quad \times 6 \quad \times 6$$

This sequence of numbers is an example of a *geometric sequence*. Each successive term is formed by multiplying by the same number, 6. In a geometric sequence, the ratio of consecutive terms is a constant. This constant is called the *common ratio*.

These are geometric sequences.

2, 10, 50, 250, . . .   common ratio 5   Each successive term

12, 6, 3, 1.5, 0.75, . . .   common ratio $\frac{1}{2}$ is formed by multiplying by the same number,

3, -12, 48, -192, . . .   common ratio -4 the common ratio.

$a, ar, ar^2, ar^3, \ldots$ common ratio r

If the first term and the common ratio of a geometric sequence are known, any other term can be found.

Example 1. In the geometric sequence 5, 15, 45, . . ., find each term.
  a) t_5 b) t_{10} c) t_n

Solution. By inspection, the common ratio is 3.
  a) t_5 can be found by extending the sequence.
      5, 15, 45, 135, 405, . . .
      t_5 is 405.
      t_5 can also be found by multiplying the first term successively by 3, four times.

$$5 \times 3 \times 3 \times 3 \times 3 = 405$$
— The number of factors is 1 less than the term number.

  b) Similarly, t_{10} is found by multiplying the first term successively by 3, nine times.
      $$5 \times 3 \times 3 \times \ldots \times 3 = 5(3)^9$$
      $$= 98\,415$$

c) An expression for t_n can be found by multiplying the first term successively by $(n - 1)$ factors of 3.

$$t_n = 5(3)^{n-1}$$

The general geometric sequence has its first term represented by a and the common ratio by r. The first few terms are shown here.

$$t_1 = a$$
$$t_2 = ar$$
$$t_3 = ar^2$$
$$t_4 = ar^3$$
$$\vdots \qquad \vdots$$
$$t_n = ar^{n-1}$$

The general term of a geometric sequence is given by:

$$t_n = ar^{n-1},$$

where a is the first term, n is the number of the term, and r is the common ratio.

Example 2. Given the geometric sequence 3, 6, 12, 24, . . .,
a) Find the 14th term.   b) Which term is 384?

Solution. Use the formula. $t_n = ar^{n-1}$
a) $t_{14} = 3(2)^{13}$ $a = 3$
$\qquad = 3(8192)$ $r = 2$
$\qquad = 24\ 576$ $n = 14$
The 14th term is 24 576.
b) $384 = 3(2)^{n-1}$ $a = 3$
$\quad 128 = 2^{n-1}$ $r = 2$
Since $128 = 2^7$, $t_n = 384$
$\quad n - 1 = 7$
$\qquad\quad n = 8$
384 is the 8th term of the sequence.

If any two terms of a geometric sequence are known, the first term and the common ratio can be found.

Example 3. In a geometric sequence, the 3rd term is 20 and the 6th term is -540. Find the first six terms.

Solution. Let the first term be a and the common ratio be r.
Since the 3rd term is 20: $ar^2 = 20$ . . . ①
Since the 6th term is -540: $ar^5 = -540$ . . . ②
To solve this system, divide each side of equation ② by the corresponding side of equation ①.

$$\frac{ar^5}{ar^2} = \frac{-540}{20}$$
$$r^3 = -27$$
$$r = -3$$

Substitute -3 for r in ①. $a(-3)^2 = 20$
$$a = \frac{20}{9}$$

The first term is $\frac{20}{9}$ and the common ratio is -3.

The first six terms of the sequence are $\frac{20}{9}$, $-\frac{20}{3}$, 20, -60, 180, -540.

If a, x, and b are in geometric sequence, then x is the *geometric mean* of a and b.

Example 4.   Between 4 and 324, insert:
   a) one geometric mean   b) three geometric means.

Solution.   a) Let the geometric mean be x. Then 4, x, and 324 are in geometric sequence.
$$\text{Hence, } \frac{x}{4} = \frac{324}{x}$$
$$x^2 = 324(4)$$
$$= 1296$$
$$x = \pm 36$$

The geometric mean of 4 and 324 is 36 or -36.

   b) We need two additional geometric means, y and z, such that 4, y, ± 36, z, 324 form a geometric sequence. But there are no real values of y and z for which 4, y, -36, z, 324 form a geometric sequence. Hence, we consider the sequence 4, y, 36, z, 324.

$$\text{Then } \frac{y}{4} = \frac{36}{y} \quad \text{and} \quad \frac{z}{36} = \frac{324}{z}$$
$$y = \pm 12 \qquad\qquad z = \pm 108$$

Hence, the three geometric means are 12, 36, 108 or -12, 36, -108.

EXERCISES 8-3

Ⓐ

1. Is each sequence geometric? If it is, what is the common ratio?
   a) 1, 2, 4, 8, 16, . . .   b) 2, 4, 6, 10, 16, . . .
   c) 4, -2, 1, $-\frac{1}{2}, \frac{1}{4}$, . . .   d) 0.6, 0.06, 0.006, . . .
   e) -3, 2, 7, 12, 17, . . .   f) 1, $-\frac{1}{3}, \frac{1}{9}, -\frac{1}{27}$, . . .

2. State the common ratio and list the next 3 terms of each geometric sequence.
   a) 1, 3, 9, 27, . . .   b) 5, -15, 45, -135, . . .
   c) 3, 6, 12, 24, . . .   d) 6, 2, $\frac{2}{3}$, $\frac{2}{9}$, . . .
   e) 36, 9, $\frac{9}{4}$, $\frac{9}{16}$, . . .   f) $\frac{1}{2}$, -2, 8, -32, . . .

3. Write the first 5 terms of each geometric sequence with the given values of *a* and *r*.
   a) $a = 2, r = 3$ b) $a = 5, r = 2$ c) $a = 3, r = -5$
   d) $a = 60, r = \frac{1}{2}$ e) $a = -4, r = -2$ f) $a = 8, r = 3$

Ⓑ

4. In the geometric sequence 3, 6, 12, ..., find each term.
   a) t_6 b) t_{11} c) t_n

5. Which of the general terms listed is the general term for each geometric sequence?
   i) $5(2)^{n-1}$ ii) $2(5)^{n-1}$ iii) $3(3)^{n-1}$
   iv) $3(-4)^{n-1}$ v) $4(-3)^{n-1}$ vi) $5(3)^{n-1}$
      a) 2, 10, 50, . . .   b) 3, -12, 48, . . .
      c) 3, 9, 27, . . .   d) 5, 15, 45, . . .

6. Is each sequence geometric?
   a) Camera shutter speeds (seconds): 1, $\frac{1}{2}$, $\frac{1}{4}$, $\frac{1}{8}$, $\frac{1}{15}$, $\frac{1}{30}$, $\frac{1}{60}$, . . .

   b) Frequencies of a piano's A notes in hertz (cycles per second): 27.5, 55, 110, 220, 440, 880, 1760, 3520

   c)

Type of sediment	Grain size (mm)
Very fine sand	$\frac{1}{16} - \frac{1}{8}$
Fine sand	$\frac{1}{8} - \frac{1}{4}$
Medium sand	$\frac{1}{4} - \frac{1}{2}$
Coarse sand	$\frac{1}{2} - 1$
Very coarse sand	$1 - 2$
Granules	$2 - 4$
Pebbles	$4 - 64$
Cobbles	$64 - 256$

d) The electromagnetic spectrum

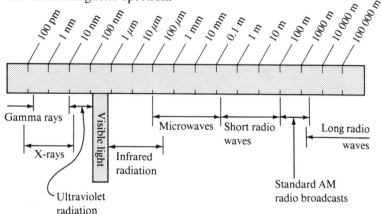

7. Find a geometric mean for each pair of numbers.
   a) 3, 48 b) 4, 64 c) 5, 80 d) 2, 1250

8. Insert three geometric means between each pair of numbers in *Exercise 7*.

9. Write the first 5 terms of each geometric sequence defined by the given terms.
   a) $t_1 = 2$, $t_2 = -6$ b) $t_1 = 20$, $t_2 = 10$ c) $t_n = 3(2)^{n-1}$

   d) $t_n = 7(3)^{n-1}$ e) $t_n = \frac{1}{8}(4)^{n-1}$ f) $t_n = -2(-5)^{n-1}$

10. For each geometric sequence, write a formula for t_n and use it to find each indicated term.
    a) 2, 4, 8, 16, . . . , t_{10} b) 5, 10, 20, 40, . . . , t_{13}

    c) -3, 15, -75, 375, . . . , t_8 d) 12, 6, 3, $\frac{3}{2}$, . . . , t_{12}

    e) 6, -2, $\frac{2}{3}$, $-\frac{2}{9}$, . . . , t_9 f) 3, 18, 108, 648, . . . , t_7

11. For the geometric sequence 3, 12, 48, 192, . . . , find:
    a) the 9th term b) which term is 12 288.

12. Find the first 5 terms of the geometric sequence with the 3rd term 18 and the 7th term 1458.

13. Find the first 4 terms of the geometric sequence with the 5th term 1536 and the 10th term 48.

14. Find the missing terms in each geometric sequence.
    a) 4, _, 16, _ b) 2, 12, _, _ c) 3, _, 12, _
    d) _, 5, _, 125 e) _, _, 2, 1 f) 3, _, _, 375

15. In a geometric sequence, $t_3 = 20$ and $t_6 = 1280$; find the first 2 terms of the sequence.

16. In a geometric sequence, $t_1 = 2$ and $t_5 = 162$; find the common ratio and the terms between t_1 and t_5.

17. Write the geometric sequence formed if, between 2 and 1458:
    a) two geometric means are inserted
    b) five geometric means are inserted.

18. How many terms are in each sequence?
    a) 2, 6, 18, . . ., 486
    b) 12, 4, $\frac{4}{3}$, . . ., $\frac{4}{729}$
    c) 3, 6, 12, . . ., 3072
    d) 64, 32, 16, . . ., $\frac{1}{256}$

19. If $x - 3$, $x + 1$, and $4x - 2$ are consecutive terms in a geometric sequence, find x.

20. If $m + 2$, $m + 4$, and $2m + 11$ are consecutive terms in a geometric sequence, find m.

21. The population of a city is 16 million and is increasing at about 4% per year. Show that the yearly populations form a geometric sequence and predict the population in 10 years.

Ⓒ

22. The arithmetic mean of two numbers is 65. The geometric mean of the same two numbers is 25. Find the numbers.

23. The sum of the first 2 terms of a geometric sequence is 3. The sum of the next 2 terms is $\frac{4}{3}$. Find the first 4 terms of the sequence.

24. In a geometric sequence, $t_3 + t_4 = 36$, and $t_4 + t_5 = 108$; find the first 5 terms of the sequence.

25. In a geometric sequence, $t_1 + t_2 + t_3 = 3$, and $t_3 + t_4 + t_5 = 12$; find the first 5 terms of the sequence.

26. Show that the arithmetic mean of two numbers is always greater than the geometric mean of those two numbers.

27. A geometric sequence has positive terms. The sum of the first 3 terms of a geometric sequence is 13. The sum of the reciprocals of the first 3 terms is $\frac{13}{9}$. Find the first 3 terms of the sequence.

28. The aperture markings on a camera lens are:
    1.4   2   2.8   4   5.6   8   11   16   22
    They form a geometric sequence but the numbers have been rounded for convenience. Determine the common ratio as accurately as possible.

29. The following sequences start with the same two terms.
    Arithmetic sequence: 3, 12, 21, . . . ①
    Geometric sequence: 3, 12, 48 . . . ②
    a) Show that t_3 of ② is the same as t_6 of ①.
    b) Which term in ① is the same as t_4 in ②?
    c) Show that every term in the geometric sequence is also a term in the arithmetic sequence.

8-4 RECURSIVE DEFINITION OF A SEQUENCE

In the arithmetic sequence 5, 7, 9, 11, . . . , the first term is 5 and every term after the first is 2 greater than the preceding term. Hence, the sequence is defined by these two equations: $t_1 = 5$, $t_n = t_{n-1} + 2$, $n > 1$. Such a definition of a sequence is called a *recursive definition*.

Example 1.   Write the first four terms of the sequence defined by
$t_1 = 3$, $t_n = 2t_{n-1} + 1$, $n > 1$.

Solution. $t_1 = 3$ $t_2 = 2t_1 + 1$ $t_3 = 2t_2 + 1$ $t_4 = 2t_3 + 1$
$= 2(3) + 1$ $= 2(7) + 1$ $= 2(15) + 1$
$= 7$ $= 15$ $= 31$

The first four terms are 3, 7, 15, 31.

Example 2.   Write a recursive definition for the geometric sequence 2, 6, 18, . . .

Solution.   The first term is 2. Each term after the first is obtained by multiplying the preceding term by 3. Hence, the recursive definition is
$t_1 = 2$, $t_n = 3t_{n-1}$, $n > 1$.

A recursive definition consists of two parts. The first part specifies the first term(s). The second part indicates how each term is calculated from preceding term(s).

EXERCISES 8-4

Ⓐ

1. Write the first 4 terms of each sequence.
    a) $t_1 = 5$, $t_n = t_{n-1} - 3$, $n > 1$
    b) $t_1 = \frac{1}{2}$, $t_n = 2t_{n-1}$, $n > 1$
    c) $t_1 = -2$, $t_n = 1 - t_{n-1}$, $n > 1$
    d) $t_1 = 1$, $t_n = 10t_{n-1} + 1$, $n > 1$
    e) $t_1 = 1$, $t_2 = 2$, $t_n = t_{n-1} + t_{n-2}$, $n > 2$

Ⓑ

2. Write a recursive definition for each sequence.
    a) 1, 6, 11, 16, . . .
    b) −2, 6, −18, 54, . . .
    c) 1, 3, 7, 15, . . .
    d) 1, 4, 9, 16, . . .
    e) 1, 1, 2, 3, 5, 8, 13, . . .
    f) 1, 2, 3, 6, 11, 20, . . .

3. Show that the recursive definition of a sequence is not necessarily unique. That is, give an example of two different recursive definitions which describe the same sequence.

8-5 WHAT IS A SERIES?

In mathematics, sequences and series have separate and distinct meanings. The following examples illustrate how they differ.

These are sequences.

1, 2, 3, 4, 5, . . .

2, 4, 8, 16, 32, . . .

1, 0.1, 0.01, 0.001, . . .

$1, \frac{1}{2}, \frac{1}{3}, \frac{1}{4}, \frac{1}{5}, \ldots$

These are series.

$1 + 2 + 3 + 4 + 5 + \ldots$

$2 + 4 + 8 + 16 + 32 + \ldots$

$1 + 0.1 + 0.01 + 0.001 + \ldots$

$1 + \frac{1}{2} + \frac{1}{3} + \frac{1}{4} + \frac{1}{5} + \ldots$

A series is obtained from a sequence by writing addition signs between the terms to indicate that the terms are to be added. A *series* is the indicated sum of the terms of a sequence.

The symbols $S_1, S_2, S_3, \ldots, S_n$ are used to represent the sums of the terms of a series. S_3 means the sum of the first three terms and S_n denotes the sum of the first n terms. We can sometimes find an expression for the first n terms of a series by looking for a pattern.

Example 1. Find a possible expression for the sum of the first n terms of the series of odd numbers $1 + 3 + 5 + \ldots + (2n - 1)$.

Solution. Evaluate $S_1, S_2, S_3, \ldots$

The first term, S_1:   1, or 1^2

Sum of first two terms, S_2: $1 + 3 = 4$, or 2^2

Sum of first three terms, S_3: $1 + 3 + 5 = 9$, or 3^2

Sum of first four terms, S_4: $1 + 3 + 5 + 7 = 16$, or 4^2

The resulting numbers are all perfect squares. This pattern suggests that a possible expression for the sum of the first n terms is $S_n = n^2$.

In *Example 1*, the expression is called "possible" because there is no guarantee that the pattern of perfect squares will continue to hold if more than four terms of the series are added.

In the same example, the values of S_3 and S_4 could have been found with fewer additions. For example, S_4 is the sum of the first three terms and the fourth term.

$S_4 = S_3 + t_4$

$\quad = 9 + 7$

$\quad = 16$

If an expression for the sum of the first n terms of a series is known, the series can easily be found.

Example 2. Given $S_n = 4n^2 + n$

    a) Find the first four terms of the series.

    b) Find the nth term of the series.

Solution.   a) Substitute 1, 2, 3, 4, in turn, in $S_n = 4n^2 + n$ to find the values of $S_1, S_2, S_3,$ and S_4.

$$S_1 = 4(1)^2 + 1, \text{ or } 5$$
$$t_1 = 5$$
$$S_2 = 4(2)^2 + 2, \text{ or } 18$$

Since $5 + t_2 = 18$, $t_2 = 18 - 5$, or 13

$$S_3 = 4(3)^2 + 3, \text{ or } 39$$

Since $18 + t_3 = 39$, $t_3 = 39 - 18$, or 21

$$S_4 = 4(4)^2 + 4, \text{ or } 68$$

Since $39 + t_4 = 68$, $t_4 = 68 - 39$, or 29

The first four terms of the series are $5 + 13 + 21 + 29$.

    b) The terms of the series appear to form an arithmetic sequence with first term 5 and common difference 8. Therefore, the nth term is

$$t_n = a + (n - 1)d$$
$$= 5 + (n - 1)8$$
$$= 8n - 3$$

In *Example 2b*, the general term can also be found by subtracting the sum of $(n - 1)$ terms from the sum of n terms.

$$t_n = S_n - S_{n-1}$$
$$= [4n^2 + n] - [4(n - 1)^2 + (n - 1)]$$
$$= [4n^2 + n] - [4n^2 - 8n + 4 + n - 1]$$
$$= 8n - 3$$

$t_1 + t_2 + t_3 + \ldots t_{n-1} + t_n$

$\leftarrow S_{n-1} \longrightarrow$

$\leftarrow S_n \longrightarrow$

In any series
- The general term is the difference between the sum of the first n terms and the sum of the first $(n - 1)$ terms.
$$t_n = S_n - S_{n-1} \quad (n > 1)$$
- The first term is the same as S_1. $t_1 = S_1$

Example 3. Given $\dfrac{1}{1 \times 3} + \dfrac{1}{3 \times 5} + \dfrac{1}{5 \times 7} + \dfrac{1}{7 \times 9} + \ldots + \dfrac{1}{(2n - 1)(2n + 1)}$

    a) Find S_1, S_2, and S_3 for this series, and from the pattern predict S_4.

    b) Find a possible expression for S_n.

Solution.   a) $S_1 = \dfrac{1}{3}$

$$S_2 = \dfrac{1}{3} + \dfrac{1}{15}$$
$$= \dfrac{5 + 1}{15}$$
$$= \dfrac{6}{15}, \text{ or } \dfrac{2}{5}$$

$$S_3 = S_2 + \dfrac{1}{35}$$
$$= \dfrac{2}{5} + \dfrac{1}{35}$$
$$= \dfrac{14 + 1}{35}$$
$$= \dfrac{15}{35}, \text{ or } \dfrac{3}{7}$$

Since the sums are $\frac{1}{3}$, $\frac{2}{5}$, $\frac{3}{7}$, . . . , S_4 might be $\frac{4}{9}$.

b) A possible expression for S_n is $S_n = \dfrac{n}{2n + 1}$.

The above method of finding an expression for the sum of the first n terms of a series applies only when we can see a pattern in the values of S_1, S_2, S_3, S_4,. . . . . If no pattern can be seen, an expression for S_n must be found by other methods. Some of these will be presented in the following sections.

EXERCISES 8-5

Ⓐ

1. Write the series corresponding to each sequence.

   a) 2, 6, 10, 14, 18, . . .   b) 9, 3, 1, $\frac{1}{3}$, $\frac{1}{9}$, . . .

2. State whether each list is a sequence or series.
   a) 2, 6, 18, 54, . . .   b) $1 + 3 + 5 + 7$
   c) $3 + 6 + 12 + 24 + \ldots$ d) $3 + 6 + 9 + 12 + \ldots$
   e) 12, 7, 2, -3, -8, . . .   f) $-2 + 3 + 1 + 4 + 5 + \ldots$

Ⓑ

3. The sum of the first 4 terms of a series is 24. Find the 4th term if the sum of the first 3 terms is:
   a) 20   b) 10   c) 8   d) 30.

4. For a given series, $S_4 = 36$; find t_5 if S_5 equals:
   a) 40   b) 60   c) 76   d) 30.

5. Find the first 5 terms of each series for which:
   a) $S_n = 3n$ b) $S_n = 2n^2 - n$ c) $S_n = n^2 - 3n$
   d) $S_n = 5n - 2$ e) $S_n = n^2 + 2n$ f) $S_n = 15 - 2n^2$.

6. Which of the expressions for S_n is the sum of the first n terms of each series?
   i) $S_n = 2n^2 - n$ ii) $S_n = n^2 + 4n$ iii) $S_n = n^2 + 2n$
   iv) $S_n = n^2 - 4n$ v) $S_n = 2n^2 + n$
   a) $3 + 5 + 7 + 9 + 11 + \ldots$ b) $1 + 5 + 9 + 13 + 17 + \ldots$
   c) $3 + 7 + 11 + 15 + 19 + \ldots$ d) $-3 - 1 + 1 + 3 + 5 + \ldots$

7. A formula for the sum of the first n terms of each series is given. Find S_{n-1} and t_n.
   a) $S_n = n^2 + n$ b) $S_n = 3n^2 - 5n$ c) $S_n = 2^n - 1$
   d) $S_n = 2n^2 - 3n$ e) $S_n = 2(3^n - 1)$ f) $S_n = n^2 - 4n$

8. For a certain series, $S_n = an$, where a is a constant. Find the first 4 terms of the series.

9. Which of the expressions for S_n is the sum of the first n terms of each series?

   i) $S_n = \dfrac{n}{6n + 4}$

   ii) $S_n = n^2(n + 1)$

   iii) $S_n = \dfrac{n(n + 1)(n + 2)(n + 3)}{4}$

   iv) $S_n = 2^n - 1$

   v) $S_n = \dfrac{n(n + 1)(n + 2)}{3}$

   vi) $S_n = (n - 1)2^n + 1$

      a) $1 \times 2 + 2 \times 3 + 3 \times 4 + \ldots + n(n + 1)$
      b) $1 \times 2 \times 3 + 2 \times 3 \times 4 + 3 \times 4 \times 5 + \ldots + n(n + 1)(n + 2)$
      c) $1 \times 1 + 2 \times 2 + 3 \times 2^2 + 4 \times 2^3 + \ldots + n(2)^{n-1}$
      d) $\dfrac{1}{2 \times 5} + \dfrac{1}{5 \times 8} + \dfrac{1}{8 \times 11} + \ldots + \dfrac{1}{(3n - 1)(3n + 2)}$

10. Find a possible expression for the sum of the first n terms of each series.
    a) $-1 + 1 + 3 + 5 + 7 + \ldots$
    b) $1 + 2 + 4 + 8 + 16 + \ldots$
    c) $1 + \dfrac{1}{2} + \dfrac{1}{4} + \dfrac{1}{8} + \dfrac{1}{16} + \ldots$
    d) $1 + 7 + 19 + 37 + 61 + 91 + \ldots$

11. a) Find S_n if t_n is equal to: i) $2n + 1$ ii) $2n + 3$ iii) $2n + 5$.
    b) Using the results of part a), predict S_n if $t_n = 2n + 7$. Show that your prediction is correct.

12. Show that only two terms of this sequence are perfect squares.
    $1, \quad 1 + (1 \times 2), \quad 1 + (1 \times 2) + (1 \times 2 \times 3),$
    $1 + (1 \times 2) + (1 \times 2 \times 3) + (1 \times 2 \times 3 \times 4)$

INVESTIGATE

Proving Series Expressions

In *Example 1* of Section 8-5, we found that a possible expression for the sum of the first n terms of the series $1 + 3 + 5 + 7 + \ldots + (2n - 1)$ is $S_n = n^2$. We can show that this expression is correct by evaluating $S_n - S_{n-1}$. It should simplify to the expression for the general term of the series.

$$S_n - S_{n-1} = n^2 - (n - 1)^2$$
$$= n^2 - (n^2 - 2n + 1)$$

That is, $S_n - S_{n-1} = 2n - 1 \ldots \textcircled{1}$

This equation is correct for all integral values of $n > 1$.

We now know these facts about the possible formula $S_n = n^2$.

When $n = 1$	S_1	$= 1$	All terms on the
When $n = 2$, ① becomes:	$S_2 - S_1$	$= 3$	left side add
When $n = 3$, ① becomes:	$S_3 - S_2$	$= 5$	to 0 except the
When $n = 4$, ① becomes:	$S_4 - S_3$	$= 7$	one term, S_n.

$$\vdots \qquad\qquad \vdots$$

For any value of n: $\qquad S_n - S_{n-1} = 2n - 1$

Add: $\qquad\qquad\qquad\quad S_n \qquad\quad = 1 + 3 + 5 + \ldots + (2n - 1)$

That is, S_n is the sum of the first n terms of the series.

This suggests a method of showing that a possible formula for the sum of the first n terms of a series is correct.

If S_n is a possible formula for the sum of the first n terms of a series, it is the correct formula if both these conditions are satisfied.
- S_1 is the first term.
- $S_n - S_{n-1}$ is equal to the general term.

---

1. Given the series $2 + 7 + 19 + 37 + \ldots + (3n^2 - 3n + 1)$; show that $S_n = n^3 + 1$.

2. Given the series $1 \times 4 + 2 \times 7 + 3 \times 10 + \ldots + n(3n + 1)$; show that $S_n = n(n + 1)^2$.

3. Determine a possible expression for the sum of the first n terms of each series, and show that the expression is correct.
   a) $2 + 4 + 6 + \ldots + 2n$
   b) $1 + 2 + 4 + 8 + \ldots + 2^{n-1}$
   c) $\dfrac{1}{1 \times 2} + \dfrac{1}{2 \times 3} + \dfrac{1}{3 \times 4} + \ldots + \dfrac{1}{n(n + 1)}$
   d) $\dfrac{1}{1 \times 4} + \dfrac{1}{4 \times 7} + \dfrac{1}{7 \times 10} + \ldots + \dfrac{1}{(3n - 2)(3n + 1)}$

4. Given $1^2 + 2^2 + 3^2 + \ldots + n^2$; show that $S_n = \dfrac{n(n + 1)(2n + 1)}{6}$.

5. Given $1^3 + 2^3 + 3^3 + \ldots + n^3$; show that $S_n = \dfrac{n^2(n + 1)^2}{4}$.

8-6 ARITHMETIC SERIES

Each of two summer jobs is for 3 months, or 12 weeks.

Job A pays $400 per month with a $100 raise each month.

Job B pays $100 per week with a $5 raise each week.

Which is the better-paying job?

Job A. Total salary for 3 months, in dollars, is $400 + 500 + 600 = 1500$

Job B. Payments, in dollars, are 100, 105, 110, . . ., t_{12}
This is an arithmetic sequence with t_{12} representing the last payment.
$t_{12} = t_1 + (n - 1)d$, where n is the number of payments, and d is the weekly increase.
$t_{12} = 100 + (11)5$
$\quad = 155$
Total salary for job B is $\$100 + \$105 + \$110 + \ldots + \$155$
This expression is an example of an *arithmetic series* because it indicates that the terms of an arithmetic sequence are to be added. Instead of adding the twelve numbers, the sum can be found as follows.
Let S represent the sum of the series.
$S = 100 + 105 + 110 + \ldots + 145 + 150 + 155 \ldots$ ①
Write the series in reverse order.
$S = 155 + 150 + 145 + \ldots + 110 + 105 + 100 \ldots$ ②
Add ① and ②.
$2S = 255 + 255 + 255 + \ldots + 255 + 255 + 255$
$\quad = 12 \times 255 \quad$ (since there are 12 terms)
$\quad = 3060$
$\ S = 1530$
Job B pays a total of $1530. It is the better-paying job.
    This method can be used to find the sum of any number of terms of an arithmetic series. The formulas for t_n can be used with both sequences and series.

Example 1. Find the sum of the first 25 terms of the arithmetic series
2 + 9 + 16 + 25 + . . .

Solution. Find the 25th term using $t_n = a + (n - 1)d$ $a = 2$
$$t_{25} = 2 + (24)7 \qquad d = 7$$
$$= 170 \qquad n = 25$$

Let S represent the sum of the series.
Then $S = \quad 2 + \quad 9 + \quad 16 + \ldots + 170$
Reversing: $S = 170 + 163 + 156 + \ldots + \quad 2$
Adding: $2S = 172 + 172 + 172 + \ldots + 172$
Since there are 25 terms,
$$2S = 25(172)$$
$$S = \frac{25(172)}{2}$$
$$= 2150$$
The sum of the first 25 terms of the series is 2150.

The method of *Example 1* can be used to find a formula for the sum of the first n terms of the general arithmetic series, using l to represent the last term $a + (n - 1)d$.

$$S_n = a \qquad + a + d \ + a + 2d + \ldots + l - d \ + l$$
$$S_n = l \qquad + l - d \ + l - 2d + \ldots + a + d \ + a$$
$$2S_n = (a + l) + (a + l) + (a + l) + \ldots + (a + l) + (a + l)$$
Since there are n terms on the right side,
$$2S_n = n(a + l)$$
$$S_n = \frac{n}{2}(a + l), \text{ or } S_n = \frac{n}{2}[2a + (n - 1)d]$$

For the general arithmetic series
$$a + a + d + a + 2d + \ldots + a + (n - 1)d$$
the sum of the first n terms is
$$S_n = \frac{n}{2}(a + l) \qquad \text{where } l = a + (n - 1)d$$
$$\text{or } S_n = \frac{n}{2}[2a + (n - 1)d]$$

Example 2. Find the sum of the first 50 terms of the arithmetic series
$3 + 4.5 + 6 + 7.5 + \ldots$.

Solution. Use the formula $S_n = \dfrac{n}{2}[2a + (n - 1)d]$ $\qquad a = 3$
$\qquad\qquad\qquad\qquad\qquad\qquad\qquad\qquad\qquad d = 1.5$
$$S_{50} = \frac{50}{2}[2(3) + (50 - 1)1.5] \qquad n = 50$$
$$= 25[6 + (49)1.5]$$
$$= 25(79.5)$$
$$= 1987.5$$
The sum of the first 50 terms is 1987.5.

Example 3. Find the sum of the arithmetic series $6 + 10 + 14 + \ldots + 50$.

Solution. The number of terms must be found before a formula for S_n can be used.
Let 50 be the nth term.
Use $t_n = a + (n - 1)d \qquad a = 6$
$\qquad 50 = 6 + (n - 1)4 \qquad d = 4$
$\qquad 4n = 48 \qquad\qquad\qquad t_n = 50$
$\qquad\quad n = 12$
There are 12 terms in the series.

To find the sum of the series, use $S_n = \dfrac{n}{2}[2a + (n - 1)d]$

$S_{12} = 6[12 + (11)4] \qquad a = 6$
$\qquad = 6[12 + 44] \qquad\quad d = 4$
$\qquad = 6(56) \qquad\qquad\quad n = 12$
$\qquad = 336$
The sum of the series is 336.

EXERCISES 8-6

Ⓐ

1. Find the sum of the first ten terms of each arithmetic series.
   a) $3 + 7 + 11 + \ldots$　　　　　b) $5 + 12 + 19 + \ldots$
   c) $2 + 8 + 14 + \ldots$　　　　　d) $45 + 39 + 33 + \ldots$
   e) $6 + 18 + 30 + \ldots$　　　　　f) $21 + 15 + 9 + \ldots$

2. Find the sum of each arithmetic series.
   a) $3 + 12 + 21 + 30 + 39 + 48 + 57 + 66$
   b) $6 + 13 + 20 + 27 + 34 + 41 + 48 + 55 + 62 + 69$
   c) $13 + 19 + 25 + 31 + 37 + 43 + 49 + 55 + 61 + 67 + 73 + 79$
   d) $19 + 31 + 43 + 55 + 67 + 79 + 91 + 103 + 115 + 127 + 139 + 151$

Ⓑ

3. For the arithmetic series $6 + 8 + 10 + 12 + \ldots$, find:
   a) the 50th term　　　　　　　b) the sum of the first 50 terms.

4. For the arithmetic series $44 + 41 + 38 + 35 + \ldots$, find the sum of the first:
   a) 15 terms　　　　　b) 30 terms　　　　　c) 60 terms.

5. Which of the expressions for S_n is the sum of the first n terms of each arithmetic series?

   i) $S_n = \dfrac{3n^2 + 5n}{2}$ ii) $S_n = 2n^2$ iii) $S_n = 3n^2 + 2n$

   iv) $S_n = 5n^2 - 2n$ v) $S_n = 2n^2 + 5n$ vi) $S_n = \dfrac{3n^2 + n}{2}$

   a) $2 + 6 + 10 + \ldots$ b) $2 + 5 + 8 + \ldots$
   c) $7 + 11 + 15 + \ldots$ d) $5 + 11 + 17 + \ldots$

6. For the three summer months (12 weeks), Job A pays $325 per month with a monthly raise of $100. Job B pays $50 per week with a weekly raise of $10. Which is the better-paying job?

7. In a supermarket, cans of apple juice are displayed in a pyramid containing 12, 11, 10, . . ., 5 cans. How many cans are displayed?

8. *Tasty Treats* finds that its profit from the sale of ice cream increases by $5 per week during the 15-week summer season. If the profit for the first week is $30, find the profit for the season.

9. Find the sum of each arithmetic series.
   a) $2 + 7 + 12 + \ldots + 92$ b) $4 + 11 + 18 + \ldots + 88$
   c) $3 + 5.5 + 8 + \ldots + 133$ d) $20 + 14 + 8 + \ldots + (-70)$

10. The sum of the first 5 terms of an arithmetic series is 85 and the sum of the first 6 terms is 123. Write the first 3 terms of the series.

11. The sum of the first 9 terms of an arithmetic series is 162 and the sum of the first 12 terms is 288. Write the first 3 terms of the series.

12. The 5th term of an arithmetic series is 16 and the sum of the first 10 terms is 145. Write the first 3 terms of the series.

13. In an arithmetic series, $t_1 = 6$ and $S_9 = 108$; find the common difference and the sum of the first 20 terms.

14. Write the first 3 terms of the arithmetic series with $S_{10} = 210$ and $S_{20} = 820$.

15. If $S_n = -441$ for the series $19 + 15 + 11 + \ldots + t_n$, find n.

16. Find an expression for the sum of:
    a) the first n even integers   b) the first n odd integers.

17. Given $3 + 7 + 11 + 15 + \ldots$
    a) Find.   i) t_{20} and t_n ii) S_{20} and S_n
    b) How many terms:
       i) are less than 500   ii) have a sum less than 500?

18. For each arithmetic series, find S_n if t_n is equal to each value.
    a) $5 + (n - 1)2$ b) $-8 + (n - 1)6$ c) $4n + 1$
    d) $5n - 2$ e) $12 - 3n$ f) $7n + 4$

Ⓒ

19. a) Verify each statement.
    b) Use the pattern to write the next line.
    c) If the pattern continues, what is the first number on the nth line?
    d) Show that the sum of the numbers on the nth line is n^3.

$$1 = 1^3$$
$$3 + 5 = 2^3$$
$$7 + 9 + 11 = 3^3$$
$$13 + 15 + 17 + 19 = 4^3$$

20. a) Verify each statement.
    b) What is the first number on the nth line?
    c) What is the sum of the numbers on the nth line?
    d) What is the general term of the sequence 1, 5, 15, 34, 65, . . .?

$$1 = 1$$
$$2 + 3 = 5$$
$$4 + 5 + 6 = 15$$
$$7 + 8 + 9 + 10 = 34$$
$$11 + 12 + 13 + 14 + 15 = 65$$

 INVESTIGATE

$$17 + 2 = 19$$
$$19 + 4 = 23$$
$$23 + 6 = 29$$
$$29 + 8 = 37$$
$$37 + 10 = 47$$
$$47 + 12 = 59$$
.
.
.

How long does this list continue to give primes?
Find other lists like this.

 INVESTIGATE

How many letters are in this snowball sentence?
I do not know where family doctors acquired illegibly perplexing handwriting; nevertheless, extraordinary pharmaceutical intellectuality, counterbalancing indecipherability, transcendentalizes intercommunications' incomprehensibleness.
Create your own snowball sentence.
Create a reverse snowball sentence.

8-7 GEOMETRIC SERIES

A favorite pastime of some people is to construct their family tree. Some families have succeeded in tracing their roots as far back as ten generations. If you go back through ten generations, how many ancestors will you find that you have?

Every person has 2 parents, 4 grandparents, 8 great-grandparents, and so on. The number of ancestors through ten generations is:

$$2 + 4 + 8 + 16 + 32 + 64 + 128 + 256 + 512 + 1024$$

Let S represent the sum of this series.

$$S = 2 + 4 + 8 + \ldots + 512 + 1024 \qquad \ldots \text{①}$$

Multiply by the common ratio 2.

Then $2S = \underline{\qquad 4 + 8 + \ldots + 512 + 1024 + 2048} \ldots \text{②}$

$$S = -2 \qquad\qquad\qquad\qquad\qquad\qquad + 2048 \quad \text{Subtracting ① from ②}$$

$$= 2046$$

The sum of the first ten terms of the series is 2046. Going back through ten generations, each person has 2046 ancestors.

In the above example, the expression for S is a *geometric series* because it indicates that the terms of a geometric sequence are to be added.

The above method can be used to find the sum of any number of terms of a geometric series.

Example 1.   Find the sum of the first 9 terms of the geometric series
$$2 + 6 + 18 + 54 + \ldots.$$

Solution.   Find t_9 using $t_n = ar^{n-1}$

$$
\begin{aligned}
t_9 &= 2(3)^8 & a &= 2 \\
&= 2(6561) & r &= 3 \\
&= 13\ 122 & n &= 9
\end{aligned}
$$

Let S represent the sum of the series.

$$S = 2 + 6 + 18 + \ldots + 13\ 122 \qquad \ldots \text{①}$$

Multiply by the common ratio 3.

Then $3S = \underline{\qquad 6 + 18 + \ldots + 13\ 122 + 39\ 366} \ldots \text{②}$

$$
\begin{aligned}
2S &= -2 \qquad\qquad\qquad\qquad\qquad + 39\ 366 \\
&= 39\ 364 \\
S &= 19\ 682 \qquad\qquad \text{Subtracting ① from ②}
\end{aligned}
$$

The sum of the first 9 terms of the series is 19 682.

The method of *Example 1* can be used to find a formula for the sum of the first n terms of the general geometric series.

Let $S_n = a + ar + ar^2 + \ldots + ar^{n-1}$ ... ①

Multiply ① by r.

$rS_n = ar + ar^2 + \ldots + ar^{n-1} + ar^n$ ... ②

Subtract ① from ②.

$rS_n - S_n = -a + ar^n$

$S_n(r - 1) = a(r^n - 1)$

$S_n = \dfrac{a(r^n - 1)}{r - 1}$

For the general geometric series $a + ar + ar^2 + \ldots + ar^{n-1}$,

the sum of the first n terms is $S_n = \dfrac{a(r^n - 1)}{r - 1}$, $r \neq 1$

Example 2. Find the sum of the first seven terms of each geometric series.

a) $5 + 10 + 20 + 40 + \ldots$

b) $12 + 6 + 3 + 1.5 + \ldots$

c) $100 - 50 + 25 - 12.5 + \ldots$

Solution. Use the formula $S_n = \dfrac{a(r^n - 1)}{r - 1}$

a) $5 + 10 + 20 + 40 + \ldots$

$S_7 = \dfrac{5(2^7 - 1)}{2 - 1}$ $a = 5$

$ = 5(128 - 1)$ $r = 2$

$ = 5(127)$ $n = 7$

$ = 635$

The sum of the first seven terms is 635.

b) $12 + 6 + 3 + 1.5 + \ldots$

$S_7 = \dfrac{12[(0.5)^7 - 1]}{0.5 - 1}$ $a = 12$

$ = -24(0.007\ 812\ 5 - 1)$ $r = 0.5$

$ = -24(-0.992\ 187\ 5)$ $n = 7$

$ = 23.8125$

The sum of the first seven terms is 23.8125.

c) $100 - 50 + 25 - 12.5 + \ldots$

$S_7 = \dfrac{100[(-0.5)^7 - 1]}{-0.5 - 1}$ $a = 100$

$ = 67.1875$ $r = -0.5$

                                      $n = 7$

The sum of the first seven terms is 67.1875.

If the numerator and the denominator of the right side of the formula $S_n = \dfrac{a(r^n - 1)}{r - 1}$ are both multiplied by -1, we obtain $S_n = \dfrac{a(1 - r^n)}{1 - r}$.

This form is more convenient to use when $|r| < 1$, as in *Example 2b)* and c).

When a calculator is used to find the value of S_n for some series, certain values of n and r may lead to a decimal approximation for the sum. This is usually sufficient for most purposes.

EXERCISES 8-7

Ⓐ

1. Using the method of *Example 1*, find the sum of each geometric series.
   a) $1 + 2 + 4 + 8 + 16 + 32$ b) $3 + 9 + 27 + 81 + 243 + 729$
   c) $2 + 8 + 32 + 128 + 512$ d) $40 + 20 + 10 + 5 + 2.5$

2. Use the formula for S_n to find the sum of the first 5 terms of each geometric series.
   a) $2 + 10 + 50 + \ldots$ b) $4 + 12 + 36 + \ldots$
   c) $3 + 6 + 12 + \ldots$ d) $24 + 12 + 6 + \ldots$
   e) $5 + 15 + 45 + \ldots$ f) $80 + 40 + 20 + \ldots$

Ⓑ

3. Which of the expressions for S_n is the sum of the first n terms of each geometric series?

   i) $S_n = \dfrac{2(1 - 6^n)}{3}$ ii) $S_n = -(1 - 4^n)$ iii) $S_n = \dfrac{5(3^n - 1)}{2}$

   iv) $S_n = \dfrac{2(1 - 6^n)}{-5}$ v) $S_n = 4(2^n - 1)$ vi) $S_n = 6(2^n - 1)$

   a) $2 + 12 + 72 + \ldots$ b) $6 + 12 + 24 + \ldots$
   c) $3 + 12 + 48 + \ldots$ d) $4 + 8 + 16 + \ldots$

4. For the geometric series $6 + 3 + 1.5 + 0.75 + \ldots$, find:
   a) the 7th term   b) the sum of the first 7 terms.

5. For the geometric series $6 + 18 + 54 + \ldots$, find:
   a) the 6th term   b) the sum of the first 6 terms.

6. a) How many ancestors does a person have in:
      i) 12 generations   ii) 15 generations?
   b) Write a formula for the number of ancestors a person has in n generations.

7. A doctor prescribes 200 mg of medication on the first day of treatment. The dosage is halved on each successive day for one week. To the nearest milligram, what is the total amount of medication administered?

8. Sixty-four players are entered in a tennis tournament. When a player loses a match, he or she drops out; the winners go on to the next round. What is the total number of matches that must be played before a winner is decided?

9. If you are paid $0.01 on the first day, $0.02 on the second day, $0.04 on the third day, $0.08 on the fourth day, and so on, how much money would you have at the end of a 30-day month?

10. Find the sum of each geometric series.
    a) $2 + 6 + 18 + \ldots + 1458$
    b) $1 + 5 + 25 + \ldots + 3125$
    c) $48 + 24 + 12 + \ldots + \frac{3}{8}$
    d) $\frac{1}{3} + 1 + 3 + \ldots + 6561$
    e) $5 + 20 + 80 + \ldots + 20\,480$
    f) $32 + 16 + 8 + \ldots + \frac{1}{8}$

11. How many generations must a person go back to have at least 1000 ancestors?

12. The sum of the first two terms of a geometric series is 12 and the sum of the first 3 terms is 62. Find the first 3 terms of the series.

13. In a geometric series, $t_1 = 3$ and $S_3 = 21$; find the common ratio and the sum of the first 7 terms.

14. The second term of a geometric series is 15 and the sum of the first 3 terms is 93. Find the first 3 terms of the series.

15. Find S_n for a series with t_n equal to each value.
    a) $2(3)^{n-1}$
    b) $5(2)^{n-1}$
    c) $3(4)^{n-1}$
    d) 2^{n+1}

Ⓒ

16. Show that for the series $1 + \frac{1}{2} + \frac{1}{4} + \frac{1}{8} + \ldots$, S_n is never greater than 2.

17. Find the sum of the factors of 2^{10}.

 INVESTIGATE

Is it possible to find 3 numbers that form an arithmetic series and a geometric series?

THE MATHEMATICAL MIND

Population and Food

Thomas R. Malthus was a man of many talents. A mathematics graduate of Cambridge University, he was also a minister of the Church of England and a professor of history and political economy. In 1798, he published his famous "Essay on the Principle of Population As It Affects the Future Improvement of Society".

In this essay, Malthus set forth his theory that the rate of increase of the world's population was fast exceeding the development of food supplies. He reasoned that the population, if left unchecked, doubles about every 25 years, or increases geometrically. But the food supply increases, at best, only arithmetically. Thus, sooner or later, there will be widespread starvation unless a limit is placed on the population.

Malthus' essay provoked considerable controversy because it offended those who believed that society would eventually be perfect; they thought a time would come when suffering, crime, disease, and war would be eliminated. Malthus held the opposite view, and felt that the basic structure of society would always remain unchanged. Although his essay was written almost 200 years ago, the truth of his theory is even more evident today than in his time. Here is an excerpt from Malthus' essay:

"Taking the whole earth. . . . and, supposing the present population to equal a thousand millions, the human species would increase [every 25 years] as the numbers 1, 2, 4, 8, 16, 32, 64, 128, 256, and subsistence as 1, 2, 3, 4, 5, 6, 7, 8, 9. In two centuries the population would be to the means of subsistence as 256 to 9; in three centuries 4096 to 13; and in two thousand years the difference would be almost incalculable."

QUESTIONS

1. Use Malthus' figures to predict the ratio of population to food supply after:
   a) four centuries
   b) five centuries.

2. If Malthus' reasoning and figures were correct, the world population today would be about 256 billion.
   a) Give reasons why this is far in excess of the present world population.
   b) Does this negate the essential validity of his theory?

3. Use a calculator to find the "almost incalculable" figures for the ratio of population to food supply after two thousand years.

8-8 INFINITE GEOMETRIC SERIES

In the 4th century B.C. the Greek philosopher Zeno of Elea made certain statements concerning motion that have come to be known as Zeno's paradoxes. A paradox is a statement that appears to be absurd, yet its explanation seems logical.

In Zeno's *racecourse paradox*, he argued that a runner can never reach the end of a racecourse! For example, consider a racecourse 100 m long, represented by segment AB. Let us assume that the runner can run at a uniform rate of 10 m/s.

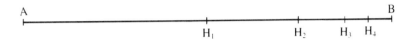

Zeno argued as follows:

The runner must reach the halfway point, H_1. This takes 5 s.

Then the runner must reach H_2, halfway between H_1 and B. This takes 2.5 s.

Then the runner must reach H_3, halfway between H_2 and B. This takes 1.25 s.

Then the runner must reach H_4, the next halfway point. This takes 0.625 s.

And so on . . .

There are infinitely many steps like this, and each will take a certain time. Since the total time is the sum of infinitely many times, the runner will never reach point B.

Yet common experience tells us that the runner does reach point B. At 10 m/s, this will take only 10 s. But it took mathematicians and philosophers almost two thousand years to find the flaw in the reasoning.

The times to reach the various halfway points are terms of a geometric series with first term 5 and common ratio 0.5.

$$5 + 2.5 + 1.25 + 0.625 + \ldots$$

Since there is always a next term, this is an example of an *infinite geometric series*. The time to reach each halfway point is the sum of a corresponding number of terms of this series.

Time to reach H_1: $S_1 = 5$

Time to reach H_2: $S_2 = 7.5$

Time to reach H_3: $S_3 = 8.75$

Time to reach H_4: $S_4 = 9.375$

Time to reach H_{10}: $S_{10} = 9.990\ 234\ 375$

Time to reach H_{20}: $S_{20} \doteq 9.999\ 990\ 463$

Notice that as *n* gets larger, S_n gets closer and closer to 10. By adding enough terms of the series we can make the sum as close to 10 as we like. Hence, we say that the sum of the infinite series is 10, and we write:

$$5 + 2.5 + 1.25 + 0.625 + \ldots = 10$$

The error in Zeno's argument is his statement that the sum of an infinite number of times is infinite. We have just shown that this particular sum is not infinite.

We can apply the above analysis to an infinite geometric series with first term *a* and common ratio *r*.

$$a + ar + ar^2 + ar^3 + \ldots + ar^{n-1} + \ldots$$

For this series,

$$S_1 = a$$
$$S_2 = a + ar$$
$$S_3 = a + ar + ar^2$$
$$S_4 = a + ar + ar^2 + ar^3$$

$$S_n = a + ar + ar^2 + ar^3 + \ldots + ar^{n-1}$$

But $S_n = \dfrac{a(r^n - 1)}{r - 1}$, provided that $r \neq 1$

$$= \left(\frac{ar^n}{r - 1}\right) - \left(\frac{a}{r - 1}\right)$$

If $|r| < 1$, then r^n becomes smaller and smaller as *n* increases. We can make r^n as small as we please by taking a sufficiently large value of *n*. Hence, if $|r| < 1$, the sum of the infinite geometric series is

$$S = 0 - \left(\frac{a}{r - 1}\right)$$

$$= \frac{a}{1 - r}$$

> The sum of the infinite geometric series
> $$a + ar + ar^2 + \ldots + ar^{n-1} + \ldots$$
> is $S = \dfrac{a}{1 - r}$, provided that $|r| < 1$.

Example 1.   Which infinite geometric series has a sum? What is the sum?

  a) $4 - 6 + 9 - 13.5 + \ldots$

  b) $6 + 2 + \dfrac{2}{3} + \dfrac{2}{9} + \ldots$

Solution.   a) $4 - 6 + 9 - 13.5 + \ldots$
   For this series, $a = 4$ and $r = -1.5$; since $|r| > 1$, this series has no sum.

b) $6 + 2 + \frac{2}{3} + \frac{2}{9} + \ldots$

For this series, $a = 6$ and $r = \frac{1}{3}$; since $|r| < 1$, this series does have a sum. Use the formula.

$$S = \frac{a}{1 - r}$$

$$= \frac{6}{1 - \frac{1}{3}}$$

$$= \frac{6}{\frac{2}{3}}$$

$$= 9$$

The sum of the series is 9.

Example 2. Express the repeating decimal $2.\overline{37}$ as a rational number in the form $\frac{m}{n}$.

Solution. $2.\overline{37} = 2 + 0.37 + 0.0037 + 0.000\,037 + \ldots$
$\qquad\quad\ = 2 + 0.37 + 0.37(0.01) + 0.37(0.0001) + \ldots$

The terms after the first term form an infinite geometric series with first term 0.37 and common ratio 0.01. Using the above formula with $a = 0.37$ and $r = 0.01$, we obtain

$$2.\overline{37} = 2 + \frac{0.37}{1 - 0.01}$$

$$= 2 + \frac{0.37}{0.99}$$

$$= 2 + \frac{37}{99}$$

$$= \frac{235}{99}$$

EXERCISES 8-8

(A)

1. Which infinite geometric series have a sum? What is the sum?
   a) $8 + 4 + 2 + 1 + \ldots$
   b) $27 + 18 + 12 + 8 + \ldots$
   c) $3 + 7 + 11 + 15 + \ldots$
   d) $50 - 40 + 32 - 25.6 + \ldots$
   e) $2 + 6 + 18 + 54 + \ldots$
   f) $-16 + 12 - 9 + 6.75 - \ldots$

(B)

2. Find the sum of each infinite geometric series.
   a) $60 + 30 + 15 + 7.5 + \ldots$
   b) $5 + 2.5 + 1.25 + 0.625 + \ldots$
   c) $20 - 15 + 11.25 - 8.4375 + \ldots$
   d) $8 + 2 + \frac{1}{2} + \frac{1}{8} + \ldots$

3. Express each repeating decimal as an infinite series. Then find the sum of the series, and use it to express the number in the form $\frac{m}{n}$.

   a) $2.\overline{3}$ b) $3.\overline{18}$ c) $1.5\overline{21}$ d) $6.0\overline{85}$

4. The general term of an infinite geometric series is given. Determine the sum of the series, if it exists.

   a) $12\left(\frac{2}{3}\right)^{n-1}$ b) $32\left(\frac{3}{8}\right)^{n-1}$ c) $9\left(\frac{3}{2}\right)^{n-1}$ d) $8\left(-\frac{5}{6}\right)^{n-1}$

5. The sum of an infinite geometric series is 63 and the first term is 21. Find the common ratio.

6. The sum of an infinite geometric series is $\frac{24}{7}$ and the common ratio is $-\frac{3}{4}$. Find the first term.

7. a) Find the sum of the series $12 - 6 + 3 - 1.5 + \ldots$
   b) Find the difference between the sum of the series in part a) and the sum of the first eight terms of the series.

8. A ball is dropped from a height of 2 m to a floor. On each bounce the ball rises to 50% of the height from which it fell. Calculate the total distance the ball travels before coming to rest.

9. Repeat *Exercise 8* if the ball rises to 70% of the height from which it fell on each bounce.

10. The midpoints of a square with sides 1 m long are joined to form another square. Then the midpoints of the sides of the second square are joined to form a third square. This process is continued indefinitely to form an infinite set of smaller and smaller squares converging on the centre of the original square. Determine the total length of the segments forming the sides of all the squares.

Ⓒ

11. Determine the values of x such that each series has a sum.

   a) $1 + x + x^2 + x^3 + \ldots$ b) $1 + \frac{1}{2}x + \frac{1}{4}x^2 + \frac{1}{8}x^3 + \ldots$

   c) $1 - \frac{1}{3}x^2 + \frac{1}{9}x^4 - \frac{1}{27}x^6 + \ldots$ d) $\frac{1}{x} + \frac{1}{x^2} + \frac{1}{x^3} + \ldots$

THE MATHEMATICAL MIND

Infinity

The concept of infinity has intrigued mathematicians and non-mathematicians alike for centuries.

Infinity in Language

Great fleas have little fleas upon
  their backs to bit 'em
And little fleas have lesser fleas,
  and so *ad infinitum*,
And the great fleas themselves, in turn,
  have greater fleas to go on,
While these again have greater still,
  and greater still, and so on.

           A. de Morgan

I could be bounded in a nutshell and count myself a king of infinite space.

           William Shakespeare

The notion of infinity is our greatest friend; it is also the greatest enemy of our peace of mind.

           James Pierpont

Infinity in Art

Circle Limit III
By Maurits Escher

Infinity in Mathematics

About two hundred years ago mathematicians noticed some strange results when they began to work with infinite quantities. Here is a small sample of some of the difficulties they encountered. Some of the world's greatest mathematicians were surprised by results such as these, and it was many years before the concept of infinity was understood.

In arithmetic

Natural numbers: 1, 2, 3, 4, . . .
Even numbers: 2, 4, 6, 8, . . .
Since the natural numbers include both odd and even numbers, there appear to be twice as many natural numbers as even numbers. But the natural numbers can be paired with the even numbers as shown above. This suggests that there are the same number of even numbers as natural numbers!

In geometry

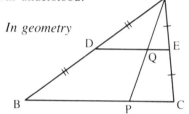

D and E are midpoints of two sides of △ABC. Since BC is twice as long as DE, it contains twice as many points as DE. But any point P on BC can be paired with a corresponding point Q on DE by joining PA. This suggests that DE contains the same number of points as BC!

Examples like the two above convinced mathematicians that when they deal with infinite sets, they need to define what is meant by the "number" of quantities in those sets.

In arithmetic

$$\frac{1}{3} = 0.333\ 333 \ldots , \text{ or } 0.\overline{3}$$

$$\frac{2}{3} = 0.666\ 666 \ldots , \text{ or } 0.\overline{6}$$

Add. $\overline{1} = \overline{0.999\ 999} \ldots , \text{ or } 0.\overline{9}$

But 0.999 999 . . . is never exactly equal to 1; no matter how many 9s we take, this expression will always be less than 1. How can a quantity that is less than 1 be equal to 1? The answer is that we can make 0.999 999 . . . as close to 1 as we like by taking enough 9s. This is what we mean when we write $1 = 0.999\ 999 \ldots$, or $0.\overline{9}$.

In algebra

Consider the infinite series
1 + 2 + 4 + 8 + 16 + . . .
Let $S = 1 + 2 + 4 + 8 + 16 + \ldots$
$\quad S = 1 + 2(1 + 2 + 4 + 8 + 16 + \ldots)$
$\quad S = 1 + 2S$
Hence, $S = -1$
But, how can a series of infinitely many positive terms have a sum of −1? The answer, of course, is that it can't. Yet, the algebra above appears correct. Hence, mathematicians began to realize that they cannot assume that familiar algebraic operations can always be performed with infinite quantities.

QUESTIONS

1. Consider the quotation by A. de Morgan. What does de Morgan mean by "ad infinitum?"

2. In his quotation, A. de Morgan describes the infinitely large and the infinitely small. How does Escher's print, Circle Limit III, illustrate the infinitely large and the infinitely small?

3. This quotation appeared in Readers' Digest magazine some years ago.

   "High up in the North, in the land called Svetjod, there stands a rock. It is a thousand miles long and a thousand miles high. Once every thousand years a little bird comes to sharpen its beak. When the rock has thus been worn away, then a single day of eternity will have gone by."

   According to this quotation, how long is a "single day of eternity"? Make any assumptions that seem reasonable.

4. Here is another example of an infinite series that can lead to absurd results.
   Let $S = 1 - 1 + 1 - 1 + 1 - 1 + \ldots$
   $\quad S = (1 - 1) + (1 - 1) + (1 - 1) + \ldots$
   $\quad S = 0 + 0 + 0 + \ldots$
   $\quad S = 0$
   Assuming that the rules of algebra apply, demonstrate that:
   a) $S = 0.5$ b) $S = 1$.

In *Question 4*, and the series on the previous page, one reason for the absurd results is that the sum S does not exist. But there are other examples of series for which the corresponding sum S *does* exist, and yet similar contradictory results can be obtained!

5. Here is a "proof" of the formula for the sum of an infinite geometric series.
   Let $S = a + ar + ar^2 + ar^3 + \ldots$
   $\quad S = a + r(a + ar + ar^2 + \ldots)$
   $\quad S = a + rS$
   $S(1 - r) = a$
   $$S = \frac{a}{1 - r} \quad (\text{if } r \neq 1)$$
   Although this "proof" leads to the correct formula, it is not a valid proof of the formula. Explain the error.

8-9 SIGMA NOTATION FOR A SERIES

There is a special notation that is used to represent a series. For example, the arithmetic series with 6 terms, $1 + 4 + 7 + 10 + 13 + 16$, has general term $t_n = a + (n - 1)d$

$$= 1 + (n - 1)3$$
$$= 3n - 2$$

Each term in the series can be expressed in this form.

$t_1 = 3(1) - 2 \qquad t_2 = 3(2) - 2 \qquad t_3 = 3(3) - 2$
$t_4 = 3(4) - 2 \qquad t_5 = 3(5) - 2 \qquad t_6 = 3(6) - 2$

The series is the sum of all the terms. This is abbreviated to:

The sum of . . . $\longrightarrow \displaystyle\sum_{k=1}^{6} (3k - 2) \longleftarrow$ . . . all numbers of the form $3k - 2$ . . .

. . . for values of k from 1 to 6.

The symbol Σ is the capital Greek letter *sigma*, which corresponds to S, the first letter of Sum. When Σ is used as shown, it is called *sigma notation*. In sigma notation, k is often used as the variable under the Σ sign and in the expression following it. Although any letter can be used for this purpose, n should be avoided because n usually represents the number of terms in a series.

Example 1. Write the series corresponding to $\displaystyle\sum_{j=1}^{3} (j^2 + 2j + 5)$.

Solution. Substitute values from 1 to 3, in turn, for j in the expression $j^2 + 2j + 5$ and add the results.

$$\sum_{j=1}^{3} (j^2 + 2j + 5)$$
$$= [1^2 + 2(1) + 5] + [2^2 + 2(2) + 5] + [3^2 + 2(3) + 5]$$
$$= 8 + 13 + 20$$

Example 2. Write each series using sigma notation.
a) $3 + 9 + 15 + 21 + 27$ b) $5 + 10 + 20 + 40 + 80 + 160$

Solution. a) $3 + 9 + 15 + 21 + 27$
This is an arithmetic series with $a = 3$ and $d = 6$.
The general term is $t_n = a + (n - 1)d$
$$= 3 + (n - 1)6$$
$$= 6n - 3$$

Since there are 5 terms, the series can be written $\displaystyle\sum_{k=1}^{5} (6k - 3)$.

b) $5 + 10 + 20 + 40 + 80 + 160$
This is a geometric series with $a = 5$ and $r = 2$.
The general terms is $t_n = ar^{n-1}$
$$= 5(2)^{n-1}$$

Since there are 6 terms, the series can be written $\sum_{k=1}^{6} 5(2)^{k-1}$.

The formulas for the sums of an arithmetic series or a geometric series can sometimes be used to simplify expressions involving sigma notation.

Example 3. Simplify. a) $\sum_{i=1}^{20} (3i + 1)$ b) $\sum_{k=1}^{7} 2^k$ c) $\sum_{k=1}^{\infty} \left(\frac{1}{2}\right)^{k-4}$

Solution.   a) $\sum_{i=1}^{20} (3i + 1) = 4 + 7 + 10 + \ldots + 61$

This is an arithmetic series with $a = 4$, $d = 3$, $n = 20$.

The sum of the series is $S_n = \frac{n}{2}(a + l)$

$$S_{20} = \frac{20}{2}(4 + 61)$$
$$= 10(65)$$
$$= 650$$

Therefore, $\sum_{i=1}^{20} (3i + 1) = 650$

b) $\sum_{k=1}^{7} 2^k = 2 + 2^2 + 2^3 + \ldots + 2^7$

This is a geometric series with $a = 2$, $r = 2$, $n = 7$.

The sum of the series is $S_n = \frac{a(r^n - 1)}{r - 1}$

$$S_7 = \frac{2(2^7 - 1)}{2 - 1}$$
$$= 2(2^7 - 1)$$
$$= 2(127)$$
$$= 254$$

Therefore, $\sum_{k=1}^{7} 2^k = 254$

c) $\sum_{k=1}^{\infty} \left(\frac{1}{2}\right)^{k-4} = 8 + 4 + 2 + \cdots$

This is an infinite geometric series with $a = 8$ and $r = \frac{1}{2}$.

The sum of the series is $S = \dfrac{a}{1-r}$

$$= \dfrac{8}{1 - \dfrac{1}{2}}$$

$$= 16$$

Therefore, $\displaystyle\sum_{k=1}^{\infty} \left(\dfrac{1}{2}\right)^{k-4} = 16$

When sigma notation is used to represent an infinite series, both notations $\displaystyle\sum_{k=1}^{\infty}$ and $\displaystyle\sum_{k}$ can be used.

EXERCISES 8-9

Ⓐ

1. Write the series corresponding to each expression.

   a) $\displaystyle\sum_{k=1}^{5} (k + 3)$

   b) $\displaystyle\sum_{j=1}^{4} (4j + 1)$

   c) $\displaystyle\sum_{m=1}^{6} 2m$

   d) $\displaystyle\sum_{j=1}^{5} (3j - 8)$

   e) $\displaystyle\sum_{i=1}^{\infty} \left(\dfrac{1}{3}\right)^{i-2}$

   f) $\displaystyle\sum_{k=1}^{4} (5k - 12)$

2. Write each series using sigma notation.

   a) $2 + 5 + 8 + 11 + \ldots + 20$

   b) $3 + 5 + 7 + 9 + 11 + 13$

   c) $5 + 1 + \dfrac{1}{5} + \dfrac{1}{25} + \ldots$

   d) $24 + 18 + 12 + 6$

Ⓑ

3. Which of the expressions in sigma notation is correct for each series?

   i) $\displaystyle\sum_{k=1}^{5} (3k + 1)$

   ii) $\displaystyle\sum_{k=1}^{5} (2k - 3)$

   iii) $\displaystyle\sum_{k=1}^{5} (3k - 2)$

   iv) $\displaystyle\sum_{k=1}^{5} (2k + 3)$

   v) $\displaystyle\sum_{k=1}^{5} (3 - 2k)$

   vi) $\displaystyle\sum_{k=1}^{5} (5k - 1)$

   a) $5 + 7 + 9 + 11 + 13$

   b) $-1 + 1 + 3 + 5 + 7$

   c) $1 + 4 + 7 + 10 + 13$

   d) $4 + 9 + 14 + 19 + 24$

4. Simplify.

   a) $\displaystyle\sum_{k=1}^{12} (2k + 3)$

   b) $\displaystyle\sum_{j=1}^{8} (j - 2)$

   c) $\displaystyle\sum_{k=1}^{10} (4k - 1)$

5. Simplify.

   a) $\displaystyle\sum_{i=1}^{7} 3(2)^i$

   b) $\displaystyle\sum_{k=1}^{6} 2^{k+1}$

   c) $\displaystyle\sum_{i=1}^{6} 3^i$

6. Write the series corresponding to each expression.

a) $\displaystyle\sum_{j=1}^{5} (j^2 - 2j)$

b) $\displaystyle\sum_{i=1}^{7} (i^2 + 3)$

c) $\displaystyle\sum_{k=1}^{4} (3k^2 + 2k - 5)$

d) $\displaystyle\sum_{m=1}^{6} (2m^2 - 5m)$

e) $\displaystyle\sum_{k=1}^{5} (3k - k^2)$

f) $\displaystyle\sum_{i=1}^{7} (i^2 + 5i - 2)$

7. Write each series using sigma notation.
a) $2 + 5 + 8 + \ldots + (3n - 1)$
b) $18 + 13 + 8 + \ldots$
c) $3 + 9 + 15 + \ldots + 93$
d) $2 + 6 + 10 + \ldots + 46$
e) $2 + 6 + 18 + \ldots$
f) $3 + 6 + 12 + \ldots + 768$

8. Write the series corresponding to each expression.

a) $\displaystyle\sum_{k=1}^{4} a^k$

b) $\displaystyle\sum_{k=1}^{4} ka^k$

c) $\displaystyle\sum_{k=1}^{4} ak^k$

d) $\displaystyle\sum_{k=1}^{4} (-ak)^k$

9. Write each series using sigma notation.
a) $3 + 6 + 9 + 12 + 15$
b) $2 + 4 + 8 + 16 + 32 + 64$
c) $1 + \dfrac{1}{2} + \dfrac{1}{3} + \dfrac{1}{4} + \dfrac{1}{5}$
d) $-3 + 6 - 12 + 24 - 48$

10. Simplify.

a) $\displaystyle\sum_{j=3}^{15} (3j - 1)$

b) $\displaystyle\sum_{k=2}^{11} (2k + 5)$

c) $\displaystyle\sum_{i=4}^{14} (4i - 3)$

11. Simplify.

a) $\displaystyle\sum_{i=2}^{6} 2^{i-1}$

b) $\displaystyle\sum_{j=3}^{7} 2^{2j-3}$

c) $\displaystyle\sum_{k=1}^{5} 2^{1-k}$

12. Write each series using sigma notation.
a) $1 + 2 + 3 + 4 + \ldots + n$
b) $1 + 4 + 9 + 16 + \ldots$
c) $1 + 4 + 27 + 256 + \ldots + n^n$
d) $3 + 6 + 12 + \ldots + 3(2)^{n-1}$

13. Find the sum of the series $\displaystyle\sum_{i=1}^{n} (-)^i$ if:

a) n is odd

b) n is even.

14. Write each series using sigma notation.
a) $a + a + d + a + 2d + a + 3d + \ldots + a + (n - 1)d$
b) $a + ar + ar^2 + ar^3 + \ldots + ar^{n-1}$

 INVESTIGATE

Π, the capital Greek letter P, is the first letter of *Product*. Make up some examples to show what pi notation would mean.

 COMPUTER POWER

The Snowflake Curve and Fractal Geometry

About a hundred years ago, mathematicians devised some strange curves to serve as counterexamples to disprove certain intuitive ideas about geometry. For example, we might think that a figure cannot have an infinite perimeter. But in 1906, Helge von Koch came up with a curve to show that it can! To visualize this curve, we construct a sequence of polygons $S_1, S_2, S_3, \ldots$ as follows.

S_1 is an equilateral triangle.

To obtain S_2, construct an equilateral triangle on each side of S_1 and remove the base.

S_3 is obtained from S_2 in the same way as S_2 is obtained from S_1.

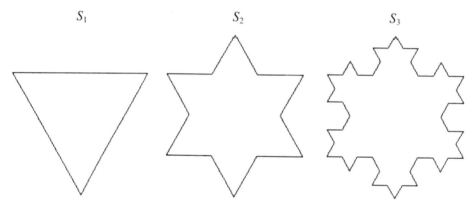

Continue in the same way to obtain the other polygons of the sequence.

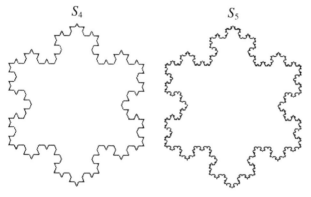

It can be proved that these polygons come closer and closer to a certain limiting curve, called the *snowflake curve*.

QUESTIONS

1. Assume that the equilateral triangle S_1 has sides 3 cm long.
   a) Calculate the perimeters of the five polygons shown.
   b) Calculate the areas of the five polygons.
   c) Calculate the area of the region enclosed by the snowflake curve, and explain why this region has an infinite perimeter.

2. Write recursive definitions for the sequence of:
   a) polygons S_1, S_2, S_3, . . .   b) perimeters P_1, P_2, P_3, . . .
   c) areas A_1, A_2, A_3, . . .

Some computer languages are well suited for displaying figures defined recursively on the screen. The two LOGO procedures below define a command called SNOWFLAKE. (On some computers it may be necessary to replace SETPOS in the second line with SETXY:)

```
TO SNOWFLAKE :X
CS PU SETPOS [-90 52] RT 90 PD
MAKE "SIZE 180
MAKE "N 5 - :X
MAKE "X 1
REPEAT :N [MAKE "X :X * 3]
REPEAT 3 [DRAW :SIZE :X RT 120]
END

TO DRAW :SIZE :X
IF :SIZE < :X [FD :SIZE STOP]
DRAW :SIZE / 3 :X LT 60
DRAW :SIZE / 3 :X RT 120
DRAW :SIZE / 3 :X LT 60
DRAW :SIZE / 3 :X
END
```

3. If you have a computer with LOGO, experiment with the SNOWFLAKE command. For example, to display the polygon S_3 on the screen, type SNOWFLAKE 3. Try to get the best example you can within the limitations of your computer screen.

   The snowflake curve is one of several weird curves that were introduced early in the 20th century. Another curve passes through every point inside a square! Still another intersects itself at every one of its points! At the time, these curves were dismissed by mathematicians as little more than pathological curiosities. No one would have thought that 70 years later they would be an important part of a new kind of geometry called *fractal geometry*.

Fractal geometry was introduced in 1977 by Benoit B. Mandelbrot for the purpose of modelling natural phenomena that are irregular (or crinkled) over several different size scales. Examples include coastlines, the surface of the lungs, the network of arteries and veins in the body, the branching structure of plants, the thermal agitation of molecules in a fluid (Brownian motion), sponges, and even the rings of Saturn.

Fractal geometry deals with novel kinds of curves and surfaces with a fractional dimension! For example, the snowflake curve is not two-dimensional because it does not include the points inside it. And, it is not one-dimensional either because it zigzags infinitely often. We can find the dimension of the snowflake curve as follows.

A key feature of the snowflake curve is its self-similarity. This means that parts of it are similar to larger copies of themselves. For example, the two parts shown are similar. The larger part is a $3\times$ enlargement of the smaller, and 4 copies of the smaller part are needed to make the enlargement.

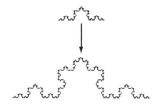

Consider what happens with simpler self-similar figures such as a line segment, a square, or a cube.

- In *1 dimension*, to make a $3\times$ enlargement of a line segment, we used 3^1, or 3 copies.

- In *2 dimensions*, to make a $3\times$ enlargement of a square, we need 3^2, or 9 copies.

- In *3 dimensions*, to make a $3\times$ enlargement of a cube, we need 3^3, or 27 copies.

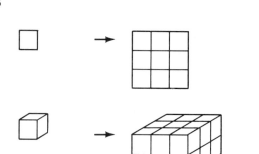

Observe that, in each case, the number of copies needed to make the enlargement is a power of the scale factor, and the exponent is the number of dimensions.

4. Let x represent the dimension of the snowflake curve. Use the above observation to write an exponential equation in x. Solve the equation to obtain the dimension of the snowflake curve.

Fractal geometry is a new and complicated branch of geometry that is accessible only with computers. Computers are needed to handle the enormous computations involved in recursive processes, and to display the intricate results. The example below provides one small glimpse of this new world. It is a set of points that is studied in fractal geometry.

5. Examine the illustration carefully.
   a) Describe as many patterns in it as you can find.
   b) Find as many examples of self-similarity as you can.

PROBLEM SOLVING

Creative Problem Posing

"For both problem solving and the teaching of problem solving, Polya's advice is most appropriate — practice, practice, practice."

Linda J. DeGuire

What happens if the constants in the equation $Ax + By + C = 0$ are in arithmetic sequence?

Think of a strategy and carry it out

- Write an example of an equation in which the constants are in arithmetic sequence.
- Write another equation like it, and then solve the system formed by the two equations.
- Repeat with another pair of equations.
- Compare your results with those of other students. What do you notice?

OR

- Write an example of an equation in which the constants are in arithmetic sequence.
- Draw the graph of the equation.
- Write some other equations like it and draw their graphs on the same grid.
- Compare your results with those of other students. What do you notice?

Look back

- Can you prove your results?
- Would it matter if the equation were written in the form $Ax + By = C$?
- Write a report of your discoveries.

The quotation below is taken from an essay entitled, "How Much Mathematics Can There Be?".

"All experience so far seems to show that there are two inexhaustible sources of new mathematical questions. One source is the development of science and technology, which makes ever new demands on mathematics for assistance. The other source is mathematics itself. As it becomes more elaborate and complex, each new, completed result becomes the potential starting point for several new investigations. Each pair of seemingly unrelated mathematical specialties pose an implicit challenge: to find a fruitful connection between them."

The last sentence of the quotation, and the above example, suggest that one method of posing problems in mathematics is to try to find connections between apparently unrelated topics. This can often be done by matching or linking certain constants or numbers that occur in the two topics.

For example, in the problem about linear equations and arithmetic sequences we matched the coefficients in the equation with the terms of an arithmetic sequence.

Many topics in mathematics can be linked in this way to create problems to investigate. To assist with this, the table below is useful. For example, cell A links the topics which suggested the problem discussed above. Each cell links two different topics and represents a potential source of problems for investigation.

Consecutive numbers

Perfect squares

Prime numbers

Coordinates of a point

Sides of a triangle

Angles of a triangle

Line $y = mx + b$

Line $Ax + By + C = 0$

Parabola $y = ax^2 + bx + c$

$ax^2 + bx + c = 0$

Arithmetic sequence

Geometric sequence

A

Choose one or more of the cells. Create problems based on the topics linked by each cell, and then solve the problems.

PROBLEMS

1. Find an expression for the sum of the squares of the terms of the finite arithmetic series $a + (a + d) + (a + 2d) + \ldots + [a + (n - 1)d]$.

2. Write the numbers from 1 to 9 in the spaces such that a correct addition of two 3-digit numbers is illustrated, and consecutive digits are in adjacent spaces.

3. Sketch the curve $y = 2 \sin x \, |\cos x|$.

4. A card 12 cm long and 6 cm wide is cut along a diagonal to form two congruent triangles. Then, the triangles are arranged as shown. Find the area of the region where the triangles overlap.

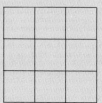

5. Prove that there is no infinite arithmetic sequence of natural numbers whose terms are all prime numbers, except for the trivial case when the common difference is 0.

6. In pentagon ABCDE, all five sides have the same length. If O is the midpoint of AB, and $\angle EOC = 90°$, determine the measures of $\angle BCD$ and $\angle AED$.

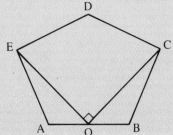

7. a) Prove that x, y, and z are consecutive terms of a geometric sequence if, and only if, $(x^2 + y^2)(y^2 + z^2) = (xy + yz)^2$.
   b) Determine whether or not a similar result holds for four consecutive terms of a geometric sequence.

8. Calculate the coordinates of all the points on the ellipse defined by $4x^2 + 9y^2 = 36$ which are twice as far from one vertex as from the other vertex.

9. In $\triangle ABC$, $AB = AC$, and $\angle A = 20°$. M is a point on AB such that $\angle MCB = 50°$, and N is a point on AC such that $\angle NBC = 60°$. Calculate $\angle BNM$.

1. Write the first 4 terms of each sequence defined by the given term.
   a) $t_n = 3n + 1$
   b) $t_n = (n - 1)^2$
   c) $t_n = 5n^2 - 2n$
   d) $t_n = \dfrac{n - 2}{n + 1}$

2. Find the indicated terms of each sequence.
   a) $t_n = 3 + 5n$, t_4 and t_{11}
   b) $t_n = 2^n - 3$, t_5 and t_{10}
   c) $t_n = \dfrac{n}{3n - 1}$, t_3 and t_8
   d) $t_n = 10 - 2^{n-1}$, t_4 and t_7

3. Write the first 4 terms of each sequence with the given values of a and d or r.
   a) $a = 2$, $d = 7$
   b) $a = 1$, $r = 3$
   c) $a = 21$, $d = -4$
   d) $a = -2$, $r = 5$

4. Classify each sequence as arithmetic or geometric, and find the value of d or r.
   a) $13, 9, 5, 1, \ldots$
   b) $\dfrac{1}{4}, \dfrac{1}{2}, 1, 2, \ldots$
   c) $18, -9, 4.5, -2.25, \ldots$
   d) $5, 13, 21, 29, \ldots$

5. Find an expression for the general term of each sequence.
   a) $2, 6, 10, 14, \ldots$
   b) $2, 6, 18, 54, \ldots$
   c) $1, 8, 27, 64, \ldots$
   d) $\dfrac{3}{2}, \dfrac{8}{3}, \dfrac{15}{4}, \dfrac{24}{5}, \ldots$

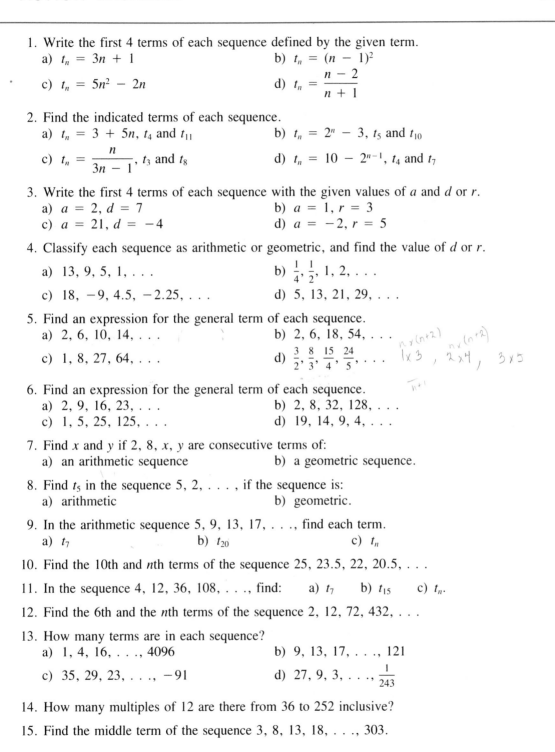

6. Find an expression for the general term of each sequence.
   a) $2, 9, 16, 23, \ldots$
   b) $2, 8, 32, 128, \ldots$
   c) $1, 5, 25, 125, \ldots$
   d) $19, 14, 9, 4, \ldots$

7. Find x and y if $2, 8, x, y$ are consecutive terms of:
   a) an arithmetic sequence
   b) a geometric sequence.

8. Find t_5 in the sequence $5, 2, \ldots$, if the sequence is:
   a) arithmetic
   b) geometric.

9. In the arithmetic sequence $5, 9, 13, 17, \ldots$, find each term.
   a) t_7
   b) t_{20}
   c) t_n

10. Find the 10th and nth terms of the sequence $25, 23.5, 22, 20.5, \ldots$

11. In the sequence $4, 12, 36, 108, \ldots$, find: a) t_7 b) t_{15} c) t_n.

12. Find the 6th and the nth terms of the sequence $2, 12, 72, 432, \ldots$

13. How many terms are in each sequence?
    a) $1, 4, 16, \ldots, 4096$
    b) $9, 13, 17, \ldots, 121$
    c) $35, 29, 23, \ldots, -91$
    d) $27, 9, 3, \ldots, \dfrac{1}{243}$

14. How many multiples of 12 are there from 36 to 252 inclusive?

15. Find the middle term of the sequence $3, 8, 13, 18, \ldots, 303$.

16. In an arithmetic sequence, the third term is 19 and the fifteenth term is -17. Find the first 3 terms of the sequence.

17. In a geometric sequence, the third term is 50 and the sixth term is 6250. Find the first 3 terms of the sequence.

18. In an arithmetic sequence, $t_4 + t_5 + t_6 = 300$, and $t_{15} + t_{16} + t_{17} = 201$; find t_{18}.

19. In a geometric sequence, $t_1 + t_2 + t_3 = 21$, and $t_4 + t_5 + t_6 = 168$; find the first 3 terms of the sequence.

20. Write the first 4 terms of each sequence.
    a) $t_1 = 1, t_n = 3t_{n-1} + 4, n > 1$ b) $t_1 = -0.5, t_n = -4t_{n-1}, n > 1$

21. Classify each series as arithmetic, geometric, or other.
    a) $1 + 7 + 13 + 19 + \ldots$ b) $1 + 4 + 9 + 16 + \ldots$
    c) $1 + 3 + 9 + 27 + \ldots$ d) $64 + 32 + 16 + 8 + \ldots$
    e) $21 + 13 + 5 + (-3) + \ldots$ f) $\frac{1}{2} + \frac{2}{3} + \frac{3}{4} + \frac{4}{5} + \ldots$

22. The sum of the first 3 terms of a series is 32. Find the fourth term if the sum of the first 4 terms is:
    a) 40   b) 55   c) 25.

23. Write the first 4 terms of the series for which:
    a) $S_n = 2n$ b) $S_n = n^2 + 2n$ c) $S_n = 3n + 1$ d) $S_n = 2n^2 - n$.

24. Find S_5 and S_n for each series.
    a) $2 + 5 + 8 + \ldots$ b) $12 + 5 + (-2) + \ldots$ c) $6 + 10 + 14 + \ldots$
    d) $5 + 10 + 20 + \ldots$ e) $12 + 6 + 3 + \ldots$ f) $2 + 6 + 18 + \ldots$

25. For the series $-3 + 1 + 5 + 9 + \ldots$, find: a) t_{10} b) S_{16}.

26. For the series $1 + 2 + 4 + 8 + \ldots$, find: a) t_8 b) S_{21}.

27. How many terms of the series $1 + 3 + 5 + 7 + \ldots$ add to 144?

28. How many terms of the series $3 + 6 + 12 + 24 + \ldots$ add to 765?

29. In an arithmetic series, if the fifth term is 74 and the twelfth term is 116, find:
    a) the first 3 terms of the series   b) the sum of the first 30 terms.

30. In a geometric series, $t_3 = 18$ and $t_6 = 486$; find:
    a) the first 3 terms of the series   b) S_{17}.

31. Find the sum of the first 15 terms of an arithmetic series if the middle term is 92.

32. Find the sum of each infinite geometric series.
    a) $40 + 20 + 10 + 5 + \ldots$ b) $-30 + 20 - \frac{40}{3} + \frac{80}{9} - \ldots$

33. Simplify.
    a) $\sum_{i=1}^{6} (4i + 3)$ b) $\sum_{i=2}^{10} (-3i + 5)$ c) $\sum_{j=3}^{7} 2^{2-j}$

9 Geometry

A mixing bowl has the shape of a truncated hemisphere, with diameter 25 cm and height 10 cm. It contains milk to a depth of 5 cm. Through what angle must the bowl be tipped before the milk spills? (See Section 9-2 *Example 2*.)

9-1 REVISITING PROPERTIES OF LINES AND TRIANGLES

Many theorems in geometry are statements which appear to be self-evident. We can sometimes apply simple constructions, manipulations or plausible arguments to suggest why they are true. However, the importance of Euclidean geometry lies in its power to prove such theorems in the general case and to establish theorems which are not immediately evident.

The following theorem is not self-evident, though it was demonstrated by the ancient Greek mathematician Pythagoras over 2500 years ago!

> **The Pythagorean Theorem**
> The square of the length of the hypotenuse of a right triangle is equal to the sum of the squares of the lengths of the other two sides.

This theorem asserts that if $\triangle$ABC is a right triangle with right angle at A, then the shortest distance from B to C (denoted by a) is related to the distances from B to A and A to C by this equation: $a^2 = b^2 + c^2$.

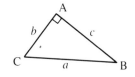

Using deductive reasoning we can prove this theorem; that is, we can establish that it is true for any lengths b and c.

In our previous study of geometry we learned various properties of angles, lines, polygons, and circles and used these properties to complete proofs of theorems. In this chapter we will review these properties and then apply them to the construction of complete proofs. In this section, we shall revisit some of the properties of lines and triangles which are embodied in the following familiar theorems.

Theorems About Lines

> **Opposite Angles Theorem**
> When two lines intersect, the opposite angles are congruent.

When two lines intersect, two pairs of *opposite angles* are formed. In the diagram, AB and CD intersect at point P, forming these pairs of opposite angles:
$\angle$CPB and $\angle$APD; $\angle$CPA and $\angle$BPD.
The Opposite Angles Theorem asserts that:
$\angle$CPB = $\angle$APD
$\angle$CPA = $\angle$BPD

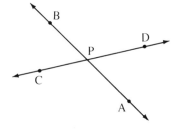

The Opposite Angles Theorem identifies pairs of equal angles formed when one line intersects another. We now consider pairs of equal angles formed when one line intersects a pair of parallel lines.

Any line which intersects a pair of lines is called a *transversal*. In the diagram below, XY is a transversal intersecting lines l_1 and l_2. The Parallel Lines Theorem identifies 6 pairs of congruent angles and 2 pairs of supplementary angles formed when a transversal intersects two parallel lines.

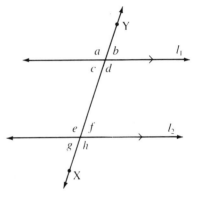

Parallel Lines Theorem
When a transversal intersects two parallel lines:
- the corresponding angles are congruent
- the alternate angles are congruent
- the interior angles are supplementary.

In this diagram,

Corresponding Angles	Alternate Angles	Interior Angles
$\angle a = \angle e$ $\angle b = \angle f$ $\angle c = \angle g$ $\angle d = \angle h$	$\angle c = \angle f$ $\angle e = \angle d$	$\angle d + \angle f = 180°$ $\angle c + \angle e = 180°$

Converse of Parallel Lines Theorem
If a transversal intersects lines l_1 and l_2 so that corresponding or alternate angles are equal, then l_1 is parallel to l_2.

Theorems About Triangles
When 3 lines intersect to form a triangle, the interior angles of the triangle are related in accordance with the Sum of the Angles Theorem.

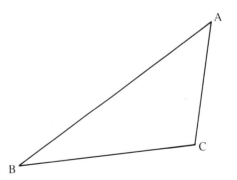

Sum of the Angles Theorem
The sum of the measures of the angles in a triangle is 180°.

This theorem asserts that for any $\triangle ABC$, $\angle A + \angle B + \angle C = 180°$.

The following Isosceles Triangle Theorem was also called "Pons Asinorum" (Bridge of Fools) by ancient mathematicians who believed that only those who were not fools could successfully cross this bridge into deductive thinking.

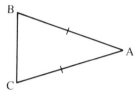

> **Isosceles Triangle Theorem**
> If two sides of a triangle are congruent, then the angles opposite the congruent sides are congruent.

Hence, if △ABC is isosceles with AB = AC, then ∠B = ∠C

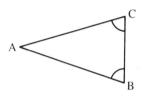

> **Converse of the Isosceles Triangle Theorem**
> If two angles of a triangle are congruent, then the sides opposite the congruent angles are congruent.

Hence, if ∠B = ∠C, then AB = AC

When a statement and its converse are both true, we can combine them into a single *biconditional statement* using the "if and only if" construction.

We can combine the Isosceles Triangle Theorem and its converse into a biconditional statement as follows.

> Two angles of a triangle are congruent if and only if the sides opposite the congruent angles are congruent.

The statement 'if and only if' is abbreviated to 'iff'.

When two figures can be positioned so that they coincide, we say that they are *congruent*. Congruent figures have the same shape and size.

If △ABC and △DEF are congruent, we write △ABC ≅ △DEF and this congruence represents the following six equations.
Corresponding angles are congruent.
∠A = ∠D
∠B = ∠E
∠C = ∠F
Corresponding sides are congruent.
AB = DE
BC = EF
AC = DF

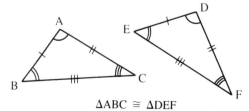

△ABC ≅ △DEF

When we know that two triangles are congruent, everything we know
about one triangle is also known to be true of the other triangle. It is
therefore helpful to know what conditions are sufficient to prove two
triangles congruent. Each of the following theorems provides a simple
set of conditions which are sufficient to establish that two triangles are
congruent.

Side-Angle-Side Theorem   (SAS)
If two sides and the contained
angle of one triangle are congruent
to two sides and the contained
angle of another triangle, then the
triangles are congruent.

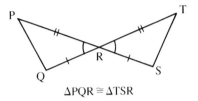

$\triangle PQR \cong \triangle TSR$

Angle-Side-Angle Theorem   (ASA)
If two angles and the contained
side of one triangle are congruent
to two angles and the contained
side of another triangle, then the
triangles are congruent.

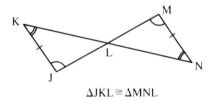

$\triangle JKL \cong \triangle MNL$

Side-Side-Side Theorem   (SSS)
If the sides of one triangle are
congruent to the corresponding sides
of another triangle, then the triangles are congruent.

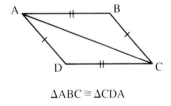

$\triangle ABC \cong \triangle CDA$

In the exercises that follow, you will be able to apply the theorems
above to find lengths of line segments or measures of angles. You will
also be able to express such lengths or measures relative to lengths and
measures of corresponding segments or angles.

EXERCISES 9-1

Ⓐ

1. Find the values of x and y.
   a)

   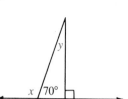

   b)

   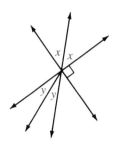

   c)

   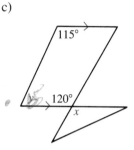

2. If you knew each value of x, how could you find the corresponding value of y? Write an equation relating x and y.
   a)

   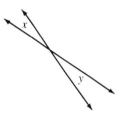

   b)

   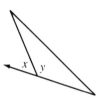

   c)

   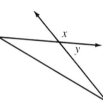

   d)

   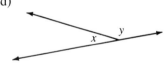

   e)

   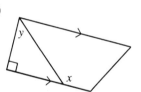

   f)

   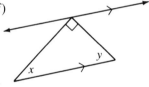

3. Write an equation relating x, y, and z in each diagram.
   a)

   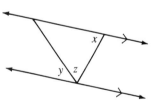

   b)

   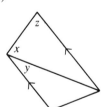

   c)

   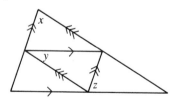

4. When light passes from air into water, parallel rays are refracted (bent) through the same angle. Parallel rays AB and DE are bent into rays BC and EF respectively. Are BC and EF parallel? Explain your answer.

   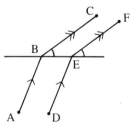

5. Explain why proving two triangles mutually equiangular (that is, corresponding angles are equal) does not guarantee that the triangles are congruent.

6. Suppose that three straws of different lengths are joined to form a triangle. Can these three straws be joined in a different way to make a triangle of a different shape? Explain your answer.

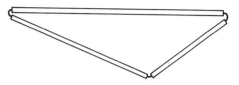

7. For each pair of triangles, name two pairs of sides which if equal would be sufficient to prove that the triangles are congruent.

a)

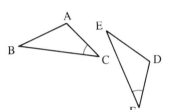

b)

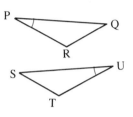

c)

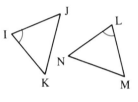

8. For each pair of triangles, name a pair of angles which if equal would be sufficient to prove the triangles congruent.

a)

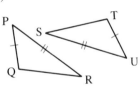

b)

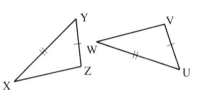

c)

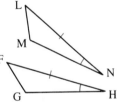

9. In each diagram, name a pair of congruent triangles. State the theorem that guarantees each congruence.

a)

b)

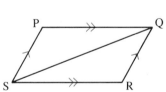

c)

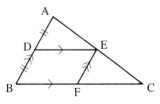

Ⓑ

10. Calculate the measures of the angles marked *x*, *y*, and *z*.

a)

b)

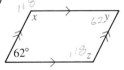

c)

11. Calculate the measures of the angles marked *x*, *y*, and *z*.

a)

b)

c)

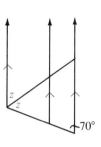

70°

12. Name two pairs of equal angles in each diagram. Name the theorems which support your answers.

a)

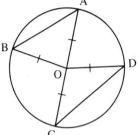

b)

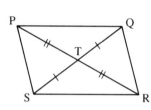

c)

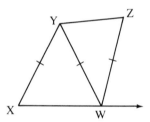

13. Triangle PQR represents an A-frame chalet with base QR 18 m, slant heights PQ = PR = 15 m, and height PS.

a) Does PS bisect QR? Explain your answer.

b) How long is SR?

c) What is the height of the chalet?

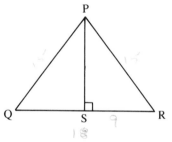

14. Right △ABC has sides of length 3 cm, 4 cm, and 5 cm. Explain why any triangle with sides of length 3 cm, 4 cm, and 5 cm must be a right triangle.

15. Write the measure of each ∠ABC in terms of *x* and *y*.

a)

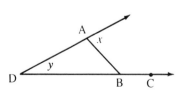

b)

c)

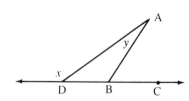

16. Express the length of OA in the diagram (below left) as a function of x if AB = BC = CD = 1.

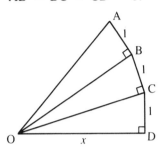

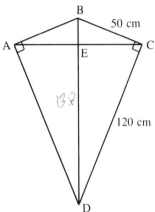

17. The kite ABCD (above right) has $\angle A = \angle C = 90°$, DC = 120 cm, and BC = 50 cm. Calculate the length of AC.

18. a) Use the Pythagorean Theorem to write expressions for the lengths PA and PB shown in the diagram.
    b) Use your result in part a) to prove that any point P on the perpendicular bisector of a line segment AB is equidistant from the ends of that line segment.

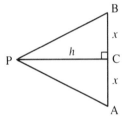

19. A room shaped like a rectangular prism has dimensions x metres by y metres by z metres. Write an expression for the distance from any vertex A to the diagonally opposite vertex B, in terms of x, y, and z.

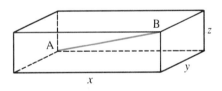

20. Write a logical argument which uses the Pythagorean Theorem to prove that the hypotenuse is the longest side of a right triangle.

9-2 REVISITING PROPERTIES OF CIRCLES

We have previously learned many theorems about properties of tangents, chords, and angles in circles. In the previous section we combined the Isosceles Triangle Theorem and its converse into a biconditional statement using the "iff" construction. In this section we shall use biconditional statements to consolidate and review the circle properties we have previously studied. This table shows a familiar theorem and its converse.

Theorem	If a line through the centre of a circle bisects a chord, then that line is perpendicular to the chord.
Converse Theorem	If a line through the centre of a circle is perpendicular to a chord, then that line bisects the chord.

Theorem   **Converse Theorem**

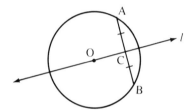   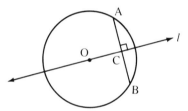

If AC = BC, then *l* is perpendicular   If *l* is perpendicular to AB, then
to AB.   AC = BC.

We can combine these theorems into a single theorem using a biconditional statement.

Chord Perpendicular Bisector Theorem
A line through the centre of a circle bisects a chord iff it is perpendicular to that chord.

Each of the following biconditional statements combines a theorem and its converse.

Equal Chords Theorem
Chords of a circle are equal iff they are equidistant from the
centre.

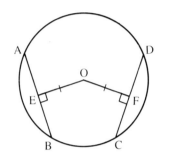   AND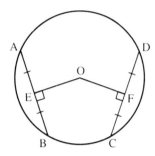

If OE = OF, then AB = CD   If AB = CD, then OE = OF

Before presenting the next theorem we review some terminology.
If C is a point on the circumference of a circle and AB is any chord,
then ∠ACB is an angle subtended at the circumference of the circle by
chord AB.

Angle in a Semicircle Theorem
The angle subtended by a chord at the circumference of a circle
is a right angle iff the chord is a diameter.

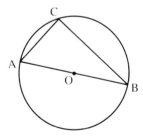   AND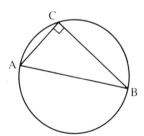

If AB is a diameter, then ∠ACB = 90°.   If ∠ACB = 90°, then AB is a diameter.

A quadrilateral that has all its vertices on the same circle is called a *cyclic* quadrilateral.

> ## Cyclic Quadrilateral Theorem
> A quadrilateral is cyclic iff its opposite angles are supplementary.

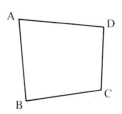   AND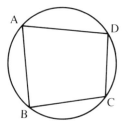

If ∠A + ∠C = 180° or ∠B + ∠D = 180°, then A, B, C, and D lie on the same circle.

If A, B, C, and D lie on the same circle, then ∠A + ∠C = 180° and ∠B + ∠D = 180°.

A *tangent* to a circle is a straight line that touches the circle in exactly one point. Using this definition of a tangent we can deduce the following biconditional theorem.

> ## Tangent-Radius Theorem
> A line is a tangent to a circle iff it is perpendicular to the radius of the circle at a point of intersection.

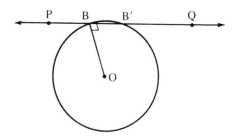   AND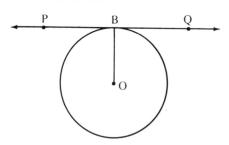

If PQ is perpendicular to OB, then B and B′ coincide.

If PQ is a tangent to the circle, then OB is perpendicular to PQ.

> ## Theorem
> Equal chords subtend equal angles at the circumference of a circle and at the centre of a circle.

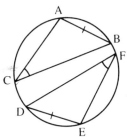

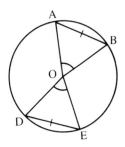

If AB = DE, then ∠ACB = ∠DFE   If AB = DE, then ∠AOB = ∠DOE

In addition to those presented above, we have the following theorems.

Angles in a Circle Theorem
If the angle at the centre of a circle
and an angle at the circumference
are subtended by the same chord
and lie on the same side of that
chord, then the angle at the centre
has twice the measure of the angle
at the circumference.

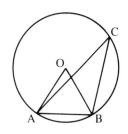

∠AOB = 2∠ACB

Equal Tangents Theorem
From a point P outside a circle
there are exactly two tangents which
can be drawn. Furthermore,
PQ = PR where Q and R are the
points of tangency

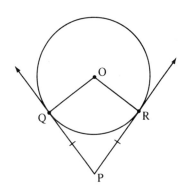

Tangent-Chord Theorem
The angle between a tangent to a
circle and a chord of the circle
is equal to one-half the angle subtended by the chord at the centre
of the circle.

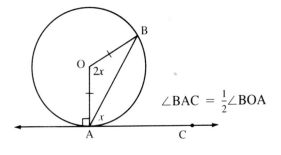

∠BAC = ½∠BOA

We may regard the Tangent-Radius Theorem given above, as a special case of the Tangent-Chord Theorem for the former deals with the angle between a tangent and a diameter, while the latter theorem deals with the angle between a tangent and *any* chord which it intersects at the point of tangency.

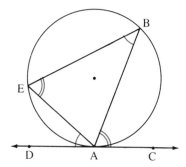

> **Corollary of the Tangent-Chord Theorem**
>
> The angle between a tangent to a circle and a chord is equal to the angle subtended on the opposite side of the chord.

$\angle EAD = \angle EBA$
$\angle BAC = \angle BEA$

The following example suggests how the theorems above can be used to find measures of angles or lengths of chords or tangents associated with circles.

Example 1. Find an expression for the length *l* of a chord which is *d* units from the centre of a circle of radius *r*.

Solution. The diagram shows a chord PQ, length *l*, which is *d* units from the centre O of a circle with radius *r*.

It follows from the Chord Perpendicular Bisector Theorem that since OR is perpendicular to PQ, then RQ = PR; that is, $l = 2RQ$.

Using the Pythagorean Theorem

$$l = 2\sqrt{r^2 - d^2}$$

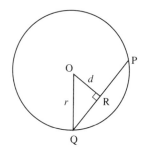

While the circle is of particular interest, many of the applications which use the properties of circles derive from the fact that the circle is the shape of a cross section of a sphere, a circular cylinder, and a cone.

Example 2. A mixing bowl has the shape of a truncated hemisphere with diameter 25 cm and height 10 cm. It contains milk to a depth of 5 cm. Through what angle must the bowl be tipped before the milk spills?

Solution. The bowl may be represented in cross section by part of a circle with radius 12.5 cm. The surface of the milk may be represented by a chord 5 cm below the centre of the circle. The milk will spill when the diagram is tipped through angle θ where

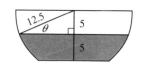

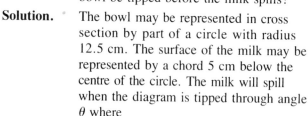

$$\sin \theta = \frac{5}{12.5}$$
$$= 0.4$$
$$\theta \doteq 23.6°$$

To the nearest degree, the bowl must be tilted 24° before the milk spills.

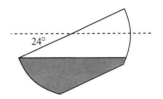

EXERCISES 9-2

1. In the diagram (below left), name a pair of parallel line segments. Name theorems to support your answer.

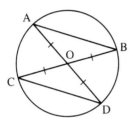

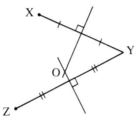

2. Explain why a circle with centre O can be drawn to pass through the points X, Y, and Z (above right).

3. How many circles can be drawn which pass through:
   a) 2 given points   b) 3 given points?

4. Explain why the centre of a circle which passes through points P and Q lies on the perpendicular bisector of line segment PQ.

5. Find the values of *x* and *y*. (O is the centre of each circle.)

   a)   b)   c)

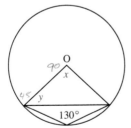

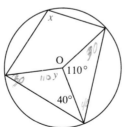

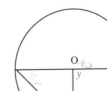

Ⓑ

6. Find the value of *x* to 1 decimal place. (O is the centre of each circle.)
   a)   b)   c)

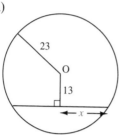
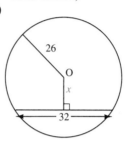
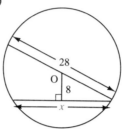

7. Find each value of *x*. O is the centre of the circle and P is a point of tangency.
   a)   b)   c)

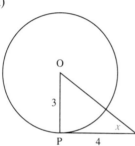
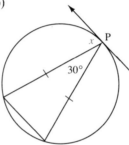
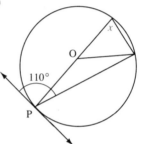

8. A chord AB of length 24 cm is constructed in a circle of diameter 26 cm. How far is the chord from the centre of the circle?

9. Find the distance between each pair of parallel chords to 2 decimal places.
   a)   b)   c)

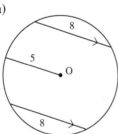
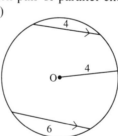

10. Find the area of each shaded polygon to 2 decimal places.
    a)   b)   c)

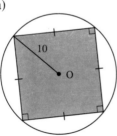
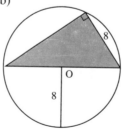
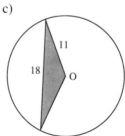

11. Find each value of θ to 1 decimal place. (O is the centre of each circle.)

a)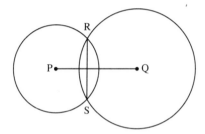

b)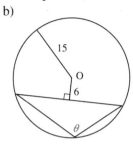

c)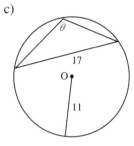

12. Two circles with centres P and Q intersect at points R and S (below left). Explain how you know that PQ bisects RS at right angles.

13. Two circles with centres P and Q and radii 7 and 5 units respectively intersect at points R and S (above right). If RS has length 6 units, find the distance between P and Q to 2 decimal places.

14. Do two circles always intersect in exactly two points? Explain your answer.

15. Find the measure of each angle if PQ and PR are tangents to the circle with centre O.
    a) ∠QPO   b) ∠PQR   c) ∠QPR

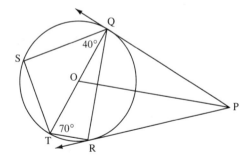

16. Find the angle subtended at the circumference of a circle of radius 20 cm by a chord of length 24 cm:
    a) when the angle at the circumference is on the same side of the chord as the centre of the circle
    b) when the angle at the circumference, and the centre of the circle are on opposite sides of the chord.

17. a) The shaded portion of the circle of radius *r* is bounded by a chord which is *d* units from the centre. Find an algebraic expression for θ in terms of *r* and *d*, where θ is the angle shown in the diagram.

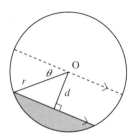

   b) A hemispherical bowl with radius 30 cm contains molten iron to a depth of 8 cm. Through what angle must the bowl be tipped before the iron begins to spill? (Use the expression developed in part a).)

Ⓒ

18. A part of a circle bounded by two radii and an arc of the circle is called a *sector*. Find an expression for the area of the sector with sector angle θ degrees (below left) in a circle of radius *r*.

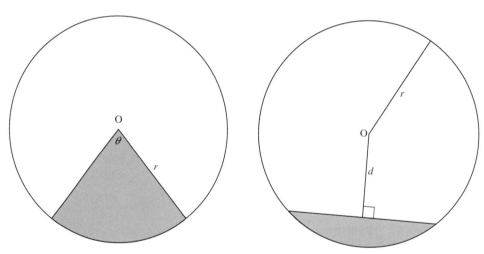

19. A part of a circle bounded by a chord and an arc of the circle is called a *segment*. Use the expression from *Exercise 18* to find an expression for the area of a segment of a circle of radius *r* bounded by a chord *d* units from the centre of the circle.

20. A cylindrical tank (lying on its side) of diameter 1.2 m and length 3.0 m is partly filled with oil to a depth of 30 cm. Use the expression from *Exercise 19* to find the volume of oil in the tank.

9-3 COMPLETING GUIDED PROOFS

In their quest for knowledge and ultimate truth, the ancient Greeks cultivated and developed the art of careful logical argument and step-by-step deductive thinking. Their mathematical investigations required detailed, carefully expressed ideas supported by basic assumptions or facts which were already known to be true.

To *prove* a theorem is to display the theorem as a logical consequence of some basic facts. In such a proof, we start with the facts which we know and then deduce the statement of the theorem.

The layout below shows the parts which comprise the statement of a theorem and its proof.

Formal statement ⟶ of the theorem

> **Theorem**
> If a point is on the perpendicular bisector of a line segment, then it is equidistant from the ends of the line segment.

Information in ⟶ the "if" clause of the theorem expressed in terms of a labelled diagram

Given: P is any point on the perpendicular bisector of AB. O is the point of intersection of the perpendicular with AB.

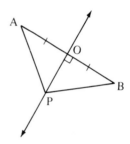

Information in ⟶ the "then" clause of the theorem

Required to Prove: PA = PB

Proof:

Sequence of statements which form the logical argument

Statement	Reason	
In △POA and △POB		
OA = OB	PO is the perpendicular bisector.	
∠POA = ∠POB	PO is the perpendicular bisector.	Known facts which support each statement
PO is common.		
Therefore, △POA ≅ △POB	SAS	
PA = PB	Congruent triangles	

Final statement in the proof ⟶ should be the same as the statement opposite the heading *Required to Prove.*

PA and PB are congruent because they are corresponding parts of congruent triangles.

We observe in the proof of the theorem above, the statements

OA = OB

∠POA = ∠POB

We know these statements to be true because they express in mathematical notation the statements under the heading *Given*.

We observe also the statement △POA ≅ △POB.

The reason used to support this statement is given as SAS.

This means that the three preceding statements assert that two sides and the contained angle of △POA are respectively congruent to the corresponding sides and angle of △POB.

The final statement, PA = PB, is the statement opposite the heading *Required to Prove*. The reason "Congruent triangles" will usually appear immediately below a congruence condition such as SSS, SAS or ASA, because triangles are proved congruent in order to prove the congruence of corresponding sides or angles.

As an intermediate step toward the construction of complete proofs, we shall in this section, practise the completion of guided proofs. The description above suggests some clues (listed below) for filling in missing statements or missing reasons.

Clues for providing missing statements and reasons

- The last statement in a proof should be identical to the statement opposite the heading *Required to Prove*.
- A missing statement followed by a congruence condition such as SSS, SAS, or ASA must be a statement of the form △ _?_ ≅ △ _?_ , where the triangles (represented by question marks) can be determined by examining the 3 statements immediately preceding.
- A missing statement followed by "Congruent triangles" must be an equation relating corresponding angles or corresponding sides of the two congruent triangles identified in an earlier statement.
- One of SSS, SAS or ASA is usually required when a minimum of 3 lines above are related to the congruence rule.
- "Congruent triangles" is usually what is required on the line below a congruence rule.
- The final reason is related to the statement on the previous line.

In the following example we shall use some of these clues to help us complete a proof of the converse of the theorem above.

Example. Copy this proof and fill in the missing statements and reasons.

Given: AB is any line segment.
    P is any point such that PA = PB.
    PO is the bisector of ∠APB.

Required to Prove: P is on the perpendicular bisector of AB.

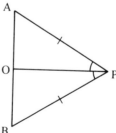

Proof:

Statement	Reason
In △POA and △POB 　　PA = PB 　　∠APO = ∠BPO 　　PO is common.	Given _____
_____ OA = OB ∠AOP = ∠BOP = 90° OP ⊥ AB	SAS _____ Congruent triangles Property of a straight angle OA = OB and OP ⊥ AB

Solution.

Congruence condition SAS prompts us to look at the 3 preceding statements to determine which triangles are congruent.

The last statement should match the *Required to Prove* statement.

Proof:

Statement	Reason
In △POA and △POB 　　PA = PB 　　∠APO = ∠BPO 　　PO is common. Therefore, △POA ≅ △POB OA = OB ∠AOP = ∠BOP = 90° OP ⊥ AB Therefore, P is on the perpendicular bisector of AB.	Given Given ⟵ We see equal angles marked on the diagram. SAS Congruent triangles ⟵ This usually follows a congruence condition and we see that OA and OB are corresponding parts of △POA and △POB. Congruent triangles Property of a straight angle OA = OB and OP ⊥ AB

In the exercises of this section, you will have an opportunity to complete guided proofs. In each case, attempt to read and understand the proof before you apply the clues. You may find you can complete many proofs without using the clues above. The clues should be applied only when you encounter difficulty.

EXERCISES 9-3

Ⓐ

1. A theorem is expressed using an "if" clause followed by a "then" clause. What heading in a complete proof of the theorem contains the information:
   a) in the "then" clause
   b) in the "if" clause?

2. Above a missing statement in a proof is the statement △ABC ≅ △DEF. The reason corresponding to the missing statement is "Congruent triangles." What are the 6 possibilities for the missing statement?

3. What statement in the proof of a theorem is usually identical to the statement in what is *Required to Prove?*

4. What reason would probably accompany the statement PQ ∥ RS? Why?

Ⓑ

5. Copy the statements in this proof and write the reasons.
   Given: MN is a diameter of a circle with centre O, and ML ∥ OK
   Required to Prove: ∠LOK = ∠NOK

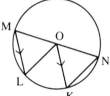

   Proof:

Statement	Reason
1. OM = OL	_____
2. ∠OML = ∠OLM	_____
3. ML ∥ OK	_____
4. ∠OML = ∠NOK	_____
5. ∠OLM = ∠LOK	_____
6. ∠OLM = ∠NOK	Statements __and __
7. ∠LOK = ∠NOK	Statements __and __

6. Copy the statements in this proof and write the reasons.
   Given: △ABC is isosceles with AB = AC. BE and CD are medians drawn to AC and AB respectively.
   Required to Prove: BE = CD

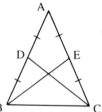

   Proof:

Statement	Reason
AB = AC	Given
In △BDC and △CEB	
BD = CE	_____
∠ABC = ∠ACB	_____
BC is common.	
Therefore, △BDC ≅ △CEB	_____
CD = BE	_____

7. Copy the statements in this proof and write the reasons.
   Given: △ABC with ∠B = ∠C
         AD is the perpendicular from A to BC.
   Required to Prove: AB = AC

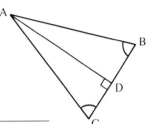

Proof:

Statement	Reason
In △ABD and △ACD	
∠B = ∠C	_____
∠ADB = ∠ADC	_____
AD is common.	
Therefore, △ABD ≅ △ACD	_____
AB = AC	_____

8. Copy the statements in this proof and write the reasons.
   Given: △QTS and △RTS share a common side
         TS, with QS = RT and QT = RS
   Required to Prove: ∠TQS = ∠SRT

Proof:

Statement	Reason
In △QTS and △RST	
QS = RT	_____
QT = RS	_____
TS is common.	
Therefore, △QTS ≅ △RST	_____
∠TQS = ∠SRT	_____

9. Given two quadrilaterals ABCD and
   WXYZ such that: AB = WX;
   BC = XY; CD = YZ; DA = ZW
   a) Are quadrilaterals ABCD and
   WXYZ congruent? Explain your
   answer.
   b) If the quadrilaterals are congruent,
   is AC = WY?
   c) If the quadrilaterals are not congruent, name a condition that would
   guarantee congruence.

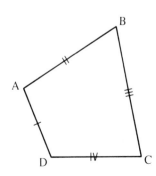
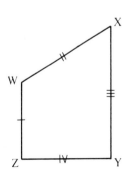

10. Copy this proof and fill in the missing statements and reasons.
    Given: Quadrilateral WXYZ such that ZW = XW
    and ZY = XY
    Required to Prove: ∠ZWY = ∠XWY

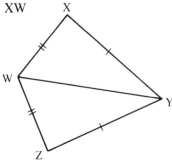

Proof:

Statement	Reason
In △WZY and △WXY	
ZW = XW	_____
ZY = XY	_____
WY is common.	
Therefore, _____	_____
_____	Congruent triangles

11. Copy the statements in this proof and write the reasons.
    Given: Chord AB of a circle with centre O, D the mid-
    point of AB, AO and OB are radii.
    Required to Prove: OD is perpendicular to AB.

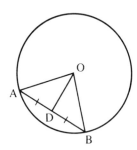

Proof:

Statement	Reason
In △OAD and △OBD	
OA = OB	_____
DA = DB	_____
OD is common.	
Therefore, △OAD ≅ △OBD	_____
∠ODA = ∠ODB	_____
But ∠ODA + ∠ODB = 180°	_____
Therefore, ∠ODA = ∠ODB = 90°	
Hence, OD ⊥ AB	

12. Copy the statements in this proof and write the reasons.

Given: Quadrilateral ABCD with diagonals AC and
BD intersecting at G; AD = DC and
AB = BC

Required to Prove: AG = CG and ∠CGD = 90°

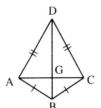

Proof:

Statement	Reason
1. In △ABD and △CBD	
AB = CB	_____
AD = CD	_____
BD is common.	
2. Therefore, △ABD ≅ △CBD	_____
3. In △ADG and △CDG	
AD = CD	_____
∠ADG = ∠CDG	Statement ___
DG is common.	
4. Therefore, △ADG ≅ △CDG	_____
5. AG = CG	_____
6. ∠AGD = ∠CGD	_____
7. ∠CGD = 90°	Straight angle and Statement ___

13. Copy this proof and fill in the missing statements and reasons.

Given: ABCD is a rectangle. E and F
are points on AB such that
DE = CF.

Required to Prove: ∠DEF = ∠CFE

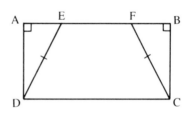

Proof:

Statement	Reason
∠DAE = ∠CBF = 90°	_____
In △DAE and △CBF	
_____	Given
_____	Property of rectangles
_____	Pythagorean Theorem
Therefore, _____	_____
_____	Congruent triangles
_____	Property of a straight angle

14. Copy this proof and fill in the missing statements and reasons.
    Given: Triangle ABC with line segment
          AD from A to BC such that
          ∠BAD = ∠ACD and
          ∠ABD = ∠DAC
    Required to Prove: AD is perpendicular to BC.

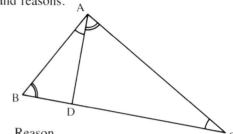

Proof:

Statement	Reason
Let ∠BAD = ∠ACD = x	
And ∠ABD = ∠DAC = y	
∠A + ∠B + ∠C = 180°	
_____	Substituting
$x + y = 90°$	_____
∠ADC = _____	_____
= 90°	_____
Therefore, _____	

15. Write a proof giving a reason for each statement.
    Given: Chord AB of a circle subtends ∠ACB and ∠ADB on the circumference,
          so that AC = BD
    Required to Prove: △AEB is isosceles.

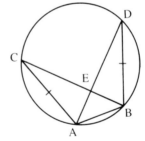

16. Write a proof giving a reason for each statement.
    Given: Any △ABC
    Required to Prove: The perpendicular bisectors of the three sides of △ABC are
          concurrent.

17. Write a proof giving a reason for each statement.
    Given: Isosceles triangle ABC inscribed in a circle with AB = AC
          AE is a line segment through point D in the triangle such that
          ∠ABD = ∠ACD.
    Required to Prove: AE passes through the centre of the circle.

9-4 BUILDING THE PARTS TO PRESENT A PROOF

In our previous work, we completed guided proofs by filling in missing statements and missing reasons. In the remainder of this chapter, we will study how to construct and present a proof. The following flow chart shows the steps we follow in presenting a proof.

To present a proof

List the facts we know under the heading *Given*, and sketch a diagram marking congruent angles and segments equal.	→	State what we need to prove, under the heading *Required to Prove*.	→	Apply the given facts or other theorems to deduce the required fact under the heading *Proof*.

The proof in the following example uses only the fact that there are 180° in a straight angle. It is merely a logical argument set out in a two-column format.

Example 1. Prove that if two lines AB and CD intersect at a point P, then ∠DPB = ∠APC.

Solution. We follow the steps outlined in the flow chart above.

Given: AB and CD intersect at point P.

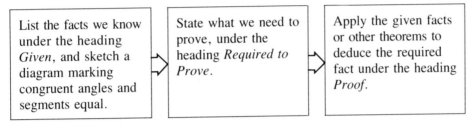

Required to Prove: ∠DPB = ∠APC

Proof:

Statement	Reason
∠DPB + ∠APD = 180°	Supplementary angles
∠APC + ∠APD = 180°	Supplementary angles
∠DPB − ∠APC = 0°	Subtracting the equations
∠DPB = ∠APC	

Sometimes, as shown in the next example, we refer to other theorems to deduce new facts.

Example 2. Prove that if △ABC and △DEF are two right triangles such that AB = DE, AC = DF, and ∠B = ∠E = 90°, then △ABC ≅ △DEF.

Solution. *Given:* △ABC and △DEF such that AB = DE, AC = DF, and ∠B = ∠E = 90°

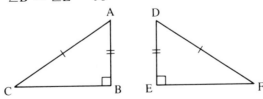

Required to Prove: $\triangle ABC \cong \triangle DEF$
Proof:

Statement	Reason
In $\triangle ABC$ and $\triangle DEF$	
$\quad AB = DE$	Given
$\quad AC = DF$	Given
$\quad \angle B = \angle E = 90°$	Given
$\quad BC = \sqrt{AC^2 - AB^2}$	Pythagorean Theorem
$\quad EF = \sqrt{DF^2 - DE^2}$	Pythagorean Theorem
$\quad BC = EF$	Since $AB = DE$ and $AC = DF$
Therefore, $\triangle ABC \cong \triangle DEF$	SSS

In *Example 2*, we used the Pythagorean Theorem to deduce that the third sides of the triangles were congruent, and then applied the SSS congruence condition. This result can be written as a congruence theorem.

Hypotenuse-Side Theorem   (HS)
If the hypotenuse and one side of a right triangle are congruent to the hypotenuse and one side of another right triangle, then the triangles are congruent.

We now apply the Hypotenuse-Side Theorem to prove the Equal Chords Theorem.

Example 3.   OA, OB, OD, and OE are radii of a circle with centre O. OF and OG are perpendiculars from O to chords AB and DE respectively, such that OF = OG. Prove that AB = DE.

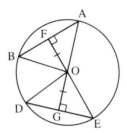

Solution.   *Given:* Chords AB and DE are equidistant from O. That is, OF = OG; OF $\perp$ AB; OG $\perp$ ED
Required to Prove: AB = DE

Proof:

Statement	Reason
In $\triangle OFB$ and $\triangle OGD$	
$\quad OF = OG$	Given
$\quad OB = OD$	Radii
$\quad \angle OFB = \angle OGD = 90°$	Given
Therefore, $\triangle OFB \cong \triangle OGD$	HS
$\quad FB = GD$	Congruent triangles
$\quad FB = \frac{1}{2}AB$ and $GD = \frac{1}{2}DE$	Chord Perpendicular Bisector Theorem
Therefore, AB = DE	

In the exercises of this section, you will practise presenting proofs by drawing and labelling diagrams, writing the appropriate information under the headings *Given* and *Required to Prove*, and providing statements and reasons for simple proofs.

EXERCISES 9-4

Ⓐ

1. Explain how you would prove that BD bisects ∠B and ∠D in the quadrilateral ABCD (below left).

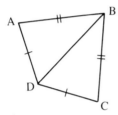 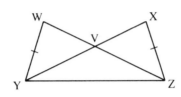

2. In the diagram (above right) WZ = XY and WY = XZ; explain why △VZY is isosceles.

3. Explain how you could use this diagram to prove the Sum of the Angles Theorem.

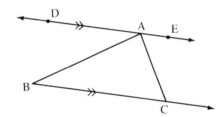

4. Explain why each statement is true.
   a) If 2 angles of one triangle are respectively congruent to 2 angles of another triangle, then the third angles are congruent.
   b) Each angle of a triangle with all angles congruent has a measure of 60°.
   c) If one angle of a triangle is congruent to the sum of the other two, then that angle is a right angle.

Ⓑ

5. For each theorem, draw and label a diagram marking all the given information. Then state the information which is given and that which it is required to prove.
   a) Theorem: In an isosceles triangle, the angles opposite the congruent sides are congruent.
   b) Theorem: Any point on the perpendicular bisector of a line segment is equidistant from the ends of the line segment.
   c) Theorem: A point is on the perpendicular bisector of a line segment if it is equidistant from the ends of the line segment.

6. For each theorem, draw and label a diagram marking all the given information. Then state the information which is given and that which it is required to prove.
   a) Theorem: If two sides of a triangle are congruent, then the median drawn to the third side is perpendicular to it.
   b) Theorem: Chords which are equidistant from the centre of a circle are equal in length.
   c) Theorem: A line segment joining the midpoints of 2 sides of a triangle is parallel to the third side and equal to one-half of its length.
   d) Theorem: The diagonals of a rhombus bisect each other at right angles.

7. Suppose you were asked to prove each statement. Draw a diagram and write the information that is given and what is required to prove.
   a) The diagonals of a rhombus intersect at right angles.
   b) The line segment from the centre of a circle to the midpoint of a chord is perpendicular to the chord.
   c) If a triangle has two congruent angles, then the sides opposite the congruent angles are congruent.

8. Write a proof for each statement in *Exercise 7*.

For Exercises 9 to 16, present complete proofs.

9. In $\triangle ABC$ and $\triangle PQR$ (below left) $\angle A = \angle P$ and $\angle B = \angle Q$; prove that $\angle C = \angle R$.

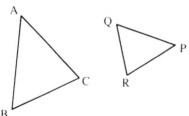 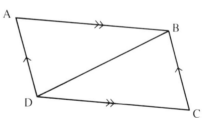

10. In parallelogram ABCD, diagonal BD is drawn (above right). Prove that $\triangle DAB$ and $\triangle BCD$ are mutually equiangular.

11. Parallelogram DEFB is inscribed in $\triangle ABC$ (below left). Prove that $\triangle ADE$ and $\triangle EFC$ are mutually equiangular.

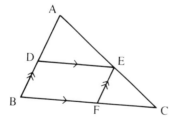 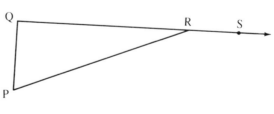

12. Prove that the measure of the exterior $\angle PRS$ of $\triangle PQR$ (above right) is equal to the sum of the measures of the two interior opposite angles, $\angle PQR$ and $\angle QPR$.

13. AB is a chord of a circle and DE is a tangent with point of tangency C (below left). If AC = BC, prove that DE is parallel to chord AB.

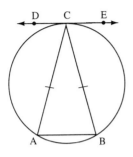

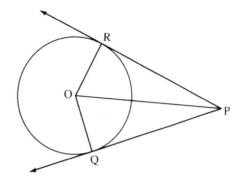

14. PQ and PR are tangents to a circle with centre O (above right). If R and Q are the points of tangency, prove that OQPR is a cyclic quadrilateral.

15. Points D and E are located on the base of △ABC so that AD = AE and BD = CE (below left). Prove that △ABC is isosceles.

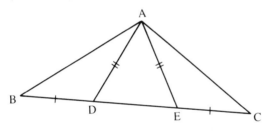

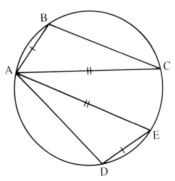

16. Two triangles ABC and ADE are inscribed in a circle such that AC = AE and AB = DE (above right). Prove that △ABC ≅ △EDA.

Ⓒ

17. a) Prove that if the radius of a circle bisects a chord, then it is perpendicular to the chord.
    b) State and prove the converse of the statement in part a).
    c) Write the statement and its converse as a biconditional statement.

18. The Equal Chords Theorem states that the chords of a circle are equal iff they are equidistant from the centre.
    a) Write the Equal Chords Theorem as a statement and its converse.
    b) Prove the statement in part a) and then prove the converse.

9-5 USING STRATEGIES TO CONSTRUCT COMPLETE PROOFS

In the previous section we practised presenting a proof by sketching and labelling a diagram using the given information. We proceeded to write the appropriate information under the *Given* and *Required to Prove* headings. To construct the proof, we prepared a set of logically-sequenced statements leading from the information given to the desired conclusion.

The following example demonstrates a problem-solving strategy which is often effective in constructing proofs.

Prove that the diagonals of a parallelogram bisect each other.

First, we express the general statement in specific terms by drawing a parallelogram and labelling its vertices A, B, C, D, and the intersection of the diagonals as point E. We can then name parts of the parallelogram using letters.

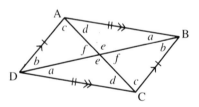

Given: The diagonals AC and BD of parallelogram ABCD intersect at E.

Required to Prove: AE = CE and DE = BE

The following first two steps in presenting a proof are an important foundation for constructing the proof.

Step 1. First work forwards.
Deduce all the information you can from what is given, and mark it on the diagram.

We think: Apply the Parallel Lines Theorem and mark alternate angles equal.
Apply the Opposite Angles Theorem and mark opposite angles equal.
Apply the property of a parallelogram that opposite sides are equal, and mark these.

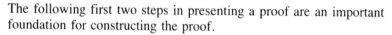

We observe: △AED and △CEB are congruent (ASA).

Step 2. Then work backwards.
We are required to prove that AE = CE and BE = ED. We can prove that △AED and △CEB are congruent, and hence AE and CE (as well as BE and DE) are corresponding sides.

Now we can write the proof.

Proof:

Statement	Reason
AB ∥ DC	Property of a parallelogram
AD ∥ BC	Property of a parallelogram
In △AED and △CEB	
∠EDA = ∠EBC	Parallel Lines Theorem, alternate angles
BC = DA	Property of parallelogram
∠EAD = ∠ECB	Parallel Lines Theorem, alternate angles
Therefore, △AED ≅ △CEB	ASA
AE = CE and DE = EB	Congruent triangles

The above example demonstrates an effective strategy for constructing complete proofs. We summarize this strategy in a flow chart.

To construct a proof

Step 1: Work forwards   *Step 2:* Work backwards   *Step 3:* Present the proof

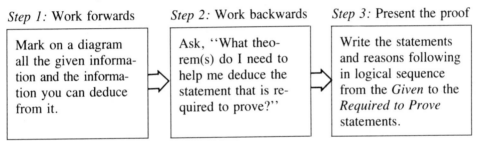

| Mark on a diagram all the given information and the information you can deduce from it. | Ask, "What theorem(s) do I need to help me deduce the statement that is required to prove?" | Write the statements and reasons following in logical sequence from the *Given* to the *Required to Prove* statements. |

The example above demonstrates the power of the congruence conditions in proving line segments congruent. The congruence conditions are equally useful in proving angles equal. By applying congruence conditions we use three known facts to deduce three more facts that may have been previously unknown. That is, knowing two sides and the contained angle (SAS) of one triangle are congruent to those of another triangle is sufficient to deduce that the triangles have 3 corresponding angles congruent and 3 corresponding sides congruent.

In the exercises of this section you will find it useful to apply the congruence conditions.

EXERCISES 9-5

Ⓐ

1. For each diagram, name the triangles that must be proved congruent to prove what is required.

   a) *Required to Prove:*
      BD = DC

   b) *Required to Prove:*
      ∠Q = ∠S

   c) *Required to Prove:*
      ∠ADO = ∠ODB

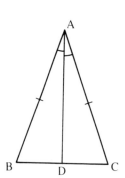

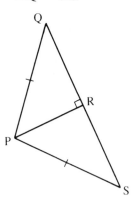

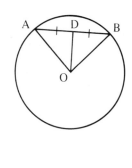

2. Name the congruence condition that can be used to prove the triangles congruent in each part of *Exercise 1*.

3. For each diagram, name two congruent triangles and give the congruence condition that can be used to prove what is required.

   a) *Required to Prove:*
      AD = AE

   b) *Required to Prove:*
      KN = LM

   c) *Required to Prove:*
      ∠QTS = ∠TSR

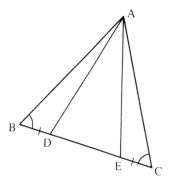

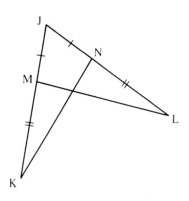

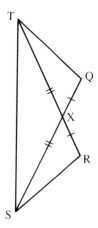

B

4. Triangle XYZ (below left) is equilateral and XU = YW = ZV. Prove that △UVW is equilateral.

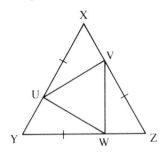

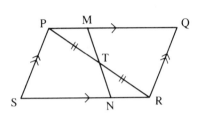

5. Given parallelogram PQRS (above right) with diagonal PR and points M and N on PQ and RS respectively, such that MN bisects PR at point T; prove that MT = TN.

6. Triangle PQR (below left) is isosceles with PQ = PR. Prove that the altitudes QS and RT are equal.

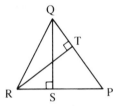

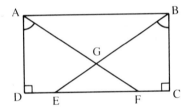

7. In rectangle ABCD (above right), ∠DAF = ∠CBE; prove that GE = GF.

For each of Exercises 8 to 11, draw and label a diagram, and then write the appropriate information under the headings *Given*, *Required to Prove*, and *Proof*.

8. Triangle PQO has points R and S on OP and OQ respectively, such that RS is parallel to PQ, and OR = OS. Prove that △OPQ is isosceles.

9. In △ABC, points E and D are located on sides AC and BC respectively, such that DE is parallel to BA and DA = DB. Prove that DE bisects ∠ADC.

10. Cyclic quadrilateral ABCD with AB parallel to DC has a tangent at B which meets DC extended at E. Prove that ∠ADB = ∠BEC.

11. A billiard ball reflects off two adjacent banks of a billiard table. Prove that the lines of approach and reflection are parallel.

Ⓒ

12. Points A and B lie on a circle of radius 8 km (below left). The angle between A and B as measured from another point X on the circle, is 38°. What is the distance between A and B?

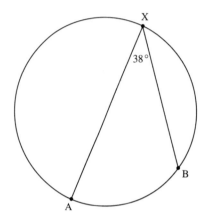

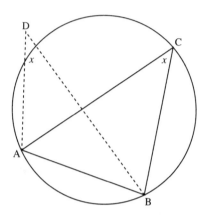

13. A, B, and C are any three points on a circle (above right). If D is any point situated on the same side of chord AB as point C, such that ∠ADB = ∠ACB, prove that D is on the circle also.

14. Two circles with equal radii 1 unit, and centres A and C are externally tangent (below left). AB and AD are tangents. Find the area of the shaded region.

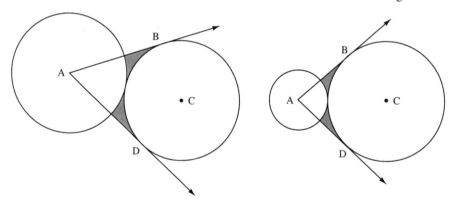

15. Two circles with centres A and C are externally tangent (above right). The radius of one circle is twice that of the other. If AB and AD are tangents, find the area of the shaded region.

9-6 WRITING COMPLETE PROOFS

While the congruence conditions embody a powerful technique for proving line segments or angles congruent, there are cases where they either cannot be applied or where they must be applied along with other theorems. For example, we cannot prove lines parallel using congruency conditions alone. The only device we have for proving parallelism is the Parallel Lines Theorem. The following example shows how we use the SSS congruence condition along with the Parallel Lines Theorem.

Example 1. Prove that a quadrilateral with all sides equal is a parallelogram.

Solution. *Given:* Quadrilateral ABCD with
    AB = BC = CD = DA
Required to Prove: BC is parallel to AD
            and AB is parallel
            to DC.

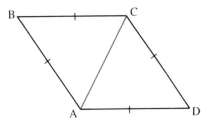

We think:
To prove AB ∥ DC we must apply the Parallel Lines Theorem. Therefore, we require a transversal intersecting AB and DC. We must draw line segment AC and prove ∠BAC = ∠DCA.
Similarly, to prove BC ∥ AD, we must prove ∠BCA = ∠DAC.

Statement	Reason
In △ABC and △CDA	
AB = CD	Given
BC = DA	Given
AC is common.	
Therefore, △ABC ≅ △CDA	SSS
∠BCA = ∠DAC	Congruent triangles
∠BAC = ∠DCA	Congruent triangles
Therefore, BC ∥ AD and AB ∥ DC	Parallel Lines Theorem

We observe in *Example 1* that it was not only necessary to use a theorem in addition to the congruent triangle condition, but it was also necessary to construct an *auxilliary line segment* to create congruent triangles.

The next example shows that sometimes we can construct proofs without using congruent triangle theorems.

Example 2. Prove that if the opposite angles of a quadrilateral are supplementary, then the quadrilateral is cyclic.

Solution. *Given:* Quadrilateral PQRS such that ∠S + ∠Q = 180° and
        ∠P + ∠R = 180°

Required to Prove: PQRS is a cyclic quadrilateral.

We think:

Construct a circle through 3 points P, Q, and R.
Choose a point T and draw cyclic quadrilateral TRQP.
Try to prove that S also lies on the constructed circle.

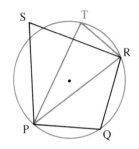

Proof:

Statement	Reason
∠S + ∠Q = 180°	Given
∠T + ∠Q = 180°	P, Q, R, T are concyclic
Therefore, ∠S = ∠T	
Since PR subtends equal angles at S and T, then P, R, T, and S are concyclic	Converse of Angles in a Circle Theorem
Therefore, S lies on the circle through P, R, and T	Definition of concyclic points
But Q lies on the circle through P, R, and T	Result of construction
Therefore, PQRS is a cyclic quadrilateral	

The proof in *Example 2* used only circle theorems to prove line segments equal. Furthermore, we observe that while an auxilliary line segment was drawn in the proof in *Example 1*, an auxilliary *circle* was drawn in the proof of *Example 2*.

In the exercises of this section you may need to draw auxilliary lines to construct proofs. Sometimes the auxilliary line(s) may be needed to form congruent triangles. In other cases they may be radii of a circle or transversals intersecting parallel lines. When an auxilliary line is drawn, it should be used to facilitate the application of one or more known theorems such as those shown in the two examples above.

To help you organize the theorems you already know, you should make a list (like the one below) for proving angles congruent and add to your list as you discover new properties.

To prove line segments congruent, look for:	Apply:
• isosceles or equilateral triangles • radii of a circle • corresponding parts of congruent triangles • a perpendicular to a chord • two chords equidistant from the centre of a circle • tangents from an external point to a circle • chords subtended by congruent angles at the centre or circumference	Isosceles Triangle Theorem Cyclic Quadrilateral Theorem ASA, SAS, SSS, AAS, HS Chord Perpendicular Bisector Theorem Equal Chords Theorem Equal Tangents Theorem Angles in a Circle Theorem

As you construct proofs in the exercises of this section, use your lists to help you work backwards from the *Required to Prove* statement to the given information.

EXERCISES 9-6

1. What auxilliary line segment would you need to draw to prove that the sum of the interior angles of quadrilateral ABCD is 360°?

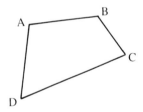

2. What auxilliary line segment would you need to draw to prove that in parallelogram PQRS, ∠P = ∠R (below left)?

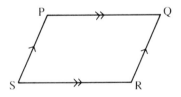

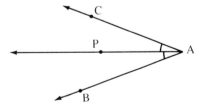

3. What auxilliary line segments would you draw to prove that any point P on the bisector of ∠BAC is equidistant from AB and AC (above right)?

Ⓑ

In each of Exercises 4 to 7, draw one or more auxilliary line segments to facilitate your proof.

4. P is a point on the bisector of ∠BAC (below left). Prove that P is equidistant from AB and AC.

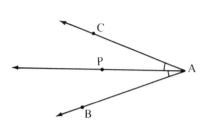
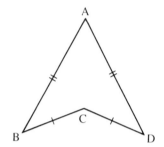

5. In the diagram (above right) AB = AD and BC = DC; prove that ∠B = ∠D.

6. In quadrilateral WXYZ (below left) XY = ZY and ∠X = ∠Z; prove that WX = WZ.

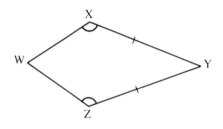
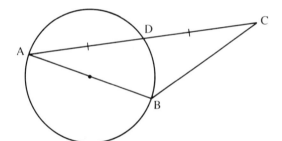

7. AB is a diameter of a circle with chord AD such that D is the midpoint of AC (above right). Prove that AB = BC.

In each of Exercises 8 to 21, draw a diagram before completing a proof.

8. A quadrilateral with all sides of equal length is called a rhombus. Prove that a rhombus is a parallelogram; that is, the opposite sides are parallel.

9. Quadrilateral PQRS has ∠P = ∠R, ∠Q = ∠S, and PQ parallel to SR. Prove that PQRS is a parallelogram.

10. Quadrilateral EFGH has EF = HG and EF parallel to HG. Prove that EFGH is a parallelogram.

11. Prove that if two opposite angles of a quadrilateral are right angles, then the bisectors of the other two angles are parallel.

12. Two distinct lines l_1 and l_2 are both parallel to line l_3. Prove that l_1 is parallel to l_2.

13. In quadrilateral ABCD, ∠A = ∠D and ∠B = ∠C. Prove that AD is parallel to BC.

14. Prove that any radius of a circle which bisects a chord is perpendicular to the chord.

15. AB and AD are equal chords of a circle with centre O. Prove that ∠OAD = ∠OBA.

16. AB and AD are equal chords in a circle with diameter AE. Prove that ∠BAE = ∠DAE.

17. WXYZ is a quadrilateral inscribed in a circle and WX = YZ. Prove that the diagonals of WXYZ are equal in length.

18. Isosceles △DEF has DE = DF. Prove that the median from D to EF is also an altitude of △DEF.

19. Prove that any point that is equidistant from the arms of an angle lies on the bisector of that angle.

20. Prove that if all the medians of a triangle are altitudes, then the triangle is equilateral.

21. a) Prove that if equal angles are subtended by the same chord but on opposite sides of that chord, then the chord is a diameter.
    b) Use part a) to prove that any parallelogram inscribed in a circle is a rectangle.

Ⓒ

22. In the circle (below left) with centre O, AB is a diameter, DE is a tangent, and AD is parallel to OE. Prove that EB is a tangent to the circle.

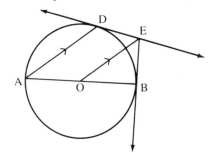 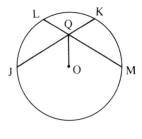

23. Two chords JK and LM of a circle with centre O intersect at point Q (above right). Prove that OQ bisects ∠JQM if and only if LM = JK.

24. Through the midpoint D of side AB of △ABC a line is drawn parallel to the side BC to intersect AC at F. Prove that AF = FC.

25. In parallelogram PQRS, T and U are the midpoints of PS and QR respectively. TR and PU intersect SQ at V and W respectively. Prove that SW = QV.

26. The Pythagorean Theorem states that if c is the length of the hypotenuse of a right triangle, and a and b are the lengths of the remaining sides, then $c^2 = a^2 + b^2$. Prove the converse of the Pythagorean Theorem; that is, if a triangle has sides of length a, b, and c such that $c^2 = a^2 + b^2$, then the triangle is a right triangle with hypotenuse of length c.

PROBLEM SOLVING

Solve the Problem in Different Ways

Carl Friedrich Gauss was one of the greatest mathematicians of all time. At age 24, he published his treatise on the theory of numbers, *Disquisitiones Arithmeticae*, which contained his proof of an important theorem that had baffled other mathematicians. Gauss wrote, with a touch of arrogance:

"The ... theorem must certainly be regarded as one of the most elegant of its type. No one has thus far presented it in as simple a form as we have done ... our demonstration must be regarded as the first. Below we shall give *two other demonstrations* of this most important theorem, which are totally different from the preceding and from each other."

Gauss later gave five other proofs of the same theorem. Hence, he proved, in eight different ways, a theorem that other mathematicians had been unable to prove once!

Problems in mathematics can frequently be solved in different ways. If you can give more than one solution to a problem, you will enhance your problem-solving skills and gain a deeper insight into the nature of mathematics.

Here is another important theorem in mathematics. Three different proofs are suggested on the next page. Try to complete each proof.

The altitudes of a triangle are concurrent.
Given: AM, BN, and CP are the altitudes of any △ABC.
Required to Prove: AM, BN, and CP intersect at a common point, O.

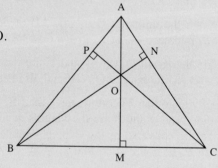

A proof using properties of a circle

Let the altitudes BN and CP intersect at O. Join AO, and extend to meet BC at M. Then we must prove that AM is perpendicular to BC.

- Notice that BPNC is a cyclic quadrilateral.
- Is there another cyclic quadrilateral on the diagram?
- Complete the proof that the altitudes of △ABC are concurrent.

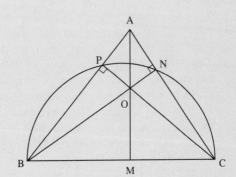

A proof using perpendicular bisectors

Through each vertex of △ABC draw a line parallel to the opposite side. This creates △PQR as shown.

- How are the perpendicular bisectors of the sides of △PQR related to the altitudes of △ABC?
- Can you prove that the perpendicular bisectors of the sides of a triangle are concurrent?

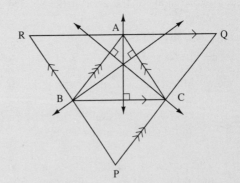

A proof using coordinates

Introduce a system of coordinates such that AM lies along the *y*-axis.

- How should the *y*-intercepts of the altitudes BN and CP be related? Can you prove this?
- Complete the proof that the altitudes of △ABC are concurrent.

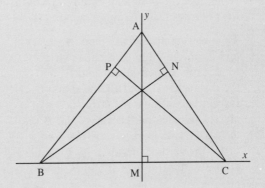

Can you prove that the altitudes of a triangle are concurrent in other ways?

PROBLEMS

1. ABCD is any rectangle. M and N are points on sides AB and AD such that the areas of △AMN, △MBC, and △CDN are all equal.

   a) Determine the ratio in which M and N divide AB and AD respectively.

   b) Determine the ratio of the area of △CMN to the area of △AMN.

   c) Under what condition does MC = NC?

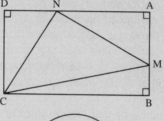

2. Each circle has radius *r*. Find an expression for the area of the shaded region.

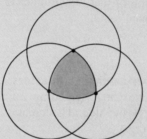

3. a) Show that a triangle with sides of length 3 units, 7 units, and 8 units contains a 60° angle.

   b) Find another example of a non-right triangle which has all three sides and one angle with integral measures.

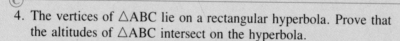

4. The vertices of △ABC lie on a rectangular hyperbola. Prove that the altitudes of △ABC intersect on the hyperbola.

5. Prove that the perimeter of any △ABC is given by the expression $(a + b) \cos C + (b + c) \cos A + (c + a) \cos B$.

6. To construct an ellipse, mark points A and B on the edge of a paper strip. Mark point C between A and B, and let the distances AC and BC be *a* and *b*, respectively. Move the strip such that A always remains on the *y*-axis and B on the *x*-axis, and mark several positions of C. Prove that the locus of C is an ellipse with semi-axes *a* and *b*.

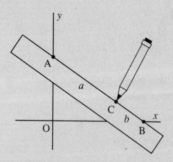

7. In △ABC, the incircle, with centre I, is tangent to BC at P. If M is the midpoint of BC and N is the midpoint of AP, prove that M, I, and N are collinear.

1. Calculate the measures of the angles marked x, y, and z.

a)

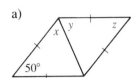

50°

b)

60° y

c)

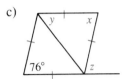

y x

76° z

2. Write the measure of each $\angle$ABC in terms of x and y.

a)

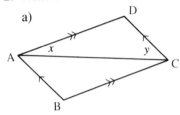

D

A x y C

B

b)

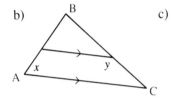

B

x y

A   C

c)

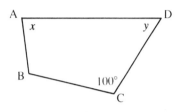

A   D

x y

B

100°

C

3. Find each value of x. O is the centre of each circle.

a)

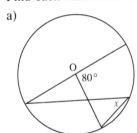

O

80°

x

b)

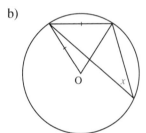

O

x

c)

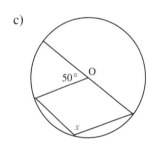

50°   O

x

4. a) What is the measure of the angle at the centre of a circle of radius 25 cm subtended by a chord of length 35 cm?

   b) What is the measure of an angle at the circumference of the circle subtended by the chord in part a), if the angle is on the opposite side of the chord from the centre?

5. Copy this proof and fill in the missing statements and reasons.
   Given: PA and PB are tangents to a circle with centre O. AO and OB are radii.
   Required to Prove: $\angle$APO = $\angle$BPO

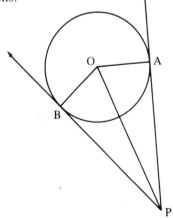

Proof:

Statement	Reason
In △PAO and △PBO	
PA = PB	_____
_____	Radii
OP is common.	
Therefore, _____	_____
_____	Congruent triangles

6. Two line segments AC and BD bisect each other (below left). Prove that ABCD is a parallelogram.

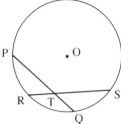

7. PQ and RS are equal chords in a circle, centre O (above right).
   a) If T is the point of intersection of PQ and RS, prove that:
      i) PT = ST   ii) QT = RT.
   b) Prove part a) by obtaining algebraic expressions for PT, ST, QT, and RT, where PQ = RS = *l* and OP = *r*.

8. Cyclic quadrilateral PQRS (below left) is such that ∠PSQ = ∠RSQ. Prove that △PQR is isosceles.

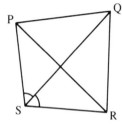

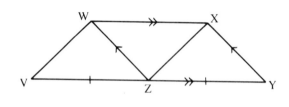

9. Parallelogram WXYZ is such that Z is the midpoint of VY (above right). Prove that VW = ZX.

10. In the diagram (below left) PQ = RS and PS = RQ; prove that PT = RT.

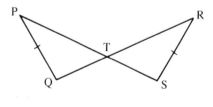

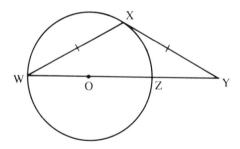

11. XY is a tangent to a circle (centre O) at X, and XW = XY (above right). Prove that WZ = OY.

12. Prove that two chords of a circle that are equal in length must be equidistant from the centre of the circle.

A stroboscopic photograph, such as this one, enables us to study a golfer's swing. Since the elapsed time between flashes is known, we can calculate the club's changing velocity, and the velocity of the ball. In a similar way, calculus is a mathematical tool for describing motion quantitatively.

10-1 WHAT IS CALCULUS?

Much of our understanding of the world in which we live depends on
our ability to describe how things change. Whether we are concerned with
the motion of a pitched baseball or the path of a planet; whether the
temperatures and currents of the oceans or the fluctuations of the stock
market; whether the propagation of radio waves or the power produced
by a chemical reaction; we are constantly forced to analyze relationships
among quantities which change with time.

Algebra and geometry are useful tools for describing relationships
among *static* quantities, but they do not involve concepts appropriate
for describing how a quantity changes. For this we need new mathematical
operations which go beyond the algebraic operations of addition, subtraction, multiplication, division, and the taking of powers and roots.
We require operations which measure the way related quantities change.

Calculus provides the tools for describing motion quantitatively. It
introduces two new operations called *differentiation* and *integration*
which, like addition and subtraction, are opposites of one another; what
differentiation does, integration undoes.

For example, consider the motion of a falling rock. The height of
the rock depends on time so it can be expressed as a function of time,
say $h = f(t)$. The process of differentiation enables us to find a new
function, which we denote $f'(t)$ and call the *derivative* of $f(t)$, and which
represents the *rate of change* of the height of the rock; that is, its *velocity*.
Inversely, if we know the velocity of the rock as a function of time,
integration enables us to find the height function $f(t)$.

Calculus was invented independently and in somewhat different
ways by two 17th century mathematicians, Sir Isaac Newton and Gottfried
Wilhelm Leibniz. Newton's motivation was a desire to analyze the
motion of moving objects. Using his calculus he was able to formulate
his laws of motion and gravitation, and to calculate from them that
the planets must move around the sun in elliptical orbits. This fact had
been discovered half a century earlier by Johannes Kepler. Kepler's
discovery was empirical, made from years of study of numerical data
on the positions of planets.

Many of the most fundamental and important "laws of nature" are
conveniently expressed as equations involving rates of change of quantities. Such equations are called *differential equations* and techniques
for their study and solution are at the heart of calculus. In the falling rock
problem the appropriate law is Newton's second law of motion:
Force $=$ mass $\times$ acceleration
The *acceleration* is the rate of change (the derivative) of the velocity,
which is in turn the rate of change (the derivative) of the height
function.

Much mathematics is related indirectly to the study of motion. We regard lines and curves as geometric figures but the ancient Greeks thought of them as paths traced out by moving points. The study of curves involves determining slopes and tangents as well as arc lengths. To solve such problems it is useful to regard curves in such a dynamic way, rather than consider them as merely static objects.

We can only scratch the surface of the calculus in this introductory chapter, and will begin by looking at the problem of finding a tangent to a curve. It may seem that this problem is of limited interest, but it is fundamental; all of calculus can be developed from a study of tangency. The solution of the problem will force us to consider the idea of a *limit* of a varying quantity. In the remainder of the chapter we will develop some of the techniques of differential calculus and use them to solve various kinds of mathematical and applied problems.

EXERCISES 10-1

Ⓑ

1. A ball is released from point A, and falls to the floor at point B in one second. The picture shows the position of the ball at intervals of 0.2 s.
   a) If 1 mm represents 0.5 cm, determine the height of the ball after 0 s, 0.2 s, 0.4 s, 0.6 s, 0.8 s, and 1.0 s.
   b) Draw a graph showing the height of the ball as a function of time.

2. In the photograph on page 427, the flashes were at intervals of 0.01 s. The scale of the photograph is 1 cm to 16 cm. By taking measurements from the photograph, determine the speed of:
   a) the clubhead just before it hit the ball
   b) the clubhead just after it hit the ball
   c) the ball.

Ⓒ

3. Using the photograph in *Exercise 1*, make a graph showing the speed of the ball as a function of time.

4. In the photograph on page 427, let $d(t)$ represent the distance the clubhead has travelled since it became visible at the left of the golfer's head. Let $v(t)$ represent the speed of the clubhead. By taking measurements from the photograph, obtain sufficient information to sketch the graphs of $d(t)$ and $v(t)$.

10-2 TANGENTS TO CURVES

In geometry a tangent to a circle is a
straight line that intersects the circle in
exactly one point. Such a line is perpendicular to the radius drawn from the
centre of the circle to that point.

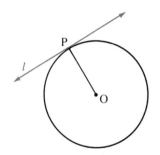

Line *l* is a tangent to the circle at P.

Curves other than circles can also have tangents. The term "tangent"
is derived from the Latin verb *tangere* which means "to touch." This
suggests that a straight line just touches the curve at a point rather than
crossing it at an angle.

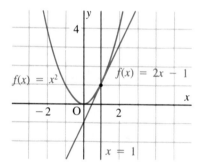

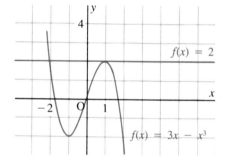

The line $f(x) = 2x - 1$ is a tangent to
the parabola $f(x) = x^2$ at the point (1,1).
The line $x = 1$ intersects the parabola
only at (1,1), but is not a tangent to it.

The line $f(x) = 2$ intersects the graph
$f(x) = 3x - x^3$ at $(-2,2)$ and at (1,2).
It is a tangent to the curve at (1,2) but
not at $(-2,2)$.

The examples above show that we cannot define a tangent to a
general curve as a line that intersects the curve at exactly one point. There
may be many lines that intersect a curve at only one point P, but at
most, only one of them can be a tangent to the curve at P. On the other
hand, a line may be a tangent to the curve at P and still intersect the
curve at more than one point. Therefore, we need a new definition of
tangency.

It happens that, except for special curves like circles, tangency
cannot be defined by a simple static geometric condition such as that
used for the circle. Instead we need a dynamic condition; we need to
consider what happens to a secant joining two points on the curve as
one of those points moves towards the other along the curve.

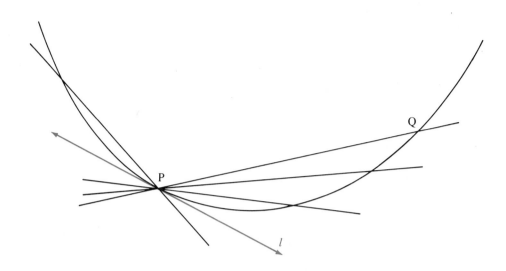

Definition: Let P be a fixed point on a curve. Let Q be any other point on the curve.
We will think of Q as moving along the curve towards P. The line PQ
is called a *secant* to the curve. If there exists a straight line *l* through P such
that the secant PQ *approaches* this line *arbitrarily closely* as Q approaches
P (from either side) along the curve, then we say that the line *l* is a tangent
to the curve at P.

What do we mean by the phrase, "PQ *approaches the line l* arbitrarily
closely as Q approaches P"? This can be made more precise in several
ways:
- the angle between PQ and *l* approaches 0 as Q approaches P, and
- the slope of PQ approaches the slope of *l* as Q approaches P.

Calculus involves the study of such dynamic *limit* operations, where
we investigate what happens to one quantity as another quantity
approaches a certain value.

If we can find the limiting value, say *m*, of the slope of PQ as Q
approaches P along the curve, then *m* will be the slope of the tangent to
the curve at P. If P has coordinates (x_1, y_1), then we can write the
equation of the tangent to the curve at P using the point-slope form of
the equation of a straight line: $y - y_1 = m(x - x_1)$.

Example.   Find an equation of the tangent to the parabola $f(x) = x^2$ at the point
P(1,1).

Solution.   Since $f(x) = x^2$ is the graph of a function, a different point Q on the
curve has a different *x*-coordinate, say $x = 1 + h$ where $h \neq 0$. Thus,
Q has coordinates $(1 + h, (1 + h)^2)$.

The slope of the secant PQ is

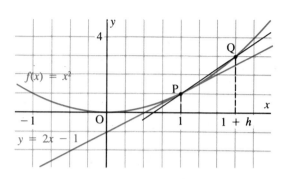

$$m = \frac{y_2 - y_1}{x_2 - x_1}$$

$$= \frac{(1 + h)^2 - 1}{(1 + h) - 1}$$

$$= \frac{1 + 2h + h^2 - 1}{h}$$

$$= \frac{h(2 + h)}{h}$$

$$= 2 + h$$

h approaches 0 as Q approaches P along the parabola. In this case, the slope $2 + h$ of PQ approaches the limiting value 2, so the tangent at $(1,1)$ must have slope 2. Therefore, its equation is
$y - 1 = 2(x - 1)$, or $y = 2x - 1$.

EXERCISES 10-2

Ⓐ

1. In which diagram(s) is the line l a tangent to the curve?

a)   b)   c)

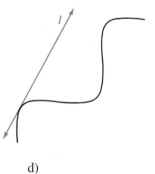
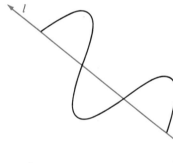
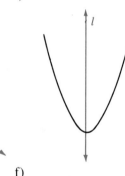

d)   e)   f)

2. a) What is the tangent to a straight line at a point on that line?
   b) What is the equation of the tangent to the graph of $f(x) = 2x + 3$:
      i)   at the point $(1,5)$ ii)   at the point $(0,3)$ iii) at the point $(-1,1)$?

(B)

3. For which curve(s) is it true that every line which intersects the curve at exactly one point is a tangent to the curve?

a) an ellipse

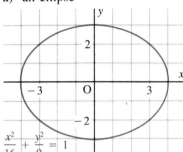

$$\frac{x^2}{16} + \frac{y^2}{9} = 1$$

b) a hyperbola

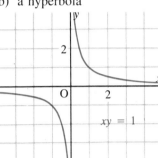

$xy = 1$

c) a parabola

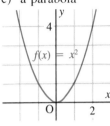

$f(x) = x^2$

d) a cubic function

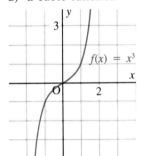

$f(x) = x^3$

e) a quartic function

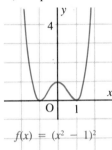

$f(x) = (x^2 - 1)^2$

f) a sine function

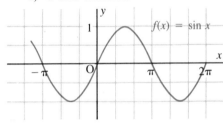

$f(x) = \sin x$

4. For which curves in *Exercise 3* is it true that every tangent to the curve intersects the curve at exactly one point?

5. a) Sketch the graph of $f(x) = |x|$.
   b) What is the equation of the tangent to the graph at $(1,1)$?
   c) What is the equation of the tangent to the graph at $(-1,1)$?
   d) Does the graph have a tangent at the origin?

6. Find the slope of the secant to the graph of the function $f(x) = x^2 - 3x$ passing through the points with x-coordinates 2 and 5.

7. Find the slope and the equation of the tangent to each curve at the point indicated.
   a) $f(x) = x^2 + x$ at $(0,0)$
   b) $f(x) = 2x^2 - 3x + 5$ at $(2,7)$
   c) $f(x) = x^2 - 2x + 1$ at $(1,0)$
   d) $f(x) = (x + 2)^2 - 3$ at $(0,1)$
   e) $f(x) = x^3$ at $(1,1)$
   f) $f(x) = x^3 - x^2 - x + 1$ at $(-1,0)$

8. a) Find the slope of the tangent to the curve with equation $f(x) = x^2$ at the point (a, a^2).
   b) What is the equation of the tangent to $f(x) = x^2$ at (a, a^2)?
   c) What line with slope -4 is a tangent to the curve $f(x) = x^2$?
   d) Find two points on the curve $f(x) = x^2$ such that the tangents to the curve at these points pass through the point $(1, -3)$.

Ⓒ

9. Find the equation of the tangent to each curve at the point indicated.

a) $f(x) = \dfrac{1}{x}$ at $\left(\dfrac{1}{2}, 2\right)$

b) $f(x) = \sqrt{x}$ at $(4, 2)$

c) $f(x) = \dfrac{2}{x^2 + 1}$ at $(1, 1)$

d) $f(x) = \dfrac{x + 2}{x - 1}$ at $(0, -2)$

10. By considering slopes of secants, find the slope of the tangent to the circle $x^2 + y^2 = 25$ at the point $(3, 4)$. Check your result by verifying that the line you have found is perpendicular to the line from the origin to $(3, 4)$. (Remember that lines are perpendicular if the product of their slopes is -1).

11. Find the slope of the tangent to the parabola $x = y^2 - 2y$ at the origin. What is an equation of the tangent?

INVESTIGATE

A tangent to a circle meets the circle at exactly one point. It is also perpendicular to the radius to that point. However, neither of these conditions can be used to define tangency for a general curve.

Try to formulate various geometric conditions which might guarantee that a line *l* is a tangent to a curve at a point P. Then test your conditions on a variety of curves you can draw to see whether they hold up in all cases.

For example, consider the condition that the line *l* intersects the curve at one point P, and the curve lies on one side of *l*, near P. Does this guarantee that *l* is a tangent to the curve? Can *l* be a tangent to the curve at P and still cross the curve at P?

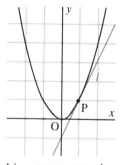

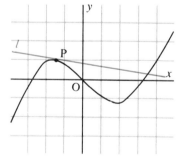

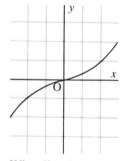

l is a tangent to the curve at P; the curve lies above *l*.

l is a tangent to the curve at P; near P, the curve lies below *l*.

What line is a tangent to the curve at the origin O? Near O, does the curve lie on one side of this tangent?

10-3 LIMITS OF SEQUENCES

M.C. Escher was a famous Dutch artist who made many designs involving mathematics. This print, called Circle Limit III, illustrates the concept of a limit. As you go from the centre of the design towards the circumference of the circle, the fish become smaller and smaller, without going outside the circle.

All of calculus is based on the process of finding limits. This process can most easily be understood in the context of numerical sequences. Consider, for example, this sequence.

$$\frac{1}{2}, \frac{2}{3}, \frac{3}{4}, \frac{4}{5}, \ldots$$

We can represent the sequence graphically by plotting points whose x-coordinates are the natural numbers 1, 2, 3, . . ., and whose y-coordinates are the terms of the sequence.

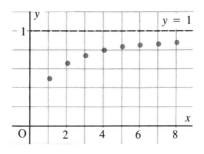

The *n*th term of the sequence is $\frac{n}{n+1}$ and corresponds, on the graph, to

the point with coordinates $\left(n, \frac{n}{n+1}\right)$. Consider the value of the *n*th term

as *n* grows large.

When $n = 100$, $\frac{n}{n+1} = \frac{100}{101}$

$$\doteq 0.990\ 099$$

When $n = 1000$, $\frac{n}{n+1} = \frac{1000}{1001}$

$$\doteq 0.999\ 001$$

It is clear that this *n*th term gets closer and closer to 1 in value, as *n* gets larger and larger. In fact, if we divide the numerator and denominator by *n* we can write the *n*th term in this form:

$$\frac{n}{n+1} = \frac{1}{1+\frac{1}{n}}$$

As *n* grows large, the fraction $\frac{1}{n}$ approaches zero, so the *n*th term of the

sequence must approach $\frac{1}{1+0} = 1$. We express this fact by saying

that $\frac{n}{n+1}$ approaches the limit 1 as *n* approaches infinity.

We write $\lim\limits_{n\to\infty} \dfrac{n}{n+1} = 1$

We also say that the sequence $\frac{1}{2}, \frac{2}{3}, \frac{3}{4}, \frac{4}{5}, \ldots$, has the limit 1.

We can define the limit of a sequence as follows.

Definition: If the *n*th term a_n of the sequence $a_1, a_2, a_3, \ldots$, approaches arbitrarily close to the real number L as *n* grows larger and larger, then we say that the sequence has limit L, and we write
$$\lim\limits_{n\to\infty} a_n = L$$

This is not a very good definition. We should really make precise what we mean by such fuzzy expressions as *approaches arbitrarily close to* and *grows larger and larger*. We wish to ensure that a_n is *as close as we want* to L by taking *n large enough*.

One important observation must be made. A sequence may or may not have a limit, but it cannot have more than one limit. a_n cannot approach two different numbers as *n* gets large. For example, the sequence
$-1, 1, -1, 1, -1, 1, \ldots$,
which has *n*th term $(-1)^n$, does not have a limit. There is no unique number to which all the terms draw arbitrarily close as *n* becomes very large. Graphically, the points representing the terms of the sequence do not get closer to a single horizontal line as we move to the right.

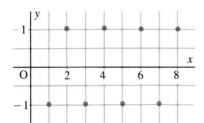

A sequence may also fail to have a limit because its terms grow arbitrarily large in size (either positive or negative) as n increases. For example, the sequence 1, 4, 9, 16, . . ., has nth term n^2 which can be made larger than any number we like if we take n large enough. This sequence has no limit.

We conclude this section with several examples to help you better understand the idea of limit of a sequence.

Example 1. What is the limit of the sequence $\frac{1}{2}, \frac{1}{4}, \frac{1}{8}, \frac{1}{16}, \ldots$?

Solution. The nth term of the sequence is $\frac{1}{2^n}$ which becomes smaller and smaller, and approaches 0 as n gets larger and larger. Thus, the sequence has limit 0, and we write

$$\lim_{n \to \infty} \frac{1}{2^n} = 0$$

In *Example 1*, observe how we can ensure that $\frac{1}{2^n}$ is as close as we like to 0 by taking n sufficiently large. The distance from $\frac{1}{2^n}$ to 0 is $\left| \frac{1}{2^n} - 0 \right| = \frac{1}{2^n}$. If we want this distance to be less than, say, $\frac{1}{1\ 000\ 000}$ we need only take n large enough that $2^n > 1\ 000\ 000$. This is so if $n \log 2 > \log 1\ 000\ 000 = 6$ so we need

$$n > \frac{6}{\log 2} \doteq \frac{6}{0.301\ 03}$$
$$\doteq 19.93$$

$n = 20$ will do.

As in Example 1, we can usually tell what the limit of a sequence will be by inspecting its general term. Sometimes a little algebraic manipulation is useful.

Consider this limit. $\lim_{n \to \infty} \dfrac{2n + 3n^2}{n^2 + 5}$

Using a calculator we can evaluate some terms of the sequence.

n	$\dfrac{2n + 3n^2}{n^2 + 5}$
1	0.833 333 33
10	3.047 619 05
100	3.018 490 76
1000	3.001 984 99
10 000	3.000 199 85

It appears that the limit should be 3. We can obtain this directly. Both the numerator and denominator grow large as n grows large. If we divide the numerator and denominator by n^2 (the largest power of n which appears in the denominator), then we obtain an equivalent fraction for which the numerator and denominator approach finite limits as n gets large:

$$\lim_{n\to\infty} \frac{2n + 3n^2}{n^2 + 5} = \lim_{n\to\infty} \frac{\dfrac{2}{n} + 3}{1 + \dfrac{5}{n^2}}$$

$$= \frac{0 + 3}{1 + 0}$$

$$= 3$$

Example 2. Find. $\displaystyle\lim_{n\to\infty} \frac{n - 2n^2}{n + 5}$

Solution. Divide the numerator and the denominator by n, the highest power of n in the denominator.

$$\lim_{n\to\infty} \frac{n - 2n^2}{n + 5} = \lim_{n\to\infty} \frac{1 - 2n}{1 + \dfrac{5}{n}}$$

The numerator $1 - 2n$ becomes large negative as n increases, but the denominator $1 + \dfrac{5}{n}$ approaches 1. Therefore, the fraction becomes large negative and has no limit.

Example 3. A regular polygon with n sides is inscribed in a circle of radius r. If P_n and A_n denote respectively the perimeter and the area of the polygon, determine:

a) $\displaystyle\lim_{n\to\infty} P_n$ b) $\displaystyle\lim_{n\to\infty} A_n$.

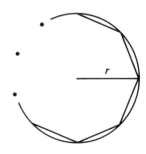

Solution. As n grows large, all points on the polygon get closer and closer to the circle. Therefore, P_n approaches the circumference of the circle and A_n approaches the area of the circle.

a) $\displaystyle\lim_{n\to\infty} P_n = 2\pi r$ b) $\displaystyle\lim_{n\to\infty} A_n = \pi r^2$

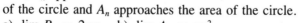

EXERCISES 10-3

Ⓐ

1. State whether each limit exists, and give the value of the limit if it does exist. Graph the first 5 terms of each sequence.

   a) $\lim_{n \to \infty} \dfrac{1}{n}$

   b) $\lim_{n \to \infty} n$

   c) $\lim_{n \to \infty} \dfrac{n + 1}{n + 1}$

   d) $\lim_{n \to \infty} (-3)^n$

   e) $\lim_{n \to \infty} \left(\dfrac{-1}{3} \right)^n$

   f) $\lim_{n \to \infty} \dfrac{n^2}{n^3 + 1}$

Ⓑ

2. The sequence $a_1, a_2, a_3, \ldots$, has the following possible nth terms. For each case, evaluate the terms for several very large values of n, and try to guess whether the sequence has a limit and what the limit is. Then confirm your guess by manipulating the general term a_n.

   a) $a_n = \dfrac{2n + 1}{3n + 1}$

   b) $a_n = \dfrac{2 - n^2}{3n^2 + 5}$

   c) $a_n = \dfrac{n + 1}{n^2 + 1}$

   d) $a_n = \dfrac{n + 2}{10}$

   e) $a_n = \dfrac{21 - n^2}{n}$

   f) $a_n = \dfrac{(-1)^n n}{n + 4}$

3. a) What is the nth term of the sequence $2, \dfrac{3}{2}, \dfrac{4}{3}, \dfrac{5}{4}, \ldots$?

   b) What is the limit of this sequence?

   c) How large does n have to be to ensure that the distance from the nth term to the limit is less than $\dfrac{1}{1000}$?

4. Two tangents are drawn to the circle with equation $x^2 + y^2 = 1$ from the point with coordinates $(2n, 0)$. They meet the circle at points A_n and B_n. If O is the origin, find $\lim_{n \to \infty} \angle A_n O B_n$.

Ⓒ

5. A mathematically-inclined artist created a design by starting with a circle inscribed in a square of side s and painting the corners of the square which lie outside the circle. She repeated this basic pattern over and over again inside the circle. Assume that she is capable of repeating the pattern indefinitely.

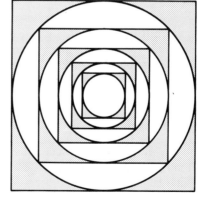

   a) Determine, as a function of s, the total area of the canvas covered with paint.

   b) What percent of the area of the canvas is covered with paint?

   c) What is the smallest number of basic circle-in-square patterns required to cover at least 42% of the canvas with paint?

6. Consider the infinite series $1 + \dfrac{1}{2} + \dfrac{1}{3} + \dfrac{1}{4} + \ldots$, which is called a *harmonic series*.

a) If $S_n = 1 + \dfrac{1}{2} + \dfrac{1}{3} + \ldots + \dfrac{1}{n}$ is the sum of the first n terms of the series,

   show that $S_2 = \dfrac{3}{2}$, $S_4 > \dfrac{4}{2}$, $S_8 > \dfrac{5}{2}$, $S_{16} > \dfrac{6}{2}, \ldots$.

b) Does the harmonic series have a sum? Explain your answer.

7. a) Find the values of $\sqrt{n^2 + n} - n$ for $n = 10$, $n = 100$, and $n = 1000$. Can you guess the value of $\lim\limits_{n \to \infty} \sqrt{n^2 + n} - n$?

b) Evaluate that limit by first writing

$$\sqrt{n^2 + n} - n = (\sqrt{n^2 + n} - n)\left(\frac{\sqrt{n^2 + n} + n}{\sqrt{n^2 + n} + n}\right)$$

$$= \frac{n^2 + n - n^2}{\sqrt{n^2 + n} + n}$$

$$= \frac{n}{\sqrt{n^2 + n} + n}$$

8. a) Using the fact that $\dfrac{1}{n(n + 1)} = \dfrac{1}{n} - \dfrac{1}{n + 1}$ for $n = 1, 2, 3, \ldots$, find a simple

   expression for the sum $S_n = \dfrac{1}{1 \times 2} + \dfrac{1}{2 \times 3} + \dfrac{1}{3 \times 4} + \ldots + \dfrac{1}{n(n + 1)}$.

b) Hence, find the sum $S = \lim\limits_{n \to \infty} S_n$ of the infinite series

$$\frac{1}{1 \times 2} + \frac{1}{2 \times 3} + \frac{1}{3 \times 4} + \ldots .$$

 INVESTIGATE

Use a scientific calculator, set to calculate trigonometric functions of angles expressed in radians, to complete the table of values for

the function $f(h) = \dfrac{\sin h}{h}$.

Can you guess the value of $\lim\limits_{h \to 0} \dfrac{\sin h}{h}$?

Assuming your guess is correct, what is the equation of the tangent to the graph of $y = \sin x$ (x in radians) at $(0,0)$?

h	$\dfrac{\sin h}{h}$
± 1	
± 0.1	
± 0.01	
± 0.001	
± 0.0001	

10-4 LIMITS OF FUNCTIONS

Consider the function $f(x) = \dfrac{x^2 - 4}{x - 2}$.

This function is defined for all real numbers x except $x = 2$; we are not allowed to divide by zero.

Consider also the function $g(x) = x + 2$, which is defined for all real numbers x without exception.

For all $x \neq 2$, we have
$$
\begin{aligned}
f(x) &= \frac{x^2 - 4}{x - 2} \\
&= \frac{(x - 2)(x + 2)}{x - 2} \\
&= x + 2 \\
&= g(x)
\end{aligned}
$$

So, $f(x) = g(x)$ wherever $f(x)$ is defined.

Therefore, the graph of $y = f(x)$ coincides with the graph of $y = g(x)$; that is, with the straight line $y = x + 2$, except that it has a point removed, the point $(2,4)$. We emphasize this missing point by showing it as an obvious "hole" in the graph.

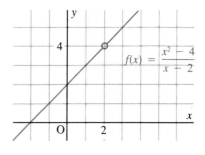

What happens to the value of $f(x)$ as x moves along the x-axis getting closer and closer to 2 (but never actually becoming equal to 2)? Since $f(x) = x + 2$ for $x \neq 2$, the answer is $2 + 2$, or 4.

We write
$$
\begin{aligned}
\lim_{x \to 2} f(x) &= \lim_{x \to 2} \frac{x^2 - 4}{x - 2} \\
&= \lim_{x \to 2} (x + 2) \\
&= 2 + 2 \\
&= 4
\end{aligned}
$$

We say that $f(x)$ has the limit 4 (or approaches the limit 4) as x approaches 2.

Definition: To have a limit at the point $x = a$, a function $f(x)$ must satisfy the following conditions.

- $f(x)$ must be defined for all points near $x = a$ except possibly at $x = a$ itself, and
- there must exist a finite real number L such that the number $f(x)$ becomes arbitrarily close to L as x approaches a from either side.

If both conditions are satisfied we say that $f(x)$ *approaches the limit L* (or *has the limit L*) as x approaches a, and we write
$$\lim_{x \to a} f(x) = L.$$

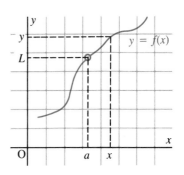

$y = f(x)$ approaches L
as x approaches a.

Once again, we have a definition with some fuzzy phrases such as *near* and *arbitrarily close to*, but the intent is clear for the examples we will be considering.

The function $g(x) = x + 2$ also has a limit 4 as x approaches 2. We write $\lim_{x \to 2} g(x) = \lim_{x \to 2} (x + 2)$

$$= 2 + 2$$
$$= 4$$

In this case, the limit is simply $g(2)$, and we say that $g(x)$ is *continuous at* $x = 2$. This means that we can draw the graph of $y = g(x)$ through the point (2,4) without any break or hole in it at that point. A function $f(x)$ is continuous at $x = a$ if $\lim_{x \to a} f(x) = f(a)$.

All polynomials in x are continuous at every real number x; the graph of a polynomial has no breaks in it anywhere.

As an example of a function that is defined everywhere but is not continuous at a certain point, consider

$$H(x) = \begin{cases} 1 & \text{if } x \geqslant 0 \\ 0 & \text{if } x < 0 \end{cases}$$

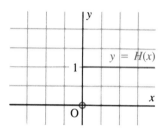

$H(x)$ is called the Heaviside function. It occurs frequently in the analysis of electrical circuits. For example, $V H(t)$ can represent the voltage V applied to a circuit when a switch is turned on at time $t = 0$.

The Heaviside function is discontinuous at $x = 0$, because $\lim_{x \to 0} H(x)$ does not exist. (If we approach 0 from the left, $H(x) = 0$; if we approach from the right, $H(x) = 1$.) You cannot draw the graph of $y = H(x)$ without lifting your pen from the paper at $x = 0$.

Examine the graph of the function $y = f(x)$. Observe that $f(x)$ is defined for all real numbers x satisfying $a < x < e$, and that $f(x)$ is continuous at all such points except at b, c, and d. Although $\lim_{x \to b} f(x)$ exists and $f(b)$ exists, these two values are not equal: $\lim_{x \to b} f(x) > f(b)$. Thus, $f(x)$

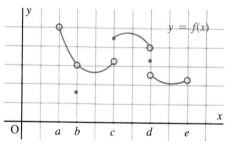

is not continuous at b.

The limit $\lim_{x \to c} f(x)$ does not exist because $f(x)$ approaches different values as x approaches c from opposite sides.

The limit $\lim_{x \to d} f(x)$ does not exist either, for the same reason.

Hence, $f(x)$ is not continuous at c or d.

In calculus, we frequently encounter limits of fractions where the numerator and denominator both approach 0. The fraction $\frac{0}{0}$ is not defined, but such limits can still exist.

For example, consider the function $f(x) = \frac{2x}{3x}$. $f(x)$ is not defined at $x = 0$ but, as $f(x) = \frac{2}{3}$ whenever $x \neq 0$, we can still say that $\lim_{x \to 0} f(x) = \frac{2}{3}$.

Limits of fractions which appear to be $\frac{0}{0}$ can usually be found by cancelling common factors from the numerator and denominator.

Example 1. Evaluate. $\lim_{x \to -2} \dfrac{x^2 - x - 6}{x^2 - 4}$

Solution. Factor the numerator and denominator and cancel the common factors.

$$\lim_{x \to -2} \frac{x^2 - x - 6}{x^2 - 4} = \lim_{x \to -2} \frac{(x - 3)(x + 2)}{(x - 2)(x + 2)}$$

$$= \lim_{x \to -2} \frac{x - 3}{x - 2}$$

$$= \frac{-2 - 3}{-2 - 2}$$

$$= \frac{5}{4}$$

Example 2. Evaluate. a) $\lim_{x \to 0} \dfrac{1}{x - 1}$ b) $\lim_{x \to 1} \dfrac{1}{x - 1}$ c) $\lim_{x \to 2} \dfrac{1}{x - 1}$

Solution. a) $\lim_{x \to 0} \dfrac{1}{x - 1} = \dfrac{1}{0 - 1}$ b) $\lim_{x \to 1} \dfrac{1}{x - 1}$ does not exist, since when

$\qquad\qquad = -1$ $\qquad\qquad\qquad x = 1$, the denominator is zero.

c) $\lim_{x \to 2} \dfrac{1}{x - 1} = \dfrac{1}{2 - 1}$

$\qquad\qquad = 1$

From the results of *Example 2*, the function

$f(x) = \dfrac{1}{x - 1}$ is defined and continuous everywhere except at $x = 1$ where it also does not have a limit because its value grows very large in absolute value as x approaches 1.

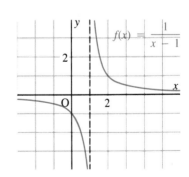

Observe that the graph $f(x) = \dfrac{1}{x - 1}$ approaches the straight line $x = 1$ as x approaches 1. We call the line $x = 1$ a *vertical asymptote* of the graph.

Rational functions are functions of the form $\frac{P(x)}{Q(x)}$, where $P(x)$ and $Q(x)$ are polynomials. Such functions are continuous wherever they are defined; that is, everywhere except at the values of x where $Q(x) = 0$. The graph of a rational function will have vertical asymptotes at these values of x except possibly if $P(x) = 0$ there, too.

Functions can also have limits as x approaches infinity (this is analogous to n approaching infinity for a sequence) or as x approaches negative infinity.

In *Example 2*, we have $\lim\limits_{x \to \infty} \dfrac{1}{x-1} = 0$ and $\lim\limits_{x \to -\infty} \dfrac{1}{x-1} = 0$

The graph approaches the horizontal line $y = 0$ (the x-axis) to the far right and the far left. We call the line $y = 0$ a *horizontal asymptote* of the graph.

EXERCISES 10-4

1. The graph of the function $y = f(x)$ is shown.
   a) For what values of x is $f(x)$ defined?
   b) Find each value.
      i) $f(x_1)$ ii) $f(x_2)$
      iii) $f(x_3)$ iv) $f(x_4)$
   c) Which of these limits exist, and what are their values?
      i) $\lim\limits_{x \to x_1} f(x)$ ii) $\lim\limits_{x \to x_2} f(x)$ iii) $\lim\limits_{x \to x_3} f(x)$ iv) $\lim\limits_{x \to x_4} f(x)$ v) $\lim\limits_{x \to x_5} f(x)$
   d) At what real numbers x satisfying $a < x < b$ does $f(x)$ fail to be continuous? Why is $f(x)$ discontinuous at each number?

2. Evaluate each limit, where possible. If the limit does not exist, state why.
   a) $\lim\limits_{x \to 0} x^2$
   b) $\lim\limits_{x \to 0} (x^2 - 5x + 2)$
   c) $\lim\limits_{x \to 2} (x^2 - 5x + 2)$
   d) $\lim\limits_{x \to -2} \dfrac{1}{x^2}$
   e) $\lim\limits_{x \to 0} \dfrac{1}{x^2}$
   f) $\lim\limits_{x \to \infty} x^2$
   g) $\lim\limits_{x \to \infty} \dfrac{x^2}{100 + 10x - x^2}$
   h) $\lim\limits_{x \to 3} \dfrac{x-3}{x-3}$
   i) $\lim\limits_{x \to 3} \dfrac{(x-3)^2}{x-3}$

3. a) Find the values of the function $f(x) = \dfrac{x^2 + x - 2}{x^2 - 1}$ corresponding to $x = 0$, 0.9, 0.99, 0.999, 0.9999, and also $x = 2$, 1.1, 1.01, 1.001, 1.0001.
   b) Guess the value of $\lim\limits_{x \to 1} f(x)$ and verify your guess by factoring the numerator and denominator, and cancelling.

4. Repeat *Exercise 3* for $f(x) = \dfrac{x^2 - 4x + 4}{x^2 - 4}$ and several points getting closer and closer to $x = 2$ from either side.

5. Evaluate each limit, where possible. If the limit does not exist, state why.

a) $\displaystyle\lim_{x \to 1} \frac{x^2 - 1}{x - 1}$

b) $\displaystyle\lim_{x \to -2} \frac{x + 2}{x^2 - 4}$

c) $\displaystyle\lim_{x \to 6} \frac{x^2 - 8x + 12}{x^2 - x + 30}$

d) $\displaystyle\lim_{x \to -5} \frac{x^2 + 2x - 15}{x^2 + x - 20}$

e) $\displaystyle\lim_{x \to 1} \frac{x - 1}{x^3 - 1}$

f) $\displaystyle\lim_{x \to \frac{1}{2}} \frac{2x^2 - 5x + 2}{4x^2 - 1}$

g) $\displaystyle\lim_{x \to 1} \frac{x^2 + x - 2}{x^2 - 2x + 1}$

h) $\displaystyle\lim_{x \to -1} \frac{x^2 - 1}{x^2 - 4}$

i) $\displaystyle\lim_{x \to \frac{3}{2}} \frac{2x^2 - x - 3}{(2x - 3)^3}$

j) $\displaystyle\lim_{x \to -2} \frac{x^4 - 16}{x^3 + 8}$

k) $\displaystyle\lim_{h \to 0} \frac{(2 + h)^3 - 8}{h}$

l) $\displaystyle\lim_{h \to 0} \frac{\frac{1}{4 + h} - \frac{1}{4}}{h}$

6. a) Let $f(x) = \dfrac{x}{|x|}$. What is the domain of $f(x)$?

b) Sketch the graph of $y = f(x)$. Where is $f(x)$ continuous?

c) Evaluate. i) $\displaystyle\lim_{x \to -1} f(x)$ ii) $\displaystyle\lim_{x \to 1} f(x)$ iii) $\displaystyle\lim_{x \to 0} f(x)$

d) The function $f(x)$ is frequently called the *signum* function and denoted *sgn x*. Signum is a Latin noun meaning "sign." Can you see why this is an appropriate name for the function?

7. a) At what points does each function fail to be continuous?

b) Where does each graph have vertical asymptotes? horizontal asymptotes?

i) $f(x) = \dfrac{1}{x^2 + 1}$

ii) $f(x) = \dfrac{1}{x^2 - 1}$

iii) $f(x) = \dfrac{x - 1}{x^2 - 1}$

iv) $f(x) = \dfrac{x^4 - 1}{x^2}$

8. A parking lot charges $1.00 for each hour or part of an hour that a car is parked. Let $C(t)$ denote the cost of parking for t hours, where t is a positive real number.

a) Sketch the graph of $y = C(t)$ for $0 < t \leqslant 6$.

b) Where does $C(t)$ fail to be continuous?

c) Does $C(t)$ have a limit as $t \to 3.4$? as $t \to 4$?

Ⓒ

9. Evaluate. $\displaystyle\lim_{x \to 1} \frac{x + \sqrt{x} - 2}{x - 1}$

10-5 THE DERIVATIVE OF A FUNCTION

Let $f(x)$ be a function whose graph is a smooth curve with equation $y = f(x)$. In Section 10-2 we learned how to find the slope of a tangent to such a curve at any point P on it. Unless the curve is a straight line, this slope will vary from point to point along the curve. Let us repeat the Example of Section 10-2 to find the slope of the tangent to the parabola $f(x) = x^2$ but this time at an arbitrary point instead of the specific point $(1,1)$ considered in that example.

Example 1. Find the slope of the tangent to the graph of $f(x) = x^2$ at the point $P(x,x^2)$.

Solution. A different point Q on the graph has coordinates $(x+h, (x+h)^2)$, where $h \neq 0$.

The slope of the tangent at P is the limit of the slope of the secant PQ as Q approaches P; that is, as h approaches 0.

$$
\begin{aligned}
\lim_{h \to 0} (\text{slope of PQ}) &= \lim_{h \to 0} \frac{(x+h)^2 - x^2}{h} \\
&= \lim_{h \to 0} \frac{x^2 + 2xh + h^2 - x^2}{h} \\
&= \lim_{h \to 0} \frac{h(2x + h)}{h} \\
&= \lim_{h \to 0} 2x + h \\
&= 2x
\end{aligned}
$$

The slope of the tangent to $f(x) = x^2$ at $P(x,x^2)$ is $2x$.

In general, the slope of the tangent to the curve with equation $y = f(x)$ is itself another function of x called the *derivative of $f(x)$*, and denoted $f'(x)$. (This is pronounced, "*f* prime of *x*"). As shown in *Example 1*, the derivative of the function $f(x) = x^2$ is the function $f'(x) = 2x$. The process of calculating the derivative of a function is called *differentiation*.

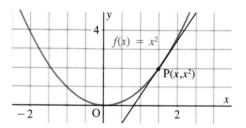

The tangent to $f(x) = x^2$ at $P(x,x^2)$ has slope $2x$.

We can mimic the solution to Example 1 to find a formula for the derivative of any function $f(x)$. If P is a point on the graph $y = f(x)$ with coordinates $(x, f(x))$, then a different point Q on the graph will have coordinates $(x+h, f(x+h))$, where $h \neq 0$. The slope of the secant PQ is

$$\frac{f(x+h) - f(x)}{(x+h) - x} = \frac{f(x+h) - f(x)}{h}$$

This is called the *Newton quotient* for the function $f(x)$ at x.

Definition: The derivative $f'(x)$ of the function $f(x)$ is the limit of the Newton quotient as h approaches 0.

$$f'(x) = \lim_{h \to 0} \frac{f(x + h) - f(x)}{h}$$

We say that the function $f(x)$ is *differentiable* at x if the limit of the Newton quotient exists at x. That is, $f(x)$ is differentiable at exactly those points where its graph has a tangent which is not vertical.

If we know the derivative $f'(x)$ of a function $f(x)$, we can write the equation of the tangent to the graph $y = f(x)$ at the point with x-coordinate x_1. The y-coordinate is $f(x_1)$ and the slope is $f'(x_1)$, so the equation of the tangent is
$y - f(x_1) = f'(x_1)(x - x_1)$.

It is also common to refer to the value of the derivative of $f(x)$ at x_1; that is, to $f'(x_1)$, as the slope of the curve $y = f(x)$ at x_1. The slope of a curve at a point is the slope of its tangent there.

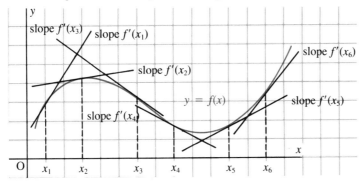

The slope of $y = f(x)$ at x_i is $f'(x_i)$.

If $f(x) = -3x + 4$, then the graph of $y = f(x)$ is a straight line with slope -3. Thus, $f'(x) = -3$; the derivative has a constant value in this case.

In general, if $f(x) = Ax + B$, then the graph of $y = f(x)$ is a straight line with slope A. Thus, $f'(x) = A$; the derivative has a constant value. We can also calculate this from the definition of derivative given above.

$$f'(x) = \lim_{h \to 0} \frac{f(x + h) - f(x)}{h}$$
$$= \lim_{h \to 0} \frac{A(x + h) + B - (Ax + B)}{h}$$
$$= \lim_{h \to 0} \frac{Ah}{h}$$
$$= \lim_{h \to 0} A$$
$$= A$$

Note that if $f(x) = B$ (a constant), then $f'(x) = 0$ everywhere. A horizontal line has slope 0 at all points.

We can use the definition of derivative to calculate the derivatives of some more elementary functions.

Example 2. Find the derivative of $f(x) = x^3$.

Solution. The required derivative is

$$f'(x) = \lim_{h \to 0} \frac{f(x+h) - f(x)}{h}$$

$$= \lim_{h \to 0} \frac{(x+h)^3 - x^3}{h}$$

$$= \lim_{h \to 0} \frac{x^3 + 3x^2h + 3xh^2 + h^3 - x^3}{h}$$

$$= \lim_{h \to 0} \frac{h(3x^2 + 3xh + h^2)}{h}$$

$$= \lim_{h \to 0} (3x^2 + 3xh + h^2)$$

$$= 3x^2$$

Example 3. Find the slope of $f(x) = \dfrac{1}{x}$ at $\left(x, \dfrac{1}{x}\right)$.

Solution. From the definition of derivative

$$f'(x) = \lim_{h \to 0} \frac{f(x+h) - f(x)}{h}$$

$$= \lim_{h \to 0} \frac{\dfrac{1}{x+h} - \dfrac{1}{x}}{h}$$

$$= \lim_{h \to 0} \frac{1}{h}\left(\frac{x - (x+h)}{(x+h)x}\right)$$

$$= \lim_{h \to 0} \frac{-h}{h(x+h)x}$$

$$= \lim_{h \to 0} \frac{-1}{(x+h)x}$$

$$= -\frac{1}{x^2}$$

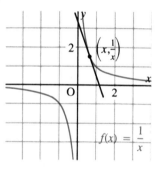

The slope of $f(x) = \dfrac{1}{x}$ at the point $\left(x, \dfrac{1}{x}\right)$ is $-\dfrac{1}{x^2}$.

Note that in all of the above examples, the Newton quotient was simplified algebraically to a point where the h in the denominator could be cancelled with an h in the numerator before the limit was evaluated. Sometimes this process can be difficult. In the following example, we reverse the usual process of "rationalizing the denominator" of a radical expression, and rationalize the numerator instead.

Example 4. Calculate the derivative of $f(x) = \sqrt{x}$ using the definition.

Solution.

$$f'(x) = \lim_{h \to 0} \frac{f(x + h) - f(x)}{h}$$

$$= \lim_{h \to 0} \frac{\sqrt{x + h} - \sqrt{x}}{h}$$

$$= \lim_{h \to 0} \frac{\sqrt{x + h} - \sqrt{x}}{h} \times \frac{\sqrt{x + h} + \sqrt{x}}{\sqrt{x + h} + \sqrt{x}}$$

$$= \lim_{h \to 0} \frac{(x + h) - x}{h(\sqrt{x + h} + \sqrt{x})}$$

$$= \lim_{h \to 0} \frac{1}{\sqrt{x + h} + \sqrt{x}}$$

$$= \frac{1}{2\sqrt{x}}$$

Observe that the function $f(x) = \sqrt{x}$ is not differentiable at $x = 0$; that is, its derivative is not defined there. The slope of $y = \sqrt{x}$ at $(x, \sqrt{x})$ is $\frac{1}{2\sqrt{x}}$, which becomes infinite as x decreases towards 0.

Frequently we want to refer to the derivative of a function expressed without the use of the function notation. For example, we may want to find the slope of the curve $y = x^3$ at the point $(2, 8)$. We could let $f(x) = x^3$ so that the required slope would be $f'(2)$. It is, however, more convenient to have a notation for the slope of the curve which doesn't require introducing f.

The derivative of $y = f(x)$ can be expressed in any of the following ways.

$$y' = \frac{dy}{dx} = \frac{d}{dx} f(x) = f'(x)$$

The expression $\frac{dy}{dx}$ is called *Leibniz notation* after one of the inventors of calculus. We pronounce this, "dee y by dee x."

$\frac{dy}{dx}$ is a single symbol denoting the derivative of y with respect to x. It is not a quotient of dy and dx, and dy does not mean d times y.

Example 5. Find an equation of the tangent to $y = x^3$ at the point $(2,8)$.

Solution. From Example 2, we know that the derivative of $y = x^3$ is $\dfrac{dy}{dx} = 3x^2$

Therefore, the tangent has slope $3(2)^2 = 12$
Its equation is $y - 8 = 12(x - 2)$, or $y = 12x - 16$

Finally, let us try to guess a formula for $\dfrac{d}{dx} x^n$, where n is a positive integer.
We already know the answer if $n = 1$, $n = 2$ or $n = 3$:

$$\frac{d}{dx}(x) = 1 \qquad \frac{d}{dx}(x^2) = 2x \qquad \frac{d}{dx}(x^3) = 3x^2$$

In Exercise 2 c), you will calculate $\dfrac{d}{dx}(x^4) = 4x^3$.

The pattern in these formulas suggests that $\dfrac{d}{dx}(x^n) = nx^{n-1}$, which is, in fact, true in general. We will not attempt to prove it at this point. Observe that Examples 3 and 4 suggest that the formula remains true even when n is negative or a fraction.

That is, if $f(x) = \dfrac{1}{x}$, or x^{-1}, then $f'(x) = -\dfrac{1}{x^2}$, or $-x^{-2}$

And, if $f(x) = \sqrt{x}$, or $x^{\frac{1}{2}}$, then $f'(x) = \dfrac{1}{2\sqrt{x}}$, or $\dfrac{1}{2}x^{-\frac{1}{2}}$

EXERCISES 10-5

Ⓐ
1. What is the derivative $f'(x)$ of each function?
   a) $f(x) = 17$ b) $f(x) = 2x$ c) $f(x) = 1 - x$
   d) $f(x) = 3 + 4x$ e) $f(x) = 0$ f) $f(x) = -3x + 2$

Ⓑ
2. Use the definition of derivative to calculate the derivative $f'(x)$ of each function.
   a) $f(x) = 2x^2 - 3x$ b) $f(x) = x^3 - 4x^2 + 1$ c) $f(x) = x^4$
   d) $f(x) = \dfrac{1}{x^2}$ e) $f(x) = \dfrac{1}{x^2 + 1}$ f) $f(x) = \dfrac{x}{x + 1}$

3. Use the definition of derivative to find the slope of each curve at the point indicated. Write an equation of the tangent to the curve at that point.
   a) $f(x) = 1 - x^2$ at $(1,0)$ b) $f(x) = 3x - x^2$ at $(-1,-4)$
   c) $f(x) = x^3$ at $(-1,-1)$ d) $f(x) = \dfrac{1}{1 - 2x}$ at $(1,-1)$
   e) $f(x) = (2x - 3)^2$ at $(2,1)$ f) $f(x) = \sqrt{x + 6}$ at $(3,3)$

4. Use the definition of derivative to calculate $\dfrac{d}{dx}\sqrt{x^2 + 5}$.

Ⓒ

5. Sketch the graph of the derivative of each function $f(x)$ whose graph is given.

a)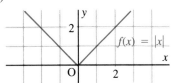

b)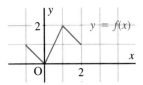

6. Let $sgn\, x = \dfrac{x}{|x|}$. Show that $\dfrac{d}{dx}|x| = sgn\, x$.

7. a) Try to find functions having the following derivatives: $x^0 = 1$, $x^1 = x$, x^2, x^3, x^{-2}, x^{-3}.

   b) If k is any integer, can a function of the form ax^n be found whose derivative is x^k?

 INVESTIGATE

1. Can the graph of a function have a vertical tangent?
   Consider the two functions $f(x) = x^{\frac{1}{3}}$ and $g(x) = x^{\frac{2}{3}}$. Does the graph of either of these functions have a tangent at the origin?

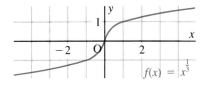

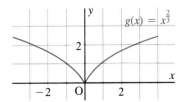

2. Try to calculate:

   a) $f'(0) = \lim\limits_{h \to 0} \dfrac{f(h) - f(0)}{h}$

   b) $g'(0) = \lim\limits_{h \to 0} \dfrac{g(h) - g(0)}{h}$.

   i) Does either limit exist?
   ii) Is either one infinite?
   iii) Is either $f(x)$ or $g(x)$ differentiable at $x = 0$?
   iv) Under what condition does the graph of a function have a tangent?

   The graph of $y = g(x)$ has a *cusp* at the origin. A cusp is a point where a graph forms an infinitely sharp angle (a zero angle) with itself.

10-6 DIFFERENTIATING POLYNOMIALS

In the previous section we calculated the derivatives of several functions directly, from the definition of derivative as a limit of the Newton quotient. For complicated functions, such calculations can be very long and difficult. Fortunately, there is an easier way to find derivatives of complicated functions. Such functions are usually built up by combining simpler functions (for example, powers of *x*) using addition, subtraction, multiplication, division, and composition. If we already know the derivatives of the simple component functions, the derivative of these combinations can be obtained by applying various *differentiation rules*.

In this section we will develop rules for differentiating sums and constant multiples of functions. These rules, summarized in the following theorem, will enable us to calculate the derivative of any polynomial.

Theorem

Suppose that functions $f(x)$ and $g(x)$ have derivatives $f'(x)$ and $g'(x)$ respectively. Let C be any constant. Then the sum $f(x) + g(x)$ and the multiple $Cf(x)$ have derivatives given by:

$$\frac{d}{dx}\Big(f(x) + g(x)\Big) = f'(x) + g'(x) \quad \text{and} \quad \frac{d}{dx}\Big(Cf(x)\Big) = Cf'(x).$$

Both of these formulas are easy to prove using the definition of derivative. We give a proof of the first one here and leave the second one as an exercise.

From the definition

$$\frac{d}{dx}\Big(f(x) + g(x)\Big) = \lim_{h \to 0} \frac{\Big(f(x + h) + g(x + h)\Big) - \Big(f(x) + g(x)\Big)}{h}$$

$$= \lim_{h \to 0} \left(\frac{f(x + h) - f(x)}{h} + \frac{g(x + h) - g(x)}{h}\right)$$

$$= \lim_{h \to 0} \frac{f(x + h) - f(x)}{h} + \lim_{h \to 0} \frac{g(x + h) - g(x)}{h}$$

$$= f'(x) + g'(x)$$

The limit of a sum of functions is the sum of the limits of those functions.

Together, the rules for differentiating sums and multiples imply a corresponding rule for differentiating differences:

$$\frac{d}{dx}\Big(f(x) - g(x)\Big) = \frac{d}{dx}\Big(f(x) + (-1)g(x)\Big)$$

$$= \frac{d}{dx}f(x) + \frac{d}{dx}\Big((-1)g(x)\Big)$$

$$= f'(x) + (-1)g'(x)$$

$$= f'(x) - g'(x)$$

Although the rule for differentiating sums was expressed for sums of only two functions, it extends to sums with any finite number of terms. The derivative of any such sum is the sum of the derivatives of the individual terms.

In the following examples it is assumed that we already know these derivatives, which should be memorized.

$$\frac{d}{dx}(1) = 0 \qquad \frac{d}{dx}(x) = 1 \qquad \frac{d}{dx}(x^2) = 2x$$

$$\frac{d}{dx}(x^3) = 3x^2 \qquad \frac{d}{dx}\left(\frac{1}{x}\right) = -\frac{1}{x^2} \qquad \frac{d}{dx}\sqrt{x} = \frac{1}{2\sqrt{x}}$$

All of these derivatives are special cases of the general power rule.

General Power Rule

If r is any real number, then $\dfrac{d}{dx}(x^r) = rx^{r-1}$

Example 1. Find the derivative of each function.

      a) $7x^2$ b) $x^3 + \sqrt{x}$

Solution.   a) The derivative of $7x^2$ is $7\dfrac{d}{dx}x^2 = 7(2x)$

$$= 14x$$

    b) The derivative of $x^3 + \sqrt{x}$ is $\dfrac{d}{dx}x^3 + \dfrac{d}{dx}\sqrt{x} = 3x^2 + \dfrac{1}{2\sqrt{x}}$

Example 2. Find the derivative of each function.

      a) $3x^2 - 5x + 6$ b) $2x^3 - 4x^2 + 6x - 8$

      c) $2\sqrt{x} - \dfrac{3}{x}$ d) $\dfrac{x^2}{3} - \dfrac{\sqrt{x}}{5}$

Solution.   a) $\dfrac{d}{dx}(3x^2 - 5x + 6) = \dfrac{d}{dx}(3x^2) + \dfrac{d}{dx}(-5x) + \dfrac{d}{dx}(6)$

$$= 3\frac{d}{dx}(x^2) - 5\frac{d}{dx}(x) + 6\frac{d}{dx}(1)$$

$$= 3(2x) - 5(1) + 6(0)$$

$$= 6x - 5$$

In the first line we applied the differentiation rule for sums (twice); in the second line we applied the rule for multiples (twice). Normally we would accomplish the whole differentiation in one step and write

$$\frac{d}{dx}(3x^2 - 5x + 6) = 3(2x) - 5(1) + 6(0)$$

$$= 6x - 5$$

b) $\dfrac{d}{dx}(2x^3 - 4x^2 + 6x - 8) = 2(3x^2) - 4(2x) + 6(1) - 8(0)$

$$= 6x^2 - 8x + 6$$

c) $\dfrac{d}{dx}\left(2\sqrt{x} - \dfrac{3}{x}\right) = 2\left(\dfrac{1}{2\sqrt{x}}\right) - 3\left(-\dfrac{1}{x^2}\right)$

$$= \dfrac{1}{\sqrt{x}} + \dfrac{3}{x^2}$$

d) $\dfrac{d}{dx}\left(\dfrac{x^2}{3} - \dfrac{\sqrt{x}}{5}\right) = \dfrac{1}{3}(2x) - \dfrac{1}{5}\left(\dfrac{1}{2\sqrt{x}}\right)$

$$= \dfrac{2x}{3} - \dfrac{1}{10\sqrt{x}}$$

EXERCISES 10-6

Ⓐ

1. State the derivative of each function.

a) $-x^2$

b) $3x^3$

c) $\dfrac{4}{x}$

d) $x^2 + 17$

e) $2x - 5$

f) $3 - x^3$

g) $100x$

h) $x^3 + x^2$

i) $\dfrac{x^3}{3} - \dfrac{x^2}{2}$

2. Assuming the general power rule is true, state the derivative of each expression.

a) $4x^{-\frac{1}{2}}$

b) $3x^{\frac{1}{3}}$

c) $3x^{-\frac{2}{3}}$

Ⓑ

3. Find the derivative of each function.

a) $x^2 + 4x - 1$

b) $2x - 5x^2$

c) $-2x^3 + 3x^2 - 6$

d) $x^3 + x^2 + x + 1$

e) $5x^2 - 4x - 1$

f) $10\sqrt{x} - \sqrt{10}x$

g) $\dfrac{1}{6} - \dfrac{x}{6} + \dfrac{x^2}{6} - \dfrac{x^3}{6}$

h) $\dfrac{1 + \sqrt{x}}{3}$

i) $\dfrac{x}{2} - \dfrac{2}{x} + 1$

4. Find the derivative of each function. You may assume that the general power rule is valid.

a) $x^{1000} + x^{100} + x^{10} + 1$

b) $\dfrac{1}{60}(2x^6 - 3x^5 + 4x^4 - 3x^3)$

c) $x^{-2} + x^{-3} - x^{-4}$

d) $\sqrt{x} + \dfrac{1}{\sqrt{x}}$

e) $x^{\frac{4}{3}} + x^{\frac{1}{3}} + x^{-\frac{2}{3}}$

f) $2(x^2 - x^{\frac{3}{2}} + x - x^{\frac{1}{2}} + 1)$

5. Find an equation of the tangent to the curve $y = 2x^3 - 3x^2$ at the point $(-1, -5)$.

6. At what points does the curve $y = x^3 - 12x + 1$ have a horizontal tangent?

7. Use the definition of derivative to prove the rule for differentiating multiples:

$$\dfrac{d}{dx}\Big(Cf(x)\Big) = Cf'(x).$$

10-7 THE PRODUCT AND QUOTIENT RULES

There are differentiation rules for calculating the derivatives of products and quotients of functions whose derivatives are already known. These rules are a little more complicated than the rules for differentiating sums and constant multiples of functions developed in the last section.
For example, if $f(x) = x^2 + 2$ and $g(x) = x^3 + 3$, then
$f(x)g(x) = (x^2 + 2)(x^3 + 3) = x^5 + 2x^3 + 3x^2 + 6$,

which has derivative $\dfrac{d}{dx}\Big(f(x)g(x)\Big) = 5x^4 + 6x^2 + 6x$

However, $f'(x) = 2x$, and $g'(x) = 3x^2$, so $f'(x)g'(x) = 6x^3$
Thus, the derivative of the product $f(x)g(x)$ of two functions is *not* the product $f'(x)g'(x)$ of their derivatives.

To see what the product rule should give for the derivative of $f(x)g(x)$, we begin by applying the definition of derivative to express the derivative as the limit of the Newton quotient.

$$\frac{d}{dx}\Big(f(x)g(x)\Big) = \lim_{h\to 0}\frac{f(x + h)g(x + h) - f(x)g(x)}{h}$$

We know that $f(x)$ has derivative $f'(x)$ and $g(x)$ has derivative $g'(x)$; that is, we know

$$\lim_{h\to 0}\frac{f(x + h) - f(x)}{h} = f'(x) \qquad \text{and} \qquad \lim_{h\to 0}\frac{g(x + h) - g(x)}{h} = g'(x)$$

The problem is to manipulate the Newton quotient for $f(x)g(x)$ so that it involves the Newton quotients for $f(x)$ and $g(x)$. To do this, add $f(x)g(x + h)$ to the numerator of the Newton quotient for $f(x)g(x)$ and then subtract it (so as not to change the numerator). Then group pairs of terms and factor.

$$\frac{d}{dx}\Big(f(x)g(x)\Big) = \lim_{h\to 0}\frac{f(x + h)g(x + h) - f(x)g(x)}{h}$$

$$= \lim_{h\to 0}\frac{f(x + h)g(x + h) - f(x)g(x + h) + f(x)g(x + h) - f(x)g(x)}{h}$$

$$= \lim_{h\to 0}\left(\frac{f(x + h) - f(x)}{h}g(x + h) + f(x)\frac{g(x + h) - g(x)}{h}\right)$$

The two fractions in the line above approach $f'(x)$ and $g'(x)$ respectively as h approaches 0. Also, $g(x + h)$ must approach $g(x)$. This is because $g(x)$ is continuous; we are assuming $g'(x)$ exists and if the graph of $g(x)$ is smooth enough to have a nonvertical tangent at x, it certainly cannot have a break there. Finally $f(x)$, which does not depend on h, just keeps on being $f(x)$ as h approaches 0. Now we know the limits of all the components in the expanded Newton quotient, so we can conclude that

$$\frac{d}{dx}\Big(f(x)g(x)\Big) = f'(x)g(x) + f(x)g'(x).$$ This is known as the product rule.

Product Rule

$$\frac{d}{dx}\Big(f(x)g(x)\Big) = f'(x)g(x) + f(x)g'(x)$$

The derivative of a product of two factors has two terms. Each term is of the same sort as the original product but has one of the factors replaced by its derivative.

Example 1. Find the derivative of $(x^2 + 2)(x^3 + 3)$.

Solution. There are two ways to do this. We could multiply out the product to get a single polynomial, $x^5 + 2x^3 + 3x^2 + 6$ which has derivative $5x^4 + 6x^2 + 6x$.

Alternatively, we could apply the product rule to give the derivative of the product directly.

$$\frac{d}{dx}(x^2 + 2)(x^3 + 3) = (2x + 0)(x^3 + 3) + (x^2 + 2)(3x^2 + 0)$$

$$= 2x^4 + 6x + 3x^4 + 6x^2$$

$$= 5x^4 + 6x^2 + 6x$$

For simple products, as in Example 1, using the product rule may seem to complicate the solution, but the rule considerably simplifies the calculation for more complicated products.

There are two useful rules for differentiating quotients. The first of these, called the *reciprocal rule*, applies to the reciprocal of a function $g(x)$ whose derivative, $g'(x)$, is known.

Reciprocal Rule

At any point where $g(x) \neq 0$, we have

$$\frac{d}{dx}\left(\frac{1}{g(x)}\right) = -\frac{g'(x)}{\big(g(x)\big)^2}$$

This rule can be proved using the definition of derivative, and its proof is left as an exercise.

Example 2. Find. $\dfrac{d}{dx}\left(\dfrac{1}{x^2 + 3x}\right)$

Solution. By the reciprocal rule, $\dfrac{d}{dx}\left(\dfrac{1}{x^2 + 3x}\right) = \dfrac{-(2x + 3)}{(x^2 + 3x)^2}$

Example 3. Find an equation of the tangent to the curve $y = \dfrac{2}{1 + \sqrt{x}}$ at $(1,1)$.

Solution. To use the reciprocal rule, write the right side of the given equation as a reciprocal.

$$y = \frac{2}{1 + \sqrt{x}} \times \frac{\frac{1}{2}}{\frac{1}{2}}$$

$$= \frac{1}{\frac{1}{2} + \frac{1}{2}\sqrt{x}}$$

Here, $g(x) = \dfrac{1}{2} + \dfrac{1}{2}\sqrt{x}$

$$= \frac{1}{2} + \frac{1}{2}x^{\frac{1}{2}}$$

$$g'(x) = 0 + \frac{1}{4}x^{-\frac{1}{2}}$$

$$= \frac{1}{4\sqrt{x}}$$

Using the reciprocal rule,

$$\frac{dy}{dx} = \frac{d}{dx}\left(\frac{1}{g(x)}\right)$$

$$= -\frac{g'(x)}{(g(x))^2}$$

$$= -\frac{\frac{1}{4\sqrt{x}}}{\left(\frac{1}{2} + \frac{1}{2}\sqrt{x}\right)^2}$$

$$= -\frac{\frac{1}{\sqrt{x}}}{(1 + \sqrt{x})^2}$$

The slope of the tangent is the value of this derivative at $x = 1$, namely

$$-\frac{1}{(1 + 1)^2} = -\frac{1}{4}$$

Thus, the tangent has equation

$$y - 1 = -\frac{1}{4}(x - 1) \quad \text{or} \quad x + 4y = 5$$

When we calculate the derivative of a function we try to simplify the answer algebraically as much as possible. However, if we want to evaluate the derivative at a particular number, we substitute that number as soon as the derivative has been calculated, and then simplify the resulting numerical expression. This is usually easier than simplifying the algebraic expression and then substituting the number.

The *quotient rule* enables us to differentiate quotients of the form $\dfrac{f(x)}{g(x)}$ when we know the derivatives of $f(x)$ and $g(x)$.

Quotient Rule

At any point where $g(x) \neq 0$, we have
$$\frac{d}{dx}\left(\frac{f(x)}{g(x)}\right) = \frac{g(x)f'(x) - f(x)g'(x)}{\left(g(x)\right)^2}$$

This rule can be proved by applying the product and reciprocal rules to the expression $f(x) \times \dfrac{1}{g(x)}$.

Example 4. Calculate the derivative of each function.

a) $\dfrac{2x + 1}{3x + 2}$

b) $\dfrac{\sqrt{x}}{x^2 + 1}$

Solution.

a)
$$\frac{d}{dx}\left(\frac{2x + 1}{3x + 2}\right) = \frac{(3x + 2)(2) - (2x + 1)(3)}{(3x + 2)^2}$$
$$= \frac{6x + 4 - 6x - 3}{(3x + 2)^2}$$
$$= \frac{1}{(3x + 2)^2}$$

b)
$$\frac{d}{dx}\left(\frac{\sqrt{x}}{x^2 + 1}\right) = \frac{(x^2 + 1)\left(\frac{1}{2\sqrt{x}}\right) - \sqrt{x}(2x)}{(x^2 + 1)^2}$$
$$= \frac{\frac{x^2 + 1 - 4x^2}{2\sqrt{x}}}{(x^2 + 1)^2}$$
$$= \frac{1 - 3x^2}{2\sqrt{x}(x^2 + 1)^2}$$

Students often have trouble remembering the quotient rule because of the minus sign in the numerator. Try to remember, and apply, the quotient rule in the following form:

The derivative of $\dfrac{\text{numerator}}{\text{denominator}}$ is

$$\frac{(\text{denominator}) \times (\text{derivative of numerator}) - (\text{numerator}) \times (\text{derivative of denominator})}{(\text{denominator})^2}$$

EXERCISES 10-7

Ⓑ

1. Use the product rule or reciprocal rule to find the derivative of each power of x.

   a) $x^{-\frac{1}{2}} = \dfrac{1}{\sqrt{x}}$

   b) $x^{\frac{3}{2}} = x\sqrt{x}$

   c) $x^{\frac{5}{2}} = x^2\sqrt{x}$

   d) $x^{-2} = \dfrac{1}{x^2}$

   e) $x^{-3} = \dfrac{1}{x^3}$

   f) $x^{-\frac{3}{2}} = \left(\dfrac{1}{x}\right)\left(\dfrac{1}{\sqrt{x}}\right)$

   Observe that all these derivatives satisfy the general power rule $\dfrac{d}{dx}(x^r) = rx^{r-1}$.

2. Find the derivative of each function. Simplify your answers wherever appropriate.

   a) $(2x + 3)(3x - 2)$

   b) $\sqrt{x}(x^2 - 3x + 7)$

   c) $y = \dfrac{2}{\sqrt{x}} - \dfrac{1}{2x^2}$

   d) $f(x) = (1 + \sqrt{x})(2 + \sqrt{x})$

   e) $g(x) = \dfrac{1}{2 - x}$

   f) $y = \dfrac{1}{x + \sqrt{x}}$

   g) $F(x) = \dfrac{x^2 - 1}{x^2 + 1}$

   h) $G(x) = \dfrac{1 - \sqrt{x}}{1 + \sqrt{x}}$

   i) $f(t) = \dfrac{4 - 3t}{3 + 4t}$

   j) $y = \dfrac{2}{3 + \dfrac{4}{x}}$

   k) $g(s) = \dfrac{(s + 1)(s^2 + 1)}{s^3 + 1}$

   l) $f(x) = \dfrac{(2x + 1)(3x + 1)}{4x + 1}$

3. Find the slope of the curve $y = \dfrac{(1 + \sqrt{x})(2 + \sqrt{x})}{5 + \sqrt{x}}$ at the point $(1,1)$.

Ⓒ

4. Prove the reciprocal rule: $\dfrac{d}{dx}\left(\dfrac{1}{g(x)}\right) = -\dfrac{g'(x)}{(g(x))^2}$. You may assume that if $g(x) \neq 0$,

   then $\displaystyle\lim_{h \to 0} \dfrac{1}{g(x + h)} = \dfrac{1}{g(x)}$.

5. Prove the quotient rule by writing $\dfrac{f(x)}{g(x)} = f(x) \times \dfrac{1}{g(x)}$ and applying the product rule and the reciprocal rule to differentiate the latter expression.

6. Let $p(x) = f(x)g(x)$ and $q(x) = \dfrac{f(x)}{g(x)}$. Prove that:

   a) $\dfrac{p'(x)}{p(x)} = \dfrac{f'(x)}{f(x)} + \dfrac{g'(x)}{g(x)}$

   b) $\dfrac{q'(x)}{q(x)} = \dfrac{f'(x)}{f(x)} - \dfrac{g'(x)}{g(x)}$.

7. Use the definition of the derivative to prove the "square-root rule":

   $\dfrac{d}{dx}\sqrt{f(x)} = \dfrac{f'(x)}{2\sqrt{f(x)}}$, and use it to find the derivative of each function.

   a) $y = \sqrt{x^2 + 1}$

   b) $y = \sqrt{1 + \sqrt{x}}$

   c) $y = \sqrt{\sqrt{x}}$

The Principle of Mathematical Induction

"Throughout history, mathematics has been investigated by observation and quasi-experiments."

Betty J. Krist

We have not yet proved that the derivative of x^n is nx^{n-1}. Here is a method of *proving* that this is true. Recall that we used the definition of the derivative to establish the derivatives of certain power functions.

$f(x)$	$f'(x)$
x	1
x^2	$2x$
x^3	$3x^2$
x^4	$4x^3$

We can use the definition of the derivative to prove that the derivative of $f(x) = x^5$ is $f'(x) = 5x^4$. A more efficient method is to write x^5 as a product and use the product rule.

$$f(x) = x^4 \times x$$
$$f'(x) = 4x^3 \times x + x^4 \times 1$$
$$= 4x^4 + x^4$$
$$= 5x^4$$

Hence, the derivative of x^5 is $5x^4$. We can prove that the derivative of $f(x) = x^6$ is $f'(x) = 6x^5$ in the same way. Then, we can prove that the derivative of x^7 is $7x^6$, and so on. But instead, we generalize the method as follows. Suppose that we have already proved that the derivative of $f(x) = x^k$ is $f'(x) = kx^{k-1}$ for some value of k. Then we prove that the derivative of $f(x) = x^{k+1}$ is $f'(x) = (k+1)x^k$.

$$f(x) = x^{k+1}$$
$$= x^k \times x$$
$$f'(x) = kx^{k-1} \times x + x^k \times 1$$
$$= kx^k + x^k$$
$$= (k+1)x^k$$

When $k = 5$, these calculations reduce to those above. When $k = 6$, they prove that the derivative of x^6 is $6x^5$; when $k = 7$ they prove that the derivative of x^7 is $7x^6$, and so on. Since the calculations have been given in the general case, we have proved that the pattern in the derivative function holds for all natural numbers. That is, the derivative of x^n is nx^{n-1} for all natural numbers n. We have proved this using what is called the *principle of mathematical induction*.

> **The Principle of Mathematical Induction**
> A statement involving natural numbers is true for all natural
> numbers if *both* of the following are true.
> 1. The statement is true when $n = 1$.
> 2. *If* the statement is true when $n = k$, *then* it is true for
> $n = k + 1$.

We can use the principle of mathematical induction to prove
statements involving natural numbers. Here is another example.

Prove that the sum of the first n terms of the series

$$\frac{1}{1 \times 2} + \frac{1}{2 \times 3} + \frac{1}{3 \times 4} + \ldots + \frac{1}{n(n + 1)} \text{ is } \frac{n}{n + 1}.$$

Think of a strategy
- Since the problem involves natural numbers, we try the principle of
  mathematical induction.

Carry out the strategy
- *Step 1.* Is the statement true when $n = 1$?
- *Step 2.* Given that the statement is true when $n = k$, try to prove
  that it is true when $n = k + 1$. It may help to set out the
  work as follows.

  Given: $S_k = \dfrac{k}{k + 1}$

  Required to prove: $S_{k+1} = \dfrac{k + 1}{k + 2}$

  Proof:
- Complete the proof. Then you have solved the problem using the
  principle of mathematical induction.

Look back
- In *Step 2*, are we assuming that the statement we are trying to prove
  is true?

Any statement that can be proved using the principle of mathematical
induction can also be proved in other ways. For example, it can be
proved that the derivative of x^n is nx^{n-1} using a theorem called the
Binomial Theorem. And, there are other methods of proving that the sum
of the first n terms of the series in the above example is $\dfrac{n}{n + 1}$ (see
Exercises 10-3, *Exercise 8*).

Mathematical induction is a very powerful method of proof, but it can only be used to solve certain kinds of problems. The statement to be proved must involve natural numbers. And, the statement to be proved must be known in advance. We cannot use mathematical induction to make discoveries.

Induction and Mathematical Induction
Establish a formula for the sum of the first n terms of this series.
$$\frac{1}{1 \times 3} + \frac{1}{3 \times 5} + \frac{1}{5 \times 7} + \cdots + \frac{1}{(2n - 1)(2n + 1)}$$

Understand the problem
- What does "establish a formula" mean?

Think of a strategy and carry it out
- Try finding S_1, S_2, S_3, . . ., and look for a pattern.
- If you can guess a formula, try to prove it by mathematical induction.

Look back
- When you guessed the formula, you used a method of reasoning called "induction". The following quotation from "How to Solve It" by George Polya explains the difference between induction and mathematical induction.

"Induction" is the process of discovering general laws by the observation and combination of particular instances. It is used in all sciences and in mathematics. "Mathematical induction" is used in mathematics alone to prove theorems of a certain kind. It is rather unfortunate that their names are similar because there is very little logical connection between the two processes. There is, however, some practical connection; we often use both methods together.

This was done in the above example. The result to be proved was *discovered* by induction and *proved* by mathematical induction. To use mathematical induction we must know what assertion is to be proved. It may come from any source, and it does not matter what that source is. In many cases, as in the above, the source is induction — the assertion is found experimentally.

PROBLEMS

Ⓑ

1. Prove by mathematical induction.
   a) $1 + 3 + 5 + \ldots + (2n - 1) = n^2$
   b) $1 + 2 + 2^2 + 2^3 + \ldots + 2^{n-1} = 2^n - 1$

   c) $1 \times 2 + 2 \times 3 + 3 \times 4 + \ldots + n(n + 1) = \frac{1}{3}n(n + 1)(n + 2)$

   d) $1 \times 1 + 2 \times 2 + 3 \times 4 + 4 \times 8 + \ldots + n \times 2^{n-1} = 1 + (n - 1)2^n$

2. Prove by mathematical induction.

   a) $1 + 2 + 3 + \ldots + n = \frac{1}{2}n(n + 1)$

   b) $1^2 + 2^2 + 3^2 + \ldots + n^2 = \frac{1}{6}n(n + 1)(2n + 1)$

   c) $1^3 + 2^3 + 3^3 + \ldots + n^3 = \left[\frac{1}{2}n(n + 1)\right]^2$

3. Prove that $2n < n!$ for $n = 4, 5, 6, \ldots$

4. Prove each statement by mathematical induction, where n is any natural number.
   a) $n^3 + 2n$ is always divisible by 3.
   b) $n(n + 1)(n + 2)$ is always divisible by 6.
   c) The product of four consecutive numbers is always divisible by 24.

Ⓒ

5. Establish a formula for the sum of each series.

   a) $\dfrac{1}{2 \times 4} + \dfrac{1}{4 \times 6} + \dfrac{1}{6 \times 8} + \ldots + \dfrac{1}{2n(2n + 2)}$

   b) $\dfrac{1}{1 \times 4} + \dfrac{1}{4 \times 7} + \dfrac{1}{7 \times 10} + \ldots + \dfrac{1}{(3n - 2)(3n + 1)}$

   c) $1 + 2 \times 2 + 3 \times 2^2 + 4 \times 2^3 + \ldots + n \times 2^{n-1}$
   d) $1 + 2 \times 2! + 3 \times 3! + 4 \times 4! + \ldots + n \times n!$
   e) $1 \times 4 + 2 \times 7 + 3 \times 10 + \ldots + n(3n + 1)$

6. Establish a formula for each product.

   a) $\left(1 - \frac{1}{2}\right)\left(1 - \frac{1}{3}\right)\left(1 - \frac{1}{4}\right) \ldots \left(1 - \frac{1}{n}\right)$

   b) $\left(1 - \frac{1}{4}\right)\left(1 - \frac{1}{9}\right)\left(1 - \frac{1}{16}\right) \ldots \left(1 - \frac{1}{n^2}\right)$

   c) $\left(1 + \frac{1}{2}\right)\left(1 + \frac{1}{3}\right)\left(1 + \frac{1}{4}\right) \ldots \left(1 + \frac{1}{n}\right)$

7. Prove that $(1 + x)^n \geq 1 + nx$, for all $n \in N$, where $x \in R$ and $x \geq -1$.

8. Prove that $x^{2n+1} + y^{2n+1}$ is divisible by $x + y$ for $n = 0, 1, 2, \ldots$

9. Prove that $(\cos \theta + i \sin \theta)^n = \cos n\theta + i \sin n\theta$, where $i^2 = -1$, and n is any natural number.

10. The terms of the *Fibonacci Sequence* 1, 1, 2, 3, 5, 8, 13, . . . , can be defined recursively as follows:
$t_1 = 1, t_2 = 1, t_n = t_{n-1} + t_{n-2}$
Establish a formula for the sum of the first n terms of the sequence.

11. A sequence is defined recursively as follows. $t_1 = 1, t_{n+1} = \sqrt{1 + 2t_n}$
    a) Determine the first five terms of the sequence.
    b) Prove that every term of the sequence is less than 3.
    c) Prove that every term of the sequence is greater than the preceding term.

12. Given that $x^{-1} + y^{-1} + z^{-1} = (x + y + z)^{-1}$, prove that
$x^n + y^n + z^n = (x + y + z)^n$, where n is any odd integer.

13. The "nth derivative", $f^{(n)}(x)$, of a function $f(x)$ can be defined recursively as follows:

$$f^{(0)}(x) = f(x), f^{(n+1)}(x) = \frac{d}{dx}f^{(n)}(x)$$

Thus, $f^{(1)}(x) = \dfrac{d}{dx}f^{(0)}(x) = \dfrac{d}{dx}f(x) = f'(x)$ (the first derivative of $f(x)$)

$\qquad f^{(2)}(x) = \dfrac{d}{dx}f^{(1)}(x) = \dfrac{d}{dx}f'(x) = f''(x)$ (the derivative of the first derivative, or the second derivative)

$\qquad f^{(3)}(x) = \dfrac{d}{dx}f^{(2)}(x) = \dfrac{d}{dx}f''(x) = f'''(x)$ (the derivative of the second derivative, or the third derivative)

$\qquad\qquad\qquad\qquad\vdots$

Establish a formula for the nth derivative of each function.

   a) $f(x) = \dfrac{1}{x}$ b) $f(x) = \sqrt{x}$ c) $f(x) = \dfrac{x}{1 + x}$

Ⓓ

14. Let $S_n = \dfrac{1}{\sqrt{1} + \sqrt{2}} + \dfrac{1}{\sqrt{2} + \sqrt{3}} + \dfrac{1}{\sqrt{3} + \sqrt{4}} + \ldots + \dfrac{1}{\sqrt{n} + \sqrt{n + 1}}$.
Prove that S_n is irrational if, and only if, $n + 1$ is not a perfect square.

10-8 VELOCITY AND ACCELERATION

A rock falling from a height of 100 m is at a height of H metres, t seconds after it begins to fall, given by $H(t) = 100 - 4.9t^2$. This formula is valid only for $0 \leqslant t \leqslant T$, where $T \doteq 4.52$. This is the positive root of the equation $100 - 4.9t^2 = 0$; the rock presumably stops falling when it strikes the ground.

In the time interval from $t = 1$ s to $t = 4$ s, the rock falls from a height $H(1) = 95.1$ m to a height $H(4) = 21.6$ m.
Its change in height is
$H(4) - H(1) = -73.5$ m over this 3-s time interval.
We say that the *average velocity* of the rock between $t = 1$ and $t = 4$ is

$$v_{\text{average}} = \frac{H(4) - H(1)}{4 - 1}$$

$$= -\frac{73.5}{3}$$

$$= -24.5$$

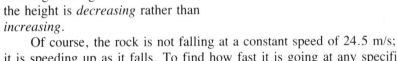

The average velocity is 24.5 m/s.
The negative sign reflects the fact that the height is *decreasing* rather than *increasing*.

Of course, the rock is not falling at a constant speed of 24.5 m/s; it is speeding up as it falls. To find how fast it is going at any specific instant of time, say $t = 2$, we take the limit of its average velocity over shorter and shorter time intervals starting at $t = 2$.
Over the time interval from $t = 2$ to $t = 2 + h$, the average velocity is $\dfrac{H(2 + h) - H(2)}{h}$.

The *instantaneous velocity* $v(2)$ of the falling rock at time $t = 2$ is the limit of this average velocity as the length h of the time interval approaches 0. Thus, it is the derivative of the height function $H(t)$ at $t = 2$.

$$v(2) = \lim_{h \to 0} \frac{H(2 + h) - H(2)}{h}$$

$$= H'(2)$$

Since $H'(t) = -4.9(2t)$

$$v(t) = -9.8t,$$

the velocity at $t = 2$ s is $v(2) = -19.6$
The instantaneous velocity at $t = 2$ is 19.6 m/s.

The concepts of average velocity and instantaneous velocity extend in an obvious way to any kind of motion in a straight line. Suppose an object is moving along a straight path, say the x-axis, so that its position x at time t is given by the function $x = x(t)$. (In the past, we used a different letter for the function, and wrote $x = f(t)$, but it is common to use the same symbol for both the dependent variable and the function.) The average velocity of the object over the time interval from $t = a$ to $t = b$ is equal to the change in position divided by the change in time,

$$v_{average} = \frac{x(b) - x(a)}{b - a}$$

The average velocity will be positive or negative depending on whether the object's change of position is in the positive or negative x-direction. If the object is at the same position at time b as it was at time a, then its average velocity is zero.

The instantaneous velocity (usually just called the velocity) of the object at time t is the limit of the average velocity over shorter and shorter time intervals starting at time t; thus it is the derivative of the position with respect to time.

Instantaneous Velocity

The velocity v at time t is given by

$$v(t) = \lim_{h \to 0} \frac{x(t + h) - x(t)}{h}$$

$$= \frac{dx}{dt}$$

$$= x'(t)$$

The velocity is positive, negative or zero at an instant if the object is moving in the positive x-direction, the negative x-direction, or is momentarily standing still at that instant. The absolute value of the velocity is called the *speed*.

Speed

The speed s at time t is given by

$$s(t) = |v(t)|$$

$$= |x'(t)|$$

Make a distinction in your use of the terms *velocity* and *speed*; velocity involves direction, speed does not. If a car travels eastward 140 km along a straight road in 2 h, then its average velocity for the trip is $\frac{140}{2}$, or 70 km/h due east. Its average speed is simply 70 km/h. The instantaneous speed is shown by the speedometer, at any given time.

Example 1. An object moves along the *x*-axis so that its position at time *t* is $x = t^3 - 3t$. Suppose *t* is measured in seconds and *x* is measured in metres.

    a) At what times is the object:
        i) moving to the right; that is, in the positive *x*-direction
        ii) moving to the left
        iii) stopped?
    b) What is its average velocity over the time interval:
        i) from $t = 0$ to $t = 1$ ii) from $t = 0$ to $t = 2$?
    c) What is its velocity at: i) time $t = 0$ ii) time $t = 2$?

Solution. The velocity at time *t* is $v = \dfrac{dx}{dt}$

$$= 3t^2 - 3$$
$$= 3(t^2 - 1)$$

    a) i) The object is moving to the right if $v > 0$;
            that is, $3(t^2 - 1) > 0$
            Solve this inequality.
            3 is always greater than 0, so consider when
$$t^2 - 1 > 0$$
$$(t - 1)(t + 1) > 0$$
            The left side is positive if:
            Either $t - 1 > 0$ and $t + 1 > 0$
                        $t > 1$ $t > -1$
            Hence, $t > 1$
            Or $t - 1 < 0$ and $t + 1 < 0$
                      $t < 1$ $t < -1$
            Hence, $t < -1$
            The object is moving to the right if $t < -1$ or $t > 1$.
      ii) The object is moving to the left when
$$3(t^2 - 1) < 0 \quad \text{or}$$
$$(t - 1)(t + 1) < 0$$
            The left side is negative if:
            Either $t - 1 > 0$ and $t + 1 < 0$
                        $t > 1$ $t < -1$
            This is not possible.
            Or $t - 1 < 0$ and $t + 1 > 0$
                      $t < 1$ $t > -1$
            Hence, $-1 < t < 1$
            The object is moving to the left if $-1 < t < 1$.
     iii) The object is stopped when its velocity is zero.
            That is, $3t^2 - 3 = 0$
$$3t^2 = 3$$
$$t^2 = 1$$
$$t = \pm 1$$
            The object is stopped at times $t = 1$ and $t = -1$.

b) i) The average velocity from $t = 0$ to $t = 1$ is

$$\frac{x(1) - x(0)}{1 - 0} = \frac{1^3 - 3(1) - (0^3 - 3(0))}{1}$$

$$= \frac{1 - 3}{1}$$

$$= -2$$

The average velocity is -2 m/s.

ii) The average velocity from $t = 0$ to $t = 2$ is

$$\frac{x(2) - x(0)}{2 - 0} = \frac{2^3 - 3(2) - (0^3 - 3(0))}{2}$$

$$= \frac{8 - 6}{2}$$

$$= 1$$

The average velocity is 1 m/s.

c) i) The velocity at $t = 0$ is $v(0)$.

$$v(0) = 3(0)^2 - 3$$

$$= -3$$

The velocity at $t = 0$ is -3 m/s.

ii) The velocity at $t = 2$ is $v(2)$.

$$v(2) = 3(2)^2 - 3$$

$$= 12 - 3$$

$$= 9$$

The velocity at $t = 2$ is 9 m/s.

For *Example 1*, the graph of $x(t)$ is shown here. Since the x-axis is vertical in the graph, the positive x-direction is "up" rather than "right." Observe that the average velocity over any interval is the slope of the secant to the graph over that interval. The velocity at time t is the slope of the tangent at t.

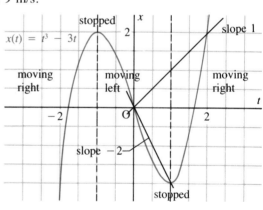

The velocity $v(t)$ of a moving object is itself a function of time which can be differentiated. Its derivative is called the *acceleration* of the object and denoted $a(t)$.

Acceleration

$$a(t) = v'(t)$$

$$= (x')'(t)$$

$$= x''(t)$$

The notation $x''(t)$ stands for the *derivative of the derivative* of $x(t)$. It is also called the *second derivative* of $x(t)$.

Taken together, the signs of the acceleration and velocity tell us whether the object is speeding up or slowing down. If $a(t)$ and $v(t)$ have the same sign (both positive or both negative), then the object is speeding up. If they have opposite signs, then the object is slowing down. When the acceleration is zero, the object is (at least momentarily) moving with constant velocity.

Example 2. An object is thrown upwards at time $t = 0$ with an initial speed of 49 m/s. It has a height y metres, given by $y = -4.9t^2 + 49t$, t seconds later, until it falls back to the ground again.
a) What is its acceleration at any time t?
b) How high does the object get?
c) How long does it remain in the air?

Solution.   The velocity is $v(t) = \dfrac{dy}{dt}$

$$= -9.8t + 49$$

a) The acceleration is $a(t) = \dfrac{dv}{dt}$

$$= -9.8$$

The acceleration is -9.8 m/s² at any time the object is in the air.

b) At its highest point the object has zero velocity; it is not going higher and it is not yet falling back.
When $v = 0$, $-9.8t + 49 = 0$

$$t = \frac{49}{9.8}, \text{ or } 5$$

When $t = 5$, the height $y = -4.9(5)^2 + 49(5)$, or 122.5
The greatest height is 122.5 m.

c) The object is at ground level when $y = 0$.
That is, $-4.9t^2 + 49t = 0$
$$t(-4.9t + 49) = 0$$
$$t = 0 \text{ or } t = 10$$
The object was thrown up at $t = 0$ and returned to the ground at $t = 10$. Hence, it was in the air for 10 s.

EXERCISES 10-8

Ⓐ

1. a) If Winnipeg is 2000 km east of Vancouver and an aircraft flies from Vancouver to Winnipeg in 2.5 h, what is its average velocity for the trip?
   b) If it returns immediately to Vancouver, arriving 6 h after it left, what is its average speed for the round trip?

2. An object falls from rest a distance $4.9t^2$ metres in t seconds. What is its speed after it has been falling for one second?

Ⓑ

3. The position x centimetres of a moving object is given in terms of time t seconds. Determine:
   i) the velocity of the object at time t
   ii) the time intervals during which the object is moving to the left; that is, in the negative x-direction
   iii) the time intervals during which the object is moving to the right
   iv) all times when the velocity is zero
   v) the average velocity from time $t = 0$ to time $t = 4$
   vi) the acceleration at time t.

a) $x = t^2 - 4t + 1$	b) $x = 2 + 3t - t^2$
c) $x = t^3 + 3t^2 + 3t$	d) $x = t^4 - 8t^2 + 16$

4. a) Find the average velocity over the time interval from $t = a$ to $t = b$ of a moving object whose position x metres at time t seconds is $x = t^2$.
   b) Find the velocity at the midpoint of the time interval.

5. Repeat *Exercise 4* for $x = t^3$.

6. The distance travelled by an aircraft along a runway before takeoff is given by $D = t^2$, where D is measured in metres from the start of the takeoff run, and t is measured in seconds from the time the brake is released.
   a) If the aircraft becomes airborne when its speed reaches 60 m/s, how long will it take to become airborne?
   b) What distance will it travel along the runway before becoming airborne?

7. A ball is thrown downward from the top of a 50-m high building with an initial speed of 3 m/s. Its height in metres above the ground t seconds later is $50 - 3t - 4.9t^2$.
   a) How long does it take to fall to the ground?
   b) What is its speed when it reaches the ground?

👤 INVESTIGATE

Suppose $y = f(x)$ is a function with a smooth graph. Draw such a graph. If A and B are two points on the graph, is there a point C on the graph between A and B such that the tangent to the graph at C is parallel to the line AB? Is there more than one such point C?

Consider these questions for several possible smooth graphs, and try to formulate a general principle based on your observations.

The average velocity of a moving object over the time interval from $t = a$ to $t = b$ is v. Must the (instantaneous) velocity of the object ever be exactly v? How is this question related to those in the above paragraph?

THE MATHEMATICAL MIND

Newton and Leibniz

Isaac Newton was born in Lincolnshire, England, on Christmas Day, 1642, and he died in London on March 20, 1727. His most important contribution to mathematics was the creation of calculus, which he called the *method of fluxions*. In it he developed techniques for differentiation; that is, for determining rates of change (which he called *fluxions* and we now call derivatives) of varying quantities (which he called *fluents* and we call functions). Newton used the method of fluxions to find tangents to curves, and maximum and minimum values of functions. More importantly, fluxions contributed to his demonstration that planets move in elliptical orbits (as Kepler had claimed) precisely because the force attracting them to the sun varies inversely with the square of the distance. Newton realized that the inverse problem of finding the fluent having a given fluxion (integration) was equivalent to the problem of determining an area bounded by a curve. This equivalence is known as the Fundamental Theorem of Calculus.

Gottfried Wilhelm Leibniz was born in Leipzig, Germany, in 1646, and died in Hanover in 1716. He created *differential calculus* as a system of calculating differentials (or infinitely small increments) of quantities. Leibniz regarded the slope of a curve as a quotient $\frac{dy}{dx}$ of differentials representing the run and the rise between two points on the curve infinitely close together. He also used his calculus to determine tangents, and maximum and minimum values, but his understanding of dynamics was far inferior to Newton's, and his contributions to that field were inconsequential.

Newton and Leibniz both created their versions of calculus at almost the same time, and it seems independently. Newton first used fluxions about 1666, and Leibniz used differentials about 1674. Though he lectured on his work and communicated it in letters to colleagues at the time, Newton did not publish an account of the method of fluxions until 1693. Leibniz published in 1684. There ensued a lengthy controversy as to whether or not Leibniz had got the idea by seeing a manuscript of Newton's.

Whatever the origin of the idea, the differential notation invented by Leibniz gained ascendancy over the next 200 years. It was (and is) very well suited to the situations in which calculus is applied. If x depends on t, Leibniz would have used the notation $\frac{dx}{dt}$ for what Newton called the fluxion $\dot{x}$ of the fluent x. Newton's notation $\dot{x}$ is close to our function notation $x'(t)$, which only came into general use in the twentieth century.

Do you think Newton's or Leibniz's notation is better? What are the advantages and disadvantages of each?

10-9 USING DERIVATIVES TO SKETCH GRAPHS

We can graph $y = f(x)$ by making a table of values of $f(x)$ for many different values of x, plotting the corresponding points, and joining them with a "suitable" curve. However, the derivative $f'(x)$ contains much useful information about the shape of the graph, and if we exploit this source of information we can usually get by with the coordinates of very few points and still get a good graph.

Example 1. Sketch the graph of $y = f(x) = x^2 - 2x$.

Solution. Find the x-intercepts.

Substitute $y = 0$.
$$x^2 - 2x = 0$$
$$x(x - 2) = 0$$
$$x = 0 \text{ and } 2$$

The graph crosses the x-axis at $(0,0)$ and $(2,0)$.

Since $f(x)$ is a polynomial in x, there will be points on the graph for every value of x.

Consider the derivative.
$$f'(x) = 2x - 2$$
$$= 2(x - 1)$$

When $x < 1$, we have $f'(x) < 0$.

This means that the graph has negative slope; we say that $f(x)$ is *decreasing* for $x < 1$.

Similarly, if $x > 1$, then $f'(x) > 0$ and the graph has positive slope; we say that $f(x)$ is *increasing* for $x > 1$.

At $x = 1$, the graph has zero slope; its tangent is horizontal.

We call $x = 1$ a *critical point* of the function $f(x)$.

Since $f(1) = -1$, the corresponding point on the graph has coordinates $(1, -1)$. The graph slopes down to the left of this point and up to the right, so the point must be the lowest point on the graph. We say that $f(x)$ has a *minimum value* -1 at $x = 1$.

All this information we get from $f'(x)$ is conveniently summarized in a chart portraying the x-axis with the critical point $x = 1$ shown on it. The intervals to the left and right are labelled with the sign of $f'(x)$. The consequent behaviour of $f(x)$ is indicated with sloping arrows $\searrow$ and $\nearrow$ to indicate "decreasing" and "increasing." The graph $y = f(x)$ is sketched using the information on this chart and the coordinates of the three points found.

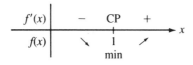

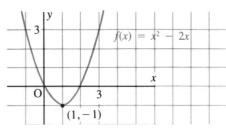

Example 2. Sketch the graph $y = 2x^2 - x^3$.

Solution. Find the x-intercepts.

Substitute $y = 0$.
$$2x^2 - x^3 = 0$$
$$x^2(2 - x) = 0$$
$$x = 0 \text{ twice and } x = 2$$

This means that the graph touches the x-axis at $(0,0)$ and crosses it at $(2,0)$.

Consider the derivative. $\dfrac{dy}{dx} = 4x - 3x^2$

When $\dfrac{dy}{dx} = 0$, the graph has zero slope.

$$4x - 3x^2 = 0$$
$$x(4 - 3x) = 0$$
$$x = 0 \text{ and } \frac{4}{3}$$

These are two critical points.

When $x = 0$, $y = 0$

When $x = \frac{4}{3}$, $y = 2\left(\frac{4}{3}\right)^2 - \left(\frac{4}{3}\right)^3$

$$= \frac{32}{9} - \frac{64}{27}$$

$$= \frac{32}{27}$$

The corresponding points on the curve are $(0,0)$ and $\left(\frac{4}{3}, \frac{32}{27}\right)$.

Consider what happens to the curve on either side of each critical point.

When $x < 0$, say $x = -1$, $f'(-1) = -4 - 3 < 0$

The graph has negative slope and $f(x)$ is decreasing for $x < 0$.

When $x > 0$ but less than $\frac{4}{3}$, say $x = 1$, $f'(1) = 4 - 3 > 0$

The graph has positive slope and $f(x)$ is increasing for $0 < x < \frac{4}{3}$

When $x > \frac{4}{3}$, say $x = 2$, $f'(2) = 8 - 12 < 0$

The graph has negative slope and $f(x)$ is decreasing for $x > \frac{4}{3}$.

We make a chart, as in *Example 1*.

y has a local minimum value at $x = 0$, and a local maximum at $x = \frac{4}{3}$.

We call these extreme values local because the corresponding points on the graph are the lowest and highest in their immediate neighbourhoods, but there are lower and higher points elsewhere on the curve.

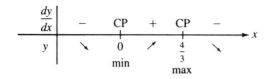

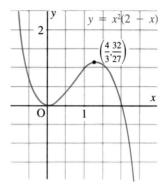

Much new terminology is introduced in the examples above. Let us review it in a more general context. We shall consider a function $f(x)$ such as the one shown. The domain of $f(x)$ is the set of numbers between a and b: $\{x \mid a \leqslant x \leqslant b, x \in R\}$. This set of numbers is called an *interval*. In this case, the *endpoints* of the interval are a and b.

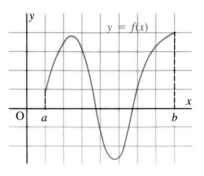

At any point or on any interval where $f'(x) > 0$, the graph $y = f(x)$ will be sloping upward to the right, and we say that $f(x)$ is increasing there. Similarly, $f(x)$ is decreasing wherever $f'(x) < 0$.

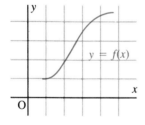

$f(x)$ is increasing

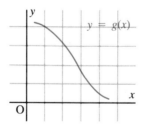

$g(x)$ is decreasing

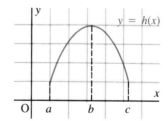

$h(x)$ increases for $a < x < b$
$h(x)$ decreases for $b < x < c$

We call a point x in the domain of $f(x)$ a *critical point* of $f(x)$ if $f'(x) = 0$. The graph $y = f(x)$ has a horizontal tangent at a critical point.

Of special importance are points where the graph $y = f(x)$ is higher or lower than it is at nearby points. These are called *local maximum points* and *local minimum points* of $f(x)$, and we say that $f(x)$ has *local maximum values* and *local minimum values* at them. Also, there may be points where the graph of $y = f(x)$ is highest and lowest for all points in the domain. These are the *global maximum* and *global minimum* points.

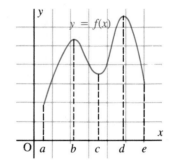

$f(x)$ has local minimum values at a, c, and e
$f(x)$ has local maximum values at b and d
$f(x)$ has a global maximum at d
$f(x)$ has a global minimum at a

A function need not have any local maximum or minimum values, and even it is does, it need not have any global ones.

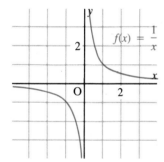

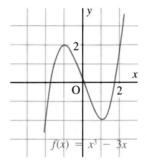

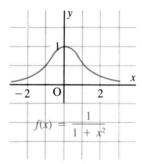

$f(x) = \dfrac{1}{x}$ has no local or global maximum or minimum values.

$f(x) = x^3 - 3x$ has a local maximum at $x = -1$ and a local minimum at $x = 1$, but it has no global maximum or minimum.

$f(x) = \dfrac{1}{1 + x^2}$ has a local and global maximum value 1 at $x = 0$, but no local or global minimum values.

A function cannot have a maximum or minimum value where it is increasing or decreasing. Therefore, to find such extreme values we need only look at:
- the endpoints of the domain,
- the critical points of $f(x)$; that is, solutions of $f'(x) = 0$,
- the points in the domain of $f(x)$ where $f'(x)$ does not exist.

$f(x)$ may not have extreme values at such points, but if it has any extreme values, these are the only places they can be. We will deal only with differentiable functions, so will not encounter any point where $f'(x)$ does not exist. Many of the functions we will encounter do not have endpoints either; for example, there were no endpoints in *Examples 1* or *2*.

Example 3.   Sketch the graph of $f(x) = \dfrac{x}{x^2 + 1}$.

Solution.   Find the y-intercept. When $x = 0$, $y = 0$
Hence, $(0,0)$ lies on the graph.
Consider what happens when x gets numerically very large.

$$\lim_{x \to \pm\infty} \frac{x}{x^2 + 1} = 0$$

When x gets numerically very large, $f(x)$ approaches zero. So, the line $f(x) = 0$ is a horizontal asymptote.
Consider the derivative.

$$f'(x) = \frac{(x^2 + 1)(1) - x(2x)}{(x^2 + 1)^2}$$

$$= \frac{1 - x^2}{(x^2 + 1)^2}$$

The critical points occur where $f'(x) = 0$.
That is, $1 - x^2 = 0$

$$x = \pm 1$$

When $x = 1$, $f(1) = \dfrac{1}{1 + 1}$, or $\dfrac{1}{2}$

When $x = -1$, $f(-1) = \dfrac{-1}{1 + 1}$, or $-\dfrac{1}{2}$

The corresponding points are $\left(1, \dfrac{1}{2}\right)$ and $\left(-1, -\dfrac{1}{2}\right)$.

Consider what happens to the curve on either side of each critical point.

When $x < -1$, say $x = -2$, $f'(-2) < 0$

The graph has negative slope and $f(x)$ is decreasing for $x < -1$.

When $x > -1$, but less than 1, say $x = 0$, $f'(0) = \dfrac{1}{1} > 0$

The graph has positive slope and $f(x)$ is increasing for $-1 < x < 1$.

When $x > 1$, say $x = 2$, $f'(2) < 0$

The graph has negative slope and $f(x)$ is decreasing for $x > 1$.

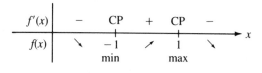

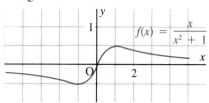

EXERCISES 10-9

(A)

1. For each function, specify its domain, and any endpoints of the domain.

   a) $f(x) = \sqrt{x}$

   b) $f(x) = \sqrt{x + 2}$

   c) $f(x) = \sqrt{1 - x^2}$

   d) $f(x) = \sqrt{x^2 - 1}$

   e) $f(x) = \dfrac{1}{\sqrt{x - 1}}$

   f) $f(x) = \dfrac{1}{x^2}$

(B)

2. For each function

   i) Determine where it is increasing and decreasing.

   ii) Classify the critical points as maxima or minima.

   iii) Sketch its graph.

   a) $f(x) = 4 - 3x - x^2$

   b) $g(x) = 2x^2 + 3x - 2$

   c) $f(x) = x^3 - 12x$

   d) $f(x) = x^3 + x$

   e) $f(x) = x^4 - 4x$

   f) $F(x) = (x^2 - 1)^2 = x^4 - 2x^2 + 1$

   g) $h(x) = x^3(4 - x)$

   h) $g(x) = x^2(x - 4)^2$

(C)

3. Sketch a graph of each function. Do not overlook any vertical or horizontal asymptotes.

   a) $y = \dfrac{x^2}{x^2 + 1}$

   b) $y = \dfrac{x^2}{1 + x^4}$

   c) $y = \dfrac{x^3}{1 + x^4}$

   d) $y = \dfrac{x + 1}{x - 1}$

   e) $y = \dfrac{x^2}{x^2 - 1}$

 INVESTIGATE

The sign of the *second derivative*, $f''(x)$, of a function $f(x)$ will tell you whether the first derivative $f'(x)$ is increasing or decreasing.

What implications does this have for the graph of $y = f(x)$? Consider special cases such as $f(x) = x^2$, $f(x) = -x^2$ and $f(x) = x^3$.

Can you formulate a general principle?

10-10 PROBLEMS INVOLVING EXTREME VALUES

Some of the most interesting applications of differential calculus are concerned with finding maximum and minimum values of functions arising in various concrete situations. In this section we look at a selection of such problems and the techniques used to solve them.

Example 1.   You want to construct a rectangular pigpen having one side along an existing long wall and the other three sides fenced. If you have 100 m of fence, what is the largest possible area your pigpen can have?

Solution.   Let the length and width of the enclosure be x and y metres respectively.
Then, the area is $A = xy$.
Since we have 100 m of fence to enclose three sides, $x + 2y = 100$.
Thus, $x = 100 - 2y$, and we can write A as a function of y alone:
$$A = A(y)$$
$$= (100 - 2y)y$$
$$=. 100y - 2y^2$$

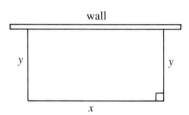

We must have $x \geq 0$ and $y \geq 0$ for the problem to make sense; we cannot have negative lengths of fence.
Since $x \geq 0$ and $x = 100 - 2y$, then $100 - 2y \geq 0$
$$\text{or} \qquad 100 \geq 2y$$
$$y \leq 50$$
Therefore, $0 \leq y \leq 50$ is the domain for $A(y)$.
It has two endpoints, 0 and 50.
However, $A(y)$ has value 0 at these endpoints, and is positive for values of y between them, so the maximum value of $A(y)$ cannot occur at either endpoint. Being a polynomial in y, $A(y)$ is differentiable. Thus, its maximum value must occur at a critical point.
Critical points are found by equating the derivative to zero.
$$0 = \frac{dA}{dy}$$
$$= 100 - 4y$$
$$= 4(25 - y)$$
$$y = 25$$
$y = 25$ is the only critical point.
Since $\dfrac{dA}{dy} > 0$ if $y < 25$ and $\dfrac{dA}{dy} < 0$ if $y > 25$, this critical point must indeed give a maximum value to $A(y)$.
The largest pigpen has area $A(25) = 100(25) - 2(25)^2$, or 1250 m²

In *Example 1*, we could have obtained the answer without using calculus. Complete the square of $A(y)$.

$$
\begin{aligned}
A(y) &= -2(y^2 - 50y) \\
&= -2[(y - 25)^2 - 625] \\
&= 1250 - 2(y - 25)^2
\end{aligned}
$$

We can see that $A(y)$ has maximum value 1250 when $y = 25$. This only works because $A(y)$ is a quadratic function. The calculus method is much better in general.

Example 2.   Find two positive numbers whose sum is 15 if the product of one and the square of the other is as large as possible.

Solution.   Let the two numbers be x and y.

Thus $x + y = 15$, or $x = 15 - y$

The required product is $P = xy^2$, which can be written as a function of y alone:

$$
\begin{aligned}
P &= P(y) \\
&= (15 - y)y^2 \\
&= 15y^2 - y^3
\end{aligned}
$$

Since $x > 0$ and $y > 0$, we must have $0 < y < 15$.

In this case there are no endpoints (0 and 15 do not belong to the domain) but, from the equation, $P(y) \to 0$ as $y \to 0$ or $y \to 15$ so the maximum value of $P(y)$ must occur at a critical point between 0 and 15. Equate the derivative to zero.

$$
\begin{aligned}
0 &= \frac{dP}{dy} \\
&= 30y - 3y^2 \\
&= 3y(10 - y)
\end{aligned}
$$

$y = 0$ or $y = 10$

Since $\dfrac{dP}{dy} > 0$ if $y < 10$ and $\dfrac{dP}{dy} < 0$ if $y > 10$, this critical point gives a maximum value to $P(y)$.

When $y = 10$, $x = 15 - 10$, or 5

The two required numbers are 5 and 10.

Observe the approach taken in the two examples above. When trying to solve an extreme-value problem it is helpful to organize your solution along these lines:

- Draw a diagram, if appropriate, to illustrate the problem.
- Define any symbols you need for various quantities in the problem. Show them on the diagram.
- Identify the quantity to be maximized or minimized. Express it as a function of *one variable only*. If it naturally depends on more than one variable, use relationships among the variables (provided by the problem) to eliminate all but one of the variables.
- Determine the domain of the function to be maximized or minimized in terms of that variable. This will depend on the context of the problem.

- Search for maximum or minimum values occurring at any endpoints or critical points.
- Justify your selection of one particular value to give the required maximum or minimum value. Sometimes it is useful to check where the function is increasing and decreasing.
- Make a concluding statement answering the question asked.

We complete this section with a few more examples.

Example 3. A billboard must have 100 m² of printed area with margins of 2 m at the top and bottom and 4 m on each side. Find the outside dimensions of the billboard if its total area is a minimum.

Solution. Let the width and height of the billboard be x metres and y metres respectively. The dimensions of the printed area are $(x - 8)$ metres and $(y - 4)$ metres.

So $(x - 8)(y - 4) = 100$

$$y - 4 = \frac{100}{x - 8}$$

$$y = 4 + \frac{100}{x - 8}$$

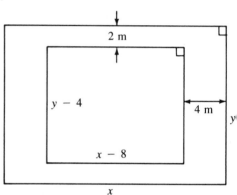

The total area of the billboard is $A = xy$, which we can express as a function of x alone:

$$A = A(x)$$

$$= x\left(4 + \frac{100}{x - 8}\right)$$

$$= 4x + \frac{100x}{x - 8}$$

We must have $x > 8$ and $y > 4$; so we should consider $A(x)$ to be defined for $8 < x$.

Observe that $A(x)$ grows very large as x grows large or x approaches 8. Thus, $A(x)$ will be a minimum at a critical point.

Consider the derivative.

$$\frac{dA}{dx} = 4 + 100\left(\frac{(x - 8) - x}{(x - 8)^2}\right)$$

$$= 4\left(\frac{(x - 8)^2 - 200}{(x - 8)^2}\right)$$

For critical points, $\dfrac{dA}{dx} = 0$

That is, $(x - 8)^2 - 200 = 0$

$$(x - 8)^2 = 200$$

$$x - 8 = \pm\sqrt{200}$$

$$x = 8 \pm 10\sqrt{2}$$

Since $x > 8$, we use the solution with the plus sign: $x = 8 + 10\sqrt{2}$
This critical point must give the minimum value of $A(x)$.

We have $\quad y = 4 + \dfrac{100}{10\sqrt{2}}$

$\qquad\quad = 4 + 5\sqrt{2}$

The smallest billboard will be $(8 + 10\sqrt{2})$ m wide and $(4 + 5\sqrt{2})$ m high, or about 22.1 m by 11.1 m.

Example 4. The volume of a circular cylinder of base radius r and height h is $\pi r^2 h$. Find the volume of the largest such cylinder that will fit inside a sphere of radius R centimetres.

Solution. The diagram shows a cylinder of radius r and height h inscribed in a sphere of radius R. From the right triangle, we have

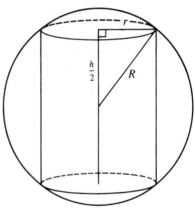

$$r^2 + \left(\frac{h}{2}\right)^2 = R^2$$

$$r^2 = R^2 - \frac{h^2}{4}$$

The volume of the cylinder can be expressed in terms of h alone.

$$V = \pi r^2 h$$

$$= \pi h\left(R^2 - \frac{h^2}{4}\right)$$

$$= \pi R^2 h - \frac{\pi}{4}h^3$$

V is defined for $0 \le h \le 2R$.
Since $V = 0$ if $h = 0$ or $h = 2R$, and $V > 0$ if $0 < h < 2R$, the maximum value of V must occur at a critical point.
For critical points

$$0 = \frac{dV}{dh} = \pi R^2 - \frac{3}{4}\pi h^2$$

$$\pi R^2 - \frac{3}{4}\pi h^2 = 0$$

$$h^2 = \frac{4}{3}R^2$$

$$h = \frac{2}{\sqrt{3}}R$$

The only critical point in the domain is $h = \dfrac{2}{\sqrt{3}}R$.

The volume of the largest cylinder that will fit inside the sphere is

$$\pi R^2\left(\frac{2}{\sqrt{3}}R\right) - \frac{\pi}{4}\left(\frac{2}{\sqrt{3}}R\right)^3 = \frac{4}{3\sqrt{3}}\pi R^3$$

Our final example shows that it is dangerous to assume the solution occurs at a critical point.

Example 5. You have a piece of wire 24 cm long. You cut off x centimetres and bend it into a circle. The remaining $(24 - x)$ centimetres you bend into a square. How should you choose x if you want the sum of the areas of the circle and the square to be as large as possible?

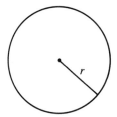 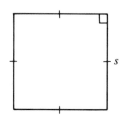

Solution. If the circle has radius r centimetres and the square has side s centimetres, then the circle has circumference $C = 2\pi r = x$ and the square has perimeter $P = 4s = 24 - x$.

Thus, $r = \dfrac{x}{2\pi}$ and $s = \dfrac{24 - x}{4}$

The sum of the areas of the circle and the square is

$$A(x) = \pi r^2 + s^2$$

$$= \frac{x^2}{4\pi} + \frac{(24 - x)^2}{16}$$

$$= \frac{x^2}{4\pi} + \frac{1}{16}(24^2 - 48x + x^2)$$

We have two endpoints to consider: $x = 0$ and $x = 24$

$$A(0) = \frac{24^2}{16} \qquad A(24) = \frac{24^2}{4\pi}$$

$$= 36 \qquad\qquad \doteq 45.84$$

Evidently $A(24) > A(0)$; if we use the whole wire for the circle we get a larger area than if we use it all for the square.

Now look for critical points.

$$0 = \frac{dA}{dx} = \frac{x}{2\pi} - \frac{48}{16} + \frac{x}{8}$$

$$\frac{x}{2\pi} - 3 + \frac{x}{8} = 0$$

$$x\left(\frac{1}{2\pi} + \frac{1}{8}\right) = 3$$

$$\frac{x(4 + \pi)}{8\pi} = 3$$

$$x = \frac{24\pi}{\pi + 4}$$

The solution $x = \dfrac{24\pi}{\pi + 4}$ lies between 0 and 24.

The corresponding area is

$$\frac{1}{4\pi}\left(\frac{24^2\pi^2}{(\pi+4)^2}\right) + \frac{1}{16}\left(576 - \frac{48 \times 24\pi}{\pi+4} + \frac{24^2\pi^2}{(\pi+4)^2}\right) \doteq 20.16$$

Observe that this value is even smaller than $A(0)$.

    The largest total area for the circle and square occurs at the endpoint $x = 24$ when we use the whole wire for the circle. In this case, the critical point $x = \dfrac{24\pi}{\pi+4}$ gives the *minimum* possible total area. The other endpoint $x = 0$ gives a local (but not global) maximum.

EXERCISES 10-10

Ⓑ

1. The sum of two numbers is 13. What is the largest possible value for their product?

2. The product of two positive numbers is 8. What is the smallest possible value for their sum?

3. Show that among all rectangles having a given area A, the one with the least perimeter is a square.

4. Show that among all isosceles triangles with given perimeter P, the one with the largest area is equilateral. (Hint: maximize the square of the area.)

5. Triangle PQR has a right angle at R and area A square centimetres. Find the maximum area of a rectangle which will fit inside the triangle if:
   a) one vertex of the rectangle lies at R
   b) one side of the rectangle lies along PQ.

6. A rectangular box with no top is made from a square of cardboard 20 cm on each side by cutting equal squares of side x centimetres from the four corners and bending up the four resulting flaps to form the sides of the box. What should x be to give the box with the largest possible volume?

7. Repeat *Exercise 6* starting with a rectangular sheet of cardboard 70 cm by 150 cm.

8. Find the shortest distance from the origin to the point (x,y) on the straight line $3x - 4y = 5$ by minimizing the square of the distance expressed as a function of either x or y.

9. Find the shortest distance from the origin to points on the curve $x^2y^4 = 32$. (Hint: minimize the square of the distance from $(0,0)$ to (x,y) on the curve expressed as a function of y alone.)

10. A circular cone of base radius r and height h has volume $V = \frac{1}{3}\pi r^2 h$. Find the base radius and height of the cone of largest volume which will fit inside a sphere of radius R centimetres.

Review Exercises

1. Find the limit of each sequence whose nth term is given. If the limit does not exist, explain why.

   a) $4 - \dfrac{2}{n}$

   b) $\dfrac{3 - n}{2n + 1}$

   c) $\dfrac{3 - n^2}{2n + 1}$

   d) $\left(\dfrac{2n}{n + 1}\right)^3$

   e) $\dfrac{8 + 2n^2 - 3n^3}{5n^3 + 6n + 7}$

   f) $\dfrac{\sqrt{3 + n^2}}{n}$

2. Evaluate each limit.

   a) $\displaystyle\lim_{x \to 0} \dfrac{4 - x^2}{16 - x^4}$

   b) $\displaystyle\lim_{x \to 2} \dfrac{4 - x^2}{16 - x^4}$

   c) $\displaystyle\lim_{x \to -2} \dfrac{4 - x^2}{x^2 + 2x}$

   d) $\displaystyle\lim_{x \to -1} \dfrac{x^3 + 1}{x^2 + 3x + 2}$

   e) $\displaystyle\lim_{h \to 0} \dfrac{(1 + h)^2 - (1 - h)^2}{h}$

   f) $\displaystyle\lim_{h \to 3} \dfrac{\sqrt{6 + h} - 3}{\sqrt{1 + h} - 1}$

3. Find the derivative of each function using the definition of derivative as the limit of the Newton quotient.

   a) $x^2 - x$ b) $2x - x^3$ c) $(x + 1)^2$ d) $\dfrac{1}{x + 1}$ e) $\dfrac{x}{x + 1}$ f) $\sqrt{1 + x}$

4. Find the equation of the tangent to each curve at the point specified.

   a) $y = 3x^2 - x$ at $(1, 2)$

   b) $y = \sqrt{x}$ at $(4, 2)$

   c) $y = x^3 - 5x + 1$ at $(2, -1)$

   d) $y = \dfrac{-2}{x}$ at $(-2, 1)$

5. Use differentiation rules to find each derivative.

   a) $1 + 2x + 3x^2 + 4x^3$

   b) $2\sqrt{x} - \dfrac{4}{x}$

   c) $\dfrac{x^3}{3} + \dfrac{x^2}{4} - \dfrac{x}{5} - \dfrac{1}{6}$

   d) $(3 + 2x^2 + x^3)(1 + x - x^2)$

   e) $\dfrac{1}{x^2 + 3x + 5}$

   f) $\dfrac{x^2 - 1}{x^2 + 2}$

6. The position x of a moving particle is given at time t by $x = t^3 - 3t^2 + 2t$. At what times is the particle:

   a) moving to the left   b) stopped   c) moving to the right?

7. What is the acceleration at time t of the moving particle of *Exercise 6*?

8. Use the derivative to help you sketch the graph of each function.

   a) $y = x^2 + 4x$ b) $y = 1 + x - x^2$ c) $y = x^3 + x^2$

   d) $y = x^3 - x + 1$ e) $y = x^4 - 2x^2 - 1$ f) $y = 4x^3 - x^4$

9. The sum of two positive numbers is 10. What is the smallest possible value for the sum of their squares?

1. If a principal P dollars is invested in an account which pays $r\%$ interest per annum compounded semi-annually, then the amount A dollars in the account after n years is given by this formula.

$$A = P\left(1 + \frac{r}{200}\right)^{2n}$$

Find the amount of each investment.
a) \$1000 at 8% compounded semi-annually for 3 years
b) \$5000 at 9.5% compounded semi-annually for 6 years
c) \$4250 at 12.5% compounded semi-annually for 7.5 years

2. Evaluate.
   a) $9^{\frac{3}{2}}$
   b) $64^{\frac{1}{3}}$
   c) $125^{-\frac{2}{3}}$
   d) $(2.75)^0$

3. Simplify.
   a) $\dfrac{12x^3y^{-2} \times 5x^{-7}y^5}{15xy^{-3}}$
   b) $\dfrac{-18m^{-4}n^{-2} \times 15m^2n^{-7}}{-10m^2n^{-3} \times 6m^9n^{-4}}$

4. Evaluate to the nearest thousandth.
   a) $5.7^{3.1}$
   b) $12.8^{-1.7}$
   c) $127^{0.68}$
   d) $\log 68$
   e) $\log_8 256$
   f) $\log_{\sqrt{5}} 0.04$
   g) $\log_{2.3} 17.6$
   h) $\log_{0.4} 2.13$

5. Solve.
   a) $\log x = -2$
   b) $\log_x 27 = \dfrac{3}{2}$
   c) $\log_4 x = \dfrac{7}{2}$
   d) $3^x = 12$
   e) $5^{x+3} = 83$
   f) $7^{x-3} = 3^{x+1}$

6. Express as a single logarithm.
   a) $\log 12 + \log 8 - \log 16$
   b) $\log_4 (x + 5) + \log_4 (2x - 3) - \log_4 (x + 4)$

7. If $\log 12 = x$ and $\log 4 = y$, write each logarithm in terms of x and y.
   a) $\log 3$
   b) $\log 0.75$
   c) $\log 480$
   d) $\log \left(\dfrac{16}{3}\right)$

8. If $\log 11 \doteq 1.0414$, find an approximation for each logarithm.
   a) $\log 121$
   b) $\log \sqrt{11}$
   c) $\log 110$
   d) $\log \left(\dfrac{1}{11}\right)$

9. Solve and check.
   a) $\log_3 x + \log_3 (x + 24) = 4$
   b) $\log_{\sqrt{7}} (x + 4) + \log_{\sqrt{7}} (x - 2) = 2$

10. Classify each sequence as arithmetic or geometric, and find the value of d or r.
   a) 2, 6, 18, 54, . . .
   b) 3, 7, 11, 15, . . .
   c) 15, 9, 3, −3, . . .
   d) 45, 30, 20, $\dfrac{40}{3}$, . . .

11. Write the first 4 terms of the sequence defined by each expression.

    a) $t_n = 5n - 2$ b) $t_n = 2n^2 - 3n$ c) $t_n = \dfrac{n + 2}{2n - 1}$

    d) $t_n = 3 + 2^{n-1}$ e) $a = -4, d = -2$ f) $a = -16, r = -\dfrac{1}{2}$

12. Write an expression for the general term of each sequence.
    a) $-5, 3, 11, 19, \ldots$ b) $3, 15, 75, 375, \ldots$
    c) $25, 18, 11, 4, \ldots$ d) $48, 36, 27, \dfrac{81}{4}$

13. Find: i) t_5 ii) t_{11} iii) t_n for each sequence.
    a) $5, 15, 45, 135, \ldots$ b) $56, 45, 34, 23, \ldots$
    c) $3, 15, 27, 39, \ldots$ d) $40, 20, 10, 5, \ldots$

14. Find x and y if $3, x, 27, y$ are consecutive terms of:
    a) an arithmetic sequence   b) a geometric sequence.

15. Find how many terms there are in each sequence.
    a) $2, 10, 50, \ldots, 781\ 250$ b) $3, 11, 19, \ldots, 171$
    c) $172, 164, 156, \ldots, -124$ d) $729, 243, 81, \ldots, \dfrac{1}{729}$

16. Find the first 4 terms of each sequence.

    a) $t_1 = 2, t_n = 2t_{n-1} + 3, n > 1$ b) $t_1 = 12, t_n = \dfrac{1}{2}t_{n-1} + 4$

17. Find S_6 and S_n for each series.
    a) $-5 + 1 + 7 + 13 + \ldots$ b) $2 + 4 + 8 + 16 + \ldots$
    c) $27 - 9 + 3 - 1 + \ldots$ d) $42 + 31 + 20 + 9 + \ldots$

18. Find the sum of each infinite geometric series.

    a) $24 + 12 + 6 + 3 + \ldots$ b) $72 + 48 + 32 + \dfrac{64}{3} + \ldots$

19. How many terms of the series $-24 - 15 - 6 + 3 + \ldots$ add to 3696?

20. Simplify.

    a) $\displaystyle\sum_{i=1}^{6} (2i + 3)$ b) $\displaystyle\sum_{n=1}^{8} (10 - 2n)$ c) $\displaystyle\sum_{k=1}^{7} (3 + 2^{k-1})$

21. Two circles share a common tangent GF, where E is the point of tangency. AB and CD are line segments through E with endpoints on the circles. Prove that AC is parallel to DB.

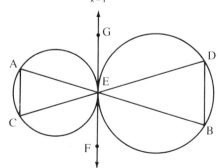

22. For each diagram, name the triangles that must be proved congruent to prove what is required, and name the congruence condition.
    a) *Required to Prove:*   b) *Required to Prove:*   c) *Required to Prove:*
        FG = HK   JM = KL   XU = VW

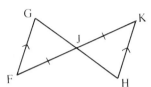 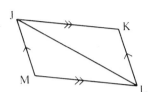 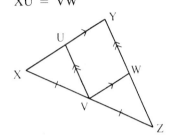

23. PA and PB are tangents to a circle with centre O. Prove that $\angle APO = \angle BPO$.

24. The bisectors of $\angle Q$ and $\angle R$ of $\triangle PQR$ meet at point S. Prove that S is equidistant from all three sides of $\triangle PQR$.

25. Prove that in any parallelogram the opposite angles are congruent and the opposite sides are congruent.

26. Find the slope and the equation of the tangent to the curve at each point indicated.
    a) $f(x) = 2x^3 - x^2 + 3x + 5$ at $(-1, -1)$
    b) $f(x) = 3(x - 1)^2 + 4$ at $(2, 7)$

27. Find the limit of each sequence whose nth term is given. If the limit does not exist, explain why.
    a) $\dfrac{2n + 3}{n}$ b) $\dfrac{n^2 + n - 8}{2n^2 + 7n + 5}$ c) $\dfrac{n^2 + 5}{n - 1}$

28. Evaluate each limit.
    a) $\displaystyle\lim_{x\to\infty} \dfrac{3x + 7}{x - 2}$ b) $\displaystyle\lim_{x\to 0} \dfrac{x^2 + 3x}{2x}$ c) $\displaystyle\lim_{x\to\infty} \dfrac{3^x}{4^x}$

29. Find the derivative of each expression.
    a) $5x^3 + 2x^2 - x + 7$ b) $3\sqrt{x} + \dfrac{5}{x}$

    c) $(2x + 7)(x^2 - 3x + 5)$ d) $\dfrac{x^2 - 7x + 3}{2x^2 - 5x}$

30. The position x metres of a particle after t seconds of motion is given by $x = t^3 + 6t^2 - 15t$. Determine:
    a) the velocity and acceleration after 2 s
    b) the times when the velocity is zero
    c) the average velocity from $t = 1$ to $t = 3$.

31. Two equal rectangular playing fields have one side in common. They are enclosed and divided with 600 m of fencing. Find the largest possible area for each field.

Answers

Chapter 1

1. a) Function
2. a) Domain: February to October; range, about 75.5¢ to 80.2¢
   b) Domain: 0 km to 50 km; range: 20°C to 29°C
3. a), c) Functions
4. a) R; R   b) R; $\{y \mid y \geq 0, y \in R\}$
   c) $\{x \mid x \geq -1, x \in R\}$; $\{y \mid y \geq 0, y \in R\}$
   d), f) Not functions   e) R; $\{y \mid y > 0, y \in R\}$
5. a), b) R; R
   c) $\{x \mid x \leq 1, x \in R\}$; $\{y \mid y \geq 0, y \in R\}$
   d) $\{x \mid x \neq 0, x \in R\}$; $\{y \mid y \neq 0, y \in R\}$
   e) $\{x \mid x \neq \pm 1, x \in R\}$; $\{y \mid y \neq 0, y \in R\}$
   f) $\{x \mid x \neq \pm 2, x \in R\}$;
      $\{y \mid y \leq 0 \text{ or } y > 1, y \in R\}$
6. a) 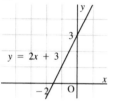   b)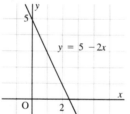

c) 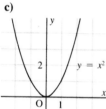   d)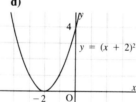

e)   f)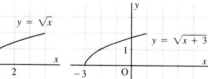

7. a) i) 100 kPa   ii) 85 kPa   iii) 80 kPa
   iv) 40 kPa   v) 28 kPa   b) 6.5 km
   c) Domain: 0 km to 14 km;
      range: 23 kPa to 100 kPa
8. a) 560 km, 360 km, 272 km, 240 km
   b) Domain: 0.025 m² to 0.6 m²;
      range: 28 km/h to 100 km/h

c) Domain would not change; the highest and lowest values of the range would increase.

9. a) 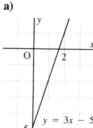   b)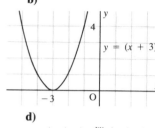

c) 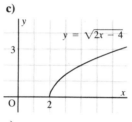   d)

e) 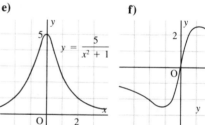   f)

10. a) Hammer-fist strike   i) 2.5 m/s, 5 m/s
    ii) 12 m/s Forward karate punch
    i) 3.8 m/s, 5.1 m/s   ii) 6.8 m/s
    b) Speed decreases because it's after the punch; speed increasing before the strike.

1. a) 4   b) 7   c) 3   d) 4   e) 7   f) 12
2. a) -1 b) 5   c) 11   d) 1   e) -11 f) 2
3. a) $-17, 18, -4.5$ b) 4, 11, -4.75
   c) 6, 20, -0.25
4. a) $-3, 2, -2$ b) 4, $-2, -1$
5. a) 30   b) 24   c) 0   d) 10   e) 2   f) 1.25
6. a) -5 b) -8 c) -20 d) -6
   e) -50 f) -8

7. a) i) 1 **ii)** 2 **iii)** 3 **b) i)** 9 **ii)** 90 **iii)** 900
8. a) $2a + 1$ **b)** $6a + 1$ **c)** $3 + 2y$
d) $2x + 3$ **e)** $3 - y$ **f)** $1 + y$
g) $4 - z$ **h)** $6 - 2x$ **i)** $4x + 2$
j) $15 - 5n$ **k)** $-6x - 3$ **l)** $2a - 6$
9. a) R; R **b)** R; $\{y \mid y \geq 0, y \in R\}$

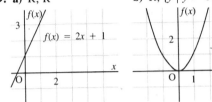

c) $\{x \mid x \geq 0; x \in R\}$; $\{y \mid y \geq 0, y \in R\}$

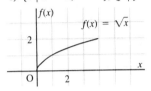

10. a) -4 **b)** -7 **c)** 8 **d)** 6 **e)** 6 **f)** 3
11. a) $\dfrac{2x + 1}{2x - 1}, x \neq \dfrac{1}{2}$ **b)** $\dfrac{x - 1}{x + 1}, x \neq -1$

c) $\dfrac{1 + x}{1 - x}, x \neq 1$ **d)** $\dfrac{1 + x}{1 - x}, x \neq 1$

e) $\dfrac{x + 2}{x}, x \neq 0$ **f)** $\dfrac{-x}{x - 2}, x \neq 2$

g) $\dfrac{x + 1}{x}, x \neq 0$ **h)** $\dfrac{x - 1}{x}, x \neq 0$

12. a) $\frac{2}{3}$ **b)** -2 **c)** 2 **d)** 1 **e)** $\frac{1}{4}$
13. a) $\frac{5}{3}$ **b)** 2 **c)** $\frac{1}{3}$ **d)** 0 **e)** No solution
14. a) i) 6 **ii)** 14 **iii)** 14
b) i) 1, 10, 100, 1000, etc.
ii) 2, 11, 20, 200, 101, 110, etc.
c) i), ii) Infinite number
16. a) i) 0 **ii)** 2 **iii)** 1 **iv)** 2 **b) i)** 30 **ii)** 210
17. b) i) 4, 6, 8, 10, 12, etc. **ii)** 3, 5, 7, 9, etc.
18. a) i) 1, 4, 9, 16 **ii)** 1, 4, 9, 16 **b)** $f(x) = x^2$
20. Answers may vary; for example, 2^x, 2^y

Mathematics Around Us, page 13

1. 4.5, 18 **2.** 4 km
3. The graph would be stretched vertically by a factor of 4.

Exercises 1-3, page 16

1. a) 7 **b)** 22 **c)** 10 **d)** 21
2. $6x + 4$; $6x + 3$
3. a) 5 **b)** 10 **c)** 4 **d)** 17
4. $2x^2 + 2$; $4x^2 + 1$
5. a) $-6x + 19$; $-6x - 3$
b) $4x^2 + 14x + 6$; $2x^2 + 10x + 1$
c) $32x^2 - 100x + 78$; $-8x^2 + 12x + 3$
6. a) $3x^2 + 12x + 11$; $3x^2 + 1$
b) $12x^2 - 12x + 2$; $3 - 6x^2$
c) $3x^4 - 1$; $9x^4 - 6x^2 + 1$
d) $3x^4 + 6x^3 + 3x^2 - 1$; $9x^4 - 3x^2$
e) $12x^4 - 36x^3 + 27x^2 - 1$; $18x^4 - 21x^2 + 5$
f) $\dfrac{3}{x^2} - 1$; $\dfrac{1}{3x^2 - 1}$

7. $A = \dfrac{\pi d^2}{4}$ **8.** $\dfrac{\pi d^3}{6}$

9. a) -11 **b)** -8 **c)** 5 **d)** 16
10. a) $1 - 6x$ **b)** $4 - 6x$ **c)** $4x - 3$
d) $9x - 2$
11. a) 4 **b)** 30 **c)** -1 **d)** 0
12. a) $4 - x - x^2$ **b)** $20 - 9x + x^2$ **c)** x
d) $x^4 + 2x^3 + 2x^2 + x$
13. a) $\sqrt{4 - 2x}$; $4 - 2\sqrt{x}$; $\sqrt[4]{x}$; $4x - 4$
b) $\sqrt{2 + 6x}$; $1 + 3\sqrt{2x}$; $\sqrt{2\sqrt{2x}}$; $9x + 4$
c) $\dfrac{x^2 - 1}{x^2}$; $\dfrac{x^2}{(x + 1)^2} - 1$; $\dfrac{x}{2x + 1}$; $x^4 - 2x^2$
d) 2^{3x-4}; $3(2^x) - 4$; 2^{2x}; $9x - 16$

14. $A = \dfrac{P^2}{16}$ **15.** $A = \dfrac{d^2}{2}$ **17. b)** No

18. $T = 0.05t + 20$ **19. a)** 0, -6 **b)** -1
20. a) $f(k(x))$ **b)** $g(e(x))$ **c)** $f(e(x))$
d) $k(e(x))$ or $e(k(x))$
21. Answers may vary; for example,
a) $f(x) = x^2$; $g(x) = x^3 + 1$; $f(g(x))$
b) $f(x) = x^2 + 3x + 4$; $g(x) = x - 4$; $f(g(x))$
c) $f(x) = \sqrt{x}$; $g(x) = 3x - 2$; $f(g(x))$
d) $f(x) = \dfrac{1}{x}$; $g(x) = x + 3$; $f(g(x))$

22. a) $\sqrt{x} - 3$ **b)** $\{x \mid x \geq 0, x \in R\}$
c) $\{y \mid y \geq -3, y \in R\}$ **d)** $\sqrt{x - 3}$
e) $\{x \mid x \geq 3, x \in R\}$ **f)** $\{y \mid y \geq 0, y \in R\}$
23. a) x **b)** R **c)** R **d)** $\sqrt{x^2}$
e) R **f)** $\{y \mid y \geq 0, y \in R\}$

24. a) $\dfrac{x - 1}{x}, x \neq 0$ **b)** $\dfrac{1}{x}, x \neq 0$

25. a) i) $4x + 3$ **ii)** $8x + 7$ **iii)** $16x + 15$
b) i) $32x + 31$ **ii)** $2^n x + 2^n - 1$

26. a) i) $\dfrac{x}{2x + 1}, x \neq -\dfrac{1}{2}$ **ii)** $\dfrac{x}{3x + 1}, x \neq -\dfrac{1}{3}$

iii) $\dfrac{x}{4x + 1}, x \neq -\dfrac{1}{4}$

b) i) $\dfrac{x}{5x + 1}, x \neq -\dfrac{1}{5}$ **ii)** $\dfrac{x}{nx + 1}, x \neq -\dfrac{1}{n}$

27. $d(a - 1) = b(c - 1)$

Exercises 1-4, page 24

1. a), b) Yes **c)** No

2. a) $y = \dfrac{x - 5}{2}$, yes **b)** $y = \pm\sqrt{\dfrac{4 + x}{3}}$, no

c) $y = \dfrac{10 - 2x}{5}$, yes **d)** $y = \pm\dfrac{\sqrt{x + 1}}{2}$, no

e) $f^{-1}(x) = \dfrac{3}{1 - x}$, yes **f)** $f^{-1}(x) = \dfrac{4x - 3}{2}$, yes

3. a)   **b)**

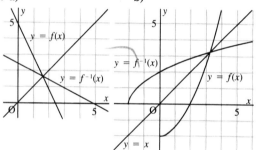

c)   **d)**

4. a) $f^{-1}(x) = \dfrac{x - 3}{2}$; R; R

b) $y = \pm\sqrt{\dfrac{x + 3}{2}}$; not a function

c) $h^{-1}(x) = \dfrac{1}{x} - 1$; $\{x \mid x \neq 0, x \in R\}$;
$\{y \mid y \neq -1, y \in R\}$
d) $y = -1 \pm \sqrt{x}$; not a function
e) $g^{-1}(x) = \dfrac{1}{x - 1}$; $\{x \mid x \neq 1, x \in R\}$;
$\{y \mid y \neq 0, y \in R\}$
f) $y = x^2 + 2$; $\{x \mid x \geq 0, x \in R\}$;
$\{y \mid y \geq 2, y \in R\}$

5. Answers may vary. Typical answers are:
a) $y = x^2 - 2, x \geq 0$

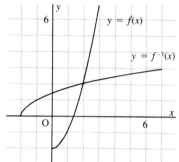

b) $y = 2(x + 1)^2 - 3, x \geq -1$

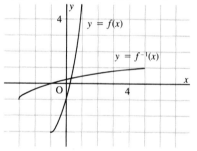

c) $y = -x^2 + 5, x \geq 0$

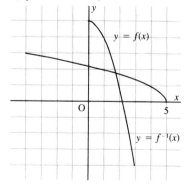

d) $y = -\frac{1}{2}x^2 + 2,\ x \geqslant 0$

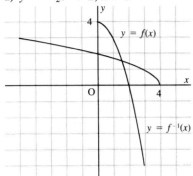

e) $y = (x - 1)^2 - 1,\ x \geqslant 1$

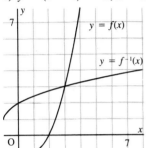

f) $y = -(x - 3)^2 + 4,\ x \geqslant 3$

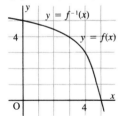

6. a) $f^{-1}(x) = \dfrac{x - 1}{x},\ x \neq 0$

b) $f^{-1}(x) = \dfrac{2x + 2}{1 - x},\ x \neq 1$

c) $y = \pm\sqrt{\dfrac{4x}{x - 2}},\ x \neq 2$

d) $y = \pm\sqrt{\dfrac{1 - 4x}{3x}},\ x \neq 0$

7. a) Yes   **b)** No   **c)** Yes   **d)** Yes

8. a) $\dfrac{x - 5}{2}$ **b)** x **c)** x

9. a) $\dfrac{1 + x}{1 - x}$ **b)** x **c)** x **10.** The line $y = x$

12. Yes, except $y = k$, whose inverse is $x = k$, which is not a function.

13. Yes, the inverse of the inverse is the original function.

14. a) $x \geqslant -1$ or $x \leqslant -1$ **b)** $x \geqslant 0$ or $x \leqslant 0$

c) $x \geqslant -\frac{3}{2}$ or $x \leqslant -\frac{3}{2}$

Exercises 1-5, page 29

1. a) $\pm\,2.74$ **b)** $\pm\,5.66$ **c)** $\pm\,2.24$
d) $\pm\,6.93$ **e)** $\pm\,2.26$ **f)** $\pm\,3.92$

2. a) $2, 7$ **b)** $5, -3$ **c)** $3, 11$ **d)** $-4, -8$
e) $2, -9$ **f)** $-6, -9$

3. a) $-2, -3$ **b)** $0, 4$ **c)** $\frac{1}{2}, -3$ **d)** $-\frac{2}{3}, 1$

e) $-\frac{1}{3}, \frac{3}{2}$ **f)** 2

4. a)

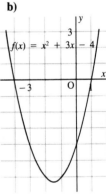

b)

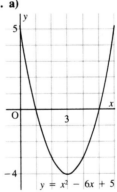

c)

d)

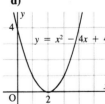

e)

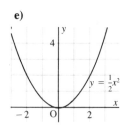

f)

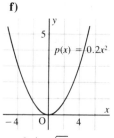

5. a) $\frac{2}{3}, 1$ **b)** $-\frac{1}{5}, -1$ **c)** $\frac{3 \pm \sqrt{11}}{2}$ **d)** 3

e) $\frac{13 \pm \sqrt{89}}{4}$ **f)** $-\frac{1}{2}, \frac{3}{2}$

6. a) $\frac{-7 \pm \sqrt{97}}{2}$ **b)** $4 \pm \sqrt{2}$ **c)** $\frac{-5 \pm \sqrt{13}}{6}$

d) $\frac{5}{4}, 1$ **e), f)** No real roots

7. a) $\frac{-5 \pm \sqrt{15}}{2}$ **b)** $-\frac{3}{2}, -\frac{7}{2}$ **c)** $-\frac{5}{2}$

8. a) $(x-3)(x-7) = 0$ **b)** $(x+4)(x-9) = 0$

c) $(x-\frac{2}{3})(x+5) = 0$

9. Answers may vary.

a) $f(x) = (x-4)(x+1)$; $g(x) = 2(x-4)(x+1)$

b) $f(x) = (x+3)(x-2)$; $g(x) = 2(x+3)(x-2)$

c) $f(x) = (x-\frac{3}{5})(x+\frac{4}{3})$; $g(x) = 15(x-\frac{3}{5})(x+\frac{4}{3})$

10. a) $f(x) = \frac{8}{3}(x-1)(x-3)$ **b)** $f(x) = \frac{4}{3}(x-1)(x-3)$

11. a) $f(x) = 2(x+1)(x-1)$

b) $f(x) = -(x+1)(x-1)$

c) $f(x) = 4(x+1)(x-1)$

12. a) $s = \sqrt{\dfrac{d}{0.05}}$ **b) i)** 4.5 m/s   **ii)** 6.3 m/s

iii) 10.0 m/s   **c) i)** Increased by a factor $\sqrt{2}$
ii) Increased by a factor $\sqrt{3}$

13. a) 629.757 184 3 or -635.157 184 3
b) 3461.401 917 or -3466.801 917

14. a) 1   **b)** 73   **c)** -39 **d)** 0   **e)** 121
f) -68

15. a) a, b, and e   **b)** d   **c)** c and f

16. a) $(3\sqrt{5} - 3)$ cm   **b)** $(27\sqrt{5} - 45)$ cm²

17. a), b), d) 2 different real roots
e) 2 equal real roots   **c), f)** no real roots

18. a) $-1, 0.2$ **b)** $\frac{4 \pm \sqrt{6}}{2}$ **c)** $\frac{-5 \pm \sqrt{13}}{6}$

d) No real roots   **e)** $2, \frac{2}{3}$ **f)** No real roots

19. a) $-4 \pm \sqrt{15}$ **b)** $-0.8, -1$ **c)** $-\frac{2}{3}$
d) $8 \pm \sqrt{102}$

20. a) $5, -3.5$ **b)** $\frac{1 \pm \sqrt{217}}{4}$ **c)** $\frac{11 \pm \sqrt{185}}{2}$
d) $0.8, 2$

21. $4\sqrt{3}$

22. 3 cm, 5 cm; two different triangles can be drawn from the given information

23. $4\sqrt{3}$ cm

24. No   **25. b)** $\frac{2n + 1}{n}$

Problem Solving, page 35

1. a) $1 + \sqrt{5}$

2. Answers will vary. Two answers are $5 = 9 - 4$ and $20 = 36 - 16$. All odd numbers, and all even numbers which are divisible by 4 can be expressed as the difference of two squares.

3. $\frac{37}{64}$

5. $5x + 12y - 13 = 0$

6. 2^{97}

7. 733

8. $4x - 6y + 5 = 0$

9. $\left(\dfrac{x_1(1 - m^2) + 2m(y_1 - b)}{1 + m^2}, \dfrac{y_1(m^2 - 1) + 2(mx_1 + b)}{1 + m^2} \right)$

Exercises 1-6, page 39

1. a) $\sqrt{5}i$ **b)** $7i$ **c)** $2 - 3i$ **d)** $-3 + 8i$
e) $13 - i$ **f)** $33 - 56i$

5. a) $\pm 2i$ **b)** $\pm 3i$ **c)** $\pm 5i$ **d)** $\pm 2\sqrt{3}i$
e) $\pm 3\sqrt{2}i$ **f)** $1 \pm i$

6. a) $10 + 6i$ **b)** 34   **c)** $7 - 4i$ **d)** $43 - 18i$
e) $8 - 16i$ **f)** $-60 - 63i$

7. a) $\frac{-3 \pm \sqrt{11}i}{2}$ **b)** $2 \pm i$ **c)** $\frac{-1 \pm \sqrt{7}i}{2}$

d) $1 \pm \sqrt{2}i$ **e)** $\frac{5 \pm \sqrt{3}i}{2}$ **f)** $\frac{-3 \pm \sqrt{7}i}{4}$

8. a) $\frac{2 \pm \sqrt{2}i}{3}$ **b)** $\frac{1 \pm \sqrt{5}i}{3}$ **c)** $\frac{-\sqrt{2}}{2}$

d) $1 \pm 2i$ **e)** $\frac{2 \pm \sqrt{10}i}{7}$ **f)** $-2 \pm \sqrt{11}$

9. $1 + i, 1 - i$

Investigate, page 39

$-\frac{1}{5} + \frac{8}{5}i$

Yes, provided the divisor is not 0.

Review Exercises, page 40

1. a) R; R

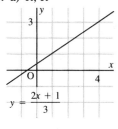

$y = \frac{2x + 1}{3}$

b) R; $\{y \mid y \geq -3, y \in R\}$

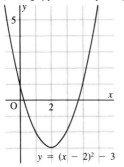

$y = (x - 2)^2 - 3$

c) $\{x \mid x \geq 0, x \in R\}$; $\{y \mid y \geq 1, y \in R\}$

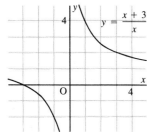

$y = \frac{x + 3}{x}$

2. a) -17 **b)** $10a - 2$ **c)** $5x + 3$
  d) $15n - 12$

3. a) -2 **b)** -2 **c)** $1 - 6x^2$ **d)** $x^2 - 6$
  e) $19 - 6x - 3x^2$ **f)** $9x^2 - 30x + 19$
  g) $x^2 - 4x + 3$ **h)** $x^2 + 5x - 9$

4. a) $\frac{1}{2}, 2$ **b)** $-\frac{3}{2}, 4$ **c)** $-\frac{3}{4}, 2$

5. a) 2   **b)** $\frac{a + 2}{a - 2}, a \neq 2$ **c)** $\frac{3x - 1}{x - 1}, x \neq 1$
  d) $\frac{x + 1}{x - 1}, x \neq 1$

6. a) 11   **b)** -9 **c)** 35   **d)** -7
  e) $6x - 1$ **f)** $\frac{2x - 3}{3}$ **g)** $\frac{2x - 7}{3}$
  h) $\frac{3x + 3}{2}$

7. a) $2x^2 - 6x + 9$ **b)** $4x^2 + 14x + 12$
  c) $4x + 15$ **d)** $x^4 - 6x^3 + 10x^2 - 3x$
  e) $\frac{x^2 - 3x - 3}{2}$ **f)** $\frac{x^2 - 16x + 63}{4}$
  g) x **h)** $\frac{x - 15}{4}$

8. a) $y = -3x + 7$, yes
  b) $y = \pm \sqrt{\dfrac{5x + 1}{2}}$, no
  c) $y = \dfrac{2x + 1}{x - 3}$, yes

9. a) R; R; yes   **b)** $\{x \mid x \geq 3, x \in R\}$; R; no

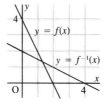

$y = f(x)$
$y = f^{-1}(x)$

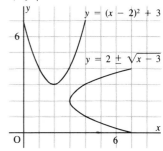

$y = (x - 2)^2 + 3$
$y = 2 \pm \sqrt{x - 3}$

c) $\{x \mid x \geq -2, x \in R\}$; $\{y \mid y \geq -1, y \in R\}$; yes

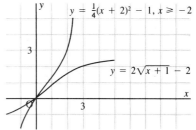

$y = \frac{1}{4}(x + 2)^2 - 1, x \geq -2$
$y = 2\sqrt{x + 1} - 2$

10. a) $-1.5, 4$ **b)** $-2.5, 0.5$ **c)** $-4, -\frac{2}{3}$

11. a) No real roots   **b)** 2 different real roots
  c) 2 equal real roots

12. a) $\frac{6 \pm \sqrt{6}}{6}$ **b)** $\frac{-3 \pm \sqrt{177}}{14}$

13. a) $-9 + 6i$ **b)** 13   **c)** $28 - 21i$

14. a) $\frac{1 \pm \sqrt{11}i}{2}$ **b)** $\frac{7 \pm \sqrt{35}i}{6}$ **c)** $\frac{-3 \pm \sqrt{23}i}{4}$

Chapter 2

Exercises 2-1, page 44

1. a) 1.7   **b)** 2.3   **c)** −2.7, −1.1, 0.5, 3.3
   d) −2.9, −1.4, 0, 1.4, 2.9

2. a) 0, ± 3.2   **b)** −3.6, 2

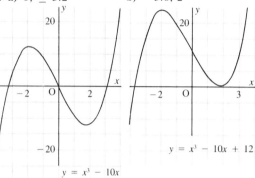

$$y = x^3 - 10x$$

$$y = x^3 - 10x + 12$$

c) −2, −1.5, 3.7   **d)** 4

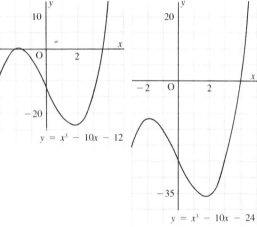

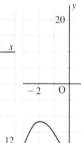

$$y = x^3 - 10x - 12$$

$$y = x^3 - 10x - 24$$

3. a) −3.5, −0.7, 4.2   **b)** 2.3

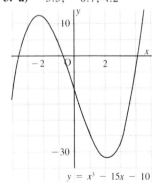

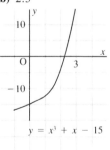

$$y = x^3 - 15x - 10$$

$$y = x^3 + x - 15$$

c) ± 1.2, ± 3.7

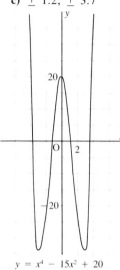

$$y = x^4 - 15x^2 + 20$$

d) −2.3, 3.2

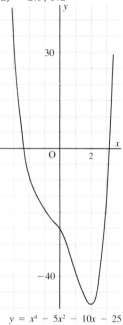

$$y = x^4 - 5x^2 - 10x - 25$$

4. a) 1.6   **b)** 3.5

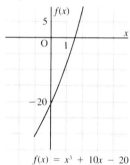

$$f(x) = x^3 + 10x - 20$$

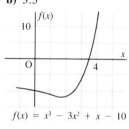

$$f(x) = x^3 - 3x^2 + x - 10$$

c) $-3.3, -0.6, 1.2, 2.7$ **d)** $-2.1, 3.2$

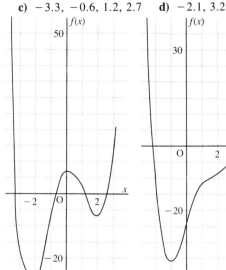

$f(x) = x^4 - 10x^2 + 5x + 7$

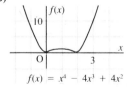

$f(x) = x^4 - 4x^3 + 16x - 25$

5. There could be 2 negative zeros which are approximately equal, or there could be no zeros.

6. Answers may vary.

7. Answers may vary.

a)

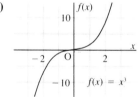

b) See *Exercise 2b*.   **c)** See *Example 2b*.
d) See *Exercise 2d*.

8. Answers may vary.

a)

b)

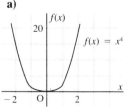

$f(x) = x^4 - 4x^3 + 4x^2$

c)

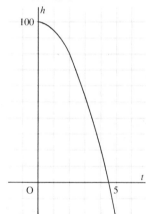

$f(x) = x^4 - 6x^3 + 8x^2$

d)

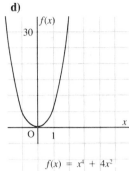

$f(x) = x^4 + 4x^2$

9. About 4.5 s

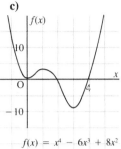

$h = 0.015t^3 - 4.9t^2 + 100$

10. a) i) $x^3 - 12x + 10 = 0$
ii) $x^3 - 12x + 20 = 0$, $x^3 - 12x - 20 = 0$
b) i) $-16 < k < 16$ **ii)** $k = \pm 16$
iii) $k > 16; k < -16$

11. a)

n	1	2	3	4	5	6
$n^3 + n^2$	2	12	36	80	150	252

n	7	8	9	10
$n^3 + n^2$	392	576	810	1100

b) 7   **c)** No

12. About 7.9 cm by 5.3 cm by 11.8 cm

Computer Power, page 47

1. a) $((5x + 2)x - 7)x + 8$; 8, 42, 140, 332, 648
b) $((2x - 5)x + 3)x - 9$; -9, -7, 9, 51, 131
c) $((6x + 1)x - 4)x + 12$; 15, 56, 171, 396, 767
d) $(((2x + 3)x - 5)x + 6)x - 11$; -5, 37, 205, 637, 1519

2. a) 24, 39, 56, 75, 96, 119, 144, 171, 200, 231
b) 7   **c) i)** 3   **ii)** 9   **iii)** 12

3. d) Linear function

Exercises 2-2, page 52

1. a) $x + 4$, R 2   **b)** $x - 1$, R 3
c) $c - 2$, R 4   **d)** $n - 16$, R 86

2. a) $x^2 - 2x + 4$, R -3
b) $m^2 - 3m - 7$, R -24
c) $3s^2 - s - 2$, R -2
d) $2x^2 - 5x - 12$

3. $x^3 - 2x^2 - 7x + 10$

4. $x^3 - x^2 - 11x + 12$

5. a) $2x + 3$, R -4 **b)** $3x + 8$, R 11
c) $5u - 3$, R 10   **d)** $3x - 6$, R 21
e) $4x + 3$, R 20   **f)** $3m - 2$, R -1

6. a) $c^2 + 4c + 3$, R -7
b) $x^2 - 6x - 11$, R 15
c) $1 + n - 2n^2$ **d)** $x^2 - 2x - 8$, R -4
e) $5a^2 + 8a + 3$, R 6
f) $m^2 + 3m - 10$, R -54

7. a) $x^2 - x - 2$, R 1   **b)** $-a^2 - 5a + 14$, R 2
c) $-3m^2 + 13m + 10$, R -3
d) $2s^2 - s - 6$

8. a) $(x - 3)(x - 4)$ **b)** $(3x + 1)(x - 1)$
c) $-(x + 1)^2$ **d)** $(5x - 2)(x + 5)$
e) $(2x + 3)(8x + 3)$ **f)** $(2x + 1)(-5x + 3)$

9. a) $x - 2$ **b)** $y - 3$, R $13y + 6$
c) $2a^2 - a + 3$, R 8   **d)** $3t^2 + 2t + 1$

10. a) $x^2 + 5x + 6$ **b)** $m^2 - 2m - 3$
c) $3x^2 - x - 10$, R -2 **d)** $a^2 - 4a - 12$, R 7

11. a) $(x - 3y)(x + 3y)$ **b)** $-(x + 4y)(x + 2y)$
c) $-(8a + 3b)(a - 3b)$
d) $-(3m + n)(m - 3n)$

12. a) $x^2 - 3$ **b)** $2a^2 + 3$ **c)** $3m^2 + 2$
d) $2x^2 + 3$

13. $(4x + 3)(x + 5)$

14. $(2a + 3)(3a - 2)$

15. a) $x^2 - x + 1$ **b)** $-5 - 2a + 3a^2$
c) $s^2 - 2s + 3$

16. a) $x^2 - x + 1$ **b)** $a^4 + a^3 + a^2 + a + 1$
c) $s^2 - st + t^2$ **d)** $m^2 - 2mn + 2n^2$

17. -21, -3 **18.** -8 **19.** $x^2 + bx + c$

20. a) $x^2 + (b + c)x + bc$
b) i) $x^2 + (a + c)x + ac$
ii) $x^2 + (a + b)x + ab$.

Investigate, page 53

1. a) 2   **b)** 2   **c)** 10, -70
d) When $f(x)$ is divided by $x - a$, the remainder is $f(a)$.

Exercises 2-3, page 56

1. a) $a^2 - 2a - 13 = (a + 3)(a - 5) + 2$
b) $x^3 + x^2 + x + 11 = (x + 2)(x^2 - x + 3) + 5$
c) $2p^3 + 5p^2 - 2p - 3$
$= (p + 1)(2p^2 + 3p - 5) + 2$
d) $2s^3 - 7s^2 + 16s - 22$
$= (2s - 3)(s^2 - 2s + 5) - 7$

2. a) 3   **b)** 14   **c)** 43   **d)** 11   **e)** 18   **f)** 19

3. a) -4 **b)** 11   **c)** 0   **d)** 16   **e)** 21
f) -43

4. a) 4   **b)** 44   **c)** 27   **d)** 7   **e)** 37   **f)** -1

5. a) 0   **b)** -6 **c)** 8   **d)** 1   **e)** 0   **f)** 2

6. a) 9   **b)** -9 **c)** 18   **d)** 43   **e)** 0
f) -16

7. a) 4   **b)** 2   **c)** 3

8. 3, -1 **9.** 1   **10. a)** 4   **b)** 3   **c)** 6

12. a) 11   **b)** -4 **c)** 5   **d)** $-\frac{3}{2}$

13. a) i), ii) No   **iii)** Yes   **b)** $7x - 5$

14. a) 1   **b)** $x + 10$ **c)** $x^2 - 2$

15. a) $f\left(-\dfrac{b}{a}\right)$ **b)** $\left(\dfrac{f(a) - f(b)}{a - b}\right)x + \dfrac{af(b) - bf(a)}{a - b}$

Exercises 2-4, page 61

4. 0   **5.** $x - 5$ **6.** a, b, d   **7.** a, c, d   **8.** b

9. a) $x^3 + 7x^2 + 7x - 15$
b) $x^3 - 5x^2 - 17x + 21$

10. $(y + 1)(y - 2)(y + 3)$ **11.** a, c   **12.** c, d

13. a) Yes   **b)** Yes   **c)** No

14. a) $(a - 2)(a - 1)(a - 3)$
b) $(a + 2)(a - 2)(a + 3)$
c) $(x + 3)(x + 2)(x - 1)$

15. a) Yes   **b)** No   **c)** Yes   **d)** No   **e)** Yes
f) Yes

16. a) $x - 1$ **b)** $x + 1$ **c)** $y + 1$ **d)** $x - 3$
e) $y - 2$ **f)** $x + 1$

17. b) $x - 4$ **18. b)** $2x - 1$

19. a) $(x - 1)(x - 3)(x - 4)$
b) $x^3 - 3x^2 + 3x - 1$; $x^3 - 3x + 2$

20. a) $(x-1)(x+2)(x+4)$
b) $(x+1)(x+3)(x+5)$
c) $(x+1)(x-4)(x+5)$
d) $(x+1)(x+2)(x-3)$
e) $(x-1)^2(5x+3)$ **f)** $(x-2)(x^2-7x+3)$
g) $(x+1)(x+2)(x+5)$
h) $(x+2)(x-3)(2x+1)$
21. a) $(x-3)(x^2-5x+2)$ **b)** $(x+2)^2(x-7)$
c) $(x+1)(x-4)(x+9)$
d) $(x+2)(x+4)(x-6)$
e) $(x+1)(x-2)(3x+5)$
f) $(x-2)(2x+1)(5x-3)$
g) $(x+2)(x+5)(x-7)$
h) $(x-3)(x+4)(3x+1)$
22. a) 11 **b)** -8 **c)** -4
23. Yes **24.** Yes **25.** Yes
26. a) $1, 5, -4$ **b)** $-2, 3, 7$ **c)** $1, -3, -\frac{1}{6}$
d) $-2, 5, -\frac{2}{5}$

Exercises 2-5, page 66

1. a) $0, 2, -5$ **b)** $0, -\frac{3}{2}, 4$ **c)** $0, -3, -7$
d) $0, -\frac{7}{3}, \frac{3}{2}$ **e)** $0, \pm 2$ **f)** $0, -2, -3$
2. a) 0 **b) i)** $-\frac{1}{2}, 3$ **ii)** $\pm\frac{3}{2}$ **iii)** $\frac{5}{2}, 3$
iv) $0, -\frac{2}{3}, -4$ **v)** $0, \pm\frac{5}{3}$ **vi)** $3, 4$
3. a) 2 **b)** $-5, \pm 3$ **c)** $-2, \frac{1}{2}, 3$ **d)** $\pm 2, \frac{2}{3}$
4. a) $-2, 3, -4$ **b)** 1 **c)** $1, 2, -\frac{3}{2}$
d) $-\frac{1}{2}, \pm\frac{3}{2}$
5. a) 2 **b)** $\pm 3, 2$ **c)** $-1, \dfrac{-4 \pm \sqrt{6}}{2}$ **d)** $\frac{2}{3}$
6. a) $-2, -3, -4$ **b)** $-4, -5, -6$
7. a) 3 **b)** -5
8. 10 cm by 6 cm by 1 cm or $\left(\dfrac{9-\sqrt{21}}{2}\right)$ cm by
$(3+\sqrt{21})$ cm by $(\sqrt{21}-1)$ cm
9. $\pm 22, \pm 23$
10. a) $x^3 - 8x^2 + 17x - 10 = 0$
b) $x^3 - 3x^2 - 3x + 1 = 0$
c) $2x^4 - x^3 - 19x^2 + 9x + 9 = 0$
d) $4x^3 - 8x^2 - 23x - 11 = 0$
11. a) $13; 5, -\frac{1}{2}$ **b)** $-104; \pm\frac{2}{5}, -2$
c) $20; \dfrac{9 \pm \sqrt{57}}{6}$ **d)** $23; -\frac{1}{3}, 3 \pm \sqrt{2}$

12. a) $\pm 1, \pm 2$ **b)** $2, -1 \pm i$
13. a) $1, 5, 14, 30$ **b)** 24

Computer Power, page 70

1. 0.694 593, 3.064 178
2. a) 1.1409 **b)** 1.5897 **c)** 2.2790
3. a) $-4.2916, -0.4283, 2.7180$
b) $-2.0205, 0.0636, 1.9364, 4.0204$
c) -2.4233
4. 88.7 m

The Mathematical Mind, page 71

1. a) 0.327 480 0 **b)** $-0.673 593 1$
c) $-0.568 946 4$

Exercises 2-6, page 76

1. a) 3 **b)** 2 **c)** 3 **d)** 4 **e)** 3 **f)** 5
2. a) $(x-1)(x-2)(x-3) = 0$
b) $(x-2)^2(x-5) = 0$ **c)** $x(x+4)(x-1) = 0$
d) $(x-2)^3 = 0$
3. a) $(x-1)(x-2)(x-3)(x-4) = 0$
b) $(x-5)(x+2)(x-1)(x-2) = 0$
c) $(x-1)^2(x-2)^2(x-3)^2 = 0$
4. a) Degree 4 **b)** Degree 3 **c)** Degree 5
d) Degree 6 **e)** Degree 2 **f)** Degree 7
5.

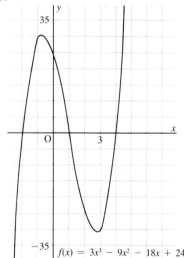

$f(x) = 3x^3 - 9x^2 - 18x + 24$

6. a)

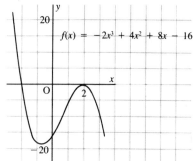

$f(x) = -2x^3 + 4x^2 + 8x - 16$

b)

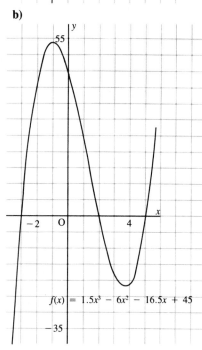

$f(x) = 1.5x^3 - 6x^2 - 16.5x + 45$

c)

$f(x) = 5x^4 - 25x^2 + 20$

d)

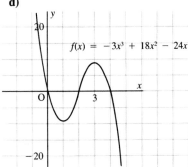

$f(x) = -3x^3 + 18x^2 - 24x$

7. a) 1

8. a) $\pm 1, \pm 5$ **b)** $\pm 1, \pm 2, \pm 4$
   c) $\pm 1, \pm 3, \pm 9$ **d)** $\pm 1, \pm 2, \pm 3, \pm 6$

9. a) $\pm 1, \pm 3$ **b)** $\pm 1, \pm 2, \pm 3, \pm 6$
   c) $\pm 1, \pm 2, \pm 5, \pm 10$ **d)** ± 1

12. a) $\pm 1, \pm \frac{1}{5}$ **b)** $\pm 1, \pm \frac{1}{2}$ **c)** $\pm 1, \pm 2, \pm \frac{1}{2}$

   d) $\pm 1, \pm \frac{1}{4}, \pm \frac{1}{2}$ **e)** $\pm 1, \pm 3, \pm \frac{1}{5}, \pm \frac{3}{5}$

   f) $\pm 1, \pm 2, \pm 4, \pm \frac{1}{2}, \pm \frac{1}{3}, \pm \frac{1}{6}, \pm \frac{2}{3}, \pm \frac{4}{3}$

13. a) ii, v   **b)** iii, iv, v   **c)** ii   **d)** i, ii, iii, iv, v
   e) iii, iv

14. a) $\frac{1}{2}, 2, -3$ **b)** $1, \dfrac{-1 \pm \sqrt{-3}}{2}$

   c) $-\frac{5}{2}, \dfrac{-3 \pm \sqrt{5}}{2}$ **d)** $1, -\frac{2}{3}, -\frac{3}{2}$

15. Answers may vary.

16. a) $y = x^3 - 9x^2 + 26x - 18$,
$y = x^3 - 9x^2 + 27x - 19$,
$y = x^3 - 9x^2 + 28x - 20$
b) Answers may vary.
c) $y = x^3 - 9x^2 + 22x - 14$,
$y = x^3 - 9x^2 + 21x - 13$,
$y = x^3 - 9x^2 + 20x - 12$
d) Answers may vary.

Exercises 2-7, page 80

1. a) i) $\{x \mid -2 < x < 3\}$
ii) $\{x \mid x < -2 \text{ or } x > 3\}$
b) i) $\{x \mid x < -2\}$
ii) $\{x \mid x > -2, x \neq 3\}$
2. a) $\{x \mid x > 2 \text{ or } x < -2\}$
b) $\{x \mid -2 \leq x \leq -1\}$
c) $\{x \mid x > 5 \text{ or } x < 0\}$
d) $\{x \mid x \leq 0 \text{ or } 2 \leq x \leq 4\}$
e) $\{a \mid a < 1 \text{ or } 2 < a < 3\}$
f) $\{n \mid -5 \leq n \leq -1 \text{ or } n \geq 3\}$
3. a) $\{x \mid -2 < x < 2 \text{ or } x > 6\}$ **b)** $\{c \mid c < -4\}$
c) $\{s \mid s \geq 0 \text{ or } -5 \leq s \leq -3\}$
d) $\{x \mid -4 \leq x \leq 0 \text{ or } 2 \leq x \leq 4\}$
e) $\{x \mid x \in R, x \neq -2, x \neq 5\}$ **f)** $\{u \mid u < 1\}$
4. a) $\{x \mid 0 < x < 5\}$ **b)** $\{m \mid m \leq -2 \text{ or } m \geq 4\}$
c) $\{y \mid -6 \leq y \leq 3\}$ **d)** $x \mid x \neq 2\}$
e) $\{x \mid x > 4\}$ **f)** $\{a \mid a \leq -5 \text{ or } 1 \leq a \leq 3\}$
5. a) $\{z \mid -2 < z < \frac{1}{2} \text{ or } z > 2\}$
b) $\{x \mid x < -3 \text{ or } -3 < x < 3\}$
c) $\{x \mid x < 0\}$ **d)** $n \in R$
e) $\{x \mid x \leq -3 \text{ or } -1 \leq x \leq 1 \text{ or } x \geq 3\}$
f) $\{r \mid 1 \leq r \leq 3\}$
6. $\{x \mid x < 1 \text{ or } x > 5\}$
7. $\{x \mid x > -1\}$
8. All real numbers between 0 and 1
10. Answers may vary; one example is $x^2 + 1 > 0$
11. Answers may vary; typical examples are:
a) $(x - 3)^2 > 0$ **b)** $(x^2 - 9)^2 > 0$
12. a) $(x + 2)(x - 3) \leq 0$ **b)** $(x + 1)(x - 2) < 0$
c) $(x + 2)(x - 1)(x - 4) < 0$
d) $x(x + 2)(x - 2)(x - 4) \leq 0$
e) $(x + 1)(x - 2)^2 \leq 0$
f) $x^2(x + 3)(x - 3) < 0$

Problem Solving, page 83

1. a) Circular ring with outside radius $(x + y)$ cm
and inside radius $(x - y)$ cm
b) Circle with radius $(x + y)$ cm
2. b) Answers will vary. Typical answers are: $a = 2$,
$b = 3, c = -2, d = -3; a = 0, b = 3, c = 0$,
$d = 5$.
3. Not possible
4. $3\sqrt{3}$ cm
5. 72

Review Exercises, page 84

1. a) -2.9 **b)** $0, \pm 3$

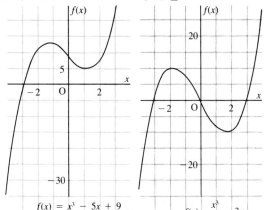

$f(x) = x^3 - 5x + 9$

$f(x) = \dfrac{x^3}{3} - 3x$

2. a) $(2a - 3)(a - 3)$ **b)** $(x + 2)(2x - 5)$
c) $(3x - 2y)(2x - y)$
d) $16x^2 - 16x - 1$, R 10
3. a) 5 **b)** -3 **c)** 5
4. 2 **5.** b, c, d
6. a) $(x - 2)(x + 2)(x + 3)$
b) $(x + 1)(x + 1)(x - 2)$
c) $(x - 1)(x + 2)(x + 4)$
d) $(x + 1)(x - 3)(x + 3)$
7. -16
8. a) $-1, -3, -6, 2$ **b)** $-1, 2, 3$ **c)** $1, \pm 2$
d) $1, \pm 2$
9. Answers may vary. $(x + 4)(x - 2)(x - 5) = 0$

10.

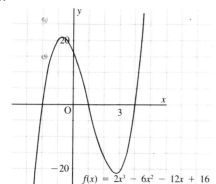

$f(x) = 2x^3 - 6x^2 - 12x + 16$

11. a) $\pm 1, \pm 2, \pm 5, \pm 10, \pm \frac{10}{3}, \pm \frac{2}{3}, \pm \frac{5}{3}, \pm \frac{1}{3}$

   b) $\pm 1, \pm 3, \pm \frac{3}{2}, \pm \frac{3}{4}, \pm \frac{1}{2}, \pm \frac{1}{4}$

12. a) $\{x \mid -6 < x < -3 \text{ or } x > 4\}$
   b) $\{a \mid a \leq -2 \text{ or } 1 \leq a \leq 5\}$

Chapter 3

Exercises 3-1, page 89

1. a) 10   **b)** $\sqrt{106}$ **c)** 17   **d)** $2\sqrt{17}$
   e) $\sqrt{157}$ **f)** $2\sqrt{41}$

2. a) $\sqrt{145}$ **b)** $\sqrt{274}$ **c)** $5\sqrt{2}$ **d)** $\sqrt{346}$
   e) $\sqrt{149}$ **f)** 25

3. a) $(-2,-2)$ **b)** $(9,1)$ **c)** $(-1,-1)$
   d) $(8,-2.5)$ **e)** $(1.5,4.5)$ **f)** $(3,3)$

4. a) D(0,1), E(4,-2), F(2,5)
   b) The length of each side of ΔDEF is half the length of the corresponding side of ΔABC.

5. a) PQ = $\sqrt{8}$, QR = $\sqrt{72}$, PR = $\sqrt{80}$;
   $PQ^2 + QR^2 = PR^2$
   b) Midpoint M of PR is $(-3,1)$.
   MP = MQ = MR = $2\sqrt{5}$

6. a) i) (9,0)   **ii)** (0,1)
   b) i) (1,0)   **ii)** (0,-1.4)
   c) i) $\left(\frac{1}{8}, 0\right)$ **ii)** $\left(0,-\frac{1}{6}\right)$
   d) i) $\left(\frac{97}{26},0\right)$ **ii)** $\left(0,-\frac{97}{16}\right)$

7. a) Isosceles   **b)** Scalene, right

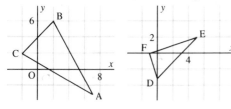

c) Scalene   **d)** Isosceles, right

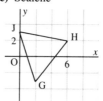
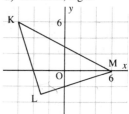

e) Scalene   **f)** Isosceles

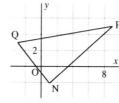
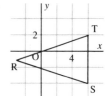

8. a) i) $\sqrt{17}, 2\sqrt{17}$ **ii)** $\sqrt{85}$ **iii)** $6\sqrt{17}$
   iv) 34
   b) i) $6\sqrt{5}, 2\sqrt{5}$ **ii)** $10\sqrt{2}$ **iii)** $16\sqrt{5}$
   iv) 60
   c) i) $2\sqrt{13}, 2\sqrt{13}$ **ii)** $2\sqrt{26}$ **iii)** $8\sqrt{13}$
   iv) 52
   d) i) $\sqrt{10}, 3\sqrt{10}$ **ii)** 10   **iii)** $8\sqrt{10}$
   iv) 30

9. a) $(-2,2), (2,0), (6,-2)$
   b) $(-2,6), (-6,3), (-10,0)$
   c) $\left(-\frac{5}{2},6\right), (2,7), \left(\frac{13}{2},8\right)$
   d) $\left(-\frac{3}{4},-7\right), \left(\frac{5}{2},-5\right), \left(\frac{23}{4},-3\right)$

10. a) $(8,-2)$ **b)** 17,8)_   **c)** $(-7,-3)$
   d) $(-9,8)$

11. Q(0,-3), M$\left(\frac{9}{2},0\right)$

12. $\left(\frac{7}{2},-2\right)$ is the midpoint of both diagonals.
   Therefore, they bisect each other.

13. $\sqrt{73}, \sqrt{82}, \sqrt{85}$

14. a) Isosceles   **b)** 90°   **c)** 40 units²

15. About 532 km   **16.** Freighter

17. $(-40,80), (160,320), (360,560)$

18. $(8,4), (9,2), (0,0), (1,-2)$

Exercises 3-2, page 93

1. a) The locus is a circle with centre $(0,0)$ and radius 2.
b) The locus is a circle with centre $(0,2)$ and radius 2.
c) The locus is a straight line with zero slope and y-intercept 3.
d) The locus is a straight line with slope $\frac{1}{2}$ and y-intercept 3.
e) The locus is a straight line with slope -1 and y-intercept 1.
f) The locus is a pair of parallel lines with infinite slope and x-intercepts 2 and -2.

2. a) The locus is a straight line parallel to the x-axis, with y-intercept -5.
b) The locus is a straight line parallel to the y-axis, with x-intercept -2.
c) The locus is a circle, centre the origin and radius 7.
d) The locus is a straight line with slope 1 and y-intercept 2.
e) The locus is a circle, centre $(1,-4)$ and radius 4.
f) The locus is a circle, centre $(1,0)$ and radius 1.

3. a) A circle, centre $B(0,3)$ and radius 6
b) $x^2 + (y-3)^2 = 36$

4. a) $(x+1)^2 + (y-2)^2 = 25$
b) A circle, centre $C(-1,2)$ and radius 5

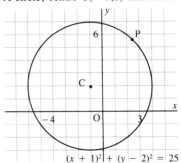

c) $5,-1$

5. a) A straight line with slope $\frac{2}{3}$, passing through $M(3,-1)$.

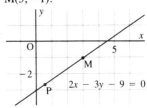

b) A parabola with vertex $(0,0)$ and axis of symmetry the y-axis. The parabola opens up.

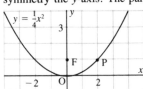

c) A parabola with vertex $(3,0)$ and axis of symmetry $x = 3$; it opens down, and is congruent to $y = -\frac{1}{4}x^2$.

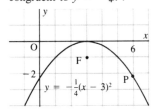

6. a) $y = \frac{1}{4}(x-2)^2 + 4$
b) A parabola with vertex $(2,4)$ and axis of symmetry $x = 2$; it opens up and is congruent to $y = \frac{1}{4}x^2$.

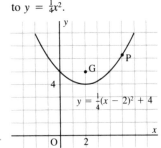

c) 13

7. a) $5x - 2y - 13 = 0$; the perpendicular bisector of AB

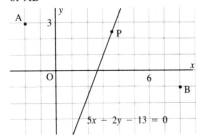

b) $x^2 + y^2 = 16$; a circle, centre (0,0) radius 4

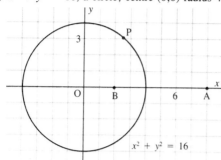

c) $x + y = 3$; a straight line through A and B

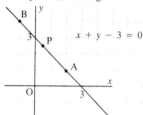

8. a) $y = \frac{1}{2}x^2 - 2$

b) A parabola, vertex $(0, -2)$, axis of symmetry the y-axis, which opens up and is congruent to $y = \frac{1}{2}x^2$

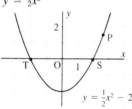

c) ± 6

9. a) $x^2 + y^2 = 25$

b) A circle, centre (0,0) and radius 5

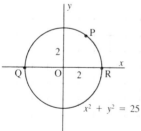

c) $\pm\sqrt{21}$

10. a) $x^2 + y^2 = 16$

b) A circle, centre (0,0) and radius 4

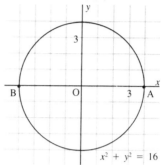

11. $x^2 + y^2 = 25$. See graph of *Exercise 9c*).

12. a)

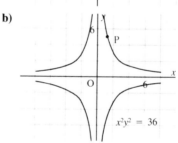

b)

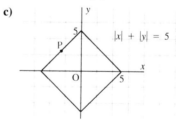

c)

d)

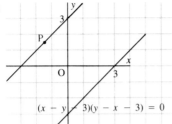

$(x - y - 3)(y - x - 3) = 0$

e)

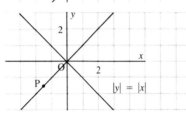

$|y| = |x|$

f)

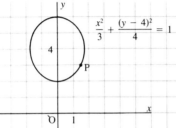

$\dfrac{x^2}{3} + \dfrac{(y - 4)^2}{4} = 1$

13.

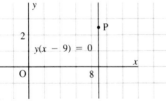

$y(x - 9) = 0$

14. a) $3x^2 + 4y^2 = 48$ **b)** $15x^2 - y^2 = 15$
15. $5x + 3y - 17 = 0$

Exercises 3-3, page 99

1. a, c, e, f
2. a) Circle **b)** Ellipse

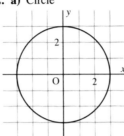

$x^2 + y^2 = 9$

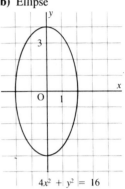

$4x^2 + y^2 = 16$

c) Hyperbola

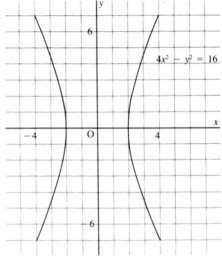

$4x^2 - y^2 = 16$

d) Parabola

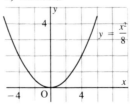

$y = \dfrac{x^2}{8}$

e) Ellipse

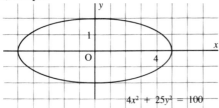

f) Hyperbola

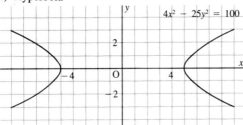

3. a) i)

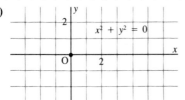

ii)

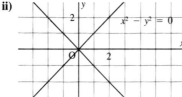

iii)

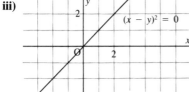

b) Answers may vary.
4. a) Hyperbola   **b)** Hyperbola, parabola or ellipse
    c) Hyperbola

Exercises 3-4, page 102

1. a), c) Yes   **b), d)** No
2. Centre (0,0); asymptotes $y = \pm x$ **a)** $(\pm 5,0)$
    b) $(\pm 8,0)$ **c)** $(0, \pm 9)$ **d)** $(\pm\sqrt{2},0)$
    e) $(0, \pm\sqrt{5})$ **f)** $(0, \pm 2\sqrt{5})$
3. a) $x^2 - y^2 = 49$ **b)** $x^2 - y^2 = -16$
    c) $x^2 - y^2 = -36$ **d)** $x^2 - y^2 = 100$
4.

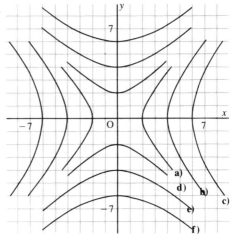

5. a) $x^2 - y^2 = -144$
    b)

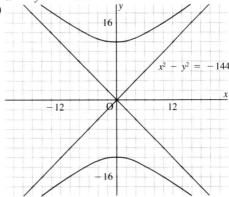

6. a) $x^2 - y^2 = 60$ **b)** ± 16
7. a) $x^2 - y^2 = -15$ **b)** ± 4
8. a) $x^2 - y^2 = -5625$ **b)** 44 m
9. a) $B < 0$, $A = |B|$, $C < 0$ or $A < 0$,
    $B = |A|$, $C > 0$
    b) $B < 0$, $A = |B|$, $C > 0$ or $A < 0$,
    $B = |A|$, $C < 0$

Exercises 3-5, page 108

1. a) Ellipse **b)** Hyperbola **c)** Ellipse
   d) Circle **e)** Parabola **f)** Hyperbola

2. Descriptions may vary.

a)

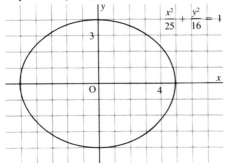

$$\frac{x^2}{25}+\frac{y^2}{16}=1$$

b)

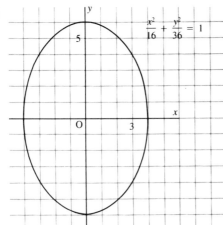

$$\frac{x^2}{16}+\frac{y^2}{36}=1$$

c)

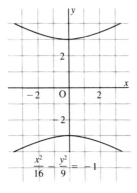

$$\frac{x^2}{16}-\frac{y^2}{9}=-1$$

d)

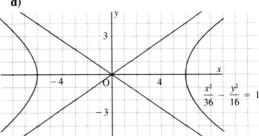

$$\frac{x^2}{36}-\frac{y^2}{16}=1$$

e)

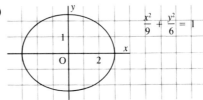

$$\frac{x^2}{9}+\frac{y^2}{6}=1$$

f)

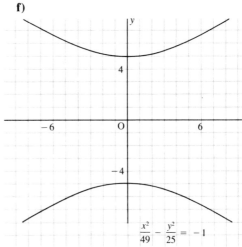

$$\frac{x^2}{49}-\frac{y^2}{25}=-1$$

g)

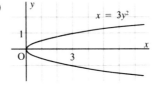

$$x=3y^2$$

h)

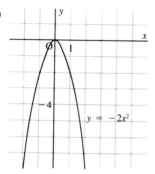

$y = -2x^2$

i)

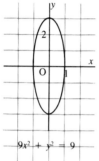

$9x^2 + y^2 = 9$

3. Descriptions may vary.

a)

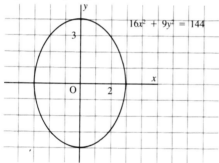

$16x^2 + 9y^2 = 144$

b)

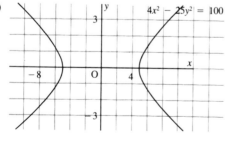

$4x^2 - 25y^2 = 100$

c)

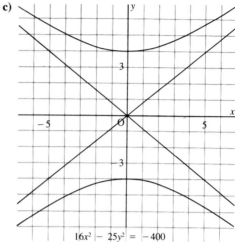

$16x^2 - 25y^2 = -400$

d)

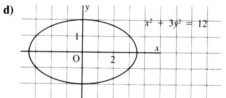

$x^2 + 3y^2 = 12$

e)

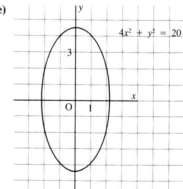

$4x^2 + y^2 = 20$

f)

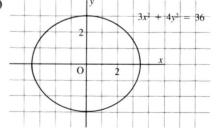

$3x^2 + 4y^2 = 36$

g)

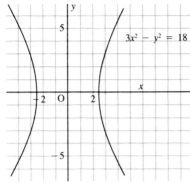

$3x^2 - y^2 = 18$

h)

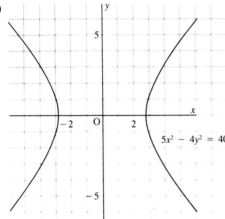

$5x^2 - 4y^2 = 40$

i)

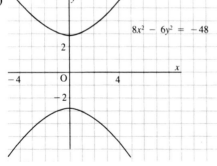

$8x^2 - 6y^2 = -48$

4. a) $\dfrac{x^2}{36} + \dfrac{y^2}{9} = 1$ **b)** $\dfrac{x^2}{25} + \dfrac{y^2}{4} = 1$

c) $\dfrac{x^2}{25} + \dfrac{y^2}{4} = 1$

5. a) $\dfrac{x^2}{9} - \dfrac{y^2}{4} = 1$ **b)** $\dfrac{x^2}{4} - \dfrac{y^2}{9} = 1$

c) $\dfrac{x^2}{36} - \dfrac{y^2}{144} = 1$

6. a) $\dfrac{x^2}{4} - \dfrac{y^2}{9} = -1$ **b)** $\dfrac{x^2}{9} - \dfrac{y^2}{4} = -1$

c) $\dfrac{x^2}{9} - \dfrac{y^2}{36} = -1$

7. No. The equation $2x^2 + 3y^2 = 24$ does represent an ellipse.

8. a) $\dfrac{4a^2b^2}{b^2 + a^2}$ **b)** Only when $b > a$; $\dfrac{4a^2b^2}{b^2 - a^2}$

Exercises 3-6, page 111

1. a) $y = \frac{1}{2160}x^2$ **b)** 42 cm

2. $y = -\frac{1}{64}x^2$

3. Typical answers: **a)** $y = -\frac{15.3}{1225}x^2$ **b)** 14 m

4. a) $9x^2 + 25y^2 = 225$ **b)** About 5.50 m

5. a) $15\ 625x^2 + 22\ 500y^2 = 351\ 562\ 500$
   b) About 123.9 m

6. 5.4 m

7. 44 m

8. a) 800 km   **b)** 2000 km   **c)** About 1352 km

Problem Solving, page 114

1. 12 edges, 8 vertices

3. a)

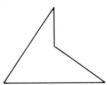

   b) One of the angles is a reflex angle.

4. 6%

5. DE = $\sqrt{\dfrac{x}{2}}$

7. Approximately 2.0565

Exercises 3-7, page 118

1. a) $\dfrac{(x-3)^2}{4} - (y-2)^2 = 1$

b) $\dfrac{(x-3)^2}{9} + \dfrac{(y+2)^2}{4} = 1$

2. Descriptions may vary.

a)

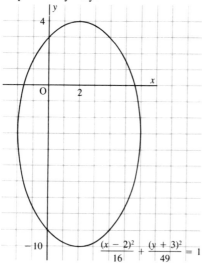

$$\dfrac{(x-2)^2}{16} + \dfrac{(y+3)^2}{49} = 1$$

b)

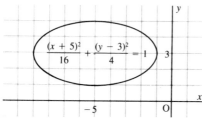

$$\dfrac{(x+5)^2}{16} + \dfrac{(y-3)^2}{4} = 1$$

c)

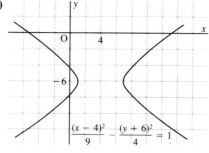

$$\dfrac{(x-4)^2}{9} - \dfrac{(y+6)^2}{4} = 1$$

d)

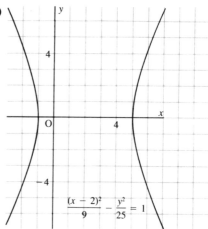

$$\dfrac{(x-2)^2}{9} - \dfrac{y^2}{25} = 1$$

e)

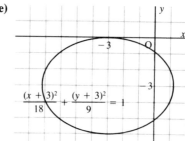

$$\dfrac{(x+3)^2}{18} + \dfrac{(y+3)^2}{9} = 1$$

f)

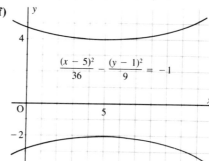

$$\dfrac{(x-5)^2}{36} - \dfrac{(y-1)^2}{9} = -1$$

g)

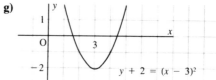

$$y + 2 = (x-3)^2$$

h)

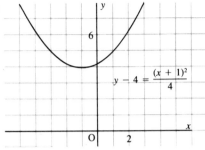

$$y - 4 = \frac{(x + 1)^2}{4}$$

3. Descriptions may vary.

a)

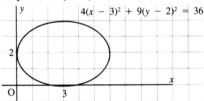

$$4(x - 3)^2 + 9(y - 2)^2 = 36$$

b)

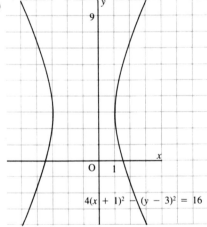

$$4(x + 1)^2 - (y - 3)^2 = 16$$

c)

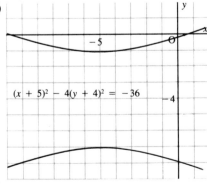

$$(x + 5)^2 - 4(y + 4)^2 = -36$$

d)

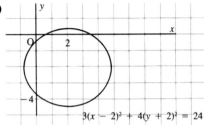

$$3(x - 2)^2 + 4(y + 2)^2 = 24$$

e)

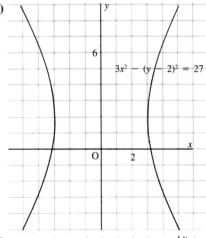

$$3x^2 - (y - 2)^2 = 27$$

f)

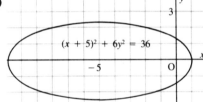

$$(x + 5)^2 + 6y^2 = 36$$

g)

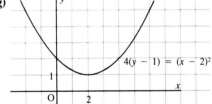

$$4(y - 1) = (x - 2)^2$$

h)

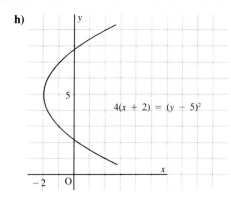

$$4(x + 2) = (y - 5)^2$$

Exercises 3-8, page 121

1. a) $3x^2 + y^2 - 6x + 4y - 2 = 0$
b) $x^2 - 2y^2 + 10x + 4y + 13 = 0$
c) $3x^2 - 24x - y + 50 = 0$
d) $4x^2 + 9y^2 + 16x - 54y + 61 = 0$
e) $3x^2 - 6y^2 + 6x - 24y - 3 = 0$
f) $2y^2 + x - 12y + 22 = 0$

2. a) Ellipse   **b)** Hyperbola   **c)** Parabola
d) Circle

3. a)

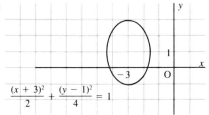

$$\frac{(x + 3)^2}{2} + \frac{(y - 1)^2}{4} = 1$$

b)

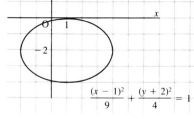

$$\frac{(x - 1)^2}{9} + \frac{(y + 2)^2}{4} = 1$$

c)

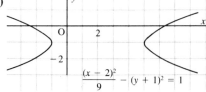

$$\frac{(x - 2)^2}{9} - (y + 1)^2 = 1$$

d)

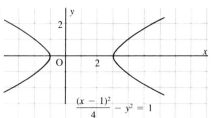

$$\frac{(x - 1)^2}{4} - y^2 = 1$$

e)

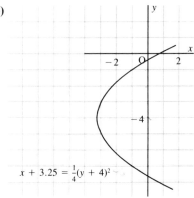

$$x + 3.25 = \frac{1}{4}(y + 4)^2$$

f)

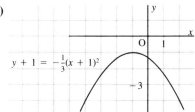

$$y + 1 = -\frac{1}{3}(x + 1)^2$$

4. a) $(x-4)^2 + (y+3)^2 = 16$; a circle, centre $(4,-3)$, radius 4

b) $\dfrac{(x-1)^2}{4} + (y+2)^2 = 1$; an ellipse, centre $(1,-2)$, length of major axis 4, length of minor axis 2

c) $\dfrac{(x+3)^2}{4} + \dfrac{(y-2)^2}{3} = 1$; an ellipse, centre $(-3,2)$, length of major axis 4, length of minor axis $2\sqrt{3}$

d) $\dfrac{(x-6)^2}{4} - \dfrac{y^2}{6} = 1$; a hyperbola, centre $(6,0)$, length of transverse axis (which is horizontal) 4, length of conjugate axis $2\sqrt{6}$

e) $x+2 = \frac{1}{8}(y-4)^2$; a parabola, vertex $(-2,4)$, opening to the right, congruent to $x = \frac{1}{8}y^2$

f) $y + 5 = 6(x+2)^2$; a parabola, vertex $(-2,-5)$, opening up, congruent to $y = 6x^2$

5. a) $y + 3 = \frac{1}{6}(x - 3)^2$

b)

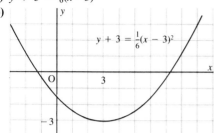

$y + 3 = \frac{1}{6}(x - 3)^2$

6. $y = -\frac{1}{8}(x - 3)^2 + 4$

7. $\frac{(x - 4)^2}{25} + \frac{(y - 3)^2}{9} = 1$

8. a) The lines $x = 1$ and $y = -4$
  b) There is no graph.
  c) The lines $2x - y + 2 = 0$ and
      $2x + y + 6 = 0$
  d) There is no graph.

Exercises 3-9, page 125

1. $3x^2 + 2y^2 - 6x + 8y - 1 = 0$

2. $5x^2 - 4xy + 8y^2 + 2x - 44y + 29 = 0$

3. a) Parabola   **b)** Ellipse   **c)** Hyperbola
  d) Hyperbola   **e)** Parabola   **f)** Ellipse

4. Descriptions may vary.
  a) See Exercises 3-2, *Exercise 12b*).
  b)

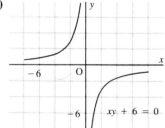

$xy + 6 = 0$

c) The graph $xy - 6 = 0$ translated 4 units right and 3 units down.

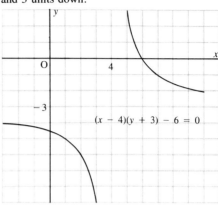

$(x - 4)(y + 3) - 6 = 0$

d) The graph $xy - 6 = 0$ translated 4 units left and 3 units up.

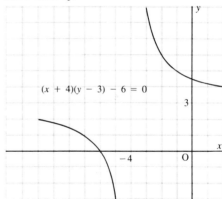

$(x + 4)(y - 3) - 6 = 0$

5. $x^2 + 2xy + y^2 - 22x + 10y - 7 = 0$

6. $x^2 - 2xy - y^2 + 10x - 10y = 0$

7. a) The equation is an ellipse if $AC - \frac{B^2}{4} > 0$

The equation is a hyperbola if $AC - \frac{B^2}{4} < 0$

The equation is a parabola if $AC - \frac{B^2}{4} = 0$

  b) Answers may vary.

8. a) $3x^2 - 2xy + 3y^2 - 8 = 0$
  b) $3x^2 - 2xy + 3y^2 - 4x - 4y - 4 = 0$

10. No; explanations may vary.

11. Assume that the first non-zero coefficient in the equation is positive. If it is not, then multiply both sides by -1.
a) $H = 0, A = B$, and $G^2 + F^2 - AC \geqslant 0$
b) i) $B > A > 0, H = F = 0$, and $G^2 - AC > 0$
ii) $A > B > 0, H = G = 0$, and $F^2 - BC > 0$
c) i) $A > 0, B < 0, H = F = 0$, and $G^2 - AC > 0$
ii) $A > 0, B < 0, H = G = 0$, and $F^2 - BC > 0$
d) i) $A = H = 0$ **ii)** $H = B = 0$

Review Exercises, page 127

1. a) 5   **b)** 13   **c)** $\sqrt{137}$
2. a) $(-1.5, 2)$ **b)** $(3, -4.5)$ **c)** $(-4, 1.5)$
3. a)

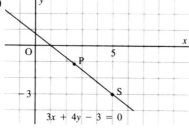

$(x + 2)^2 + (y - 1)^2 = 9$

b)

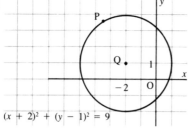

$3x + 4y - 3 = 0$

c)

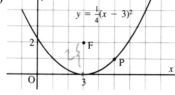

$y = \frac{1}{4}(x - 3)^2$

d)

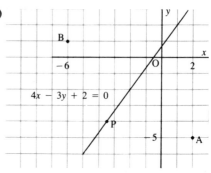

$4x - 3y + 2 = 0$

4. a) Ellipse

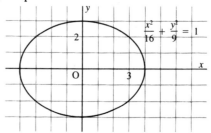

$\dfrac{x^2}{16} + \dfrac{y^2}{9} = 1$

b) Parabola   **c)** Circle

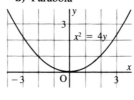

$x^2 = 4y$

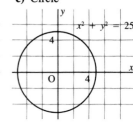

$x^2 + y^2 = 25$

d) Hyperbola

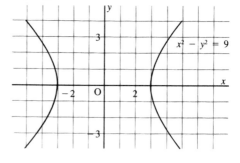

$x^2 - y^2 = 9$

e) Circle

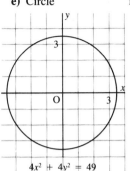

$$4x^2 + 4y^2 = 49$$

f) Hyperbola

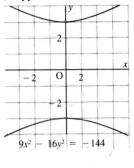

$$9x^2 - 16y^2 = -144$$

5. Yes

6. a) $\dfrac{x^2}{9} + \dfrac{y^2}{25} = 1$ **b)** $\dfrac{x^2}{9} + \dfrac{y^2}{36} = 1$

7. a) $\dfrac{x^2}{16} - \dfrac{y^2}{64} = 1$ **b)** $\dfrac{x^2}{16} - \dfrac{y^2}{49} = 1$

8. $y = -\frac{1}{64}x^2$

9. $\dfrac{x^2}{900} + \dfrac{y^2}{625} = 1$ **10.** $x^2 - y^2 = -380.25$

11. a)

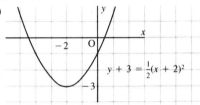

$$y + 3 = \frac{1}{2}(x + 2)^2$$

b)

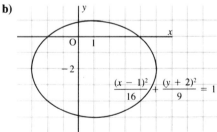

$$\frac{(x-1)^2}{16} + \frac{(y+2)^2}{9} = 1$$

c)

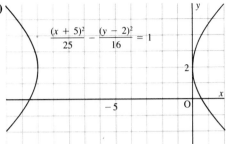

$$\frac{(x+5)^2}{25} - \frac{(y-2)^2}{16} = 1$$

d)

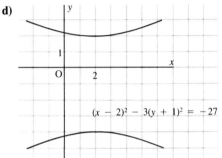

$$(x-2)^2 - 3(y+1)^2 = -27$$

12. a) $(x+2)^2 + (y-5)^2 = 49$; a circle, centre $(-2,5)$, radius 7

b) $\dfrac{(x-1)^2}{16} + \dfrac{(y+3)^2}{9} = 1$; an ellipse, centre $(1,-3)$, major axis length 8, minor axis length 6

c) $x + 7 = \frac{1}{6}(y-4)^2$; a parabola, vertex $(-7,4)$, opening to the right, congruent to $x = \frac{1}{6}y^2$

d) $\dfrac{(x-3)^2}{4} - \dfrac{(y+2)^2}{5} = -1$; a hyperbola, centre $(3,-2)$, transverse axis is vertical with length $2\sqrt{5}$, conjugate axis length 4

Cumulative Review, Chapters 1-3, page 128

1. a) R; R

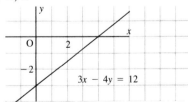

$$3x - 4y = 12$$

b) R; $\{y \mid y \geqslant 5, y \in R\}$

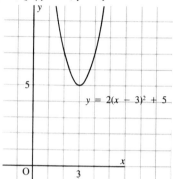

$y = 2(x - 3)^2 + 5$

c) $\{x \mid x \neq 0, x \in R\}$; $\{y \mid y \neq 2, y \in R\}$

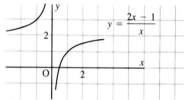

$y = \dfrac{2x - 1}{x}$

2. a) 13 **b)** -3 **c)** $12a - 2$ **d)** $3x^2 - 5$
e) $4x^2 + 2x - 3$ **f)** $3x^2 + 9x - 5$

3. a) R; R; yes

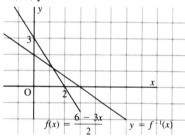

$f(x) = \dfrac{6 - 3x}{2}$ $y = f^{-1}(x)$

b) $\{x \mid x \neq 3, x \in R\}$; $\{y \mid y \neq 0, y \in R\}$; yes

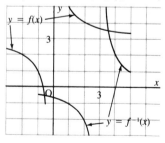

$y = f(x)$

$y = f^{-1}(x)$

4. a) 2 different real roots **b)** No real roots
c) 2 equal real roots

5. a) $\dfrac{5 \pm \sqrt{57}}{2}$ **b)** $\dfrac{-3 \pm \sqrt{23}i}{4}$ **c)** $-1.8, 1$

6. a) $1.4, -3.4$ **b)** 0

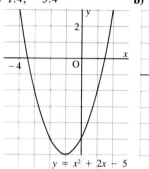 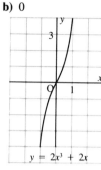

$y = x^2 + 2x - 5$ $y = 2x^3 + 2x$

7. a) $(x-5)(x+2)$ **b)** $(2x-1)(2x+1)$
c) $(x-1)(x+1)(x+2)$
8. a) Yes **b)** No; -2
9. a) $(x-1)(x+3)(x+5)$
b) $(x-1)(x-2)(x+2)(x+3)$
10. a) $\pm 1, \pm 2, \pm 3, \pm 4, \pm 6, \pm 12$
b) $\pm 1, \pm 3, \pm \frac{1}{2}, \pm \frac{3}{2}$
11. a) $\{x \mid x < -3 \text{ or } -2 < x < 1\}$
b) $\{x \mid x \leqslant -2 \text{ or } -1 \leqslant x \leqslant 1 \text{ or } x \geqslant 3\}$
12. a) $\sqrt{65}$; $(1.5, -1)$ **b)** $\sqrt{265}$; $(-2, 3.5)$
c) $3\sqrt{2}$; $(6.5, -5.5)$
13. a) The perpendicular bisector of AB

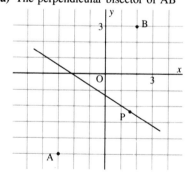

b) A circle, centre Q$(-2, -3)$, radius 4 units

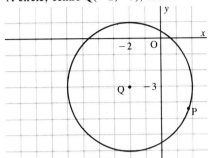

14. a) $\dfrac{x^2}{16} + y^2 = 1$ **b)** $\dfrac{x^2}{36} + \dfrac{y^2}{16} = 1$

15. $x^2 - y^2 = -28$

Chapter 4

Exercises 4-1, page 132

1. a) 2 points   **b)** No points   **c)** 2 points
  d) 1 point

2. a) 2 points   **b)** No points   **c)** No points
  d) 1 point

3. a) $(3,4), (-3, -4)$ **b)** $(-4, -3)$
  c) No points

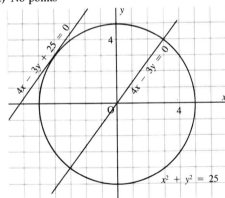

4. a) $(-1,1)$ **b)** $(1,1)$ **c)** No points

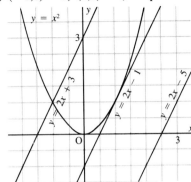

5. a) $(8,6), (-6, -8)$

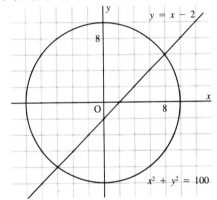

b) No points

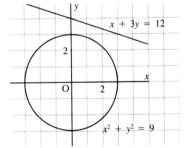

c) $(3,2)$, $(-4,-1.5)$

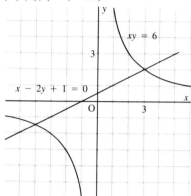

d) $(1,3)$

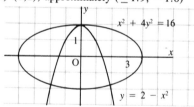

e) $(0,2)$, approximately $(\pm 1.9, -1.8)$

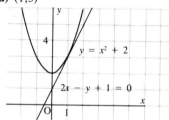

f) Approximately $(3.2,1.2)$, $(-3.2,-1.2)$

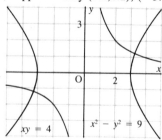

6. Answers may vary.   **a)** $y = x$
  b) $x + y = 100$
7. Answers may vary.   **a)** $y = x^2 - 3$
  b) $y = x^2 - 2$ **c)** $y = x^2$ **d)** $y = x^2 + 2$
  e) $y = x^2 + 3$
8. a) Yes   **b)** Yes   **c)** No   **d)** No   **e)** Yes
  f) Yes
9. a) i) $0 < k < 2$ **ii)** $k = 2$ **iii)** $2 < k < 8$
  iv) $k = 8$ **v)** $k > 8$ **b)** Answers may vary.
10. a) $r < 2$ **b)** $r = 2$ **c)** $2 < r < 4$
  d) $r = 4$ **e)** $r > 4$
11. a) $b \leqslant r \leqslant a$ **b)** $r \geqslant a$

Mathematics Around Us, page 135

1. a) i) 10 000   **ii)** 14 000   **iii)** 18 000 ·
  b) i) 3.50   **ii)** 4.75   **iii)** 6.20   **c)** 0.50
2. a) i) 4500   **ii)** 3000   **iii)** 1500   **b) i)** 0.80
  ii) 1.25   **iii)** 2.20   **c)** 2.50   **d)** 7500
3. a) 0.80   **b)** 4400

Exercises 4-2, page 139

1. a) $(1,2)$, $(-1,-2)$ **b)** $(2,-1)$
  c) $(3,1)$, $(1,-3)$ **d)** No points
2. a) $(0,-5)$, $(3,4)$ **b)** $(-1,1)$, $(2,4)$
  c) $(4,-2)$ **d)** $(3,4)$, $(-2,-6)$
3. 3,7   **4.** 4 cm, 2.5 cm
5. a) About 7.1 s   **b)** About 113 m

6. a) $(-2,3)$, $\left(\frac{46}{13}, -\frac{9}{13}\right)$ **b)** $(2,3)$

  c) $(-3,-4)$, $\left(-\frac{10}{3}, -\frac{35}{9}\right)$

  d) $\left(-\frac{4}{\sqrt{3}}, \frac{2}{\sqrt{3}}\right)$, $\left(\frac{4}{\sqrt{3}}, -\frac{2}{\sqrt{3}}\right)$

  e) No solution   **f)** $(-2,2)$, $\left(-\frac{4}{3},3\right)$
7. $(9.6,-2.8)$, $(6,8)$

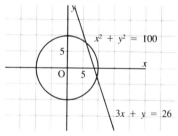

8. $(-40,0)$, $(-24,32)$

10. 8,12 **11.** 6,10 **12.** 90 m, 160 m

13. $\left(6 + \sqrt{14}\right)$ cm, $\left(6 - \sqrt{14}\right)$ cm

14. $x + 6y - 18 = 0$ or $2x + 3y - 18 = 0$

15. a) P_1 (3,7), P_2 (−2.5,1.5)

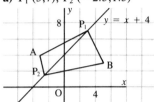

16. a) i)

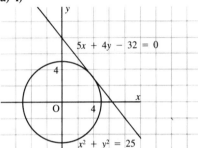

ii)

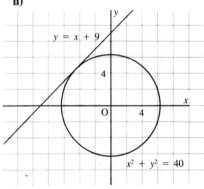

b) i) $\left(\frac{156}{41}, \frac{133}{41}\right)$, (4,3) **ii)** No solution

17. b) D(0, −5), E(3, −4)

18. a) D(4, −3), E(3, −4), F(0, −5)

Exercises 4-3, page 143

1. a) (0,0), (1,1) **b), c)** No solution

d) (4,0), (−4,0) **e)** (0, −1), (1,0), (−1,0)

f) (2,2), (−2,2), (−2, −2), (2, −2)

2. a) i) (0,2), (0, −2)

ii) (3,1), (−3,1), (3, −1), (−3, −1)

iii) $(2\sqrt{3},0)$, $(-2\sqrt{3},0)$

b) Answers may vary. A circle with radius less than 2; for example, $x^2 + y^2 = 1$

3. a) (2,4), (−2,4) **b)** (2,0), (−2,0), (0, −4)

c) (4,1), (4, −1), (−4,1), (−4, −1)

d) $(\sqrt{7.5}, -2.5)$, $(\sqrt{7.5}, 2.5)$, (−2,1), (2,1)

e) (0,0), (4, −2)

f) $\left(\sqrt{2}, \frac{3}{\sqrt{2}}\right)$, $\left(-\sqrt{2}, -\frac{3}{\sqrt{2}}\right)$

4. a) (−2, −2), (−2,2), (1,4), (1, −4)

b) $\left(3, 2\sqrt{2}\right)$, $\left(3, -2\sqrt{2}\right)$, (−1,0)

c) (−1,6), (−3,2) **d)** (0,0), (−12,18)

e) (0, −2), $\left(\frac{4\sqrt{2}}{3}, \frac{14}{9}\right)$, $\left(-\frac{4\sqrt{2}}{3}, \frac{14}{9}\right)$

5. a) There appear to be 2 solutions.

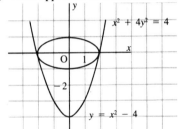

b) There are 4 solutions: (2,0), (−2,0),

$\left(\frac{\sqrt{15}}{2}, -\frac{1}{4}\right)$, $\left(-\frac{\sqrt{15}}{2}, -\frac{1}{4}\right)$

6. a) $\left(3\sqrt{2}, \sqrt{2}\right)$, $\left(-3\sqrt{2}, -\sqrt{2}\right)$

b)

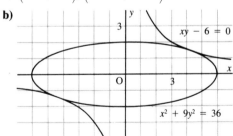

7. About (35,32)

8. $\sqrt{10}$ cm, $\sqrt{10}$ cm

9. $\sqrt{20}$, $2\sqrt{20}$; $-\sqrt{20}$, $-2\sqrt{20}$

10. $3\sqrt{3}$, $2\sqrt{3}$; $-3\sqrt{3}$, $-2\sqrt{3}$

11. 1.5 h

12. a) 2.8, 9.6   **b)** 2.8, 9.6

13. Theorem: Two congruent right triangles can be joined along their legs to form isosceles triangles in two different ways. The length of an altitude to the equal sides in one triangle is equal to the length of an altitude to the equal sides in the other triangle.

14. a) $r^2 \geqslant a^2$ **b)** $r^2 \geqslant 2k$

15. a) $(2,1)$ **b)** $\left(3\sqrt{\dfrac{5}{13}}, 2\sqrt{\dfrac{5}{13}}\right)$

16. a) $(2,-4), (-2,4), (4,-2)$
b) $(0,0), (4,0), (6,3), (-2,3)$

Exercises 4-4, page 147

1. a) $x - y < 4$ **b)** $y < -2x$ **c)** $x^2 + y^2 < 4$
d) $x^2 + 4y^2 \geqslant 4$ **e)** $xy > 1$ **f)** $y^2 + x \geqslant 2$

2. a)

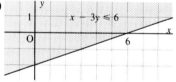

b)

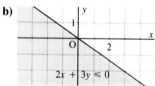

c)

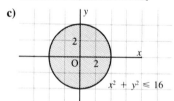

d)

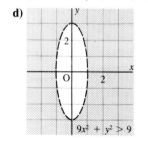

e)

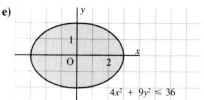

f)

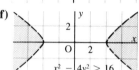

3. a)

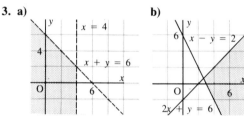

b)

c)

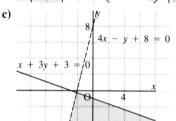

d)

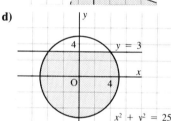

e)

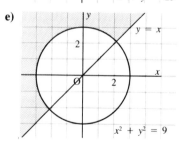

f)

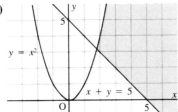

4. a)

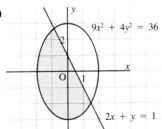

b)

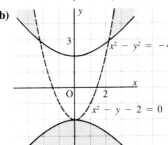

c)

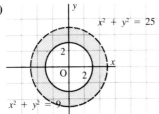

d)

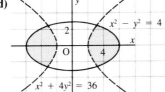

e)

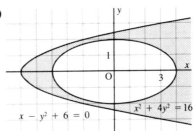

f)

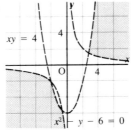

5. Answers may vary. Typical answers are:
  a) $x^2 + y^2 \leqslant 1$; $x^2 + y^2 \geqslant 4$
  b) $x^2 + y^2 \leqslant 1$; $y \geqslant x^2 + 1$
  c) $x^2 + 4y^2 \geqslant 4$; $x^2 + y^2 \leqslant 1$

Problem Solving, page 150

1. 12 714 km

4. $x = \dfrac{s}{2 + \sqrt{2}}$

5. $x = \sqrt{\tfrac{1}{3}}\, s,\ y = \sqrt{\tfrac{2}{3}}\, s$

6. Yes, twin primes

7. $(3 + \sqrt{3}, 5 + 2\sqrt{3})$ and $(3 - \sqrt{3}, 5 - 2\sqrt{3})$

8. $x = (36 - 36\sqrt{3} + 12\pi)$ cm,
  $y = (-36 + 18\sqrt{3} - 3\pi)$ cm,
  $z = (36 - 9\sqrt{3} - 6\pi)$ cm

Exercises 4-5, page 152

1. a) ± 5 **b)** 0 **c)** $9, -5$ **d)** 6,2 **e)** $4, -6$
  f) 5
2. a) $\{x \mid -3 < x < 3\}$ **b)** $\{x \mid x \geqslant 4 \text{ or } x \leqslant -4\}$
  c) $\{x \mid -3 < x < 7\}$ **d)** $\{x \mid -1 \leqslant x \leqslant 3\}$
  e) $\{x \mid x < -8 \text{ or } x > 6\}$ **f)** $\{x \mid -10 < x < 8\}$
3. a) 3,7 **b)** $7, -3$ **c)** $1, -3$ **d)** $-1, -3$
  e) $-6,12$ **f)** $-1,7$

4. a) $\{x \mid 2 \leqslant x \leqslant 4\}$

b) $\{x \mid x > 5 \text{ or } x < 1\}$

c) $\{x \mid -8 < x < 4\}$

d) $\{x \mid x \geqslant 9 \text{ or } x \leqslant 1\}$

e) $\{x \mid x \leqslant -11 \text{ or } x \geqslant 9\}$

f) $\{x \mid -14 \leqslant x \leqslant 4\}$

5. a) $3.5, -0.5$ **b)** $1, -2$ **c)** $1, \frac{7}{3}$
d) $0.75, -2.25$ **e)** $1, \frac{1}{3}$ **f)** $0, -0.5$

6. a) $\{x \mid -5 \leqslant x \leqslant 4\}$ **b)** $\{x \mid -\frac{4}{3} < x < \frac{8}{3}\}$
c) $\{x \mid x > -0.5 \text{ or } x < -3.5\}$
d) $\{x \mid x \geqslant 0.2 \text{ or } x \leqslant -1\}$
e) $\{x \mid -6 \leqslant x \leqslant 2\}$ **f)** $\{x \mid -\frac{1}{3} < x < \frac{5}{3}\}$

7. Answers may vary. Typical inequalities are:
a) $|x| \leqslant 3$ **b)** $|x| \geqslant 3$ **c)** $|x - 1| < 2$
d) $|x - 1| > 2$

8. Answers may vary. Typical inequalities are:
a) $|x - 4| \leqslant 3$ **b)** $|x - 1| \leqslant 3$
c) $|x - 0.5| < 1.5$ **d)** $|x - 4| > 2$
e) $|x - 2| > 2$ **f)** $|x - 2| > 0$

9. Answers may vary. Typical inequalities are:
a) $|2 - 3x| < 3x - 4$ **b)** $|x + 1| > x - 1$
c) $|6 - 3x| \leqslant x - 2$

10. a) $5 - x + \dfrac{1}{x - 2}$ **b)** $2 < x \leqslant 3.7808$

Review Exercises, page 154

1. a) i **b)** iii **c)** ii
2. Answers may vary.
a) $(2.2, 3.4), (-1.4, -3.8)$

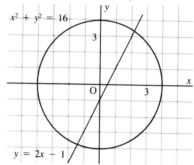

b) $(4.9, 5.2), (-0.2, 1.9)$

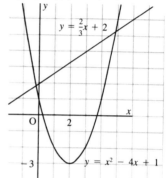

c) No solution

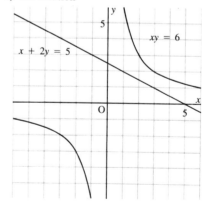

d) $(0, -2)$, $(-2.1, -1.8)$, $(1.2, 1.9)$, $(-3.2, 1.7)$

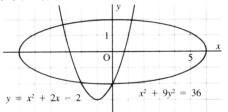

$y = x^2 + 2x - 2$
$x^2 + 9y^2 = 36$

e) $(4.0, 2.7)$, $(-4.0, -2.7)$

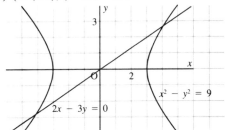

$x^2 - y^2 = 9$
$2x - 3y = 0$

f) $(0.3, 3.9)$, $(1.9, 0.6)$, $(-1.9, -0.6)$, $(-0.3, -3.9)$

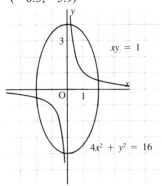

$xy = 1$
$4x^2 + y^2 = 16$

3. a) $(1.86, -0.73)$, $(0.54, 1.93)$ **b)** $\left(-\frac{4}{3}, \frac{22}{9}\right)$, $(3, 1)$

   c) $(1.23, 3.24)$, $(-1.23, -3.24)$
   d) $(2.71, 0.86)$, $(-1.99, -1.50)$

4. 7, 4 or -7, -4

5. $-40 \le x \le 40$

6. 3 cm by 6 cm

7. a)

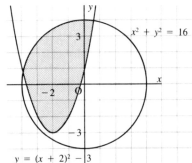

$x^2 + y^2 = 16$

$y = (x + 2)^2 - 3$

b)

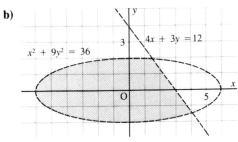

$x^2 + 9y^2 = 36$
$4x + 3y = 12$

c)

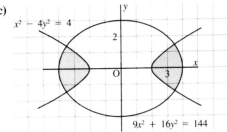

$x^2 - 4y^2 = 4$

$9x^2 + 16y^2 = 144$

8. a) $3, -7$ **b)** $6, 2$ **c)** $2.5, -5.5$

9. a) $-3 \le x \le 5$ **b)** $x \ge 4$ or $x \le -10$
   c) $-3 < x < 2$ **d)** $-3.5 \le x \le 3$
   e) $x > 4$ or $x < \frac{4}{3}$ **f)** $2 \le x \le 3$

Chapter 5

Section 5-1, page 156

Estimates may vary.

1. a) i) 17:00 h   **ii)** 20:00 h   **iii)** 17:00 h
   b) Approximate dates: **i)** May 20, July 23
   ii) April 12, Aug. 30   **iii)** Mar. 13, Sept. 29
   iv) Feb. 20, Oct. 24

2. Answers may vary.

3. 10 to 11 years

4. Typical answers: **a)** 173 m, 58 m   **b)** 6 h

5. Answers may vary.   **6.** Answers may vary.

7. 5 s

8. Answers may vary.

9. Sunsets: 1 year; sunspots; 10.5 years; volume and pressure of blood: 0.8 s; volume of air: 5 s

10. 15   **11.** Sunspots

Exercises 5-2, page 162

1. a) $\dfrac{\pi}{6}$ **b)** $\dfrac{\pi}{4}$ **c)** $\dfrac{\pi}{3}$ **d)** $\dfrac{\pi}{2}$ **e)** $\dfrac{2\pi}{3}$ **f)** $\dfrac{3\pi}{4}$

g) $\dfrac{5\pi}{6}$ **h)** π **i)** $\dfrac{7\pi}{6}$ **j)** $\dfrac{5\pi}{4}$ **k)** $\dfrac{4\pi}{3}$

l) $\dfrac{3\pi}{2}$ **m)** $\dfrac{5\pi}{3}$ **n)** $\dfrac{7\pi}{4}$ **o)** $\dfrac{11\pi}{6}$ **p)** 2π

q) $\dfrac{13\pi}{6}$ **r)** $\dfrac{9\pi}{4}$

2. a) 90°   **b)** 135°   **c)** −120°   **d)** 210°
e) 45°   **f)** −270°   **g)** 315°   **h)** 360°
i) −300°   **j)** 225°   **k)** 30°   **l)** −330°

3. a) 1.75   **b)** 3.93   **c)** 1.00   **d)** −2.18
e) $1.31x$ **f)** 0.33   **g)** −1.13   **h)** $0.43x$
i) 2.62   **j)** 0.52   **k)** 1.00   **l)** $-1.57x$

4. a) 114.6°   **b)** −286.5°   **c)** 183.3°
d) 103.1°   **e)** −40.1°   **f)** $80.2\theta°$ **g)** 383.9°
h) $-360x°$

5. a) 10 cm   **b)** 15 cm   **c)** 9 cm   **d)** 30.5 cm
e) 21 cm   **f)** 3 cm

6. a) 28.3 cm   **b)** 15.7 cm   **c)** 22.0 cm
d) 34.6 cm   **e)** 50.3 cm   **f)** 37.7 cm
g) 64.9 cm   **h)** 41.9 cm

7. a) i) 15 m   **ii)** 26 m   **b) i)** 47 cm
ii) 353 cm   **c) i)** 509 mm   **ii)** 1131 mm

8. a) 2π **b)** π **c)** $\dfrac{\pi}{2}$

9. 15 m

10. 51 cm

11. $\dfrac{\pi x}{50}$

12. a) About 0.0172   **b)** 2 560 000 km

13. a) About 87 rad/s   **b)** $\dfrac{500x}{9d}$ rad/s

14. a) i) $R\sqrt{2}$ **ii)** $\dfrac{\pi R}{2}$ **b)** $\dfrac{\pi}{2\sqrt{2}}$ **c)** $\dfrac{R^2(\pi - 2)}{4}$

d) $\dfrac{R\sqrt{2}}{2}$

Exercises 5-3, page 169

1. a) 0.939 69   **b)** −0.898 79   **c)** −4.331 48
d) −0.374 61   **e)** −0.809 02   **f)** −0.139 17
g) −0.424 47   **h)** −0.998 63

2. a) 0.295 52   **b)** 0.764 84   **c)** 5.797 88
d) 0.999 57   **e)** −0.998 29   **f)** −2.848 59
g) −0.345 89   **h)** −0.656 39

3. a) P is in the 4th quadrant.
b) −0.447 21; 0.894 43, −0.500 00

4. a) P is in the 2nd quadrant.
b) 0.832 05, −0.554 70, −1.500 00

5. a) 0.75, 5.53   **b)** 0.47, 3.61   **c)** 1.41, 4.88
d) 1.57, 4.71   **e)** 0.34, 2.80   **f)** 0.90, 5.38

6. a) P is in the 4th quadrant; $-\dfrac{6}{\sqrt{157}}, \dfrac{11}{\sqrt{157}}, -\dfrac{6}{11}$

b) P is in the 3rd quadrant; $-\dfrac{1}{\sqrt{26}}, -\dfrac{5}{\sqrt{26}}, \dfrac{1}{5}$

c) P is in the 2nd quadrant; $\dfrac{1}{\sqrt{5}}, -\dfrac{2}{\sqrt{5}}, -\dfrac{1}{2}$

d) P is in the 3rd quadrant; $-\dfrac{5}{\sqrt{41}}, -\dfrac{4}{\sqrt{41}}, \dfrac{5}{4}$

e) P is in the 4th quadrant; $-\dfrac{3}{\sqrt{34}}, \dfrac{5}{\sqrt{34}}, -\dfrac{3}{5}$

f) P is in the 1st quadrant; $\dfrac{8}{\sqrt{73}}, \dfrac{3}{\sqrt{73}}, \dfrac{8}{3}$

g) P is on the positive y-axis; 1, 0, undefined
h) P is on the negative x-axis; 0, −1, 0

7. a) 0.707 11
b) Answers may vary. 45°, 405°, 495°

8. a) −0.813 94
b) Answers may vary; to 5 decimal places, 8.741 59, 2.458 41, 11.883 19

9. a) 203°, 337°   **b)** 139°, 221°   **c)** 17°, 197°
d) 319°, 139°   **e)** 119°, 241°   **f)** 14°, 166°

10. a) 2.83, 5.98   **b)** 3.69, 5.73   **c)** 2.51, 3.77
d) 1.31, 4.98   **e)** 2.55, 5.69   **f)** 0.51, 2.63

11. a) i) 43°, 223°   **ii)** 125°, 305°   **iii)** 116°, 296°
b) i) 0.74, 3.88   **ii)** 2.18, 5.32
iii) 2.03, 5.17

12. b) P has coordinates (5,4), (10,8), (15,12), etc.
c) $\sin \theta = \dfrac{4}{\sqrt{41}}, \cos \theta = \dfrac{5}{\sqrt{41}}$

13. b) P has coordinates (−3,5), (−6,10), (−9,15), etc.
c) $\sin \theta = \dfrac{5}{\sqrt{34}}, \cos \theta = -\dfrac{3}{\sqrt{34}}$

14. b) P has coordinates (−1,3), (−2,6), (−3,9), etc.
c) $\cos \theta = -\dfrac{1}{\sqrt{10}}, \tan \theta = -3$

15. Answers may vary.

Exercises 5-4, page 173

1. a) 3.420 **b)** 1.804 **c)** 2.281 **d)** 0.158
e) 1.836 **f)** 1.058 **g)** 5.145 **h)** 1.012
i) 0.754 **j)** 1.589 **k)** 1.086 **l)** 1.006

2. a) $\sin 25° = 0.423$, $\csc 25° = 2.366$;
$\cos 25° = 0.906$, $\sec 25° = 1.103$;
$\tan 25° = 0.466$, $\cot 25° = 2.145$
b) $\sin 50° = 0.766$; $\csc 50° = 1.305$;
$\cos 50° = 0.643$, $\sec 50° = 1.556$;
$\tan 50° = 1.192$, $\cot 50° = 0.839$
c) $\sin 75° = 0.966$, $\csc 75° = 1.035$;
$\cos 75° = 0.259$, $\sec 75° = 3.864$;
$\tan 75° = 3.732$, $\cot 75° = 0.268$
d) $\sin 30° = 0.500$, $\csc 30° = 2.000$;
$\cos 30° = 0.866$, $\sec 30° = 1.155$;
$\tan 30° = 0.577$, $\cot 30° = 1.732$
e) $\sin 45° = \cos 45° = 0.707$;
$\csc 45° = \sec 45° = 1.414$;
$\tan 45° = \cot 45° = 1.000$
f) $\sin 60° = 0.866$, $\csc 60° = 1.155$;
$\cos 60° = 0.500$, $\sec 60° = 2.000$;
$\tan 60° = 1.732$, $\cot 60° = 0.577$

3. a) 38° **b)** 56° **c)** 19° **d)** 61° **e)** 41°
f) 50° **g)** 15° **h)** 74° **i)** 23° **j)** 67°
k) 12° **l)** 52°

4. a), b) $\sin A = \cos B = \dfrac{a}{c}$; $\cos A = \sin B = \dfrac{b}{c}$;

$\tan A = \cot B = \dfrac{a}{b}$; $\csc A = \sec B = \dfrac{c}{a}$;

$\sec A = \csc B = \dfrac{c}{b}$; $\cot A = \tan B = \dfrac{b}{a}$

5. $\sin A = \cos B$, $\cos A = \sin B$, $\tan A = \cot B$,
$\csc A = \sec B$, $\sec A = \csc B$, $\cot A = \tan B$

6. a) $AB = 16.1$, $\angle A = 43.0°$; $\angle C = 47.0°$
b) $\angle N = 33°$, $PM = 26.1$, $PN = 40.3$
c) $\angle S = 57°$, $VS = 22.4$, $TS = 41.1$

7. a) $\sin \theta = \dfrac{q}{p}$, $\cos \theta = \dfrac{\sqrt{p^2 - q^2}}{p}$,

$\tan \theta = \dfrac{q}{\sqrt{p^2 - q^2}}$, $\sec \theta = \dfrac{p}{\sqrt{p^2 - q^2}}$,

$\cot \theta = \dfrac{\sqrt{p^2 - q^2}}{q}$

b) $\sin \phi = \dfrac{2\sqrt{x}}{x + 1}$, $\cos \phi = \dfrac{x - 1}{x + 1}$,

$\tan \phi = \dfrac{2\sqrt{x}}{x - 1}$, $\csc \phi = \dfrac{x + 1}{2\sqrt{x}}$,

$\cot \phi = \dfrac{x - 1}{2\sqrt{x}}$

c) $\sin \alpha = \dfrac{a + 1}{\sqrt{5a^2 + 2a + 1}}$,

$\cos \alpha = \dfrac{2a}{\sqrt{5a^2 + 2a + 1}}$, $\tan \alpha = \dfrac{a + 1}{2a}$,

$\csc \alpha = \dfrac{\sqrt{5a^2 + 2a + 1}}{a + 1}$,

$\sec \alpha = \dfrac{\sqrt{5a^2 + 2a + 1}}{2a}$

8. a) 31 cm **b)** 7.85 m **c)** 196.23 m
d) 9613 m

Exercises 5-5, page 177

1. a) 1 **b)** $\dfrac{2}{\sqrt{3}}$ **c)** $\dfrac{\sqrt{3}}{2}$ **d)** 0 **e)** 2 **f)** 1

g) $\sqrt{2}$ **h)** $\dfrac{1}{\sqrt{2}}$ **i)** $\sqrt{3}$ **j)** $\dfrac{\sqrt{3}}{2}$ **k)** 0

l) 1

2. a) $-\sqrt{2}$ **b)** $\dfrac{1}{2}$ **c)** 0 **d)** $\dfrac{1}{2}$ **e)** 1

f) Undefined **g)** $\dfrac{1}{\sqrt{2}}$ **h)** -2 **i)** $\dfrac{2}{\sqrt{3}}$

j) -1 **k)** $-\dfrac{1}{\sqrt{3}}$ **l)** $\dfrac{1}{\sqrt{3}}$

3. a) 3 **b)** 4 **c)** $\dfrac{1}{4}$ **d)** $\dfrac{4}{3}$ **e)** $-\dfrac{1}{2\sqrt{2}}$ **f)** $\dfrac{1}{3}$

4. a) $\dfrac{7\pi}{6}, \dfrac{11\pi}{6}$ **b)** $\dfrac{\pi}{4}, \dfrac{7\pi}{4}$ **c)** $\dfrac{2\pi}{3}, \dfrac{5\pi}{3}$ **d)** $\dfrac{\pi}{6}, \dfrac{5\pi}{6}$
e) $\dfrac{\pi}{4}, \dfrac{7\pi}{4}$ **f)** $\dfrac{3\pi}{4}, \dfrac{7\pi}{4}$ **g)** $\dfrac{\pi}{4}, \dfrac{3\pi}{4}$ **h)** $\dfrac{\pi}{6}, \dfrac{7\pi}{6}$
i) $\dfrac{2\pi}{3}, \dfrac{4\pi}{3}$ **j)** $\dfrac{3\pi}{2}$ **k)** $\dfrac{2\pi}{3}, \dfrac{4\pi}{3}$ **l)** $\dfrac{2\pi}{3}, \dfrac{5\pi}{3}$

5. a) $\dfrac{\pi}{4}, \dfrac{3\pi}{4}, \dfrac{5\pi}{4}, \dfrac{7\pi}{4}$ **b)** $\dfrac{\pi}{3}, \dfrac{2\pi}{3}, \dfrac{4\pi}{3}, \dfrac{5\pi}{3}$ **c)** $\dfrac{\pi}{4}, \dfrac{3\pi}{4}, \dfrac{5\pi}{4}, \dfrac{7\pi}{4}$
d) $\dfrac{\pi}{3}, \dfrac{2\pi}{3}, \dfrac{4\pi}{3}, \dfrac{5\pi}{3}$ **e)** $\dfrac{\pi}{3}, \dfrac{2\pi}{3}, \dfrac{4\pi}{3}, \dfrac{5\pi}{3}$ **f)** $\dfrac{2\pi}{3}, \dfrac{4\pi}{3}$
g) $\dfrac{7\pi}{6}, \dfrac{11\pi}{6}$ **h)** $\dfrac{\pi}{4}, \dfrac{3\pi}{4}, \dfrac{5\pi}{4}, \dfrac{7\pi}{4}$

6. a) $\csc \theta = -\dfrac{\sqrt{3}}{2}$, $\cos \theta = \pm\dfrac{1}{2}$, $\sec \theta = \pm 2$,

$\tan \theta = \pm\sqrt{3}$, $\cot \theta = \pm\dfrac{1}{\sqrt{3}}$

b) $\cot \theta = \dfrac{1}{\sqrt{3}}$, $\sin \theta = \pm\dfrac{\sqrt{3}}{2}$, $\csc \theta = \pm\dfrac{2}{\sqrt{3}}$,

$\cos \theta = \pm\dfrac{1}{2}$, $\sec \theta = \pm 2$

c) $\cos \theta = -\dfrac{\sqrt{3}}{2}$, $\sin \theta = \pm\dfrac{1}{2}$,

$\csc \theta = \pm 2$, $\tan \theta = \pm\dfrac{1}{\sqrt{3}}$, $\cot \theta = \pm\sqrt{3}$

7. a) $\sin(\pi + \theta) = -\dfrac{y}{r}$, $\csc(\pi + \theta) = -\dfrac{r}{y}$

$\cos(\pi + \theta) = -\dfrac{x}{r}$, $\sec(\pi + \theta) = -\dfrac{r}{x}$

$\tan(\pi + \theta) = \dfrac{y}{x}$, $\cot(\pi + \theta) = \dfrac{x}{y}$

b) $\sin(2\pi - \theta) = -\dfrac{y}{r}$, $\csc(2\pi - \theta) = -\dfrac{r}{y}$,

$\cos(2\pi - \theta) = \dfrac{x}{r}$, $\sec(2\pi - \theta) = \dfrac{r}{x}$,

$\tan(2\pi - \theta) = -\dfrac{y}{x}$, $\cot(2\pi - \theta) = -\dfrac{x}{y}$

Exercises 5-6, page 181

2. a) $\cos\theta = 1, 0.5, 0, -0.5, -1$
b) $\cos\theta = -0.5, 0, 0.5, 1$

5. a) $y = 1$ when $\theta = \dfrac{\pi}{2}$ and $-\dfrac{3\pi}{2}$

b) $y = -1$ when $\theta = \dfrac{3\pi}{2}$ and $-\dfrac{\pi}{2}$

c) $\{y \mid -1 \leqslant y \leqslant 1\}$ **d)** 0
e) $0, \pm\pi, \pm2\pi$

6. a) $y = 1$ when $\theta = 0$ and $\pm2\pi$
b) $y = -1$ when $\theta = \pm\pi$
c) $\{y \mid -1 \leqslant y \leqslant 1\}$ **d)** 1 **e)** $\pm\dfrac{\pi}{2}, \pm\dfrac{3\pi}{2}$

7. Answers may vary.
10. a)

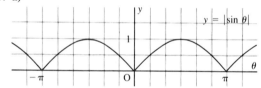

b)

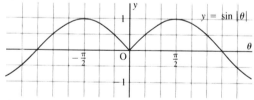

c)

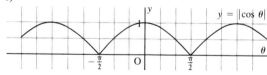

d)

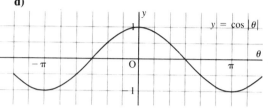

Exercises 5-7, page 186

3. a) No, explanations may vary; the graph goes to infinity at the asymptotes.
b) The domain is any angle in standard position. The range is any real number.
c) 0 **d)** $0, \pm\pi, \pm2\pi$, etc.

4. Answers may vary.
6. Odd
7. a)

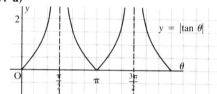

b)

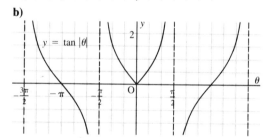

Exercises 5-8, page 192

2. a) $y = 1.5\sin\theta$; 1.5; -1.5; 1.5
b) $y = 2.5\sin\theta$; 2.5; -2.5; 2.5
c) $y = 0.5\cos\theta$; 0.5, -0.5, 0.5

3. a) $y = \sin\theta + 0.5$; 0.5; 1.5; -0.5; 0.5
b) $y = \cos\theta - 1$; -1; 0; -2; 0

4. a) 5; -5; $\{y \mid -5 \leqslant y \leqslant 5\}$

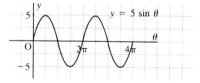

b) 3; -3; $\{y \mid -3 \leqslant y \leqslant 3\}$

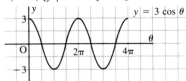

c) 7; 1; $\{y \mid 1 \leqslant y \leqslant 7\}$

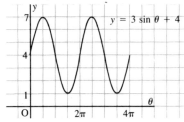

d) -1; -5; $\{y \mid -5 \leqslant y \leqslant -1\}$

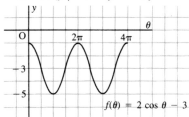

e) 2; -6; $\{y \mid -6 \leqslant y \leqslant 2\}$

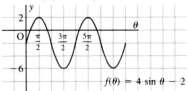

f) 3.5; 2.5; $\{y \mid 2.5 \leqslant y \leqslant 3.5\}$

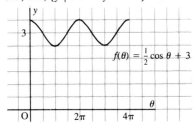

g) -0.5; -1.5; $\{y \mid -1.5 \leqslant y \leqslant -0.5\}$

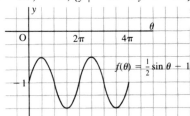

h) 4; 0; $\{y \mid 0 \leqslant y \leqslant 4\}$

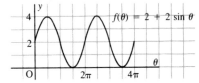

i) 6; 0; $\{y \mid 0 \leqslant y \leqslant 6\}$

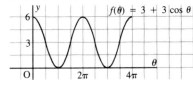

5. a) $a + q$; $\frac{\pi}{2}, \frac{5\pi}{2}, \ldots$ **b)** $q - a$; $\frac{3\pi}{2}, \frac{7\pi}{2}, \ldots$

6. a) $a + q$; 0, π, 2π, $\ldots$
  b) $q - a$; π, 3π, $\ldots$

7. $y = \sin \theta + 1$; $y = \sin \theta - 1$

Exercises 5-9, page 197

2. Typical answers: $\frac{\pi}{3}$, $y = \sin \left(\theta - \frac{\pi}{3} \right)$;

  $-\frac{5\pi}{3}$, $y = \sin \left(\theta + \frac{5\pi}{3} \right)$

3. Typical answers: $\frac{5\pi}{6}$, $y = \cos \left(\theta - \frac{5\pi}{6} \right)$;

  $-\frac{7\pi}{6}$, $y = \cos \left(\theta + \frac{7\pi}{6} \right)$

4. a)

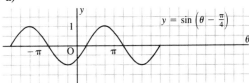

b)

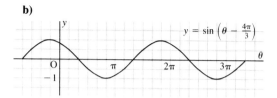

$$y = \sin\left(\theta - \frac{4\pi}{3}\right)$$

c)

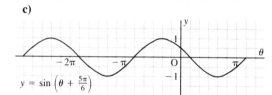

$$y = \sin\left(\theta + \frac{5\pi}{6}\right)$$

d)

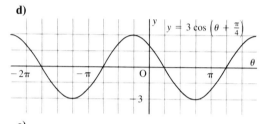

$$y = 3\cos\left(\theta + \frac{\pi}{4}\right)$$

e)

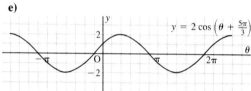

$$y = 2\cos\left(\theta + \frac{5\pi}{3}\right)$$

f)

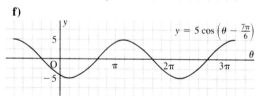

$$y = 5\cos\left(\theta - \frac{7\pi}{6}\right)$$

5. a)

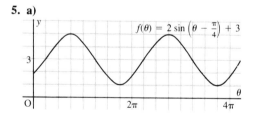

$$f(\theta) = 2\sin\left(\theta - \frac{\pi}{4}\right) + 3$$

b)

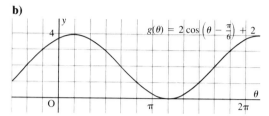

$$g(\theta) = 2\cos\left(\theta - \frac{\pi}{6}\right) + 2$$

c)

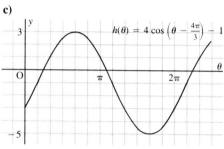

$$h(\theta) = 4\cos\left(\theta - \frac{4\pi}{3}\right) - 1$$

d)

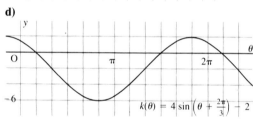

$$k(\theta) = 4\sin\left(\theta + \frac{2\pi}{3}\right) - 2$$

6. a)

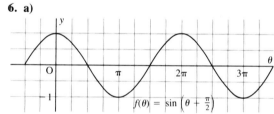

$$f(\theta) = \sin\left(\theta + \frac{\pi}{2}\right)$$

b)

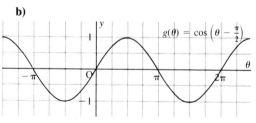

$$g(\theta) = \cos\left(\theta - \frac{\pi}{2}\right)$$

$f(\theta) = \sin\left(\theta + \frac{\pi}{2}\right)$ is the same graph as
$f(\theta) = \cos\theta$.
$g(\theta) = \cos\left(\theta - \frac{\pi}{2}\right)$ is the same graph as
$g(\theta) = \sin\theta$.

7. Answers may vary.   **a)** $\pm 2\pi$, $\pm 4\pi$, . . .

　b) $-\frac{\pi}{2}$, $\frac{3\pi}{2}$, . . .

8. Answers may vary.   **a)** $\frac{\pi}{2}$, $\frac{5\pi}{2}$, . . .

　b) $\pm 2\pi$, $\pm 4\pi$, . . .

9. a) $f(\theta) = a + q$ when $\theta = p + \frac{\pi}{2}$; $p - \frac{3\pi}{2}$; . . .

　b) $f(\theta) = -a + q$ when $\theta = p + \frac{3\pi}{2}$;

　　$p - \frac{\pi}{2}$; . . .

10. a) $f(\theta) = a + q$ when $\theta = p$; $\pm 2\pi + p$; . . .
　b) $f(\theta) = -a + q$ when $\theta = \pm \pi + p$; . . .

11. Typical answer: $f(\theta) = \sin\left(\theta + \frac{\pi}{2}\right) + 2$

12. Typical answer: $f(\theta) = \cos(\theta + \pi) - 4$

Exercises 5-10, page 203

2. a) $y = \sin 3\theta$ **b)** $y = \sin 6\theta$
3. a) 2, π **b)** 3, 4π

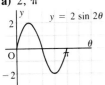

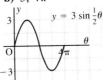

c) 4, π **d)** 4, 4π

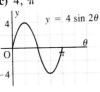

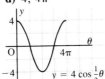

e) 5, π **f)** 3, $\frac{2\pi}{3}$

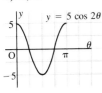

4. a) 5; $\frac{2\pi}{3}$; π **b)** 2; $\frac{\pi}{2}$; $-\frac{\pi}{2}$ **c)** 2.5; $\frac{\pi}{3}$; $\frac{2\pi}{3}$

　d) 0.5; $\frac{2\pi}{5}$; $-\frac{5\pi}{4}$

5. a) 1; π; $\frac{\pi}{3}$

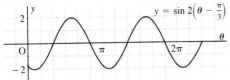

b) 2; $\frac{2\pi}{3}$; $\frac{\pi}{2}$

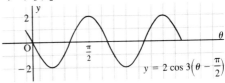

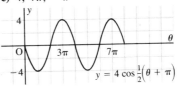

c) 4; 4π; $-\pi$

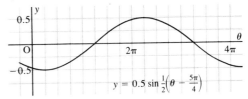

d) 0.5; 4π; $\frac{5\pi}{4}$; only 1 cycle shown

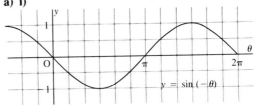

6. a) i)

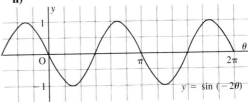

ii)

iii)

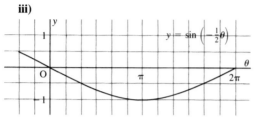

b) Answers may vary.

c) For $y = \sin k\theta$, see the graphs in part a).

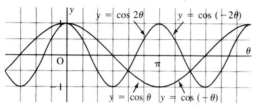

d) Answers may vary.

7. a) $\frac{2\pi}{3}$

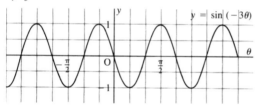

b) 4π

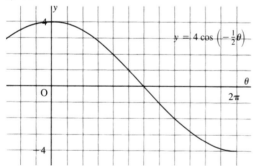

c) π

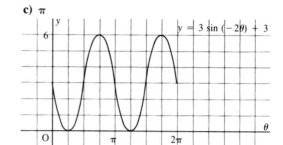

8. a) $y = \sin(-\theta)$ is a reflection of $y = \sin\theta$ in the y-axis.

b) $y = \cos(-\theta)$ is the same graph as $y = \cos\theta$.

The Mathematical Mind, page 205

1. a) 6   **b)** 120   **c)** 5040   **d)** 40 320
e) 362 880   **f)** 3 628 800

2. $\sin x = x - \dfrac{x^3}{6} + \dfrac{x^5}{120} - \dfrac{x^7}{5040}$
$+ \dfrac{x^9}{362\ 880} - \dfrac{x^{11}}{39\ 916\ 800}$,

$\cos x = 1 - \dfrac{x^2}{2} + \dfrac{x^4}{24} - \dfrac{x^6}{720} + \dfrac{x^8}{40\ 320}$
$- \dfrac{x^{10}}{3\ 628\ 800}$

4. a) 3   **b)** 4   **c)** 5

Exercises 5-11, page 209

1. a) i) 2   **ii)** 2π
  iii) Typical answer: $\frac{\pi}{4}$ for cosine function
  iv) $y = 5$ when $\theta = \frac{\pi}{4}, \frac{9\pi}{4}, \dots$
  v) $y = 1$ when $\theta = \frac{5\pi}{4}, \dots$ **vi)** 3
  b) i) 3   **ii)** π
  iii) Typical answer: $\frac{\pi}{2}$ for sine function
  iv) $y = 6$ when $\theta = -\frac{\pi}{4}, \frac{3\pi}{4}, \frac{7\pi}{4}, \dots$
  v) $y = 0$ when $\theta = \frac{\pi}{4}, \frac{5\pi}{4}, \dots$ **vi)** 3
  c) i) 5   **ii)** 2π
  iii) Typical answer: $\frac{\pi}{6}$ for cosine function
  iv) $y = 20$ when $\theta = \frac{\pi}{6}, \frac{13\pi}{6}, \dots$
  v) $y = 10$ when $\theta = \frac{7\pi}{6}, \frac{19\pi}{6}, \dots$ **vi)** 15

2. Typical answers: **a)** $y = 2\cos\left(\theta - \frac{\pi}{4}\right) + 3$

b) $y = 3 \sin 2\left(\theta - \frac{\pi}{2}\right) + 3$

c) $y = 5 \cos \left(\theta - \frac{\pi}{6}\right) + 15$

3. a) $\frac{\pi}{3}$; π **b)** 4; 2

c)

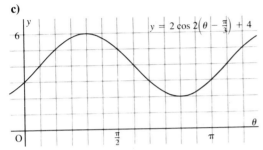

4. a) $\frac{\pi}{4}$, π **b)** 3; 3

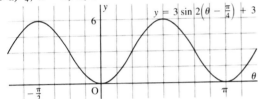

5. a) $\frac{\pi}{2}$; $\frac{2\pi}{3}$

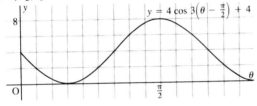

b) $-\pi$; $\frac{\pi}{2}$

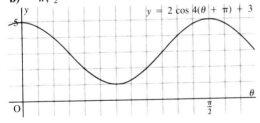

c) $-\dfrac{\pi}{6}$; π

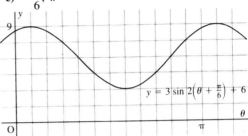

d) $\frac{\pi}{6}$, $\frac{2\pi}{3}$

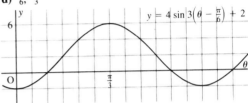

6. a)

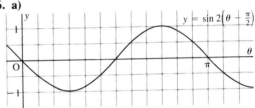

b)

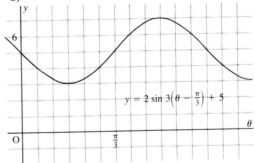

c)

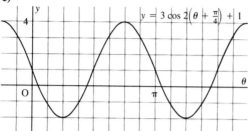

$y = 3 \cos 2\left(\theta + \frac{\pi}{4}\right) + 1$

d)

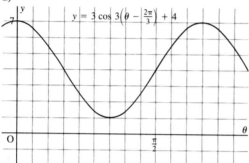

$y = 3 \cos 3\left(\theta - \frac{2\pi}{3}\right) + 4$

7. Answers may vary.

8. a) $\frac{\pi}{2}$; π

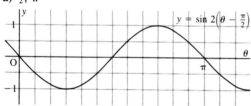

$y = \sin 2\left(\theta - \frac{\pi}{2}\right)$

b) $\frac{\pi}{3}$; $\frac{2\pi}{3}$

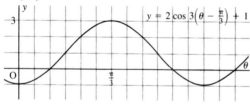

$y = 2 \cos 3\left(\theta - \frac{\pi}{3}\right) + 1$

c) $\frac{\pi}{3}$; $\frac{2\pi}{3}$; same shape as part b) but shifted 3 units up.

d) $-\frac{\pi}{4}$; $\frac{\pi}{2}$

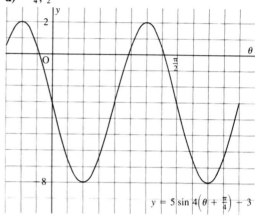

$y = 5 \sin 4\left(\theta + \frac{\pi}{4}\right) - 3$

9. a)

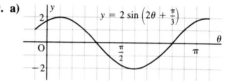

$y = 2 \sin\left(2\theta + \frac{\pi}{3}\right)$

b)

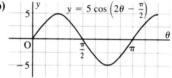

$y = 5 \cos\left(2\theta - \frac{\pi}{2}\right)$

c) Same shape as part b), but y-axis labelled with 3 in place of 5

d) Same shape as part a), but y-axis labelled with 5 in place of 2

10. a and c   **11.** a and b

12. a) Typical answers: 0, $\pm\pi$, $\pm 2\pi$, $\pm 3\pi$
   b) $n\pi$, where n is an integer

13. a) Typical answers:

$-\frac{11\pi}{4}$, $-\frac{7\pi}{4}$, $-\frac{3\pi}{4}$, $\frac{\pi}{4}$, $\frac{5\pi}{4}$, $\frac{9\pi}{4}$

   b) $n\pi + \frac{\pi}{4}$, where n is an integer

14. Answers may vary.

15. a) 0; 1
b)

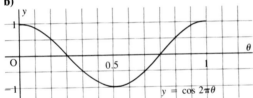

16. a) 0; 1

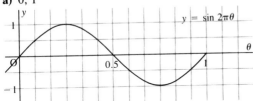

b) 0; 4

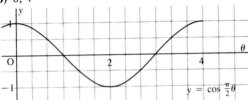

c) 0; 4

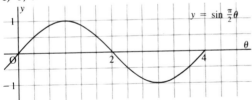

Exercises 5-12, page 216

1. a) 3; 5; 1; 4   **b)** 2; 4; 5; 6
2. a) 2; 12; typical answer: 2; 3
   b) 6; 4; typical answer: 0; 8
   c) 10; 40; typical answer: −5; 20
3. a) $y = 2 \sin \dfrac{2\pi(t - 2)}{12} + 3$
   b) $y = 6 \cos \dfrac{2\pi t}{4} + 8$
   c) $y = 10 \cos \dfrac{2\pi(t + 5)}{40} + 20$

4. a) $y = \sin \pi t$ **b)** $y = \cos \pi t$ **c)** $y = \cos \frac{\pi t}{2}$
   d) $y = \sin \frac{\pi t}{2}$
5. a) $y = 5 \cos 2\pi(t - 9) + 4$
   b) $y = 12 \cos 4\pi(t + 3) + 1.5$
   c) $y = 2.4 \cos \dfrac{2\pi(t - 19)}{27} + 15.1$

6. a)

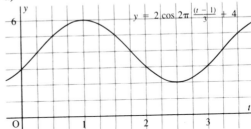

b)

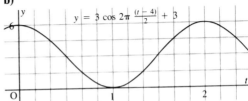

c)

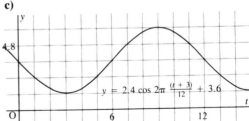

d)

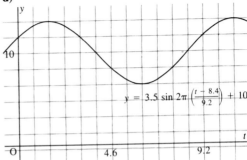

7. a) See page 212.

b)

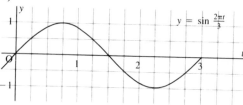

$$y = \sin \frac{2\pi t}{3}$$

c)

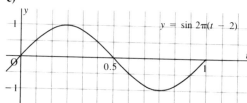

$$y = \sin 2\pi(t - 2)$$

d)

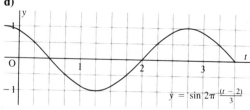

$$y = \sin 2\pi \frac{(t - 2)}{3}$$

e) See page 212.

f)

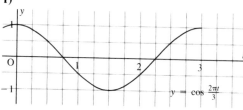

$$y = \cos \frac{2\pi t}{3}$$

g)

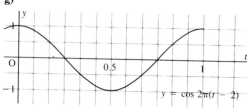

$$y = \cos 2\pi(t - 2)$$

h)

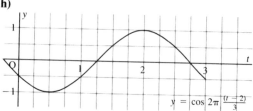

$$y = \cos 2\pi \frac{(t - 2)}{3}$$

8. a) $y = 5$ when $t = -5, -2, 1, 4$;
$y = 1$ when $t = -3.5, -0.5, 2.5$
b) $y = 0$ when $t = -0.75, 4.25$;
$y = -8$ when $t = -3.25, 1.75$
c) $y = 8$ when $t = -4.25, -1.25, 1.75, 4.75$;
$y = 4$ when $t = -2.75, 0.25, 3.25$
d) $y = 7$ when $t = -3, 3$; $y = -3$ when $t = 0$

9. a) $y = 6 \sin \dfrac{2\pi(t - 9)}{5} + 17$

b) $y = 4.3 \sin \dfrac{2\pi(t - 4.7)}{3.9} + 12.9$

10. Typical answer: $y = 2000 \sin \frac{\pi t}{5} + 3000$

11. a)

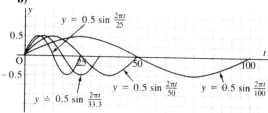

$$y = 80 \sin \frac{2\pi t}{10}$$

b) Typical answer: $y = 80 \sin \frac{\pi t}{5}$

12. a) i) 40 cm   **ii)** 0 cm   **iii)** 0.05 s   **b)** 72 000

13. a) $y = 0.5 \sin \frac{\pi t}{50}$; $y = 0.5 \sin \frac{\pi t}{25}$; $y = 0.5 \sin \frac{3\pi t}{50}$;
$y = 0.5 \sin \frac{2\pi t}{25}$

b)

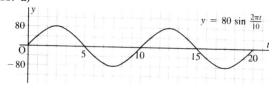

$$y = 0.5 \sin \frac{2\pi t}{25}$$

$$y = 0.5 \sin \frac{2\pi t}{50}$$

$$y = 0.5 \sin \frac{2\pi t}{100}$$

$$y \doteq 0.5 \sin \frac{2\pi t}{33.3}$$

14. b and c

Exercises 5-13, page 223

1. **a)** About 4.0 m; 1.7 m
   b) 4.9 m at 7:06 A.M. and 7:30 P.M.

2. About 2.3 m

3. **a)** $y = 4 \cos \dfrac{2\pi(t - 8.00)}{12.4}$ **b)** About 2.1 m

4. **a)** $y = 4.6 \cos \dfrac{2\pi(t - 4.50)}{12.4} + 5$
   b) 1.2 m, 7.7 m

5. **a)** $y = 1.4 \cos \dfrac{2\pi(t - 4.50)}{12.4} + 5$
   b) 3.9 m, 5.8 m

6. **a)**

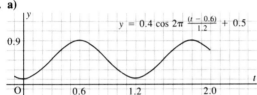

$$y = 0.4 \cos 2\pi \tfrac{(t - 0.6)}{1.2} + 0.5$$

   b) Typical answer:
   $$y = 0.4 \cos \dfrac{2\pi(t - 0.6)}{1.2} + 0.5 \text{ or}$$
   $$y = 0.4 \sin \dfrac{2\pi(t - 0.3)}{1.2} + 0.5$$
   c) i) 0.50 m   **ii)** About 0.85 m   **iii)** 0.10 m

7. **a)**

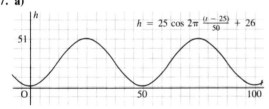

$$h = 25 \cos 2\pi \tfrac{(t - 25)}{50} + 26$$

   b) Typical answer: $h = 25 \cos \dfrac{2\pi(t - 25)}{50} + 26$
   c) i) 18 m   **ii)** 46 m   **iii)** 18 m   **iv)** 18 m

8. **a)**

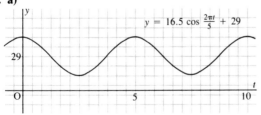

$$y = 16.5 \cos \tfrac{2\pi t}{5} + 29$$

   b) Typical answer: $y = 16.5 \cos \dfrac{2\pi t}{5} + 29$
   c) i) 45.5 cm   **ii)** 15.7 cm   **iii)** 15.7 cm

9. **a)** Typical answer:
   $$t = 2.5 \cos \dfrac{2\pi(n - 172)}{365} + 17.7$$
   b) i) 7:34 P.M.   **ii)** 8:10 P.M.   **iii)** 5:50 P.M.
   iv) 3:20 P.M.

10. **a)** Typical answer: $t = 2 \cos \dfrac{2\pi(n - 172)}{365} + 18.3$
    b) i) 5:19 P.M.   **ii)** 7:05 P.M.   **iii)** 7:58 P.M.
    iv) 4:53 P.M.

11. **a)** 5:28 A.M.   **b)** Answers may vary.

12. **a)** Typical answer:
    $$d = 2.5 \cos \dfrac{2\pi(n - 172)}{365} + 149.7$$
    b) i) 148.8 million km   **ii)** 151.3 million km
    iii) 150.5 million km

15. **a)** Answers may vary.   **b)** Feb. 16 and Oct. 23

16. **a)** 6:56 A.M.   **b)** 9:02 A.M.

Problem Solving, page 227

1. $y^2 = 2p(x + a^2)$

2. 4

3. $\dfrac{|Ax_1 + By_1 + C|}{\sqrt{A^2 + B^2}}$

4. 55°, 83°, 42°

7. **b)** Yes   **c) i)** $\tfrac{1}{2}\sqrt{2b^2 + 2c^2 - a^2}$
   ii) $\sqrt{bc\left(1 - \dfrac{a^2}{(b + c)^2}\right)}$
   iii) $\sqrt{c^2 - \dfrac{(a^2 - b^2 + c^2)^2}{2a}}$

8. 1:5

Review Exercises, page 228

1. **a)** 60°   **b)** −315°   **c)** 150°   **d)** 269.3°

2. **a)** $\tfrac{3\pi}{4}$ **b)** $\tfrac{3\pi}{2}$ **c)** $\tfrac{11\pi}{6}$ **d)** −0.82

3. About 35 cm

4. **a)** 0.914, 0.406, 2.250
   b) −0.882, 0.471, −1.875
   c) 0.868, −0.496, −1.75
   d) −0.640, −0.768, 0.833

5. a) i) 66.0° **ii)** 1.153
  b) i) 298.1° **ii)** 5.202
  c) i) 119.7° **ii)** 2.090
  d) i) 219.8° **ii)** 3.836

6. a) 47°, 133° **b)** 113°, 293° **c)** 101°, 281°

7. a) 1.30, 4.98 **b)** 0.82, 3.96 **c)** 5.80, 3.63

8. a) $\csc \theta = \dfrac{b}{a}$; $\cos \theta = \dfrac{\sqrt{b^2 - a^2}}{b}$;

  $\sec \theta = \dfrac{b}{\sqrt{b^2 - a^2}}$; $\tan \theta = \dfrac{a}{\sqrt{b^2 - a^2}}$;

  $\cot \theta = \dfrac{\sqrt{b^2 - a^2}}{a}$

  b) $\sin \theta = \dfrac{p}{\sqrt{2p^2 + 2pq + q^2}}$;

  $\csc \theta = \dfrac{\sqrt{2p^2 + 2pq + q^2}}{p}$;

  $\cos \theta = \dfrac{p + q}{\sqrt{2p^2 + 2pq + q^2}}$;

  $\sec \theta = \dfrac{\sqrt{2p^2 + 2pq + q^2}}{p + q}$; $\cot \theta = \dfrac{p + q}{p}$

  c) $\sin \theta = \dfrac{\sqrt{3m^2 - 10m - 8}}{2m - 1}$;

  $\csc \theta = \dfrac{2m - 1}{\sqrt{3m^2 - 10m - 8}}$; $\cos \theta = \dfrac{m + 3}{2m - 1}$;

  $\tan \theta = \dfrac{\sqrt{3m^2 - 10m - 8}}{m + 3}$;

  $\cot \theta = \dfrac{m + 3}{\sqrt{3m^2 - 10m - 8}}$

9. a) $\sin \dfrac{5\pi}{6} = \dfrac{1}{2}$; $\csc \dfrac{5\pi}{6} = 2$;

  $\cos \dfrac{5\pi}{6} = -\dfrac{\sqrt{3}}{2}$; $\sec \dfrac{5\pi}{6} = -\dfrac{2}{\sqrt{3}}$;

  $\tan \dfrac{5\pi}{6} = -\dfrac{1}{\sqrt{3}}$; $\cot \dfrac{5\pi}{6} = -\sqrt{3}$

  b) $\sin \dfrac{\pi}{3} = \dfrac{\sqrt{3}}{2}$; $\csc \dfrac{\pi}{3} = \dfrac{2}{\sqrt{3}}$;

  $\cos \dfrac{\pi}{3} = \dfrac{1}{2}$; $\sec \dfrac{\pi}{3} = 2$;

  $\tan \dfrac{\pi}{3} = \sqrt{3}$; $\cot \dfrac{\pi}{3} = \dfrac{1}{\sqrt{3}}$

  c) $\sin \dfrac{7\pi}{4} = -\dfrac{1}{\sqrt{2}}$; $\csc \dfrac{7\pi}{4} = -\sqrt{2}$;

  $\cos \dfrac{7\pi}{4} = \dfrac{1}{\sqrt{2}}$; $\sec \dfrac{7\pi}{4} = \sqrt{2}$;

  $\tan \dfrac{7\pi}{4} = -1$; $\cot \dfrac{7\pi}{4} = -1$

d) $\sin \dfrac{4\pi}{3} = -\dfrac{\sqrt{3}}{2}$; $\csc \dfrac{4\pi}{3} = -\dfrac{2}{\sqrt{3}}$;

  $\cos \dfrac{4\pi}{3} = -\dfrac{1}{2}$; $\sec \dfrac{4\pi}{3} = -2$;

  $\tan \dfrac{4\pi}{3} = \sqrt{3}$; $\cot \dfrac{4\pi}{3} = \dfrac{1}{\sqrt{3}}$

  e) $\sin \dfrac{11\pi}{6} = -\dfrac{1}{2}$; $\csc \dfrac{11\pi}{6} = -2$;

  $\cos \dfrac{11\pi}{6} = \dfrac{\sqrt{3}}{2}$; $\sec \dfrac{11\pi}{6} = \dfrac{2}{\sqrt{3}}$;

  $\tan \dfrac{11\pi}{6} = -\dfrac{1}{\sqrt{3}}$; $\cot \dfrac{11\pi}{6} = -\sqrt{3}$

10. See page 180.

  a) $\sin \theta$: 1 at $-\dfrac{3\pi}{2}, \dfrac{\pi}{2}$; $\cos \theta$; 1 at 0, $\pm 2\pi$

  b) $\sin \theta$: -1 at $-\dfrac{\pi}{2}, \dfrac{3\pi}{2}$; $\cos \theta$: -1 at $\pm \pi$

  c) $\sin \theta$: y-intercept 0, θ-intercepts $\pm 2\pi$, $\pm \pi$, 0; $\cos \theta$: y-intercept 1, θ-intercepts $\pm \dfrac{3\pi}{2}, \pm \dfrac{\pi}{2}$, 0

11. a) 3; π; $\dfrac{\pi}{4}$; 4 **b)** 2; $\dfrac{2\pi}{5}$; $-\dfrac{\pi}{3}$; 1

12. a)

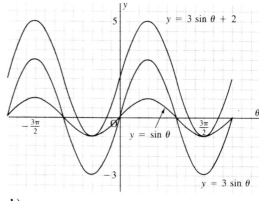

b)

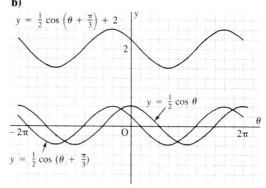

13. a)

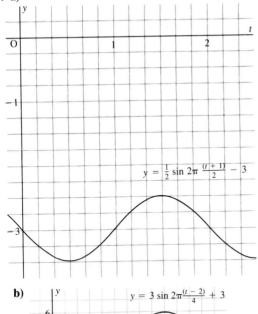

$$y = \tfrac{1}{2} \sin 2\pi \, \frac{(t+1)}{2} - 3$$

b)

$$y = 3 \sin 2\pi \frac{(t-2)}{4} + 3$$

Chapter 6

Exercises 6-1, page 233

5. b) $\dfrac{\sin \theta + \tan \theta}{\csc \theta + \cot \theta} = \sin \theta \tan \theta$

6. b) $\dfrac{\cot \theta}{\csc \theta + 1} = \dfrac{\csc \theta - 1}{\cot \theta}$

7. b) $\dfrac{1}{1 + \cos \theta} + \dfrac{1}{1 - \cos \theta} = 2 \csc^2\theta$

8. b) $\cot^2\theta(1 + \tan^2\theta) = \csc^2\theta$

15. a) $r\sqrt{2 - 2 \cos \theta}$; $r\sqrt{2 + 2 \cos \theta}$

16. $0, \pi, 2\pi$

Exercises 6-2, page 239

1. a) $-\tfrac{1}{2}$ **b)** $\tfrac{1}{\sqrt{2}}$ **c)** -1 **d)** -1 **e)** $-\tfrac{\sqrt{3}}{2}$
f) $\tfrac{1}{\sqrt{2}}$ **g)** $\tfrac{\sqrt{3}}{2}$ **h)** $-\tfrac{1}{2}$

3. a) $-\sqrt{3}$ **b)** $\sqrt{2}$ **c)** -2 **d)** $-\tfrac{1}{\sqrt{3}}$
  e) $-\tfrac{\sqrt{3}}{2}$ **f)** $-\tfrac{1}{2}$ **g)** $-\tfrac{1}{2}$ **h)** 1

4. $\sin \theta = \sin (\pi - \theta)$;
$\sin (\pi - \theta) = -\sin (\pi + \theta)$

6. $\sin \theta = \cos \left(\tfrac{\pi}{2} - \theta\right)$

7. b) $\sin (\pi + \theta) = -\sin (\pi - \theta)$;
$\sin \left(\tfrac{3\pi}{2} + \theta\right) = \sin \left(\tfrac{3\pi}{2} - \theta\right)$;

$\sin (2\pi + \theta) = -\sin (2\pi - \theta)$;
$\cos (\pi + \theta) = \cos (\pi - \theta)$;

$\cos \left(\tfrac{3\pi}{2} + \theta\right) = -\cos \left(\tfrac{3\pi}{2} - \theta\right)$;

$\cos (2\pi + \theta) = \cos (2\pi - \theta)$

Exercises 6-3, page 245

2. a) 1 **b)** 0 **c)** $\tfrac{1}{2}$ **d)** $\tfrac{1}{2}$

3. a), b), c) $-\tfrac{1}{2}$

4. a), b), c) $\tfrac{1}{\sqrt{2}}$

5. b) $\cos \tfrac{\pi}{12} = \dfrac{\sqrt{3} + 1}{2\sqrt{2}}$

6. a) $\dfrac{1 - \sqrt{3}}{2\sqrt{2}}$ **b)** $\dfrac{\sqrt{3} - 1}{2\sqrt{2}}$ **c)** $\dfrac{\sqrt{3} - 1}{2\sqrt{2}}$
  d) $\dfrac{\sqrt{3} + 1}{2\sqrt{2}}$

9. a) $-\cos \theta$ **b)** $\cos \theta$ **c)** $\sin x$ **d)** $\sin x$

10. a) $\dfrac{4\sqrt{3} + 3}{10}$ **b)** $\dfrac{7}{5\sqrt{2}}$ **c)** $\dfrac{3 + 4\sqrt{3}}{10}$

11. a) $\dfrac{\sqrt{15} - 2}{6}$ **b)** $\dfrac{-2 - \sqrt{15}}{6}$ **c)** $\dfrac{\sqrt{5} - 2}{3\sqrt{2}}$

12. a) $\dfrac{3 - \sqrt{21}}{8}$ **b)** $\dfrac{3 - \sqrt{21}}{8}$ **c)** $\dfrac{-\sqrt{7} - 3}{4\sqrt{2}}$

13. b) i) $\cos \theta$ **ii)** $\sqrt{3} \cos \theta$
  c) $\sin (x + y) + \sin (x - y) = 2 \sin x \cos y$

14. a) $-\tfrac{16}{65}$ **b)** $\tfrac{56}{65}$ **c)** $\tfrac{63}{65}$ **d)** $-\tfrac{33}{65}$

15. a) $\dfrac{4\sqrt{5} - 6}{15}$ **b)** $\dfrac{4\sqrt{5} + 6}{15}$ **c)** $\dfrac{-3\sqrt{5} - 8}{15}$
  d) $\dfrac{-3\sqrt{5} + 8}{15}$

16. Values do exist; some examples are:
  a) $\beta = 0$ **b)** $\alpha = \tfrac{\pi}{3}, \beta = -\tfrac{\pi}{3}$ **c)** $\beta = 0$

Exercises 6-4, page 249

3. a) sin 1.2   **b)** sin 6   **c)** sin 4   **d)** cos 0.9
e) cos 10   **f)** cos 6

4. a) sin $\frac{\pi}{3}$ **b)** cos $\frac{\pi}{3}$ **c)** cos 1

5. $\frac{\sqrt{3}}{2}, -\frac{1}{2}$

6. 1, 0

7. Answers may vary.

8. a) $\frac{4\sqrt{2}}{9}$ **b)** $\frac{7}{9}$ **c)** $\frac{4\sqrt{2}}{7}$

9. a) $-\frac{\sqrt{3}}{2}, -\frac{1}{2}, \sqrt{3}$ **b)** $\frac{4\sqrt{5}}{9}, \frac{1}{9}, 4\sqrt{5}$

c) $\frac{24}{25}, \frac{7}{25}, \frac{24}{7}$

11. b) $\frac{1 + \cos 2\theta}{2}$

13. b) $\frac{(\sin \theta - \cos \theta)^2}{\sin 2\theta}$

14. a) tan θ **b)** tan θ **c)** cot θ

15. a) $-\frac{3}{4}$

16. a)

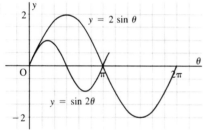

b) The graphs do not coincide.
c) $\theta = 0, \pm\pi, \pm 2\pi, \ldots$

17. a)

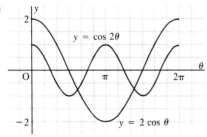

b) The graphs do not coincide.
c) Approximately 1.95, 4.34, . . .

Exercises 6-5, page 255

1. a) 0.52, 1.57, 2.62   **b)** 1.05, 5.24
c) 0.46, 0.79, 3.61, 3.93
d) 0.99, 2.43, 4.14, 5.57

2. a) 0, 1.05, 3.14, 5.24
b) 0.45, 2.69, 4.02, 5.41
c) 0.72, 5.56   **d)** 1.24, 2.03, 4.25, 5.04

3. a) $\frac{\pi}{3}, \frac{2\pi}{3}$ **b)** $\frac{\pi}{6}, \frac{5\pi}{6}, \frac{3\pi}{2}$ **c)** $\frac{3\pi}{4}, \frac{7\pi}{4}$ **d)** 0, π

4. a) $\frac{7\pi}{12} + n\pi, \frac{11\pi}{12} + n\pi$ **b)** $\frac{7\pi}{24} + \frac{n\pi}{2}, \frac{11\pi}{24} + \frac{n\pi}{2}$
c) No solution
d) $\pi + n\pi$, 0.244 978 7 + $n\pi$

5. 7:26 A.M., 7:50 P.M.

6. a)

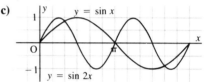

b) $\frac{\pi}{3}, \pi, \frac{5\pi}{3}$
c)

$0, \frac{2\pi}{3}, \pi, \frac{4\pi}{3}$

7. 46°

8. Answers may vary. Typical answers are:
a) sin $x = 2$
b) cos $x = x^2 + 1$
c) sin $x = \frac{1}{2}x$

9. a) 0   **b)** 0.739 085   **c)** 0

Problem Solving, page 258

2. a) i) 2   **ii)** 4   **iii)** 7   **b)** No
c) Answers may vary.
5. $3x - 4y - 9 = 0$ and $3x - 4y - 29 = 0$
6. $4x - 3y + 6 = 0, 4x - 3y + 21 = 0$; or
$4x - 3y - 6 = 0, 4x - 3y - 21 = 0$
7. 22 square units

Review Exercises, page 259

3. a) $-\frac{\sqrt{3}}{2}$ **b)** $\sqrt{2}$ **c)** $\sqrt{3}$ **d)** $-\frac{\sqrt{3}}{2}$

4. a) $\frac{\sqrt{3}-1}{2\sqrt{2}}$ **b)** $\frac{\sqrt{3}-1}{2\sqrt{2}}$ **c)** $\frac{\sqrt{3}}{2}$ **d)** $\frac{\sqrt{3}}{2}$

5. a) $\frac{\sqrt{3}-1}{2\sqrt{2}}$ **b)** $\frac{-1-\sqrt{3}}{2\sqrt{2}}$ **c)** $\frac{1-\sqrt{3}}{2\sqrt{2}}$

d) $\frac{1-\sqrt{3}}{2\sqrt{2}}$

6. a) $\frac{3\sqrt{7}-2}{10}$ **b)** $\frac{\sqrt{21}-2}{5\sqrt{2}}$

7. a) $\frac{3\sqrt{7}-12}{20}$ **b)** $\frac{3\sqrt{7}+12}{20}$ **c)** $\frac{-9-4\sqrt{7}}{20}$

d) $\frac{-9+4\sqrt{7}}{20}$

8. a) $\cos\frac{\pi}{3}$ **b)** $\sin 1.6$ **c)** $\cos 0.7$

9. a) $-\frac{\sqrt{15}}{8}$ **b)** $\frac{7}{8}$ **c)** $-\frac{\sqrt{15}}{7}$

11. a) 0.25, 0.52, 2.62, 2.89 **b)** 2.30, 3.98
  c) 1.57, 3.67, 4.71, 5.76
  d) 1.15, 1.99, 4.29, 5.13

Cumulative Review, Chapters 4-6, page 260

1. a) (7.5,1.5) **b)** (0,4) **c)** (1,0), (5,8)

2. 3,8; $-3,-8$

3. 5 cm by 12 cm

4. a) 3, -4 **b)** $-\frac{8}{3} \leqslant x \leqslant 4$
  c) $x \leqslant -3$ or $x \geqslant 8$

5. a) 135° **b)** $-210°$ **c)** 154.70° **d)** $-660°$

6. a) $\frac{7\pi}{6}$ **b)** $-\frac{5\pi}{4}$ **c)** 2.57 radians **d)** $\frac{3\pi}{2}$

7. a) i) $\frac{1}{\sqrt{10}}, \frac{3}{\sqrt{10}}, \frac{1}{3}$ **ii)** $-\frac{2}{\sqrt{29}}, -\frac{5}{\sqrt{29}}, \frac{2}{5}$
  iii) $-\frac{2}{\sqrt{13}}, \frac{3}{\sqrt{13}}, -\frac{2}{3}$
  b) i) 18.4° **ii)** 201.8° **iii)** 326.3°

8. a) 0.87, 2.27 **b)** 2.16, 5.30 **c)** 0.52, 5.76

9. a) $\csc\theta = \frac{b-c}{a}$; $\cos\theta = \frac{\sqrt{(b-c)^2-a^2}}{b-c}$;
  $\sec\theta = \frac{b-c}{\sqrt{(b-c)^2-a^2}}$;
  $\tan\theta = \frac{a}{\sqrt{(b-c)^2-a^2}}$;
  $\cot\theta = \frac{\sqrt{(b-c)^2-a^2}}{a}$

b) $\tan\theta = \frac{q}{2p}$; $\sin\theta = \frac{q}{\sqrt{4p^2+q^2}}$;
  $\csc\theta = \frac{\sqrt{4p^2+q^2}}{q}$;
  $\cos\theta = \frac{2p}{\sqrt{4p^2+q^2}}$; $\sec\theta = \frac{\sqrt{4p^2+q^2}}{2p}$

10. a) 2, $\frac{2\pi}{3}$, $\frac{\pi}{6}$, 0 **b)** $\frac{1}{2}$, π, $-\frac{\pi}{4}$, -1

12. a) $\frac{1+\sqrt{3}}{2\sqrt{2}}$ **b)** $\frac{1+\sqrt{3}}{2\sqrt{2}}$ **c)** $\frac{\sqrt{3}+1}{1-\sqrt{3}}$

13. a) $\frac{\sqrt{5}-2\sqrt{15}}{12}$ **b)** $\frac{5\sqrt{3}-2}{12}$ **c)** $\frac{1}{9}$
  d) $\frac{\sqrt{5}+2\sqrt{15}}{12}$

14. a) $\frac{\pi}{6}$, $\frac{5\pi}{6}$, 3.87, 5.55 **b)** 0.72, 1.23, 5.05, 5.56

Chapter 7

Exercises 7-1, page 264

1. a) About 9 years **b)** About 14 years

3. About 45 years **5.** About 6 bounces

7. About 27 m **9.** $P = 80(2)^{\frac{n}{20}}$

10. $P = 300(2)^{\frac{d}{5}}$

11. $P = 100(0.95)^n$

12. $C = 100(0.5)^n$

Exercises 7-2, page 269

1. a) 1 **b)** $\frac{1}{5}$ **c)** $\frac{8}{125}$ **d)** $\frac{1}{8}$ **e)** $\frac{1}{16}$ **f)** 1
  g) 4 **h)** $\frac{16}{81}$ **i)** $\frac{1}{64}$ **j)** $\frac{9}{25}$ **k)** 81 **l)** $\frac{64}{27}$

2. a) 3 **b)** $\frac{1}{9}$ **c)** 2.5 **d)** 5 **e)** 5 **f)** $\frac{1}{2}$
  g) $\frac{1}{1000}$ **h)** 2 **i)** $\frac{7}{5}$ **j)** $\frac{1}{9}$ **k)** 0.5 **l)** 2

3. a) $\frac{1}{216}$ **b)** 9 **c)** 4 **d)** $\frac{1}{32}$ **e)** $\frac{1}{243}$ **f)** $\frac{27}{8}$
  g) $\frac{125}{27}$ **h)** $\frac{1}{1000}$ **i)** $\frac{4}{25}$ **j)** $\frac{125}{27}$ **k)** 32 **l)** $\frac{1}{27}$

4. a) 32 **b)** $\frac{1}{125}$ **c)** $\frac{1}{243}$ **d)** 8000 **e)** 8
  f) 8 **g)** 1 **h)** $\frac{32}{3125}$ **i)** 2 **j)** $\frac{16}{81}$ **k)** $\frac{8}{27}$
  l) 1

5. a) 3.278 **b)** 16.442 **c)** 5.481 **d)** 8.000
  e) 121.268 **f)** 3.386 **g)** 0.48 **h)** 0.17
  i) 68.47 **j)** 10.60 **k)** 0.15 **l)** 0.70

6. a) m^{-6} **b)** x^5 **c)** $-45a^7$ **d)** $-14s^{15}$
  e) $-9m^5$ **f)** $\frac{64n}{5}$

7. a) x^{-1} **b)** $s^{-\frac{1}{4}}$ **c)** $-3m^{-2}$ **d)** $-3a^{\frac{3}{5}}$
e) $n^{\frac{49}{60}}$ **f)** $-4x^{\frac{3}{4}}$

8. a) 5 **b)** 7 **c)** $\frac{17}{72}$ **d)** 0 **e)** 11 **f)** $\frac{1}{2}$
g) 256 **h)** $\frac{33}{16}$ **i)** 2.7

9. a) i) 8000 **ii)** 22 627 **iii)** 2828
b) i) 1000 **ii)** 1414 **iii)** 630

10. a) $P = 24.3(1.0185)^t$ **b)** 20.2 million

11. a) $N = 100(10)^{\frac{t}{7}}$ **b)** 3.7×10^8

12. a) $-7a^9b^{-8}$ **b)** $20m^{-7}n^3$ **c)** $9x^9y^{-12}$
d) $12a^3b^{-4}c^{-4}$ **e)** $10n^4$ **f)** $\frac{15x^{-4}z^5}{2}$

13. a) $-4b^{\frac{1}{3}}$ **b)** $\frac{5mn^{-1}}{2}$ **c)** $x^{\frac{4}{5}}y^{\frac{3}{5}}$ **d)** $a^{-\frac{9}{2}}b^{\frac{11}{4}}$
e) $m^{-\frac{5}{6}}n^{\frac{8}{9}}$ **f)** $a^{-1}b^2$

14. a) $-3m^{\frac{1}{3}}n^{-\frac{1}{2}}$ **b)** $-42a^{\frac{1}{6}}b^{\frac{1}{6}}$ **c)** $-2x^{-\frac{5}{4}}$
d) $2a^{-1}b^{\frac{3}{10}}c^{-\frac{7}{15}}$ **e)** $-\frac{2a^{\frac{1}{4}}c^{-3}}{21}$ **f)** $-\frac{40x^{-\frac{7}{4}}z^{\frac{7}{4}}}{9}$

15. a) 16 **b)** 32 **c)** $\frac{1}{1024}$ **d)** $\frac{1}{4096}$

16. a) $-\frac{16}{9}$ **b)** $\frac{59\,049}{4096}$ **c)** 1.5 **d)** 2187

17. a) $a^{\frac{9}{2}}$ **b)** $4a^{-4}$ **c)** $216a^{39}$

18. a) $6x^9$ **b)** $\frac{4x^{-12}}{27}$ **c)** $\frac{9x^3}{4}$

19. a) 1 **b)** s^{8n} **c)** a **d)** $m^{bc-ac-ab}$ **e)** x^{-2a+2}
f) $\frac{a^{x-4y}}{9}$ **g)** $x^{-\frac{a}{6}}$ **h)** $m^{-\frac{5n}{6}}n^{-\frac{3m}{4}}$ **i)** $a^{-\frac{10x}{3}}$

20. a) 31.544 **b)** 36.462 **c)** 25.955 **d)** 1.823
e) 0.013 **f)** 0.064 **g)** 3.416 **h)** 3.040

21. a) i) 4 **ii)** 0.25 **iii)** 0.25 **iv)** 4 **v)** 2
vi) 0.5 **vii)** 0.5 **viii)** 2

22. a) $5^{\frac{4}{3}}$ **b)** 2^{2x+1} **c)** 2^{2x+2}

Problem Solving, page 273

1. 7.75 cm²
2. a) Powers of 6 **b)** Powers of 12
3. $(20 + 10\sqrt{3})$ cm
4. $3x - 4y + 2 = 0,\ 3x - 4y + 22 = 0$
5. There are two angles such that one is double the other.
6. a) $n!$ **c)** $\frac{(2n)!}{2^n(n!)}$
7. $\frac{b}{a}$

Exercises 7-3, page 277

1. a) iv **b)** iii **c)** i **d)** ii
2. Answers may vary.

3. a)

x	-2	-1	0	1	2
3^x	0.11	0.33	1	3	9
$\left(\frac{1}{3}\right)^x$	9	3	1	0.33	0.11

b)

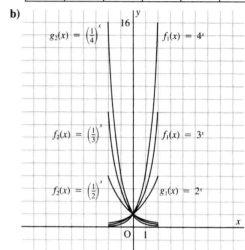

4.

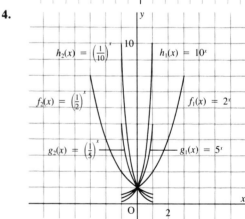

5. a) 6 **b)** 2 **c)** 8 **d)** 4 **e)** $\frac{1}{8}$ **f)** 6
g) 7 **h)** 27

8.

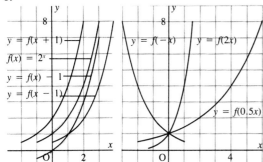

9. a) $a \in R$, $x = 0$ or $a = 1$, $x \in R$
b) $a > 1$, $x > 0$ or $0 < a < 1$, $x < 0$
c) $0 < a < 1$, $x > 0$ or $a > 1$, $x < 0$

10.

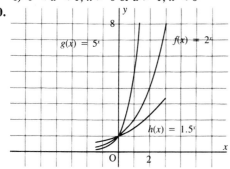

11. Answers may vary.

12. a)

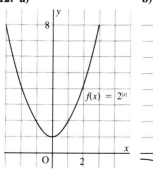

b)

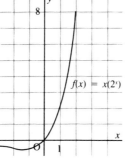

c)

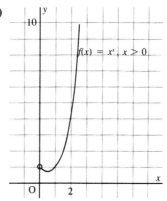

Exercises 7-4, page 281

1. a) 2 **b)** 3 **c)** 6 **d)** 1 **e)** −1 **f)** −3
g) 0 **h)** $\frac{1}{3}$ **i)** 5 **j)** $\frac{1}{5}$ **k)** $\frac{2}{3}$ **l)** n

2. a) $10^{0.6990}$ **b)** $10^{1.2553}$ **c)** $10^{1.7952}$ **d)** $10^{3.6882}$
e) $10^{-0.6021}$ **f)** $10^{-0.0969}$ **g)** $10^{-1.6990}$
h) $10^{2.2218}$

3. a) 5 **b)** 9 **c)** 1

4. a) 12 **b)** −7 **c)** −12

5. a) $10\ 000 = 10^4$ **b)** $10 = 10^1$
c) $0.01 = 10^{-2}$

6. a) $\log 1000 = 3$ **b)** $\log 1 = 0$
c) $\log 0.001 = -3$

7. 600

8. a) 100 **b)** 100 000 **c)** 0.001 **d)** 1 **e)** 10
f) 10^{10}

9. a) 4 **b)** 5 **c)** −3 **d)** 100 **e)** 20
f) 0.2

10. a) i) 0.301 03 **ii)** 1.301 03 **iii)** 2.301 03
iv) 3.301 03 **v)** −0.698 97 **vi)** −1.698 97
vii) −2.698 97 **viii)** −3.698 97
b) Answers may vary.

Exercises 7-5, page 285

1. a) $\log 42$ **b)** $\log 4$ **c)** $\log 24$ **d)** $\log 7$
e) $\log 84$ **f)** $\log 0.5$ **g)** $\log 10$ **h)** $\log 90$
i) $\log 21$ **j)** $\log 28$

2. Answers may vary. Typical answers:
a) $\log 2 + \log 5$ **b)** $\log 3 + \log 7$
c) $\log 4 + \log 7$ **d)** $\log 3 + \log 12$
e) $\log 3 + \log 3$ **f)** $\log 4 + \log 11$
g) $\log 3 + \log 19$ **h)** $\log 11 + \log 11$

3. Answers may vary. Typical answers:
   a) $\log 10 - \log 2$ b) $\log 16 - \log 2$
   c) $\log 24 - \log 2$ d) $\log 26 - \log 2$
   e) $\log 20 - \log 2$ f) $\log 42 - \log 2$
   g) $\log 34 - \log 2$ h) $\log 80 - \log 2$

4. a) $2 \log 3$ b) $2 \log 5$ c) $3 \log 2$
   d) $3 \log 3$ e) $3 \log 10$ f) $5 \log 2$
   g) $3 \log 7$ h) $7 \log 2$

5. a) $\log 36$ b) $\log 64$ c) $\log 81$ d) $\log 49$
   e) $\log 243$ f) $\log 16$ g) $\log 216$
   h) $\log 100\ 000$

6. a) $1.477\ 12$ b) $3.477\ 12$ c) $-0.522\ 88$
   d) $-2.522\ 88$ e) $0.954\ 24$ f) $1.908\ 48$
   g) $0.238\ 56$ h) $0.095\ 42$

7. a) $2.795\ 88$ b) $0.232\ 99$ c) $-0.698\ 97$
   d) $-1.397\ 94$

8. a) 0.8451 b) 2.8451 c) -1.1549
   d) -0.1549 e) 5.8451 f) -2.1549

9. a) $3 + \log a + \log b$ b) $2 \log a + \log b$
   c) $\log a + \frac{1}{2} \log b$ d) $\log a - 2 \log b$
   e) $\frac{1}{2} \log a - \log b$ f) $\frac{1}{3} \log a - 2 \log b$

10. a) $1 + 2 \log x$ b) $\frac{1}{2} \log x$ c) $\frac{1}{2} + \log x$
    d) $\frac{1}{2} + \frac{1}{2} \log x$ e) $1 + \frac{1}{2} \log x$

11. a) $\log \left(\dfrac{xy}{z} \right)$ b) $\log \left(\dfrac{m}{np} \right)$ c) $\log \left(\dfrac{ab}{cd} \right)$
    d) $\log \left(\dfrac{a^2 + ab}{a - b} \right)$

12. a) $\log (a^2 b^5)$ b) $\log (x^3 y^{\frac{1}{2}})$ c) $\log \left(\dfrac{m^2 n}{p^5} \right)$
    d) $\log \left(\dfrac{x^{\frac{1}{2}}}{y^2 z} \right)$ e) $\log \left(\dfrac{a^3 b^{\frac{1}{2}}}{c^{\frac{5}{4}}} \right)$ f) $\log \left(\dfrac{a^{10} c^{\frac{1}{2}}}{b^3 d} \right)$

13. a) $\log \left(\dfrac{x + 3}{x - 1} \right), x \neq 1$
    b) $\log \left(\dfrac{2x - 7}{x + 3} \right), x \neq -3$
    c) $\log \left(\dfrac{a + 2}{a - 2} \right), a \neq 2$
    d) $\log \left(\dfrac{8a + 15}{2a + 3} \right), a \neq -1.5$

14. a) $x + y$ b) $y - x$ c) $1 + x + y$
    d) $2x + y$ e) $x + 2y$ f) $2x + 2y$
    g) $2x + 2y - 1$ h) $-x - y$

15. a) $3^{1.7712437}$ b) $2^{2.3219281}$ c) $2^{4.8579809}$
    d) $8^{2.0889288}$ e) $0.5^{-1.5849625}$ f) $6^{-0.4456556}$

16. a) 3.459 b) 2.579 c) 0.898 d) 2.365
    e) -0.415 f) -0.398

17. a) $0.630\ 929\ 8$ b) $1.160\ 964$ c) $-0.564\ 575$
    d) $-0.464\ 973\ 5$ e) $-1.547\ 952\ 1$
    f) $0.769\ 124$

18. a) $\log y = 1 + \log x$ b) $\log y = -\log x$
    c) $\log y = 2 \log x$ d) $\log y = \frac{1}{2} \log x$
    e) $\log y = 1 + \frac{1}{2} \log x$
    f) $\log y = \frac{1}{2} + \frac{1}{2} \log x$

19. a) $x > 2$ b) $x > 0$ c) $x > 5$

20. a) 3 b) 6 c) 101

21. a) $y = \dfrac{x + 2}{3x}; \{x \mid x > 0, x \in R\}$
    b) $y = 100 + \dfrac{100}{x}; \{x \mid x > 0, x \in R\}$
    c) $y = 10^x;\ R$

22. a) 3376 b) 6533 c) $39\ 751$ d) $65\ 050$

23. a) $3.056\ 912 \times 10^{79}$ b) 80

24. a) 218 b) 2083 c) $20\ 734$
    d) Answers may vary.

Mathematics Around Us, page 288

1. a) It's the logarithm of the distance in metres.
   b) The number increases by 3, the distance is 10^3 times as great

2. a) 3 b) 39

3. a) 5 b) km and cm

4. 2 cm   5. 1 week   7. 4.8

8. a) 6 b) 8 c) 12

9. 1.3×10^{26} m   10. 2.0×10^{26} m   11. 99.9%

Exercises 7-6, page 294

1. a) $x \doteq 3.3 \log \left(\dfrac{y}{5} \right)$ b) $x = \log \left(\dfrac{y}{1.3} \right)$
   c) $x \doteq 78 \log \left(\dfrac{y}{8.2} \right)$ d) $x \doteq -3.3 \log \left(\dfrac{y}{6.4} \right)$
   e) $x \doteq 2.3 \log \left(\dfrac{y}{3.5} \right)$
   f) $x \doteq -5.7 \log \left(\dfrac{y}{2.75} \right)$

2. a) $n \doteq 30 \log \left(\dfrac{A}{500} \right)$

   b) i) 11.9 years; $500 will amount to $1250 in
       nearly 12 years

   ii) −4.6 years; $350 invested about 4.6 years ago
      will amount to $500 now

   c)

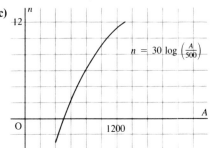

   d) $\{ A \mid A > 0,\ A \in \mathrm{R} \}$; R

3. a) $n \doteq -6.5 \log \left(\dfrac{h}{2} \right)$

   b) i) 3; after 3 bounces, the height is about 0.7 m

   ii) 8; after 8 bounces, the height is about 0.12 m

   c)

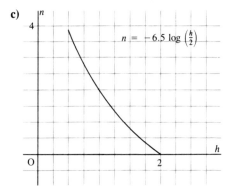

   d) N

4. a) $P = 6800(1.018)^{n}$ **b)** $n \doteq 129 \log \left(\dfrac{P}{6800} \right)$

   c) i) 17   **ii)** −12

d) They are inverses of each other.

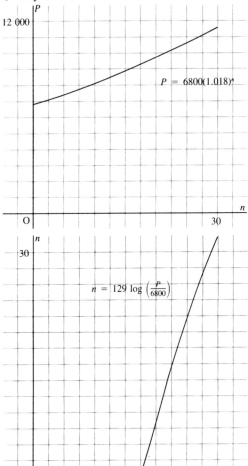

5. a) 3:20 P.M.   **b)** 5:04 P.M.   **c)** 8:57 A.M.

6.

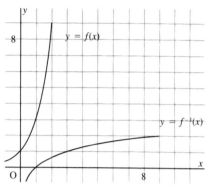

7. a) See page 296.

b)

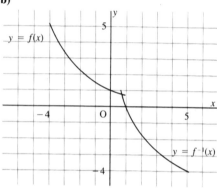

Exercises 7-7, page 298

1. a) $f^{-1}(x) = \log x$ **b)** $g^{-1}(x) = \log_3 x$
   c) $h^{-1}(x) = \log_7 x$ **d)** $f^{-1}(x) = \log_{0.4} x$
   e) $g^{-1}(x) = \log_{\frac{3}{2}} x$ **f)** $h^{-1}(x) = \log_{15} x$

2. a) $f^{-1}(x) = 10^x$ **b)** $g^{-1}(x) = 2^x$
   c) $h^{-1}(x) = 6^x$ **d)** $f^{-1}(x) = \left(\frac{1}{2}\right)^x$

   e) $g^{-1}x = \left(\frac{5}{4}\right)^x$ **f)** $h^{-1}(x) = 21^x$

3. a) $f^{-1}(x) = \log_5 x$

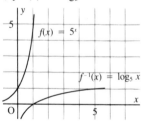

b) $g^{-1}(x) = \log_{\frac{3}{4}} x$

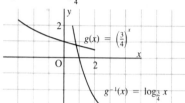

4. a), b) See Exercises 7-6, *Exercise 6*.
   c) $f^{-1}(x) = \log_3 x$

5. a), b)

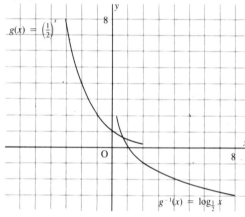

c) $g^{-1}(x) = \log_{\frac{1}{2}} x$

6. a)   **b)**

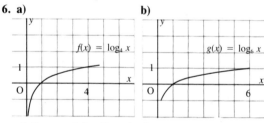

c) See graph for *Exercise 5*.

d)

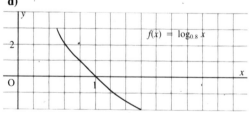

e)

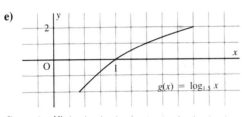

$g(x) = \log_{1.5} x$

f)

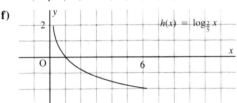

$h(x) = \log_{\frac{2}{5}} x$

9. (0.548, 0.548)

10. a) $0 < a < 1$ **b)** Answers may vary.

Exercises 7-8, page 301

1. a) $8 = 2^3$ **b)** $32 = 2^5$ **c)** $\frac{1}{4} = 2^{-2}$
d) $625 = 5^4$ **e)** $9 = 3^2$ **f)** $3 = 9^{\frac{1}{2}}$

2. a) 4 **b)** 2 **c)** 3 **d)** 2 **e)** -1 **f)** 1
g) 0 **h)** 4

3. a) 8; 6; 2; 1; -4, -8 **b)** 4; 3; 1; 0.5; -2, -4

4. a) $\frac{1}{2}$ **b)** 4 **c)** 2 **d)** 4 **e)** -3 **f)** -2
g) 1.5 **h)** 6

5. a) 1.465 **b)** 0.712 **c)** 5.644 **d)** 1.544
e) 2.377 **f)** 0.750

6. a) $\log_6 36 = 2$ **b)** $\log_4 \left(\frac{1}{16}\right) = -2$
c) $\log_3 243 = 5$ **d)** $\log_7 343 = 3$
e) $\log_8 2 = \frac{1}{3}$ **f)** $\log_2 1 = 0$
g) $\log_5 0.04 = -2$ **h)** $\log_4 \left(\frac{1}{2}\right) = -\frac{1}{2}$
i) $\log_{\frac{1}{2}} \left(\frac{1}{4}\right) = 2$ **j)** $\log_{\frac{2}{3}} \left(\frac{3}{2}\right) = -1$
k) $\log_{\frac{1}{9}} \left(\frac{1}{81}\right) = 2$ **l)** $\log_x z = y$

7. a) $400 = 20^2$ **b)** $\frac{1}{49} = 7^{-2}$ **c)** $4 = 8^{\frac{2}{3}}$
d) $36^2 = 6^4$ **e)** $8 = (0.5)^3$ **f)** $s = r^t$

8. a) 2 **b)** 0 **c)** 4 **d)** 9 **e)** 8 **f)** 81

9. a) 512 **b)** $\frac{1}{4}$ **c)** -1 **d)** 10 **e)** $\frac{1}{4}$ **f)** $\frac{1}{5}$

10. a) $3x + 2y$ **b)** $6x + 2y$

11. a) $2^x - x$ **b)** $\dfrac{2^x}{x}$

12. a) 0 **b)** 14

13. a) i) $3; \frac{1}{3}$ **ii)** $2; \frac{1}{2}$ **b)** $\log_a b = \dfrac{1}{\log_b a}$

Exercises 7-9, page 307

1. a) 2 **b)** 1 **c)** 3 **d)** 3 **e)** 3 **f)** 4

2. Answers may vary. Typical answers:
a) $\log_3 10 + \log_3 2$ **b)** $\log_7 5 + \log_7 9$
c) $\log_5 10 + \log_5 9$ **d)** $\log_{12} 2 + \log_{12} 3$
e) $\log_8 5 + \log_8 15$ **f)** $\log_{20} 3 + \log_{20} 13$

3. Answers may vary. Typical answers:
a) $\log_4 22 - \log_4 2$ **b)** $\log_3 24 - \log_3 2$
c) $\log_9 10 - \log_9 2$ **d)** $\log_6 14 - \log_6 2$
e) $\log_{11} 42 - \log_{11} 2$ **f)** $\log_2 26 - \log_2 2$

4. a) 2 **b)** 3 **c)** 2 **d)** 5

5. a) 7 **b)** 7 **c)** 6 **d)** 3 **e)** 2 **f)** 1

6. a) $3 \log_3 2$ **b)** $2 \log_5 6$ **c)** $3 \log_2 3$
d) $5 \log_6 2$ **e)** $4 \log_{12} 3$ **f)** $3 \log_4 5$

7. a) $\log_2 125$ **b)** $\log_7 16$ **c)** $\log_3 262\ 144$
d) $\log_{12} 1024$ **e)** $\log_2 14\ 348\ 907$

8. a) 4 **b)** $\frac{5}{3}$ **c)** 1.5 **d)** 2.5 **e)** 1
f) -1.5 **g)** 1.5 **h)** 3.5

9. a) 4.3219 **b)** 4.6438 **c)** 1.3219 **d)** 1.1610

10. a) 5 **b)** 3 **c)** 2 **d)** 1

11. a) 6.2877 **b)** 3.0959 **c)** $-0.547\ 95$
d) 2.1918

12. a) $y = x^2; \{x \mid x > 0, x \in R\}$
b) $y = (x + 1)^2(x - 1); \{x \mid x > 1, x \in R\}$
c) $y = 3(x + 3)^2 + 3; \{x \mid x > -3, x \in R\}$

13. a) i) 11.550 747 **ii)** 8.228 819 **iii)** 4.906 891
iv) 1.584 963 **v)** $-1.736\ 966$
vi) $-5.058\ 894$ **vii)** $-8.380\ 822$
viii) $-11.702\ 750$

14. a) $3x$ **b)** $1 + 3x$ **c)** $0.5x$ **d)** $1 + 1.5x$

15. a) $2 + x$ **b)** $2 + 2x$ **c)** $1 + 1.5x$
d) $\frac{1}{3}x - 1$

16. a) 6 **b)** 4 **c)** 10 **d)** 12

17. a) 7 **b)** 11 **c)** 0 **d)** 4

18. a) 8 **b)** 9 **c)** 2 **d)** 6 **e)** 2 **f)** 5

19. a) 100 **b)** 18 **c)** 3 **d)** 4 **e)** 3 **f)** 2

20. a) 10.079 **b)** 114.036

21. b) $\dfrac{1}{\log_a x} + \dfrac{1}{\log_b x} = \dfrac{1}{\log_{ab} x}$

Exercises 7-10, page 312

1. $3814.48
2. About 12.9%
3. In 1990, about 3.52×10^{13}
4. Between 10 and 11 years
5. Between 6 and 7 years
6. a) $P = 100(0.65)^d$; $P = 100(0.95)^d$; $P = 100(0.975)^d$ b) 1.6 m; 13.5 m; 27.4 m
   c) 10.7 m; 89.8 m; 181.9 m
7. a) About 60%   b) About 90
8. 11 300   9. About 1.9%   10. 3960
11. 2620   12. 48 min
14. a) 93 years   b) 186 years
15. a)

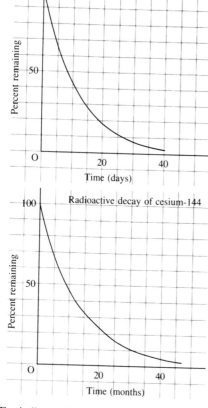

Radioactive decay of iodine-131

Percent remaining vs Time (days)

Radioactive decay of cesium-144

Percent remaining vs Time (months)

For iodine − 131   b) i) $P = 100(0.5)^n$
ii) $P = 100(0.5)^{\frac{t}{8.1}}$ c) i) 55%   ii) 7.7%
iii) 2.7×10^{-12}%   d) i) 27 days   ii) 807 days
For cesium − 144   b) i) $P = 100(0.5)^n$
ii) $P = 100(0.5)^{\frac{t}{282}}$ c) i) 98%   ii) 93%
iii) 41%   d) i) 937 days   ii) 21 810 days

16. a) 99.7%   b) 97.2%   c) 74.9%   d) 5.6%
17. a) 8.8 g   b) 15 g   c) 4.1 g   d) 2.0 g
18. Between 9 and 10 years
19. a) $T = 80(0.5)^{\frac{t}{5}} + 20$ b) 15 min
20. a) $c = 100(0.5)^{\frac{t}{5}}$ b) i) 16.6 h   ii) 33.2 h
21. a) $L = 2.00(1.2)^n$ b) 18
22. a) $\frac{5}{6}$ b) $t = 0.120\left(\frac{5}{6}\right)^n$ c) 27   d) 240 m
23. a) 2018   b) i) 2065   ii) 2050
    iii) 2142 is the year when demand exceeds supply

Exercises 7-11, page 318

1. a) i) $P_4 = P_0(5)$ ii) $P_6 = P_0(5)^{1.5}$
   b) About 2.2
2. About 1.9   3. About 2.6   4. 5
5. a) About 4   b) About 3   c) About 13
6. a) 6 or 7 times as frequent   b) 36 to 49 times as frequent   c) 216 to 343 times as frequent
7. 20
8. a) 10   b) Answers may vary
   c) i) 50   ii) 501
9. 8
10. a) $\frac{P_2}{P_1} = (0.95)^{\frac{h_2 - h_1}{300}}$ b) About 15.7%
11. a) $\frac{N_2}{N_1} = 4^{\frac{t_2 - t_1}{3}}$ b) i) 10 times as many
    ii) 102 times as many   iii) 1024 times as many

Investigate, page 319

2.718 281 8

The Mathematical Mind, page 321

1. a) $e^{0.6931471} \doteq 2$ b) $e^{1.3862944} \doteq 4$
   c) $e^{3.4011974} \doteq 30$ d) $e^{4.6051702} \doteq 100$
   e) $e^{9.0768090} \doteq 8750$ f) $e^{-0.6931472} \doteq 0.5$
   g) $e^{-2.3025851} \doteq 0.1$ h) $e^{-7.7287358} \doteq 0.000\ 44$
2. a) 1.609 437 9   b) 2.708 050 2
   c) 3.987 130 5   d) 5.583 496 3   e) 0
   f) −1.386 294 4   g) −2.385 966 7
   h) −8.111 728 1
3. a) 2.718 281 8   b) 4.953 032 4
   c) 20.085 537   d) 90.017 131   e) 1.390 968 1
   f) 0.367 879 4   g) 0.246 597 0
   h) 0.110 803 2
4. a) ln 15   b) ln 20   c) ln 36   d) ln 9
   e) ln 7   f) ln 5
5. a) i) 1   ii) 2   iii) −3   iv) 0.2
   b) $\ln e^n = n$

6. a) 4   **b)** 22   **c)** 145   **d)** 72 382
e) 48 254 942
7. a) 4   **b)** 9   **c)** 42   **d)** 10 478
e) 4 657 079
8. a) 3.912 023

Mathematics Around Us, page 324

1. a) 57 million; 0.7%   **b)** 20 million; 3.0%
c) 2.6 million; 3.8%
2. a) $P = 770e^{0.016t}$ **b) i)** 903.6 million
ii) 2001   **iii)** 1958
3. a) 99.8%   **b)** 4.53×10^9 years
4. a) 17 600 m; 25 500 m   **b)** 5.9 kPa
c) $h \doteq -6452 \ln \left(\dfrac{P}{130}\right)$

Review Exercises, page 325

1. a) $\frac{1}{4}$ **b)** 3   **c)** 8   **d)** 25   **e)** 3.375
f) 3.375   **g)** 1   **h)** 0.000 32
2. a) i) 4000   **ii)** 45 255   **b) i)** 125   **ii)** 44
3. a) $5x^3y^{-2}$ **b)** $\dfrac{m^2n}{2}$ **c)** $\dfrac{25a^{-4}b^{-7}}{8}$
d) $\dfrac{9y^{-\frac{4}{3}}}{25}$ **e)** $-\dfrac{3a^{-\frac{1}{4}}b^{-\frac{1}{3}}}{5}$ **f)** $\dfrac{3m^{-\frac{5}{2}}n^{-\frac{1}{6}}}{2}$
4. a) 1   **b)** $\dfrac{2m^{6x-4y}}{3}$ **c)** $a^x b^{\frac{x}{2}}$
5. \$2351.18   **6.** About 20.7%
7. About 12.25 years
8. a) $1000 = 10^3$ **b)** $\sqrt{10} = 10^{\frac{1}{2}}$ **c)** $81 = 3^4$
9. a) $\log 10\,000 = 4$ **b)** $\log 0.001 = -3$
c) $\log_5 625 = 4$
10. a) 100   **b)** 0.000 01   **c)** 8   **d)** 27   **e)** -2
f) 32
11. a) $\log x + 2 \log y$ **b)** $\log x + \frac{1}{2} \log y$
c) $1 + 3 \log x + 2 \log y$
d) $\frac{1}{3}[\log x + 2 \log y]$
e) $\log x - \frac{1}{2} \log y$
f) $2 \log x - \frac{1}{3} \log y$
12. a) $\log \left(\dfrac{xy}{z}\right)$ **b)** $\log \left(\dfrac{x^2}{y}\right)$ **c)** $\log (x^3y^5)$
d) $\log (x^{\frac{1}{2}}y^3)$ **e)** $\log (2x - 3)(y + 5)$
f) $\log \dfrac{(x + y)^3}{x - y}$

13. a) $3^{1.8927893}$ **b)** $6^{1.7737056}$ **c)** $1.3^{9.4712085}$
d) $2^{-0.358454}$
14. a) 1.3652   **b)** 0.7879   **c)** 1.9650   **d)** 2.2541
e) 2.2876   **f)** 0.8072   **g)** -0.5204
h) 3.5547
15. a) 4   **b)** 4   **c)** 5   **d)** -3 **e)** -3 **f)** 10
g) -3 **h)** 3
16. a) 4   **b)** 4   **c)** 3   **d)** 3
17. a) See graph for Exercises 7-6, *Exercise 6*.
b) See answers for Exercises 7-7, *Exercise 3a)*.
c) See *Example 1*, page 297.
18. a) 76 days   **b)** 116 days
19. a) 64.7%   **b)** 536 days
20. a) $N = 1000(2)^{\frac{n}{2}}$ **b)** 1991
21. 19

Chapter 8

Exercises 8-1, page 329

1. Answers may vary.
2. a) K M O   **b)** K P V   **c)** F B G
3. a) Add 2: 10, 12, 14
b) Multiply by 3: 81, 243, 729
c) Add 5: 25, 30, 35
d) Add the previous amount, plus 1: 16, 22, 29
e) Divide by 2: 1, 0.5, 0.25
f) Add 3: 14, 17, 20
4. a) 2, 4, 6, 8, 10   **b)** 11, 12, 13, 14, 15
c) 3, 6, 9, 12, 15   **d)** 2, 4, 8, 16, 32
e) 9, 8, 7, 6, 5   **f)** 1, 2, 3, 4, 5
5. a) Add 2: $2n-1$ **b)** Add 5: $5n$
c) Add 5: $5n-1$ **d)** Multiply by 10: 10^n
6. a) 1, 4, 7, 10, 13   **b)** 1, 3, 7, 15, 31
c) 18, 15, 12, 9, 6   **d)** 7, 9, 11, 13, 15
e) $\frac{1}{4}, \frac{2}{7}, \frac{3}{10}, \frac{4}{13}, \frac{5}{16}$ **f)** 2, $\frac{5}{2}, \frac{8}{3}, \frac{11}{4}, \frac{14}{5}$
7. a) 24, 34   **b)** 17, 53   **c)** 11, 76   **d)** 4, -32
8. a) v   **b)** ii   **c)** vi   **d)** iii
9. a) $2n$ **b)** $2n + 3$ **c)** $2n - 5$ **d)** 2^n
e) $2^n - 1$ **f)** $19 - 3n$ **g)** $\dfrac{n}{2n - 1}$
h) $\dfrac{n}{n + 1}$
10. Answers may vary.
11. b and d are correct.
12. a) $f(x) = x^5, f(x) = x^6$
b) $f(x) = ax^4 + bx^3 + cx^2 + dx + e$;
$f(x) = ax^5 + bx^4 + cx^3 + dx^2 + ex + f$

13. a) 3, 4, 5

b) $t_n = n - 1$, where n is the number of the polygon in the table; or $t_n = n - 3$, where n is the number of sides in the polygon

14. a) 120°, approximately 128.57°, 135°

b) $t_n = 180° - \dfrac{360°}{n + 2}$, where n is the number of the polygon; or $t_n = 180° - \dfrac{360°}{n}$, where n is the number of sides

15. a) i) 3 **ii)** 7 **iii)** 15 **iv)** 31

b) Answers may vary.

Investigate, page 331

i) The prime numbers greater than 1

ii) The difference between consecutive terms increases by 1.

iii) Beyond the second term, add the 2 previous terms to get the next term.

iv) Beyond the second term, add all the preceding terms to get the next term.

v) Beginning at 2, all numbers except those which are perfect squares

vi) Beyond the second term, multiply the 2 preceding terms and subtract 1.

Investigate, page 331

Another similar sequence is: 1, 31, 331, 3331, 33 331, 333 331, 3 333 331, 33 333 331, 333 333 331. The first 8 terms are prime; the 9th term is not prime since 333 333 331 = 17 × 19 607 843.

Exercises 8-2, page 334

1. a) No **b)** Yes, 3 **c)** Yes, −1 **d)** No

e) Yes, 0 **f)** Yes, 8

2. a) 3; 13, 16, 19 **b)** 4; 11, 15, 19

c) −2; 8, 6, 4 **d)** −6; −26, −32, −38

e) 5; 22, 27, 32 **f)** −3; −6, −9, −12

3. a) 2, 5, 8, 11, 14 **b)** 7, 11, 15, 19, 23

c) −1, −4, −7, −10, −13

d) 12, 8, 4, 0, −4 **e)** −8, −3, 2, 7, 12

f) 25, 20, 15, 10, 5

4. a) 17 **b)** 51 **c)** $2n + 1$

5. a) −4 **b)** −46 **c)** $-3n + 14$

6. a) Answers may vary. 91 million years, 39 million years, 13 million years

b) About 13 million years from now

7. a) i) No **ii)** Yes

b) It is the 24th term of the sequence, with 1st term 1896 and common difference 4.

8. a) ii **b)** iv **c)** i **d)** v

9. a) 3, 10, 17, 24, 31 **b)** −3, 1, 5, 9, 13

c) 5, 7, 9, 11, 13 **d)** 16, 11, 6, 1, −4

e) −4, −1, 2, 5, 8

f) −10, −14, −18, −22, −26

10. a) 71, 104 **b)** 51st term

11. a) 72, 202 **b)** 67th term

12. a) $4n - 3$; 65 **b)** $3n$; 63 **c)** $5n - 9$; 56

d) $47 - 6n$; −61 **e)** $1 - 3n$; −29

f) $17 - 8n$; −351

13. −3, 4 **14.** 7, 11, 15 **15.** 87, 81, 75

16. 3, 8, 13 **17.** 4, 11, 18

18. a) 24 **b)** 37 **c)** 20 **d)** 25

19. a) 2; 23; 30 **b)** 20; 14; −4 **c)** 17; 27; 32

d) 10; 17; 31 **e)** 8; 0; −4 **f)** 6; −3; −12

20. $\frac{10}{3}$ **21.** $5x - 8y + 1 = 0$

22. 30 **23.** 10 or −2

24. a) $(2n - 1)(3n - 2)$ **b)** $6n^2$ **c)** $\dfrac{n}{2n + 1}$

d) $\dfrac{(2n - 1)(2n + 1)}{2n(2n + 2)}$; none of the sequences is arithmetic.

25. a) 4th **b)** 3rd **c)** 1st **d)** 2nd

26. a) 3, 6, 11, 14, 19, 22, 27, 30, 35, 38

b) i) 3rd **ii)** 4th **iii)** 3rd **iv)** 3rd

Investigate, page 336

There is an infinite number of 3 perfect squares in arithmetic sequence. Some examples are: 49, 169, 289; 4, 100, 196; 289, 625, 961; 1, 25, 49.

Computer Power, page 337

1. Answers may vary; for example, 5, 11, 17, 23, 29; 41, 47, 53, 59; 61, 67, 73, 79

2. Answers may vary.

3. 7, 157, 307, 457, 607, 757, 907

4. a) 5, 7; 11, 13; 17, 19 and 17, 19; 29, 31; 41, 43

b) 41, 43; 461, 463; 881, 883; 1301, 1303; 1721, 1723; 2141, 2143

5. 276 615 587 107

6. $2 \times 3^2 \times 5 \times 7 \times 11^2 \times 13 \times 17 \times 19 \times 31$

Exercises 8-3, page 341

1. a) Yes, 2   b) No   c) Yes, $-\frac{1}{2}$ d) Yes, 0.1
   e) No   f) Yes, $-\frac{1}{3}$
2. a) 3; 81, 243, 729   b) -3; 405, -1215, 3645
   c) 2; 48, 96, 192   d) $\frac{1}{3}, \frac{2}{27}, \frac{2}{81}, \frac{2}{243}$
   e) $\frac{1}{4}; \frac{9}{64}, \frac{9}{256}, \frac{9}{1024}$ f) -4; 128, -512, 2048
3. a) 2, 6, 18, 54, 162   b) 5, 10, 20, 40, 80
   c) 3, -15, 75, -375, 1875
   d) 60, 30, 15, $\frac{15}{2}, \frac{15}{4}$
   e) -4, 8, -16, 32, -64
   f) 8, 24, 72, 216, 648
4. a) 96   b) 3072   c) $3(2)^{n-1}$
5. a) ii   b) iv   c) iii   d) vi
6. a) No   b) Yes   c) No   d) Yes
7. a) ± 12 b) ± 16 c) ± 20 d) ± 50
8. a) ± 6, 12, ± 24 b) ± 8, 16, ± 32
   c) ± 10, 20, ± 40 d) ± 10, 50, ± 250
9. a) 2, -6, 18, -54, 162
   b) 20, 10, 5, 2.5, 1.25   c) 3, 6, 12, 24, 48
   d) 7, 21, 63, 189, 567   e) $\frac{1}{8}, \frac{1}{2}$, 2, 8, 32
   f) -2, 10, -50, 250, -1250
10. a) 2^n; 1024   b) $5(2)^{n-1}$; 20 480
    c) $-3(-5)^{n-1}$; 234 375   d) $12\left(\frac{1}{2}\right)^{n-1}$; $\frac{3}{512}$
    e) $6\left(-\frac{1}{3}\right)^{n-1}$; $\frac{2}{2187}$ f) $3(6)^{n-1}$; 139 968
11. a) 196 608   b) 7th term
12. 2, ± 6, 18, ± 54, 162
13. 24 576, 12 288, 6144, 3072
14. a) ± 8; ± 32 b) 72, 432   c) ± 6; ± 24
    d) ± 1; ± 25 e) 8, 4   f) 15, 75
15. 1.25, 5   16. ± 3; ± 6, 18, ± 54
17. a) 2, 18, 162, 1458
    b) 2, ± 6, 18, ± 54, 162, ± 486, 1458
18. a) 6   b) 8   c) 11   d) 15
19. $\frac{1}{3}$ or 5   20. -1 or -6
21. About 22.8 million
22. 5, 125   23. $\frac{9}{5}, \frac{6}{5}, \frac{4}{5}, \frac{8}{15}$ or 9, -6, 4, $-\frac{8}{3}$
24. 1, 3, 9, 27, 81
25. $\frac{3}{7}, \frac{6}{7}, \frac{12}{7}, \frac{24}{7}, \frac{48}{7}$ or 1, -2, 4, -8, 16
27. 1, 3, 9 or 9, 3, 1   28. 1.41   29. b) t_{22}

Exercises 8-4, page 345

1. a) 5, 2, -1, -4 b) $\frac{1}{2}$, 1, 2, 4
   c) -2, 3, -2, 3   d) 1, 11, 111, 1111
   e) 1, 2, 3, 5
2. a) $t_1 = 1$, $t_n = t_{n-1} + 5$, $n > 1$
   b) $t_1 = 2$, $t_n = -3t_{n-1}$, $n > 1$
   c) $t_1 = 1$, $t_n = t_{n-1} + 2^{n-1}$, $n > 1$
   d) $t_1 = 1$, $t_n = t_{n-1} + 2n - 1$, $n > 1$
   e) $t_1 = 1$, $t_2 = 1$, $t_n = t_{n-1} + t_{n-2}$, $n > 2$
   f) $t_1 = 1$, $t_2 = 2$, $t_3 = 3$,
      $t_n = t_{n-1} + t_{n-2} + t_{n-3}$, $n > 3$
3. Examples may vary; for example, the sequence
   1, 4, 9, 16, ... can be defined by
   $t_1 = 1$, $t_n = t_{n-1} + 2n - 1$, $n > 1$ and by
   $t_1 = 1$, $t_n = (\sqrt{t_{n-1}} + 1)^2$, $n > 1$

Exercises 8-5, page 348

1. a) $2 + 6 + 10 + 14 + 18 + \ldots$
   b) $9 + 3 + 1 + \frac{1}{3} + \frac{1}{9} + \ldots$
2. a) Sequence   b) Series   c) Series   d) Series
   e) Sequence   f) Series
3. a) 4   b) 14   c) 16   d) -6
4. a) 4   b) 24   c) 40   d) -6
5. a) $3 + 3 + 3 + 3 + 3$
   b) $1 + 5 + 9 + 13 + 17$
   c) $-2 + 0 + 2 + 4 + 6$
   d) $3 + 5 + 5 + 5 + 5$
   e) $3 + 5 + 7 + 9 + 11$
   f) $13 - 6 - 10 - 14 - 18$
6. a) iii   b) i   c) v   d) iv
7. a) $n(n - 1)$; $2n$ b) $(n - 1)(3n - 8)$; $6n - 8$
   c) $2^{n-1} - 1$; 2^{n-1} d) $(n - 1)(2n - 5)$; $4n - 5$
   e) $2(3^{n-1} - 1)$; $4(3)^{n-1}$
   f) $(n - 1)(n - 5)$; $2n - 5$
8. $a + a + a + a + \ldots$
9. a) v   b) iii   c) vi   d) i
10. a) $n^2 - 2n$ b) $2^n - 1$ c) $\dfrac{2^n - 1}{2^{n-1}}$ d) n^3
11. a) i) $n^2 + 2n$ ii) $n^2 + 4n$ iii) $n^2 + 6n$
    b) $n^2 + 8n$

Investigate, page 349

3. a) $n^2 + n$ b) $2^n - 1$ c) $\dfrac{n}{n + 1}$ d) $\dfrac{n}{3n + 1}$

Exercises 8-6, page 353

1. a) 210 **b)** 365 **c)** 290 **d)** 180 **e)** 600
f) −60
2. a) 276 **b)** 375 **c)** 552 **d)** 1020
3. a) 104 **b)** 2750
4. a) 345 **b)** 15 **c)** −2670
5. a) ii **b)** vi **c)** v **d)** iii
6. Job A **7.** 68 **8.** $975
9. a) 893 **b)** 598 **c)** 3604 **d)** −400
10. 3 + 10 + 17 **11.** 2 + 6 + 10
12. 28 + 25 + 22
13. 1.5; 405 **14.** 3 + 7 + 11 **15.** 21
16. a) $n(n + 1)$ **b)** n^2
17. a) i) 79; $4n - 1$ **ii)** 820; $n(2n + 1)$
b) i) 125 **ii)** 15
18. a) $n(n + 4)$ **b)** $n(3n - 11)$ **c)** $n(2n + 3)$
d) $\frac{n}{2}(5n + 1)$ **e)** $\frac{n}{2}(21 - 3n)$ **f)** $\frac{n}{2}(15 + 7n)$
19. b) $21 + 23 + 25 + 27 + 29 = 5^3$
c) $n^2 - n + 1$
20. b) $\frac{1}{2}(n^2 - n + 2)$ **c)** $\frac{1}{2}n(n^2 + 1)$
d) $\frac{1}{2}n(n^2 + 1)$

Investigate, page 355

The list continues to give primes to 227 + 30 = 257;
the next sum is 257 + 32 = 289 = 17^2.
Another example: 11 + 2 = 13; 13 + 4 = 17;
17 + 6 = 23; etc., gives primes up to 57 + 16 = 73;
the next sum is 73 + 18 = 91 = 13 × 7.

Investigate, page 355

210 letters

Exercises 8-7, page 358

1. a) 63 **b)** 1092 **c)** 682 **d)** 77.5
2. a) 1562 **b)** 484 **c)** 93 **d)** 46.5 **e)** 605
f) 155
3. a) iv **b)** vi **c)** ii **d)** v
4. a) 0.093 75 **b)** 11.906 25
5. a) 1458 **b)** 2184
6. a) i) 8190 **ii)** 65 534 **b)** $2^{n+1} - 2$
7. 397 mg **8.** 63 **9.** $10 737 418.23
10. a) 2186 **b)** 3906 **c)** 95.625 **d)** $9841.\overline{3}$
e) 27 305 **f)** 63.875
11. 9 **12.** 2 + 10 + 50 or 72 − 60 + 50

13. 2; 381 or −3; 1641
14. 3 + 15 + 75 or 75 + 15 + 3
15. a) $3^n - 1$ **b)** $5(2^n - 1)$ **c)** $4^n - 1$
d) $4(2^n - 1)$
17. 2047

The Mathematical Mind, page 360

1. a) 65 536 : 17 **b)** 1 048 576 : 21
2. Answers may vary. **3.** 1.2×10^{24} : 81

Exercises 8-8, page 363

1. a) Yes, 16 **b)** Yes, 81 **c)** Not geometric
d) Yes, $\frac{250}{9}$ **e)** No **f)** Yes, $-\frac{64}{7}$
2. a) 120 **b)** 10 **c)** $\frac{80}{7}$ **d)** $\frac{32}{3}$
3. a) $\frac{7}{3}$ **b)** $\frac{35}{11}$ **c)** $\frac{1520}{999}$ **d)** $\frac{1205}{198}$
4. a) 36 **b)** 51.2 **c)** Sum does not exist **d)** $\frac{48}{11}$
5. $\frac{2}{3}$ **6.** 6
7. a) 8 **b)** 0.031 25
8. 6 m **9.** About 11.3 m **10.** $(8 + 4\sqrt{2})$ m
11. a) $|x| < 1$ **b)** $|x| < 2$ **c)** $|x| < \sqrt{3}$
d) $|x| > 1$

Exercises 8-9, page 370

1. a) 4 + 5 + 6 + 7 + 8 **b)** 5 + 9 + 13 + 17
c) 2 + 4 + 6 + 8 + 10 + 12
d) −5 − 2 + 1 + 4 + 7
e) $3 + 1 + \frac{1}{3} + \frac{1}{9} + \ldots$
f) −7 − 2 + 3 + 8
2. a) $\sum_{i=1}^{7}(3i - 1)$ **b)** $\sum_{i=1}^{6}(2i + 1)$ **c)** $\sum_{i=1}^{\infty}\left(\frac{1}{5}\right)^{i-2}$
d) $\sum_{i=1}^{4}(30 - 6i)$
3. a) iv **b)** ii **c)** iii **d)** vi
4. a) 192 **b)** 20 **c)** 210
5. a) 762 **b)** 252 **c)** 1092
6. a) −1 + 0 + 3 + 8 + 15
b) 4 + 7 + 12 + 19 + 28 + 39 + 52
c) 0 + 11 + 28 + 51
d) −3 − 2 + 3 + 12 + 25 + 42
e) 2 + 2 + 0 − 4 − 10
f) 4 + 12 + 22 + 34 + 48 + 64 + 82

7. a) $\sum_{i=1}^{n}(3i - 1)$ **b)** $\sum_{i}(23 - 5i)$

c) $\sum_{i=1}^{16}(6i - 3)$ **d)** $\sum_{i=1}^{12}(4i - 2)$

e) $\sum_{i}2(3)^{i-1}$ **f)** $\sum_{i=1}^{9}3(2)^{n-1}$

8. a) $a + a^2 + a^3 + a^4$
b) $a + 2a^2 + 3a^3 + 4a^4$
c) $a + 4a + 27a + 256a$
d) $-a + 4a^2 - 27a^3 + 256a^4$

9. a) $\sum_{i=1}^{5}3i$ **b)** $\sum_{i=1}^{6}2^i$ **c)** $\sum_{i=1}^{5}\frac{1}{i}$ **d)** $\sum_{i=1}^{5}(-3)(-2)^{n-1}$

10. a) 338   **b)** 180   **c)** 363

11. a) 62   **b)** 2728   **c)** 1.9375

12. a) $\sum_{i=1}^{n}i$ **b)** $\sum_{i}^{n}i^2$ **c)** $\sum_{i=1}^{n}i^i$ **d)** $\sum_{i=1}^{n}3(2)^{i-1}$

13. a) -1 **b)** 0

14. a) $\sum_{i=1}^{n}[a + (i - 1)d]$ **b)** $\sum_{i=1}^{n}ar^{i-1}$

Computer Power, page 373

1. a) 9 cm, 12 cm, 16 cm, $21.\overline{3}$ cm, $28.\overline{4}$ cm
b) Approximately 3.897 11 cm², 6.495 19 cm²,
7.072 54 cm², 7.200 84 cm², 7.229 35 cm²
c) $\dfrac{117\sqrt{3}}{28}$ cm²

2. a) Descriptions may vary.

b) $P_1 = 9$ cm, $P_n = \frac{4}{3}P_{n-1}$, $n > 1$

c) $A_1 = \dfrac{9\sqrt{3}}{4}$, $A_2 = \dfrac{15\sqrt{3}}{4}$, $A_n = A_{n-1} + \frac{2}{9}B_{n-1}$,

where $B_2 = \dfrac{6\sqrt{3}}{4}$, $n > 2$

4. 1.261 859 5

Problem Solving, page 378

1. $na^2 + adn(n - 1) + \dfrac{d^2n(n - 1)(2n - 1)}{6}$

2. 129
438
567

3.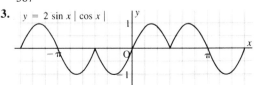
$y = 2 \sin x \,|\cos x|$

4. 24 cm²
6. Both approximately 41.4°
7. b) Yes
8. $(\pm 1.410\ 533\ 616,\ \pm 1.765\ 143\ 358)$
9. 30°

Review Exercises, page 379

1. a) 4, 7, 10, 13   **b)** 0, 1, 4, 9   **c)** 3, 16, 39, 72
d) $-\frac{1}{2}, 0, \frac{1}{4}, \frac{2}{5}$

2. a) 23; 58   **b)** 29; 1021   **c)** $\frac{3}{8}; \frac{8}{23}$ **d)** 2; -54

3. a) 2, 9, 16, 23   **b)** 1, 3, 9, 27
c) 21, 17, 13, 9   **d)** $-2, -10, -50, -250$

4. a) Arithmetic; -4 **b)** Geometric; 2
c) Geometric; -0.5 **d)** Arithmetic; 8

5. a) $4n - 2$ **b)** $2(3)^{n-1}$ **c)** n^3 **d)** $\dfrac{n(n + 2)}{n + 1}$

6. a) $7n - 5$ **b)** $2(4)^{n-1}$ **c)** 5^{n-1} **d)** $24 - 5n$

7. a) 14, 20   **b)** 32, 128

8. a) -7 **b)** 0.128

9. a) 29   **b)** 81   **c)** $4n + 1$

10. 11.5; $26.5 - 1.5n$

11. a) 2916   **b)** 19 131 876   **c)** $4(3)^{n-1}$

12. 15 552; $2(6)^{n-1}$

13. a) 7   **b)** 29   **c)** 22   **d)** 9

14. 19   **15.** 153   **16.** 25, 22, 19

17. 2, 10, 50   **18.** 61   **19.** 3, 6, 12

20. a) 1, 7, 25, 79   **b)** $-0.5, 2, -8, 32$

21. a) Arithmetic   **b)** Other   **c)** Geometric
d) Geometric   **e)** Arithmetic   **f)** Other

22. a) 8   **b)** 23   **c)** -7

23. a) $2 + 2 + 2 + 2$ **b)** $3 + 5 + 7 + 9$
c) $4 + 3 + 3 + 3$ **d)** $1 + 5 + 9 + 13$

24. a) 40; $\dfrac{n}{2}(3n + 1)$ **b)** -10; $\dfrac{n}{2}(31 - 7n)$
c) 70; $n(2n + 4)$ **d)** 155; $5(2^n - 1)$
e) 23.25; $24(1 - (0.5)^n)$ **f)** 242; $3^n - 1$

25. a) 33   **b)** 432

26. a) 128   **b)** 2 097 151

27. 12   **28.** 8

29. a) $50 + 56 + 62$ **b)** 4110

30. a) $2 + 6 + 18$ **b)** 129 140 162

31. 1380   **32. a)** 80   **b)** -18

33. a) 102   **b)** -117 **c)** 0.968 75

Chapter 9

Exercises 9-1, page 386

1. a) 110°, 20°   **b)** 45°, 22.5°   **c)** 120°, 65°
2. a) $y = x$ **b)** $x + y = 180°$
  c) $x + y = 180°$ **d)** $x + y = 180°$
  e) $x - y = 90°$ **f)** $x + y = 90°$
3. a) $x + y + z = 180°$ **b)** $x + y + z = 180°$
  c) $x + y + z = 180°$
4. Yes   **6.** No
7. a) AC = DF and BC = EF
  b) QP = SU and RP = TU
  c) IJ = LM and IK = LN or IJ = LN and
    IK = LM
8. a) $\angle P = \angle U$ **b)** $\angle Y = \angle U$
  c) $\angle L = \angle F$ or $\angle M = \angle G$
9. a) $\triangle ABC \cong \triangle EDC$ (ASA)
  b) $\triangle PQS \cong \triangle RSQ$ (SSS or SAS or AAS or
    ASA)   **c)** $\triangle ADE \cong \triangle EFC$ (AAS)
10. a) 23°   **b)** 118°, 62°, 118°   **c)** 45°, 45°
11. a) 36°, 36°   **b)** 60°, 30°   **c)** 55°
12. a) $\angle OBA = \angle OAB$; $\angle OCD = \angle ODC$
    (Isosceles Triangle Theorem)
  b) $\angle PTS = \angle QTR$; $\angle PTQ = \angle STR$
    (Opposite Angles Theorem)
  c) $\angle YXW = \angle YWX$; $\angle WYZ = \angle WZY$
    (Isosceles Triangle Theorem)
13. a) Yes   **b)** 9 m   **c)** 12 m
15. a) $180° - x + y$ **b)** $180° - 2x - y$
  c) $180° - x + y$
16. $\sqrt{x^2 + 3}$ **17.** About 92 cm
18. a) PA = PB = $\sqrt{h^2 + x^2}$ **19.** $\sqrt{x^2 + y^2 + z^2}$

Exercises 9-2, page 395

1. AB ∥ CD   ($\triangle OAB \cong \triangle OCD$ (SAS))
3. a) Infinite number   **b)** At most 1; no circle can
    be drawn if the points are collinear.
5. a) 100°, 40°   **b)** 105°, 110°   **c)** 42°, 96°
6. a) 19.0   **b)** 23.0   **c)** 20.5
7. a) Approximately 36.9°   **b)** 75°   **c)** 70°
8. 5 cm   **9. a)** 6.00   **b)** 6.11   **c)** 2.72
10. a) 200.00   **b)** 55.43   **c)** 56.92
11. a) 42.0°   **b)** 113.6°   **c)** 129.4°
13. 10.32 units   **15. a)** 20°   **b)** 70°   **c)** 40°
16. a) Approximately 36.9°
  b) Approximately 143.1°

17. a) $\sin \theta = \dfrac{d}{r}$ **b)** Approximately 47.2°

18. $\dfrac{\pi r^2 \theta}{360°}$ **19.** $\dfrac{\pi r^2 \theta}{360°} - \dfrac{1}{2} r^2 \sin \theta$
20. Approximately 0.66 m³

Exercises 9-3, page 402

1. a) Required to Prove   **b)** Given
2. AB = DE, BC = EF, AC = DF, $\angle A = \angle D$,
    $\angle B = \angle E$, $\angle C = \angle F$
3. The final statement   **4.** Parallel Lines Theorem
9. a) No, they have different shapes   **b)** Yes
  c) Answers may vary: for example,
    $\angle ADC = \angle WZY$

Exercises 9-4, page 409

1. Prove $\triangle ABD \cong \triangle CBD$, then $\angle ABD = \angle CBD$.
2. $\triangle WYZ \cong \triangle XZY$ (SSS); subtracting equal angles
    or parts of angles

Exercises 9-5, page 414

1. a) $\triangle ABD \cong \triangle ACD$ **b)** $\triangle QRP \cong \triangle SRP$
  c) $\triangle ADO \cong \triangle BDO$
2. a) SAS   **b)** HS   **c)** SSS or SAS
3. a) $\triangle ABD \cong \triangle ACE$ (SAS)
  b) $\triangle JNK \cong \triangle JML$ (SAS)
  c) First prove $\triangle TQX \cong \triangle SRX$ (SAS),
    then QT = RS; and $\angle Q = \angle R$;
    so $\triangle TQS \cong \triangle SRT$ (SAS)
12. Approximately 9.85 km
14. $\left(\sqrt{3} - \frac{\pi}{2}\right)$ square units
15. Approximately $0.378r^2$ square units, where r is the
    radius of the smaller circle

Exercises 9-6, page 419

1. Either AC or BD   **2.** QS
3. Perpendiculars from P to AC and AB

Problem Solving, page 424

1. a) $\dfrac{1 + \sqrt{5}}{2}$ (the golden ratio)   **b)** $\sqrt{5}$
  c) When ABCD is a square
2. $\dfrac{\pi - \sqrt{3}}{2} r^2$
3. b) Answers will vary; two examples are: sides 3,
    5, 7 angle 120°; sides 7, 15, 13 angle 60°

Review Exercises, page 425

1. a) 65°, 65°, 50°   **b)** 30°, 60°   **c)** 76°, 52°, 76°
2. a) $180° - x - y$ **b)** $y - x$ **c)** $260° - x - y$
3. a) 50°   **b)** 30°   **c)** 115°
4. a) Approximately 88.9°   **b)** Approximately 136°

Chapter 10

Exercises 10-1, page 429

1. a) 49 cm, 47 cm, 41 cm, 31.5 cm, 17.5 cm, 0 cm
   b)

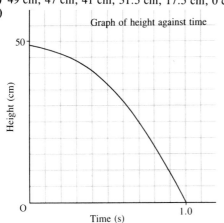

2. a) 4320 cm/s   **b)** 3520 cm/s   **c)** 7200 cm/s
3.

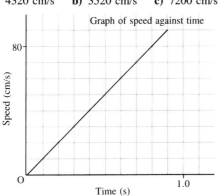

4.

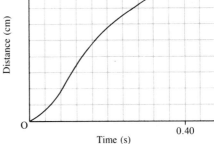

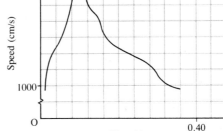

Exercises 10-2, page 432

1. a, d, e, f
2. a) The straight line   **b) i), ii), iii)** $f(x) = 2x + 3$
3. a   **4.** a, b, c
5. a)

b) $y = x$ **c)** $y = -x$ **d)** No
6. 4
7. a) 1; $y = x$ **b)** 5; $y = 5x - 3$ **c)** 0; $y = 0$
   d) 4; $y = 4x + 1$ **e)** 3; $y = 3x - 2$
   f) 4; $y = 4x + 4$
8. a) $2a$ **b)** $y = 2ax - a^2$ **c)** $y = -4x - 4$
   d) (3,9), (−1,1)
9. a) $y = -4x + 4$ **b)** $y = \frac{1}{4}x + 1$
   c) $y = -x + 2$ **d)** $y = -3x - 2$
10. $-\frac{3}{4}$ **11.** $-\frac{1}{2}$; $y = -\frac{1}{2}x$

Exercises 10-3, page 439

1. a) 0

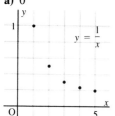

$y = \dfrac{1}{x}$

b) No limit

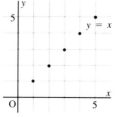

$y = x$

c) 1

$y = \dfrac{x + 1}{x + 1}$

d) No limit

e) 0

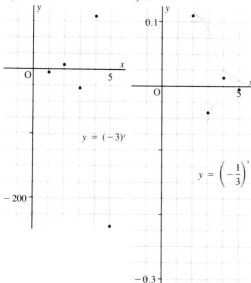

$y = (-3)^x$

$y = \left(-\dfrac{1}{3}\right)^x$

f) 0

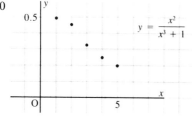

$y = \dfrac{x^2}{x^3 + 1}$

2. a) $\dfrac{3}{4}, \dfrac{21}{31}, \dfrac{201}{301}, \dfrac{2001}{3001}, \dfrac{20\,001}{30\,001}; \dfrac{2}{3}$

b) $\dfrac{1}{8}, -\dfrac{98}{305}, -\dfrac{9998}{30\,005}, -\dfrac{999\,998}{3\,000\,005}, -\dfrac{99\,999\,998}{300\,000\,005}; -\dfrac{1}{3}$

c) $1, \dfrac{11}{101}, \dfrac{101}{10\,001}, \dfrac{1001}{1\,000\,001}, \dfrac{10\,001}{100\,000\,001}; 0$

d) 0.3, 1.2, 10.2, 100.2, 1000.2; no limit

e) 20, -7.9, -99.79, -999.979, -9999.9979; no limit **f)** $-\dfrac{1}{5}, \dfrac{5}{7}, \dfrac{25}{26}, \dfrac{250}{251}, \dfrac{2500}{2501}$; no limit

3. a) $\dfrac{n + 1}{n}$ **b)** 1 **c)** Greater than 1000

4. π

5. a) $2\left(1 - \dfrac{\pi}{4}\right)s^2$ **b)** About 42.92% **c)** 6

6. b) The harmonic series has no sum.

7. a) $\sqrt{110} - 10$, or 0.4881; $\sqrt{10\,100} - 100$, or 0.4988; $\sqrt{1\,001\,000} - 1000$, or 0.4999; limit 0.5

8. a) $\dfrac{n}{n + 1}$ **b)** 1

Investigate, page 440

0.841 471 0; 0.998 334 2; 0.999 983 3; 0.999 999 8; 0.999 999 9
Limit appears to be 1; $y = x$

Exercises 10-4, page 444

1. a) $a \leqslant x < b, x \neq x_5$
b) i) B **ii)** B **iii)** C **iv)** C
c) i) No limit **ii)** B **iii)** C **iv)** No limit
v) B **d)** x_1, x_2, x_4, x_5

2. a) 0 **b)** 2 **c)** -4 **d)** $\dfrac{1}{4}$ **e)** No limit
f) No limit **g)** -1 **h)** 1 **i)** 0

3. a) $2; \dfrac{2.9}{1.9}, \dfrac{2.99}{1.99}, \dfrac{2.999}{1.999}, \dfrac{2.9999}{1.9999}, \dfrac{4}{3}; \dfrac{3.1}{2.1}, \dfrac{3.01}{2.01}, \dfrac{3.001}{2.001}, \dfrac{3.0001}{2.0001}$ **b)** $\dfrac{3}{2}$

4. a) Answers may vary. **b)** 0

5. a) 2 **b)** $-\dfrac{1}{4}$ **c)** $\dfrac{4}{11}$ **d)** $\dfrac{8}{9}$ **e)** $\dfrac{1}{3}$ **f)** $-\dfrac{3}{4}$
g) No limit **h)** 0 **i)** No limit **j)** $-\dfrac{8}{3}$
k) 12 **l)** $-\dfrac{1}{16}$

6. a) $\{x \mid x \neq 0, x \in R\}$
b) $f(x)$ is continuous at all points except $x = 0$

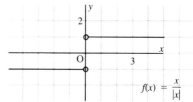

$f(x) = \dfrac{x}{|x|}$

c) i) -1 **ii)** 1   **iii)** No limit
d) Answers may vary.
7. i) a) Continuous at all points
   b) Asymptote at $y = 0$
   ii) a) Discontinuous at $x = \pm 1$
   b) Asymptotes at $x = \pm 1$, $y = 0$
   iii) a) Discontinuous at $x = \pm 1$
   b) Asymptotes at $x = -1$, $y = 0$
   iv) a) Discontinuous at $x = 0$
   b) Asymptote at $x = 0$

8. a)

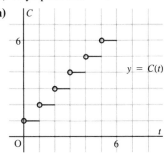

b) $t = 1, 2, 3, 4, 5, 6$ **c)** Yes; no

9. $\frac{3}{2}$

Exercises 10-5, page 450

1. a) 0   **b)** 2   **c)** -1 **d)** 4   **e)** 0   **f)** -3

2. a) $4x - 3$ **b)** $3x^2 - 8x$ **c)** $4x^3$ **d)** $-\dfrac{2}{x^3}$

   e) $-\dfrac{2x}{(x^2 + 1)^2}$ **f)** $\dfrac{1}{(x + 1)^2}$

3. a) $-2; y = -2x + 2$ **b)** $5; y = 5x + 1$
   c) $3; y = 3x + 2$ **d)** $2; y = 2x - 3$
   e) $4; y = 4x - 7$ **f)** $\frac{1}{6}; y = \frac{1}{6}x + \frac{5}{2}$

4. $\dfrac{x}{\sqrt{x^2 + 5}}$

5. a)

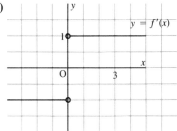

b)

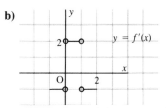

7. a) $\dfrac{d}{dx}(x) = x^0; \dfrac{d}{dx}\left(\dfrac{x^2}{2}\right) = x^1; \dfrac{d}{dx}\left(\dfrac{x^3}{3}\right) = x^2;$

$\dfrac{d}{dx}\left(\dfrac{x^4}{4}\right) = x^3; \dfrac{d}{dx}(-x^{-1}) = x^{-2}; \dfrac{d}{dx}\left(\dfrac{-x^{-2}}{2}\right) = x^{-3}$

b) Yes, except for x^{-1}, which is not a derivative of a function of the form ax^n.

Exercises 10-6, page 454

1. a) $-2x$ **b)** $9x^2$ **c)** $-\dfrac{4}{x^2}$ **d)** $2x$ **e)** 2
   f) $-3x^2$ **g)** 100   **h)** $3x^2 + 2x$ **i)** $x^2 - x$

2. a) $-2x^{-\frac{3}{2}}$ **b)** $x^{-\frac{2}{3}}$ **c)** $-2x^{-\frac{5}{3}}$

3. a) $2x + 4$ **b)** $2 - 10x$ **c)** $-6x^2 + 6x$
   d) $3x^2 + 2x + 1$ **e)** $10x - 4$
   f) $\dfrac{5}{\sqrt{x}} - \sqrt{10}$ **g)** $-\dfrac{1}{6} + \dfrac{x}{3} - \dfrac{x^2}{2}$ **h)** $\dfrac{1}{6\sqrt{x}}$
   i) $\dfrac{1}{2} + \dfrac{2}{x^2}$

4. a) $1000x^{999} + 100x^{99} + 10x^9$
   b) $\dfrac{x^5}{5} - \dfrac{x^4}{4} + \dfrac{4x^3}{15} - \dfrac{9x^2}{60}$
   c) $-2x^{-3} - 3x^{-4} + 4x^{-5}$ **d)** $\dfrac{1}{2\sqrt{x}} - \dfrac{1}{2\sqrt{x^3}}$
   e) $\frac{4}{3}x^{\frac{1}{3}} + \frac{1}{3}x^{-\frac{2}{3}} - \frac{2}{3}x^{-\frac{5}{3}}$ **f)** $4x - 3x^{\frac{1}{2}} + 2 - x^{-\frac{1}{2}}$

5. $y = 12x + 7$ **6.** $(2, -15), (-2, 17)$

Exercises 10-7, page 459

1. a) $-\frac{1}{2}x^{-\frac{3}{2}}$ **b)** $\frac{3}{2}x^{\frac{1}{2}}$ **c)** $\frac{5}{2}x^{\frac{3}{2}}$ **d)** $-2x^{-3}$
   e) $-3x^{-4}$ **f)** $-\frac{3}{2}x^{-\frac{5}{2}}$

2. a) $12x + 5$ **b)** $\frac{5}{2}x^{\frac{3}{2}} - \frac{9}{2}x^{\frac{1}{2}} + \frac{7}{2}x^{-\frac{1}{2}}$
   c) $-\dfrac{1}{x^{\frac{3}{2}}} + \dfrac{1}{x^3}$ **d)** $\dfrac{3}{2\sqrt{x}} + 1$ **e)** $\dfrac{1}{(2 - x)^2}$
   f) $-\dfrac{1 + 2\sqrt{x}}{2\sqrt{x}(x + \sqrt{x})^2}$ **g)** $\dfrac{4x}{(x^2 + 1)^2}$
   h) $\dfrac{-1}{\sqrt{x}(1 + \sqrt{x})^2}$ **i)** $\dfrac{-25}{(3 + 4t)^2}$ **j)** $\dfrac{8}{x^2\left(3 + \frac{4}{x}\right)^2}$

k) $\dfrac{1 - s^2}{(s^2 - s + 1)^2}$ **l)** $\dfrac{24x^2 + 12x + 1}{(4x + 1)^2}$

3. $\frac{1}{3}$

7. a) $\dfrac{x}{\sqrt{x^2 + 1}}$ **b)** $\dfrac{1}{4\sqrt{x}\sqrt{1 + \sqrt{x}}}$ **c)** $\dfrac{1}{4\sqrt{x}\sqrt{\sqrt{x}}}$

Problem Solving, page 463

5. a) $\dfrac{n}{4(n + 1)}$ **b)** $\dfrac{n}{3n + 1}$ **c)** $(n - 1)2^n + 1$
  d) $(n + 1)! - 1$ **e)** $n(n + 1)^2$

6. a) $\dfrac{1}{n}$ **b)** $\dfrac{n + 1}{2n}$ **c)** $\dfrac{n + 1}{2}$

10. $S_n = t_{n+2} - 1$

11. a) 1, 1.732 050 8, 2.112 842 1, 2.285 975 5,
  2.360 498 1

13. a) $(-1)^n(n!)(x)^{-(n+1)}$, where $n! = n(n-1)(n-2)$
  $\ldots 3 \times 2 \times 1$
  b) $\dfrac{(-1)^{n+1}(1)(3)(5)\ldots(2n-3)}{2^n}x^{-\frac{(2n-1)}{2}}$
  c) $\dfrac{(-1)^{n+1}(n!)}{(1+x)^{n+1}}$

Exercises 10-8, page 469

1. a) 800 km/h due East   **b)** 667 km/h
2. 9.8 m/s
3. a) i) $(2t - 4)$ cm/s   **ii)** $t < 2$ s   **iii)** $t > 2$ s
  iv) 2 s   **v)** 0 cm/s   **vi)** 2 cm/s^2
  b) i) $(3 - 2t)$ cm/s   **ii)** $t > 1.5$ s   **iii)** $t < 1.5$ s
  iv) 1.5 s   **v)** -1 cm/s   **vi)** -2 cm/s^2
  c) i) $(3t^2 + 6t + 3)$ cm/s   **ii)** At no time
  iii) At all times except $t = -1$ **iv)** -1 s
  v) 31 cm/s   **vi)** $(6t + 6)$ cm/s^2
  d) i) $(4t^3 - 16t)$ cm/s   **ii)** $t < -2$ s or
  0 s $< t < 2$ s   **iii)** -2 s $< t < 0$ s or $t > 2$ s
  iv) 0 s, 2 s, -2 s   **v)** 32 cm/s
  vi) $(12t^2 - 16)$ cm/s^2
4. a) $(b + a)$ m/s   **b)** $(a + b)$ m/s
5. a) $(b^2 + ab + a^2)$ m/s   **b)** $\frac{3}{4}(a + b)^2$ m/s
6. a) 30 s   **b)** 900 m
7. a) About 2.9 s   **b)** About 31.4 m/s

Exercises 10-9, page 477

1. a) $\{x \mid x \geqslant 0,\ x \in R\}$; endpoint at 0
  b) $\{x \mid x \geqslant -2,\ x \in R\}$; endpoint at -2
  c) $\{x \mid -1 \leqslant x \leqslant 1,\ x \in R\}$; endpoints at ± 1
  d) $\{x \mid x \leqslant -1$ or $x \geqslant 1,\ x \in R\}$; endpoints at ± 1
  e) $\{x \mid x > 1,\ x \in R\}$ **f)** $\{x \mid x \neq 0,\ x \in R\}$
2. a) i) Increasing for $x < -1.5$; decreasing
  for $x > -1.5$ **ii)** Maximum $(-1.5, 6.25)$
  iii)

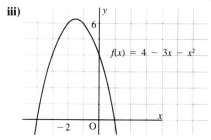
$f(x) = 4 - 3x - x^2$

  b) i) Decreasing for $x < -0.75$; increasing
  for $x > -0.75$
  ii) Minimum $(-0.75, -3.125)$
  iii)

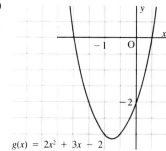
$g(x) = 2x^2 + 3x - 2$

  c) i) Increasing for $x < -2$ and $x > 2$; decreasing
  for $-2 < x < 2$
  ii) $(-2, 16)$ maximum; $(2, -16)$ minimum

iii)

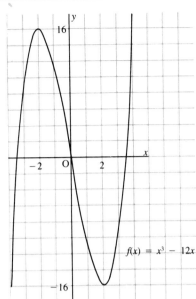

$f(x) = x^3 - 12x$

d) i) Increasing for all values of x
ii) No critical points
iii)

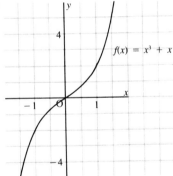

$f(x) = x^3 + x$

e) i) Decreasing for $x < 1$; increasing for $x > 1$
ii) Minimum $(1, -3)$

iii)

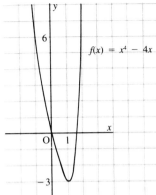

$f(x) = x^4 - 4x$

f) i) Decreasing for $x < -1$ and $0 < x < 1$;
increasing for $-1 < x < 0$ and $x > 1$
ii) $(-1, 0)$ and $(1, 0)$ minimum; $(0, 1)$ maximum
iii)

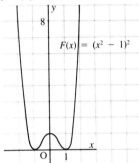

$F(x) = (x^2 - 1)^2$

g) i) Increasing for $x < 0$ and $0 < x < 3$;
decreasing for $x > 3$ **ii)** Minimum $(3, 27)$
iii)

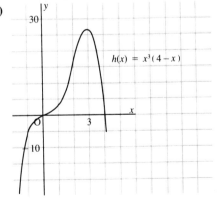

$h(x) = x^3(4 - x)$

h) i) Decreasing for $x < 0$ and $2 < x < 4$; increasing for $0 < x < 2$ and $x > 4$

ii) Minimum $(0,0)$, $(4,0)$; maximum $(2,16)$

iii)

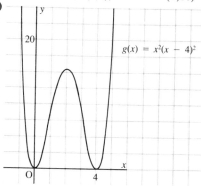

$g(x) = x^2(x - 4)^2$

3. a)

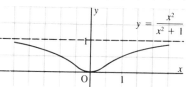

$y = \dfrac{x^2}{x^2 + 1}$

b)

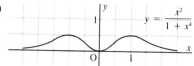

$y = \dfrac{x^2}{1 + x^4}$

c)

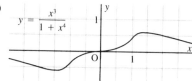

$y = \dfrac{x^3}{1 + x^4}$

d)

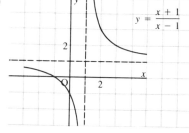

$y = \dfrac{x + 1}{x - 1}$

e)

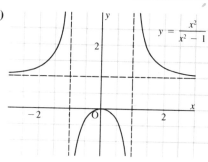

$y = \dfrac{x^2}{x^2 - 1}$

Exercises 10-10, page 483

1. 42.25 **2.** $4\sqrt{2}$

5. a) $\dfrac{A}{2}$ **b)** $\dfrac{A}{2}$ **6.** $3.\overline{3}$ cm

7. 15 cm   **8.** 1 **9.** $\sqrt{6}$ **10.** $\dfrac{2\sqrt{2}}{3}R, \dfrac{4}{3}R$

Review Exercises, page 484

1. a) 4 **b)** $-\dfrac{1}{2}$ **c)** No limit   **d)** 8 **e)** $-\dfrac{3}{5}$
f) 1

2. a) $\dfrac{1}{4}$ **b)** $\dfrac{1}{8}$ **c)** -2 **d)** 3 **e)** 4 **f)** 0

3. a) $2x - 1$ **b)** $2 - 3x^2$ **c)** $2x + 2$
d) $-\dfrac{1}{(x + 1)^2}$ **e)** $\dfrac{1}{(x + 1)^2}$ **f)** $\dfrac{1}{2\sqrt{1 + x}}$

4. a) $y = 5x - 3$ **b)** $y = \dfrac{1}{4}x + 1$
c) $y = 7x - 15$ **d)** $y = \dfrac{1}{2}x + 2$

5. a) $2 + 6x + 12x^2$ **b)** $\dfrac{1}{\sqrt{x}} + \dfrac{4}{x^2}$
c) $x^2 + \dfrac{x}{2} - \dfrac{1}{5}$
d) $-5x^4 - 4x^3 + 9x^2 - 2x + 3$
e) $\dfrac{-2x - 3}{(x^2 + 3x + 5)^2}$ **f)** $\dfrac{6x}{(x^2 + 2)^2}$

6. a) Approximately $0.42 < t < 1.58$
b) Approximately 0.42 and 1.58
c) Approximately $t < 0.42$ and $t > 1.58$

7. $6t - 6$

8. a)

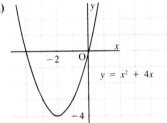

$y = x^2 + 4x$

b)

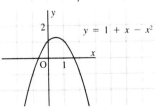

$y = 1 + x - x^2$

c)

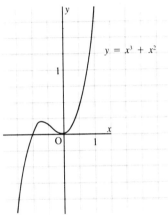

$y = x^3 + x^2$

d)

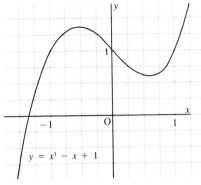

$y = x^3 - x + 1$

e)

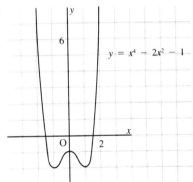

$y = x^4 - 2x^2 - 1$

f)

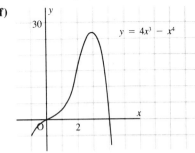

$y = 4x^3 - x^4$

9. 50

Cumulative Review, Chapters 7-10, page 485

1. a) \$1265.32   **b)** \$8726.06   **c)** \$10 551.71

2. a) 27   **b)** 4   **c)** $\frac{1}{25}$ **d)** 1

3. a) $4ax^{-2}y^6$ **b)** $\dfrac{9m^{-13}n^{-2}}{2}$

4. a) 220.400   **b** 0.013   **c)** 26.952   **d)** 1.833
   e) 2.667   **f)** -4.000 **g)** 3.443   **h)** -0.8252

5. a) 0.01   **b)** 9   **c)** 128   **d)** 2.261 859 5
   e) -0.254 412   **f)** 8.186 427 8

6. a) $\log 6$ **b)** $\log\left(\dfrac{2x^2 + 7x - 15}{x + 4}\right)$

7. a) $x - y$ **b)** $x - 2y$ **c)** $1 + x + y$
   d) $3y - x$

8. a) 2.0828   **b)** 0.5207   **c)** 2.0414
   d) -1.0414 **9. a)** 3   **b)** 3

10. a) Geometric, $r = 3$ **b)** Arithmetic, $d = 4$
   c) Arithmetic, $d = -6$ **d)** Geometric, $r = \frac{2}{3}$

11. a) 3, 8, 13, 18   **b)** $-1, 2, 9, 20$ **c)** 3, $\frac{4}{3}$, 1, $\frac{6}{7}$
   d) 4, 5, 7, 11   **e)** $-4, -6, -8, -10$
   f) $-16, 8, -4, 2$

12. a) $t_n = 8n - 13$ **b)** $t_n = 3(5)^{n-1}$

   c) $t_n = -7n + 32$ **d)** $t_n = 48\left(\dfrac{3}{4}\right)^{n-1}$

13. a) i) 405   **ii)** 295 245   **iii)** $5(3)^{n-1}$ **b) i)** 12

   ii) -54 **iii)** $-11n + 67$ **c) i)** 51   **ii)** 123

   iii) $12n - 9$ **d) i)** 2.5   **ii)** 0.039 062 5

   iii) $40\left(\dfrac{1}{2}\right)^{n-1}$

14. a) 15; 39   **b)** 9; 81

15. a) 9   **b)** 22   **c)** 38   **d)** 13

16. a) 2, 7, 17, 37   **b)** 12, 10, 9, 8.5

17. a) 60; $3n^2 - 8n$ **b)** 126; $2^{n+1} - 2$

   c) $\dfrac{364}{9}$; $\dfrac{81\left(1 - \left(-\frac{1}{3}\right)^n\right)}{2}$ **d)** 87; $\frac{11}{2}n^2 - \frac{95}{2}n$

18. a) 48   **b)** 216

19. 32

20. a) 60   **b)** 8   **c)** 148

22. Congruence conditions may vary.

   a) $\triangle GJF \cong \triangle HJK$ (ASA)

   b) $\triangle JML \cong \triangle LKJ$ (ASA)

   c) $\triangle XUV \cong \triangle VWZ$ (AAS)

26. a) 11; $y = 11x + 10$ **b)** 6; $y = 6x - 5$

27. a) 2   **b)** $\frac{1}{2}$ **c)** No limit

28. a) 3   **b)** $\frac{3}{2}$ **c)** 0

29. a) $15x^2 + 4x - 1$ **b)** $\dfrac{3}{2\sqrt{x}} - \dfrac{5}{x^2}$

   c) $6x^2 + 2x - 11$ **d)** $\dfrac{9x^2 - 12x + 15}{(2x^2 - 5x)^2}$

30. a) 21 m/s; 24 m/s²   **b)** -5; 1   **c)** 22 m/s

31. 7500 m²

Index